The Sacred Writings of Saint Ambrose

SAINT AMBROSE

The Sacred Writings of Saint Ambrose
Jazzybee Verlag Jürgen Beck
86450 Altenmünster, Loschberg 9
Deutschland

ISBN: 9783849675370

www.jazzybee-verlag.de
admin@jazzybee-verlag.de

Cover Design: © Sue Colvil - Fotolia.com

Printed by Createspace, North Charleston, SC, USA

CONTENTS:

PROLEGOMENA TO ST. AMBROSE.

I. Literature.

§1. Editions.

All the Editions of the works of St. Ambrose which preceded that of the Benedictines are very inadequate. Of these the chief are the following:

1.   Venice, a.d. 1485.

2.   Cribellius, a.d. 1490.

3.   Auerbach, Basel, a.d. 1492, reprinted in 1506, with a full Index. These are very faulty Editions.

4.   Erasmus, Basel, a.d. 1527, reprinted and re-edited by different persons, in various places [by Baronius amongst others, a.d. 1549].

5.   Gillot Campanus, Paris, a.d. 1568.

6.   Felix de Montalto [afterwards Pope Sixtus V.], Rome, a.d. 1580–1585, reprinted at Paris, a.d. 1603.

7.   The Benedictines of St. Maur, Paris, a.d. 1686–1690, reprinted at Venice, a.d. 1748 and 1781, as well as with additions by Migne, Patres Latini, Vols. XIV.-XVII.

8.   A new edition by Ballerini, Milan, a.d. 1875–1886, founded on that of the Benedictines, but by no means superior to it.

There is still room for a critical edition of the works of this great Father, which are unfortunately very corrupt, but in many points it is not likely that the work of the Benedictine editors can be improved upon.

9.   There are separate editions of some of the treatises of St. Ambrose, as of the *Hexaëmeron* and *De Officiis Clericorum*, in the Bibliotheca Patrum Eccl. Latinae Selecta, Leipzig, Tauchnitz. The *De Officiis* has also been edited, with considerable improvements in the text, by Krabinger, Tübingen, 1857, and the *De Fide* and *De Poenitentia*, by Hurter in the Vienna selections from the Fathers.

§2. Translations.

There seems to have never been any attempt to translate the works of this great Christian Father and Doctor in full.

Some few treatises, *De Officiis, De excessu fratris Satyri, De Virginitate,* and several other short ones, appear in German, in the select writings of the Fathers, published by Kosel of Kempten. The Epistles have been translated into French by Bonrecueil, Paris, a.d. 1746; and the *De Officiis* and Epistles into English, the former by Humfrey, London, a.d. 1637; the latter in the Oxford "Library of the Fathers," revised by E. Walford, London, 1881; whilst the *De Mysteriis* appears in a little volume of Sacramental Treatises, published by Messrs. J. Parker & Co., Oxford, under the supervision of the Editor of this volume. There is a very valuable little monograph entitled *Studia Ambrosiana*, chiefly critical, and unfortunately brief, by Maximilian Ihm. Leipzig, Teubner, 1889.

§3. Biographies and Authorities for the Life of St. Ambrose.

(a.) Ancient.

Many of his own writings.—Life of St. Ambrose by Paulinus, a deacon of the Church of Milan.—St. Augustine, Confessions, V. 23, 24; VI. 1–6; IX. 13–16; and many other passages in his writings.—St. Jerome, *De Scriptoribus Ecclesiasticis,* c. 134.—Rufinus, Ecclesiastical History, XI, 11, 15, 16, 18.—Socrates, Eccl. History, IV. 30; V. 11.—Sozomen, Eccl. History, VI, 24; VII. 13, 25.

(B.) Modern.

Baronius, Annals, a.d. 397, n. 25–35; Life of St. Ambrose in the prolegomena to the Roman Edition of his works.—The Life of St. Ambrose gathered from his own writings, in the Benedictine Edition (excellent).—Hermant, *Vie de St. Ambroise,* Paris, 1678.—Tillemont, *Mémoires,* etc., Tome X. St. Ambroise [pp. 78–386], and notes, pp. 729–770.—Ceillier, *Histoire générale des Auteurs sacrés,* Tome V. pp. 328 ff. Ed. 2, Paris, 186c.—Dupin, Tome ii. pp. 438–515.

[This writer says that the text of St. Ambrose is more corrupt than that of any other Father. See Alzog, *Patrologie*, p. 296. Ed. i.]—Cave, *Hist. Lit.* Vol. I. 262.—Schoeneman, *Bibliotheca historica PP. Lat.* I. 388–419.—Silbert, *Leben des heiligen Ambrosius*, Vienna, 1841—Baunard, *Histoire de St. Ambroise*, Paris, 1872 [translated into German, Freiburg, 1873].—Life of St. Ambrose, by Archdeacon Thornton, London, and other shorter sketches.—Fessler [Jungmann], *Institutiones Patrologiae*, I. 655 [also Patrologies of Moehler, Alzog, etc.]. Articles in the Freiburg Kirchen-Lexikon, the Dictionary of Christian Biography, and other encyclopaedias.

II. Notes on Secular and Church History During the Latter Part of the Fourth Century.

After the Council of Nicaea, a.d. 325, the faith of the Catholic Church was established, but a considerable time was to elapse, and the tide of heterodoxy was to ebb and flow many times before peace should finally ensue. The "conversion" of the Emperor Constantine, though not followed, till he was dying, by baptism, led not merely to the toleration but to the protection and, as it were, the "establishment" of the Christian religion. This very naturally was followed by a large influx of worldliness into the Church, and bishops began to be time-servers and courtiers. St. Ambrose, however, was not of this number, but whether in defence of the Catholic faith, of the property of the Church, or, as in his legations to Maximus, for the protection of those in peril or anxiety who sought his aid, he braved every danger, even that of death itself.

During the greater part of the life of St. Ambrose many of those in power, amongst others the empress mother Justina, were Arians. Julian, though too early to affect the actions of the bishop, apostatized to paganism, which also numbered many supporters of high station. On the other hand, the influence of St. Ambrose, exercised even with severe strictness, was all-powerful with Theodosius, known as the emperor who subdued the Arian heresy and abolished the worship of idols in the Roman Empire.

The various historical events during the lifetime of St. Ambrose will be found entered under the different years in the subjoined table; it remains only here to give some account of his burial-place.

St. Ambrose having discovered the bodies of SS. Cosmas and Damian, a.d. 389, placed them under the right side of the altar in his basilica, and desired that he should be himself buried near them to the left, which was done a.d. 397. In the year 835 the Archbishop of Milan, Angilbert II., caused a large porphyry sarcophagus to be made in which he laid the body of St. Ambrose between the other two under the altar. In 1864 some excavations and repairs revealed *in situ* a magnificent sarcophagus nearly four and a half feet in length, three in width, and nearly two in height, without the covering, placed lengthwise. Further excavations brought to view two other tombs, one to the right and one to the left, lined with marble and placed east and west, not as the sarcophagus, north and south. In the one to the left were a few pieces of money, one of Flavius Victor, one of Theodosius, with some fragments of cloth of gold and other things. These were evidently the original resting-places of St. Ambrose and of SS. Cosmas and Damian, and the sarcophagus that constructed under Lothair, a.d. 835, by Angilbert.

a.d.

340.

Birth of St. Ambrose (probably at Treèves), youngest son of Ambrose, Prefect of the Gauls. Constantine II. killed at Aquieleia. Death of Eusebius.

341.

Seventh Council of Antioch. Second exile of St. Athanasius.

343.

Photinus begins teaching his heresy.

347.

Birth of St. John Crysostom. Council of Sardica. St. Athanasius restored.

348.

Birth of Prudentius the Christian poet.

349.

Synod of Sirmium against Photinus.

350.

Death of the Emperor Constans. St. Hilary, Bishop of Poitiers. Magnentius proclaimed Emperor of the West.

351.

Photinus condemned by a semi-Arian synod.

352.

Liberius, Pope in succession to Julius.

353–4.

About this date St. Ambrose is taken by his mother to live at Rome, where his sister Marcellina received the veil at the hands of Liberius at Christmas, either a.d. 353, or more probably 354. Suicide of Magnentius the Emperor.

354.

Birth of St. Augustine. Death of the Emperor Gallus.

355.

Liberius the Pope, Dionysius, Bishop of Milan, and Lucifer, Bishop of Cagliari, banished by an Arian synod at Milan. Third exile of St. Athanasius.

356.

Banishment of St. Hilary of Poitiers.

357.

Liberius subscribes (as the Arians say> an Arian Creed, and returns to Rome a.d. 358.

359.

Council of Ariminum. Macedonius of Constantinople deposed. Eudoxius consecrated Bishop.

361.

Julian Emperor.

362.

Fourth exile of St. Athanasius.

363.

Death of the Emperor Julian. St. Athanasius restored. Felix Pope.

364.

Death of the Emperor Jovian. Valentinian and Valens Emperors.

366.

Death of Liberius in September. Damasus elected in his place, but the see is also claimed by Ursinus.

367.

Gratian, though only a boy, declared Augustus by his father Valentinian.

368–74.

Successful career of St. Ambrose in legal business and as "consular."

370.

St. Basil, Bishop of Caesarea.

372.

St. Gregory of Nazianzus, Bishop of Susium.

373.

Death of St. Athanasius.

374.

Death of Auxentius, the Arian Bishop of Milan, and election of St. Ambrose, though still only a catechumen, by acclamation. St. Martin Bishop of Tours.

374–5.

St. Ambrose sends a deputation of clerics to St. Basil to ask for the body of St. Dionysius, late Catholic Bishop of Milan. [St. Basil, Ep. 197.]

375.

Death of Valentinian in November. His son Valentinian is admitted by Gratian to be Emperor of the East, though only four years old.

377.

St. Ambrose writes the three books, *De Virginibus;* one, *De Viduis;* which is followed by the book, *De Virginitate.*

378.

The first two books, De Fide, written at the request of Gratian, who was setting out to the relief of Valens against the Goths. Valens is overcome and killed at Adrianople. Many Christians having been made captives, St. Ambrose sells Church plate to redeem them.

379.

Theodosius is proclaimed Augustus. Death of St. Basil and of St. Ephrem Syrum. Gratian, on his way back from Thrace, requests St. Ambrose to come to meet him and receives the first two books of the treatise De Fide, and asks for a further one of the Holy Spirit; the latter was written two years later. Death of Satyrus, brother of St. Ambrose. The two treatises on his death written.

379–80.

Famine in Rome.—See De Off. III. 46–48.

380.

Baptism of Theodosius at Thessalonica. Books III.–V. of the De Fide written about this time. The basilica which had been sequestered by Gratian is restored to the Church.

380.

Synod at Rome under Damasus at which St. Ambrose was present. Probably in the same year St. Ambrose consecrated Anemius Bishop of Sirmium in spite of Arian opposition.

381.

Death at Constantinople of Athanaricus, leader of the Goths. The three books, De Spiritu Sancto, written. Death of Peter, Bishop of Alexandria. The Oecumenical Council of Constantinople commences under the presidency of Meletius of Antioch. Also at Aquileia a council, at which St. Ambrose took a leading part, was held against the heretics Palladius and Secundianus. An account is given of the proceedings in Epistles 9–12.

381–2.

St. Ambrose presides over a council of Italian bishops to take into consideration the troubles at Antioch and Constantinople. Epistles 13, to Theodosius, and 14, his reply, state the proceedings. Theodosius summoned a council to consider the same matters at Constantinople.

382.

Gratian orders the removal of the image of Victory from the forum at Rome. [Ep. 17, 18.] Acholius, Bishop of Thessalonica, dies and is succeeded by Anysius.

383.

The Priscillianists endeavour in vain to gain Damasus and St. Ambrose to their side by means of a visit to Rome and Milan. On the 25th of August Gratian is assassinated at Lyons by the instigation of Maximus. A great dearth at Rome. [De Off. III. 7, 49; Ep. 18.]

383–4.

First legation of St. Ambrose to Maximus on behalf of Justina the Empress and her son Valentinian II.384. The memorial of Symmachus the prefect of the city to Valentinian, requesting the restoration of the Altar of Victory, and the reply of St. Ambrose. [Ep. 17, 18.] A synod at Bordeaux against the Priscillianists. Death of Damasus, who is succeeded by Siricius as Pope.

385.

Priscillian and his companions are condemned to death at Trèves at the instigation of the Spanish Bishops Idacius and Ithacius. The Ithacians consecrate Felix as Bishop. [Ep. 42–51.] The persecution at Milan of Catholics by Justina in Holy Week. [Ep. 20.] The law of Valentinian II., granting Arians equal rights with Catholics. Auxentius claims the see of Milan. [Sermon against Auxentius and Ep. 21.] The deposit which a widow had entrusted to the Church at Trent having been carried off by imperial order, St. Ambrose succeeds in procuring its restitution. [De Off. II. 29, 150, 151.] New basilica at Milan consecrated.

386.

Finding of the bodies of St. Gervasius and Protasius [Ep. 22]. Epistle 23 to the bishops of the province of Aemilia on the right day for the observance of Easter.

386–7.

The exposition of the Gospel according to St. Luke written.387.   Baptism of St. Augustine at Milan by St. Ambrose at Easter. Second mission of St. Ambrose to Maximus. [Ep. 24.] Expulsion of St. Ambrose from Trèves because of his refusal to communicate with the murderer of his sovereign. In the later part of the year Maximus crosses into Italy and enters Milan.

388.

At Constantinople the Arians destroy the residence of the Catholic Bishop Nectarius. [Ep. 40, §13.] Death of Justina, and conversion of Valentinian II. by Theodosius. Theodosius marches against Maximus, who is everywhere defeated [Ep. 40, §23], and executed at Aquileia. Third application concerning the Altar of Victory.

390.

The excessive cruelty with which Theodosius punished a sedition at Thessalonica brought on him exclusion from communion, and a severe rebuke at the hands of St. Ambrose. The Emperor's penitence and readmission to communion. A synod is held at Milan against the Ithacian heretics, and Felix, Bishop of Trèves. [Ep. 51.]

391–2.

The deputation of part of the Roman Senate to Valentinian to request the restoration of the Altar of Victory in the Forum. [Ep. 57, §5.] The treatise De institutione Virginis, written about this time, as also, De Officiis.

392.

Valentinian II. killed at Vienne by Arbogastes [Ep. 53, §2; De ob. Valent. 25 ff.]. His body is brought to Milan. The address, Consolatio de ob. Val. A further delegation from the Senate is sent to Eugenius respecting the Altar of Victory [Ep. 57, §6 ff.].

393.

On the arrival of Eugenius at Milan St. Ambrose leaves the city for Bononia Faventia and Florence. The letters to Eugenius and Sabinus written about this time.

393–4.

At Florence St. Ambrose dedicates a basilica, in which he deposits the bodies of the martyrs Vitalis and Agricola, which he had brought from Bononia. His address on this occasion was that which is inscribed, Exhortatio Virginitatis. He writes Ep. 59.

394.

Theodosius sets out from Constantinople against Eugenius. About the beginning of August St. Ambrose returns to Milan. Eugenius defeated by Theodosius and slain, Sept. 6. St. Ambrose intercedes and obtains pardon for the followers of Eugenius. After this St. Ambrose writes the Enarrationes on Psalms 35–40 and Ep. 61, 62.

395.

Death of Theodosius at Milan. St. Ambrose's oration De obitu Theodosii. Honorius and Arcadius Emperors. St. Augustine, Bishop of Hippo. Death of Rufinus.

396.

Dissensions at Vercellae, the occasion of writing Ep. 63, and of a visit to that Church.

397.

St. Ambrose consecrates a bishop for Ticinum, and shortly after falls ill. He commenced the Enarratio on Psalm 43, which he left unfinished; and died in the night between Good Friday and Easter Eve,

III. On the Doctrine of St. Ambrose.

There is a very complete agreement on the part of St. Ambrose with the Catholic teaching of the universal Church. St. Augustine speaks of him as "a faithful teacher of the Church, and even at the risk of his life a most strenuous defender of Catholic truth," "whose skill, constancy, labours, and perils, both on account of what he did and what he wrote, the Roman world unhesitatingly proclaims." In matters both of faith and morals by his words and writings he greatly benefited the Church and was called by St. Jerome "a pillar of the Church."

In his dogmatic treatises, more particularly in his books on the Faith, he shows great skill and penetration, and his reasoning is full and clear, meeting the most subtle objections with patient industry. Scarcely any ancient writer has treated the mystery of the Holy Trinity and the theological difficulties connected with it more clearly and convincingly than St. Ambrose in his *De Fide* and *De Spiritu Sancto.*

In his expositions of Holy Scripture he treats of the threefold sense, the literal, the moral, and the mystical, devoting more pains, however, and time to the latter than to the former. He gives special consideration to the mystical interpretation of such passages as may seem to contain in a literal sense anything diverging from sound morality. Many of his other mystical interpretations of plain, simple matters of fact have much beauty, as in his treatment of the story of the building of the ark, the marriage of Isaac, and the blessings of the Patriarchs. The literal sense is followed specially in the *Hexaëmeron,* the treatise on Paradise, Noah and the Ark, and the Exposition of the Gospel according to St. Luke. The moral sense, though referred to throughout his writings, is more particularly sought out in the Expositions of the Psalms.

St. Ambrose was a diligent student of the Greek writers, whom he often follows largely, especially Origen and Didymus, as also St. Basil the Great and St. Athanasius, and he has also adapted many points of allegorical interpretation from Philo. He is fond of alleging scriptural proofs, and when he argues from reason often confirms his argument by some quotation or reference, a task easy for him who, from his consecration, was so diligent a student of holy Scripture.

As to justification, St. Ambrose ascribes the whole work to the Holy Spirit, Who seals us in our hearts, as we receive the outward sign in our bodies. Through the Holy Spirit we receive a share of the grace of adoption. Christ was perfect according to the fulness of His Majesty; we are perfected by a continual progress in virtue.

With regard to baptism, he taught in accordance with the received belief of his day that it is the sacrament of adoption and regeneration, wherein sin is forgiven, and the Holy Spirit confers new life upon the soul and joins it mystically to Christ. As to the Real Presence in the Sacrament of the Eucharist, his doctrine is no less definite. In his treatise on the Faith he says of the elements that they "are transfigured [*transfigurantur*] by the mystery of the sacred prayer in to flesh and blood." He interprets various texts, also, in many places in the same sense. In a like spirit he maintains that the power of forgiving sins on repentance is vested in the ministry of the Church. The intercession of the saints, and up to a certain point their invocation, is likewise upheld.

There was a Latin version made from the Septuagint, including the Apocrypha, in Africa, and in use there at the end of the second century, very barbarous, and copying even Greek constructions. Of this text SS. Ambrose and Augustine used a recension. But our author seems to have been very independent, and to have made use of several different versions of holy Scripture, translating, as it would seem, often for himself from the Septuagint, referring also to Symmachus, Theodotion, and Aquila, though thinking less of the latter. When the prophets, he says, were moved by the Holy Spirit, they were troubled and darkened with their own ignorance. Prayer, he asserts, is necessary for understanding holy Scripture. Each Testament is not equally easy, and we are not to criticise what we do not understand. He speaks of the Hebrew as the truth, but states that the Septuagint added much that is useful.

The Arians are repeatedly charged by St. Ambrose with falsifying and manipulating Scripture for their own ends, not always, it would seem, very justly, but the same charge is a common one against all heretical bodies in early days. As to the Canon, he would seem to have no very definite rule. He admits Tobit as prophetic, Judith as canonical, nor does he distinguish between canonical and deuterocanonical, while the sapiential books are all attributed to Solomon. He quotes Baruch as Jeremiah, and refers to the History of Susanna, Bel and the Dragon, and other apocryphal works as "Scripture." Ezra, he says, re-established holy Scripture by memory, and he quotes the fourth book of Esdras.

IV. Life of St. Ambrose.

St. Ambrose, Bishop of Milan, one of the four Latin doctors of the Church, was descended from a Roman family of some distinction, some time Christian, and counting martyrs as well as state officials amongst its members.

His father, likewise named Ambrosius, was prefect of the Gauls, an office the jurisdiction of which extended over Spain, Britain, Cis- and Trans-Alpine Gaul. His chief official residence was Trèves, where probably St. Ambrose was born, as seems most likely, a.d. 340.

After his father's death, his mother and his elder brother, Satyrus, went with St. Ambrose to Rome, not earlier than 353, where his elder sister, Marcellina, received the veil at Christmas from Pope Liberius, the exact year being uncertain.

Here the future bishop devoted himself to legal studies, in which he met with great success. His skill in law and general reputation soon led to his advancement, and about a.d. 370 he was appointed by the Praetorian Prefect Probus governor of Liguria and Aemilia, with the rank of consular. On this occasion Probus is said to have closed an address to St. Ambrose with the words, "Go and act, not as a judge, but as a bishop." This advice was so well followed by Ambrose, that owing to his equity and kindness the people came to look up to him rather as a father than as a judge.

After some few years Auxentius, the intended Arian Bishop of Milan, died, a.d. 374, and it is said that during the discussion as to the appointment of his successor a child cried out in the assembly, "Ambrose Bishop," and, although he was but a catechumen and so canonically unqualified, the multitude immediately elected him by acclamation.

St. Ambrose did all in his power, even, if we accept the statements if his biographer Paulinus, probably a clerk of Milan, resorting to some questionable expedients, to escape from the dignity laid upon him, but when his election was ratified by the Emperor Valentinian, he recognized his appointment as being the will of God, and insisted on being baptized by a Catholic priest. Eight days later, December 7, a.d. 374, he was consecrated Bishop.

The first care of the new bishop was at once to divest himself of his worldly property, giving his silver and gold to the poor and the Church, and committing the management of his estates, except a life interest for his sister, to his brother Satyrus, who gave up his own office to come to his assistance, and enable him to devote himself wholly to theological study and his other episcopal duties.

His chief studies were holy Scripture and ecclesiastical writers, especially St. Basil the Great and Didymus of Alexandria, from whom no less a man than St. Jerome accused him of plagiarizing. His natural abilities and thorough knowledge of Greek stood him in good stead, when, as he says himself, he had to learn and to teach at the same time.

The life of St. Ambrose was a pattern of the discharge of episcopal duties. He spent much time daily in study and devotion, besides the more public duties of his office. He preached every Sunday and at certain seasons daily. His labours in preparing catechumens for baptism were blessed with great success, amongst those taught by him being St. Augustine.

But the zeal and courage of the new Bishop were soon tried. The Empress mother Justina was still an Arian, but had little influence during the life of the Emperor Gratian, who was much attached to St. Ambrose. After his murder, however, a.d. 383, his brother Valentinian II., a boy of only twelve years of age, ascended the throne and was naturally much under his mother's influence. Justina led him to support a demand of the Arians for the use of the Portian basilica, situated outside the walls of Milan. This being refused, a second application was made for the large and newer basilica within the city. Ambrose replied, "The Emperor has his palaces, let him leave the churches to the Bishop." Soldiers were sent to secure the delivery of the basilica, but

St. Ambrose with the faithful occupied the building and remained within, singing psalms and hymns till the soldiers retired.

St. Ambrose was no less successful in his zeal against the expiring heathenism of Italy than against Arianism. One of the many remnants till recent times of heathen worship had been the Altar of Victory in the Senate-house at Rome, which was removed under Gratian; the prefect of Rome, Symmachus, himself a heathen but a friend of St. Ambrose, appealed to Valentinan II. that it might be restored, and Ambrose successfully opposed this appeal in two Epistles (17, 18) addressed to the young Emperor. Yet again, when Theodosius assumed the imperial power [a.d. 387], a renewed attempt was made and once more frustrated. Later on, Eugenius the usurper judged it politic to take the heathen's side, the Altar of Victory was once more set up, and the temples stood open as in the days of old. But this triumph lasted only for a brief period. When Theodosius defeated the usurper at Aquileia, in the spring of 394, he also defeated paganism, which sank to rise no more as a public religion, though it long lingered in private amidst indifference, toleration, and at times persecution.

The influence exercised by Ambrose upon the rulers of his day is sufficiently manifested by these facts, but he had the courage to use not only influence, but, when needed, rebuke and Church discipline.

Only a few months after his elevation to the see of Milan, he remonstrated with Valentinian I. concerning the severity of his rule and other abuses, and required amendment. The Emperor's reply did him honour: "Well, if I have offended, prescribe for me the remedies which the law of God requires." Again, on another occasion, in 390, Theodosius had put down a seditious movement in Thessalonica with great severity, causing some 7,000 persons to be slain. St. Ambrose at once, disregarding the possible consequences to himself, wrote him a letter (Ep. 51) on the subject, exhorting him to repentance, and pointing out that he could not permit him to be present at the celebration of the Mysteries, till he had openly testified his sorrow. At another time when the same Emperor had ventured into the sanctuary or chancel of the church, which was the right of the clergy alone, St. Ambrose rebuked him and caused him to retire.

These acts of ecclesiastical discipline were also accompanied by others in which the great Bishop was able in temporal matters to assist the imperial family.

Twice on behalf of the young Emperor Valentinian II. he undertook a mission to Trèves, to see the usurper Maximus, and when Valentinian died, St. Ambrose delivered a striking oration at his funeral, recording his many virtues. Theodosius did not survive his victory over Eugenius for many months. In January of the following year [a.d. 395], he died at Milan, and the funeral oration which St. Ambrose pronounced over him is also extant.

Yet whilst thus devoting much time to weighty affairs of State, the Bishop never neglected the duties of his office. He preached every Sunday, at great festivals, once or more often, every day. He celebrated the Holy Mysteries daily. His life was marked by perfect purity, sympathy, energy, and devotion. He was always ready to help those requiring assistance, and so when Augustine came to Milan to teach rhetoric, a.d. 384, he was kindly received and fascinated. Probably he owed his conversion even more to the life and character than to the teaching of St. Ambrose.

On subject St. Ambrose never tired of recommending was Virginity; and such was the power of his exhortations that mothers used to forbid their daughters to attend his sermons and addresses.

The indefatigable zeal of the great Bishop further exhibited itself in the number of his writings. Many of them consist of addresses subsequently worked up into treatises, and are on all subjects, dogmatic, controversial, exegetical, and ascetic. There remain also a large number of valuable letters, and some hymns, probably from four to twelve of those ascribed to him being genuine, and in use to the present day.

But besides his writings and his resistance to the attacks of Arianism, heathenism, or the secular power, St. Ambrose devoted himself to actively defending the cause of the Church and

8

of orthodoxy wherever he had the opportunity. Although the death of Satyrus, a.d. 379, must have greatly added to the troubles of St. Ambrose, he was as watchful as ever against all possibilities of heretical aggression. To his care and opposition to the party of the Empress Justina it was owing that the city of Sirmium was preserved in a.d. 381 from receiving an Arian bishop. And in the same year, when the Arians, hoping for large support from the East, had almost persuaded the Emperor to summon a general council at Aquileia, St. Ambrose prevailed upon him to summon only the neighbouring bishops, and what might have been a serious evil was avoided.

In such ways the holy man, embracing in his far-seeing care the interests of religion far and wide, spent his days in unceasing labour till his health failed in the year 397, when, as is related by Paulinus, Count Stilicho, saying that the loss of such a man threatened destruction to Italy, persuaded the nobles of the city to request St. Ambrose that he would pray for longer life. But the Saint replied: "I have not so lived amongst you as to be ashamed of living, and I do not fear to die, for we have a good Lord." As some of the bystanders were discussing in whispers who would be St. Ambrose's successor, and mentioned Simplicianus, he overheard them, and said, "An old man, but good." For the last few hours of his life Ambrose lay with his arms extended in the form of a cross, praying. Honoratus, Bishop of Vercellae, lying in another room, heard himself called thrice, and coming down, offered him the Body of the Lord, after receiving which St. Ambrose breathed his last, on Good Friday night, April 4–5, a.d. 397, and was laid to rest on Easter morning in the Ambrosian basilica at Milan, where he still is reverenced, and in which the Ambrosian liturgy and rites, differing considerably from the Roman use of the rest of the churches of Italy, continue to this day, though doubtless with many modifications subsequent to the time of St. Ambrose.

V. Writings of St. Ambrose.

The extant writings of St. Ambrose may be divided under six heads. I. Dogmatic; II. Exegetic; III. Moral; IV. Sermons; V. Letters; VI. A few Hymns.

I. Dogmatic and Controversial Works.

1. *De Fide.* The chief of these are the Five Books on the Faith, of which the two first were written in compliance with a request of the Emperor Gratian, a.d. 378. Books III.-V. were written in 379 or 380, and seem to have been worked up from addresses delivered to the people [V. prol. 9, 11; III. 143; IV. 119]. This treatise vindicates the Divinity of Christ from the attacks of the Arians, and has always enjoyed the highest reputation, being quoted and referred to again and again.

2. *De Spiritu Sancto.* The three books on the Holy Spirit may be considered as a continuation of the above treatise, and were also addressed to Gratian in compliance with his request, a.d. 381. In this treatise St. Ambrose shows that the Holy Spirit is God, and of one nature and substance with the Father and the Son. He makes use of the Greek writers, SS. Didymus, Basil the Great, and Athanasius, and was on this ground attacked by St. Jerome. See Rufinus, *Apol. adv. Hieron.* II. 23–25.

3. *De Incarnationis Dominicae Sacramento.* The book on the Mystery of the Lord's Incarnation owed its origin to a challenge to dispute publicly given to St. Ambrose by two Arian chamberlains of Gratian. On the day appointed they were, as Paulinus relates in his life of St. Ambrose, thrown out of the chariot which was conveying them and killed. On the next day, that the people might not be disappointed, this discourse was delivered, but the reference made to the absence of the challengers hardly suits the story of Paulinus. The treatise is a very valuable argument in defence of our Lord's Divinity and Eternity, and that He is perfect God and perfect Man. In rewriting the address the Bishop added a refutation of the argument that the Begotten and the Unbegotten could not be of one nature and substance. The treatise may be considered as a supplement to that concerning the Faith.

4. *De Mysteriis.* A valuable treatise on the Mysteries, under which title St. Ambrose includes Baptism, with its complement, Confirmation, and the Eucharist. It is somewhat similar to the *Catecheses Mystagogicae* of St. Cyril of Jerusalem, expounding the doctrine and ceremonies of these sacraments. On doctrinal grounds the authenticity of the work has been impugned by some modern writers, but there is no sufficient foundation for their arguments, as the teaching may be paralleled in many other passages of St. Ambrose. The date is not certain, but may be about a.d. 387.

5. *Libri duo de paenitentia.* These books on Penitence were written about a.d. 384, against the Novatians. In the first book the writer proves that the power of forgiving sins was left by Christ to His Church. In the second book, insisting on the necessity of repentance and confession, he also refutes the Novatian interpretations of Heb. vi. 4–6 and St. Matt. xii. 31–32. This treatise has also underservedly been questioned on doctrinal grounds by some moderns.

These treatises are all translated in this volume.

II. Exegetical Works.

St. Ambrose was in the habit of explaining various books of holy Scripture in courses of lectures, which he subsequently worked up, often at the request of friends, into treatises in the shape in which they have come down to us. Of the class we have:

1. *Hexaëmeron.* This treatise, expounding the literal and moral sense of the work of the six days of creation [Gen. i. 1–26], consists of nine addresses to the people of Milan, delivered in the last week of Lent, probably a.d. 389, and is now divided into six books. The writer has studied Origen, but followed rather the teaching of St. Hippolytus and Basil the Great, though he expresses himself often quite in a different sense.

2. *De Paradiso.* This is the earliest or one of the earliest of the extant writings of St. Ambrose, though the exact date is uncertain. In it he discusses what and where Paradise was, and the question of the life of our first parents there, the temptation, fall and its results, and answers certain cavils of the Gnostics and Manichees. He also enters into an allegorical exposition comparing Paradise with the human soul.

3. *De Cain et Abel.* The treatise is now divided into two books, but the division is too inartistic to have been made by the writer. As to the date, it was later than the last treatise, but probably not many months. The interpretations are very mystical, and touch upon moral and dogmatic questions.

4. *De Noe et Arca.* This treatise has reached us in a mutilated condition. It was written probably before the *De Officiis* and *De Abraham,* but after the works on Paradise and Cain and Abel, though the exact date cannot be determined. The exposition is literal and allegorical.

5. *De Patriarchis.* Seven books preached and written at various dates about 387 or 388. The same kind of interpretation is followed in these as in the former treatises.

6. *De fuga saeculi.* Written probably about a.d. 389–390. An instructive treatise setting forth the desirability of avoiding the dangers of the world, and for those who must live in the world, showing how to pass through them most safely.

7. *De Elia et jejunio.* A treatise composed from addresses delivered during Lent, certainly after a.d. 386, possibly 389.

8. *De Tobia.* A work quoted by St. Augustine (*C. Jul. Pelag.* I. 3, 10), consisting of sermons on the story of Tobias, and chiefly directed against the practice of usury.

9. *De Nabuthe Jezraelita.* One or two sermons against avarice, probably written about a.d. 395.

10. *Libri iv. de interpellatione Job et David.* The first and third books have Job, the second and fourth David, for their subject, and formed a course of sermons the date of which is uncertain.

11. *Apologia prophetae David ad Theodosium Augustum.* A number of addresses delivered, it would seem, about a.d. 384, quoted also by St. Augustine.

12. *Enarrationes in* xii. *Psalmos Davidicos.* Commentaries on Psalms 1, 35–40, 43, 45, 47, 48, 61 (according to St. Ambrose's numbering). These seem to have been partly preached, partly dictated at various dates, and much in them is borrowed from St. Basil.

13. *Expositio Psalmi* cxviii. This treatise is one of the most carefully worked out of all the writings of St. Ambrose and consists of twenty-two addresses to the faithful, each address comprising one division of the Psalm. From various allusions, it would seem that the completed work dates from about a.d. 388.

14. *Expositio Evangelii secundum Lucam.* The ten books of this commentary consist likewise of sermons in which St. Ambrose explained the Gospel during a period of one or two years, in 386 and 387.

III. Ethical Writings.

Among the ethical or moral writings of St. Ambrose, the first place is deservedly assigned to:

1. *De Officiis Ministrorum.* In three books, which are translated in this series.

2. *De Virginibus.* Three books concerning Virgins, addressed to his sister Marcellina in the year 377, probably, like most of the treatises of St. Ambrose, revised from addresses, the first of which was delivered on the festival of St. Agnes, January 21. This would seem to have been perhaps the very earliest of the writings of St. Ambrose, judging from the opening chapter. The treatise is referred to by St. Jerome, St. Augustine, Cassian, and others.

3. *De Viduis.* This shorter work, concerning Widows, was probably written not very long after the last mentioned treatise.

4. *De Virginitate.* A treatise on Virginity, the date of which cannot certainly be fixed, but the writing *De Viduis* is referred to in chapter 9.

5. *De Institutione Virginis.* A treatise on the training and discipline of a Virgin, addressed to Eusebius, either bishop or a noble of Bologna, after St. Ambrose had admitted his niece to the rank of Virgins, probably about a.d. 391 or 392.

6. *Exhortatio Virginitatis.* A commendation of Virginity preached on the occasion of the consecration of a church at Florence by St. Ambrose, a.d. 393 or 394.

IV. Sermons and Addresses.

1. *Contra Auxentium.* A sermon against Auxentius, concerning giving up the basilicas to the Arians, usually inserted between the twenty-first and twenty-second of the letters of St. Ambrose.

2. *De Excessu fratris Satyri.* The two addresses on the occasion of the death of St. Ambrose's brother Satyrus, translated in this volume.

3. *De obitu Valentiniani Consolatio.* The Emperor Valentinian having been murdered by Arbogastes, Count of Vienne, his body was brought to Milan, and remained two months unburied. At last Theodosius sent the necessary rescript, and at the funeral solemnities St. Ambrose delivered the address entitled the "Consolation."

4. *De obitu Theodosii oratio.* A discourse delivered forty days after the death of the Emperor Theodosius before the Emperor Honorius at Milan.

V. The Letters of St. Ambrose.

The Benedictine Editors of St. Ambrose have divided his Epistles into two classes: the first comprising those to which they thought it possible to assign dates; the second those which afford no data for a conclusion. Probably in many cases the exact year is not so certain as the editors have made it appear, but they seem arranged in a fairly probable consecutive order.

The Letters.

1. To the Emperor Gratian, in reply to his request for a treatise on the Faith. Written a.d. 379, before August, as Gratian came to Milan in that month.

2. To Constantius, a bishop, on episcopal duties, and commending to him the care of the vacant see of Forum Cornelii, or Imola. Probably written about a.d. 379.

3, 4. To Cornelius, Bishop of Comum, the first a friendly letter, the second containing also an invitation to the consecration of a church by Bassianus, Bishop of Laus Pompeia, now Lodi Vecchio, near Milan. Written probably after a.d. 381.

5, 6. To Syagrius, Bishop of Verona. On a charge falsely brought against the Virgin Indicia. They may have been written a.d. 380.

7, 8. To Justus, perhaps Bishop of Lyons. On holy Scripture. If the conjecture that Justus was the Bishop of Lyons is correct, written about 380 or 381.

9–12. Letters concerning the Council of Aquileia, held a.d. 381, to the bishops of the provinces of Gaul, to the Emperor Gratian and his colleagues. Two men, Palladius and Secundianus, held Arian opinions, and the former appears to have asked Gratian to convoke a General Council, pleading that he was unjustly condemned. St. Ambrose pointed out to the Emperor that such a question as the orthodoxy of two persons could be settled by a local council in Italy; and as a result, by the Emperor's mandate, a council of Italian bishops met at Aquileia, other bishops having also permission to attend. Palladius and Secundianus were condemned, and these letters have reference to the proceedings at the council. They were probably written by St. Ambrose in the name of the council, a.d. 381.

13, 14. Two letters addressed to Theodosius, the former relating the decisions of a council, probably held at Milan, on the Meletian schism at Antioch, and the latter further expressing the desire of the bishops for a council on this subject, and also on the opinions of Apollinaris. Written a.d. 381 or 382.

15. To the Bishops of Macedonia, in reply to their notification of the death of Acholius, Bishop of Thessalonica, who baptized Theodosius, and had met St. Ambrose at a council in Rome. Written a.d. 383.

16. To Anicius, on his election to succeed Acholius, whose labours and life are commended by St. Ambrose. Written a.d. 383.

17, 18. On the occasion of the attempt of Symmachus and the heathen senators to procure the restitution of the image and Altar of Victory in the Roman Senate-house, frustrated by St. Ambrose, a.d. 384.

19. To Vigilius, Bishop of Trent, subsequently martyred, written probably about a.d. 385.

20. To his sister, Marcellina, giving an account of the frustrated attempts of the Arian and imperial party to gain possession of a basilica at Milan, a.d. 385,

21. To the Emperor Valentinian II., declining the challenge to dispute with the Arian Auxentius before lay judges. a.d. 386.

22. To his sister Marcellina, giving an account of the finding of the bodies of SS. Gervasius and Protasius, and of the consequent miracles. Written a.d. 386.

23. To the bishops of the province of Aemilia, on the proper date for the observance of Easter, in 387. Written a.d. 386.

24. To Valentinian II., with an account of St. Ambrose's second mission to Maximus on his behalf. Written probably a.d. 387.

25, 26. Inscribed the former to Studius, the second to Irenaeus, but from internal evidence these appear to be the same person. It deals with the question, how far a judge being a Christian may lawfully sentence any one to death. Written probably about a.d. 388.

27–33. Addressed to Irenaeus, on various questions. Written about a.d. 387.

34–36. To Orontianus, a cleric, on the soul and other questions. Written after 386.

37, 38. To Simplicianus, who became the successor of St. Ambrose in the see of Milan, setting forth that holiness is perfect freedom.

39. To Faustinus, on the occasion of the death of a sister. Written probably after a.d. 387.

40. To Theodosius. The Jewish synagogue at Callinicum in Mesopotamia having been destroyed by the Christians, and a meeting-house of the Valentinian heretics also burnt by the

Catholics, Theodosius ordered that the bishop should rebuild the synagogue at his own expense, and the monks be punished. St. Ambrose remonstrates with the Emperor, and it would seem, from the following letter to his sister, at first unsuccessfully.

41. To his sister Marcellina, relating the circumstances alluded to above, and telling her of his sermon before the Emperor, and of his subsequent refusal to celebrate the Eucharist, until the Emperor had promised to rescind the order. The date of the two letters is a.d. 388.

42. Reply of St. Ambrose and a synod at Milan to the notification of Pope Siricius announcing the sentence of excommunication passed upon Jovinian and his followers.

43, 44. To Horontianus, in reply to his inquiries on some points connected with the Creation.

45. To Sabinus, Bishop of Placentia, in answer to questions concerning Paradise.

46. To the same, on the subject of an Apollinarian heretic.

47–49. To the same, with books and on private matters.

50. To Chromatius, probably Bishop of Aquileia, explaining how evil men may be used to utter true prophecies.

51. To Theodosius, after the massacre at Thessalonica. Written a.d. 390.

52. A private letter to Titianus.

53. To Theodosius, to express the sorrow of St. Ambrose at the death of Valentinian II., slain by Arbogastes.

54, 55. To Eusebius, not, it would seem, the Bishop of Bologna who was present at the Council of Aquileia, but rather a lay friend to whom St. Ambrose wrote his treatise on the training of a virgin. Probably written a.d. 392 or 393.

56. To Theophilus. The troubles of the church of Antioch through the Meletian schism might have terminated on the death of Paulinus, had he not on his deathbed consecrated Evagrius as his successor in violation of the canons. Theodosius, being pressed by the Western bishops, now summoned a council at Capua, commanding Flavian to attend, which command he however disobeyed. The council referred the matter to Theophilus of Alexandria and the bishops of Egypt. But Flavian, as Theophilus had informed St. Ambrose, refused to submit to their decision. This is the reply of St. Ambrose advising Theophilus to summon Flavian once more, and communicate the result to Pope Siricius. The letter must have been written quite at the end of a.d. 391, or the beginning of 392.

57. To Eugenius the usurper, to avoid whom St. Ambrose had left Milan, and to whose letters he had sent no reply. Written a.d. 393.

58. To Sabinus, Bishop, on the resolution of Paulinus and Therasia to forsake the world. Written probably a.d. 393.

59. To Severus, Bishop probably of Naples, telling him of James, a Persian priest, who had resolved to retire from the world into Campania, and contrasting this with his own troubles, owing to the invasion of Eugenius, a.d. 393 or 394.

60. To Paternus, against a proposed incestuous marriage.

61. To Theodosius, after his victory over Eugenius. Written a.d. 394.

62. To the same, urging him to be merciful to the followers of Eugenius. Written in the same year.

63. To the Church at Vercellae.

The second division of the letters, being those which cannot be dated, begins here in the Benediction Edition.

64. To Irenaeus, on the Manna.

65. To Simplicianus, on Exodus xxiv. 6.

66. To Romulus, on Aaron's making the calf of the golden earrings.

67. To Simplicianus, showing how Moses yielded to Aaron in matters relating to his priestly character.

68. To Romulus. Explanation of the text Deut. xxviii. 23.

69. To Irenaeus, answering a question as to the prohibition under severe penalties in the Mosaic law, of disguising the sex by dress.

70, 71. To Horontianus, on part of the prophecy of Micah.

72. To Constantius, on the rite of circumcision.

73–76. To Irenaeus. Why the law was given, and the scope of the Epistle to the Ephesians. The letter numbered 75 is plainly a continuation of 74, although inscribed to Clementianus, a difficulty similar to that about letter 26.

77, 78. To Horontianus, contrasting the condition of the Jew and the Christian.

79, 80. To Bellicius, on recovery from sickness, and on the miracle of healing the man blind from his birth.

81. To certain clergy, against despondency.

82. To Marcellus, concerning a lawsuit.

83. To Sisinnius, commending him for forgiving his son, who had married without consulting him.

84. To Cynegius.

85, 86. To Siricius, with thanks for letters, and commending Priscus.

87. To Segatius [more probably Phaebadius], Bishop of Agens, and Delphinus, Bishop of Bordeaux. Polybius, mentioned in the letter, was proconsul of Africa between the years 380 and 390.

88. To Atticus. Commendation of Priscus.

89. To Alypius. Acknowledgment of letters.

90. To Antonius. On the mutual affection of himself and St. Ambrose.

91. To Candidianus, probably a fellow-bishop. A letter of affection.

VI. Hymns.

During the persecutions stirred up by the Arian Empress Justina, a.d. 385–6, referred to in his 20th letter, St. Ambrose and the faithful spent the whole night in the basilica, and the holy Bishop employed the people in singing psalms and hymns. A large number of hymns have been attributed to St. Ambrose, the number having by some editors been brought down to twelve, of which, however, only four are certainly his compositions.

1. *Eterne rerum Conditor,* referred to by St. Augustine, *Retract.* I. 21, and by St. Ambrose himself, *Hexaëm.* V. 24, 88. The hymn is still in use at Lauds on Sunday.

2. *Deus Creator omnium.* Quoted by St. Augustine, *Conf.* IX. 12, 32.

3. *Jam surigil hora tertia.* Also quoted by St. Augustine.

4. *Veni Redemptor gentium.* A Christmas hymn, quoted by Pope Celestine, a.d. 430, in a sermon against the Nestorians, preached before a synod at Rome, and also by other writers.

Of other hymns one commencing, *Illuminans Altissimus,* is quoted by Cassiodorus as an Epiphany hymn by St. Ambrose, and the same author refers to another, *Orabo mente Dominum.* The Benedictine Editors admit six other hymns, but they are supported by no authority anterior to Venerable Bede.

VII. Doubtful and Spurious Works.

This volume cannot of course comprehend the arguments and discussions necessary for any critical examination of certain works whether doubtful or certainly spurious, but their names may be given and certain conclusions stated.

1. Five books on the Jewish war, ordinarily attributed to Hegisippus. This is a translation into Latin and a condensation in part of the well-known work of Josephus. Ihm, a very thorough student of St. Ambrose, seems quite disposed to maintain after careful examination that this is the work of St. Ambrose.

2. *De lege Dei.* This treatise, a sort of compendium of Roman law in the fourth century, and comparison of it with the law of Moses, is ascribed, in a translation published by Mai, to St.

Ambrose, who is said to have undertaken the work at the command of Theodosius. On the authenticity, however, of this treatise there probably will always remain much doubt.

3. Among works more or less doubtful are *De Sacramentis*, admitted by the Benedictines, but rejected, and apparently on sufficient grounds, by Ihm.

4. *Apologia David altera.* Suspected by Erasmus, Tillemont, and Ihm.

5. *De lapsu Virginis consecratae.* A severe castigation of a fallen virgin and of her seducer. The treatise seems to have been written by a certain Bishop of Nicetas, and a ms. at speaks of it as having been revised by St. Ambrose.

6. There are further three brief addresses ascribed by some persons to St. Ambrose, touching on the question of selling all and giving to the poor. Some of the matter is like St. Ambrose, but the same cannot be said of the diction and style.

VIII. Lost Writings of St. Ambrose.

1. *Expositio Isaiae prophetiae,* referred to by St. Augustine as well as by St. Ambrose himself.

2. *Liber de Sacramento regenerationis sive de philosophia,* referred to by St. Augustine.

3. *Libellus ad Pansophium puerum,* written a.d. 393–4, according to Paulinus in his life of St. Ambrose.

4. *Libri quatuor regnorum,* referred to in the introduction to the work on the Jewish war.

5. *Expositio fidei,* quoted by Theodoret and others as a writing of St. Ambrose.

On the Duties of the Clergy. Introduction.

St. Ambrose, esteeming very highly the dignity of the ministerial office, was most desirous that the clergy of his diocese should live worthily of their high vocation, and be good and profitable examples to the people. Consequently he undertook the following treatise, setting forth the duties of the clergy, and taking as a model the treatise of Cicero, *De Officiis*.

The writer says that his object is to impress upon those whom he has ordained the lessons which he had previously taught them. Like Cicero, he treats of that which is right, becoming, or honourable [*decorum*], and what is expedient [*utile*]; but with reference not to this life but to that which is to come, teaching in the first book that which is becoming or honourable; in the second, what is expedient; and in the third, considering both in conjunction.

In the first book he divides duties into "ordinary," or the way of the commandments, binding upon all alike; and "perfect," which consist in following the counsels. After treating then of some elementary duties, such as those towards parents and elders, he touches upon the two principles which lead the mind, reason and appetite, and shows that what is becoming consists in thinking of good and right things, and in the subjection of the appetite to reason, and supplies certain rules and examples, ending with a discussion on the four Cardinal Virtues, Prudence, Justice, Fortitude, and Temperance.

In the second book, passing from what is becoming to what is expedient, he points out that we can only measure what is really expedient by reference to eternal life, in contradiction to the errors of heathen philosophers, and shows that what is expedient consists in the knowledge of God and in good living. Incidentally he shows that what is becoming is really that which is expedient, and ends the book with several chapters of practical considerations.

In the third book he treats of duties of perfection, and lays down as a rule that in everything we must inquire what is expedient, not for individuals, but for many or for all. Nothing is to be striven after which is not becoming; to this everything must give place, not only expediency but even friendship and life itself. By many examples he then proves how holy men have sought after what was becoming, and have thereby secured what was expedient.

The object of St. Ambrose in basing his treatise on the lines of that of Cicero would seem to have been the confutation of some of the false principles of heathenism, and to show how much higher Christian morality is than that of the Gentiles. The treatise was probably composed about a.d. 391.

THREE BOOKS ON THE DUTIES OF THE CLERGY.
BOOK I.

Chapter I.

A Bishop's special office is to teach; St. Ambrose himself, however, has to learn in order that he may teach; or rather has to teach what he has not learnt; at any rate learning and teaching with himself must go on together.

1. I Think I shall not seem to be taking too much on myself, if, in the midst of my children, I yield to my desire to teach, seeing that the master of humility himself has said: "Come, ye children, hearken unto me: I will teach you the fear of the Lord." Wherein one may observe both the humility and the grace of his reverence for God. For in saying "the fear of the Lord," which seems to be common to all, he has described the chief mark of reverence for God. As, however, fear itself is the beginning of wisdom and the source of blessedness—for they that fear the Lord are blessed —he has plainly marked himself out as the teacher for instruction in wisdom, and the guide to the attainment of blessedness.

2. We therefore, being anxious to imitate his reverence for God, and not without justification in dispensing grace, deliver to you as to children those things which the Spirit of Wisdom has imparted to him, and which have been made clear to us through him, and learnt by sight and by example. For we can no longer now escape from the duty of teaching which the needs of the priesthood have laid upon us, though we tried to avoid it: "For God gave some, apostles; and some, prophets; and some, evangelists; and some, pastors and teachers."

3. I do not therefore claim for myself the glory of the apostles (for who can do this save those whom the Son of God Himself has chosen?); nor the grace of the prophets, nor the virtue of the evangelists, nor the cautious care of the pastors. I only desire to attain to that care and diligence in the sacred writings, which the Apostle has placed last amongst the duties of the saints; and this very thing I desire, so that, in the endeavour to teach, I may be able to learn. For one is the true Master, Who alone has not learnt, what He taught all; but men learn before they teach, and receive from Him what they may hand on to others.

4. But not even this was the case with me. For I was carried off from the judgment seat, and the garb [*infulis*] of office, to enter on the priesthood, and began to teach you, what I myself had not yet learnt. So it happened that I began to teach before I began to learn. Therefore I must learn and teach at the same time, since I had no leisure to learn before.

Chapter II.

Manifold dangers are incurred by speaking; the remedy for which Scripture shows to consist in silence.

5. Now what ought we to learn before everything else, but to be silent, that we may be able to speak? lest my voice should condemn me, before that of another acquit me; for it is written: "By thy words thou shalt be condemned." What need is there, then, that thou shouldest hasten to undergo the danger of condemnation by speaking, when thou canst be more safe by keeping silent? How many have I seen to fall into sin by speaking, but scarcely one by keeping silent; and so it is more difficult to know how to keep silent than how to speak. I know that most persons speak because they do not know how to keep silent. It is seldom that any one is silent even when speaking profits him nothing. He is wise, then, who knows how to keep silent. Lastly, the Wisdom of God said: "The Lord hath given to me the tongue of learning, that I should know when it is good to speak." Justly, then, is he wise who has received of the Lord to know when he ought to speak. Wherefore the Scripture says well: "A wise man will keep silence until there is opportunity."

6. Therefore the saints of the Lord loved to keep silence, because they knew that a man's voice is often the utterance of sin, and a man's speech is the beginning of human error. Lastly, the Saint of the Lord said: "I said, I will take heed to my ways, that I offend not in my tongue." For he knew and had read that it was a mark of the divine protection for a man to be hid from the scourge of his own tongue, and the witness of his own conscience. We are chastised by the

silent reproaches of our thoughts, and by the judgment of conscience. We are chastised also by the lash of our own voice, when we say things whereby our soul is mortally injured, and our mind is sorely wounded. But who is there that has his heart clean from the impurities of sin, and does not offend in his tongue? And so, as he saw there was no one who could keep his mouth free from evil speaking, he laid upon himself the law of innocency by a rule of silence, with a view to avoiding by silence that fault which he could with difficulty escape in speaking.

7. Let us hearken, then, to the master of precaution: "I said, I will take heed to my ways;" that is, "I said to myself: in the silent biddings of my thoughts, I have enjoined upon myself, that I should take heed to my ways." Some ways there are which we ought to follow; others as to which we ought to take heed. We must follow the ways of the Lord, and take heed to our own ways, lest they lead us into sin. One can take heed if one is not hasty in speaking. The law says: "Hear, O Israel, the Lord thy God." It said not: "Speak," but "Hear." Eve fell because she said to the man what she had not heard from the Lord her God. The first word from God says to thee: Hear! If thou hearest, take heed to thy ways; and if thou hast fallen, quickly amend thy way. For: "Wherein does a young man amend his way; except in taking heed to the word of the Lord?" Be silent therefore first of all, and hearken, that thou fail not in thy tongue.

8. It is a great evil that a man should be condemned by his own mouth. Truly, if each one shall give account for an idle word, how much more for words of impurity and shame? For words uttered hastily are far worse than idle words. If, therefore, an account is demanded for an idle word, how much more will punishment be exacted for impious language?

Chapter III.

Silence should not remain unbroken, nor should it arise from idleness. How heart and mouth must be guarded against inordinate affections.

9. What then? Ought we to be dumb? Certainly not. For: "there is a time to keep silence and a time to speak." If, then, we are to give account for an idle word, let us take care that we do not have to give it also for an idle silence. For there is also an active silence, such as Susanna's was, who did more by keeping silence than if she had spoken. For in keeping silence before men she spoke to God, and found no greater proof of her chastity than silence. Her conscience spoke where no word was heard, and she sought no judgment for herself at the hands of men, for she had the witness of the Lord. She therefore desired to be acquitted by Him, Who she knew could not be deceived in any way. Yea, the Lord Himself in the Gospel worked out in silence the salvation of men. David rightly therefore enjoined on himself not constant silence, but watchfulness.

10. Let us then guard our hearts, let us guard our mouths. Both have been written about. In this place we are bidden to take heed to our mouth; in another place thou art told: "Keep thy heart with all diligence." If David took heed, wilt thou not take heed? If Isaiah had unclean lips—who said: "Woe is me, for I am undone, for I am a man, and have unclean lips" —if a prophet of the Lord had unclean lips, how shall we have them clean?

11. But for whom was it written, unless it was for each one of us: "Hedge thy possession about with thorns, and bind up thy silver and gold, and make a door and a bar for thy mouth, and a yoke and a balance for thy words"? Thy possession is thy mind, thy gold thy heart, thy silver thy speech: "The words of the Lord are pure words, as silver tried in the fire." A good mind is also a good possession. And, further, a pure inner life is a valuable possession. Hedge in, then, this possession of thine, enclose it with thought, guard it with thorns, that is, with pious care, lest the fierce passions of the flesh should rush upon it and lead it captive, lest strong emotions should assault it, and, overstepping their bounds, carry off its vintage. Guard thy inner self. Do not neglect or contemn it as though it were worthless, for it is a valuable possession; truly valuable indeed, for its fruit is not perishable and only for a time, but is lasting and of use for eternal salvation. Cultivate, therefore, thy possession, and let it be thy tilling ground.

12. Bind up thy words that they run not riot, and grow wanton, and gather up sins for themselves in too much talking. Let them be rather confined, and held back within their own banks. An overflowing river quickly gathers mud. Bind up also thy meaning; let it not be left slack and unchecked, lest it be said of thee: "There is no healing balsam, nor oil, nor bandage to apply." Sobriety of mind has its reins, whereby it is directed and guided.

13. Let there be a door to thy mouth, that it may be shut when need arises, and let it be carefully barred, that none may rouse thy voice to anger, and thou pay back abuse with abuse. Thou hast heard it read to-day: "Be ye angry and sin not." Therefore although we are angry (this arising from the motions of our nature, not of our will), let us not utter with our mouth one evil word, lest we fall into sin; but let there be a yoke and a balance to thy words, that is, humility and moderation, that thy tongue may be subject to thy mind. Let it be held in check with a tight rein; let it have its own means of restraint, whereby it can be recalled to moderation; let it utter words tried by the scales of justice, that there may be seriousness in our meaning, weight in our speech, and due measure in our words.

Chapter IV.

The same care must be taken that our speech proceed not from evil passions, but from good motives; for here it is that the devil is especially on the watch to catch us.

14. If any one takes heed to this, he will be mild, gentle, modest. For in guarding his mouth, and restraining his tongue, and in not speaking before examining, pondering, and weighing his words—as to whether this should be said, that should be answered, or whether it be a suitable time for this remark—he certainly is practising modesty, gentleness, patience. So he will not burst out into speech through displeasure or anger, nor give sign of any passion in his words, nor proclaim that the flames of lust are burning in his language, or that the incentives of wrath are present in what he says. Let him act thus for fear that his words, which ought to grace his inner life, should at the last plainly show and prove that there is some vice in his morals.

15. For then especially does the enemy lay his plans, when he sees passions engendered in us; then he supplies tinder; then he lays snares. Wherefore the prophet says not without cause, as we heard read to-day: "Surely He hath delivered me from the snare of the hunter and from the hard word." Symmachus said this means "the word of provocation;" others "the word that brings disquiet." The snare of the enemy is our speech—but that itself is also just as much an enemy to us. Too often we say something that our foe takes hold of, and whereby he wounds us as though by our own sword. How far better it is to perish by the sword of others than by our own!

16. Accordingly the enemy tests our arms and clashes together his weapons. If he sees that I am disturbed, he implants the points of his darts, so as to raise a crop of quarrels. If I utter an unseemly word, he sets his snare. Then he puts before me the opportunity for revenge as a bait, so that in desiring to be revenged, I may put myself in the snare, and draw the death-knot tight for myself. If any one feels this enemy is near, he ought to give greater heed to his mouth, lest he make room for the enemy; but not many see him.

Chapter V.

We must guard also against a visible enemy when he incites us by silence; by the help of which alone we can escape from those greater than ourselves, and maintain that humility which we must display towards all.

17. But we must also guard against him who can be seen, and who provokes us, and spurs us on, and exasperates us, and supplies what will excite us to licentiousness or lust. If, then, any one reviles us, irritates, stirs us up to violence, tries to make us quarrel; let us keep silence, let us not be ashamed to become dumb. For he who irritates us and does us an injury is committing sin, and wishes us to become like himself.

18. Certainly if thou art silent, and hidest thy feelings, he is wont to say: "Why are you silent? Speak if you dare; but you dare not, you are dumb, I have made you speechless." If thou art

silent, he is the more excited. He thinks himself beaten, laughed at, little thought of, and ridiculed. If thou answerest, he thinks he has become the victor, because he has found one like himself. For if thou art silent, men will say: "That man has been abusive, but this one held him in contempt." If thou return the abuse, they will say: "Both have been abusive." Both will be condemned, neither will be acquitted. Therefore it is his object to irritate, so that I may speak and act as he does. But it is the duty of a just man to hide his feelings and say nothing, to preserve the fruit of a good conscience, to trust himself rather to the judgment of good men than to the insolence of a calumniator, and to be satisfied with the stability of his own character. For that is: "To keep silence even from good words;" since one who has a good conscience ought not to be troubled by false words, nor ought he to make more of another's abuse than of the witness of his own heart.

19. So, then, let a man guard also his humility. If, however, he is unwilling to appear too humble, he thinks as follows, and says within himself: "Am I to allow this man to despise me, and say such things to my face against me, as though I could not open my mouth before him? Why should I not also say something whereby I can grieve him? Am I to let him do me wrong, as though I were not a man, and as though I could not avenge myself? Is he to bring charges against me as though I could not bring together worse ones against him?"

20. Whoever speaks like this is not gentle and humble, nor is he without temptation. The tempter stirs him up, and himself puts such thoughts in his heart. Often and often, too, the evil spirit employs another person, and gets him to say such things to him; but do thou set thy foot firm on the rock. Although a slave should abuse, let the just man be silent, and if a weak man utter insults, let him be silent, and if a poor man should make accusations, let him not answer. These are the weapons of the just man, so that he may conquer by giving way, as those skilled in throwing the javelin are wont to conquer by giving way, and in flight to wound their pursuers with severer blows.

Chapter VI.

In this matter we must imitate David's silence and humility, so as not even to seem deserving of harm.

21. What need is there to be troubled when we hear abuse? Why do we not imitate him who says: "I was dumb and humbled myself, and kept silence even from good words"? Or did David only say this, and not act up to it? No, he also acted up to it. For when Shimei the son of Gera reviled him, David was silent; and although he was surrounded with armed men he did not return the abuse, nor sought revenge: nay, even when the son of Zeruiah spoke to him, because he wished to take vengeance on him, David did not permit it. He went on as though dumb, and humbled; he went on in silence; nor was he disturbed, although called a bloody man, for he was conscious of his own gentleness. He therefore was not disturbed by insults, for he had full knowledge of his own good works.

22. He, then, who is quickly roused by wrong makes himself seem deserving of insult, even whilst he wishes to be shown not to deserve it. He who despises wrongs is better off than he who grieves over them. For he who despises them looks down on them, as though he feels them not; but he who grieves over them is tormented, just as though he actually felt them.

Chapter VII.

How admirably Ps. xxxix. [xxxviii.] takes the place of an introduction. Incited thereto by this psalm the saint determines to write on duties. He does this with more reason even than Cicero, who wrote on this subject to his son. How, further, this is so.

23. Not without thought did I make use of the beginning of this psalm, in writing to you, my children. For this psalm which the Prophet David gave to Jeduthun to sing, I urge you to regard, being delighted myself with its depth of meaning and the excellency of its maxims. For we have learnt in those words we have just shortly touched upon, that both patience in keeping silence and the duty of awaiting a fit time for speaking are taught in this psalm, as well as contempt of

riches in the following verses, which things are the chief groundwork of virtues. Whilst, therefore, meditating on this psalm, it has come to my mind to write "on the Duties."

24. Although some philosophers have written on this subject,—Panaetius, for instance, and his son amongst the Greek, Cicero amongst the Latin, writers—I did not think it foreign to my office to write also myself. And as Cicero wrote for the instruction of his son, so I, too, write to teach you, my children. For I love you, whom I have begotten in the Gospel, no less than if you were my own true sons. For nature does not make us love more ardently than grace. We certainly ought to love those who we think will be with us for evermore than those who will be with us in this world only. These often are born unworthy of their race, so as to bring disgrace on their father; but you we chose beforehand, to love. They are loved naturally, of necessity, which is not a sufficiently suitable and constant teacher to implant a lasting love. But ye are loved on the ground of our deliberate choice, whereby a great feeling of affection is combined with the strength of our love: thus one tests what one loves and loves what one has chosen.

Chapter VIII.

The word "Duty" has been often used both by philosophers and in the holy Scriptures; from whence it is derived.

25. Since, therefore, the person concerned is one fit to write on the Duties, let us see whether the subject itself stands on the same ground, and whether this word is suitable only to the schools of the philosophers, or is also to be found in the sacred Scriptures. Beautifully has the Holy Spirit, as it happens, brought before us a passage in reading the Gospel to-day, as though He would urge us to write; whereby we are confirmed in our view, that the word *officium*, "duty," may also be used with us. For when Zacharias the priest was struck dumb in the temple, and could not speak, it is said: "And it came to pass that as soon as the days of his duty [*officii*] were accomplished, he departed to his own house." We read, therefore, that the word *officium*, "duty," can be used by us.

26. And this is not inconsistent with reason, since we consider that the word *officium* (duty) is derived from *efficere* (to effect), and is formed with the change of one letter for the sake of euphony; or at any rate that you should do those things which injure [*officiant*] no one, but benefit all.

Chapter IX.

A duty is to be chosen from what is virtuous, and from what is useful, and also from the comparison of the two, one with the other; but nothing is recognized by Christians as virtuous or useful which is not helpful to the future life. This treatise on duty, therefore, will not be superfluous.

27. The philosophers considered that duties were derived from what is virtuous and what is useful, and that from these two one should choose the better. Then, they say, it may happen that two virtuous or two useful things will clash together, and the question is, which is the more virtuous, and which the more useful? First, therefore, "duty" is divided into three sections: what is virtuous, what is useful, and what is the better of two. Then, again, these three are divided into five classes; that is, two that are virtuous, two that are useful, and, lastly, the right judgment as to the choice between them. The first they say has to do with the moral dignity and integrity of life; the second with the conveniences of life, with wealth, resources, opportunities; whilst a right judgment must underlie the choice of any of them. This is what the philosophers say.

28. But we measure nothing at all but that which is fitting and virtuous, and that by the rule of things future rather than of things present; and we state nothing to be useful but what will help us to the blessing of eternal life; certainly not that which will help us enjoy merely the present time. Nor do we recognize any advantages in opportunities and in the wealth of earthly goods, but consider them as disadvantages if not put aside, and to be looked on as a burden, when we have them, rather than as a loss when expended.

29. This work of ours, therefore, is not superfluous, seeing that we and they regard duty in quite different ways. They reckon the advantages of this life among the good things, we reckon them among the evil things; for he who receives good things here, as the rich man in the parable, is tormented there; and Lazarus, who endured evil things here, there found comfort. Lastly, those who do not read their writings may read ours if they will—if, that is, they do not require great adornment of language or a skilfully-treated subject, but are satesfied with the simple charm of the subject itself.

Chapter X.

What is seemly is often found in the sacred writings long before it appears in the books of the philosophers. Pythagoras borrowed the law of his silence from David. David's rule, however, is the best, for our first duty is to have due measure in speaking.

30. We are instructed and taught that "what is seemly" is put in our Scriptures in the first place. (In Greek it is called prepon.) For we read: "A Hymn beseems Thee, O God, in Sion." In Greek this is: Soi prepei umno" o Qeo" en Siwn. And the Apostle says: "Speak the things which become sound doctrine." And elsewhere: "For it beseemed Him through Whom are all things and for Whom are all things, in bringing many sons unto glory, to make the Captain of their salvation perfect through sufferings."

31. Was Panaetius or Aristotle, who also wrote on duty," earlier than David? Why, Pythagoras himself, who lived before the time of Socrates, followed the prophet David's steps and gave his disciples a law of silence. He went so far as to restrain his disciples from the use of speech for five years. David, on the other hand, gave his law, not with a view to impair the gift of nature, but to teach us to take heed to the words we utter. Pythagoras again made his rule, that he might teach men to speak by not speaking. But David made his, so that by speaking we might learn the more how to speak. How can there be instruction without exercise, or advance without practice?

32. A man wishing to undergo a warlike training daily exercises himself with his weapons. As though ready for action he rehearses his part in the fight and stands forth just as if the enemy were in position before him. Or, with a view to acquiring skill and strength in throwing the javelin, he either puts his own arms to the proof, or avoids the blows of his foes, and escapes them by his watchful attention. The man that desires to navigate a ship on the sea, or to row, tries first on a river. They who wish to acquire an agreeable style of singing and a beautiful voice begin by bringing out their voice gradually by singing. And they who seek to win the crown of victory by strength of body and in a regular wrestling match, harden their limbs by daily practice in the wrestling school, foster their endurance, and accustom themselves to hard work.

33. Nature herself teaches us this in the case of infants. For they first exercise themselves in the sounds of speech and so learn to speak. Thus these sounds of speech are a kind of practice, and a school for the voice. Let those then who want to learn to take heed in speaking not refuse what is according to nature, but let them use all watchful care; just as those who are on a watch-tower keep on the alert by watching, and not by going to sleep. For everything is made more perfect and strong by exercises proper and suitable to itself.

34. David, therefore, was not always silent, but only for a time; not perpetually nor to all did he refuse to speak; but he used not to answer the enemy that provoked him, the sinner that exasperated him. As he says elsewhere: "As though he were deaf he heard not them that speak vanity and imagine deceit: and as though he were dumb he opened not his mouth to them." Again, in another place, it is said: "Answer not a fool according to his folly, lest thou also be like to him."

35. The first duty then is to have due measure in our speech. In this way a sacrifice of praise is offered up to God; thus a godly fear is shown when the sacred Scriptures are read; thus parents are honoured. I know well that many speak because they know not how to keep silence. But it is not often any one is silent when speaking does not profit him. A wise man, intending to

speak, first carefully considers what he is to say, and to whom he is to say it; also where and at what time. There is therefore such a thing as due measure in keeping silence and also in speaking; there is also such a thing as a due measure in what we do. It is a glorious thing to maintain the right standard of duty.

Chapter XI.
It is proved by the witness of Scripture that all duty is either "ordinary" or "perfect." To which is added a word in praise of mercy, and an exhortation to practise it.

36. Every duty is either "ordinary" or "perfect," a fact which we can also confirm by the authority of the Scriptures. For we read in the Gospel that the Lord said: "If thou wilt enter into life, keep the commandments. He saith: Which? Jesus said to him: Thou shalt do no murder, Thou shalt not commit adultery, Thou shalt not steal, Thou shalt not bear false witness, Honour thy father and thy mother, Thou shalt love thy neighbour as thyself." These are ordinary duties, to which something is wanting.

37. Upon this the young man says to Him: "All these things have I kept from my youth up, what lack I yet? Jesus said unto him: If thou wilt be perfect, go and sell all thy goods and give to the poor, and thou shalt have treasure in heaven; and come and follow Me." And earlier the same is written, where the Lord says that we must love our enemies, and pray for those that falsely accuse and persecute us, and bless those that curse us. This we are bound to do, if we would be perfect as our Father Who is in heaven; Who bids the sun to shed his rays over the evil and the good, and makes the lands of the whole universe fertile with rain and dew without any distinction. This, then, is a perfect duty (the Greeks call it katorqwma), whereby all things are put right which could have any failings in them.

38. Mercy, also, is a good thing, for it makes men perfect, in that it imitates the perfect Father. Nothing graces the Christian soul so much as mercy; mercy as shown chiefly towards the poor, that thou mayest treat them as sharers in common with thee in the produce of nature, which brings forth the fruits of the earth for use to all. Thus thou mayest freely give to a poor man what thou hast, and in this way help him who is thy brother and companion. Thou bestowest silver; he receives life. Thou givest money; he considers it his fortune. Thy coin makes up all his property.

39. Further, he bestows more on thee than thou on him, since he is thy debtor in regard to thy salvation. If thou clothe the naked, thou clothest thyself with righteousness; if thou bring the stranger under thy roof, if thou support the needy, he procures for thee the friendship of the saints and eternal habitations. That is no small recompense. Thou sowest earthly things and receivest heavenly. Dost thou wonder at the judgment of God in the case of holy Job? Wonder rather at his virtue, in that he could say: "I was an eye to the blind, and a foot to the lame. I was a father to the poor. Their shoulders were made warm with the skins of my lambs. The stranger dwelt not at my gates, but my door was open to every one that came." Clearly blessed is he from whose house a poor man has never gone with empty hand. Nor again is any one more blessed than he who is sensible of the needs of the poor, and the hardships of the weak and helpless. In the day of judgment he will receive salvation from the Lord, Whom he will have as his debtor for the mercy he has shown.

Chapter XII.
To prevent any one from being checked in the exercise of mercy, he shows that God cares for human actions; and proves on the evidence of Job that all wicked men are unhappy in the very abundance of their wealth.

40. But many are kept back from the duty of showing active mercy, because they suppose that God does not care about the actions of men, or that He does not know what we do in secret, and what our conscience has in view. Some again think that His judgment in no wise seems to be just; for they see that sinners have abundance of riches, that they enjoy honours,

health, and children; while, on the other hand, the just live in poverty and unhonoured, they are without children, sickly in body, and often in grief.

41. That is no small point. For those three royal friends of Job declared him to be a sinner, because they saw that he, after being rich, became poor; that after having many children, he had lost them all, and that he was now covered with sores and was full of weals, and was a mass of wounds from head to foot. But holy Job made this declaration to them: "If I suffer thus because of my sins, why do the wicked live? They grow old also in riches, their seed is according to their pleasure, their children are before their eyes, their houses are prosperous; but they have no fear; there is no scourge from the Lord on them."

42. A faint-hearted man, seeing this, is disturbed in mind, and turns his attention away from it. Holy Job, when about to speak in the words of such a one, began thus, saying: "Bear with me, I also will speak; then laugh at me. For if I am found fault with, I am found fault with as a man. Bear, therefore, the burden of my words." For I am going to say (he means) what I do not approve; but I shall utter wrong words to refute you. Or, to translate it in another way: "How now? Am I found fault with by a man?" That is: a man cannot find fault with me because I have sinned, although I deserve to be found fault with; for ye do not find fault with me on the ground of an open sin, but estimate what I deserve for my offences by the extent of my misfortunes. Thus the faint-hearted man, seeing that the wicked succeed and prosper, whilst he himself is crushed by misfortune, says to the Lord: "Depart from me, I desire not the knowledge of Thy ways. What good is it that we serve Him, or what use to hasten to Him? In the hands of the wicked are all good things, but He sees not their works."

43. Plato has been greatly praised, because in his book "on the State," he has made the person who undertook the part of objector against justice to ask pardon for his words, of which he himself did not approve; and to say that that character was only assumed for the sake of finding out the truth and to investigate the question at issue. And Cicero so far approved of this, that he also, in his book which he wrote "on the Commonwealth," thought something must be said against that idea.

44. How many years before these did Job live! He was the first to discover this, and to consider what excuses had to be made for this, not for the sake of decking out his eloquence, but for the sake of finding out the truth. At once he made the matter plain, stating that the lamp of the wicked is put out, that their destruction will come; that God, the teacher of wisdom and instruction, is not deceived, but is a judge of the truth. Therefore the blessedness of individuals must not be estimated at the value of their known wealth, but according to the voice of their conscience within them. For this, as a true and uncorrupted judge of punishments and rewards, decides between the deserts of the innocent and the guilty. The innocent man dies in the strength of his own simplicity, in the full possession of his own will; having a soul filled as it were with marrow. But the sinner, though he has abundance in life, and lives in the midst of luxury, and is redolent with sweet scents, ends his life in the bitterness of his soul, and brings his last day to a close, taking with him none of those good things which he once enjoyed—carrying away nothing with him but the price of his own wickedness.

45. In thinking of this, deny if thou canst that a recompense is paid by divine judgment. The former feels happy in his heart, the latter wretched; that man on his own verdict is guiltless, this one a criminal; that man again is happy in leaving the world, this man grieves over it. Who can be pronounced guiltless that is not innocent in the sight of his own conscience? "Tell me," he says, "where is the covering of his tabernacle; his token will not be found." The life of the criminal is as a dream. He has opened his eyes. His repose has departed, his enjoyment has fled. Nay, that very repose of the wicked, which even while they live is only seeming, is now in hell, for alive they go down into hell.

46. Thou seest the enjoyments of the sinner; but question his conscience. Will he not be more foul than any sepulchre? Thou beholdest his joy, thou admirest the bodily health of his children, and the amount of his wealth; but look within at the sores and wounds of his soul, the

sadness of his heart. And what shall I say of his wealth, when thou readest: "For a man's life consisteth not in the abundance of the things which he possesseth"? When thou knowest, that though he seems to thee to be rich, to himself he is poor, and in his own person refutes thy judgment? What also shall I say of the number of his children and of his freedom from pain— when he is full of grief and decides that he will have no heir, and does not wish that those who copy his ways should succeed him? For the sinner really leaves no heir. Thus the wicked man is a punishment to himself, but the upright man is a grace to himself—and to either, whether good or bad, the reward of his deeds is paid in his own person.

Chapter XIII.
The ideas of those philosophers are refuted who deny to God the care of the whole world, or of any of its parts.
47. But let us return to our point, lest we seem to have lost sight of the break we made in answering the ideas of those who, seeing some wicked men, rich, joyous, full of honours, and powerful, whilst many upright men are in want and are weak,—suppose therefore that God either cares nothing about us (which is what the Epicureans say), or that He is ignorant of men's actions as the wicked say—or that, if He knows all things, He is an unjust judge in allowing the good to be in want and the wicked to have abundance. But it did not seem out of place to make a digression to meet an idea of this kind and to contrast it with the feelings of those very persons whom they consider happy—for they think themselves wretched. I suppose they would believe themselves more readily than us.

48. After this digression I consider it an easy matter to refute the rest—above all the declaration of those who think that God has no care whatever for the world. For instance, Aristotle declares that His providence extends only to the moon. But what workman is there who gives no care to his work? Who would forsake and abandon what he believes himself to have produced? If it is derogatory to rule, is it not more so to have created? Though there is no wrong involved in not creating anything, it is surely the height of cruelty not to care for what one has created.

49. But if some deny God to be the Creator, and so count themselves amongst the beasts and irrational creatures, what shall we say of those who condemn themselves to such indignity? They themselves declare that God pervades all things, that all depend upon His power, that His might and majesty penetrate all the elements,—lands, heaven, and seas; yet they think it derogatory to Him to enter into man's spirit, whitch is the noblest thing He has given us, and to be there with the full knowledge of the divine Majesty.

50. But philosophers who are held to be reasonable laugh at the teacher of these ideas as besotted and licentious. But what shall I say of Aristotle's idea? He thinks that God is satisfied with His own narrow bounds, and lives within the prescribed limits of His kingdom. This, however, is also what the poets' tales tell us. For they relate that the world is divided between three gods, so that it has fallen to the lot of one to restrain and rule heaven, to another the sea, and to a third the lower regions. They have also to take care not to stir up war one with the other by allowing thoughts and cares about the belongings of others to take hold of them. In the same way, Aristotle also declares that God has no care for the earth, as He has none for the sea or the lower regions. How is it that these philosophers shut out of their ranks the poets whose footsteps they follow?

Chapter XIV.
Nothing escapes God's knowledge. This is proved by the witness of the Scriptures and the analogy of the sun, which, although created, yet by its light or heat enters into all things.
51. Next comes the answer to the question, whether God, not having failed to show care for His work, now fails to have knowledge of it? Thus it is written: "He that planted the ear, shall He not hear? He that made the eye, shall He not regard?"

52. This false idea was not unknown to the holy prophets. David himself introduces men to speak whom pride has filled and claimed for its own. For what shows greater pride than when men who are living in sin think it unfit that other sinners should live, and say: "Lord, how long shall the ungodly, how long shall the ungodly triumph?" And later on: "And yet they say, the Lord shall not see: neither shall the God of Jacob regard it." Whom the prophet answers, saying: "Take heed, ye unwise among the people: O ye fools, when will ye understand? He that planted the ear, shall He not hear? or He that made the eye, shall He not see? He that rebuketh the nations, shall He not punish?—He that teacheth man knowledge? The Lord knoweth the thoughts of man that they are vain." Does He Who discerns whatsoever is vain not know what is holy, and is He ignorant of what He Himself has made? Can the workman be ignorant of his own work? This one is a man, yet he discerns what is hidden in his work; and God—shall He not know His own work? Is there more depth, then, in the work than in its author? Has He made something superior to Himself; the value of which, as its Author, He was ignorant of, and whose condition He knew not, though He was its Director? So much for these persons.

53. But we are satisfied with the witness of Him Who says: "I search out the heart and the reins." In the Gospel, also, the Lord Jesus says: "Why think ye evil in your hearts? For He knew they were thinking evil." The evangelist also witnesses to this, saying: "For Jesus knew their thoughts."

54. The idea of these people will not trouble us much if we look at their actions. They will not have Him to be judge over them, Whom nothing deceives; they will not grant to Him the knowledge of things hidden, for they are afraid their own hidden things may be brought to light. But the Lord, also, "knowing their works, has given them over unto darkness. In the night," he says, "he will be as a thief, and the eye of the adulterer will watch for the darkness, saying, No eye shall see me; he hath covered up his face." For every one that avoids the light loves darkness, seeking to be hid, though he cannot be hid from God, Who knows not only what is transacted, but also what will be thought of, both in the depths of space and in the minds of men. Thus, again, he who speaks in the book Ecclesiasticus says: "Who seeth me? The darkness hath covered me, and the walls have hidden me; whom do I fear?" But although lying on his bed he may think thus, he is caught where he never thought of it. "It shall be," it says, "a shame to him because he knew not what the fear of the Lord was."

55. But what can be more foolish than to suppose that anything escapes God's notice, when the sun which supplies the light enters even hidden spots, and the strength of its heat reaches to the foundations of a house and its inner chambers? Who can deny that the depths of the earth, which the winter's ice has bound together, are warmed by the mildness of spring? Surely the very heart of a tree feels the force of heat or cold, to such an extent that its roots are either nipped with the cold or sprout forth in the warmth of the sun. In short, wherever the mildness of heaven smiles on the earth, there the earth produces in abundance fruits of different kinds.

56. If, then, the sun's rays pour their light over all the earth and enter into its hidden spots; if they cannot be checked by iron bars or the barrier of heavy doors from getting within, how can it be impossible for the Glory of God, which is instinct with life, to enter into the thoughts and hearts of men that He Himself has created? And how shall it not see what He Himself has created? Did He make His works to be better and more powerful than He Himself is, Who made them (in this event) so as to escape the notice of their Creator whensoever they will? Did He implant such perfection and power in our mind that He Himself could not comprehend it when He wished?

Chapter XV.

Those who are dissatisfied with the fact that the good receive evil, and the evil good, are shown by the example of Lazarus, and on the authority of Paul, that punishments and rewards are reserved for a future life.

57. We have fully discussed two questions; and this discussion, as we think, has not turned out quite unfavourably for us. A third question yet remains; it is this: Why do sinners have

abundance of wealth and riches, and fare sumptuously, and have no grief or sorrow; whilst the upright are in want, and are punished by the loss of wives or children? Now, that parable in the Gospel ought to satisfy persons like these; for the rich man was clothed in purple and fine linen, and dined sumptuously every day; but the beggar, full of sores, used to gather the crumbs of his table. After the death of the two, however, the beggar was in Abraham's bosom in rest; the rich man was in torment. Is it not plain from this that rewards and punishments according to deserts await one after death?

58. And surely this is but right. For in a contest there is much labour needed—and after the contest victory falls to some, to others disgrace. Is the palm ever given or the crown granted before the course is finished? Paul writes well; He says: "I have fought a good fight, I have finished my course, I have kept the faith; henceforth there is laid up for me a crown of righteousness, which the Lord, the righteous judge, shall give me at that day; and not to me only, but unto all them also that love His appearing." "In that day," he says, He will give it—not here. Here he fought, in labours, in dangers, in shipwrecks, like a good wrestler; for he knew how that "through much tribulation we must enter into the kingdom of God." Therefore no one can receive a reward, unless he has striven lawfully; nor is the victory a glorious one, unless the contest also has been toilsome.

Chapter XVI.

To confirm what has been said above about rewards and punishments, he adds that it is not strange if there is no reward reserved for some in the future; for they do not labour here nor struggle. He goes on to say also that for this reason temporal goods are granted to these persons, so that they may have no excuse whatever.

59. Is not he unjust who gives the reward before the end of the contest? Therefore the Lord says in the Gospel: "Blessed are the poor in spirit, for theirs is the kingdom of heaven." He said not: "Blessed are the rich," but "the poor." By the divine judgment blessedness begins there whence human misery is supposed to spring. "Blessed are they that hunger, for they shall be filled; Blessed are they that mourn, for they shall be comforted; Blessed are the merciful, for God will have mercy on them; Blessed are the pure in heart, for they shall see God; Blessed are they that are persecuted for righteousness' sake, for theirs is the kingdom of heaven; Blessed are ye when men shall revile you, and persecute you, and shall say all manner of evil against you for righteousness' sake. Rejoice and be exceeding glad, for plentiful is your reward in heaven." A reward future and not present,—in heaven, not on earth,—has He promised shall be given. What further dost thou expect? What further is due? Why dost thou demand the crown with so much haste, before thou dost conquer? Why dost thou desire to shake off the dust and to rest? Why dost thou long to sit at the feast before the course is finished? As yet the people are looking on, the athletes are in the arena, and thou—dost thou already look for ease?

60. Perhaps thou sayest: Why are the wicked joyous? why do they live in luxury? why do they not toil with me? It is because they who have not put down their names to strive for the crown are not bound to undergo the labours of the contest. They who have not gone down into the race-course do not anoint themselves with oil nor get covered with dust. For those whom glory awaits trouble is at hand. The perfumed spectators are wont to look on, not to join in the struggle, nor to endure the sun, the hear, the dust, and the showers. Let the athletes say to them: Come, strive with us. The spectators will but answer: We sit here now to decide about you, but you, if you conquer, will gain the glory of the crown and we shall not.

61. They, then, who have devoted themselves to pleasures, luxury, robbery, gain, or honours are spectators rather than combatants. They have the profit of labour, but not the fruits of virtue. They love their ease; by cunning and wickedness they heap up riches; but they will pay the penalty of their iniquity, though it be late. Their rest will be in hell, thine in heaven; their home in the grave, thine in paradise. Whence Job said beautifully that they watch in the tomb, for they cannot have the calm of quiet rest which he enjoys who shall rise again.

62. Do not, therefore, understand, or speak, or think as a child; nor as a child claim those things now which belong to a future time. The crown belongs to the perfect. Wait till that which is perfect is come, when thou mayest know—not through a glass as in a riddle, but face to face —the very form of truth made clear. Then will be made known why that person was rich who was wicked and a robber of other men's goods, why another was powerful, why a third had many children, and yet a fourth was loaded with honours.

63. Perhaps all this happens that the question may be asked of the robber: Thou wast rich, wherefore didst thou seize on the goods of others? Need did not force thee, poverty did not drive thee to it. Did I not make thee rich, that thou mightest have no excuse? So, too, it may be said to a person of power: Why didst thou not aid the widow, the orphans also, when enduring wrong? Wast thou powerless? Couldst thou not help? I made thee for this purpose, not that thou mightest do wrong, but that thou mightest check it. Is it not written for thee "Save him that endureth wrong?" Is it not written for thee: "Deliver the poor and needy out of the hand of the sinner"? It may be said also to the man who has abundance of good things: I have blessed thee with children and honours; I have granted thee health of body; why didst thou not follow my commands? My servant, what have I done to thee, or how have I grieved thee? Was it not I that gave thee children, bestowed honours, granted health to thee? Why didst thou deny me? Why didst thou suppose that thy actions would not come to my knowledge? Why didst thou accept my gifts, yet despise my commands?

64. We can gather the same from the example of the traitor Judas. He was chosen among the Twelve Apostles, and had charge of the money bag, to lay it out upon the poor, that it might not seem as though he had betrayed the Lord because he was unhonoured or in want. Wherefore the Lord granted him this office, that He might also be justified in him; he would be guilty of a greater fault, not as one driven to it by wrong done to him, but as one misusing grace.

Chapter XVII.
The duties of youth, and examples suitable to that age, are next put forth.

65. Since it has been made sufficiently plain that there will be punishment for wickedness and reward for virtue, let us proceed to speak of the duties which have to be borne in mind from our youth up, that they may grow with our years. A good youth ought to have a fear of God, to be subject to his parents, to give honour to his elders, to preserve his purity; he ought not to despise humility, but should love forbearance and modesty. All these are an ornament to youthful years. For as seriousness is the true grace of an old man, and ardour of a young man, so also is modesty, as though by some gift of nature, well set off in a youth.

66. Isaac feared the Lord, as was indeed but natural in the son of Abraham; being subject also to his father to such an extent that he would not avoid death in opposition to his father's will. Joseph also, though he dreamed that sun and moon and stars made obeisance to him, yet was subject to his father's will with ready obedience. So chaste was he, he would not hear even a word unless it were pure; humble was he even to doing the work of a slave, modest, even to taking flight, enduring, even to bearing imprisonment, so forgiving of wrong as even to repay it with good. Whose modesty was such, that, when seized by a woman, he preferred to leave his garment in her hands in flight, rather than to lay aside his modesty. Moses, also, and Jeremiah, chosen by the Lord to declare the words of God to the people, were for avoiding, through modesty, that which through grace they could do.

Chapter XVIII.
On the different functions of modesty. How it should qualify both speech and silence, accompany chastity, commend our prayers to God, govern our bodily motions; on which last point reference is made to two clerics in language by no means unsuited to its object. Further he proceeds to say that one's gait should be in accordance with that same virtue, and how careful one must be that nothing immodest come forth from one's mouth, or be noticed in one's body. All these points are illustrated with very appropriate examples.

67. Lovely, then, is the virtue of modesty, and sweet is its grace! It is seen not only in actions, but even in our words, so that we may not go beyond due measure in speech, and that our words may not have an unbecoming sound. The mirror of our mind often enough reflects its image in our words. Sobriety weighs out the sound even of our voice, for fear that too loud a voice should offend the ear of any one. Nay, in singing itself the first rule is modesty, and the same is true in every kind of speech, too, so that a man may gradually learn to praise God, or to sing songs, or even to speak, in that the principles of modesty grace his advance.

68. Silence, again, wherein all the other virtues rest, is the chief act of modesty. Only, if it is supposed to be a sign of a childish or proud spirit, it is accounted a reproach; if a sign of modesty, it is reckoned for praise. Susanna was silent in danger, and thought the loss of modesty was worse than loss of life. She did not consider that her safety should be guarded at the risk of her chastity. To God alone she spoke, to Whom she could speak out in true modesty. She avoided looking on the face of men. For there is also modesty in the glance of the eye, which makes a woman unwilling to look upon men, or to be seen by them.

69. Let no one suppose that this praise belongs to chastity alone. For modesty is the companion of purity, in company with which chastity itself is safer. Shame, again, is good as a companion and guide of chastity, inasmuch as it does not suffer purity to be defiled in approaching even the outskirts of danger. This it is that, at the very outset of her recognition, commends the Mother of the Lord to those who read the Scriptures, and, as a credible witness, declares her worthy to be chosen to such an office. For when in her chamber, alone, she is saluted by the angel, she is silent, and is disturbed at his entrance, and the Virgin's face is troubled at the strange appearance of a man's form. And so, though she was humble, yet it was not because of this, but on account of her modesty, that she did not return his salutation, nor give him any answer, except to ask, when she had learnt that she should conceive the Lord, how this should be. She certainly did not speak merely for the sake of making a reply.

70. In our very prayers, too, modesty is most pleasing, and gains us much grace from our God. Was it not this that exalted the publican, and commended him, when he dared not raise even his eyes to heaven? So he was justified by the judgment of the Lord rather than the Pharisee, whom overweening pride made so hideous. "Therefore let us pray in the incorruptibility of a meek and quiet spirit, which is in the sight of God of great price," as St. Peter says. A noble thing, then, is modesty, which, though giving up its rights, seizing on nothing for itself, laying claim to nothing, and in some ways somewhat retiring within the sphere of its own powers, yet is rich in the sight of God, in Whose sight no man is rich. Rich is modesty, for it is the portion of God. Paul also bids that prayer be offered up with modesty and sobriety. He desires that this should be first, and, as it were, lead the way of prayers to come, so that the sinner's prayer may not be boastful, but veiled, as it were, with the blush of shame, may merit a far greater degree of grace, in giving way to modesty at the remembrance of its fault.

71. Modesty must further be guarded in our very movements and gestures and gait. For the condition of the mind is often seen in the attitude of the body. For this reason the hidden man of our heart (our inner self) is considered to be either frivolous, boastful, or boisterous, or, on the other hand, steady, firm, pure, and dependable. Thus the movement of the body is a sort of voice of the soul.

72. Ye remember, my children, that a friend of ours who seemed to recommend himself by his assiduity in his duties, yet was not admitted by me into the number of the clergy, because his gestures were too unseemly. Also that I bade one, whom I found already among the clergy, never to go in front of me, because he actually pained me by the seeming arrogance of his gait. That is what I said when he returned to his duty after an offence committed. This alone I would not allow, nor did my mind deceive me. For both have left the Church. What their gait betrayed them to be, such were they proved to be by the faithlessness of their hearts. The one forsook his faith at the time of the Arian troubles; the other, through love of money, denied that he belonged to us, so that he might not have to undergo sentence at the hands of the Church. In

their gait was discernible the semblance of fickleness, the appearance, as it were, of wandering buffoons.

73. Some there are who in walking perceptibly copy the gestures of actors, and act as though they were bearers in the processions, and had the motions of nodding statues, to such an extent that they seem to keep a sort of time, as often as they change their step.

74. Nor do I think it becoming to walk hurriedly, except when a case of some danger demands it, or a real necessity. For we often see those who hurry come up panting, and with features distorted. But if there is no reason for the need of such hurry, it gives cause for just offence. I am not, however, talking of those who have to hurry now and then for some particular reason, but of those to whom, by the yoke of constant habit, it has become a second nature. In the case of the former I cannot approve of their slow solemn movements, which remind one of the forms of phantoms. Nor do I care for the others with their headlong speed, for they put one in mind of the ruin of outcasts.

75. A suitable gait is that wherein there is an appearance of authority and weight and dignity, and which has a calm collected bearing. But it must be of such a character that all effort and conceit may be wanting, and that it be simple and plain. Nothing counterfeit is pleasing. Let nature train our movements. If indeed there is any fault in our nature, let us mend it with diligence. And, that artifice may be wanting, let not amendment be wanting.

76. But if we pay so much attention to things like these, how much more careful ought we to be to let nothing shameful proceed out of our mouth, for that defiles a man terribly. It is not food that defiles, but unjust disparagement of others and foul words. These things are openly shameful. In our office indeed must no word be let fall at all unseemly, nor one that may give offence to modesty. But not only ought we to say nothing unbecoming to ourselves, but we ought not even to lend our ears to words of this sort. Thus Joseph fled and left his garment, that he might hear nothing inconsistent with his modesty. For he who delights to listen, urges the other on to speak.

77. To have full knowledge of what is foul is in the highest degree shameful. To see anything of this sort, if by chance it should happen, how dreadful that is! What, therefore, is displeasing to us in others, can that be pleasing in ourselves? Is not nature herself our teacher, who has formed to perfection every part of our body, so as to provide for what is necessary and to beautify and grace its form? However she has left plain and open to the sight those parts which are beautiful to look upon; among which, the head, set as it were above all, and the pleasant lines of the figure, and the appearance of the face are prominent, whilst their usefulness for work is ready to hand. But those parts in which there is a compliance with the necessities of nature, she has partly put away and hidden in the body itself, lest they should present a disgusting appearance, and partly, too, she has taught and persuaded us to cover them.

78. Is not nature herself then a teacher of modesty? Following her example, the modesty of men, which I suppose is so called from the mode of knowing what is seemly, has covered and veiled what it has found hid in the frame of our body; like that door which Noah was bidden to make in the side of the ark; wherein we find a figure of the Church, and also of the human body, for through that door the remnants of food were cast out. Thus the Maker of our nature so thought of our modesty, and so guarded what was seemly and virtuous in our body, as to place what is unseemly behind, and to put it out of the sight of our eyes. Of this the Apostle says well: "Those members of the body which seem to be more feeble are necessary, and those members of the body which we think to be less honourable, upon these we bestow more abundant honour, and our uncomely parts have more abundant comeliness." Truly, by following the guidance of nature, diligent care has added to the grace of the body. In another place I have gone more fully into this subject, and said that not only do we hide those parts which have been given us to hide, but also that we think it unseemly to mention by name their description, and the use of those members.

79. And if these parts are exposed to view by chance, modesty is violated; but if on purpose, it is reckoned as utter shamelessness. Wherefore Ham, Noah's son, brought disgrace upon himself; for he laughed when he saw his father naked, but they who covered their father received the gift of a blessing. For which cause, also, it was an ancient custom in Rome, and in many other states as well, that grown-up sons should not bathe with their parents, or sons-in-law with their fathers-in-law, in order that the great duty of reverence for parents should not be weakened. Many, however, cover themselves so far as they can in the baths, so that, where the whole body is bare, that part of it at least may be covered.

80. The priests, also, under the old law, as we read in Exodus, wore breeches, as it was told Moses by the Lord: "And thou shalt make them linen breeches to cover their shame: from the loins even to the thighs they shall reach, and Aaron and his sons shall wear them, when they enter into the tabernacle of witness, and when they come unto the altar of the holy place to offer sacrifice, that they lay not sin upon themselves and die." Some of us are said still to observe this, but most explain it spiritually, and suppose it was said with a view to guarding modesty and preserving chastity.

Chapter XLX.

How should seemliness be represented by a speaker? Does beauty add anything to virtue, and, if so, how much? Lastly, what care should we take that nothing conceited or effeminate be seen in us?

81. It has given me pleasure to dwell somewhat at length on the various functions of modesty; for I speak to you who either can recognize the good that is in it in your own cases, or at least do not know its loss. Fitted as it is for all ages, persons, times, and places, yet it most beseems youthful and childish years.

82. But at every age we must take care that all we do is seemly and becoming, and that the course of our life forms one harmonious and complete whole. Wherefore Cicero thinks that a certain order ought to be observed in what is seemly. He says that this lies in beauty, order, and in appointment fitted for action. This, as he says, it is difficult to explain in words, yet it can be quite sufficiently understood.

83. Why Cicero should have introduced beauty, I do not quite understand; though it is true he also speaks in praise of the powers of the body. We certainly do not locate virtue in the beauty of the body, though, on the other hand, we do recognize a certain grace, as when modesty is wont to cover the face with a blush of shame, and to make it more pleasing. For as a workman is wont to work better the more suitable his materials are, so modesty is more conspicuous in the comeliness of the body. Only the comeliness of the body should not be assumed; it should be natural and artless, unstudied rather than elaborated, not heightened by costly and glistening garments, but just clad in ordinary clothing. One must see that nothing is wanting that one's credit or necessity demands, whilst nothing must be added for the sake of splendour.

84. The voice, too, should not be languid, nor feeble, nor womanish in its tone,—such a tone of voice as many are in the habit of using, under the idea of seeming important. It should preserve a certain quality, and rhythm, and a manly vigour. For all to do what is best suited to their character and sex, that is to attain to beauty of life. This is the best order for movements, this the employment fitted for every action. But as I cannot approve of a soft or weak tone of voice, or an effeminate gesture of the body, so also I cannot approve of what is boorish and rustic. Let us follow nature. The imitation of her provides us with a principle of training, and gives us a pattern of virtue.

Chapter XX.

If we are to preserve our modesty we must avoid fellowship with profligate men, also the banquets of strangers, and intercourse with women; our leisure time at home should be spent in pious and virtuous pursuits.

85. Modesty has indeed its rocks—not any that she brings with her, but those, I mean, which she often runs against, as when we associate with profligate men, who, under the form of pleasantry, administer poison to the good. And the latter, if they are very constant in their attendance at banquets and games, and often join in jests, enervate that manly gravity of theirs. Let us then take heed that, in wishing to relax our minds, we do not destroy all harmony, the blending as it were of all good works. For habit quickly bends nature in another direction.

86. For this reason I think that what ye wisely do is befitting to the duties of clerics, and especially to those of the priesthood—namely, that ye avoid the banquets of strangers, but so that ye are still hospitable to travellers, and give no occasion for reproach by reason of your great care in the matter. Banquets with strangers engross one's attention, and soon produce a love for feasting. Tales, also, of the world and its pleasures often creep in. One cannot shut one's ears; and to forbid them is looked on as a sign of haughtiness. One's glass, too, even against one's will, is filled time after time. It is better surely to excuse oneself once for all at one's own home, than often at another's. When one rises sober, at any rate one's presence need not be condemned by the insolence of another.

87. There is no need for the younger clergy to go to the houses of widows or virgins, except for the sake of a definite visit, and in that case only with the elder clergy, that is, with the bishop, or, if the matter be somewhat important, with the priests. Why should we give room to the world to revile? What need is there for those frequent visits to give ground for rumours? What if one of those women should by chance fall? Why shouldst thou undergo the reproach of another's fall? How many even strong men have been led away by their passions? How many are there who have not indeed yielded to sin, but have given ground for suspicion?

88. Why dost thou not spend the time which thou hast free from thy duties in the church in reading? Why dost thou not go back again to see Christ? Why dost thou not address Him, and hear His voice? We address Him when we pray, we hear Him when we read the sacred oracles of God. What have we to do with strange houses? There is one house which holds all. They who need us can come to us. What have we to do with tales and fables? An office to minister at the altar of Christ is what we have received; no duty to make ourselves agreeable to men has been laid upon us.

89. We ought to be humble, gentle, mild, serious, patient. We must keep the mean in all things, so that a calm countenance and quiet speech may show that there is no vice in our lives.

Chapter XXI.

We must guard against anger, before it arises; if it has already arisen we must check and calm it, and if we cannot do this either, at least we should keep our tongue from abuse, so that our passions may be like boys' quarrels. He relates what Archites said, and shows that David led the way in this matter, both in his actions and in his writings.

90. Let anger be guarded against. If it cannot, however, be averted, let it be kept within bounds. For indignation is a terrible incentive to sin. It disorders the mind to such an extent as to leave no room for reason. The first thing, therefore, to aim at, if possible, is to make tranquillity of character our natural disposition by constant practice, by desire for better things, by fixed determination. But since passion is to a large extent implanted in our nature and character, so that it cannot be uprooted and avoided, it must be checked by reason, if, that is, it can be foreseen. And if the mind has already been filled with indignation before it could be foreseen or provided against in any way, we must consider how to conquer the passion of the mind, how to restrain our anger, that it may no more be so filled. Resist wrath, if possible; if not, give way, for it is written: "Give place to wrath."

91. Jacob dutifully gave way to his brother when angry, and to Rebecca; that is to say, taught by counsels of patience, he preferred to go away and live in foreign lands, rather than to arouse his brother's anger; and then to return only when he thought his brother was appeased. Thus it was that he found such great grace with God. With what offers of willing service, with what gifts, did he reconcile his brother to himself again, so that he should not remember the blessing which had been taken away from him, but should only remember the reparation now offered?

92. If, then, anger has got the start, and has already taken possession of thy mind, and mounted into thy heart, forsake not thy ground. Thy ground is patience, it is wisdom, it is reason, it is the allaying of indignation. And if the stubbornness of thy opponent rouses thee, and his perverseness drives thee to indignation: if thou canst not calm thy mind, check at least thy tongue. For so it is written: "Keep thy tongue from evil, and thy lips that they speak no guile. Seek peace and pursue it." See the peace of holy Jacob, how great it was! First, then, calm thy mind. If thou canst not do this, put a restraint upon thy tongue. Lastly, omit not to seek for reconciliation. These ideas the speakers of the world have borrowed from us, and have set down in their writings. But he who said it first has the credit of understanding its meaning.

93. Let us then avoid or at any rate check anger, so that we may not lose our share of praise, nor yet add to our list of sins. It is no light thing to calm one's anger. It is no less difficult a thing than it is not to be roused at all. The one is an act of our own will, the other is an effect of nature. So quarrels among boys are harmless, and have more of a pleasant than a bitter character about them. And if boys quickly come to quarrel one with the other, they are easily calmed down again, and quickly come together with even greater friendliness. They do not know how to act deceitfully and artfully. Do not condemn these children, of whom the Lord says: "Except ye be converted and become as this child, ye shall not enter into the kingdom of heaven." So also the Lord Himself, Who is the Power of God, as a Boy, when He was reviled, reviled not again, when He was struck, struck not back. Set then thy mind on this—like a child never to keep an injury in mind, never to show malice, but that all things may be done blamelessly by thee. Regard not the return made thee by others. Hold thy ground. Guard the simplicity and purity of thy heart. Answer not an angry man according to his anger, nor a foolish man according to his folly. One fault quickly calls forth another. If stones are rubbed together, does not fire break forth?

94. The heathen—(they are wont to exaggerate everything in speaking)—make much of the saying of the philosopher Archites of Tarentum, which he spoke to his bailiff: "O you wretched man, how I would punish you, if I were not angry." But David already before this had in his indignation held back his armed hand. How much greater a thing it is not to revile again, than not to avenge oneself! The warriors, too, prepared to take vengeance against Nabal, Abigail restrained by her prayers. From whence we perceive that we ought not only to yield to timely entreaties, but also to be pleased with them. So much was David pleased that he blessed her who intervened, because he was restrained from his desire for revenge.

95. Already before this he had said of his enemies: "For they cast iniquity upon me, and in their wrath they were grievous to me." Let us hear what he said when overwhelmed in wrath: "Who will give me wings like a dove, and I will flee away and be at rest." They kept provoking him to anger, but he sought quietness.

96. He had also said: "Be ye angry and sin not." The moral teacher who knew that the natural disposition should rather be guided by a reasonable course of teaching, than be eradicated, teaches morals, and says: "Be angry where there is a fault against which ye ought to be angry." For it is impossible not to be roused up by the baseness of many things; otherwise we might be accounted, not virtuous, but apathetic and neglectful. Be angry therefore, so that ye keep free from fault, or, in other words: If ye are angry, do not sin, but overcome wrath with reason. Or one might put it thus: If ye are angry, be angry with yourselves, because ye are roused, and ye will not sin. For he who is angry with himself, because he has been so easily roused, ceases to be angry with another. But he who wishes to prove his anger is righteous only

gets the more inflamed, and quickly falls into sin. "Better is he," as Solomon says, "that restraineth his anger, than he that taketh a city," for anger leads astray even brave men.

97. We ought therefore to take care that we do not get into a flurry, before reason prepares our minds. For oftentimes anger or distress or fear of death almost deprives the soul of life, and beats it down by a sudden blow. It is therefore a good thing to anticipate this by reflection, and to exercise the mind by considering the matter. So the mind will not be roused by any sudden disturbance, but will grow calm, being held in by the yoke and reins of reason.

Chapter XXII.
On reflection and passion, and on observing propriety of speech, both in ordinary conversation and in holding discussions.

98. There are two kinds of mental motions —those of reflection and of passion. The one has to do with reflection, the other with passion. There is no confusion one with the other, for they are markedly different and unlike. Reflection has to search and as it were to grind out the truth. Passion prompts and stimulates us to do something. Thus by its very nature reflection diffuses tranquillity and calm; and passion sends forth the impulse to act. Let us then be ready to allow reflection on good things to enter into our mind, and to make passion submit to reason (if indeed we wish to direct our minds to guard what is seemly), lest desire for anything should shut out reason. Rather let reason test and see what befits virtue.

99. And since we have said that we must aim at the observance of what is seemly, so as to know what is the due measure in our words and deeds, and as order in speech rather than in action comes first; speech is divided into two kinds: first, as it is used in friendly conversation, and then in the treatment and discussion of matters of faith and justice. In either case we must take care that there is no irritation. Our language should he mild and quiet, and full of kindness and courtesy and free from insult. Let there be no obstinate disputes in our familiar conversations, for they are wont only to bring up useless subjects, rather than to supply anything useful. Let there be discussion without wrath, urbanity without bitterness, warning without sharpness, advice without giving offence. And as in every action of our life we ought to take heed to this, in order that no overpowering impulse of our mind may ever shut out reason (let us always keep a place for counsel), so, too, ought we to observe that rule in our language, so that neither wrath nor hatred may be aroused, and that we may not show any signs of our greed or sloth.

100. Let our language be of this sort, more especially when we are speaking of the holy Scriptures. For of what ought we to speak more often than of the best subject of conversation, of its exhortation to watchfulness, its care for good instruction? Let us have a reason for beginning, and let our end be within due limits. For a speech that is wearisome only stirs up anger. But surely it is most unseemly that when every kind of conversation generally gives additional pleasure, this should give cause of offence!

101. The treatment also of such subjects as the teaching of faith, instruction on self-restraint, discussion on justice, exhortation to activity, must not be taken up by us and fully gone into all at one time, but must be carried on in course, so far as we can do it, and as the subject-matter of the passage allows. Our discourse must not be too lengthy, nor too soon cut short, for fear the former should leave behind it a feeling of aversion, and the latter produce carelessness and neglect. The address should be plain and simple, clear and evident, full of dignity and weight; it should not be studied or too refined, nor yet, on the other hand, be unpleasing and rough in style.

Chapter XXIII.

Jests, although at times they may be quite proper, should be altogether banished among clerics. The voice should be plain and frank.

102. Men of the world give many further rules about the way to speak, which I think we may pass over; as, for instance, the way jesting should be conducted. For though at times jests may be proper and pleasant, yet they are unsuited to the clerical life. For how can we adopt those things which we do not find in the holy Scriptures?

103. We must also take care that in relating stories we do not alter the earnest purpose of the harder rule we have set before us. "Woe unto you that laugh, for ye shall weep," says the Lord. Do we seek for something to laugh at, that laughing here we may weep hereafter? I think we ought to avoid not only broad jokes, but all kinds of jests, unless perchance it is not unfitting at the time for our conversation to be agreeable and pleasant.

104. In speaking of the voice, I certainly think it ought to be plain and clear. That it should be musical is a gift of nature, and is not to be won by exertion. Let it be distinct in its pronunciation and full of a manly vigour, but let it be free from a rough and rustic twang. See, too, that it does not assume a theatrical accent, but rather keeps true to the inner meaning of the words it utters.

Chapter XXIV.

There are three things to be noticed in the actions of our life. First, our passions are to be controlled by our reason; next, we ought to observe a suitable moderation in our desires; and, lastly, everything ought to be done at the right time and in the proper order. All these qualities shone forth so conspicuously in the holy men of Old Testament time, that it is evident they were well furnished with what men call the cardinal virtues.

105. I Think I have said enough on the art of speaking. Let us now consider what beseems an active life. We note that there are three things to be regarded in connection with this subject. One is, that passion should not resist our reason. In that way only can our duties be brought into line with what is seemly. For if passion yields to reason we can easily maintain what is seemly in our duties. Next, we must take care rest, either by showing greater zeal or less than the matter we take up demands, we look as though we were taking up a small matter with great parade or were treating a great matter with but little care. Thirdly, as regards moderation in our endeavours and works, and also with regard to order in doing things and in the right timing of things, I think that everything should be open and straightforward.

106. But first comes that which I may call the foundation of all, namely, that our passions should obey our reason. The second and third are really the same—moderation in either case. There is room with us for the survey of a pleasing form, which is accounted beauty, and the consideration of dignity. Next follows the consideration of the order and the timing of things. These, then, are the three points, and we must see whether we can show them in perfection in any one of the saints.

107. First there is our father Abraham, who was formed and called for the instruction of generations to come. When bidden to go forth from his own country and kindred and from his father's house, though bound and held back by many ties of relationship, did he not give proof that in him passion was subject to reason? Who does not delight in the sweet charms of his native land, his kindred, and his own home? Their sweetness then delighted him. But the thought of the heavenly command and of an eternal reward influenced him more. Did he not reflect that he could not take his wife with him without the greatest danger, unused as she was to hardships, and so tender to bear insults, and so beautiful as to be likely to arouse the lust of profligate men? Yet he decided somewhat deliberately to undergo all this rather than to escape it by making excuses. Lastly, when he had gone into Egypt, he advised her to say she was his sister, not his wife.

108. See here what passions are at work! He feared for the chastity of his wife, he feared for his own safety, he had his suspicions about the lust of the Egyptians, and yet the reasonableness

of performing his duty to God prevailed with him. For he thought that by the favour of God he could be safe everywhere, but if he offended the Lord he could not abide unharmed even at home. Thus reason conquered passion, and brought it into subjection to itself.

109. When his nephew was taken captive, without being terrified or dismayed at the hordes of so many kings, he resumed the war. And after the victory was gained he refused his share of the spoil, which he himself had really won. Also, when a son was promised him, though he thought of the lost vigour of his body, now as good as dead, and the barrenness of his wife, and his own great age, he believed God, though it was against the law of nature.

110. Note how everything meets together here. Passion was not wanting, but it was checked. Here was a mind equable in action, which neither treated great things as unimportant or little things as great. Here there was moderation in different affairs, order in things, fitness of occasion, due measure in words. He was foremost in faith, conspicuous in virtue, vigorous in battle, in victory not greedy, at home hospitable, and to his wife attentive.

111. Jacob also, his holy grandson, loved to pass his time at home free from danger; but his mother wished him to live in foreign parts, and so give place to his brother's anger. Sound counsels prevailed over natural feelings. An exile from home, banished from his parents, yet everywhere, in all he did, he observed due measure, such as was fitting, and made use of his opportunities at the right time. So dear was he to his parents at home, that the one, moved by the promptness of his compliance, gave him his blessing, the other inclined towards him with tender love. In the judgment of his brother, also, he was placed first, when he thought that he ought to give up his food to his brother. For though according to his natural inclinations he wished for food, yet when asked for it he gave it up from a feeling of brotherly affection. He was a faithful shepherd of the flock for his master, an attentive son-in-law to his father-in-law; he was active in work, sparing in his meals, conspicuous in making amends, lavish in repaying. Nay, so well did he calm his brother's anger that he received his favour, though he had feared his enmity.

112. What shall I say of Joseph? He certainly had a longing for freedom, and yet endured the bonds of servitude. How meek he was in slavery, how unchanging in virtue, how kindly in prison! Wise, too, in interpreting, and self-restrained in exercising his power! In the time of plenty was he not careful? In the time of famine was he not fair? Did he not praiseworthily do everything in order, and use opportunities at their season; giving justice to his people by the restraining guidance of his office?

113. Job also, both in prosperity and adversity, was blameless, patient, pleasing, and acceptable to God. He was harassed with pain, yet could find consolation.

114. David also was brave in war, patient in time of adversity, peaceful at Jerusalem, in the hour of victory merciful, on committing sin repentant, in his old age foreseeing. He preserved due measure in his actions, and took his opportunities as they came. He has set them down in the songs of succeeding years; and so it seems to me that he has by his life no less than by the sweetness of his hymns poured forth an undying song of his own merits to God.

115. What duty connected with the chief virtues was wanting in these men? In the first place they showed prudence, which is exercised in the search of the truth, and which imparts a desire for full knowledge; next, justice, which assigns each man his own, does not claim another's, and disregards its own advantage, so as to guard the rights of all; thirdly, fortitude, which both in warfare and at home is conspicuous in greatness of mind and distinguishes itself in the strength of the body; fourthly, temperance, which preserves the right method and order in all things that we think should either be done or said.

Chapter XXV.

A reason is given why this book did not open with a discussion of the above-mentioned virtues. It is also concisely pointed out that the same virtues existed in the ancient fathers.

116. Perhaps, as the different classes of duties are derived from these four virtues, some one may say that they ought to have been described first of all. But it would have been artificial to have given a definition of duty at the outset, and then to have gone on to divide it up into various classes. We have avoided what is artificial, and have put forward the examples of the fathers of old. These certainly offer us no uncertainty as regards our understanding them, and give us no room for subtlety in our discussion of them. Let the life of the fathers, then, be for us a mirror of virtue, not a mere collection of shrewd and clever acts. Let us show reverence in following them, not mere cleverness in discussing them.

117. Prudence held the first place in holy Abraham. For of him the Scriptures say: "Abraham believed God, and that was counted to him for righteousness;" for no one is prudent who knows not God. Again: "The fool hath said, There is no God;" for a wise man would not say so. How is he wise who looks not for his Maker, but says to a stone: "Thou art my father"? Who says to the devil as the Manichaean does: "Thou art the author of my being"? How is Arius wise, who prefers an imperfect and inferior creator to one who is a true and perfect one? How can Marcion or Eunomius be wise, who prefer to have an evil rather than a good God? And how can he be wise who does not fear his God? For: "The fear of the Lord is the beginning of wisdom." Elsewhere, too, it stands: "The wise turn not aside from the mouth of the Lord, but come near Him in their confession of His greatness." So when the Scripture says: "It was counted to him for righteousness," that brought to him the grace of another virtue.

118. The chief amongst ourselves have stated that prudence lies in the knowledge of the truth. But who of them all excelled Abraham, David, or Solomon in this? Then they go on to say that justice has regard to the whole community of the human race. So David said: "He hath dispersed abroad and given to the poor, His righteousness remaineth for ever." The just man has pity, the just man lends. The whole world of riches lies at the feet of the wise and the just. The just man regards what belongs to all as his own, and his own as common property. The man just accuses himself rather than others. For he is just who does not spare himself, and who does not suffer his secret actions to be concealed. See now how just Abraham was! In his old age he begat a son according to promise, and when the Lord demanded him for sacrifice he did not think he ought to refuse him, although he was his only son.

119. Note here all these four virtues in one act. It was wise to believe God, and not to put love for his son before the commands of his Creator. It was just to give back what had been received. It was brave to restrain natural feelings by reason. The father led the victim; the son asked where it was: the father's feelings were hardly tried, but were not overcome. The son said again: "My father," and thus pierced his father's heart, though without weakening his devotion to God. The fourth virtue, temperance, too, was there. Being just he preserved due measure in his piety, and order in all he had to carry out. And so in bringing what was needed for the sacrifice, in lighting the fire, in binding his son, in drawing the knife, in performing the sacrifice in due order; thus he merited as his reward that he might keep his son.

120. Is there greater wisdom than holy Jacob's, who saw God face to face and won a blessing? Can there be higher justice than his in dividing with his brother what he had acquired, and offering it as a gift? What greater fortitude than his in striving with God? What moderation so true as his, who acted with such moderation as regards time and place, as to prefer to hide his daughter's shame rather than to avenge himself? For being set in the midst of foes, he thought it better to gain their affections than to concentrate their hate on himself.

121. How wise also was Noah, who built the whole of the ark! How just again! For he alone, preserved of all to be the father of the human race, was made a survivor of past generations, and the author of one to come; he was born, too, rather for the world and the universe than for himself. How brave he was to overcome the flood! how temperate to endure it! When he had

entered the ark, with what moderation he passed the time! When he sent forth the raven and the dove, when he received them on their return, when he took the opportunity of leaving the ark, with what moderation did he make use of these occasions!

Chapter XXVI.

In investigating the truth the philosophers have broken through their own rules. Moses, however, showed himself more wise than they. The greater the dignity of wisdom, the more earnestly must we strive to gain it. Nature herself urges us all to do this.

122. It is said, therefore, that in investigating the truth, we must observe what is seemly. We ought to look for what is true with the greatest care. We must not put forward falsehood for truth, nor hide the truth in darkness, nor fill the mind with idle, involved, or doubtful matters. What so unseemly as to worship a wooden thing, which men themselves have made? What shows such darkness as to discuss subjects connected with geometry and astronomy (which they approve of), to measure the depths of space, to shut up heaven and earth within the limits of fixed numbers, to leave aside the grounds of salvation and to seek for error?

123. Moses, learned as he was in all the wisdom of the Egyptians, did not approve of those things, but thought that kind of wisdom both harmful and foolish. Turning away therefrom, he sought God with all the desire of his heart, and thus saw, questioned, heard Him when He spoke. Who is more wise than he whom God taught, and who brought to nought all the wisdom of the Egyptians, and all the powers of their craft by the might of his works? He did not treat things unknown as well known, and so rashly accept them. Yet these philosophers, though they do not consider it contrary to nature, nor shameful for themselves to worship, and to ask help from an idol which knows nothing, teach us that these two things mentioned in the words just spoken, which are in accordance both with nature and with virtue, ought to be avoided.

124. The loftier the virtue of wisdom is, the more I say we ought to strive for it, so that we may be able to attain to it. And that we may have no ideas which are contrary to nature, or are disgraceful, or unfitting, we ought to give two things, that is, time and care, to considering matters for the sake of investigating them. For there is nothing in which man excels all other living creatures more than in the fact that he has reason, seeks out the origin of things, thinks that the Author of his being should be searched out. For in His hand is our life and death; He rules this world by His nod. And to Him we know that we must give a reason for our actions. For there is nothing which is more of a help to a good life than to believe that He will be our judge, Whom hidden things do not escape, and unseemly things offend, and good deeds delight.

125. In all men, then, there lies, in accordance with human nature, a desire to search out the truth, which leads us on to have a longing for knowledge and learning, and infuses into us a wish to seek after it. To excel in this seems a noble thing to mankind; but there are only few who attain to it. And they, by deep thought, by careful deliberation, spend no little labour so as to be able to attain to that blessed and virtuous life, and to approach its likeness in their actions. "For not he that saith to Me Lord. Lord, shall enter into the kingdom of heaven, but he that doeth those things that I say." To have a desire for knowledge without actions to correspond—well! I do not know whether that carries anything more with it.

Chapter XXVII.

The first source of duty is prudence, from whence spring three other virtues; and they cannot be separated or torn asunder, since they are mutually connected one with the other.

126. The first source of duty, then, is prudence. For what is more of a duty than to give to the Creator all one's devotion and reverence? This source, however, is drawn off into other virtues. For justice cannot exist without prudence, since it demands no small amount of prudence to see whether a thing is just or unjust. A mistake on either side is very serious. "For he that says a just man is unjust, or an unjust man is just, is accursed with God. Wherefore does justice abound unto the wicked?" says Solomon. Nor, on the other hand, can prudence exist

without justice, for piety towards God is the beginning of understanding. On which we notice that this is a borrowed rather than an original idea among the worldly wise, for piety is the foundation of all virtues.

127. But the piety of justice is first directed towards God; secondly, towards one's country; next, towards parents; lastly, towards all. This, too, is in accordance with the guidance of nature. From the beginning of life, when understanding first begins to be infused into us, we love life as the gift of God, we love our country and our parents; lastly, our companions, with whom we like to associate. Hence arises true love, which prefers others to self, and seeks not its own, wherein lies the pre-eminence of justice.

128. It is ingrained in all living creatures, first of all, to preserve their own safety, to guard against what is harmful, to strive for what is advantageous. They seek food and converts, whereby they may protect themselves from dangers, storms, and sun,—all which is a mark of prudence. Next we find that all the different creatures are by nature wont to herd together, at first with fellows of their own class and sort, then also with others. So we see oxen delighted to be in herds, horses in droves, and especially like with like, stags, also, in company with stags and often with men. And what should I say on their desire to have young, and on their offspring, or even on their passions, wherein the likeness of justice is conspicuous?

129. It is clear, then, that these and the remaining virtues are related to one another. For courage, which in war preserves one's country from the barbarians, or at home defends the weak, or comrades from robbers, is full of justice; and to know on what plan to defend and to give help, how to make use of opportunities of time and place, is the part of prudence and moderation, and temperance itself cannot observe due measure without prudence. To know a fit opportunity, and to make return according to what is right, belongs to justice. In all these, too, large-heartedness is necessary, and fortitude of mind, and often of body, so that we may carry out what we wish.

Chapter XXVIII.

A community rests upon justice and good-will. Two parts of the former, revenge and private possession, are not recognized by Christians. What the Stoics say about common property and mutual help has been borrowed from the sacred writings. The greatness of the glory of justice, and what hinders access to it.

130. Justice, then, has to do with the society of the human race, and the community at large. For that which holds society together is divided into two parts,—justice and good-will, which also is called liberality and kindness. Justice seems to me the loftier, liberality the more pleasing, of the two. The one gives judgment, the other shows goodness.

131. But that very thing is excluded with us which philosophers think to be the office of justice. For they say that the first expression of justice is, to hurt no one, except when driven to it by wrongs received. Thisis put aside by the authority of the Gospel. For the Scripture wills that the Spirit of the Son of Man should be in us, Who came to give grace, not to bring harm.

132. Next they considered it consonant with justice that one should treat common, that is, public property as public, and private as private. But this is not even in accord with nature, for nature has poured forth all things for all men for common use. God has ordered all things to be produced, so that there should be food in common to all, and that the earth should be a common possession for all. Nature, therefore, has produced a common right for all, but greed has made it a right for a few. Here, too, we are told that the Stoics taught that all things which are produced on the earth are created for the use of men, but that men are born for the sake of men, so that mutually one may be of advantage to another.

133. But whence have they got such ideas but out of the holy Scriptures? For Moses wrote that God said: "Let us make man in our image, after our likeness, and let them have dominion over the fish of the sea, and over the fowl of the air, and over the cattle, and over every creeping thing that creepeth upon the earth." And David said: "Thou hast put all things under his feet; all sheep and oxen, yea, and the beasts of the field, the fowls of the air, and the fishes of the sea."

So these philosophers have learnt from our writings that all things were made subject to man, and, therefore, they think that all things were produced also for man's sake.

134. That man was made for the sake of man we find stated also in the books of Moses, when the Lord says: "It is not good that man should be alone, let us make him an helpmeet for him." Thus the woman was given to the man to help him. She should bear him children, that one man might always be a help to another. Again, before the woman was formed, it was said of Adam: "There was not found an help-meet for him." For one man could not have proper help but from another. Amongst all the living creatures, therefore, there was none meet for him, or, to put it plainly, none to be his helper. Hence a woman was looked for to help him.

135. Thus, in accordance with the will of God and the union of nature, we ought to be of mutual help one to the other, and to vie with each other in doing duties, to lay all our advantages as it were before all, and (to use the words of Scripture) to bring help one to the other from a feeling of devotion or of duty, by giving money, or by doing something, at any rate in some way or other; so that the charm of human fellowship may ever grow sweeter amongst us, and none may ever be recalled from their duty by the fear of danger, but rather account all things, whether good or evil, as their own concern. Thus holy Moses feared not to undertake terrible wars for his people's sake, nor was he afraid of the arms of the mightiest kings, nor yet was he frightened at the savagery of barbarian nations. He put on one side the thought of his own safety so as to give freedom to the people.

136. Great, then, is the glory of justice; for she, existing rather for the good of others than of self, is an aid to the bonds of union and fellowship amongst us. She holds so high a place that she has all things laid under her authority, and further can bring help to others and supply money; nor does she refuse her services, but even undergoes dangers for others.

137. Who would not gladly climb and hold the heights of this virtue, were it not that greed weakens and lessens the power of such a virtue? For as long as we want to add to our possessions and to heap up money, to take into our possession fresh lands, and to be the richest of all, we have cast aside the form of justice and have lost the blessing of kindness towards all. How can he be just that tries to take from another what he wants for himself?

138. The desire to gain power also enervates the perfect strength and beauty of justice. For how can he, who attempts to bring others under his own power, come forward on behalf of others? And how can a man help the weak against the strong, when he himself aspires to great power at the cost of liberty?

Chapter XXIX.

Justice should be observed even in war and with enemies. This is proved by the example of Moses and Elisha. The ancient writers learnt in turn from the Hebrews to call their enemies by a gentler term. Lastly, the foundation of justice rests on faith, and its symmetry is perfect in the Church.

139. How great a thing justice is can be gathered from the fact that there is no place, nor person, nor time, with which it has nothing to do. It must even be preserved in all dealings with enemies. For instance, if the day or the spot for a battle has been agreed upon with them, it would be considered an act against justice to occupy the spot beforehand, or to anticipate the time. For there is some difference whether one is overcome in some battle by a severe engagement, or by superior skill, or by a mere chance. But a deeper vengeance is taken on fiercer foes, and on those that are false as well as on those who have done greater wrongs, as was the case with the Midianites. For they had made many of the Jewish people to sin through their women; for which reason the anger of the Lord was poured out upon the people of our fathers. Thus it came about that Moses when victorious allowed none of them to live. On the other hand, Joshua did not attack the Gibeonites, who had tried the people of our fathers with guile rather than with war, but punished them by laying on them a law of bondage. Elisha again would not allow the king of Israel to slay the Syrians when he wished to do so. He had brought them into the city, when they were besieging him, after he had struck them with instantaneous

blindness, so that they could not see where they were going, For he said: "Thou shall not smite those whom thou hast not taken captive with thy spear and with thy sword. Set before them bread and water, that they may eat and drink and return and go to their own home." Incited by their kind treatment they should show forth to the world the kindness they had received. "Thus" (we read) "there came no more the bands of Syria into the land of Israel."

140. If, then, justice is binding, even in war, how much more ought we to observe it in time of peace. Such favour the prophet showed to those who came to seize him. We read that the king of Syria had sent his army to lie in wait for him, for he had learnt that it was Elisha who had made known to all his plans and consultations. And Gehazi the prophet's servant, seeing the army, began to fear that his life was in danger. But the prophet said to him: "Fear not, for they that be with us are more than they that be with them." And when the prophet asked that the eyes of his servant might be opened, they were opened. Then Gehazi saw the whole mountain full of horses and chariots round about Elisha. As they came down to him the prophet says: "Smite, O God, the army of Syria with blindness." And this prayer being granted, he says to the Syrians: "Follow me, and I will bring you to the man whom ye seek." Then saw they Elisha, whom they were endeavouring to lay hold of, and seeing him they could not hold him fast. It is clear from this that faith and justice should be observed even in war; and that it could not but be a disgraceful thing if faith were violated.

141. So also the ancients used to give their foes a less harsh name, and called them strangers. For enemies used to be called strangers after the customs of old. This too we can say they adopted from our writings; for the Hebrews used to call their foes "allophyllos," that is, when put into Latin, "alienigenas" (of another race). For so we read in the first book of Kings: "It came to pass in those days that they of another race put themselves in array against Israel."

142. The foundation of justice therefore is faith, for the hearts of the just dwell on faith, and the just man that accuses himself builds justice on faith, for his justice becomes plain when he confesses the truth. So the Lord saith through Isaiah: "Behold, I lay a stone for a foundation in Sion." This means Christ as the foundation of the Church. For Christ is the object of faith to all; but the Church is as it were the outward form of justice, she is the common right of all. For all in common she prays, for all in common she works, in the temptations of all she is tried. So he who denies himself is indeed a just man, is indeed worthy of Christ. For this reason Paul has made Christ to be the foundation, so that we may build upon Him the works of justice, whilst faith is the foundation. In our works, then, if they are evil, there appears unrighteousness; if they are good, justice.

Chapter XXX.

On kindness and its several parts, namely, good-will and liberality. How they are to be combined. What else is further needed for any one to show liberality in a praiseworthy manner.

143. Now we can go on to speak of kindness, which breaks up into two parts, goodwill and liberality. Kindness to exist in perfection must consist of these two qualities. It is not enough just to wish well; we must also do well. Nor, again, is it enough to do well, unless this springs from a good source even from a good, will. "For God loveth a cheerful giver." If we act unwillingly, what is our reward? Wherefore the Apostle, speaking generally, says: "If I do this thing willingly, I have a reward, but if unwillingly, a dispensation is given unto me." In the Gospel, also, we have received many rules of just liberality.

144. It is thus a glorious thing to wish well, and to give freely, with the one desire to do good and not to do harm. For if we were to think it our duty to give the means to an extravagant man to live extravagantly, or to an adulterer to pay for his adultery, it would not be an act of kindness, for there would be no good-will in it. We should be doing harm, not good, to another if we gave him money to aid him in plotting against his country, or in attempting to get together at our expense some abandoned men to attack the Church. Nor, again, does it look like liberality

to help one who presses very hardly on widows and orphans, or attempts to seize on their property with any show of violence.

145. It is no sign of a liberal spirit to extort from one what we give to another, or to gain money unjustly, and then to think it can be well spent, unless we act as Zacchaeus did, and restore fourfold what we have taken from him whom we have robbed, and make up for such heathenish crimes by the zeal of our faith and by true Christian labour. Our liberality must have some sure foundation.

146. The first thing necessary is to do kindness in good faith, and not to act falsely when the offering is made. Never let us say we are doing more, when we are really doing less. What need is there to speak at all? In a promise a cheat lies hid. It is in our power to give what we like. Cheating shatters the foundation, and so destroys the work. Did Peter grow angry only so far as to desire that Ananias and his wife should be slain? Certainly not. He wished that others, through knowing their example, should not perish.

147. Nor is it a real act of liberality if thou givest for the sake of boasting about it, rather than for mercy's sake. Thy inner feelings give the name to thy acts. As it comes forth from thee, so will others regard it. See what a true judge thou hast! He consults with thee how to take up thy work, and first of all he questions thy mind. "Let not," he says, "thy left hand know what thy right hand doth." This does not refer to our actual bodies, but means: Let not him who is of one mind with thee, not even thy brother, know what thou doest, lest thou shouldst lose the fruit of thy reward hereafter by seeking here thy price in boastfulness. But that liberality is real where a man hides what he does in silence, and secretly assists the needs of individuals, whom the mouth of the poor, and not his own lips, praises.

148. Perfect liberality is proved by its good faith, the case it helps, the time and place when and where it is shown. But first we must always see that we help those of the household of faith. It is a serious fault if a believer is in want, and thou knowest it, or if thou knowest that he is without means, that he is hungry, that he suffer distress, especially if he is ashamed of his need. It is a great fault if he is overwhelmed by the imprisonment or false accusation of his family, and thou dost not come to his help. If he is in prison, and—upright though he is—has to suffer pain and punishment for some debt (for though we ought to show mercy to all, yet we ought to show it especially to an upright man); if in the time of his trouble he obtains nothing from thee; if in the time of danger, when he is carried off to die, thy money seems more to thee than the life of a dying man; what a sin is that to thee! Wherefore Job says beautifully: "Let the blessing of him that was ready to perish come upon me."

149. God, indeed, is not a respecter of persons, for He knows all things. And we, indeed, ought to show mercy to all. But as many try to get help on false pretences, and make out that they are miserably off; therefore where the case is plain and the person well known, and no time is to be lost, mercy ought to be shown more readily. For the Lord is not exacting to demand the utmost. Blessed, indeed, is he who forsakes all and follows Him, but blessed also is he who does what he can to the best of his powers with what he has. The Lord preferred the two mites of the widow to all the gifts of the rich, for she gave all that she had, but they only gave a small part out of all their abundance. It is the intention, therefore, that makes the gift valuable or poor, and gives to things their value. The Lord does not want us to give away all our goods at once, but to impart them little by little; unless, indeed, our case is like that of Elisha, who killed his oxen, and fed the people on what he had, so that no household cares might hold him back, and that he might give up all things, and devote himself to the prophetic teaching.

150. True liberality also must be tested in this way: that we despise not our nearest relatives, if we know they are in want. For it is better for thee to help thy kindred who feel the shame of asking help from others, or of going to another to beg assistance in their need. Not, however, that they should become rich on what thou couldst otherwise give to the poor. It is the facts of the case we must consider, and not personal feeling. Thou didst not dedicate thyself to the Lord on purpose to make thy family rich, but that thou mightest win eternal life by the fruit of good

41

works, and atone for thy sins by showing mercy. They think perhaps that they are asking but little, but they demand the price thou shouldst pay for thy sins. They attempt to take away the fruits of thy life, and think they are acting rightly. And one accuses thee because thou hast not made him rich, when all the time he wished to cheat thee of the reward of eternal life.

151. So far we have given our advice, now let us look for our authority. First, then, no one ought to be ashamed of becoming poor after being rich, if this happens because he gives freely to the poor; for Christ became poor when He was rich, that through His poverty He might enrich all." He has given us a rule to follow, so that we may give a good account of our reduced inheritance; whoever has stayed the hunger of the poor has lightened his distress. "Herein I give my advice," says the Apostle, "for this is expedient for you, that ye should be followers of Christ." Advice is given to the good, but warnings restrain the wrong-doers. Again he says, as though to the good: "For ye have begun not only to do, but also to be willing, a year ago." Both of these, and not only one, is the mark of perfection. Thus he teaches that liberality without good-will, and good-will without liberality, are neither of them perfect. Wherefore he also urges us on to perfection, saying: "Now, therefore, perform the doing of it; that as the will to do it was ready enough in you, so also there may be the will to accomplish it out of that which ye have. For if the will be ready, it is accepted according to that a man hath, and not according to that he hath not. But not so that others should have plenty, and ye should be in want: but let there be equality,—your abundance must now serve for their want, that their abundance may serve for your want; that there may be equality, as it is written: "He that gathered much had nothing over, and he that gathered little had no lack."

152. We notice how the Apostle includes both good-will and liberality, as well as the manner, the fruits of right giving, and the persons concerned. The manner certainly, for he gave advice to those not perfect: For only the imperfect suffer anxiety. But if any priest or other cleric, being unwilling to burden the Church, does not give away all that he has, but does honourably what his office demands, he does not seem to me to be imperfect. I think also that the Apostle here spoke not of anxiety of mind, but rather of domestic troubles.

153. And I think it was with reference to the persons concerned that he said: "that your abundance might serve for their want, and their abundance for your want." This means, that the abundance of the people might arouse them to good works, so as to supply the want of food of others; whilst the spiritual abundance of these latter might assist the want of spiritual merits among the people themselves, and so win them a blessing.

154. Wherefore he gave them an excellent example: "He that gathered much had nothing over, and he that gathered little had no lack." That example is a great encouragement to all men to show mercy. For he that possesses much gold has nothing over, for all in this world is as nothing; and he that has little has no lack, for what he loses is nothing already. The whole matter is without loss, for the whole of it is lost already.

155. We can also rightly understand it thus. He that has much, although he does not give away, has nothing over. For however much he gets, he always is in want, because he longs for more. And he who has little has no lack, for it does not cost much to feed the poor. In like manner, too, the poor person that gives spiritual blessings in return for money, although he has much grace, has nothing over. For grace does not burden the mind, but lightens it.

156. It can further be taken in this way: Thou, O man, hast nothing over! For how much hast thou really received, though it may seem much to thee? John, than whom none was greater among those born of woman, yet was less than he who is least in the kingdom of heaven.

157. Or once more. The grace of God is never superabundant, humanly speaking, for it is spiritual. Who can measure its greatness or its breadth, which one cannot see? Faith, if it were as a grain of mustard seed, can transplant mountains—and more than a grain is not granted thee. If grace dwelt fully in thee, wouldst thou not have to fear lest thy mind should begin to be elated at so great a gift? For there are many who have fallen more terribly, from spiritual heights, than if

they had never received grace at all from the Lord. And he who has little has no lack, for it is not tangible so as to be divided; and what seems little to him that has is much to him that lacks.

158. In giving we must also take into consideration age and weakness; sometimes, also, that natural feeling of shame, which indicates good birth. One ought to give more to the old who can no longer supply themselves with food by labour. So, too, weakness of body must be assisted, and that readily. Again, if any one after being rich has fallen into want, we must assist, especially if he has lost what he had from no sin of his own, but owing to robbery or banishment or false accusation.

159. Perchance some one may say: A blind man sits here in one place, and people pass him by, whilst a strong young man often has something given him. That is true; for he comes over people by his importunity. That is not because in their judgment he deserves it, but because they are wearied by his begging. For the Lord speaks in the Gospel of him who had already closed iris door; how that when one knocks at his door very violently, he rises and gives what is wanted, because of his importunity.

Chapter XXXI.

A kindness received should be returned with a freer hand. This is shown by the example of the earth. A passage from Solomon about feasting is adduced to prove the same, and is expounded later in a spiritual sense.

160. It is also right that more regard should be paid to him who has conferred some benefit or girl upon thee, if he ever is reduced to want. For what is so contrary to one's duty as not to return what one has received? Nor do I think that a return of equal value should be made, but a greater. One ought to make up for the enjoyment of a kindness one has received from another, to such an extent as to help that person. even to putting an end to his needs. For not to be the better in returning than in conferring a kindness, is to be the inferior; for he who was the first to give was the first in point of time, and also first in showing a kind disposition.

161. Wherefore we must imitate the nature of the earth in this respect, which is wont to return the seed she has received, multiplied a thousand-fold. And so it is written: "As a field is the foolish man, and as a vineyard is the man without sense. If thou leavest him, he will be made desolate." As a field also is the wise man, so as to return the seed given him in fuller measure, as though it had been lent to him on interest. The earth either produces fruits of its own accord, or pays back and restores, what it was entrusted with, in fruitful abundance. In both these ways a return is due from thee, when thou enterest upon the use of thy father's possession, that thou mayest not be left to lie as an unfruitful field. It may be that a man can make an excuse for not giving anything, but how can he excuse himself for not returning what was given? It is hardly right not to give anything; it is certainly not right to make no return for kindness done to oneself.

162. Therefore Solomon says well: "When thou sittest to eat at the table of a ruler consider diligently what is before thee, and put forth thine hand, knowing that it behoves thee to make such preparations. But if thou art insatiable, be not desirous of his dainties, for they have but a deceptive life." I have written these words as I wish that we all should follow them. It is a good thing to do a service, but he who knows not how to return one is very hard. The earth herself supplies an example of kindliness. She provides fruits of her own accord, which thou didst not sow; she also returns many-fold what she has received. It is not right for thee to deny knowledge of money paid in to thee, and how can it be right to let a service done go without notice? In the book of Proverbs also it is said: that the repayment of kindness has such great power with God, that through it, even in the day of destruction, a man may find grace, though his sins outweigh all else. And why need I bring forward other examples when the Lord Himself promises in the Gospel a fuller reward to the merits of the saints, and exhorts us to do good works, saying: "Forgive, and ye shall be forgiven; give, and it shall be given unto you; good measure, shaken together and running over, shall men give into your bosom."

163. But the feasting that Solomon speaks of has not to do with common food only, but it is to be understood as having to do with good works. For how can the soul be feasted in better wise than on good works; or what can so easily fill the mind of the just as the knowledge of a good work done? What pleasanter food is there than to do the will of God? The Lord has told us that He had this food alone in abundance, as it is written in the Gospel, saying: "My food is to do the will of My Father which is in heaven."

164. In this food let us delight of which the prophet says: "Delight thou in the Lord." In this food they delight, who have with wonderful knowledge learnt to take in the higher delights; who can know what that delight is which is pure and which can be understood by the mind. Let us therefore eat the bread of wisdom, and let us be filled with the word of God. For the life of man made in the image of God consists not in bread alone, but in every word that cometh from God. About the cup, too, holy Job says, plainly enough: "As the earth waiteth for the rain, so did they for my words."

Chapter XXXII.

After saying what return must be made for the service of the above-mentioned feast, various reasons for repaying kindness are enumerated. Then he speaks in praise of good-will, on its results and its order.

165. It is therefore a good thing for us to be bedewed with the exhortations of the divine Scriptures, and that the word of God should come down upon us like the dew. When, therefore, thou sittest at the table of that great man, understand who that great man is. Set in the paradise of delight and placed at the feast of wisdom, think of what is put before thee! The divine Scriptures are the feast of wisdom, and the single books the various dishes. Know, first, what dishes the banquet offers, then stretch forth thy hand, that those things which thou readest, or which thou receivest from the Lord thy God, thou mayest carry out in action, and so by thy duties mayest show forth the grace that was granted thee. Such was the case with Peter and Paul, who in preaching the Gospel made some return to Him Who freely gave them all things. So that each of them might say: "By the grace of God I am what I am, and His grace in me was not in vain, but I laboured more abundantly than they all."

166. One repays the fruit of a service done him, and repays it, gold with gold, silver with silver. Another gives his labour. Another—and I do not know whether he does not do it in fuller measure—gives but the best wishes of his heart. But what if there is no opportunity to make a return at hand? If we wish to return a kindness, more depends on the spirit in which we do it than on the amount of our property, whilst people will think more of our good-will, than of our power to make a full return. For a kindness done is regarded in the light of what one has. A great thing, therefore, is good-will. For even if it has nothing to give, yet it offers the more, and though there is nothing in its own possession, yet it gives largely to many, and does that, too, without loss to itself, and to the gain of the many. Thus good-will is better than liberality itself. It is richer in character than the other is in gifts; for there are more that need a kindness than there are that have abundance.

167. But good-will also goes in conjunction with liberality, for liberality really starts from it, seeing that the habit of giving comes after the desire to give. It exists, however, also separate and distinct. For where liberality is wanting, there good-will abide's—the parent as it were of all in common, uniting and binding friendships together. It is faithful in counsel, joyful in times of prosperity, and in times of sorrow sad. So it happens that any one trusts himself to the counsels of a man of good-will rather than to those of a wise one, as David did. For he, though he was the more farseeing, agreed to the counsels of Jonathan, who was the younger. Remove good-will out of the reach of men, and it is as though one had withdrawn the sun from the world. For without it men would no longer care to show the way to the stranger, to recall the wanderer, to show hospitality (this latter is no small virtue, for on this point Job praised himself, when he said: "At my doors the stranger dwelt not, my gate was open to every one who came"), nor even to give water from the water that flows at their door, or to light another's candle at their own.

Thus good-will exists in all these, like a fount of waters refreshing the thirsty, and like a light, which, shining forth to others, fails not them who have given a light to others from their own light.

168. There is also liberality springing from good-will, that makes one tear up the bond of a debtor which one holds, without demanding any of the debt back from him. Holy Job bids us act thus by his own example. For he that has does not borrow, but he that has not does not put an end to the agreement. Why, then, if thou hast no need, dost thou save up for greedy heirs what thou canst give back immediately, and so get praise for good-will, and that without loss of money?

169. To go to the root of thereafter—good-will starts first with those at home, that is with children, parents, brothers, and goes on from one step to another throughout the world. Having started from Paradise, it has filled the world. For God set the feeling of good-will in the man and woman, saying: "They shall be one flesh," and (one may add) one spirit. Wherefore Eve also believed the serpent; for she who had received the gift of good-will did not think there was ill-will.

Chapter XXXIII.
Good-will exists especially in the Church, and nourisheskindred virtues.

170. Good-Will expands in the body of the Church, by fellowship in faith, by the bond of baptism, by kinship through grace received, by communion in the mysteries. For all these bonds claim for themselves the name of intimacy, the reverence of children, the authority and religious care of parents, the relationship of brothers. Therefore the bonds of grace clearly point to an increase of good-will.

171. The desire to attain to like virtues also stands one in good stead; just as again good-will brings about a likeness in character. For Jonathan the king's son imitated the gentleness of holy David, because he loved him. Wherefore those words: "With the holy thou shalt be holy," seem not only to be concerned with our ordinary intercourse, but also to have some connection with good-will. The sons of Noah indeed dwelt together, and yet their characters were not at all alike. Esau and Jacob also dwelt together in their father's house, but were very unlike. There was, however, no good-will between them to make the one prefer the other to himself, but rather a rivalry as to which should first get. the blessing. Since one was so hard, and the other gentle, good-will could not exist as between such different characters and conflicting desires. Add to this the fact that holy Jacob could not prefer the unworthy in son of his father's house to virtue.

172. But nothing is so harmonious as justice and impartiality. For this, as the comrade and ally of good-will, makes us love those whom we think to be like ourselves. Again, good-will contains also in itself fortitude. For when friendship springs from the fount of good-will it does not hesitate to endure the great dangers of life for a friend. "If evils come to me through him," it says, "I will bear them."

Chapter XXXIV.
Some other advantages of goodwill are here enumerated.

173. Good-Will also is wont to remove the sword of anger. It is also good-will that makes the wounds of a friend to be better than the willing kisses of an enemy. Goodwill again makes many to become one. For if many are friends, they become one; in whom there is but one spirit and one opinion. We note, too, that in friendship corrections are pleasing. They have their sting, but they cause no pain. We are pierced by the words of blame, but are delighted with the anxiety that good-will shows.

174. To conclude, the same duties are not owed to all. Nor is regard ever paid to persons, though the occasion and the circumstances of the case are generally taken into consideration, so that one may at times have to help a neighbour rather than one's brother. For Solomon also says: "Better is a neighbour that is near than a brother far off." For this reason a man generally

trusts himself to the good-will of a friend rather than to the ties of relationship with his brother. So far does good-will prevail that it often goes beyond the pledges given by nature.

Chapter XXXV.

On fortitude. This is divided into two parts: as it concerns matters of war and matters at home. The first cannot be a virtue unless combined with justice and prudence. The other depends to a large extent upon endurance.

175. We have discussed fully enough the nature and force of what is virtuous from the standpoint of justice. Now let us discuss fortitude, which (being a loftier virtue than the rest) is divided into two parts, as it concerns matters of war and matters at home. But the thought of warlike matters seems to be foreign to the duty of our office, for we have our thoughts fixed more on the duty of the soul than on that of the body; nor is it our business to look to arms, but rather to the affairs of peace. Our fathers, however, as Joshua, the son of Nun, Jerubbaal, Samson, and David, gained great glory also in war.

176. Fortitude, therefore, is a loftier virtue than the rest, but it is also one that never stands alone. For it never depends on itself alone. Moreover, fortitude without justice is the source of wickedness. For the stronger it is, the more ready is it to crush the weaker, whilst in matters of war one ought to see whether the war is just or unjust.

177. David never waged war unless he was driven to it. Thus prudence was combined in him with fortitude in the battle. For even when about to fight single-handed against Goliath, the enormous giant, he rejected the armour with which he was laden. His strength depended more on his own arm than on the weapons of others. Then, at a distance, to get a stronger throw, with one cast of a stone, he slew his enemy. After that he never entered on a war without seeking counsel of the Lord. Thus he was victorious in all wars, and even to his last years was ready to fight. And when war arose with the Philistines, he joined battle with their fierce troops, being desirous of winning renown, whilst careless of his own safety. 178. But this is not the only kind of fortitude which is worthy of note. We consider their fortitude glorious, who, with greatness of mind, "through faith stopped the mouth of lions, quenched the violence of fire, escaped the edge of the sword, out of weakness were made strong." They did not gain a victory in common with many, surrounded with comrades, and aided by the legions, but won their triumph alone over their treacherous foes by the mere courage of their own souls. How unconquerable was Daniel, who feared not the lions raging round about him. The beasts roared, whilst he was eating.

Chapter XXXVI.

One of the duties of fortitude is to keep the weak from receiving injury; another, to check the wrong motions of our own souls; a third, both to disregard humiliations, and to do what is right with an even mind. All these clearly ought to be fulfilled by all Christians, and especially by the clergy.

179. The glory of fortitude, therefore, does not rest only on the strength of one's body or of one's arms, but rather on the courage of the mind. Nor is the law of courage exercised in causing, but in driving away all harm. He who does not keep harm off a friend, if he can, is as much in fault as he who causes it. Wherefore holy Moses gave this as a first proof of his fortitude in war. For when he saw an Hebrew receiving hard treatment at the hands of an Egyptian, he defended him, and laid low the Egyptian and hid him in the sand. Solomon also says: "Deliver him that is led to death."

180. From whence, then, Cicero and Panaetius, or even Aristotle, got these ideas is perfectly clear. For though living before these two, Job had said: "I delivered the poor out of the hand of the strong, and I aided the fatherless for whom there was no helper. Let the blessing of him that was ready to perish come upon me." Was not he most brave in that he bore so nobly the attacks of the devil, and overcame him with the powers of his mind? Nor have we cause to doubt the fortitude of him to whom the Lord said: "Gird up thy loins like a man. Put on loftiness and

power. Humble every one that doeth wrong." The Apostle also says: "Ye have a strong consolation." He, then, is brave who finds consolation in any grief.

181. And in very truth, rightly is that called fortitude, when a man conquers himself, restrains his anger, yields and gives way to no allurements, is not put out by misfortunes, nor gets elated by good success, and does not get carried away by every varying change as by some chance wind. But what is more noble and splendid than to train the mind, keep down the flesh, and reduce it to subjection, so that it may obey commands, listen to reason, and in undergoing labours readily carry out the intention and wish of the mind?

182. This, then, is the first notion of fortitude. For fortitude of the mind can be regarded in two ways. First, as it counts all externals as very unimportant, and looks on them as rather superfluous and to be despised than to be sought after. Secondly, as it strives after those things which are the highest, and all things in which one can see anything moral (or as the Greeks call it, prepon,) with all the powers of the mind. For what can be more noble than to train thy mind so as not to place a high value on riches and pleasures and honours, nor to waste all thy care on these? When thy mind is thus disposed, thou must consider how all that is virtuous and seemly must be placed before everything else; and thou must so fix thy mind upon that, that if aught happens which may break thy spirit, whether loss of property, or the reception of fewer honours, or the disparagement of unbelievers, thou mayest not feel it, as though thou wert above such things; nay, so that even dangers which menace thy safety, if undertaken at the call of justice, may not trouble thee.

183. This is the true fortitude which Christ's warrior has, who receives not the crown unless he strives lawfully. Or does that call to fortitude seem to thee but a poor one: "Tribulation worketh patience, and patience, experience, and experience, hope"? See how many a contest there is, yet but one crown! That call none gives, but he who was strengthened in Christ Jesus, and whose flesh had no rest. Affliction on all sides, fighting without and fears within. And though in dangers, in countless labours, in prisons, in deaths —he was not broken in spirit, but fought so as to become more powerful through his infirmities.

184. Think, then, how he teaches those who enter upon their duties in the Church, that they ought to have contempt for all earthly things: "If, then, ye be dead with Christ from the elements of this world, why do ye act as though living in the world? Touch not, taste not, handle not, which all are to perish with the using." And further: "If ye then be risen with Christ, seek those things which are above, not those things which are on the earth." And again: "Mortify, therefore, your members which are on the earth." This, indeed, is meant for all the faithful. But thee, especially, my son, he urges to despise riches and to avoid profane and old wives fables— allowing nothing but this: "Exercise thyself unto godliness, for bodily exercise profiteth a little, but godliness is profitable unto all things."

185. Let, then, godliness exercise thee unto justice, continence, gentleness, that thou mayest avoid childish acts, and that rooted and grounded in grace thou mayest fight the good fight of faith. Entangle not thyself in the affairs of this life, for thou art fighting for God. For if he who fights for the emperor is forbidden by human laws to enter upon lawsuits, to do any legal business, or to sell merchandise; how much more ought he who enters upon the warfare of faith to keep from every kind of business, being satisfied with the produce of his own little bit of land, if he has it? If he has not that, let him be content with the pay he will get for his service. Here is a good witness to this fact, who says: "I have been young and now am old, yet have I not seen the righteous forsaken, nor his seed begging bread." That is the true rest and temperance of the mind which is not excited by the desire of gain, nor tormented by the fear of want.

Chapter XXXVII.

An even mind should be preserved in adversity as well as in prosperity. However, evil things must be avoided.

186. There is also that true freedom of the mind from vexation which makes us neither give way too much in our griefs, nor be too elated in prosperity. And if they who urge men to undertake the affairs of the state give such rules, how much more ought we who are called to do duty in the Church, to act thus and do those things which are pleasing to God, so that Christ's power may show itself forth in us. We too must prove ourselves to our Captain, so that our members may be the weapons of justice; not carnal weapons in which sin may reign, but weapons strong for God, whereby sin may be destroyed. Let our flesh die, that in it every sin may die. And as though living again after death, may we rise to new works and a new life.

187. These, then, are the services of fortitude; and full they are of virtuous and seemly duties. But in all that we do we must look to see, not only if it is virtuous, but whether it is possible, so that we may not enter upon anything that we cannot carry out. Wherefore the Lord, to use His own word, wills us to flee in the time of persecution from one city to another; so that no one, whilst longing for the crown of martyrdom, may put himself in the way of dangers which possibly the weak flesh or a mind indulged could not bear and endure.

Chapter XXXVIII.

We must strengthen the mind against troubles to come, and build it up by looking out for them beforehand. What difficulties there are in doing this.

188. But again, no one must retire through cowardice, or give up his faith from fear of danger. With what grace must the soul be equipped, and the mind trained and taught. to stand firm, so as never to be disturbed by any fears, to be broken by any troubles, or to yield to any torments! With what difficulty indeed are they borne! But as all pains seem less in the fear of greater pains, so also, if thou dost build up thy soul by quiet counsel, and dost determine not to go from thy course, and layest before thee the fear of divine judgment and the torment of eternal punishment, canst thou gain endurance of mind.

189. If a man thus prepares himself, he gives signs of great diligence. On the other hand it is a sign of natural ability, if a man by the power of his mind can foresee the future, and put as it were before his eyes what may happen, and decide what he ought to do if it should take place. It may happen, too, that he will think over two or three things at once, which he supposes may come either singly or together, and that he settles what he will do with them as he thinks will be to the most advantage, in the event of their coming either singly or together.

200. Therefore it is the duty of a brave man not to shut his eyes when anything threatens, but to put it before him and to search it out as it were in the mirror of his mind, and to meet the future with foreseeing thought, for fear he might afterwards have to say: This has come to me because I thought it could not come about. If misfortunes are not looked for beforehand, they quickly get a hold over us. In war an unexpected enemy is with difficulty resisted, and if he finds the others unprepared, he easily overcomes them; so evils unthought of readily break down the soul.

200. In these two points, then, consists the excellency of the soul: so that thy soul, trained in good thoughts, and with a pure heart, first, may see what is true and virtuous (for "blessed are the pure in heart, for they shall see God"), and may decide that only to be good which is virtuous; and, next, may never be disturbed by business of any kind, nor get tossed about by any desires.

201. Not that this is an easy thing for any one. For what is so difficult as to discern, as though from some watch-tower, the resources of wisdom and all those other things, which to most seem so great and noble? Again, what so difficult as to place one's decision on fixed grounds, and to despise what one has decided to be worthless, as of no good? Or, once more, what so difficult, when some misfortune has happened, and it is looked on as something serious and grieving, as to bear it in such a way that one considers it nothing beyond what is natural,

when one reads: "Naked was I born, naked shall I go forth. What the Lord gave, the Lord hath taken away" (he who said this had lost children and possessions), and to preserve in all things the character of a wise and upright man, as he did who says: "As the Lord pleased, so did He. Blessed be the name of the Lord." And again: "Thou speakest as one of the foolish women speaketh. Shall we receive good at the hand of God, and shall we not receive evil?"

Chapter XXXIX.
One must show fortitude in fighting againnt all vices, especially against avarice. Holy Job teaches this lesson.

202. Fortitude of soul, then, is not an unimportant thing, nor is it cut off from the other virtues, for it wages war in conjunction with the virtues, and alone defends the beauty of all the virtues, and guards their powers of discernment, and fights against all vices with implacable hate. It is unconquerable as regards labours, brave to endure dangers, stern as against pleasures, hardened against allurements, to which it knows not how to lend an ear, nor, so to speak, to give a greeting. It cares not for money, and flies from avarice as from a plague that destroys all virtue. For nothing is so much opposed to fortitude as when one allows one self to be overcome by gain. Often when the enemy is repulsed and the hosts of the foe are turned to flight, has the warrior died miserably among those whom he has laid low, whilst he is busy with the spoils of the fallen; and the legions, whilst busy with their booty, have called back upon them the enemy that had fled, and so have been robbed of their triumph.

203. Fortitude, then, must repulse so foul a plague and crush it down. It must not let itself be tempted by desires, nor shaken by fear. Virtue stands true to itself and bravely pursues all vices as though they were the poison of virtue. It must repel anger as it were with arms, for it removes counsel far off. It must avoid it as though it were some severe sickness. It must further be on its guard against a desire for glory, which often has done harm when sought for too anxiously, and always when it has been once attained.

204. What of all this was wanting in holy Job, or in his virtue, or what came upon him in the way of vice? How did he bear the distress of sickness or cold or hunger? How did he look upon the dangers which menaced his safety? Were the riches from which so much went to the poor gathered together by plunder? Did he ever allow greed for wealth, or the desire for pleasures, or lusts to rise in his heart? Did ever the unkind disputes of the three princes, or the insults of the slaves, rouse him to anger? Did glory carry him away like some fickle person when he called down vengeance on himself if ever he had hidden even an involuntary fault, or had feared the multitude of the people so as not to confess it in the sight of all? His virtues had no point of contact with any vices, but stood firm on their own ground. Who, then, was so brave as holy Job? How can he be put second to any, on whose level hardly one like himself can be placed?

Chapter XL.
Courage in war was not wanting in our forefathers, as is shown by the example of the men of old, especially by the glorious deed of Eleazar.

205. But perhaps renown in war keeps some so bound to itself as to make them think that fortitude is to be found in battle alone, and that therefore I had gone aside to speak of these things, because that was wanting in ns. But how brave was Joshua the son of Nun, who in one battle laid low five kings together with their people! Again, when he fought against the Gibeonites and feared that night might stop him from gaining the victory, he called out with deep faith and high spirit: "Let the sun stand still;" and it stood still until the victory was complete. Gideon with three hundred men gained a triumph over a great nation and a cruel foe. Jonathan when a young man showed great courage in battle, and what shall I say about the Maccabees?

206. First, I will speak of the people of our fathers. They were ready to fight for the temple of God and for their rights, and when attacked on the Sabbath day by the craft of the enemy, willingly allowed wounds to be inflicted on their unprotected bodies, rather than to join in the

fight, so that they might not defile the Sabbath. They all gladly gave themselves up to death. But the Maccabees thinking that then all the nation would perish, on the Sabbath also, when they were challenged to fight, took vengeance for the death of their innocent brethren. And afterwards when he had been roused by this to fresh exertions, King Antiochus, having begun the war afresh under the leadership of his generals Lysias, Nicanor, and Georgias, was so utterly crushed, together with his Eastern and Assyrian forces, that he left 48,000 lying on the battle-field, slain by an army of but 3,000 men.

207. Mark the courage of the leader, Judas Maccabaeus, as exemplified in the character of one of his soldiers. Eleazar, meeting with an elephant higher than all the rest, and with all the royal trappings upon it, and thinking that the king was on it, ran hastily and threw himself into the midst of the legion; and, casting away his shield, with both hands he slew those opposed to him until he reached the beast. Then he got beneath it, thrust in his sword and slew it. But the beast in falling crushed Eleazar and so killed him. What courage of mind was his then, first, in that he feared not death, next because, when surrounded by enemies, he was carried by it into the thickest of his foes and penetrated the very centre! Then, despising death, and casting away his shield, he ran beneath the huge beast, wounded it with both his hands, and let it fall upon him. He ran beneath it so as to give a more deadly blow. Enclosed by its fall, rather than crushed, he was buried in his own triumph.

208. Nor was he deceived in his intention though he was deceived by the royal ornaments. For the enemy, startled at such an exhibition of valour, dared not rush upon this single unarmed man, held fast though he was. They were so terrified after the mischance of the slaughter of the beast, that they considered themselves altogether unequal to the valour of one. Nay, King Antiochus, son of Lysias, terrified at the fortitude of one, asked for peace. He had come to the war with 120,000 armed men and with 32 elephants, which glittered and gleamed with the sheen of arms like a line of burning lamps, as the sun rose upon them, marching along one by one, like very mountains for size. Thus Eleazar left peace as the heir of his courage. These are the signs of triumphs.

Chapter XLI.

After praising Judas' and Jonathan's loftiness of mind, the constancy of the martyrs in their endurance of tortures, which is no small part of fortitude, is next brought before us.

209. But as fortitude is proved not only by prosperity but also in adversity, let us now consider the death of Judas Maceabaeus. For he, after Nicanor, the general of King Demetrius, was defeated, boldly engaged 20,000 of the king's army with 900 men who were anxious to retire for fear of being overcome by so great a multitude, but whom he persuaded to endure a glorious death rather than to retire in disgraceful flight. "Let us not leave," he says, "any stain upon our glory." Thus, then, engaging in battle after having fought from sunrise till evening, he attacks and quickly drives back the right wing, where he sees the strongest troop of the enemy to be. But whilst pursuing the fugitives from the rear he gave a chance for a wound to be inflicted. Thus he found the spot of death more full of glory for himself than any triumph.

210. Why need I further mention his brother Jonathan, who fought against the king's force, with but a small troop. Though forsaken by his men, and left with only two, he retrieved the battle, drove back the enemy, and recalled his own men, who were flying m every direction, to share in his triumph.

211. Here, then, is fortitude in war, which bears no light impress of what is virtuous and seemly upon it, for it prefers death to slavery and disgrace. But what am I to say of the sufferings of the martyrs? Not to go too far abroad, did not the children of Maccabaeus gain triumphs over the proud King Antiochus, as great as those of their fathers? The latter in truth were armed, but they conquered without arms. The company of the seven brothers stood unconquered, though surrounded by the legions of the king—tortures failed, tormentors ceased; but the martyrs failed not. One, having had the skin of his head pulled off, though changed in

appearance, grew in courage. Another, bidden to put forth his tongue, so that it might be cut off, answered: "The Lord hears not only those who speak, for He heard Moses when silent. He hears better the silent thoughts of His own than the voice of all others. Dost thou fear the scourge of my tongue—and dost thou not fear the scourge of blood spilt upon the ground? Blood, too, has a voice whereby it cries aloud to God—as it did in the case of Abel."

212. What shall I say of the mother who with joy looked on the corpses of her children as so many trophies, and found delight in the voices of her dying sons, as though in the songs of singers, noting in her children the tones of the glorious harp of her own heart, and a sweeter harmony of love than any strain of the lute could give?

213. What shall I say of those two-year-old children of Bethlehem, who received the palm of victory before they felt their natural life within them? What of St. Agnes, who when in danger as regards two great matters, that is, chastity and life, protected her chastity and exchanged life for immortality?

214. And let us not pass by St. Lawrence, who, seeing Xystus his bishop led to martyrdom, began to weep, not at his sufferings but at the fact that he himself was to remain behind. With these words he began to address him: "Whither, father, goest thou without thy son? Whither, holy priest, art thou hastening without thy deacon? Never wast thou wont to offer sacrifice without an attendant. What are thou displeased at in me, my father? Hast thou found me unworthy? Prove, then, whether thou hast chosen a fitting servant. To him to whom thou hast entrusted the consecration of the Saviour's blood, to whom thou hast granted fellowship in partaking of the Sacraments, to him dost thou refuse a part in thy death? Beware lest thy good judgment be endangered, whilst thy fortitude receives its praise. The rejection of a pupil is the loss of the teacher; or how is it that noble and illustrious men gain the victory in the contests of their scholars rather than in their own? Abraham offered his son, Peter sent Stephen on before him! Do thou, father, show forth thy courage in thy son. Offer me whom thou hast trained, that thou, confident in thy choice of me, mayest reach the crown in worthy company."

215. Then Xystus said: "I leave thee not nor forsake thee. Greater struggles yet await thee. We as old men have to undergo an easier fight; a more glorious triumph over the tyrant awaits thee, a young man. Soon shalt thou come. Cease weeping; after three days thou shalt follow me. This interval must come between the priest and his levite. It was not for thee to conquer under the eye of thy master, as though thou needest a helper. Why dost thou seek to share in my death? I leave to thee its full inheritance. Why dost thou need my presence? Let the weak disciples go before their master, let the brave follow him, that they may conquer without him. For they no longer need his guidance. So Elijah left Elisha. To thee I entrust the full succession to my own courage."

216. Such was their contention, and surely a worthy one, wherein priest and attendant strove as to who should be the first to suffer for the name of Christ. When that tragic piece is played, it is said there is great applause in the theatre as Pylades says he is Orestes, whilst Orestes declares that he is really himself. The former acted as he did, that he might die for Orestes, and Orestes, that he might not allow Pylades to be slain instead of himself. But it was not right that they should live, for each of them was guilty of parricide, the one because he had committed the crime, the other because he had helped in its commission. But here there was nothing to call holy Lawrence to act thus but his love and devotion. However, after three days he was placed upon the gridiron by the tyrant whom he mocked, and was burnt. He said: "The flesh is roasted, turn it and eat." So by the courage of his mind he overcame the power of fire.

Chapter XLII.

The powers that be are not needlessly to be irritated. One must not lend one's ears to flattery.

217. I Think we must take care, lest in being led on by too great a desire for glory, we should abuse the powers that be, and arouse the minds of the heathen, who are opposed to us, to desire

persecution, and excite them to anger. How many do some cause to perish, that they themselves may continue to the end, and overcome their tortures!

218. We must also look to it that we do not open our ears to flatterers. To allow oneself to be smoothed down by flattery seems to be a sign not only of want of fortitude, but a sign of actual cowardice.

Chapter XLIII.

On temperance and its chief parts, especially tran-quillity of mind and moderation, care for what is virtuous, and reflection on what is seemly.

219. As we have spoken of three of the virtues, there remains but the fourth for us to speak of. This is called temperance and moderation; wherein, before all else, tranquillity of mind, the attainment of gentleness, the grace of moderation, regard for what is virtuous, and reflection on what is seemly are sought and looked for.

220. We must keep to a certain order in life, so that a foundation may be laid with our first feelings of modesty, for that is the friend and ally of calmness of mind. Avoiding over-confidence, averse to all excess, it loves sobriety, guards what is honourable, and seeks only what is seemly.

221. Let choice of intercourse come next. Let us link ourselves with older men of approved goodness. For as the companionship of people of our own age is the plea-santer, so that of our elders is the safer. By their guidance and the conduct of their lives they give colour to the character of younger men, and tinge them as it were with the deep purple of probity. For if they who are ignorant of a locality are very glad to take a journey in the company of skilled guides, how much more ought young men to enter on the path of life, which is new to them, in the company of old men; so that they may not go wrong, and turn aside froth the true path of virtue. For nothing is better than to have the same men both to direct us in life, and also to be witnesses of how we live.

222. One must also in every action consider what is suitable for different persons, times, and ages, and what will also be in accordance with the abilities of individuals. For often what befits one does not befit another; one thing suits a youth, another an old man;one thing does in danger, another in good fortune.

223. David danced before the ark of the Lord. Samuel did not dance; yet David was not blamed, while the other was praised. David changed his countenance before the king, whose name was Achish. If he had done this without any fear of being recognized, he would certainly not have escaped the charge of levity. Saul also, surrounded by the company of prophets, himself prophesied. Yet of him alone, as though he were unworthy, was it said: "Is Saul also among the prophets?"

Chapter XLIV.

Every one ought to apply himself to the duties suited to his character. Many, however, are hindered by following their fathers' pursuits. Clerics act in a different way.

224. Each one knows his own powers. Therefore let each one apply himself to that which he has chosen as suitable to himself. But he must first consider what will be the consequences. He may know his good points, but he must know his faults also. He must also be a fair judge of himself, so as to aim at what is good and avoid what is bad.

225. One is more fitted for the post of reader, another does better for the singing, a third is more solicitous for exorcising those possessed with an evil spirit, another, again, is held to be more suited to have the charge of the sacred things. All these things a priest should look at. He should give each one that particular duty for which he is best fitted. For whither each one's bent of mind leads him, or whatever duty befits him, that position or duty is filled with greater grace.

226. But as this is a difficult matter in every state of life, so in our case it is most difficult. For each one is wont to follow his parent's choice in life. Thus those whose fathers were in the

army generally enter the army too. And others do the same with regard to the different professions.

227. In the clerical office, however, nothing is more rare than to find a man to follow his father's footsteps, either because the difficulties of the work hold him back, or continence in the uncertain days of youth is too difficult to hold to, or the life seems to be too quiet for the activity of youth. So they turn to those pursuits which are thought to be more showy. Most, indeed, prefer the present to the future. They are fighting for the present, we for the future. Wherefore it follows that the greater the cause in which we are engaged, the more must our attention be devoted to it.

Chapter XLV.

On what is noble and virtuous, and what the difference between them is, as stated both in the profane and sacred writers.

228. Let us then hold fast modesty, and that moderation which adds to the beauty of the whole of life. For it is no light thing in every matter to preserve due measure and to bring about order, wherein that is plainly conspicuous which we call "decorum," or what is seemly. This is so closely connected with what is virtuous, that one cannot separate the two. For what is seemly is also virtuous—and what is virtuous is seemly. So that the distinction lies rather in the words than in the things themselves. That there is a difference between them we can understand, but we cannot explain it.

229. To make an attempt to get some sort of a distinction between them, we may say that what is virtuous may be compared to the good health and soundness of the body, whilst what is seemly is, as it were, its comeliness and beauty. And as beauty seems to stand above soundness and health, and yet cannot exist without them, nor be separated from them in any way—for unless one has good health, one cannot have beauty and comeliness—so what is virtuous contains in itself also what is seemly, so as to seem to start with it, and to be unable to exist without it. What is virtuous, then, is like soundness in all our work and undertaking; what is seemly is, as it were, the outward appearance, which, when joined with what is virtuous, can only be known apart in our thoughts. For though in some cases it seems to stand out conspicuous, yet it has its root in what is virtuous, though the flower is its own. Rooted in this, it flourishes; otherwise it fails and droops. For what is virtue, but to avoid anything shameful as though it were death? And what is the opposite of virtue, except that which brings barrenness and death? If, then, the essence of virtue is strong and vigorous, seemliness will also quickly spring forth like a flower, for its root is sound. But if the root of its purpose is corrupt, nothing will grow out of it.

230. In our writings this is put somewhat more plainly. For David says: "The Lord reigneth, He is clothed with splendour." And the Apostle says: "Walk honestly as in the day." The Greek text has euschmonw"—and this really means: with good clothing, with a good appearance. When God made the first man, He created him with a good figure, with limbs well set, and gave him a very noble appearance. He had not given him remission of sins. But afterwards He, Who came in the form of a servant, and in the likeness of man, renewed him with His Spirit, and poured His grace into his heart, and put on Himself the splendour of the redemption of the human race. Therefore the Prophet said: "The Lord reigneth, He is clothed with splendour." And again he says: "A hymn beseems Thee, O God, in Sion." That is: It is right and good to fear Thee, to love Thee, to pray to Thee, to honour Thee, for it is written: "Let all things be done decently and in order." But we can also fear, love, ask, honour men; yet the hymn especially is addressed to God. This seemliness which we offer to God we may believe to be far better than other things. It befits also a woman to pray in an orderly dress, but it especially beseems her to pray covered, and to pray giving promise of purity together with a good conversation.

Chapter XLVI.

A twofold division of what is seemly is given. Next it is shown that what is according to nature is virtuous, and what is otherwise must be looked on as shameful. This division is explained by examples.

231. Seemliness, therefore, which stands conspicuous has a twofold division. For there is what we may call a general seemli-ness, which is diffused through all that is virtuous, and is seen, as one may say, in the whole body. It is also individual, and shows itself clearly in some particular part. The first has a consistent form and the perfection of what is virtuous harmonizing in every action. For all its life is consistent with itself, and there is no discrepancy in anything. The other is concerned when there is any special action done in a virtuous course of life.

232. At the same time let us note that it is seemly to live in accordance with nature, and to pass our time in accordance with it, and that whatever is contrary to nature is shameful. For the Apostle asks: "Is it comely that a woman pray unto God uncovered; doth not nature itself teach you that if a man have long hair, it is a shame unto him? For it is contrary to nature." And again he says: "If a woman have long hair, it is a glory unto her." It is according to nature, since her hair is given her for a veil, for it is a natural veil. Thus nature arranges for us both character and appearance, and we ought to observe her directions. Would that we could guard her innocence, and not change what we have received by our wickedness!

233. We have that general seemliness; for God made the beauty of this world. We have it also in its parts; for when God made the light, and marked off the day from the night, when He made heaven, and separated land and seas, when He set the sun and moon and stars to shine on the earth, He approved of them all one by one. Therefore this comeliness, which shone forth in each single part of the world, was resplendent in the whole, as the Book of Wisdom shows, saying: "I existed, in whom He rejoiced when He was glad at the completion of the world." Likewise also in the building up of the human body each single member is pleasing, but the right adjustment of the members all together delights us far more. For thus they seem to be united and fitted in one harmonious whole.

Chapter XLVII.

What is seemly should always shine forth in our life. What passions, then, ought we to allow to come to a head, and which should we restrain?

234. If any one preserves an even tenor in the whole of life, and method in all that he does, and sees there is order and consistency in his words and moderation in his deeds, then what is seemly stands forth conspicuous in his life and shines forth as in some mirror.

235. There should be besides a pleasant way of speaking, so that we may win the good-will of those who hear us, and make ourselves agreeable to all our friends and fellow-citizens, if possible. Let none show himself to be given to flattery, nor to be desirous of flattery from any one. The one is a mark of artfulness, the other of vanity.

236. Let no one ever look down on what another, least of all a good man, thinks of him, for thus he learns to give regard to the good. For to disregard the judgment of good men is a sign of conceitedness or of weakness. One of these arises from pride, the other from carelessness.

237. We must also guard against the motions of our soul. The soul must always watch and look after itself, so as to guard itself against itself. For there are motions in which there is a kind of passion that breaks forth as it were in a sort of rush. Wherefore in Greek it is called ormh, because it comes out suddenly with some force. In these there lies no slight force of soul or of nature. Its force, however, is twofold: on the one side it rests on passion, on the other on reason, which checks passion, and makes-it obedient to itself, and leads it whither it will; and trains it by careful teaching to know what ought to be done, and what ought to be avoided, so as to make it submit to its kind tamer.

238. For we ought to be careful never to do anything rashly or carelessly, or anything at all for which we cannot give a reasonable ground. For though a reason for our action is not given

to every one, yet everybody looks into it. Nor, indeed, have we anything whereby we can excuse ourselves. For though there is a sort of natural force in every passion of ours, yet that same passion is subject to reason by the law of nature itself, and is obedient to it. Wherefore it is the duty of a careful watchman so to keep a lookout, that passion may not outrun reason nor utterly forsake it, lest by outstripping it confusion be caused, and reason be shut out, and come to nothing by such desertion. Disquiet destroys consistency. Withdrawal shows cowardice and implies indolence. For when the mind is disquieted passion spreads wide and far, and in a fierce outburst endures not the reins of reason and feels not the management of its driver so as to be turned back. Wherefore as a rule not only is the soul perturbed and reason lost, but one's countenance gets inflamed by anger or by lust. it grows pale with fear, it contains not itself in pleasure, and cannot bear joy.

239. When this happens, then that natural judgment and weight of character is cast aside, and that consistency which alone in deed and thought can keep up its own authority and what is seemly, can no longer be retained.

240. But fiercer passion springs from excessive anger, which the pain of some wrong received kindles within us. The monitions of the psalm which forms the opening of our subject instruct us on this point. Beautifully; then, has it come about that, in writing on duties, we used that declaration of our opening passage which also itself has to do with the direction of duty.

241. But since (as was but right) we there only touched upon the matter, as to how each one ought to take care not to be disturbed when wrong is done him, for fear that our preliminary remarks should run to too great length, I think that I will now discuss it a little more fully. For the occasion is opportune, as we are speaking on the different parts of temperance, to see how anger may be checked.

Chapter XLVIII.

The argument for restraining anger is given again. Then the three classes of those who receive wrongs are set forth; to the most perfect of which the Apostle and David are said to have attained. He takes the opportunity to state the difference between this and the future life.

242. We wish if we can to point out three classes of men who receive wrongs in holy Scripture. One of these forms the class of those whom the sinner reviles, abuses, rides over rough-shod. And just because justice fails them, shame grows, pain increases. Very many of my own order, of my own number, are like these. For if any one does me, who am weak, an injury, perhaps, though I am weak, I may forgive the wrong done me. If he charges me with an offence I am not such an one as to be content with the witness of my own conscience, although I know I am clear of what he brings against me; but I desire, just because I am weak, to wash out the mark of my inborn shame. Therefore I demand eye for eye, and tooth for tooth, and repay abuse with abuse.

243. If, however, I am one who is advancing, although not yet perfect, I do not return the reproaches; and if he breaks out into abuse, and fills my ears with reproaches, I am silent and do not answer.

244. But if I am perfect (I say this only by way of example, for in truth I am weak), if, then, I am perfect, I bless him that curses me, as Paul also blessed, for he says: "Being reviled we bless." He had heard Him Who says: "Love your enemies, pray for them which despitefully use you and persecute you." And so Paul suffered persecution and endured it, for he conquered and calmed his human feelings for the sake of the reward set before him, namely, that he should become a son of God if he loved his enemies.

245. We call show, too, that holy David was like to Paul in this same class of virtue. When the son of Shimei cursed him, and charged him with heavy offences, at the first he was silent and humbled himself, and was silent even about his good deeds, that is, his knowledge of good works. Then he even asked to be cursed; for when he was cursed he hoped to gain divine pity.

246. But see how he stored up humility and justice and prudence so as to merit grace from the Lord! At first he said: "Therefore he cursed me, because the Lord hath said unto him that he should curse." Here we have humility; for he thought that those things which are divinely ordered were to be endured with an even mind, as though he were but some servant lad. Then he said: "Behold my son, which came forth of my bowels, seeketh my life." Here we have justice. For if we suffer hard things at the hand of our own family, why are we angry at what is done to us by strangers? Lastly he says: "Let him alone that he may curse, for the Lord hath bidden him. It may be that the Lord will look on my humiliation and requite me good for this cursing." So he bore not only the abuse, but left the man unpunished when throwing stones and following him. Nay, more I After his victory he freely granted him pardon when he asked for it.

247. I have written this to show that holy David, in true evangelical spirit, was not only not offended, but was even thankful to his abuser, and was delighted rather than angered by his wrongs, for which he thought some return would be granted to him. But, though perfect, he sought something still more perfect. As a man he grew hot at the pain of his wrongs, but like a good soldier he conquered, he endured like a brave wrestler. The end and aim of his patience was the expectation of the fulfilment of the promises, and therefore he said: "Lord, make me to know mine end and the measure of my days, what it is: that I may know what is wanting to me." He seeks, then, that end of the heavenly promises, when each one shall arise in his own order: "Christ the firstfruits, then they that are Christ's who have believed in His coming. Then cometh the end." For when the kingdom is delivered up to God, even the Father, and all the powers are put down, as the Apostle says, then perfection begins. Here, then, is the hindrance, here the weakness of the perfect; there full perfection. Thus it is he asks for those days of eternal life which are, and not for those which pass away, so that he may know what is wanting to him, what is the land of promise that bears everlasting fruits, which is the first mansion in his Father's house, which the second, which the third, wherein each one will rest according to his merits.

248. We then must strive for that wherein is perfection and wherein is truth. Here is the shadow, here the image; there the truth. The shadow is in the law, the image in the Gospel, the truth in heaven. In old times a lamb, a Calf was offered; now Christ is offered. But He is offered as man and as enduring suffering. And He offers Himself as a priest to take away our sins, here in an image, there in truth, where with the Father He intercedes for us as our Advocate Here, then, we walk in an image, we see in an image; there face to face where is full perfection.For all perfection rests in the truth.

Chapter XLIX.

We must reserve the likeness of the virtues in ourselves. The likenessofthe devil and of vice must be got rid of, and especially that of avarice; for this deprives us of liberty, and despoils those who are in the midst of vanities of the image of God.

249. Whilst, then, we are here let us preserve the likeness, that there we may attain to the truth. Let the likeness of justice exist in us, likewise that of wisdom, for we shall come to that day and shall be rewarded according to our likeness.

250. Let not the adversary find his image in thee, let him not find fury nor rage; for in these exists the likeness of wickedness. "Our adversary the devil as a roaring lion seeketh whom he may kill, whom he may devour." Let him not find desire for gold, nor heaps of money, nor the appearance of vices, lest he take from thee the voice of liberty. For the voice of true liberty is heard, when thou canst say: "The prince of this world shall come, and shall find no part in me." Therefore, if thou art sure that he will find nothing in thee, when he comes to search through thee, thou wilt say, as the patriarch Jacob did to Laban: "Know now if there is aught of thine with me." Rightly do we account Jacob blessed with whom Laban could find naught of his. For Rachel had hidden the gold and silver images of his gods.

251. If, then, wisdom, and faith, and contempt of the world, and spiritual grace, exclude all faithlessness, thou wilt be blessed; for thou regardest not vanity and folly and lying. Is it a light

thing to take away from thy adversary the opportunity to speak, so that he can have no ground to make his complaint against thee? Thus he who looks not on vanity is not perturbed; but he who looks upon it is perturbed, and that, too, all to no purpose. Is it not a vain thing to heap up riches? for surely to seek for fleeting things is vain enough. And when thou hast gathered them, how dost thou know that thou shall have them in possession?

252. Is it not vain for a merchant to journey by night and by day, that he may be able to heap up treasures? Is it not vain for him to gather merchandise, and to be much perturbed about its price, for fear he might sell it for less than he gave? that he should strive everywhere for high prices, and thus unexpectedly call up robbers against himself through their envy at his much-vaunted business; or that, without waiting for calmer winds, impatient of delays, he should meet with shipwreck whilst seeking for gain?

253. And is not he, too, perturbed in vain who with great toil amasses wealth, though he knows not what heir to leave it to? Often and often all that an avaricious man has got together with the greatest care, his spendthrift heir scatters abroad with headlong prodigality. The shameless prodigal, blind to the present, heedless of the future, swallows up as in an abyss what took so long to gather. Often, too, the desired successor gains but envy for his share of the inheritance, and by his sudden death hands over the whole amount of the succession, which he has hardly entered upon, to strangers.

254. Why, then, dost thou idly spin a web which is worthless and fruitless? And why dost thou build up useless heaps of treasures like spiders' webs? For though they overflow, they are no good; nay, they denude thee of the likeness of God, and put on thee the likeness of the earthy. If any one has the likeness of the tyrant, is he not liable to condemnation? Thou layest aside the likeness of the Eternal King, and raisest in thyself the image of death. Rather cast out of the kingdom of thy soul the likeness of the devil, and raise up the likeness of Christ. Let this shine forth in thee; let this glow brightly in thy kingdom, that is, thy soul, for it destroys the likeness of all vices. David says of this: "O Lord, in Thy kingdom thou bringest their images to nothing." For when the Lord has adorned Jerusalem according to His own likeness, then every likeness of the adversary is destroyed.

Chapter L.

The Levites ought to be utterly free from all earthly desires. What their virtues should be on the Apostle's own showing, and how great their purity must be. Also what their dignity and duty is, for the carrying out of which the chief virtues are necessary. He states that these were not unknown to the philosophers, but that they erred in their order. Some are by their nature in accordance with duty, which yet on account of what accompanies them become contrary to duty. From whence he gathers what gifts the office of the Levites demands. To conclude, he adds an exposition of Moses' words when blessing the tribe of Levi.

255. If, then, in the Gospel of the Lord the people themselves were taught and led to despise riches, how much more ought ye Levites no longer to be bound down by earthly desires. For your portion is God. For when their earthly possessions were portioned out by Moses to the people of our fathers, the Lord suffered not the Levites to have a share in that earthly possession, for He Himself would be the strength of their inheritance. Wherefore David says: "The Lord is the portion of mine inheritance and of my cup." Whence we get the name "Levite," which means: "Himself is mine," or "Himself for me." Great, then, is his honour, that God should say of him: Himself is Mine. Or, as was said to Peter about the piece of money found in the fish's mouth: "Give to them for Me and for thee." Wherefore the Apostle, when he said: "A bishop should be sober, modest, of good behaviour, given to hospitality, apt to teach, not covetous, nor a brawler, one that rules well his own house," also added: "Likewise must the deacons be grave, not double-tongued, not given to much wine, not greedy of filthy lucre, holding the mystery of the faith in a pure conscience. And let them also first be proved, and so let them serve, being found blameless."

256. We note how much is required of us. The minister of the Lord should abstain from wine, so that he may be upheld by the good witness not only of the faithful but also by those who are without. For it is right that the witness to our acts and works should be the opinion of the public at large, that the office be not disgraced. Thus he who sees the minister of the altar adorned with suitable virtues may praise their Author, and reverence the Lord Who has such servants. The praise of the Lord sounds forth where there is a pure possession and an innocent rule at home.

257. But what shall I say about chastity, when only one and no second union is allowed? As regards marriage, the law is, not to marry again, nor to seek union with another wife. It seems strange to many why impediment should be caused by a second marriage entered on before baptism, so as to prevent election to the clerical office, and to the reception of the gift of ordination; seeing that even crimes are not wont to stand in the way, if they have been put away in the sacrament of baptism. But we must learn, that in baptism sin can be forgiven, but law cannot be abolished. In the case of marriage there is no sin, but there is a law. Whatever sin there is can be put away, whatever law there is cannot be laid aside in marriage. How could he exhort to widowhood who himself had married more than once?

258. But ye know that the ministerial office must be kept pure and unspotted, and must not be defiled by conjugal intercourse; ye know this, I say, who have received the gifts of the sacred ministry, with pure bodies, and unspoilt modesty, and without ever having enjoyed conjugal intercourse. I am mentioning this, because in some out-of-the-way places, when they enter on the ministry, or even when they become priests, they have begotten children. They defend this on the ground of old custom, when, as it happened, the sacrifice was offered up at long intervals. However, even the people had to be purified two or three days beforehand, so as to come clean to the sacrifice, as we read in the Old Testament. They even used to wash their clothes. If such regard was paid in what was only the figure, how much ought it to be shown in the reality! Learn then, Priest and Levite, what it means to wash thy clothes. Thou must have a pure body wherewith to offer up the sacraments. If the people were forbidden to approach their victim unless they washed their clothes, dost thou, while foul in heart and body, dare to make supplication for others? Dost thou dare to make an offering for them?

259. The duty of the Levites is no light one, for the Lord says of them: "Behold I have taken the Levites from among the children of Israel, instead of every first-born that openeth the matrix among the children of Israel. These shall be their redemption, and the Levites shall be Mine. For I hallowed unto Me all the first-born in the land of Egypt." We know that the Levites are not reckoned among the rest, but are preferred before all, for they are chosen out of all, and are sanctified like the firstfruits and the firstlings which belong to the Lord, since the payment of vows and redemption for sin are offered by them. "Thou shalt not receive them," He says, "among the children of Israel, but thou shalt appoint the Levites over the tabernacle of testimony, and over all the vessels thereof, and over all things that belong to it. They shall bear the tabernacle and all the vessels thereof, and they shall minister in it, and shall encamp round about the tabernacle. And when the tabernacle setteth forward the Levites shall take it down, and when the camp is pitched they shall set up the tabernacle again. And the stranger that cometh nigh shall surely be put to death."

260. Thou, then, art chosen out of the whole number of the children of Israel, regarded as the firstfruits of the sacred offerings, set over the tabernacle so as to keep guard in the camp of holiness and faith, to which if a stranger approach, he shall surely die. Thou art placed there to watch over the ark of the covenant. All do not see the depths of the mysteries, for they are hid from the Levites, lest they should see who ought not to see, and they who cannot serve should take it up. Moses, indeed, saw the circumcision of the Spirit, but veiled it, so as to give circumcision only in an outward sign. He saw the unleavened bread of sincerity and truth; he saw the sufferings of the Lord, but he veiled the unleavened bread of truth in the material unleavened bread, he veiled the sufferings of the Lord in the sacrifice of a lamb or a calf. Good

Levites have ever preserved the mystery entrusted to them under the protection of their own faith, and yet dost thou think little of what is entrusted to thee? First, thou shalt see the deep things of God, which needs wisdom. Next, thou must keep watch for the people; this requires justice. Thou must defend the camp and guard the tabernacle, which needs fortitude. Thou must show thyself continent and sober, and this needs temperance.

261. These chief virtues, they who are without have recognized, but they considered that the order resting on society was higher than that resting on wisdom; though wisdom is the foundation, and justice the building which cannot stand unless it have a foundation. The foundation is Christ.

262. First stands faith, which is a sign of wisdom, as Solomon says, in following his father: "The fear of the Lord is the beginning of wisdom." And the law says: "Thou shalt love the Lord thy God, thou shalt love thy neighbour." It is a noble thing to do one's kindnesses and duties towards the whole of the human race. But it is ever most seemly that thou shouldst give to God the most precious thing thou hast, that is, thy mind, for thou hast nothing better than that. When thou hast paid thy debt to thy Creator, then thou mayest labour for men, to show them kindness, and to give help; then thou mayest assist the needy with money, or by some duty, or some service that lies in the way of thy ministry; by money to support him; by paying a debt, so as to free him that is bound; by undertaking a duty, so as to take charge of a trust, which he fears to lose, who has put it by in trust.

263. It is a duty, then, to take care of and to restore what has been entrusted to us. But meanwhile a change comes, either in time or circumstances, so that it is no longer a duty to restore what one has received. As, for instance, when a man demands back his money as an open enemy, to use it against his country, and to offer his wealth to barbarians. Or, if thou shouldst have to restore it, whilst another stood by to extort it from him by force. If thou restore money to a raving lunatic when he cannot keep it; if thou give up to a madman a sword once put by with thee, whereby he may kill himself, is it not an act contrary to duty to pay the debt? Is it not contrary to duty to take knowingly what has been got by a thief, so that he who has lost it is cheated out of it?

264. It is also sometimes contrary toduty to fulfil a promise, or to keep an oath. As was the case with Herod, who swore that whatever was asked he would give to the daughter of Herodies, and so allowed the death of John, that he might not break his word. And what shall I say of Jephthah, who offered up his daughter in sacrifice, she having been the first to meet him as he returned home victorious; whereby he fulfilled the vow which he had made that he would offer to God whatever should meet him first. It would have been better to make no promise at all, than to fulfil it in the death of his daughter.

265. Ye are not ignorant how important it is to look to this. And so a Levite is chosen to guard the sanctuary, one who shall never fail in counsel, nor forsake the faith, nor fear death, nor do anything extravagant, so that in his whole appearance he may give proof of his earnestness. For he ought to have not only his soul but even his eyes in restraint, so that no chance mishap may bring a blush to his forehead. For "whosoever looketh on a woman to desire her hath already committed adultery with her in his heart." Thus adultery is committed not only by actual committal of the foul deed, but even by the desire of the ardent gaze.

266. This seems high and somewhat severe, but in a high office it is not out of place. For the grace of the Levites is such that Moses spoke of them as follows in his blessing: "Give to Levi his men, give Levi his trusted ones, give Levi the lot of his inheritance, and his truth to the holy men whom they tempted in temptation, and reviled at the waters of contradiction. Who said to his father and mother, I know thee not, and knew not his brethren, and renounced his children. He guarded Thy word and kept Thy testimony."

267. They, then, are His men, His trusty ones, who have no deceit in their hearts, hide no treachery within them, but guard His words and ponder them in their heart, as Mary pondered them; who know not their parents so as to put them before their duty; who hate the violators of

chastity, and avenge the injury done to purity; and know the times for the fulfilling of their duty, as also which duty is the greater, which the lesser, and to what occasion each is suited. In all this they follow that alone which is virtuous. And who, where there are two virtuous duties, think that which is the more virtuous must come first. These are in truth tightly blessed.

268. If any one makes known the just works of the Lord, and offers Him incense, then: "Bless, O Lord, his strength; accept the work of his hands," that he may find the grace of the prophetic blessing with Him Who liveth and reigneth for ever and ever. Amen.

BOOK II.

Chapter I.

Happiness in life is to be gained by living virtuously, inasmuch as thus a Christian, whilst despising glory and the favour of men, desires to please God alone in what he does.

1. In the first book we spoke of the duties which we thought befitted a virtuous life, whereon no one has ever doubted but that a blessed life, which the Scripture calls eternal life, depends. So great is the splendour of a virtuous life that a peaceful conscience and a calm innocence work out a happy life. And as the risen sun hides the globe of the moon and the light of the stars, so the brightness of a virtuous life, where it glitters in true pure glory, casts into the shade all other things, which, according to the desires of the body, are considered to be good, or are reckoned in the eyes of the world to be great and noble.

2. Blessed, plainly, is that life which is not valued at the estimation of outsiders, but is known, as judge of itself, by its own inner feelings. It needs no popular opinion as its reward in any way; nor has it any fear of punishments. Thus the less it strives for glory, the more it rises above it. For to those who seek for glory, that reward in the shape of present things is but a shadow of future ones, and is a hindrance to eternal life, as it is written in the Scriptures: "Verily, I say unto you, they have received their reward." This is said of those who, as it were, with the sound of a trumpet desire to make known to all the world the liberality they exercise towards the poor. It is the same, too, in the case of fasting, which is done but for outward show. "They have," he says, "their reward."

3. It therefore belongs to a virtuous life to show mercy and to fast in secret; that thou mayest seem to be seeking a reward from thy God alone, and not from men. For he who seeks it from man has his reward, but he who seeks it from God has eternal life, which none can give but the Lord of Eternity, as it is said: "Verily, I say unto thee, to-day shalt thou be with Me in Paradise." Wherefore the Scripture plainly has called that life which is blessed, eternal life. It has not been left to be appraised according to man's ideas on the subject, but has been entrusted to the divine judgment.

Chapter II.

The different ideas of philosophers on the subject of happiness. He proves, first, from the Gospel that it rests on the knowledge of God and the pursuit of good works; next, that it may not be thought that this idea was adopted from the philosophers, he adds proofs from the witness of the prophets.

4. The philosophers have made a happy life to depend, either (as Hieronymus) on freedom from pain, or (as Herillus) on knowledge. For Herillus, hearing knowledge very highly praised by Aristotle and Theophrastus, made it alone to be the chief good, when they really praised it as a good thing, not as the only good; others, as Epicurus, have called pleasure such; others, as Callipho, and after him Diodorus, understood it in such a way as to make a virtuous life go in union, the one with pleasure, the other with freedom from pain, since a happy life could not exist without it. Zeno, the Stoic, thought the highest and only good existed in a virtuous life. But Aristotle and Theophrastus and the other Peripatetics maintained that a happy life consisted in virtue, that is, in a virtuous life, but that its happiness was made complete by the advantages of the body and other external good things.

5. But the sacred Scriptures say that eternal life rests on a knowledge of divine things and on the fruit of good works. The Gospel bears witness to both these statements. For the Lord Jesus spoke thus of knowledge: "This is eternal life, to know Thee, the only true God, and Jesus Christ Whom Thou hast sent," About works He gives this answer: "Every one that hath forsaken house, or brethren, or sisters, or father, or mother, or wife, or children, or lands, for My Name's sake, shall receive an hundred-fold, and shall inherit everlasting life."

6. Let no one think that this was but lately said, and that it was spoken of by the philosophers before it was mentioned in the Gospel. For the philosophers, that is to say,

Aristotle and Theophrastus, as also Zeno and Hieronymus, certainly lived before the time of the Gospel; but they came after the prophets. Let them rather think how long before even the names of the philosophers were heard of, both of these seem to have found open expression through the mouth of the holy David; for it is written: "Blessed is the man whom Thou instructest, O Lord, and teachest him out of Thy law." We find elsewhere also: "Blessed is the man that feareth the Lord, he will rejoice greatly in His commandments," We have proved our point as regards knowledge, the reward for which the prophet states to be the fruit of eternity, adding that in the house of the man that feareth the Lord, or is instructed in His law and rejoices greatly in the divine commandments, "is glory and riches; and his justice abideth for ever and ever." He has further also in the same psalm stated of good works, that they gain for an upright man the gift of eternal life. He speaks thus: "Blessed is the man that showeth pity and lendeth, he will guide his affairs with discretion, surely he shall not be moved for ever, the righteous shall be in everlasting remembrance," And further: "He hath dispersed, he hath given to the poor, his justice endureth for ever."

7. Faith, then, has [the promise of] eternal life, for it is a good foundation. Good works, too, have the same, for an upright man is tested by his words and acts. For if a man is always busy talking and yet is slow to act, he shows by his acts how worthless his knowledge is: besides it is much worse to know what one ought to do, and yet not to do what one has learnt should be done. On the other hand, to be active in good works and unfaithful at heart is as idle as though one wanted to raise a beautiful and lofty dome upon a bad foundation. The higher one builds, the greater is the fall; for without the protection of faith good works cannot stand. A treacherous anchorage in a harbour perforates a ship, and a sandy bottom quickly gives way and cannot bear the weight of the building placed upon it. There then will be found the fulness of reward, where the virtues are perfect, and where there is a reasonable agreement between words and acts.

Chapter III.
The definition of blessedness as drawn from the Scriptures is considered and proved. It cannot be enhanced by external good fortune, nor can it be weakened by misfortune.

8. As, then, knowledge, so far as it stands alone, is put aside either as worthless, according to the superfluous discussions of the philosophers, or as but an imperfect idea, let us now note how clearly the divine Scriptures explain a thing about which we see the philosophers held so many involved and perplexing ideas. For the Scriptures state that nothing is good but what is virtuous, and declare that virtue is blessed in every circumstance, and that it is never enhanced by either corporal or other external good fortune, nor is it weakened by adversity. No state is so blessed as that wherein one is free from sin, is filled with innocence, and is fully supplied with the grace of God. For it is written: "Blessed is the man that hath not walked in the counsel of the ungodly, and hath not stood in the way of sinners, and hath not sat in the seat of pestilence, but in the law of the Lord was his delight." And again: "Blessed are the undefiled in the way, who walk in the law of the Lord."

9. Innocence, then, and knowledge make a man blessed. We have also noted already that the blessedness of eternal life is the reward for good works. It remains, then, to show that when the patronage of pleasure or the fear of pain is despised (and the first of these one abhors as poor and effeminate, and the other as unmanly and weak), that then a blessed life can rise up in the midst of pain. This can easily be shown when we read: "Blessed are ye when men shall revile you and persecute you and shall say all manner of evil against you for righteousness' sake. Rejoice and be exceeding glad, for great is your reward in heaven; for so persecuted they the prophets which were before you." And again: "He that will come after Me, let him take up his cross and follow Me."

Chapter IV.

The same argument, namely, that blessedness is not lessened or added to by external matters, is illustrated by the example of men of old.

10. There is, then, a blessedness even in pains and griefs. All which virtue with its sweetness checks and restrains, abounding as it does in natural resources for either soothing conscience or increasing grace. For Moses was blessed in no small degree when, surrounded by the Egyptians and shut in by the sea, he found by his merits a way for himself and the people to go through the waters. When was he ever braver than at the moment when, surrounded by the greatest dangers, he gave not up the hope of safety, but besought a triumph?

11. What of Aaron? When did he ever think himself more blessed than when he stood between the living and the dead, and by his presence stayed death from passing from the bodies of the dead to the lines of the living? What shall I say of the youth Daniel, who was so wise that, when in the midst of the lions enraged with hunger, he was by no means overcome with terror at the fierceness of the beasts. So free from fear was he, that he could eat, and was not afraid he might by his example excite the animals to feed on him.

12. There is, then, in pain a virtue that can display the sweetness of a good conscience, and therefore it serves as a proof that pain does not lessen the pleasure of virtue. As, then, there is no loss of blessedness to virtue through pain, so also the pleasures of the body and the enjoyment that benefits give add nothing to it. On this the Apostle says well: "What things to me were gain, those I counted loss for Christ," and he added: "Wherefore I count all things but loss, and do count them but dung, that I may win Christ."

13. Moses, too, thought the treasures of Egypt to be his loss, and thus showed forth in his life the reproach of the Cross of the Lord. He was not rich when he had abundance of money, nor was he afterwards poor when he was in want of food, unless, perchance, there is any one who thinks he was less happy when daily food was wanting to him and his people in the wilderness. But yet manna, that is, angels' food, which surely none will dare deny to be a mark of the greatest good and of blessedness, was given him from heaven; also the daily shower of meat was sufficient to feed the whole multitude.

14. Bread for food also failed Elijah, that holy man, had he sought for it; but it seemed not to fail him because he sought it not. Thus by the daily service of the ravens bread was brought to him in the morning, meat in the evening. Was he any the less blessed because he was poor to himself? Certainly not. Nay, he was the more blessed, for he was rich toward God. It is better to be rich for others than for oneself. He was so, for in the time of famine he asked a widow for food, intending to repay it, so that the barrel of meal failed not for three years and six months, and the oil jar sufficed and served the needy widow for her daily use all that time also. Rightly did Peter wish to be there where he saw them. Rightly did they appear in the mount with Christ in glory, for He Himself became poor when He was rich.

15. Riches, then, give no assistance to living a blessed life, a fact that the Lord clearly shows in the Gospel, saying: "Blessed are ye poor, for yours is the kingdom of God. Blessed are they that hunger and thirst now, for they shall be filled. Blessed are ye that weep now, for ye shall laugh." Thus it is stated as plainly as possible that poverty, hunger, and pain, which are considered to be evils, not only are not hindrances to a blessed life, but are actually so many helps toward it.

Chapter V.

Those things which are generally looked on as good are mostly hindrances to a blessed life, and those which are looked on as evil are the materials out of which virtues grow. What belongs to blessedness is shown by other examples.

16. But those things which seem to be good, as riches, abundance, joy without pain, are a hindrance to the fruits of blessedness, as is clearly stated in the Lord's own words, when He said: "Woe to you rich, for ye have received your consolation! Woe unto you that are full, for ye

shall hunger, and to those who laugh, for they shall mourn!" So, then, corporal or external good things are not only no assistance to attaining a blessed life, but are even a hindrance to it.

17. Wherefore Naboth was blessed, even though he was stoned by the rich; weak and poor, as opposed to the royal resources, he was rich in his aim and his religion; so rich, indeed, that he would not exchange the inheritance of the vineyard received from his father for the king's money; and on this account was he perfect, for he defended the rights of his forefathers with his own blood. Thus, also, Ahab was wretched on his own showing, for he caused the poor man to be put to death, so as to take possession of his vineyard himself.

18. It is quite certain that virtue is the only and the highest good; that it alone richly abounds in the fruit of a blessed life; that a blessed life, by means of which eternal life is won, does not depend on external or corporal benefits, but on virtue only. A blessed life is the fruit of the present, and eternal life is the hope of the future.

19. Some, however, there are who think a blessed life is impossible in this body, weak and fragile as it is. For in it one must suffer pain and grief, one must weep, one must be ill. So I could also say that a blessed life rests on bodily rejoicing, but not on the heights of wisdom, on the sweetness of conscience, or on the loftiness of virtue. It is not a blessed thing to be in the midst of suffering; but it is blessed to be victorious over it, and not to be cowed by the power of temporal pain.

20. Suppose that things come which are accounted terrible as regards the grief they cause, such as blindness, exile, hunger, violation of a daughter, loss of children. Who will deny that Isaac was blessed, who did not see in his old age, and yet gave blessings with his benediction? Was not Jacob blessed who, leaving his father's house, endured exile as a shepherd for pay, and mourned for the violated chastity of his daughter, and suffered hunger? Were they not blessed on whose good faith God received witness, as it is written: "The God of Abraham, the God of Isaac, and the God of Jacob"? A wretched thing is slavery, but Joseph was not wretched; nay, clearly he was blessed, when he whilst in slavery checked the lusts of his mistress. What shall I say of holy David who bewailed the death of three sons, and, what was even worse than this, his daughter's incestuous connection? How could he be unblessed from whom the Author of blessedness Himself sprung, Who has made many blessed? For: "Blessed are they who have not seen yet have believed." All these felt their own weakness, but they bravely prevailed over it. What can we think of as more wretched than holy Job, either in the burning of his house, or the instantaneous death of his ten sons, or his bodily pains? Was he less blessed than if he had not endured those things whereby he really showed himself approved?

21. True it is that in these sufferings there is something bitter, and that strength of mind cannot hide this pain. I should not deny that the sea is deep because inshore it is shallow, nor that the sky is clear because sometimes it is covered with clouds, nor that the earth is fruitful because in some places there is but barren ground, nor that the crops are rich and full because they sometimes have wild oats mingled with them. So, too, count it as true that the harvest of a happy conscience may be mingled with some bitter feelings of grief. In the sheaves of the whole of a blessed life, if by chance any misfortune or bitterness has crept in, is it not as though the wild oats were hidden, or as though the bitterness of the tares was concealed by the sweet scent of the corn? But let us now proceed again with our subject.

Chapter VI.

On what is useful: not that which is advantageous, but that which is just and virtuous. It is to be found in losses, and is divided into what is useful for the body, and what is useful unto godliness.

22. In the first book we made our division in such a way as to set in the first place what is virtuous and what is seemly; for all duties are derived from these. In the second place we set what is useful. But as at the start we said that there was a difference between what is virtuous and what is seemly—which one can comprehend more easily than one can explain—so also

when we are thinking of what is useful, we have to give considerable thought to what is the more useful.

23. But we do not reckon usefulness by the value of any gain in money, but in acquiring godliness, as the Apostle says: "But godliness is profitable unto all things, having promise of the life that now is, and of that which is to come." Thus in the holy Scriptures, if we look carefully we shall often find that what is virtuous is called useful: "All things are lawful unto me, but all things are not profitable" [useful]. Before that he was speaking of vices, and so means: It is lawful to sin, but it is not seemly. Sins rest in one's own power, but they are not virtuous. To live wantonly is easy, but it is not right. For food serves not God but the belly.

24. Therefore, because what is useful is also just, it is just to serve Christ, Who redeemed us. They too are just who for His Name's sake have given themselves up to death, they are unjust who have avoided it. Of them it says: What profit is there in my blood? that is: what advance has my justice made? Wherefore they also say: "Let us bind the just, for he is useless to us," that is: he is unjust, for he complains of us, condemns and rebukes us. This could also be referred to the greed of impious men, which closely resembles treachery; as we read in the case of the traitor Judas, who in his longing for gain and his desire for money put his head into the noose of treachery and fell.

25. We have then to speak of that usefulness which is full of what is virtuous, as the Apostle himself has laid it down in so many words, saying: "And this I speak for your own profit, not that I may cast a snare upon you, but for that which is comely." It is plain, then, that what is virtuous is useful, and what is useful is virtuous; also that what is useful is just, and what is just is useful. I can say this, for I am speaking, not to merchants who are covetous from a desire to make gain, but to my children. And I am speaking of the duties which I wish to impress upon and impart to you, whom I have chosen for the service of the Lord; so that those things which have been already implanted and fixed in your minds and characters by habit and training may now be further unfolded to you by explanation and instruction.

26. Therefore as I am about to speak of what is useful, I will take up those words of the Prophet: "Incline my heart unto Thy testimonies and not to covetousness," that the sound of the word "useful" may not rouse in us the desire for money. Some indeed put it thus: "Incline my heart unto Thy testimonies and not to what is useful," that is, that kind of usefulness which is always on the watch for making gains in business, and has been bent and diverted by the habits of men to the pursuit of money. For as a rule most people call that only useful which is profitable, but we are speaking of that kind of usefulness which is sought in earthly loss "that we may gain Christ," whose gain is "godliness with contentment." Great, too, is the gain whereby we attain to godliness, which is rich with God, not indeed in fleeting wealth, but in eternal gifts, and in which rests no uncertain trial but grace constant and unending.

27. There is therefore a usefulness connected with the body, and also one that has to do with godliness, according to the Apostle's division: "Bodily exercise profiteth a little, but godliness is profitable unto all things." And what is so virtuous as integrity? what so seemly as to preserve the body unspotted and undefiled, and its purity unsullied? What, again, is so seemly as that a widow should keep her plighted troth to her dead husband? What more useful than this whereby the heavenly kingdom is attained? For "there are some who have made themselves eunuchs for the kingdom of heaven's sake."

Chapter VII.

What is useful is the same as what is virtuous; nothing is more useful than love, which is gained by gentleness, courtesy, kindness, justice, and the other virtues, as we are given to understand from the histories of Moses and David. Lastly, confidence springs from love, and again love from confidence.

28. There is therefore not only a close intercourse between what is virtuous and what is useful, but the same thing is both useful and virtuous. Therefore He Who willed to open the kingdom of heaven to all sought not what was useful to Himself, but what was useful for all.

Thus we must have a certain order and proceed step by step from habitual or common acts to those which are more excellent, so as to show by many examples the advancement of what is useful.

29. And first we may know there is nothing so useful as to be loved, nothing so useless as not to be loved; for to be hated in my opinion is simply fatal and altogether deadly. We speak of this, then, in order that we may take care to give cause for a good estimate and opinion to be formed of us, and may try to get a place in others' affections through our calmness of mind and kindness of soul. For goodness is agreeable and pleasing to all, and there is nothing that so easily reaches human feelings. And if that is assisted by gentleness of character and willingness, as well as by moderation in giving orders and courtesy of speech, by honour in word, by a ready interchange of conversation and by the grace of modesty, it is incredible how much all this tends to an increase of love.

30. We read, not only in the case of private individuals but even of kings, what is the effect of ready and willing courtesy, and what harm pride and great swelling words have done, so far as to make even kingdoms to totter and powers to be destroyed. If any one gains the people's favour by advice or service, by fulfilling the duties of his ministry or office, or if he encounters danger for the sake of the whole nation, there is no doubt but that such love will be shown him by the people that they all will put his safety and welfare before their own.

31. What reproaches Moses had to bear from his people! But when the Lord would have avenged him on those who reviled him, he often used to offer himself for the people that he might save them from the divine anger. With what gentle words used he to address the people, even after he was wronged I He comforted them in their labours, consoled them by his prophetic declarations of the future, and encouraged them by his works. And though he often spoke with God, yet he was wont to address men gently and pleasantly. Worthily was he considered to stand above all men. For they could not even look on his face, and refused to believe that his sepulchre was found. He had captivated the minds of all the people to such an extent; that they loved him even more for his gentleness than they admired him for his deeds.

32. There is David too who followed his steps, who was chosen from among all to rule the people. How gentle and kindly he was, humble in spirit too, how diligent and ready to show affection. Before he came to the throne he offered himself in the stead of all. As king he showed himself an equal to all in warfare, and shared in their labours. He was brave in battle, gentle in ruling, patient under abuse, and more ready to bear than to return wrongs. So dear was he to all, that though a youth, he was chosen even against his will to rule over them, and was made to undertake the duty though he withstood it. When old he was asked by his people not to engage in battle, because they all preferred to incur danger for his sake rather than that he should undergo it for theirs.

33. He had bound the people to himself freely in doing his duty; first, when he during the division among the people preferred to live like an exile at Hebron rather than to reign at Jerusalem; next, when he showed that he loved valour even in an enemy. He had also thought that justice should be shown to those who had borne arms against himself the same as to his own men. Again, he admired Abner, the bravest champion of the opposing side, whilst he was their leader and was yet waging war. Nor did he despise him when suing for peace, but honoured him by a banquet. When killed by treachery, he mourned and wept for him. He followed him and honoured his obsequies, and evinced his good faith in desiring vengeance for the murder; for he handed on that duty to his son in the charge that he gave him, being anxious rather that the death of an innocent man should not be left unavenged, than that any one should mourn for his own.

34. It is no small thing, especially in the case of a king, so to perform humble duties as to make oneself like the very lowest. It is noble not to seek for food at another's risk and to refuse a drink of water, to contless a sin, and to offer oneself to death for one's people. This latter David did, so that the divine anger might be turned against himself, when he offered himself to

the destroying angel and said: "Lo I have sinned: I the shepherd have done wickedly, but this flock, what hath it done? Let Thy hand be against me."

35. What further should I say? He opened not his mouth to those planning deceit, and, as though hearing not, he thought no word should be returned, nor did be answer their reproaches. When he was evil spoken of, he prayed, when he was cursed, he blessed. He walked in simplicity of heart, and fled from the proud. He was a follower of those unspotted from the world, one who mixed ashes with his food when bewailing his sins, and mingled his drink with weeping. Worthily, then, was he called for by all the people. All the tribes of Israel came to him saying: "Behold, we are thy bone and thy flesh. Also yesterday and the day before when Saul lived, and reigned, thou wast he that leddest out and broughtest in Israel. And the Lord said to thee, Thou shalt feed My people!" And why should I say more about him of whom the word of the Lord has gone forth to say: "I have found David according to My heart"? Who ever walked in holiness of heart and in justice as he did, so as to fulfil the will of God; for whose sake pardon was granted to his children when they sinned, and their rights were preserved to his heirs?

36. Who would not have loved him, when they saw how dear he was to his friends? For as he truly loved his friends, so he thought that he was loved as much in return by his own friends. Nay, parents put him even before their own children, and children loved him more than their parents. Wherefore Saul was very angry and strove to strike Jonathan his son with a spear because he thought that David's friendship held a higher place in his esteem than either filial piety or a father's authority.

37. It gives a very great impetus to mutual love if one shows love in return to those who love us and proves that one does not love them less than oneself is loved, especially if one shows it by the proofs that a faithful friendship gives. What is so likely to win favour as gratitude? What more natural than to love one who loves us? What so implanted and so impressed on men's feelings as the wish to let another, by whom we want to be loved, know that we love him? Well does the wise man say: "Lose thy money for thy brother and thy friend." And again: "I will not be ashamed to defend a friend, neither will I hide myself from him." If, indeed, the words in Ecclesiasticus testify that the medicine of life and immortality is in a friend; yet none has ever doubted that it is in love that our best defence lies. As the Apostle says: "It beareth all things, believeth all things, hopeth all things, endureth all things; love never faileth."

38. Thus David failed not, for he was dear to all, and wished to be loved rather than feared by his subjects. Fear keeps the watch of temporal protection, but knows not how to keep guard permanently. And so where fear has departed, boldness often creeps in; for fear does not force confidence but affection calls it forth.

39. Love, then, is the first thing to give us a recommendation. It is a good thing therefore to have our witness in the love of many. Then arises confidence, so that even strangers are not afraid to trust themselves to thy kindness, when they see thee so dear to many. So likewise one goes through confidence to love, so that he who has shown good faith to one or two has an influence as it were on the minds of all, and wins the good-will of all.

Chapter VIII.

Nothing has greater effect in gaining good-will than giving advice; but none can trust it unless it rests on justice and prudence. How conspicuous these two virtues were in Solomon is shown by his well-known judgment.

40. Two things, therefore, love and confidence, are the most efficacious in commending us to others; also this third quality if thou hast it, namely, what many consider to be worthy of admiration in thee, and think to be rightly worthy of honour [the power, in fact, of giving good advice].

41. Since the giving of good advice is a great means of gaining men's affections, prudence and justice are much needed in every case. These are looked for by most, so that confidence at once is placed in him in whom they exist, because he can give useful and trustworthy advice to whoever wants it. Who will put himself into the hands of a man whom he does not think to be

more wise than himself who asks for advice? It is necessary therefore that he of whom advice is asked should be superior to him who asks it. For why should we consult a man when we do not think that he can make anything more plain than we ourselves see it?

42. But if we have found a man that by the vigour of his character, by his strength of mind and influence, stands forth above all others, and further, is better fitted by example and experience than others; that can put an end to immediate dangers, foresee future ones, point out those close at hand, can explain a subject, bring relief in time, is ready not only to give advice but also to give help,—in such a man confidence is placed, so that he who seeks advice can say: "Though evil should happen to me through him, I will bear it."

43. To a man of this sort then we entrust our safety and our reputation, for he is, as we said before, just and prudent. Justice causes us to have no fear of deceit, and prudence frees us from having any suspicions of error. However, we trust ourselves more readily to a just than to a prudent man, to put it in the way people generally do. But, according to the definition of the philosophers, where there is one virtue, others exist too, whilst prudence cannot exist without justice. We find this stated also in our writers, for David says: "The just showeth mercy and lendeth." What the just lends, he says elsewhere: "A good man is he that showeth mercy and lendeth, he will guide his words with discretion."

44. Is not that noble judgment of Solomon full of wisdom and justice? Let us see whether it is so. "Two women," it says, "stood before King Solomon, and the one said to him, Hear me, my lord, I and this woman dwell in one house, and before the third day we gave birth and bore a son apiece, and were together, there was no witness in the house, nor any other woman with us, only we two alone. And her son died this night, because she overlaid it, and she arose at midnight, and took my son from my breast, and laid it in her bosom, and her dead child she laid at my breast, And I arose in the morning to give my child suck, and found him dead. And I considered it at dawn, and behold it was not my son. And the other woman said, Nay, but the living is my son, and the dead is thy son."

45. This was their dispute, in which either tried to claim the living child for herself, and denied that the dead one was hers. Then the king commanded a sword to be brought and the infant to be cut in half, and either piece to be given to one, one half to the one, and one half to the other. Then the woman whose the child really was, moved by her feelings, cried out: "Dividenot the child, my lord; let it rather be given to her and live, and do not kill it." But the other answered: "Let it be neither mine nor hers, divide it." Then the king ordered that the infant should be given to the woman who had said: Do not kill it, but give it to that woman; "For," as it says, "her bowels yearned upon her son."

46. It is not wrong to suppose that the mind of God was in him; for what is hidden from God? What can be more hidden than the witness that lies deep within; into which the mind of the wise king entered as though to judge a mother's feelings, and elicited as it were the voice of a mother's heart. For a mother's feelings were laid bare, when she chose that her son should live with another, rather than that he should be killed in his mother's sight.

47. It was therefore a sign of wisdom to distinguish between secret heart-thoughts, to draw the truth from hidden springs, and to pierce as it were with the sword of the Spirit not only the inward parts of the body, but even of the mind and soul. It was the part of justice also that she who had killed her own child should not take away another's, but that the real mother should have her own back again. Indeed the Scriptures have declared this. "All Israel," it says, "heard of the judgment which the king had judged, and they feared the king, for they saw that the wisdom of God was in him to do judgment." Solomon also himself had asked for wisdom, so that a prudent heart might be given him to hear and to judge with justice.

Chapter IX.

Though justice and prudence are inseparable, we must have respect to the ideas of people in general, for they make a distinction between the different cardinal virtues.

48. It is clear also, according to the sacred Scriptures, which are the older, that wisdom cannot exist without justice, for where one of these two is, there the other must be also. With what wisdom did Daniel expose the lie in the false accusation brought against him by his thorough examination, so that those false informers had no answer ready to hand! It was a mark of prudence to convict the criminals by the witness of their own words, and a sign of justice to give over the guilty to punishment, and to save the innocent from it.

49. There is therefore an inseparable union between wisdom and justice; but, generally speaking, the one special form of virtue is divided up. Thus temperance lies in despising pleasures, fortitude may be seen in undergoing labours and dangers, prudence in the choice of what is good, by knowing how to distinguish between things useful and the reverse; justice, in being a good guardian of another's rights and protector of its own, thus maintaining for each his own. We can make this fourfold division in deference to commonly received ideas; and so, whilst deviating from those subtle discussions of philosophic learning which are brought forth as though from some inner recess for the sake of investigating the truth, can follow the commonly received use and their ordinary meaning. Keeping, then, to this division, let us return to our subject.

Chapter X.

Men entrust their safety rather to a just than to a prudent man. But every one is wont to seek out the man who combines in himself the qualities of justice and prudence. Solomon gives us an example of this. (The words which the queen of Sheba spoke of him are explained.) Also Daniel and Joseph.

50. We entrust our case to the most prudent man we can find, and ask advice from him more readily than we do from others. However, the faithful counsel of a just man stands first and often has more weight than the great abilities of the wisest of men: "For better are the wounds of a friend than the kisses of others." And just because it is the judgment of a just man, it is also the conclusion of a wise one: in the one lies the result of the matter in dispute, in the other readiness of invention.

51. And if one connects the two, there will be great soundness in the advice given, which is regarded by all with admiration for the wisdom shown, and with love for its justice. And so all will desire to hear the wisdom of that man in whom those two virtues are found together, as all the kings of the earth desired to see the face of Solomon and to hear his wisdom. Nay, even the queen of Sheba came to him and tried him with questions. She came and spoke of all the things that were in her heart, and heard all the wisdom of Solomon, nor did any word escape her.

52. Who she was whom nothing escaped, and that there was nothing which the truth-loving Solomon did not tell her, learn, O man, from this which thou hearest her saying: "It was a true report that I heard in mine own land of thy words and of thy prudence, yet I did not believe those that told it me until I came, and mine eyes had seen it; and behold the half was not told me. Thou hast added good things over and above all that I heard in mine own land. Blessed are thy women and blessed thy servants, which stand before thee, and that hear all thy prudence." Recognize the feast of the true Solomon, and who are set down at that feast; recognize it wisely and think in what land all the nations shall hear the fame of true wisdom and justice, and with what eyes they shall see Him, beholding those things which are not seen. "For the things that are seen are temporal, but the things which are not seen are eternal."

53. What women are blessed but those of whom it is said "that many hear the word of God and bring forth fruit"? And again: "Whosoever doeth the word of God is My father and sister and mother." And who are those blessed servants, who stand before Him, but Paul, who said: "Even to this day I stand witnessing both to great and small;" or Simeon, who was waiting in the temple to see the consolation of Israel? How could he have asked to be let depart, except

that in standing before the Lord he had not the power of departing, but only according to the will of God? Solomon is put before us simply for the sake of example, of whom it was eagerly expected that his wisdom should be heard.

54. Joseph also when in prison was not free from being consulted about matters of uncertainty. His counsel was of advantage to the whole of Egypt, so that it felt not the seven years' famine, and he was able even to relieve other peoples from their dreadful hunger.

55. Daniel, though one of the captives, was made the head of the royal counsellors. By his counsels he improved the present and foretold the future. Confidence was put in him in all things, because he had frequently interpreted things, and had shown that he had declared the truth.

Chapter XI.

A third element which tends to gain any one's confidence is shown to have been conspicuous in Moses, Daniel, and Joseph.

56. But a third point seems also to have been noted in the case of those who were thought worthy of admiration after the example of Joseph, Solomon, and Daniel. For what shall I say of Moses whose advice all Israel always waited for, whose life caused them to trust in his prudence and increased their esteem for him? Who would not trust to the counsel of Moses, to whom the elders reserved for decision whatever they thought beyond their understanding and powers?

57. Who would refuse the counsel of Daniel, of whom God Himself said: "Who is wiser than Daniel?" How can men doubt about the minds of those to whom God has given such grace? By the counsel of Moses wars were brought to an end, and for his merit's sake food came from heaven and drink from the rock.

58. How pure must have been the soul of Daniel to soften the character of barbarians and to tame the lions! What temperance was his, what self-restraint in soul and body! Not unworthily did he become an object of admiration to all, when—and all men do admire this,—though enjoying royal friendships, he sought not for gold, nor counted the honour given him as more precious than his faith. For he was willing to endure danger for the law of God rather than to be turned from his purpose in order to gain the favour of men.

59. And what, again, shall I say of the chastity and justice of Joseph, whom I had almost passed by, whereby on the one hand he rejected the allurements of his mistress and refused rewards, on the other he mocked at death, repressed his fear, and chose a prison? Who would not consider him a fit person to give advice in a private case, whose fruitful spirit and fertile mind enriched the barrenness of the time with the wealth of his counsels and heart?

Chapter XII.

No one asks counsel from a man tainted with vice, or from one who is morose or impracticable, but rather from one of whom we have a pattern in the Scriptures.

60. We note therefore that in seeking for counsel, uprightness of life, excellence in virtues, habits of benevolence, and the charm of good-nature have very great weight. Who seeks for a spring in the mud? Who wants to drink from muddy water? So where there is luxurious living, excess, and a union of vices, who will think that he ought to draw from that source? Who does not despise a foul life? Who will think a man to be useful to another's cause whom he sees to be useless in his own life? Who, again, does not avoid a wicked, ill-disposed, abusive person, who is always ready to do harm? Who would not be only too eager to avoid him?

61. And who will come to a man however well fitted to give the best of advice who is nevertheless hard to approach? It goes with him as with a fountain whose waters are shut off. What is the advantage of having wisdom, if one refuses to give advice? If one cuts off the opportunities of giving advice, the source is closed, so as no longer to flow for others or to be of any good to oneself.

62. Well can we refer this to him who, possessing prudence, has defiled it with the foulness of a vicious life and so pollutes the water at the source. His life is a proof of a degenerate spirit. How can one judge him to be good in counsel whom one sees to be evil in character? He ought to be superior to me, if I am ready to trust myself to him. Am I to suppose that he is fit to give me advice who never takes it for himself, or am I to believe that he has time to give to me when he has none for himself, when his mind is filled with pleasures, and he is overcome by lust, is the slave of avarice, is excited by greed, and is terrified with fright? How is there room for counsel here where there is none for quiet?

63. That man of counsel whom I must admire and look up to, whom the gracious Lord gave to our fathers, put aside all that was offensive. His follower he ought to be, who can give counsel and protect another's prudence from vice; for nothing foul can mingle with that.

Chapter XIII.

The beauty_of wisdom is made plain by the divine testimony. From this he goes on to prove its connection with the other virtues.

64. Is there any one who would like to be beautiful in face and at the same time to have its charm spoilt by a beast-like body and fearful talons? Now the form of virtues is so wonderful and glorious, and especially the beauty of wisdom, as the whole of the Scriptures tell us. For it is more brilliant than the sun, and when compared with the stars far outshines any constellation. Night takes their light away in its train, but wickedness cannot overcome wisdom.

65. We have spoken of its beauty, and proved it by the witness of Scripture. It remains to show on the authority of Scripture that there can be no fellowship between it and vice, but that it has an inseparable union with the rest of the virtues. "It has a spirit sagacious, undefiled, sure, holy, loving what is good, quick, that never forbids a kindness, kind, steadfast, free from care, having all power, overseeing all things." And again: "She teacheth temperance and justice and virtue."

Chapter XIV.

Prudence is combined with all the virtues, especially with contempt of riches.

66. Prudence, herefore, works through all things, she has fellowship with all that is good. For how can she give good advice unless she have justice too, so that she may clothe herself in consistency, not fear death, be held back by no alarm, no fear, nor think it right to be turned aside from the truth by any flattery, nor shun exile, knowing that the world is the fatherland of the wise man. She fears not want, for she knows that nothing is wanting to the wise man, since the whole world of riches is his. What is greater than the man that knows not how to be excited at the thought of money, and has a contempt for riches, and looks down as from some lofty vantage-ground on the desires of men? Men think that one who acts thus is more than man: "Who is this," it says, "and we will praise him. For wonderful things hath he done in his life." Surely he ought to be admired who despises riches, seeing that most place them even before their own safety.

67. The rule of economy and the authority of self-restraint befits all, and most of all him who stands highest in honour; so that no love for his treasures may seize upon such a man, and that he who rules over free men may never become a slave to money. It is more seemly that in soul he should be superior to treasures, and in willing service be subject to his friends. For humility in- creases the regard in which one is held. It is praiseworthy and right for the chief of men to have no desire for filthy lucre incommon with Syrian traders and Gilead merchants, nor to place all their hope of good in money, or to count up their dailygains and to calculate their savings like a hireling.

Chapter XV.

Of liberality. To whom it must chiefly be shown, and how men of slender means may show it by giving their service and counsel.

68. But if it is praiseworthy to have one's soul free from this failing, how much more glorious is it to gain the love of the people by liberality which is neither too freely shown to those who are unsuitable, nor too sparingly bestowed upon the needy.

69. There are many kinds of liberality. Not only can we distribute and give away food to those who need it from our own daily supply, so that they may sustain life; but we can also give advice and help to those who are ashamed to show their want openly, so long as the common supplies of the needy are not exhausted. I am now speaking of one set over some office. If he is a priest or almoner, let him inform the bishop of them, and not withhold the name of any he knows to be in any need, or to have lost their wealth and to be now reduced to want; especially if they have not fallen into this trouble owing to wastefulness in youth, but because of another's theft, or through loss of their inheritance from no fault of their own, so that they cannot now earn their daily bread.

70. The highest kind of liberality is, to redeem captives, to save them from the hands of their enemies, to snatch men from death, and, most of all, women from shame, to restore children to their parents, parents to their children, and, to give back a citizen to his country. This was recognized when Thrace and Illyria were so terribly devastated. How many captives were then for sale all over the world! Could one but call them together, their number would have surpassed that of a whole province. Yet there were some who would have sent back into slavery those whom the Church had redeemed. They themselves were harder than slavery itself to look askance at another's mercy. If they themselves (they said) had come to slavery, they would be slaves freely. If they had been sold, they would not refuse the service of slavery. They wished to undo the freedom of others, though they could not undo their own slavery, unless perchance it should please the buyer to receive his price again, whereby, however, slavery would not be simply undone but redeemed.

71. It is then a special quality of liberality to redeem captives, especially from barbarian enemies who are moved by no spark of human feeling to show mercy, except so far as avarice has preserved it with a view to redemption. It is also a great thing to take upon oneself another's debt, if the debtor cannot pay and is hard pressed to do so, and where the money is due by right and is only left unpaid through want. So, too, it is a sign of great liberality to bring up children, and to take care of orphans.

72. There are others who place in marriage maidens that have lost their parents, so as to preserve their chastity, and who help them not only with good wishes but also by a sum of money. There is also another kind of liberality which the Apostle teaches: "If any that believeth hath widows let him relieve them, that the Church be not burdened by supplying them, that it may have enough for those that are widows indeed."

73. Useful, then, is liberality of this sort; but it is not common to all. For there are many good men who have but slender means, and are content with little for their own use, and are not able to give help to lighten the poverty of others. However, another sort of kindness is ready to their hand, whereby they can help those poorer still. For there is a twofold liberality: one that gives actual assistance, that is, in money; the other, which is busy in offering active help, is often much grander and nobler.

74. How much grander it was for Abraham to have recovered his captured son-in-law by his victorious arms, than if he had ransomed him! How much more usefully did holy Joseph help King Pharaoh by his counsel to provide for the future. than if he had offered him money! For money would not have bought back the fruitfulness of any one state; whilst he by his foresight kept the famine for five years from the whole of Egypt.

75. Money is easily spent; counsels can never be exhausted. They only grow the stronger by constant use. Money grows less and quickly comes to an end, and has failed even kindness itself;

so that the more there are to whom one wants to give, the fewer one can help; and often one has not got what one thinks ought to be given to others. But as regards the offer of advice and active help, the more there are to spend it on, the more there seems to be, and the more it returns to its own source. The rich stream of prudence ever flows back upon itself, and the more it has reached out to, so much the more active becomes all that remains.

Chapter XVI.

Due measure must be observed in liberality, that it may not be expended on worthless persons, when it is needed by worthier ones. However, alms are not to be given in too sparing and hesitating a way. One ought rather to follow the example of the blessed Joseph, whose prudence is commended at great length.

76. It is clear, then, that there ought to be due measure in our liberality, that our gifts may not become useless. Moderation must be observed, especially by priests, for fear that they should give away for the sake of ostentation, and not for justice' sake. Never was the greed of beggars greater than it is now. They come in full vigour, they come with no reason but that they are on the tramp. They want to empty the purses of the poor—to deprive them of their means of support. Not content with a little, they ask for more. In the clothes that cover them they seek a ground to urge their demands, and with lies about their lives they ask for further sums of money. If any one were to trust their tale too readily, he would quickly drain the fund which is meant to serve for the sustenance of the poor. Let there be method in our giving, so that the poor may not go away empty nor the subsistence of the needy be done away and become the spoil of the dishonest. Let there be then such due measure that kindness may never be put aside, and true need never be left neglected.

77. Many pretend they have debts. Let the truth be looked into. They bemoan the fact that they have been stripped of everything by robbers. In such a case give credit only if the misfortune is apparent, or the person is well known; and then readily give help. To those rejected by the Church supplies must be granted if they are in want of food. He, then, that observes method in his giving is hard towards none, but is free towards all, We ought not only to lend our ears to hear the voices of those who plead, but also our eyes to look into their needs. Weakness calls more loudly to the good dispenser than the voice of the poor. It cannot always be that the cries of an importunate beggar will never extort more, but let us not always give way to impudence. He must be seen who does not see thee. He must be sought for who is ashamed to be seen. He also that is in prison must come to thy thoughts; another seized with sickness must present himself to thy mind, as he cannot reach thy ears.

78. The more people see thy zeal in showing mercy, the more will they love thee, I know many priests who had the more, the more they gave, For they who see a good dispenser give him something to distribute in his round of duty, sure that the act of mercy will reach the poor. If they see him giving away either in excess or too sparingly, they contemn either of these; in the one case because he wastes the fruits of another's labours by unnecessary payments, on the other hand because he hoards them in his money bags. As, then, method must be observed in liberality, so also at times it seems as though the spur must be applied. Method, then, so that the kindness one shows may be able to be shown day by day, and that we may not have to withdraw from a needful case what we have freely spent on waste. A spur, because money is better laid out in food for the poor than on a purse for the rich. We must take care test in our money chests we shut up the welfare of the needy, and bury the life of the poor as it were in a sepulchre.

79. Joseph could have given away all the wealth of Egypt, and have spent the royal treasures; but he would not even seem to be wasteful of what was another's. He preferred to sell the corn rather than to give it to the hungry. For if he had given it to a few there would have been none for most. He gave good proof of that liberality whereby there was enough for all. He opened the storehouses that all might buy their corn supply, lest if they received it for nothing, they should

give up cultivating the ground. For he who has the use of what is another's often neglects his own.

80. First of all, then, he gathered up their money, then their implements, last of all he acquired for the king all their rights to the ground. He did not wish to deprive all of them of their property, but to support them in it. He also imposed a general tax, that they might hold their own in safety. So pleasing was this to all from whom he had taken the land, that they looked on it, not as the selling of their rights, but as the recovery of their welfare. Thus they spoke: "Thou hast saved our lives, let us find grace in the sight of our Lord." For they had lost nothing of their own, but had received a new right. Nothing of what was useful to them had failed, for they had now gained it in perpetuity.

81. O noble man! who sought not for the fleeting glory of a needless bounty, but set up as his memorial the lasting benefits of his foresight. He acted so that the people should help themselves by their payments, and should not in their time of need seek help from others. For it was surely better to give up part of their crops than to lose the whole of their rights. He fixed the impost at a fifth of their whole produce, and thus showed himself clear-sighted in making provision for the future, and liberal in the tax he laid upon them. Never after did Egypt suffer from such a famine.

82. How splendidly he inferred the future. First, how acutely, when interpreting the royal dream, he stated the truth. This was the king's first dream. Seven heifers came up out of the river well-favoured and fat-fleshed, and they fed at the banks of the river. And other bullocks ill-favoured and lean-fleshed came up out of the river after the heifers, and fed near them on the very edge of the river. And these thin and wretched bullocks seemed to devour those others which were so fat and well-favoured. And this was the second dream. Seven fat ears full and good came up from the ground. And after them seven wretched ears, blasted with the wind and withered, endeavoured to take their place. And it seemed that the barren and thin ears devoured the rich and fruitful ears.

83. This dream Joseph unfolded as follows: that the seven heifers were seven years, and the seven ears likewise were seven years,—interpreting the times by the produce of cattle and crops. For both the calving of a heifer takes a year, and the produce of a crop fills out a whole year. And they came up out of the river just as days, years, and times pass by and flow along swiftly like the rivers. He therefore states that the seven earlier years of a rich land will be fertile and fruitful but the latter seven years will be barren and unfruitful, whose barrenness will eat up the richness of the former time. Wherefore he warns them to see that supplies of corn are got together in the fruitful years that they may help out the needs of the coming scarcity.

84. What shall we admire first? His powers of mind, with which he descended to the very resting-place of truth? Or his counsel, whereby he foresaw so great and lasting a need? Or his watchfulness or justice? By his watchfulness, when so high an office was given him, he gathered together such vast supplies; and through his justice he treated all alike. And what am I to say of his greatness of mind? For though sold by his brothers into slavery, he took no revenge for this wrong, but put an end to their want. What of his gentleness, whereby by a pious fraud he sought to gain the presence of his beloved brother whom, under pretence of a well-planned theft, he declared to have stolen his property, that he might hold him as a hostage of his love?

85. Whence it was deservedly said to him by his father: "My son Joseph is enlarged, my son is enlarged, my younger son, my beloved. My God hath helped thee and blessed thee with the blessing of heaven above and the blessing of the earth, the earth that hath all things, on account of the blessings of thy father and thy mother. It hath prevailed over the blessings of the everlasting hills and the desires of the eternal hills." And in Deuteronomy: "Thou Who wast seen in the bush, that Thou mayest come upon the head of Joseph, upon his pate. Honoured among his brethren, his glory is as the firstling of his bullocks; his horns are like the horns of unicorns. With his horn he shall push the nations even to the ends of the earth. They are the ten thousands of Ephraim and the thousands of Manasseh."

Chapter XVII.

What virtues ought to exist in him whom we consult. How Joseph and Paul were equipped with them.

86. Such, then, ought he to be who gives counsel to another, in order that he may offer himself as a pattern in all good works, in teaching, in trueness of character, in seriousness. Thus his words will be wholesome and irreproachable, his counsel useful, his life virtuous, and his opinions seemly.

87. Such was Paul, who gave counsel to virgins, guidance to priests, so as to offer himself as a pattern for us to copy. Thus he knew how to be humble, as also Joseph did, who, though sprung from the noble family of the patriarchs, was not ashamed of his base slavery; rather he adorned it with his ready service, and made it glorious by his virtues. He knew how to be humble who had to go through the hands of both buyer and seller, and called them, Lord. Hear him as he humbles himself: "My lord on my account knoweth not what is in his house, and he hath committed all that he hath to my hand, neither hath he kept back anything from me but thee, because thou art his wife; how, then, can I do this great wickedness, and sin against God?" Full of humility are his words, full, too, of chastity. Of humility, for he was obedient to his Lord; of an honourable spirit, for he was grateful; full, also, of chastity, for he thought it a terrible sin to be defiled by so great a crime.

88. Such, then, ought the man of counsel to be. He must have nothing dark, or deceptive, or false about him, to cast a shadow on his life and character, nothing wicked or evil to keep back those who want advice. For there are some things which one flies from, others which one despises. We fly from those things which can do harm, or can perfidiously and quietly grow to do us hurt, as when he whose advice we ask is of doubtful honour, or is desirous of money, so that a certain sum can make him change his mind. If a man acts unjustly, we fly from him and avoid him. A man that is a pleasure seeker and extravagant, although he does not act falsely, yet is avaricious and too fond of filthy lucre; such an one is despised. What proof of hard work, what fruits of labour, can he give who gives himself up to a sluggish and idle life, or what cares and anxieties ever enter his mind?

89. Therefore the man of good counsel says: "I have learnt in whatsoever state I am therewith to be content." For he knew that the root of all evils is the love of money, and therefore he was content with what he had, without seeking for what was another's. Sufficient for me, he says, is what I have; whether I have little or much, to me it is much. It seems as though he wanted to state it as clearly as possible. He makes use of these words: "I am content," he says, "with what I have." That means: "I neither have want, nor have I too much. I have no want, for I seek nothing more. I have not too much, for I have it not for myself, but for the many." This is said with reference to money.

90. But he could have said these words about everything, for all that he had at the moment contented him; that is, he wanted no greater honour, he sought for no further services, he was not desirous of vainglory, nor did he look for gratitude where it was not due; but patient in labours, sure in his merits, he waited for the end of the struggle that he must needs endure. "I know," he says, "how to be abased." An untaught humility has no claim to praise, but only that which possesses modesty and a knowledge of self. For there is a humility that rests on fear, one, too, that rests on want of skill and ignorance. Therefore the Scripture says: "He will save the humble in spirit." Gloriously, therefore, does he say: "I know how to be abased;" that is to say, where, in what moderation, to what end, in what duty, in which office. The Pharisee knew not how to be abased, therefore he was cast down. The publican knew, and therefore he was justified.

91. Paul knew, too, how to abound, for he had a rich soul, though he possessed not the treasure of a rich man. He knew how to abound, for he sought no gift in money, but looked for fruit in grace. We can understand his words that he knew how to abound also in another way. For he could say again: "0 ye Corinthians, our mouth is open unto you, our heart is enlarged."

92. In all things he was accustomed both to be full and to be hungry. Blessed is he that knows how to be full in Christ. Not corporal, but spiritual, is that satiety which knowledge brings about. And rightly is there need of knowledge: "For man lives not by bread alone, but by every word of God." For he who knew how to be full also knew how to be hungry, so as to be always seeking something new, hungering after God, thirsting for the Lord. He knew how to hunger, for he knew that the hungry shall eat. He knew, also, how to abound, and was able to abound, for he had nothing and yet possessed all things.

Chapter XVIII.

We learn from the fact of the separation of the ten tribes from King Rehoboam what harm bad counsellors can do.

93. Justice, then, especially graces men that are set over any office; on the other hand, injustice fails them and fights against them. Scripture itself gives us an example, where it says, that when the people of Israel, after the death of Solomon, had asked his son Rehoboam to free their neck from their cruel yoke, and to lighten the harshness of his father's rule, he, despising the counsel of the old men, gave the following answer at the suggestion of the young men: "He would add a burden to the yoke of his father, and change their lighter toils for harder."

94. Angered by this answer, the people said: "We have no portion in David, nor inheritance in the son of Jesse. Return to your tents, O Israel. For we will not have this man for a prince or a leader over us." So, forsaken and deserted by the people, he could keep with him scarce two of the ten tribes for David's sake.

Chapter XIX.

Many are won by justice and benevolence and courtesy, but all this must be sincere.

95. It is plain, then, that equity strengthens empires, and injustice destroys them. How could wickedness hold fast a kingdom when it cannot even rule over a single family? There is need, therefore, of the greatest kindness, so that we may preserve not only the government of affairs in general, but also the rights of individuals. Benevolence is of the greatest value; for it seeks to embrace all in its favours, to bind them to itself by fulfilling duties, and to pledge them to itself by its charm.

96. We have also said that courtesy of speech has great effect in winning favour. But we want it to be sincere and sensible, without flattery, lest flattery should disgrace the simplicity and purity of our address. We ought to be a pattern to others not only in act but also in word, in purity, and in faith. What we wish to be thought, such let us be; and let us show openly such feelings as we have within us. Let us not say an unjust word in our heart that we think can be hid in silence, for He hears things said in secret Who made things secret, and knows the secrets of the heart, and has implanted feelings within. Therefore as though under the eyes of the Judge let us consider all we do as set forth in the light, that it may be manifest to all.

Chapter XX.

Familiarity with good men is very advantageous to all, especially to the young, as is shown by the example of Joshua and Moses and others. Further, those who are unlike in age are often alike in virtues, as Peter and John prove.

97. It is a very good thing to unite oneself to a good man. It is also very useful for the young to follow the guidance of great and wise men. For he who lives in company with wise men is wise himself; but he who clings to the foolish is looked on as a fool too. This friendship with the wise is a great help in teaching us, and also as giving a sure proof of our uprightness. Young men show very soon that they imitate those to whom they attach themselves. And this idea gains ground from the fact that in all their daily life they grow to be like those with whom they have enjoyed intercourse to the full.

98. Joshua the son of Nun became so great, because his union with Moses was the means not only of instructing him in a knowledge of the law, but also of sanctifying him to receive grace. When in His tabernacle the majesty of the Lord was seen to shine forth in its divine Presence, Joshua alone was in the tabernacle. When Moses spoke with God, Joshua too was covered by the sacred cloud. The priests and people stood below, and Joshua and Moses went up the mount to receive the law. All the people were within the camp; Joshua was without the camp in the tabernacle of witness. When the pillar of a cloud came down, and God spoke with Moses, he stood as a trusty servant beside him; and he, a young man, did not go out of the tabernacle, though the old men who stood afar off trembled at these divine wonders.

99. Everywhere, therefore, he alone kept close to holy Moses amid all these wondrous works and dread secrets. Wherefore it happens that he who had been his companion in this intercourse with God succeeded to his power. Worthy surely was he to stand forth as a man who might stay the course of the river, and who might say: "Sun, stand still," and delay the night and lengthen the day, as though to witness his victory. Why?—a blessing denied to Moses—he alone was chosen to lead the people into the promised land. A man he was, great in the wonders he wrought by faith, great in his triumphs. The works of Moses were of a higher type, his brought greater success. Either of these then aided by divine grace rose above all human standing. The one ruled the sea, the other heaven.

100. Beautiful, therefore, is the union between old and young. The one to give witness, the other to give comfort; the one to give guidance, the other to give pleasure. I pass by Lot, who when young clung to Abraham, as he was setting out. For some perhaps might say this arose rather owing to their relationship than from any voluntary action on his part. And what are we to say of Elijah and Elisha? Though Scripture has not in so many words stated that Elisha was a young man, yet we gather from it that he was the younger. In the Acts of the Apostles, Barnabas took Mark with him, and Paul took Silas and Timothy and Titus.

101. We see also that duties were divided amongst them according to their superiority in anything. The elders took the lead in giving counsel, the younger in showing activity. Often, too, those who were alike in virtue but unlike in years were greatly rejoiced at their union, as Peter and John were. We read in the Gospel that John was a young man, even in his own words, though he was behind none of the elders in merits and wisdom. For in him there was a venerable ripeness of character and the prudence of the hoarhead. An unspotted life is the due of a good old age.

Chapter XXI.

To defend the weak, or to help strangers, or to perform similar duties, greatly adds to one's worth, especially in the case of tried men. Whilst one gets great blame for love of money; wastefulness, also, in the cue of priests is very much condemned.

102. The regard in which one is held is also very much enhanced when one rescues a poor man out of the hands of a powerful one, or saves a condemned criminal from death; so long as it can be done without disturbance, for fear that we might seem to be doing it rather for the sake of showing off than for pity's sake, and so might inflict severer wounds whilst desiring to heal slighter ones. But if one has freed a man who is crushed down by the resources and faction of a powerful person, rather than overwhelmed by the deserts of his own wickedness, then the witness of a great and high opinion grows strong.

103. Hospitality also serves to recommend many. For it is a kind of open display of kindly feelings: so that the stranger may not want hospitality, but be courteously received, and that the door may be open to him when he comes. It is most seemly in the eyes of the whole world that the stranger should be received with honour; that the charm of hospitality should not fail at our table; that we should meet a guest with ready and free service, and look out for his arrival.

104. This especially was Abraham's praise, for he watched at the door. of his tent, that no stranger by any chance might pass by. He carefully kept a lookout, so as to meet the stranger,

and anticipate him, and ask him not to pass by, saying: "My lord, if I have found favour in thy sight, pass not by thy servant." Therefore as a reward for his hospitality, he received the gift of posterity.

105. Lot also, his nephew, who was near to him not only in relationship but also in virtue, on account of his readiness to show hospitality, turned aside the punishment of Sodom from himself and his family.

106. A man ought therefore to be hospitable, kind, upright, not desirous of what belongs to another, willing to give up some of his own rights if assailed, rather than to take away another's. He ought to avoid disputes, to hate quarrels. He ought to restore unity and the grace of quietness. When a good man gives up any of his own rights, it is not only a sign of liberality, but is also accompanied by great advantages. To start with, it is no small gain to be free from the cost of a lawsuit. Then it also brings in good results, by an increase of friendship, from which many advantages rise. These become afterwards most useful to the man that can despise a little something at the time.

107. In all the duties of hospitality kindly feeling must be shown to all, but greater respect must be given to the upright. For "Whosoever receiveth a righteous man, in the name of a righteous man, shall receive a righteous man's reward," as the Lord has said. Such is the favour in which hospitality stands with God, that not even the draught of cold water shall fail of getting a reward. Thou seest that Abraham, in looking for guests, received God Himself to entertain. Thou seest that Lot received the angels. And how dost thou know that when thou receivest men, thou dost not receive Christ? Christ may be in the stranger that comes, for Christ is there in the person of the poor, as He Himself says: "I was in prison and thou camest to Me, I was naked and thou didst clothe Me." .

108. It is sweet, then, to seek not for money but for grace. It is true that this evil has long ago entered into human hearts, so that money stands in the place of honour, and the minds of men are filled with admiration for wealth. Thus love of money sinks in and as it were dries up every kindly duty; so that men consider everything a loss which is spent beyond the usual amount. But even here the holy Scriptures have been on the watch against love of money, that it might prove no cause of hindrance, saying: "Better is hospitality, even though it consisteth only of herbs." And again: "Better is bread in pleasantness with peace." For the Scriptures teach us not to be wasteful, but liberal.

109. There are two kinds of free-giving, one arising from liberality, the other from wasteful extravagance. It is a mark of liberality to receive the stranger, to clothe the naked, to redeem the captives, to help the needy. It is wasteful to spend money on expensive banquets and much wine. Wherefore one reads: "Wine is wasteful, drunkenness is abusive." It is wasteful to spend one's own wealth merely for the sakeof gaining the favour of the people. This they do who spend their inheritance on thegames of the circus, or on theatrical pieces and gladiatorial shows, or even a combat of wild beasts, just to surpass the fame of their forefathers for these things. All this that they do is but foolish, for it is not right to be extravagant in spending money even on good works.

110. It is a right kind of liberality to keep due measure towards the poor themselves, that one may have enough for more; and not to go beyond the right limit for the sake of winning favour. Whatever comes forth out of a pure sincere disposition, that is seemly. It is also seemly not to enter on unnecessary undertakings, nor to omit those that are needed.

111. But it befits the priest especially to adorn the temple of God with fitting splendour, so that the court of the Lord may be made glorious by his endeavours. He ought always to spend money as mercy demands. It behoves him to give to strangers what is right. This must not be too much, but enough; not more than, but as much as, kindly feeling demands, so that he may never seek another's favour at the expense of the poor, nor show himself as either too stingy or too free to the clergy. The one act is unkind, the other wasteful. It is unkind if money should be

wanting for the necessities of those whom one ought to win back from their wretched employments. It is wasteful if there should be too much over for pleasure.

Chapter XXII.

We must observe a right standard between too great mildness and excessive harshness. They who endeavour to creep into the hearts of others by a false show of mildness gain nothing substantial or lasting. This the example of Absalom plainly enough shows.

112. Moreover, due measure befits even our words and instructions, that it may not seem as though there was either too great mildness or too much harshness. Many prefer to be too mild, so as to appear to be good. But it is certain that nothing feigned or false can bear the form of true virtue; nay, it cannot even last. At first it flourishes, then, as time goes on, like a floweret it fades and passes away, but what is true and sincere has a deep root.

113. To prove by examples our assertion that what is feigned cannot last, but flourishing just for a time quickly fails, we will take one example of pretence and falsehood from that family, from which we have already drawn so many examples to show their growth in virtue.

114. Absalom was King David's son, known for his beauty, of splendid appearance and in the heyday of youth; so that no other such man as he was found in Israel. He was without a blemish from the sole of his foot to the crown of his head. He had for himself a chariot and horses and fifty men to run before him. He rose at early dawn and stood before the gate in the way, and whoever he knew to be seeking the judgment of the king, he called to himself, saying: "From what city art thou?" And he answered: "I thy servant am of one of the tribes of Israel." And Absalom answered: "Thy words are good and right. Is there none given thee by the king to hear thee? Who will make me a judge? And whosoever will come unto me, that hath need of judgment, I will give him justice." With such words he cajoled them. And when they came to make obeisance to him, stretching forth his hand he took hold of them and kissed them. So he turned the hearts of all to himself. For flattery of this sort quickly finds its way to touch the very depths of the heart.

115. Those spoilt and ambitious men chose what for a time seemed an honour to them, and was pleasing and enjoyable. But whilst that delay took place, which the prophet, being prudent above all, thought ought to intervene, they could no longer hold out or bear it. Then David having no doubt about the victory commended his son to those who went out to fight, so that they should spare him. He would not engage in the battle himself test he should seem to be taking up arms against one who was still his son, though attempting to destroy his father.

116. It is clear, then, that those things are lasting and sound, which are true and grow out of a sincere and not a false heart. Those, however, which are brought about by pretence and adulation can never last for long.

Chapter XXIII.

The good faith of those who are easily bought over with money or flattery is a frail thing to trust to.

117. Who would suppose that those who are bought over to obedience by money, or those who are allured by adulation, would ever be faithful to them? For the former are ever ready to sell themselves, whilst the latter cannot put up with a hard rule. They are easily won with a little adulation, but if one reproves them by a word, they murmur against it, they give one up, they go away with hostile feelings, they forsake one in anger. They prefer to rule rather than to obey. They think that those whom they ought to have placed over them ought to be subject to themselves, as though indebted to them by their kindness.

118. What man is there that thinks those will be faithful to himself, whom he believes he will have to bind to himself by money or flattery? For he who takes thy money supposes that he is cheaply held, and looked down upon, unless the money is paid again and again. So he frequently expects his price; whilst the other, who is met with prayer and flattery, is always wanting to be asked.

Chapter XXIV.

We must strive for preferment only by right means. An office undertaken must be carried out wisely and with moderation. The inferior clergy should not detract from the bishop's reputation by feigned virtues; nor again, should the bishop be jealous of a cleric, but he should be just in all things and especially in giving judgment.

119. I Think, then, that one should strive to win preferment, especially in the Church, only by good actions and with a right aim; so that there may be no proud conceit, no idle carelessness, no shameful disposition of mind, no unseemly ambition. A plain simplicity of mind is enough for everything, and commends itself quite sufficiently.

120. When in office, again, it is not right to be harsh and severe, nor may one be too easy; lest on the one hand we should seem to be exercising a despotic power, and on the other to be by no means filling the office we had taken up.

121. We must strive also to win many by kindnesses and duties that we can do, and to preserve the favour already shown us. For they will with good reason forget the benefits of former times if they are now vexed at some great wrong. For it often enough happens that those one has shown favour to and allowed to rise step by step, are driven away, if one decides in some unworthy way to put another before them. But it is seemly for a priest to show such favour in his kindnesses and his decisions as to guard equity, and to show regard to the other clergy as to parents.

122. Those who once stood approved should not now become overbearing, but rather, as mindful of the grace they have received, stand firm in their humility. A priest ought not to be offended if either cleric or attendant or any ecclesiastic should win regard for himself, by showing mercy, or by fasting, or by uprightness of life, or by teaching and reading. For the grace of the Church is the praise of the teacher. It is a good thing that the work of another should be praised, if only it be done without any desire to boast. For each one should receive praise from the lips of his neighbour, and not from his own mouth, and each one should be commended by the work he has done, not merely by the wishes he had.

223. But if any one is disobedient to his bishop and wishes to exalt and upraise himself, and to overshadow his bishop's merits by a feigned appearance of learning or humility or mercy, he is wandering from the truth in his pride; for the rule of truth is, to do nothing to advance one's own cause whereby another loses ground, nor to use whatever good one has to the disgrace or blame of another.

124. Never protect a wicked man, nor allow the sacred things to be given over to an unworthy one; on the other hand, do not harass and press hard on a man whose fault is not clearly proved. Injustice quickly gives offence in every case, but especially in the Church, where equity ought to exist, where like treatment should be given to all, so that a powerful person may not claim the more, nor a rich man appropriate the more. For whether we be poor or rich, we are one in Christ. Let him that lives a holier life claim nothing more thereby for himself; for he ought rather to be the more humble for it.

125. In giving judgment let us have no respect of persons. Favour must be put out of sight, and the case be decided on its merits. Nothing is so great a strain on another's good opinion or confidence, as the fact of our giving away the cause of the weaker to the more powerful in any case that comes before us. The same happens if we are hard on the poor, whilst we make excuses for the rich man when guilty. Men are ready enough to flatter those in high positions, so as not to let them think themselves injured, or to feel vexed as though overthrown. But if thou fearest to give offence then do not undertake to give judgment. If thou art a priest or some cleric do not urge it. It is allowable for thee to be silent in the matter, if it be a money affair, though it is always due to consistency to be on the side of equity. But in the cause of God, where there is danger to the whole Church, it is no small sin to act as though one saw nothing.

Chapter XXV.

Benefits should be conferred on the poor rather than on the rich, for these latter either think a return is expected from them, or else they are angry at seeming to be indebted for such an action. But the poor man makes God the debtor in his place, and freely owns to the benefits he has received. To these remarks is added a warning to despise riches.

126. But what advantage is it to thee to show favour to a rich man? Is it that he is more ready to repay one who loves him? For we generally show favour to those from whom we expect to receive a return of favour. But we ought to think far more of the weak and helpless, because we hope to receive, on behalf of him who has it not, a recompense from the Lord Jesus, Who in the likeness of a marriage feast has given us a general representation of virtue. By this He bids us confer benefits rather on those who cannot give them to us in return, teaching us to bid to our feasts and meals, not those who are rich, but those that are poor. For the rich seem to be asked that they may prepare a banquet for us in return; the poor, as they have nothing wherewith to make return, when they receive anything, make the Lord to be our recompense Who has offered Himself as surety for the poor.

127. In the ordinary course of things, too, the conferring of a benefit on the poor is of more use than when it is conferred on the rich. The rich man scorns the benefit and is ashamed to feel indebted for a favour. Nay, moreover, whatever is offered to him he takes as due to his merits, as though only a just debt were paid him; or else he thinks it was but given because the giver expected a still greater return to be made him by the rich man. So. in accepting a kindness, the rich man, on that very ground, thinks that he has given more than he ever received. The poor man, however, though he has no money wherewith he can repay, at least shows his gratitude. And herein it is certain that he returns more than he received. For money is paid in coins, but gratitude never fails; money grows less by payment, but gratitude fails when held back, and is preserved when given to others. Next—a thing the rich man avoids—the poor man owns that he feels bound by the debt. He really thinks help has been given him, not that it has been offered in return for his honour. He considers that his children have been again given him, that his life is restored and his family preserved. How much better, then, is it to confer benefits upon the good than on the ungrateful.

128. Wherefore the Lord said to His disciples: "Take neither gold nor silver nor money." Whereby as with a sickle He cuts off the love of money that is ever growing up in human hearts. Peter also said to the lame man, who was always carried even from his mother's womb: "Silver and gold have I none, but what I have give I thee. In the Name of Jesus Christ of Nazareth, arise and walk." So he gave not money, but he gave health. How much better it is to have health without money, than money without health! The lame man rose; he had not hoped for that: he received no money; though he had hoped for that. But riches are hardly to be found among the saints of the Lord, so as to become objects of contempt to them.

Chapter XXVI.

How long standing an evil love of money is, is plain from many examples in the Old Testament. And yet it is plain, too, how idle a thing the possession of money is.

129. But man's habits have so long applied themselves to this admiration of money, that no one is thought worthy of honour unless he is rich. This is no new habit. Nay, this vice (and that makes the matter worse) grew long years ago in the hearts of men. When the city of Jericho fell at the sound of the priests' trumpets, and Joshua the son of Nun gained the victory, he knew that the valour of the people was weakened through love of money and desire for gold. For when Achan had taken a garment of gold and two hundred shekels of silver and a golden ingot from the spoils of the ruined city, he was brought before the Lord, and could not deny the theft, but owned it.

130. Love of money, then, is an old, an ancient vice, which showed itself even at the declaration of the divine law; for a law was given to check it. On account of love of money

Balak thought Balaam could be tempted by rewards to curse the people of our fathers. Love of money would have won the day too, had not God bidden him hold back from cursing. Overcome by love of money Achan led to destruction all the people of the fathers. So Joshua the son of Nun, who could stay the sun from setting, could not stay the love of money in man from creeping on. At the sound of his voice the sun stood still, but love of money stayed not. When the sun stood still Joshua completed his triumph, but when love of money went on, he almost lost the victory.

131. Why? Did not the woman Delilah's love of money deceive Samson, the bravest man of all So he who had torn asunder the roaring lion with his hands; who, when bound and handed over to his enemies, alone, without help, burst his bonds and slew a thousand of them; who broke the cords interwoven with sinews as though they were but the slight threads of a net; he, I say, having laid his head on the woman's knee, was robbed of the decoration of his victory-bringing hair, that which gave him his might. Money flowed into the lap of the woman, and the favour of God forsook the man.

132. Love of money, then, is deadly. Seductive is money, whilst it also defiles those who have it, and helps not those who have it not. Supposing that money sometimes is a help, yet it is only a help to a poor man who makes his want known. What good is it to him who does not long for it, nor seek it; who does not need its help and is not turned aside by pursuit of it? What good is it to others, if he who has it is alone the richer for it? Is he therefore more honourable because he has that whereby honour is often lost, because he has what he must guard rather than possess? We possess what we use, but what is beyond our use brings us no fruit of possession, but only the danger of watching.

Chapter XXVII.

In contempt of money there is the pattern of justice, which virtue bishops and clerics ought to aim at together with some others. A few words are added on the duty of not bringing an excommunication too quickly into force.

133. To come to an end; we know that contempt of riches is a form of justice, therefore we ought to avoid love of money, and strive with all our powers never to do anything against justice, but to guard it in all our deeds and actions.

134. If we would please God, we must have love, we must be of one mind, we must follow humility, each one thinking the other higher than himself. This is true humility, when one never claims anything proudly for oneself, but thinks oneself to be the inferior. The bishop should treat the clerics and attendants, who are indeed his sons, as members of himself, and give to each one that duty for which he sees him to be fit.

135. Not without pain is a limb of the body cut off which has become corrupt. It is treated for a long time, to see if it can be cured with various remedies. If it cannot be cured, then it is cut off by a good physician. Thus it is a good bishop's desire to wish to heal the weak, to remove the spreading ulcers, to burn some parts and not to cut them off; and lastly, when they cannot be healed, to cut them off with pain to himself. Wherefore that beautiful rule of the Apostle stands forth brightly, that we should look each one, not on his own things, but on the things of others. In this way it will never come about that we shall in anger give way to our own feelings, or concede more than is right in favour to our own wishes.

Chapter XXVIII.

Mercy must be freely shown even though it brings an odium of its own. With regard to this, reference is made to the well-known story about the sacred vessels which were broken up by Ambrose to pay for the redemption of captives; and very beautiful advice is given about the right use of the gold and silver which the Church possesses. Next, after showing from the action of holy Lawrence what are the true treasures of the Church, certain rules are laid down which ought to be observed in melting down and employing for such uses the consecrated vessels of the Church.

136. It is a very great incentive to mercy to share in others' misfortunes, to help the needs of others as far as our means allow, and sometimes even beyond them. For it is better for mercy's sake to take up a case, or to suffer odium rather than to show hard feeling. So I once brought odium on myself because I broke up the sacred vessels to redeem captives—a fact that could displease the Arians. Not that it displeased them as an act, but as being a thing in which they could take hold of something for which to blame me. Who can be so hard, cruel, iron-hearted, as to be displeased because a man is redeemed from death, or a woman from barbarian impurities, things that are worse than death, or boys and girls and infants from the pollution of idols, whereby through fear of death they were defiled?

137. Although we did not act thus without good reason, yet we have followed it up among the people so as to confess and to add again and again that it was far better to preserve souls than gold for the Lord. For He Who sent the apostles without gold also brought together the churches without gold. The Church has gold, not to store up, but to lay out, and to spend on those who need. What necessity is there to guard what is of no good? Do we not know how much gold and silver the Assyrians took out of the temple of the Lord? Is it not much better that the priests should melt it down for the sustenance of the poor, if other supplies fail, than that a sacrilegious enemy should carry it off and defile it? Would not the Lord Himself say: Why didst thou suffer so many needy to die of hunger? Surely thou hadst gold? Thou shouldst have given them sustenance. Why are so many captives brought on the slave market, and why are so many unredeemed left to be slain by the enemy? It had been better to preserve living vessels than gold ones.

138. To this no answer could be given. For what wouldst thou say: I feared that the temple of God would need its ornaments? He would answer: The sacraments need not gold, nor are they proper to gold only—for they are not bought with gold. The glory of the sacraments is the redemption of captives. Truly they are precious vessels, for they redeem men from death. That, indeed, is the true treasure of the Lord which effects what His blood effected. Then, indeed, is the vessel of the Lord's blood recognized, when one sees in either redemption, so that the chalice redeems from the enemy those whom His blood redeemed from sin. How beautifully it is said, when long lines of captives are redeemed by the Church: These Christ has redeemed. Behold the gold that can be tried, behold the useful gold, behold the gold of Christ which frees from death, behold the gold whereby modesty is redeemed and chastity is preserved.

139. These, then, I preferred to hand over to you as free men, rather than to store up the gold. This crowd of captives, this company surely is more glorious than the sight of cups. The gold of the Redeemer ought to contribute to this work so as to redeem those in danger. I recognize the fact that the blood of Christ not only glows in cups of gold, but also by the office of redemption has impressed upon them the power of the divine operation.

140. Such gold the holy martyr Lawrence preserved for the Lord. For when the treasures of the Church were demanded from him, he promised that he would show them. On the following day he brought the poor together. When asked where the treasures were which he had promised, he pointed to the poor, saying: "These are the treasures of the Church." And truly they were treasures, in whom Christ lives, in whom there is faith in Him. So, too, the Apostle says: "We have this treasure in earthen vessels." What greater treasures has Christ than those in whom He says He Himself lives? For thus it is written: "I was hungry and ye gave Me to eat, I was thirsty and ye gave Me to drink, I was a stranger and ye took Me in." And again: "What thou didst to one of these, thou didst it unto Me." What better treasures has Jesus than those in which He loves to be seen?

141. These treasures Lawrence pointed out, and prevailed, for the persecutors could not take them away. Jehoiachim, who preserved his gold during the siege and spent it not in providing food, saw his gold carried off, and himself led into captivity. Lawrence, who preferred to spend the gold of the Church on the poor, rather than to keep it in hand for the persecutor, received the sacred crown of martyrdom for the unique and deep-sighted vigour of his meaning. Or was

it perhaps said to holy Lawrence: "Thou shouldst not spend the treasures of the Church, or sell the sacred vessels"?

142. It is necessary that every one should fill this office, with genuine good faith and clear-sighted forethought. If any one derives profit from it for himself it is a crime, but if he spends the treasures on the poor, or redeems captives, he shows mercy. For no one can say: Why does the poor man live? None can complain that captives are redeemed, none can find fault because a temple of the Lord is built, none can be angry because a plot of ground has been enlarged for the burial of the bodies of the faithful, none can be vexed because in the tombs of the Christians there is rest for the dead. In these three ways it is allowable to break up, melt down, or sell even the sacred vessels of the Church.

143. It is necessary to see that the mystic cup does not go out of the Church, lest the service of the sacred chalice should be turned over to base uses. Therefore vessels were first sought for in the Church which had not been consecrated to such holy uses. Then broken up and afterwards melted down, they were given to the poor in small payments, and were also used for the ransom of captives. But if new vessels fail, or those which never seem to have been used tot such a holy purpose, then, as I have already said, I think that all might be put to this use without irreverence.

Chapter XXIX.

The property of widows or of all the faithful, that has been entrusted to the Church, ought to be defended though it brings danger to oneself. This is illustrated by the example of Onias the priest, and of Ambrose, bishop of Ticinum.

144. Great care must be taken that the property entrusted by widows remains inviolate. It should be guarded without causing complaint, not only if it belongs to widows, but to any one at all. For good faith must be shown to all, though the cause of the widow and orphans comes first.

145. So everything entrusted to the temple was preserved in the name of the widows alone, as we read in the book of the Maccabees. For when information was given of the money, which Simon treacherously had told King Antiochus could be found in large quantities in the temple at Jerusalem, Heliodorus was sent to look into the matter. He came to the temple, and made known to the high priest his hateful information and the reason of his coming.

146. Then the priest said that only means for the maintenance of the widows and orphans was laid up there. And when Heliodorus would have gone to seize it, and to claim it on the king's behalf, the, priests cast themselves before the altar, after putting on their priestly robes, and with tears called on the living God Who had given them the law concerning trust-money to show Himself as guardian of His own commands. The changed look and colour of the high priest showed what grief of soul and anxiety and tension of mind were his. All wept, for the spot would fall into contempt, if not even in the temple of God safe and faithful guardianship could be preserved. Women with breasts girded, and virgins who usually were shut in, knocked at the doors. Some ran to the walls, others looked out of the windows, all raised their hands to heaven in prayer that God would stand by His laws.

147. But Heliodorus, undeterred by this, was eager to carry out his intention, and had already surrounded the treasury with his followers, when suddenly there appeared to him a dreadful horseman all glorious in golden armour, his horse also being adorned with costly ornaments. Two other youths also appeared in glorious might and wondrous beauty, in splendour and glory and beauteous array. They stood round him, and on either side beat the sacrilegious wretch, and gave him stroke after stroke without intermission. What more need I say? Shut in by darkness he fell to the ground, and lay there nearly dead with fear at this plain proof of divine power, nor had he any hope of safety left within him. Joy returned to those who were in fear, fear fell on those who were so proud before. And some of the friends of Heliodorus in their trouble besought Onias, asking life for him, since he was almost at his last breath.

148. When, therefore, the high priest asked for this, the same youths again appeared to Heliodorus, clad in the same garments, and said to him: Give thanks to Onias the high priest, for whose sake thy life is granted thee. But do thou, having experienced the scourge of God, go and tell thy friends how much thou hast learnt of the sanctity of the temple and the power of God. With these words they passed out of sight. Heliodorus then, his life having come back to him, offered a sacrifice to the Lord, gave thanks to the priest Onias, and returned with his army to the king, saying: "If thou hast an enemy or one who is plotting against thy power, send him thither and thou wilt receive him back well scourged."

149. Therefore, my sons, good faith must be preserved in the case of trust-money, and care, too, must be shown. Your service will glow the brighter if the oppression of a powerful man, which some widow or orphan cannot withstand, is checked by the assistance of the Church, and if ye show that the command of the Lord has more weight with you than the favour of the rich.

150. Ye also remember how often we entered on a contest against the royal attacks, on behalf of the trust-money belonging to widows, yea, and to others as well. You and I shared this in common. I will also mention the late case of the Church at Ticinum, which was in danger of losing the widow's trust-money that it had received. For when he who wanted to claim it on some imperial rescript demanded it, the clergy did not maintain their rights. For they themselves, having once been called to office and sent to intervene, now supposed that they could not oppose the emperor's orders. The plain words of the rescript were read, the orders of the chief officer of the court were there, he who was to act in the matter was at hand. What more was to be said? It was handed over.

151. However, after taking counsel with me, the holy bishop took possession of the rooms to which he knew that the widow's property had been carried. As it could not be carried away, it was all set down in writing. Later on it was again demanded on proof of the document. The emperor repeated the order, and would meet us himself in his own person. We refused. And when the force of the divine law, and a long list of passages and the danger of Heliodorus was explained, at length the emperor became reasonable. Afterwards, again, an attempt was made to seize it, but the good bishop anticipated the attempt and restored to the widow all he had received. So faith was preserved, but the oppression was no longer a cause for fear; for now it is the matter itself, not good faith, that is in danger.

Chapter XXX.

The ending of the book brings an exhortation to avoid ill-will, and to seek prudence, faith, and the other virtues.

152. My sons, avoid wicked men, guard against the envious. There is this difference between a wicked and an envious man: the wicked man is delighted at his own good fortune, but the envious is tortured at the thought of an other's. The former loves evil, the latter hates good. So he is almost more bearable who desires good for himself alone, than he who desires evil for all.

153. My sons, think before you act, and when you have thought long then do what you consider right. When the opportunity of a praiseworthy death is given let it be seized at once. Glory that is put off flies away and is not easily laid hold of again.

154. Love faith. For by his devotion and faith Josiah won great love for himself from his enemies. For he celebrated the Lord's passover when he was eighteen yearsold, as no one had done it before him. As then in zeal he was superior to those who went before him, so do ye, my sons, show zeal for God. Let zeal for God search you through, and devour you, so that each one of you may say: "The zeal of thine house hath eaten me up. " An apostle of Christ was called the zealot. But why do I speak of an apostle? The Lord Himself said: "The zeal of thine house hath eaten Me up." Let it then be real zeal for God, not mean earthy zeal, for that causes jealousy.

155. Let there be peace among you, which passeth all understanding. Love one another. Nothing is sweeter than charity, nothing more blessed than peace. Ye yourselves know that I

have ever loved you and do now love you above all others. As the children of one father ye have become united under the bond of brotherly affection.

156. Whatsoever is good, that hold fast; and the God of peace and love be with you in the Lord Jesus, to Whom be honour and glory, dominion and might, together with the Holy Spirit, for ever and ever. Amen.

BOOK III.

Chapter I.

We are taught by David and Solomon how to take counsel with our own heart. Scipio is not to be accounted prime author of the saying which is ascribed to him. The writer proves what glorious things the holy prophets accomplished in their time of quiet, and shows, by examples of their and others' leisure moments, that a just man is never alone in trouble.

I. The prophet David taught us that we should go about in our heart as though in a large house; that we should hold converse with it as with some trusty companion. He spoke to himself, and conversed with himself, as these words show: "I said, I will take heed to my ways." Solomon his son also said: "Drink water out of thine own vessels, and out of the springs of thy wells; " that is: use thine own counsel. For: "Counsel in the heart of a man is as deep waters." "Let no stranger," it says, "share it with thee. Let the fountain of thy water be thine own, and rejoice with thy wife who is thine from thy youth. Let the loving hind and pleasant doe converse with thee."

2. Scipio, therefore, was not the first to know that he was not alone when he was alone, or that he was least at leisure when he was at leisure. For Moses knew it before him, who, when silent, was crying out; who, when he stood at ease, was fighting, nay, not merely fighting but triumphing over enemies whom he had not come near. So much was he at ease, that others held up his hands; yet he was no less active than others, for he with his hands at ease was overcoming the enemy, whom they that were in the battle could not conquer. Thus Moses in his silence spoke, and in his ease laboured hard. And were his labours greater than his times of quiet, who, being in the mount for forty days, received the whole law? And in that solitude there was One not far away to speak with him. Whence also David says: "I will hear what the Lord God will say within me." How much greater a thing is it for God to speak with any one, than for a man to speak with himself!

3. The apostles passed by and their shadows cured the sick. Their garments were touched and health was granted.

4. Elijah spoke the word, and the rain ceased and fell not on the earth for three years and six months. Again he spoke, and the barrel of meal failed not, and the cruse of oil wasted not the whole time of that long famine.

5. But—as many delight in warfare—which is the most glorious, to bring a battle to an end by the strength of a great army, or, by merits before God alone? Elisha rested in one place while the king of Syria waged a great war against the people of our fathers, and was adding to its terrors by various treacherous plans, and was endeavouring to catch them in an ambush. But the prophet found out all their preparations, and being by the grace of God present everywhere in mental vigour, he told the thoughts of their enemies to his countrymen, and warned them of what places to beware. And when this was known to the king of Syria, he sent an army and shut in the prophet. Elisha prayed and caused all of them to be struck with blindness, and made those who had come to besiege him enter Samaria as captives.

6. Let us compare this leisure of his with that of others. Other men for the sake of rest are wont to withdraw their minds from business, and to retire from the company and companionship of men; to seek the retirement of the country or the solitude of the fields, or in the city to give their minds a rest and to enjoy peace and quietness. But Elisha was ever active. In solitude he divided Jordan on passing over it, so that the lower part flowed down, whilst the upper returned to its source. On Carmel he promises the woman, who so far had had no child, that a son now unhoped for should be born to her. He raises the dead to life, he corrects the bitterness of the food, and makes it to be sweet by mixing meal with it. Having distributed ten loaves to the people for food, he gathered up the fragments that were left after they had been filled. He makes the iron head of the axe, which had fallen off and was sunk deep in the river

Jordan, to swim by putting the wooden handle in the water. He changes leprosy for cleanness, drought for rain, famine for plenty.

7. When can the upright man be alone, since he is always with God? When is he left forsaken who is never separated from Christ? "Who," it says, "shall separate us from the love of Christ? I am confident that neither death nor life nor angel shall do so." And when can he be deprived of his labour who never can be deprived of his merits, wherein his labour receives its crown? By what places is he limited to whom the whole world of riches is a possession? By what judgment is he confined who is never blamed by any one? For he is "as unknown yet well known, as dying and behold he lives, as sorrowful yet always rejoicing, as poor yet making many rich, as having nothing and yet possessing all things." For the upright man regards nothing but what is consistent and virtuous. And so although he seems poor to another, he is rich to himself, for his worth is taken not at the value of the things which are temporal, but of the things which are eternal.

Chapter II.

The discussions among philosophers about the comparison between what is virtuous and what is useful have nothing to do with Christians. For with them nothing is useful which is not just. What are the duties of perfection, and what are ordinary duties? The same words often suit different things in different ways. Lastly, a just man never seeks his own advantage at the cost of another's disadvantage, but rather is always on the lookout for what is useful to others.

8. As we have already spoken about the two former subjects, wherein we discussed what is virtuous and what is useful, there follows now the question whether we ought to compare what is virtuous and useful together, and to ask which we must follow. For, as we have already discussed the matter as to whether a thing is virtuous or wicked, and in another place whether it is useful or useless, so here some think we ought to find out whether a thing is virtuous or useful.

9. I am induced to do this, lest I should seem to be allowing that these two are mutually opposed to one another, when I have already shown them to be one. For I said that nothing can be virtuous but what is useful, and nothing can be useful but what is virtuous. For we do not follow the wisdom of the flesh, whereby the usefulness that consists in an abundance of money is held to be of most value, but we follow that wisdom which is of God, whereby those things which are greatly valued in this world are counted but as loss.

10. For this catorqwma, which is duty carried out entirely and in perfection, starts from the true source of virtue. On this follows another, or ordinary duty. This shows by its name that no hard or extraordinary practice of virtue is involved, for it can be common to very many. The desire to save money is the usual practice with many. To enjoy a well-prepared banquet and a pleasant meal is a general habit; but to fast or to use self-restraint is the practice of but few, and not to be desirous of another's goods is a virtue rarely found. On the other hand, to wish to deprive another of his property—and not to be content with one's due—here one will find many to keep company with one. Those (the philosopher would say) are primary duties—these ordinary. The primary are found but with few, the ordinary with the many.

11. Again, the same words often have a different meaning. For instance, we call God good and a man good; but it bears in each case quite a different meaning. We call God just in one sense, man in another. So, too, there is a difference in meaning when we call God wise and a man wise. This we are taught in the Gospel: "Be ye perfect even as your Father Who is in heaven is perfect. " I read again that Paul was perfect and yet not perfect. For when he said: "Not as though I had already attained, either were already perfect; but I follow after, if that. I may apprehend it. " Immediately he added: "We, then, that are perfect." There is a twofold form of perfection, the one having but ordinary, the other the highest worth. The one availing here, the other hereafter. The one in accordance with human powers, the other with the perfection of the world to come. But God is just through all, wise above all, perfect in all.

12. There is also diversity even among men themselves. Daniel, of whom it was said: "Who is wiser than Daniel? " was wise in a different sense to what others are. The same may be said of Solomon, who was filled with wisdom, above all the wisdom of the ancients, and more than all the wise men of Egypt. To be wise as men are in general is quite a different thing to being really wise. He who is ordinarily wise is wise for temporal matters, is wise for himself, so as to deprive another of something and get it for himself. He who is really wise does not know how to regard his own advantage, but looks with all his desire to that which is eternal, and to that which is seemly and virtuous, seeking not what is useful for himself, but for all.

13. Let this, then, be our rule, so that we may never go wrong between two things, one virtuous, the other useful. The upright man must never think of depriving another of anything, nor must he ever wish to increase his own advantage to the disadvantage of another. This rule the Apostle gives thee, saying: "All things are lawful, but all things are not expedient; all things are lawful, but all things edify not. Let no man seek his own, but each one another's." That is: Let no man seek his own advantage, but another's; let no man seek his own honour, but another's. Wherefore he says in another place: "Let each esteem other better than themselves, looking not each one to his own things, but to the things of others."

14. And let no one seek his own favour or his own praise, but another's. This we can plainly see declared in the book of Proverbs, where the Holy Spirit says through Solomon: "My son, if thou be wise, be wise for thyself and thy neighbours; but if thou turn out evil, thou alone shalt bear it." The wise man gives counsel to others, as the upright man does, and shares with him in wearing the form of either virtue.

Chapter III.

The rule given about not seeking one's own gain is established, first by the examples of Christ, next by the meaning of the word, and lastly by the very form and uses of our limbs. Wherefore the writer shows what a crime it is to deprive another of what is useful, since the law of nature as well as the divine law is broken by such wickedness. Further, by its means we also lose that gift which makes us superior to other living creatures; and lastly, through it civil laws are abused and treated with the greatest contempt.

15. If, then, any one wishes to please all, he must strive in everything to do, not what is useful for himself, but what is useful for many, as also Paul strove to do. For this is "to be conformed to the image of Christ," namely, when one does not strive for what is another's, and does not deprive another of something so as to gain it for oneself. For Christ our Lord, though He was in the form of God, emptied Himself so as to take on Himself the form of man, which He wished to enrich with the virtue of His works. Wilt thou, then, spoil him whom Christ has put on? Wilt thou strip him whom Christ has clothed? For this is what thou art doing when thou dost attempt to increase thine own advantage at another's loss.

16. Think, O man, from whence thou hast received thy name—even from the earth, which takes nothing from any one, but gives freely to all, and supplies varied produce for the use of all living things. Hence humanity is called a particular and innate virtue in man, for it assists its partner.

17. The very form of thy body and the uses of thy limbs teach thee this. Can one limb claim the duties of another? Can the eye claim for itself the duties of the ear; or the mouth the duties of the eye; or the hand the service of the feet; or the feet that of the hands? Nay, the hands themselves, both left and right, have different duties to do, so that if one were to change the use of either, one would act contrary to nature. We should have to lay aside the whole man before we could change the service of the various members: as if, for instance, we were to try to take food with the left hand, or to perform the duties of the left hand with the right, so as to remove the remains of food—unless, of course, need demanded it.

18. Imagine for a moment, and give to the eye the power to withdraw the understanding from the head, the sense of hearing from the ears, the power of thought from the mind, the sense of smell from the nose, the sense of taste from the mouth, and then to assume them itself,

would it not at once destroy the whole order of nature? Wherefore the Apostle says well: "If the whole body were an eye, where were the hearing? If the whole were hearing, where were the smelling?" So, then, we are all one body, though with many members, all necessary to the body. For no one member can say of another: "I have no need of thee." For those members which seem to be more feeble are much more necessary and require greater care and attention. And if one member suffers, all the members suffer with it.

19. So we see how grave a matter it is to deprive another, with whom we ought rather to suffer, of anything, or to act unfairly or injuriously towards one to whom we ought to give a share in our services. This is a true law of nature, which binds us to show all kindly feeling, so that we should all of us in turn help one another, as parts of one body, and should never think of depriving another of anything, seeing it is against the law of nature even to abstain from giving help. We are born in such a way that limb combines with limb, and one works with another, and all assist each other in mutual service. But if one fails in its duty, the rest are hindered. If, for instance, the hand tears out the eye, has it not hindered the use, of its work? If it were to wound the foot, how many actions would it not prevent? But how much worse is it for the whole man to be drawn aside from his duty than for one of the members only! If the whole body is injured in one member, so also is the whole community of the human race disturbed in one man. The nature of mankind is injured, as also is the society of the holy Church, which rises into one united body, bound together in oneness of faith and love. Christ the Lord, also, Who died for all, will grieve that the price of His blood was paid in vain.

20. Why, the very law of the Lord teaches us that this rule must be observed, so that we may never deprive another of anything for the sake of our own advantage. For it says: "Remove not the bounds which thy fathers have set. " It bids a neighbour's ox to be brought back if found wandering. It orders a thief to be put to death. It forbids the labourer to be deprived of his hire, and orders money to be returned without usury. It is a mark of kindly feeling to help him who has nothing, but it is a sign of a hard nature to extort more than one has given. If a man has need of thy assistance because he has not enough of his own wherewith to repay a debt, is it not a wicked thing to demand under the guise of kindly feeling a larger sum from him who has not the means to pay off a less amount? Thou dost but free him from debt to another, to bring him under thy own hand; and thou callest that human kindliness which is but a further wickedness.

21. It is in this very matter that we stand before all other living creatures, for they do not understand how to do good. Wild beasts snatch away, men share with others. Wherefore the Psalmist says: "The righteous showeth mercy and giveth." There are some, however, to whom the wild beasts do good. They feed their young with what they get, and the birds satisfy their brood with food; but to men alone has it been given to feed all as though they were their own. That is so in accordance with the claims of nature. And if it is not lawful to refuse to give, how is it lawful to deprive another? And do not our very laws teach us the same? They order those things which have been taken from others with injury to their persons or property to be restored with additional recompense; so as to check the thief from stealing by the penalty, and by the fine to recall him from his ways.

22. Suppose, however, that some one did not fear the penalty, or laughed at the fine, would that make it a worthy thing to deprive another of his own? That would be a mean vice and suited only to the lowest of the low. So contrary to nature is it, that while want might seem to drive one to it, yet nature could never urge it. And yet we find secret theft among slaves, open robbery among the rich.

23. But what so contrary to nature as to injure another for our own benefit? The natural feelings of our own hearts urge us to keep on the watch for all, to undergo trouble, to do work for all. It is considered also a glorious thing for each one at risk to himself to seek the quiet of all, and to think it far more thankworthy to have saved his country from destruction than to have kept danger from himself. We must think it a far more noble thing to labour for our country than to pass a quiet life at ease in the full enjoyment of leisure.

Chapter IV.

As it has been shown that he who injures another for the sake of his own advantage will undergo terrible punishment at the hand of his own conscience, it is referred that nothing is useful to one which is not in the same way useful to all. Thus there is no place among Christians for the question propounded by the philosophers about two shipwrecked persons, for they must show love and humility to all.

24. Hence we infer that a man who guides himself according to the ruling of nature, so as to be obedient to her, can never injure another. If he injures another, he violates nature, nor will he think that what he has gained is so much an advantage as a disadvantage. And what punishment is worse than the wounds of the conscience within? What judgment harder than that of our hearts, whereby each one stands convicted and accuses himself of the injury that he has wrongfully done against his brother? This the Scriptures speak of very plainly, saying: "Out of the mouth of fools there is a rod for wrong-doing." Folly, then, is condemned because it causes wrong-doing. Ought we not rather to avoid this, than death, or loss, or want, or exile, or sickness? Who would not think some blemish of body or loss of inheritance far less than some blemish of soul or loss of reputation?

25. It is clear, then, that all must consider and hold that the advantage of the individual is the same as that of all, and that nothing must be considered advantageous except what is for the general good. For how can one be benefited alone? That which is useless to all is harmful. I certainly cannot think that he who is useless to all can be of use to himself. For if there is one law of nature for all, there is also one state of usefulness for all. And we are bound by the law of nature to act for the good of all. It is not, therefore, right for him who wishes the interests of another to be considered according to nature, to injure him against the law of nature.

26. For if those who run in a race are, as one hears, instructed and warned each one to win the race by swiftness of foot and not by any foul play, and to hasten on to victory by running as hard as they can, but not to dare to trip up another or push him aside with their hand, how much more in the course of this life ought the victory to be won by us, without falseness to another and cheating?

27. Some ask whether a wise man ought in case of a shipwreck to take away a plank from an ignorant sailor? Although it seems better for the common good that a wise man rather than a fool should escape from shipwreck, yet I do not think that a Christian, a just and a wise man, ought to save his own life by the death of another; just as when he meets with an armed robber he cannot return his blows, lest in defending his life he should stain his love toward his neighbour. The verdict on this is plain and clear in the books of the Gospel. "Put up thy sword, for every one that taketh the sword shall perish with the sword." What robber is more hateful than the persecutor who came to kill Christ? But Christ would not be defended from the wounds of the persecutor, for He willed to heal all by His wounds.

28. Why dost thou consider thyself greater than another, when a Christian man ought to put others before himself, to claim nothing for himself, usurp no honours, claim no reward for his merits? Why, next, art thou not wont to bear thy own troubles rather than to destroy another's advantage? For what is so contrary to nature as not to be content with what one has or to seek what is another's, and to try to get it in shameful ways. For if a virtuous life is in accordance with nature—for God made all things very good—then shameful living must be opposed to it A virtuous and a shameful life cannot go together, since they are absolutely severed by the law of nature.

Chapter V.

The upright does nothing that is contrary to duty, even though there is a hope of keeping it secret. To point this out the tale about the ring of Gyges was invented by the philosophers. Exposing this, he brings forWard known and true examples from the life of David and John the Baptist.

29. To lay down here already the result of our discussion, as though we had already ended it, we declare it a fixed rule, that we must never aim at anything hut what is virtuous. The wise man

does nothing but what can be done openly and without falseness, nor does he do anything whereby he may involve himself in any wrong-doing, even where he may escape notice. For he is guilty in his own eyes, before being so in the eyes of others; and the publicity of his crime does not bring him more shame than his own consciousness of it. This we can show, not by the made-up stories which philosophers use, but from the true examples of good men.

30. I need not, therefore, imagine a great chasm in the earth, which had been loosened by heavy rains, and had afterwards burst asunder, as Plato does. For he makes Gyges descend into that chasm, and to meet there that iron horse of the fable that had doors in its sides. When these doors were opened, he found a gold ring on the finger of a dead man, whose corpse lay there lifeless. He desiring the gold took away the ring. But when he returned to the king's shepherds, to whose number he belonged, by chance having turned the stone inwards towards the palms of his hands, he saw all, yet was seen by none. Then when he turned the ring to its proper position, he was again seen by all. On becoming conscious of this strange power, by the use of the ring he committed adultery with the queen, killed the king, and took possession of the kingdom after slaying all the rest, who he thought should be put to death, so that they might be no hindrance to him.

31. Give, says Plato, this ring to a wise man, that when he commits a fault he may by its help remain unnoticed; yet he will be none the more free from the stain of sin than if he could not be hid. The hiding-place of the wise lies not in the hope of impunity but in his own innocency. Lastly, the law is not laid down for the just but for the unjust. For the just has within himself the law of his mind, and a rule of equity and justice. Thus he is not recalled from sin by fear of punishment, but by the rule of a virtuous life.

32. Therefore, to return to our subject, I will now bring forward, not false examples for true, but true examples in place of false. For why need I imagine a chasm in the earth, and an iron horse and a gold ring found on the fingers of a dead man; and say that such was the power of this ring, that he who wore it could appear at his own will, but if he did not wish to be seen, he could remove himself out of the sight of those who stood by, so as to seem to be away. This story, of course, is meant to answer the question whether a wise man, on getting the opportunity of using that ring so as to be able to hide his crimes, and to obtain a kingdom,—whether, I say, a wise man would be unwilling to sin and would consider the stain of sin far worse than the pains of punishment, or whether he would use it for doing wickedness in the hope of not being found out? Why, I say, should I need the pretence of a ring, when I can show from what has been done that a wise man, on seeing he would not only be undetected in his sin, but would also gain a kingdom if he gave way to it, and who, on the other hand, noted danger to his own safety if he did not commit the crime, yet chose to risk his own safety so as to be free from crime, rather than to commit the crime and so gain the kingdom.

33. When David fled from the face of King Saul, because the king was seeking him in the desert with three thousand chosen men to put him to death, he entered the king's camp and found him sleeping. There he not only did him no injury, but actually guarded him from being slain by any who had entered with him. For when Abishai said to him: "The Lord hath delivered thine enemy into thine hand this day, now therefore I will slay him," he answered: "Destroy him not, for who can stretch forth his hand against the Lord's anointed, and be guiltless?" And he added: "As the Lord liveth, unless the Lord shall smite him, or his day shall come to die, or he shall die in battle, and it be laid to me, the Lord forbid that I should stretch out my hand against the Lord's anointed."

34. Therefore he did not suffer him to be slain, but removed only his spear, which stood by his head, and his cruse of water. Then, whilst all were sleeping, he left the camp and went across to the top of the hill, and began to reproach the royal attendants, and especially their general Abner, for not keeping faithful watch over their lord and king. Next, he showed them where the king's spear and cruse were which had stood at his head. And when the king called to him, he restored the spear, and said: "The Lord render to every man his righteousness and faithfulness,

for the Lord delivered thee into my hand, but I would not avenge myself on the Lord's anointed." Even whilst he said this, he feared his plots and fled, changing his place in exile. However, he never put safety before innocency, seeing that when a second opportunity was given him of killing the king, he would not use the chance that came to him, and which put in his reach certain safety instead of fear, and a kingdom instead of exile.

35. Where was the use of the ring in John's case, who would not have been put to death by Herod if he had kept silence? He could have kept silence before him so as to be both seen and yet not killed. But because he not only could not endure to sin himself to protect his own safety, but could not bear and endure even another's sin, he brought about the cause of his own death. Certainly none can deny that he might have kept silence, who in the case of Gyges deny that he could have remained invisible by the help of the ring.

36. But although that fable has not the force of truth, yet it has this much to go upon, that if an upright man could hide himself, yet he would avoid sin just as though he could not conceal himself; and that he would not hide his person by putting on a ring, but his life by putting on Christ. As the Apostle says: "Our life is hid with Christ in God." Let, then, no one here strive to shine, let none show pride, let none boast. Christ willed not to be known here, He would not that His Name should be preached in the Gospel whilst He lived on earth. He came to lie hid from this world. Let us therefore likewise hide our life after the example of Christ, let us shun boastfulness, let us not desire to be made known. It is better to live here in humility, and there in glory. "When Christ," it says, "shall appear, then shall we also appear with Him in glory."

Chapter VI.

We ought not to allow the idea of profit to get hold of us. What excuses they make who get their gains by selling corn, and what answer ought to be made to them. In connection with this certain parables from the Gospels and some of the sayings of Solomon are set before our eyes.

37. Let not, therefore, expediency get the better of virtue, but virtue of expediency. By expediency here I mean what is accounted so by people generally. Let love of money be destroyed, let lust die. The holy man says that he has never been engaged in business. For to get an increase in price is a sign not of simplicity but of cunning. Elsewhere it says: "He that seeketh a high price for his corn is cursed among the people."

38. Plain and definite is the statement, leaving no room for debate, such as a disputatious kind of speaking is wont to give, when one maintains that agriculture is considered praiseworthy by all; that the fruits of the earth are easily grown; that the more a man has sown, the greater will be his meed of praise; further, that the richer returns of his active labours are not gained by fraud, and that carelessness and disregard for an uncultivated soil are wont to be blamed.

39. I have ploughed, he says, carefully. I have sown freely. I have tilled actively. I have gathered good increase. I have stored it anxiously, saved it faithfully, and guarded it with care. Now in a time of famine I sell it, and come to the help of the hungry. I sell my own corn, not another's. And for no more than others, nay, even at a less price. What fraud is there here, when many would come to great danger if they had nothing to buy? Is industry to be made a crime? Or diligence to be blamed? Or foresight to be abused? Perhaps he may even say: Joseph collected corn in a time of abundance, and sold it when it was dear. Is any one forced to buy it at too dear a price? Is force employed against the buyer? The opportunity to buy is afforded to all, injury is inflicted on none.

40. When this has been said, and one man's ideas have carried him so far, another rises and says: Agriculture is good indeed, for it supplies fruits for all, and by simple industry adds to the richness of the earth without any cheating or fraud. If there is any error, the loss is the greater, for the better a man sows, the better he will reap. If he has sown the pure grain of wheat, he gathers a purer and cleaner harvest. The fruitful earth returns what she has received in manifold measure. A good field returns its produce with interest.

41. Thou must expect payment for thy labour from the crops of the fruitful land, and must hope for a just return from the fruitfulness of the rich earth. Why dost thou use the industry of nature and make a cheat of it? Why dost thou grudge for the use of men what is grown for all? Why lessen the abundance for the people? Why make want thy aim? Why make the poor long for a barren season? For when they do not feel the benefits of a fruitful season, because thou art putting up the price, and art storing up the corn, they would far rather that nothing should be produced, than that thou shouldst do business at the expense of other people's hunger. Thou makest much of the want of corn, the small supply of food. Thou groanest over the rich crops of the soil; thou mournest the general plenty, and bewailest the garners full of corn; thou art on the lookout to see when the crop is poor and the harvest fails. Thou rejoicest that a curse has smiled upon thy wishes, so that none should have their produce. Then thou rejoicest that thy harvest has come. Then thou collectest wealth from the misery of all, and callest this industry and diligence, when it is but cunning shrewdness and an adroit trick of the trade. Thou callest it a remedy, when it is but a wicked contrivance. Shall I call this robbery or only gain? These opportunities are seized as though seasons for plunder, wherein, like some cruel waylayer, thou mayest fall upon the stomachs of men. The price rises higher as though by the mere addition of interest, but the danger to life is increased too. For then the interest of the stored-up crops grows higher. As a usurer thou hidest up thy corn, as a seller thou puttest it up for auction. Why dost thou wish evil to all, because the famine will grow worse, as though no corn should be left, as though a more unfruitful year should follow? Thy gain is the public loss.

42. Holy Joseph opened the garners to all; he did not shut them up. He did not try to get the full price of the year's produce, but assigned it for a yearly payment. He took nothing for himself, but, so far as famine could be checked for the future, he made his arrangements with careful foresight.

43. Thou hast read how the Lord Jesus in the Gospel speaks of that corn-dealer who was looking out for a high price, whose possessions brought him in rich fruits, but who, as though still in need, said: "What shall I do? I have no room where to bestow my goods. I will pull down my barns and build greater," though he could not know whether in the following night his soul would not be demanded of him. He knew not what to do, he seemed to be in doubt, just as though he were in want of food. His barns could not take in the year's supply, and yet he thought he was in need.

44. Rightly, therefore, Solomon says: "He that withholdeth corn shall leave it for the nations," not for his heirs, for the gains of avarice have nothing to do with the rights of succession. That which is not rightfully got together is scattered as though by a wind by outsiders that seize it. And he added: "He who graspeth at the year's produce is cursed among the people, but blessing shall be his that imparteth it." Thou seest, then, what is said of him who distributes the corn, but not of him that seeks for a high price. True expediency does not therefore exist where virtue loses more than expediency gains.

Chapter VII.

Strangers must never be expelled the city in a time of famine. In this matter the noble advice of a Christian sage is adduced, in contrast to which the shameful deed committed at Rome is given. By comparing the two it is shown that the former is combined with what is virtuous and useful, but the latter with neither.

45. But they, too, who would forbid the city to strangers cannot have our approval. They would expel them at the very time when they ought to help, and separate them from the trade of their common parent. They would refuse them a share in the produce meant for all, and avert the intercourse that has already begun; and they are unwilling, in a time of necessity, to give those with whom they have enjoyed their rights in common, a share in what they themselves have. Beasts do not drive out beasts, yet man shuts out man. Wild beasts and animals consider food which the earth supplies to be common to all. They all give assistance to those like

themselves; and man, who ought to think nothing human foreign to himself, fights against his own.

46. How much better did he act who, having already reached an advanced age, when the city was suffering from famine, and, as is common in such cases, the people demanded that strangers should be forbidden the city, having the office of the prefectship of the city, which is higher than the rest, called together the officials and richer men, and demanded that they should take counsel for the public welfare. He said that it was as cruel a thing for the strangers to be expelled as for one man to be cast off by another, and to be refused food when dying. We do not allow our dogs to come to our table and leave them unfed, yet we shut out a man. How unprofitable, again, it is for the world that so many people perish, whom some deadly plague carries off. How unprofitable for their city that so large a number should perish, who were wont to be helpful either in paying contributions or in carrying on business. Another's hunger is profitable to no man, nor to put off the day of help as long as possible and to do nothing to check the want. Nay more, when so many of the cultivators of the soil are gone, when so many labourers are dying, the corn supplies will fail for the future. Shall we then expel those who are wont to supply us with food, are we unwilling to feed in a time of need those who have fed us all along? How great is the assistance which they supply even at this time. "Not by bread alone does man live." They are even our own family; many of them even are our own kindred. Let us make some return for what we have received.

47. But perhaps we fear that want may increase. First of all, I answer, mercy never fails, but always finds means of help. Next, let us make up for the corn supplies which are to be granted to them, by a subscription. Let us put that right with our gold. And, again, must we not buy other cultivators of the soil if we lose these? How much cheaper is it to feed than to buy a working-man. Where, too, can one obtain, where find a man to take the place of the former? And suppose one finds him, do not forget that, with an ignorant man used to different ways, one may fill up the place in point of numbers, but not as regards the work to be done.

48. Why need I say more? When the money was supplied corn was brought in. So the city's abundance was not diminished, and yet assistance was given to the strangers. What praise this act won that holy man from God! What glory among men! He, indeed, had won an honoured name, who, pointing to the people of a whole province, could truly say to the emperor: All these I have preserved for thee; these live owing to the kindness of the senate; these thy council has snatched from death!

49. How much more expedient was this than that which was done lately at Rome. There from that widely extended city were those expelled who had already passed most of their life in it. In tears they went forth with their children, for whom as being citizens they bewailed the exile, which, as they said, ought to be averted; no less did they grieve over the broken bonds of union, the severed ties of relationship. And yet a fruitful year had smiled upon us. The city alone needed corn to be brought into it. It could have got help, if it had sought corn from the Italians whose children they were driving out. Nothing is more shameful than to expel a man as a foreigner, and yet to claim his services as though he belonged to us. How canst thou expel a man who lives on his own produce? How canst thou expel him who supplies thee with food? Thou retainest thy servant, and thrustest out thy kindred! Thou takest the corn, but showest no good feeling! Thou takest food by force, but dost not show gratitude!

50. How wretched this is, how useless! For how can that be expedient which is not seemly. Of what great supplies from her corporations has Rome at times been deprived, yet she could not dismiss them and yet escape a famine, while waiting for a favourable breeze, and the provisions in the hoped-for ships.

51. How far more virtuous and expedient was that first-mentioned management! For what is so seemly or virtuous as when the needy are assisted by the gifts of the rich, when food is supplied to the hungry, when daily bread fails none? What so advantageous as when the cultivators are kept for the land, and the country people do not perish?

52. What is virtuous, then, is also expedient, and what is expedient is virtuous. On the other hand, what is not expedient is unseemly, and what is unseemly is also not expedient.

Chapter VIII.

That those who put what is virtuous before what is useful are acceptable to God is shown by the example of Joshua, Caleb, and the other spies.

53. When could our fathers ever have thrown off their servitude, unless they had believed that it was not only shameful but even useless to serve the king of Egypt?

54. Joshua, also, and Caleb, when sent to spy out the land, brought back the news that the land was indeed rich, but that it was inhabited by very fierce nations. The people, terrified at the thought of war, refused to take possession of their land. Joshua and Caleb, who had been sent as spies, tried to persuade them that the land was fruitful. They thought it unseemly to give way before the heathen; they chose rather to be stoned, which is what the people threatened, than to recede from their virtuous standpoint. The others kept dissuading, the people exclaimed against it. saying they would have to fight against cruel and terrible nations; that they would fall in battle, and their wives and children would be left for a prey.

55. The anger of the Lord burst forth, so that He would kill all, but at the prayer of Moses He softened His judgment and put off His vengeance, knowing that He had already sufficiently punished those who were faithless, even if He spared them meanwhile and did not slay the unbelievers. However, He said they should not come to that land which they had refused, as a penalty for their unbelief; but their children and wives, who had not murmured, and who, owing to their sex and age, were guiltless, should receive the promised inheritance of that land. So the bodies of those of twenty years old and upwards fell in the desert. The punishment of the rest was put aside. But they who had gone up with Joshua, and had thought fit to dissuade the people, died forthwith of a great plague. Joshua and Caleb entered the land of promise together with those who were innocent by reason of age or sex.

56. The better part, therefore, preferred glory to safety; the worse part safety to virtue. But the divine judgment approved those who thought virtue was above what is useful, whilst it condemned those who preferred what seemed more in accordance with safety than with what is virtuous.

Chapter IX.

Cheating and dishonest ways of making money are utterly unfit for clerics whose duty is to serve all. They ought never to be involved in a money affair, unless it is one affecting a man's life. For them the example of David is given, that they should injure none, even when provoked; also the death of Naboth, to keep them from preferring life to virtue.

57. Nothing is more odious than for a man to have no love for a virtuous life, but instead to be kept excited by an unworthy business in following out a low line of trade, or to be inflamed by an avaricious heart, and by day and by night to be eager to damage another's property, not to raise the soul to the splendour of a virtuous life, and not to regard the beauty of true praise.

58. Hence rise inheritances sought by cunning words and gained under pretence of being self-restrained and serious. But this is absolutely abhorrent to the idea of a Christian man. For everything gained by craft and got together by cheating loses the merit of openness. Even amongst those who have undertaken no duty in the ranks of the clergy it is considered unfitting to seek for the inheritance of another. Let those who are reaching the end of their life use their own judgment, so that they may freely make their wills as they think best, since they will not be able to amend them later. For it is not honourable to divert the savings that belong to others or have been got together for them. It is further the duty of the priest or the cleric to be of use if possible to all and to be harmful to none.

59. If it is not possible to help one without injuring another, it is better to help neither than to press hard upon one. Therefore it is not a priest's duty to interfere in money affairs. For here

it must often happen that he who loses his case receives harm; and then he considers that he has been worsted through the action of the intervener. It is a priest's duty to hurt no one, to be ready to help all. To be able to do this is in God's power alone. In a case of life and death, without doubt it is a grave sin to injure him whom one ought to help when in danger. But it is foolish to gain others' hate in taking up money matters, though for the sake of a man's safety great trouble and toil may often be undertaken. It is glorious in such a case to run risks. Let, then, this be firmly held to in the priestly duties, namely, to injure none, not even when provoked and embittered by some injury. Good was the man who said: "If I have rewarded evil to those who did me good." For what glory is it if we do not injure him who has not injured us? But it is true virtue to forgive when injured.

60. What a virtuous action was that, when David wished rather to spare the king his enemy, though he could have injured him! How useful, too, it was, for it helped him when he succeeded to the throne. For all learnt to observe faith to their king and not to seize the kingdom, but to fear and reverence him. Thus what is virtuous was preferred to what was useful, and then usefulness followed on what was virtuous.

61. But that he spared him was a small matter; he also grieved for him when slain in war, and mourned for him with tears, saying: "Ye mountains of Gilboa, let neither dew nor rain fall upon you; ye mountains of death, for there the shield of the mighty is cast away, the shield of Saul. It is not anointed with oil, but with the blood of the wounded and the fat of the warriors. The bow of Jonathan turned not back and the sword of Saul returned not empty. Saul and Jonathan were lovely and very dear, inseparable in life, and in death they were not divided. They were swifter than eagles, they were stronger than lions. Ye daughters of Israel, weep over Saul, who clothed you in scarlet with your ornaments, who put on gold upon your apparel. How are the mighty fallen in the midst of the battle! Jonathan was wounded even to death. I am distressed for thee, my brother Jonathan; very pleasant hast thou been unto me. Thy love came to me like the love of women. How have the mighty fallen and the longed-for weapons perished!

62. What mother could weep thus for her only son as he wept here for his enemy? Who could follow his benefactor with such praise as that with which he followed the man who plotted against his life? How affectionately he grieved, with what deep feeling he bewailed him! The mountains dried up at the prophet's curse, and a divine power filled the judgment of him who spoke it. Therefore the elements themselves paid the penalty for witnessing the king's death.

63. And what, in the case of holy Naboth, was the cause of his death, except his regard for a virtuous life? For when the king demanded the vineyard from him, promising to give him money, he refused the price for his father's heritage as unseemly, and preferred to shun such shame by dying. "The Lord forbid it me, that I should give the inheritance of my fathers unto thee;" that is, that such reproach may not fall on me, that God may not allow such wickedness to be attained by force. He is not speaking about the vines—nor has God care for vines or plots of ground—but he says it of his fathers' rights. He could have received another or the king's vineyards and been his friend, wherein men think there is no small usefulness so far as this world is concerned. But because it was base he thought it could not be useful, and so he preferred to endure danger with honour intact, rather than gain what was useful to his own disgrace. I am here again speaking of what is commonly understood as useful, not that in which there is the grace of virtuous life.

64. The king could himself have taken it by force, but that he thought too shameless; then when Naboth was dead he grieved. The Lord also declared that the woman's cruelty should be punished by a fitting penalty, because she was unmindful of virtue and preferred a shameful gain.

65. Every kind of unfair action is shameful. Even in common things, false weights and unjust measures are accursed. And if fraud in the market or in business is punished, can it seem free from reproach if found in the midst of the performance of the duties of virtue? Solomon

says: "A great and a little weight and divers measures are an abomination before the Lord. " Before that it also says: "A false balance is abomination to the Lord, but a just weight is acceptable to Him. "

Chapter X.

We are warned not only in civil law, but also in the holy Scriptures, to avoid fraud in every agreement, as is clear from the example of Joshua and the Gibeonites.

66. In everything, therefore, good faith is seemly, justice is pleasing, due measure in equity is delightful. But what shall I say about contracts, and especially about the sale of land, or agreements, or covenants? Are there not rules just for the purpose of shutting out all false deceit, and to make him whose deceit is found out liable to double punishment? Everywhere, then, does regard for what is virtuous take the lead; it shuts out deceit, it expels fraud. Wherefore the prophet David has rightly stated his judgment in general, saying: "He hath done no evil to his neighbour." Fraud, then, ought to be wanting not only in contracts, in which the defects of those things which are for sale are ordered to be recorded (which contracts, unless the vendor has mentioned the defects, are rendered void by an action for fraud, although he has conveyed them fully to the purchaser), but it ought also to be absent in all else. Candour must be shown, the truth must be made known.

67. The divine Scriptures have plainly stated (not indeed a legal rule of the lawyers but) the ancient judgment of the patriarchs on deceit, in that book of the Old Testament which is ascribed to Joshua the son of Nun. When the report had gone forth among the various peoples that the sea was dried up at the crossing of the Hebrews; that water had flowed from the rock; that food was supplied daily from heaven in quantities large enough for so many thousands of the people; that the walls of Jericho had fallen at the sound of the holy trumpets, being overthrown by the noise of the shouts of the people; also, that the king of Ai was conquered and had been hung on a tree until the evening; then the Gibeonites, fearing his strong hand, came with guile, pretending that they were from a land very far away, and by travelling so long had rent their shoes and worn out their clothing, of which they showed proofs that it was growing old. They said, too, that their reason for undergoing so much labour was their desire to obtain peace and to form friendship with the Hebrews, and began to ask Joshua to form an alliance with them. And he, being as yet ignorant of localities, and not knowing anything of the inhabitants, did not see through their deceit, nor did he enquire of God, but readily believed them.

68. So sacred was one's plighted word held in those days that no one would believe that others could try to deceive. Who could find fault with the saints in this, namely, that they should consider others to have the same feelings as themselves, and suppose no one would lie because truth was their own companion? They know not what deceit is, they gladly believe of others what they themselves are, whilst they cannot suspect others to be what they themselves are not. Hence Solomon says: "An innocent man believeth every word." We must not blame his readiness to believe, but should rather praise his goodness. To know nothing of aught that may injure another, this is to be innocent. And although he is cheated by another, still he thinks well of all, for he thinks there is good faith in all.

69. Induced, therefore, by such considerations to believe them, he made an agreement, he gave them peace, and formed a union with them. But when he came to their country and the deceit was found out,—for though they lived quite close they pretended to be strangers,—the people of our fathers began to be angry at having been deceived. Joshua, however, thought the peace they had made could not be broken (for it had been confirmed by an oath), for fear that, in punishing the treachery of others, he should. be breaking his own pledge. He made them pay the penalty, however, by forcing them to undertake the lowest kind of work. The judgment was mild indeed, but it was a lasting one, for in their duties there abides the punishment of their ancient cunning, handed down to this day in their hereditary service.

Chapter XI.

Having adduced examples of certain frauds found in a few passages of the rhetoricians, he shows that these and all others are more fully and plainly condemned in Scripture.

70. I Shall say nothing of the snapping of fingers, or the naked dancing of the heir, at entering on an inheritance. These are well-known things. Nor will I speak of the mass of fishes gathered up at a pretended fishing expedition to excite the buyer's desires. For why did he show himself so eager for luxuries and delicacies as to allow a fraud of this character?

71. What need is there for me to speak of that well-known story of the pleasant and quiet retreat at Syracuse and of the cunning of a Sicilian? For he having found a stranger, and knowing that he was anxious to buy an estate, asked him to his grounds for a meal. He accepted, and on the following day he came. There the sight of a great number of fishermen met his eyes, and a banquet laid out in the most splendid profusion. In the sight of the guests, fishers were placed in the garden-grounds, where no net had ever been laid before. Each one in turn presented to the guests what he had taken, the fish were placed upon the table, and caught the glance of those who sat there. The stranger wondered at the large quantity of fish and the number of boats there were. The answer given was, that this was the great water supply, and that great numbers of fish came there because of the sweetness of the water. To be brief, he drew on the stranger to be urgent in getting the grounds, he willingly allows himself to be induced to sell them, and seemingly with a heavy heart he receives the money.

72. On the next day the purchaser comes to the grounds with his friends, but finds no boat there. On asking whether perhaps the fishermen were observing a festival on that day, he is told that, with the exception of yesterday, they were never wont to fish there; but what power had he to proceed against such a fraud, who had so shamefully grasped at such luxuries? For he who convicts another of a fault ought himself to be free from it. I will not therefore include such trifles as these under the power of ecclesiastical censure, for that altogether condemns every desire for dishonourable gain, and briefly, with few words, forbids every sharp and cunning action.

73. And what shall I say of him who claims to be the heir or legatee, on the proof of a will which, though falsified by others, yet was known to be so by him, and who tries to make again through another's crime, though even the laws of the state convict him who knowingly makes use of a false will, as guilty of a wrong action. But the law of justice is plain, namely, that a good man ought not to go aside from the truth, nor to inflict an unjust loss on any one, nor to act at all deceitfully or to take part in any fraud.

74. What is clearer, however, on this point than the case of Ananias? He acted falsely as regards the price he got for his land, for he sold it and laid at the apostles' feet part of the price, pretending it was the whole amount. For this he perished as guilty of fraud. He might have offered nothing and have acted so without committing a fraud. But as deceit entered into his action, he gained no favour for his liberality, but paid the penalty for his artifice.

75. The Lord also in the Gospel rejected those coming to Him with guile, saying: "The foxes have holes," for He bids us live in simplicity and innocency of heart. David also says: "Thou hast used deceit as a sharp razor," pointing out by this the treacherous man, just as an implement of this kind is used to help adorn a man, yet often wounds him. If any one makes a show of favour and yet plans deceit after the example of the traitor, so as to give up to death him whom he ought to guard, let him be looked on in the light of that instrument which is wont to wound owing to the vice of a drunken mind and a trembling hand. Thus that man drunk with the wine of wickedness brought death on the high priest Ahimelech, through a terrible act of treachery, because he had received the prophet with hospitality when the king, roused by the stings of envy, was following him.

Chapter XII.

We may make no promise that is wrong, and if we have made an unjust oath, we may not keep it. It is shown that Herod sinned in this respect. The vow taken by Jephtha is condemned, and so are all others which God does not desire to have paid to Him. Lastly, the daughter of Jephtha is compared with the two Pythagoreans and is placed before them.

76. A Man's disposition ought to be undefiled and sound, so that he may utter words without dissimulation and possess his vessel in sanctification; that he may not delude his brother with false words nor promise aught dishonourable. If he has made such a promise it is far better for him not to fulfil it, rather than to fulfil what is shameful.

77. Often people bind themselves by a solemn oath, and, though they come to know that they ought not to have made the promise, fulfil it in consideration of their oath. This is what Herod did, as we mentioned before. For he made a shameful promise of reward to a dancer— and cruelly performed it. It was shameful, for a kingdom was promised for a dance; and it was cruel, for the death of a prophet is sacrificed for the sake of an oath. How much better perjury would have been than the keeping of such an oath, if indeed that could be called perjury which a drunkard had sworn to in his wine-cups, or an effeminate profligate had promised whilst the dance was going on. The prophet's head was brought in on a dish, and this was considered an act of good faith when it really was an act of madness!

78. Never shall I be led to believe that the leader Jephtha made his vow otherwise than without thought, when he promised to offer to God whatever should meet him at the threshold of his house on his return. For he repented of his vow, as afterwards his daughter came to meet him. He rent his clothes and said: "Alas, my daughter, thou hast entangled me, thou art become a source of trouble unto me." And though with pious fear and reverence he took upon himself the bitter fulfilment of his cruel task, yet he ordered and left to be observed an annual period of grief and mourning for future times. It was a hard vow, but far more bitter was its fulfilment, whilst he who carried it out had the greatest cause to mourn. Thus it became a rule and a law in Israel from year to year, as it says: "that the daughters of Israel went to lament the daughter of Jephtha the Gileadite four days in a year." I cannot blame the man for holding it necessary to fulfil his vow, but yet it was a wretched necessity which could only be solved by the death of his child.

79. It is better to make no vow than to vow what God does not wish to be paid to Him to Whom the promise was made. In the case of Isaac we have an example, for the Lord appointed a ram to be offered up instead of him. Therefore it is not always every promise that is to be fulfilled. Nay, the Lord Himself often alters His determination, as the Scriptures point out. For in the book called Numbers He had declared that He would punish the people with death and destroy them, but afterwards, when besought by Moses, He was reconciled again to them. And again, He said to Moses and Aaron: "Separate yourselves from among this congregation that I may consume them in a moment." And when they separated from the assembly the earth suddenly clave asunder and opened her mouth and swallowed up Dathan and Abiram.

80. That example of Jephtha's daughter is far more glorious and ancient than that of the two Pythagoreans, which is accounted so notable among the philosophers. One of these, when condemned to death by the tyrant Dionysius, and when the day of his death was fixed, asked for leave to be granted him to go home, so as to provide for his family. But for fear that he might break his faith and not return, he offered a surety for his own death, on condition that if he himself were absent on the appointed day, his surety would be ready to die in his stead. The other did not refuse the conditions of suretyship which were proposed and awaited the day of death with a calm mind. So the one did not withdraw himself and the other returned on the day appointed. This all seemed so wonderful that the tyrant sought their friendship whose destruction he had been anxious for.

81. What, then, in the case of esteemed and learned men is full of marvel, that in the case of a virgin is found to be far more splendid, far more glorious, as she says to her sorrowing father:

"Do to me according to that which hath proceeded out of thy mouth." But she asked for a delay of two months in order that she might go about with her companions upon the mountains to bewail fitly and dutifully her virginity now given up to death. The weeping of her companions did not move her, their grief prevailed not upon her, nor did their lamentations hold her back. She allowed not the day to pass, nor did the hour escape her notice. She returned to her father as though returning according to her own desire, and of her own will urged him on when he was hesitating, and acted thus of her own free choice, so that what was at first an awful chance became a pious sacrifice.

Chapter XIII.
Judith, after enduring many dangers for virtue's sake, gained very many and great benefits.

82. See! Judith presents herself to thee as worthy of admiration. She approaches Holophernes, a man feared by the people, and surrounded by the victorious troops of the Assyrians. At first she makes an impression on him by the grace of her form and the beauty of her countenance. Then she entraps him by the refinement of her speech. Her first triumph was that she returned from the tent of the enemy with her purity unspotted. Her second, that she gained a victory over a man, and put to flight the people by her counsel.

83. The Persians were terrified at her daring. And so what is admired in the case of those two Pythagoreans deserves also in her case our admiration, for she trembled not at the danger of death, nor even at the danger her modesty was in, which is a matter of greater concern to good women. She feared not the blow of one scoundrel, nor even the weapons of a whole army. She, a woman, stood between the lines of the combatants—right amidst victorious arms—heedless of death. As one looks at her overwhelming danger, one would say she went out to die; as one looks at her faith, one says she went but out to fight.

84. Judith then followed the call of virtue, and as she follows that, she wins great benefits. It was virtuous to prevent the people of the Lord from giving themselves up to the heathen; to prevent them from betraying their native rites and mysteries, or from yielding up their consecrated virgins, their venerable widows, and modest matrons to barbarian impurity, or from ending the siege by a surrender. It was virtuous for her to be willing to encounter danger on behalf of all, so as to deliver all from danger.

85. How great must have been the power of her virtue, that she, a woman, should claim to give counsel on the chiefest matters and not leave it in the hands of the leaders of the people! How great, again, the power of her virtue to reckon for certain upon God to help her! How great her grace to find His help!

Chapter XIV.
How virtuous and useful was that which Elisha did. This is compared with that oft-recounted act of the Greeks. John gave up his life for virtue's sake, and Susanna for the same reason exposed herself to the danger of death.

86. What did Elisha follow but virtue, when he brought the army of Syria who had come to take him as captive into Samaria, after having covered their eyes with blindness? Then he said: "O Lord, open their eyes that they may see." And they saw. But when the king of Israel wished to slay those that had entered and asked the prophet to give him leave to do so, he answered that they whose captivity was not brought about by strength of hand or weapons of war must not be slain, but that rather he should help them by supplying food. Then they were refreshed with plenty of food. And after that those Syrian robbers thought they must never again return to the land of Israel.

87. How much nobler was this than that which the Greeks once did! For when two nations strove one with the other to gain glory and supreme power, and one of them had the opportunity to burn the ships of the other secretly, they thought it a shameful thing to do so, and preferred to gain a less advantage honourably than a greater one in shameful wise. They,

indeed, could not act thus without disgrace to themselves, and entrap by this plot those who had banded together for the sake of ending the Persian war. Though they could deny it in word, yet they could never but blush at the thought of it. Elisha, however, wished to save, not destroy, those who were deceived indeed, though not by some foul act, and had been struck blind by the power of the Lord. For it was seemly to spare an enemy, and to grant his life to an adversary when indeed he could have taken it, had he not spared it.88. It is plain, then, that whatever is seemly is always useful. For holy Judith by seemly disregard for her own safety put an end to the dangers of the siege, and by her own virtue won what was useful to all in common. And Elisha gained more renown by pardoning than he would have done by slaying, and preserved those enemies whom he had taken for greater usefulness.

89. And what else did John have in mind but what is virtuous, so that he could not endure a wicked union even in the king's case, saying: "It is not lawful for thee to have her to wife." He could have been silent, had he not thought it unseemly for himself not to speak the truth for fear of death, or to make the prophetic office yield to the king, or to indulge in flattery. He knew well that he would die as he was against the king, but he preferred virtue to safety. Yet what is more expedient than the suffering which brought glory to the saint.

90. Holy Susanna, too, when threatened with the fear of false witness, seeing herself hard pressed on one side by danger, on the other by disgrace, preferred to avoid disgrace by a virtuous death rather than to endure and live a shameful life in the desire to save herself. So while she fixed her mind on virtue, she also preserved her life. But if she had preferred what seemed to her to be useful to preserve life, she would never have gained such great renown, nay, perhaps—and that would have been not only useless but even dangerous—she might even not have escaped the penalty for her crime. We note, therefore, that whatsoever is shameful cannot be useful, nor, again, can that which is virtuous be useless. For usefulness is ever the double of virtue, and virtue of usefulness.

Chapter XV.

After mentioning a noble action of the Romans, the writer shows from the deeds of Moses that he had the greatest regard for what is virtuous.

91. It is related as a memorable deed of a Roman general, that when the physician of a hostile king came to him and promised to give him poison, he sent him back bound to the enemy. In truth, it is a noble thing for a man to refuse to gain the victory by foul acts, after he has entered on the struggle for power. He did not consider virtue to lie in victory, but declared that to be a shameful victory unless it was gained with honour.

92. Let us return to our hero Moses, and to loftier deeds, to show they were both superior as well as earlier. The king of Egypt would not let the people of our fathers go, Then Moses bade the priest Aaron to stretch his rod over all the waters of Egypt. Aaron stretched it out, and the water of the river was turned into blood. None could drink the water, and all the Egyptians were perishing with thirst; but there was pure water flowing in abundance for the fathers. They sprinkled ashes toward heaven, and sores and burning boils came upon man and beast. They brought down hail mingled with flaming fire, and all things were destroyed upon the land. Moses prayed, and all things were restored to their former beauty. The hail ceased, the sores were healed, the rivers gave their wonted draught.

93. Then, again, the land was covered with thick darkness for the space of three days, because Moses had raised his hand and spread out the darkness. All the first-born of Egypt died, whilst all the offspring of the Hebrews was left unharmed. Moses was asked to put an end to these horrors, and he prayed and obtained his request. In the one case it was a fact worthy of praise that he checked himself from joining in deceit; in the other it was noteworthy how, by his innate goodness, he turned aside from the foe those divinely ordered punishments. He was indeed, as it is written, gentle and meek. He knew that the king would not keep true to his

promises, yet he thought it right and good to pray when asked to do so, to bless when wronged, to forgive when besought.

94. He cast down his rod and it became a serpent which devoured the serpents of Egypt; this signifying that the Word should become Flesh to destroy the poison of the dread serpent by the forgiveness and pardon of sins. For the rod stands for the Word that is true—royal—filled with power—and glorious in ruling. The rod became a serpent; so He Who was the Son of God begotten of the Father became the Son of man born of a woman, and lifted, like the serpent, on the cross, poured His healing medicine on the wounds of man. Wherefore the Lord Himself says: "As Moses lifted up the serpent in the wilderness, so must the Son of Man be lifted up."

95. Again, another sign which Moses gave points to our Lord Jesus Christ. He put his hand into his bosom, and drew it out again, and his hand was become as snow. A second time he put it in and drew it out, and it was again like the appearance of human flesh. This signified first the original glory of the Godhead of the Lord Jesus, and then the assumption of our flesh, in which truth all nations and peoples must believe. So he put in his hand, for Christ is the right hand of God; and whosoever does not believe in His Godhead and Incarnation is punished as a sinner; like that king who, whilst not believing open and plain signs, yet afterwards, when punished, prayed that he might find mercy. How great, then, Moses' regard for virtue must have been is shown by these proofs, and especially by the fact that he offered himself on behalf of the people, praying that God would either forgive the people or blot him out of the book of the living.

Chapter XVI.

After saying a few words about Tobit he demonstrates that Raguel surpassed the philosophers in virtue.

96. Tobit also clearly portrayed in his life true virtue, when he left the feast and buried the dead, and invited the needy to the meals at his own poor table. And Raguel is a still brighter example. For he, in his regard for virtue, when asked to give his daughter in marriage, was not silent regarding his daughter's faults, for fear of seeming to get the better of the suitor by silence. So when Tobit the son of Tobias asked that his daughter might be given him, he answered that, according to the law, she ought to be given him as near of kin, but that he had already given her to six men, and all of them were dead. This just man, then, feared more for others than for himself, and wished rather that his daughter should remain unmarried than that others should run risks in consequence of their union with her.

97. How simply he settled all the questions of the philosophers! They talk about the defects of a house, whether they ought to be concealed or made known by the vendor. Raguel was quite certain that his daughter's faults ought not to be kept secret. And, indeed, he had not been eager to give her up—he was asked for her. We can have no doubt how much more nobly he acted than those philosophers, when we consider how much more important a daughter's future is than some mere money affair.

Chapter XVII.

With what virtuous feelings the fathers of old hid the sacred fires when on the point of going into captivity.

98. Let us consider, again, that deed done at the time of the captivity, which has attained the highest degree of virtue and glory. Virtue is checked by no adversities, for it rises up among them, and prevails here rather than in prosperity. 'Mid chains or arms, 'mid flames or slavery (which is harder for freemen to bear than any punishment), 'midst the pains of the dying, the destruction of their country, the fears of the living, or the blood of the slain,—amidst all this our forefathers failed not in their care and thought for what is virtuous. Amidst the ashes and dust of their fallen country it glowed and shone forth brightly in pious efforts.

99. For when our fathers were carried away into Persia, certain priests, who then were in the service of Almighty God, secretly buried in the valley the fire taken from the altar of the Lord. There was there an open pit, with no water in it, and not accessible for the wants of the people,

in a spot unknown and free from intruders. There they sealed the hidden fire with the sacred mark and in secret. They were not anxious to bury gold or to hide up silver to preserve it for their children, but in their own great peril, thinking of all that was virtuous, they thought the sacred fire ought to be preserved so that impure men might not defile it, nor the blood of the slain extinguish it, nor the heaps of miserable ruins cover it.

100. So they went to Persia, free only in their religion; for that alone could not be torn from them by their captivity. After a length of time, indeed, according to God's good pleasure, He put it into the Persian king's heart to order the temple in Judea to be restored, and the regular customs to be again rebuilt at Jerusalem. To carry out this work of his the Persian king appointed the priest Nehemiah. He took with him the grandchildren of those priests who on leaving their native soil had hidden the sacred fire to save it from perishing. But on arriving, as we are told in the history of the fathers, they found not fire but water. And when fire was wanting to burn upon the altars, the priest Nehemiah bade them draw the water, to bring it to him, and to sprinkle it upon the wood. Then, O wondrous sight! though the sky had been overcast with clouds, suddenly the sun shone forth, a great fire flamed forth, so that all, wonder-stricken at such a clear sign of the favour of the Lord, were filled with joy. Nehemiah prayed; the priests sang a hymn of praise to God, when the sacrifice was completed. Nehemiah again bade the remainder of the water to be poured upon the larger stones. And when this was done a flame burst forth whilst the light shining from off the altar shone more brightly yet.

101. When this sign became known, the king of Persia ordered a temple to be built on that spot where the fire had been hidden and the water afterwards found, to which many gifts were made. They who were with holy Nehemiah called it Naphthar, —which means cleansing—by many it is called Nephi. It is to be found also in the history of the prophet Jeremiah, that he bade those who should come after him to take of the fire. That is the fire which fell on Moses' sacrifice and consumed it, as it is written: "There came a fire out from the Lord and consumed upon the altar all the whole burnt-offering." The sacrifice must be hallowed with this fire only. Therefore, also, fire went out from the Lord upon the sons of Aaron who wished to offer strange fire, and consumed them, so that their dead bodies were cast forth without the camp.

101. Jeremiah coming to a spot found there a house like a cave, and brought into it the tabernacle, the ark, and the altar of incense, and closed up the entrance. And when those who had come with him examined it rather closely to mark the spot, they could not discover nor find it. When Jeremiah understood what they wanted he said: "The spot will remain unknown until God shall gather His people together and be gracious to them. Then God shall reveal these things and the majesty of the Lord shall appear."

Chapter XVIII.

In the narration of that event already mentioned, and especially of the sacrifice offered by Nehemiah, is typified the Holy Spirit and Christian baptism. The sacrifice of Moses and Elijah and the history of Noah are also referred to the same.

102. We form the congregation of the Lord. We recognize the propitiation of our Lord God, which our Propitiator wrought in His passion. I think, too, we cannot leave out of sight that fire when we read that the Lord Jesus baptizes with the Holy Spirit and with fire, as John said in his Gospel. Rightly was the sacrifice consumed, for it was for sin. But that fire was a type of the Holy Spirit Who was to come down after the Lord's ascension, and forgive the sins of all, and Who like fire inflames the mind and faithful heart. Wherefore Jeremiah, after receiving the Spirit, says: "It became in my heart as a burning fire flaming in my bones, and I am vile and cannot bear it." In the Acts of the Apostles, also, when the Holy Spirit descended upon the apostles and those others who were waiting for the Promise of the Father, we read that tongues as of fire were distributed among them. The soul of each one was so uplifted by His influence that they were supposed to be full of new wine, who instead had received the gift of a diversity of tongues.

103. What else can this mean—namely, that fire became water and water called forth fire—but that spiritual grace burns out our sins through fire, and through water cleanses them? For sin is washed away and it is burnt away. Wherefore the Apostle says: "The fire shall try every man's work of what sort it is." And further on: "If any man's work shall be burned, he shall suffer loss: but he himself shall be saved; yet so as by fire."

104. This, then, we have stated, so as to prove that sins are burnt out by means of fire. We know now that this is in truth the sacred fire which then, as a type of the future remission of sins, came down upon the sacrifice.

105. This fire is hidden in the time of captivity, during which sin reigns, but in the time of liberty it is brought forth. And though it is changed into the appearance of water, yet it preserves its nature as fire so as to consume the sacrifice. Do not wonder when thou readest that God the Father said: "I am a consuming fire." And again: "They have forsaken Me, the fountain of living water." The Lord Jesus, too, like a fire inflamed the hearts of those who heard Him, and like a fount of waters cooled them. For He Himself said in His Gospel that He came to send fire on the earth and to supply a draught of living waters to those who thirst.

106. In the time of Elijah, also, fire came down when he challenged the prophets of the heathen to light up the altar without fire. When they could not do so, he poured water thrice over his victim, so that the water ran round about the altar; then he cried out and the fire fell from the Lord from heaven and consumed the burnt-offering.

107. Thou art that victim. Contemplate in silence each single point. The breath of the Holy Spirit descends on thee, He seems to burn thee when He consumes thy sins. The sacrifice which was consumed in the time of Moses was a sacrifice for sin, wherefore Moses said, as is written in the book of the Maccabees: "Because the sacrifice for sin was not to be eaten, it was consumed." Does it not seem to be consumed for thee when in the sacrament of baptism the whole outer man perishes? "Our old man is crucified," the Apostle exclaims. Herein, as the example of the fathers teaches us, the Egyptian is swallowed up—the Hebrew arises renewed by the Holy Spirit, as he also crossed the Red Sea dryshod—where our fathers were baptized in the cloud and in the sea.

108. In the flood, too, in Noah's time all flesh died, though just Noah was preserved together with his family. Is not a man consumed when all that is mortal is cut off from life? The outer man is destroyed, but the inner is renewed. Not in baptism alone but also in repentance does this destruction of the flesh tend to the growth of the spirit, as we are taught on the Apostle's authority, when holy Paul says: "I have judged as though I were present him that hath so done this deed, to deliver him unto Satan for the destruction of the flesh, that the spirit may be saved in the day of our Lord Jesus Christ."

109. We seem to have made a somewhat lengthy digression for the sake of regarding this wonderful mystery, in desiring to unfold more fully this sacrament which has been revealed to us, and which, indeed, is as full of virtue as it is full of religious awe.

Chapter XIX.
The crime committed by the inhabitants of Gibeah against the wife of a certain Levite is related, and from the vengeance taken it is inferred how the idea of virtue must have filled the heart of those people of old.

110. What regard for virtue our forefathers had to avenge by a war the wrongs of one woman which had been brought on her by her violation at the hands of profligate men! Nay, when the people were conquered, they vowed that they would not give their daughters in marriage to the tribe of Benjamin! That tribe had remained without hope of posterity, had they not received leave of necessity to use deceit. And this permission does not seem to fail in giving fitting punishment for violation, since they were only allowed to enter on a union by a rape, and not through the sacrament of marriage. And indeed it was right that they who had broken another's intercourse should themselves lose their marriage rites.

111. How full of pitiful traits is this story! A man, it says, a Levite, had taken to himself a wife, who I suppose was called a concubine from the word "concubitus." She some time afterwards, as is wont to happen, offended at certain things, betook herself to her father, and was with him four months. Then her husband arose and went to the house of his father-in-law, to reconcile himself with his wife, to win her back and take her home again. The woman ran to meet him and brought her husband into her father's house.

112. The maiden's father rejoiced and went to meet him, and the man stayed with him three days, and they ate and rested. On the next day the Levite arose at daybreak, but was detained by his father-in-law, that he might not so quickly lose the pleasure of his company. Again on the next and the third day the maiden's father did not suffer his son-in-law to start, until their joy and mutual regard was complete. But on the seventh day, when it was already drawing to a close, after a pleasant meal, having urged the approach of the coming night, so as to make him think he ought to sleep amongst friends rather than strangers, he was unable to keep him, and so let him go together with his daughter.

113. When some little progress was made, though night was threatening to come on, and they were close by the town of the Jebusites, on the slave's request that his lord should turn aside there, he refused, because it was not a city of the children of Israel. He meant to get as far as Gibeah, which was inhabited by the people of the tribe of Benjamin. But when they arrived there was no one to receive them with hospitality, except a stranger of advanced age—When he had looked upon them he asked the Levite: Whither goest thou and whence dost thou come? On his answering that he was travelling and was making for Mount Ephraim and that there was no one to take him in, the old man offered him hospitality and prepared a meal.

114. And when they were satisfied and the tables were removed, vile men rushed up and surrounded the house. Then the old man offered these wicked men his daughter, a virgin, and the concubine with whom she shared her bed, only that violence might not be inflicted on his guest. But when reason did no good and violence prevailed, the Levite parted from his wife, and they knew her and abused her all that night. Overcome by this cruelty or by grief at her wrong, she fell at the door of their host where her husband had entered, and gave up the ghost, with the last effort of her life guarding the feelings of a good wife so as to preserve for her husband at least her mortal remains.

115. When this became known (to be brief) almost all the people of Israel broke out into war. The war remained doubtful with an uncertain issue, but in the third engagement the people of Benjamin were delivered to the people of Israel, and being condemned by the divine judgment paid the penalty for their profligacy. The sentence, further, was that none of the people of the fathers should give his daughter in marriage to them. This was confirmed by a solemn oath. But relenting at having laid so hard a sentence on their brethren, they moderated their severity so as to give them in marriage those maidens that had lost their parents, whose fathers had been slain for their sins, or to give them the means of finding a wife by a raid. Because of the villainy of so foul a deed, they who have violated another's marriage rights were shown to be unworthy to ask for marriage. But for fear that one tribe might perish from the people, they connived at the deceit.

116. What great regard our forefathers had for virtue is shown by the fact that forty thousand men drew the sword against their brethren of the tribe of Benjamin in their desire to avenge the wrong done to modesty, for they would not endure the violation of chastity. And so in that war on both sides there fell sixty-five thousand warriors, whilst their cities were burnt. And when at first the people of Israel were defeated, yet unmoved by fear at the reverses of the war, they disregarded the sorrow the avenging of chastity cost them. They rushed into the battle ready to wash out with their own blood the stains of the crime that had been committed.

Chapter XX.

After the terrible siege of Samaria was ended in accordance with Elisha's prophecy, he relates what regard the four lepers showed for what was virtuous.

117. Why need we wonder that the people of the Lord had regard for what was seemly and virtuous when even the lepers—as we read in the books of the Kings—showed concern for what is virtuous?

118. There was a great famine in Samaria, for the army of the Syrians was besieging it. The king in his anxiety was making the round of the guards on the walls when a woman addressed him, saying: This woman persuaded me to give up my son—and I gave him up, and we boiled him and did eat him. And she promised that she would afterwards bring her son and that we should eat his flesh together, but now she hath hidden her son and will not bring him. The king was troubled because these women seemed to have fed not merely on human bodies, but on the bodies of their own children; and being moved by an example of such awful misery, threatened the prophet Elisha with death. For he believed it was in his power to break up the siege and to avert the famine; or else he was angry because the prophet had not allowed the king to smite the Syrians whom he had struck with blindness.

119. Elisha sat with the elders at Bethel, and before the king's messenger came to him he said to the elders: "See ye how the son of that murderess hath sent to take away mine head?" Then the messenger entered and brought the king's command threatening instant danger to his life. Him the prophet answered: "To-morrow about this time shall a measure of fine flour be sold for a shekel, and two measures of barley for a shekel in the gate of Samaria." Then when the messenger sent by the king would not believe it, saying: "If the Lord would rain abundance of corn from heaven, not even so would that come about," Elisha said to him: "Because thou hast not believed, thou shall see it with thine eyes, but shall not eat of it."

120. And suddenly in the camp of Syria was there heard, as it were, a sound of chariots and a loud noise of horses and the noise of a great host, and the tumult of some vast battle. And the Syrians thought that the king of Israel had called to his help in the battle the king of Egypt and the king of the Amorites, and they fled at dawn leaving their tents, for they feared that they might be crushed by the sudden arrival of fresh foes, and would not be able to withstand the united forces of the kings. This was unknown in Samaria, for they dared not go out of the town, being overcome with fear and also being weak through hunger.

121. But there were four lepers at the gate of the city to whom life was a misery, and to die would be gain. And they said one to another: "Behold we sit here and die. If we enter into the city, we shall die with hunger; if we remain here, there are no means of living at hand for us. Let us go to the Syrian camp, either they will quickly kill us or grant us the means of safety." So they went and entered into the camp, and behold, all was forsaken by the enemy. Entering the tents, first of all on finding food they satisfied their hunger, then they laid hold of as much gold and silver as they could. But whilst they were intent on the booty alone, they arranged to announce to the king that the Syrians had fled, for they thought this more virtuous than to withhold the information and keep for themselves the plunder gained by deceit.

122. At this information the people went forth and plundered the Syrian camp. The supplies of the enemy produced an abundance, and brought about cheapness of corn according to the prophet's word: "A measure of fine flour for a shekel, and two measures of barley for a shekel." In this rejoicing of the people, that officer on whose hand the king leaned died, being crushed and trodden under foot by the people as the crowds kept hurrying to go out or returned with great rejoicing.

Chapter XXI.

Esther in danger of her life followed the grace of virtue; nay, even a heathen king did so, when death was threatened to a man most friendly to him, For friendship must ever be combined with virtue, as the examples of Jonathan and Ahimelech show.

123. Why did Queen Esther expose herself to death and not fear the wrath of a fierce king? Was it not to save her people from death, an act both seemly and virtuous? The king of Persia himself also, though fierce and proud, yet thought it seemly to show honour to the man who had given information about a plot which had been laid against himself, to save a free people from slavery, to snatch them from death, and not to spare him who had pressed on such unseemly plans. So finally he handed over to the gallows the man that stood second to himself, and whom he counted chief among all his friends, because he considered that he had dishonoured him by his false counsels.

124. For that commendable friendship which maintains virtue is to be preferred most certainly to wealth, or honours, or power. It is not wont to be preferred to virtue indeed, but to follow after it. So it was with Jonathan, who for his affection's sake avoided not his father's displeasure nor the danger to his own safety. So, too, it was with Ahimelech, who, to preserve the duties of hospitality, thought he must endure death rather than betray his friend when fleeing.

Chapter XXII.

Virtue must never be given up for the sake of a friend. If, however, one has to bear witness against a friend, it must be done with caution. Between friends what candour is needed in opening the heart, what magnanimity in suffering, what freedom in finding fault! Friendship is the guardian of virtues, which are not to be found but in men of like character. It must be mild in rebuking and averse to seeking its own advantage; whence it happens that true friends are scarce among the rich. What is the dignity of friendship? The treachery of a friend, as it is worse, so it is also more hateful than another's, as is recognized from the example of Judas and of Job's friends.

125. Nothing, then, must be set before virtue; and that it may never be set aside by the desire for friendship, Scripture also gives us a warning on the subject of friendship. There are, indeed various questions raised among philosophers; for instance whether a man ought for the sake of a friend to plot against his country or not, so as to serve his friend? Whether it is right to break one's faith, and so aid and maintain a friend's advantage?

126. And Scripture also says: "A maul, and a sword, and a sharp arrow, so is a man that beareth false witness against his friend." But note what it adds. It blames not witness given against a friend, but false witness. For what if the cause of God or of one's country compels one to give witness? Ought friendship to take a higher place than our religion, or our love for our fellow-citizens? In these matters, however, true witness is required so that a friend may not be assailed by the treachery of a friend, by whose good faith he ought to be acquitted. A man, then, ought never to please a friend who desires evil, or to plot against one who is innocent.

127. Certainly, if it is necessary to give witness, then, when one knows of any fault in a friend, one ought to rebuke him secretly—if he does not listen, one must do it openly. For rebukes are good, and often better than a silent friendship. Even if a friend thinks himself hurt, still rebuke him; and if the bitterness of the correction wounds his mind, still rebuke him and fear not. "The wounds of a friend are better than the kisses of flatterers:" Rebuke, then, thy erring friend; forsake not an innocent one. For friendship ought to be steadfast and to rest firm in true affection. We ought not to change our friends in childish fashion at some idle fancy.

128. Open thy breast to a friend that he may be faithful to thee, and that thou mayest receive from him the delight of thy life. "For a faithful friend is the medicine of life and the grace of immortality." Give way to a friend as to an equal, and be not ashamed to be beforehand with thy friend in doing kindly duties. For friendship knows nothing of pride. So the wise man says: "Do not blush to greet a friend." Do not desert a friend in time of need, nor forsake him nor fail him, for friendship is the support of life. Let us then bear our burdens as the Apostle has taught: for he spoke to those whom the charity of the same one body had embraced together. If friends in prosperity help friends, why do they not also in times of adversity offer their support? Let us aid by giving counsel, let us offer our best endeavours, let us sympathize with them with all our heart.

129. If necessary, let us endure for a friend even hardship. Often enmity has to be borne for the sake of a friend's innocence; oftentimes revilings, if one defends and answers for a friend who is found fault with and accused. Do not be afraid of such displeasure, for the voice of the just says: "Though evil come upon me, I will endure it for a friend's sake." In adversity, too, a friend is proved, for in prosperity all seem to be friends. But as in adversity patience and endurance are needed, so in prosperity strong influence is wanted to check and confute the arrogance of a friend who becomes overbearing.

130. How nobly Job when he was in adversity said: "Pity me, my friends, pity me." That is not a cry as it were of misery, but rather one of blame. For when he was unjustly reproached by his friends, he answered: "Pity me, my friends," that is, ye ought to show pity, but instead ye assail and overwhelm a man with whose sufferings ye ought to show sympathy for friendship's sake.

131. Preserve, then, my sons, that friendship ye have begun with your brethren, for nothing in the world is more beautiful than that. It is indeed a comfort in this life to have one to whom thou canst open thy heart, with whom thou canst share confidences, and to whom thou canst entrust the secrets of thy heart. It is a comfort to have a trusty man by thy side, who will rejoice with thee in prosperity, sympathize in troubles, encourage in persecution. What good friends those Hebrew children were whom the flames of the fiery furnace did not separate from their love of each other! Of them we have already spoken. Holy David says well: "Saul and Jonathan were lovely and pleasant, inseparable in their life, in death they were not divided."

132. This is the fruit of friendship; and so faith may not be put aside for the sake of friendship. He cannot be a friend to a man who has been unfaithful to God. Friendship is the guardian of pity and the teacher of equality, so as to make the superior equal to the inferior, and the inferior to the superior. For there can be no friendship between diverse characters, and so the good-will of either ought to be mutually suited to the other. Let not authority be wanting to the inferior if the matter demands it, nor humility to the superior. Let him listen to the other as though he were of like position—an equal, and let the other warn and reprove like a friend, not from a desire to show off, but with a deep feeling of love.

134. Let not thy warning be harsh, nor thy rebuke bitter, for as friendship ought to avoid flattery, so, too, ought it to be free from arrogance. For what is a friend but a partner in love, to whom thou unitest and attachest thy soul, and with whom thou blendest so as to desire from being two to become one; to whom thou entrustest thyself as to a second self, from whom thou fearest nothing, and from whom thou demandest nothing dishonourable for the sake of thine own advantage. Friendship is not meant as a source of revenue, but is full of seemliness, full of grace. Friendship is a virtue, not a way of making money. It is produced, not by money, but by esteem; not by the offer of rewards, but by a mutual rivalry in doing kindnesses.

134. Lastly, the friendships of the poor are generally better than those of the rich, and often the rich are without friends, whilst the poor have many. For true friendship cannot exist where there is lying flattery. Many try fawningly to please the rich, but no one cares to make pretence to a poor man. Whatsoever is stated to a poor man is true, his friendship is free from envy.

135. What is more precious than friendship which is shared alike by angels and by men? Wherefore the Lord Jesus says: "Make to yourselves friends of the mammon of unrighteousness, that they may receive you into eternal habitations." God Himself makes us friends instead of servants, as He Himself says: "Ye are My friends if ye do whatsoever I command you." He gave us a pattern of friendship to follow. We are to fulfil the wish of a friend, to unfold to him our secrets which we hold in our own hearts, and are not to disregard his confidences. Let us show him our heart and he will open his to us. Therefore He says: "I have called you friends, for I have made known unto you all things whatsoever I have heard of My Father." A friend, then, if he is a true one, hides nothing; he pours forth his soul as the Lord Jesus poured forth the mysteries of His Father.

136. So he who does the will of God is His friend and is honoured with this name. He who is of one mind with Him, he too is His friend. For there is unity of mind in friends, and no one is more hateful than the man that injures friendship. Hence in the traitor the Lord found this the worst point on which to condemn his treachery, namely, that he gave no sign of gratitude and had mingled the poison of malice at the table of friendship. So He says: "It was thou, a man of like mind, My guide and Mine acquaintance, who ever didst take pleasant meals with Me." That is: it could not be endured, for thou didst fall upon Him Who granted grace to thee. "For if My enemy had reproached Me I could have borne it, and I would have hid Myself from him who hated Me." An enemy can be avoided; a friend cannot, if he desires to lay a plot. Let us guard against him to whom we do not entrust our plans; we cannot guard against him to whom we have already entrusted them. And so to show up all the hatefulness of the sin He did not say: Thou, My servant, My apostle; but thou, a man of like mind with Me; that is: thou art not My but thy own betrayer, for thou didst betray a man of like mind with thyself.

137. The Lord Himself, when He was displeased with the three princes who had not deferred to holy Job, wished to pardon them through their friend, so that the prayer of friendship might win remission of sins. Therefore Job asked and God pardoned. Friendship helped them whom arrogance had harmed.

138. These things I have left with you, my children, that you may guard them in your minds—you yourselves will prove whether they will be of any advantage. Meanwhile they offer you a large number of examples, for almost all the examples drawn from our forefathers, and also many a word of theirs, are included within these three books; so that, although the language may not be graceful, yet a succession of old-time examples set down in such small compass may offer much instruction.

Introduction to the Three Books of St. Ambrose on the Holy Spirit

The three books on the Holy Spirit are, as St. Ambrose says himself, a sequel to those on the Faith, and the two treatises together have been sometimes quoted as if one, with the title, *De Trinitate*. But we see from Gratian's letter to St. Ambrose, and from the reply, that each treatise is separate, and the *De Spiritu Sancto* was written some years later, a.d. 381.

In the first book St. Ambrose commences by allegorizing the history of Gideon and the fleece, seeing in the drying of the fleece and the moistening of the threshing-floor a type of the Holy Spirit leaving the Jews and being poured out on the Gentiles. Passing to his more immediate subject, he proves that the Holy Spirit is above the whole Creation and is truly God, alleging as a special argument that the sin against the Holy Spirit can never be forgiven, here or hereafter. He shows how the Holy Spirit is in Scripture called the Spirit of God; that He spake by the prophets and apostles; that He sanctifies men, and is typified by the mystical ointment spoken of in Scripture. Next, St. Ambrose treats of His oneness with the other two Persons of the Holy Trinity, and shows that His mission in no way detracts from this oneness, but that there is in all the Divine Persons a perfect unity of peace, love, and other virtues.

The second book commences with a treatment of the history of Samson in the same way as that of Gideon in Book I. Samson always succeeded so long as the Holy Spirit was with him, but fell into misfortune so soon as he was forsaken. It is shown that the power of the Holy Spirit is the same as that of the Father and the Son, and that there is an agreement in design and working, and in vivifying man. He is Creator and therefore to be worshipped, and He worked with the Father and the Son in founding the Church, and in conclusion is proved the unity of operation in the Three Persons.

The third book continues the same argument, showing that the mission of prophets and apostles, and even of the Son Himself, is to be referred to the Spirit, yet without any subjection on the part of the Son, seeing that the Spirit also receives His mission from the Father and the Son. The Godhead of the Holy Spirit is next taken up and proved, when occasion is taken also to show that there are not three Gods or three Lords, for the Three Divine Persons are one in holiness and nature; and the work is concluded with a summary of some of the principal arguments.

There can be but little doubt that this is the work, and St. Ambrose the author, bitterly attacked by St. Jerome; the whole passage may be read in the *Apology* of Rufinus, p. 470, in vol. iii. of this series. St. Ambrose is compared to a daw decked in another bird's plumage, and charged with writing "bad things in Latin taken from good things in Greek," and St. Jerome even took the trouble to translate a work of St. Didymus on the Holy Spirit (from the preface to which the above extracts are taken), in order that those who did not know Greek might, St. Jerome hoped, recognize the plagiarisms.

Rufinus vigorously defends St. Ambrose, and, pointing out many inconsistencies in his opponent, says: "The saintly Ambrose wrote his book on the Holy Spirit not in words only but with his own blood, for he offered his life-blood to his persecutors, and shed it within himself, though God preserved his life for future labours."

The truth is that St. Ambrose being a good Greek scholar, and having undertaken to write on the Holy Spirit, studied what others had written before him, and made use of what had been urged by SS. Basil, Didymus, and other. The opinion of the great St. Augustine concerning this treatise may be set against that of St. Jerome. "St. Ambrose when treating of the deep subject of the Holy Spirit, and showing that He is equal with the Father and the Son, yet makes use of a simple style of discourse; inasmuch as his subject required no the embellishments of language, but proofs to move the minds of his readers."

THREE BOOKS ON THE HOLY SPIRIT.

To the Emperor Gratian.

BOOK I.

The choice of Gideon was a figure of our Lord's Incarnation, the sacrifice of a kid, of the satisfaction for sins in the body of Christ; that of the bullock, of the abolition of profane rites; and in the three hundred soldiers was a type of the future redemptic through the cross. The seeking of various signs by Gideon was also a mystery, for by the dryness and moistening of the fleece was signified the falling away of the Jews and the calling of the Gentiles, by the water received in a baSin the washing of t apostles' feet. St. Ambrose prays that his own pollution may be washed away, and praises the loving-kindness of Christ. The same water sent forth by the Son of God effects marvellous conversions; it cannot, however, be sent by any other, since it is the pouring forth of the Holy Spirit, Who is subject to no external power.

1. When Jerubbaal, as we read, was beating out wheat under an oak, he received a message from God in order that he might bring the people of God from the power of strangers into liberty. Nor is it a matter of wonder if he was chosen for grace, seeing that even then, being appointed under the shadow of the holy cross and of the adorable Wisdom in the predestined mystery of the future Incarnation, he was bringing forth the visible grains of the fruitful corn from their hiding places, and was [mystically] separating the elect of the saints from the refuse of the empty chaff. For these elect, as though trained with the rod of truth, laying aside the superfluities of the old man together with his deeds, are gathered in the Church as in a winepress. or the Church is the winepress of the eternal fountain, since from her wells forth the juice of the heavenly Vine.

2. And Gideon, moved by that message, when he heard that, though thousands of the people failed, God would deliver His own from their enemies by means of one man, offered a kid, and according to the word of the Angel, laid its flesh and the unleavened cakes upon the rock, and poured the broth upon them. And as soon as the Angel touched them with the end of the staff which he bore, fire burst forth out of the rock, and so the sacrifice which he was offering was consumed. By which it seems clear that that rock was a figure of the Body of Christ, for it is written: "They drank of that rock that followed them, and that rock was Christ." Which certainly refers not to His Godhead, but to His Flesh, which watered the hearts of the thirsting people with the perpetual stream of His Blood.

3. Even at that time was it declared in a mystery that the Lord Jesus in His Flesh would, when crucified, do away the sins of the whole world, and not only the deeds of the body, but the desires of the soul. For the flesh of the kid refers to sins of deed, the broth to the enticements of desire as it is written: "For the people lusted' an evil lust, and said, Who shall give us flesh to eat?" That the Angel then stretched forth his staff, and touched the rock, from which fire went out, shows that the Flesh of the Lord, being filled with the Divine Spirit, would burn away all the sins of human frailty. Wherefore, also, the Lord says: "I am come to send fire upon the earth."

4. Then the man, instructed and fore-knowing what was to be, observes the heavenly mysteries, and therefore, according to the warning, slew the bullock destined by his father to idols, and himself offered to God another bullock seven years old. By doing which he most plainly showed that after the coming of the Lord all Gentile sacrifices should be done away, and that only the sacrifice of the Lord's passion should be offered for the redemption of the people. For that bullock was, in a type, Christ, in Whom, as Esaias said, dwelt the fulness of the seven gifts of the Spirit. This bullock Abraham also offered when he saw the day of the Lord and was glad. He it is Who was offered at one time in the type of a kid, at another in that of a sheep, at another in that of a bullock. Of a kid, because He is a sacrifice for sin; of a sheep, because He is an unresisting victim; of a bullock, because He is a victim without blemish.

5. Holy Gideon then saw the mystery beforehand. Next he chose out three hundred for the battle, so as to show that the world should be freed from the incursion of worse enemies, not by the multitude of their number, but by the mystery of the cross. And yet, though he was brave and faithful, he asked of the Lord yet fuller proofs of future victory, saying: "If Thou wilt save Israel by mine hand, O Lord, as Thou hast said, behold I will put a fleece of wool on the threshing-floor, and if there shall be dew on the fleece and dryness on all the ground, I shall know that Thou wilt deliver the people by my hand according to Thy promise. And it was so." Afterwards he asked in addition that dew should descend on all the earth and dryness be on the fleece.

6. Some one perhaps will enquire whether he does not seem to have been wanting in faith, seeing that after being instructed by many signs he asked still more. But how can he seem to have asked as if doubting or wanting in faith, who was speaking in mysteries? He was not then doubtful, but careful that we should not doubt. For how could he be doubtful whose prayer was effectual? And how could he have begun the battle without fear, unless he had understood the message of God? for the dew on the fleece signified the faith among the Jews, because the words of God come down like the dew.

7. So when the whole world was parched with the drought of Gentile superstition, then came that dew of the heavenly visits on the fleece. But after that the lost sheep of the house of Israel (whom I think that the figure of the Jewish fleece shadowed forth), after that those sheep, I say, "had refused the fountain of living water," the dew of moistening faith dried up in the breasts of the Jews, and that divine Fountain turned away its course to the hearts of the Gentiles. Whence it has come to pass that now the whole world is moistened with the dew of faith, but the Jews have lost their prophets and counsellors.

8. Nor is it strange that they should suffer the drought of unbelief, whom the Lord deprived of the fertilising of the shower of prophecy, saying: "I will command My clouds that they rain not upon that vineyard." For there is a health-giving shower of salutary grace, as David also said: "He came down like rain upon a fleece. and like drops that drop upon the earth." The divine Scriptures promised us this rain upon the whole earth, to water the world with the dew of the Divine Spirit at the coming of the Saviour. The Lord, then, has now come, and the rain has come; the Lord has come bringing the heavenly drops with Him, and so now we drink, who before were thirsty, and with an interior draught drink in that Divine Spirit.

9. Holy Gideon, then, foresaw this, that the nations of the Gentiles also would drink by the reception of faith, and therefore he enquired more diligently, for the caution of the saints is necessary. Insomuch that also Joshua the son of Nun, when he saw the captain of the heavenly host, enquired: "Art thou for us, or for our adversaries?" lest, perchance, he might be deceived by some stratagem of the adversary.

10. Nor was it without a reason that he put the fleece neither in a field nor in a meadow, but in a threshing-floor, where is the harvest of the wheat: "For the harvest is plenteous, but the labourers are few;" because that, through faith in the Lord, there was about to be a harvest fruitful in virtues.

11. Nor, again, was it without a reason that he dried the fleece of the Jews, and put the dew from it into a basin, so that it was filled with water, yet he did not himself wash his feet in that dew. The prerogative of so great a mystery was to be given to another. He was being waited for Who alone could wash away the filth of all. Gideon was not great enough to claim this mystery for himself, but "the Son of Man came not to be ministered unto, but to minister." Let us, then, recognize in Whom these mysteries are seen to be accomplished. Not in holy Gideon, for they were still at their commencement. Therefore the Gentiles were surpassed, for dryness was still upon the Gentiles, and therefore did Israel surpass them, for then did the dew remain on the fleece.

12. Let us come now to the Gospel of God. I find the Lord stripping Himself of His garments, and girding Himself with a towel, pouring water into a basin, and washing the

disciples' feet. That heavenly dew was this water, this was foretold, namely, that the Lord Jesus Christ would wash the feet of His disciples in that heavenly dew. And now let the feet of our minds be stretched out. The Lord Jesus wills also to wash our feet, for He says, not to Peter alone, but to each of the faithful: "If I wash not thy feet thou wilt have no part with Me."

13. Come, then, Lord Jesus, put off Thy garments, which Thou didst put on for my sake; be Thou stripped that Thou mayest clothe us with Thy mercy. Gird Thyself for our sakes with a towel, that Thou mayest gird us with Thy gift of immortality. Pour water into the basin, wash not only our feet but also the head, and not only of the body, but also the footsteps of the soul. I wish to put off all the filth of our frailty, so that I also may say: "By night I have put off my coat, how shall I put it on? I have washed my feet, how shall I defile them?")

14. How great is that excellence! As a servant, Thou dost wash the feet of Thy disciples; as God, Thou sendest dew from heaven. Nor dost Thou wash the feet only, but also invitest us to sit down with Thee, and by the example of Thy dignity dost exhort us, saying: "Ye call Me Master and Lord, and ye do well, for so I am. If, then, I the Lord and Master have washed your feet, ye ought also to wash one another's feet."

15. I, then, wish also myself to wash the feet of my brethren, I wish to fulfil the commandment of my Lord, I will not be ashamed in myself, nor disdain what He Himself did first. Good is the mystery of humility, because while washing the pollutions of others I wash away my own. But all were not able to exhaust this mystery. Abraham was, indeed, willing to wash feet, but because of a feeling of hospitality. Gideon, too, was willing to wash the feet of the Angel of the Lord who appeared to him, but his willingness was confined to one; he was willing as one who would do a service, not as one who would confer fellowship with himself. This is a great mystery which no one knew. Lastly, the Lord said to Peter: "What I do thou knowest not now, but shalt know hereafter." This, I say, is a divine mystery which even they who wash will enquire into. It is not, then, the simple water of the heavenly mystery whereby we attain to be found worthy of having part with Christ.

16. There is also a certain water which we put into the basin of our soul, water from the fleece and from the Book of Judges; water, too, from the Book of Psalms. It is the water of the message from heaven. Let, then, this water, O Lord Jesus, come into my soul, into my flesh, that through the moisture of this rain the valleys of our minds and the fields of our hearts may grow green. May the drops from Thee come upon me, shedding forth grace and immortality. Wash the steps of my mind that I may not sin again. Wash the heel of my soul, that I may be able to efface the curse, that I feel not the serpent's bite on the foot of my soul, but, as Thou Thyself hast bidden those who follow Thee, may tread on serpents and scorpions with uninjured foot. Thou hast redeemed the world, redeem the soul of a single sinner.

17. This is the special excellence of Thy loving-kindness, wherewith Thou hast redeemed the whole world one by one. Elijah was sent to one widow; Elisha cleansed one; Thou, O Lord Jesus, hast at this day cleansed a thousand. How many in the city of Rome, how many at Alexandria, how many at Antioch, how many also at Constantinople! For even Constantinople has received the word of God, and has received evident proofs of Thy judgment. For so long as she cherished the Arians' poison in her bosom, disquieted by neighbouring wars, she echoed with hostile arms around. But so soon as she rejected those who were alien from the faith she received as a suppliant the enemy himself, the judge of kings, whom she had always been wont to fear, she buried him when dead, and retains him entombed. How many, then, hast Thou cleansed at Constantinople, how many, lastly, at this day in the whole world!

18. Damasus cleansed not, Peter cleansed not, Ambrose cleansed not, Gregory cleansed not; for ours is the ministry, but the sacraments are Thine. For it is not in man's power to confer what is divine, but it is, O Lord, Thy gift and that of the Father, as Thou hast spoken by the prophets, saying: "I will pour out of My Spirit upon all flesh, and their sons and their daughters shall prophesy." This is that typical dew from heaven, this is that gracious rain, as we read: "Agracious rain, dividing for His inheritance." For the Holy Spirit is not subject to any foreign

power or law, but is the Arbiter of this own freedom, dividing all things according to the decision of His own will, to each, as we read, severally as He wills.

Chapter I.

St. Ambrose commences his argument by complimenting the Emperor, both for his faith and for the restitution of the Basilica to the Church; then having urged that his opponents, if they affirm that the Holy Spirit is not a servant, cannot deny Him to be above all, adds that the same Spirit, when He said, "All things serve Thee," showed plainly that He was distinct from creatures; which point he also establishes by other evidence.

19. The Holy Spirit, then, is not amongst but above all things. For (since you, most merciful Emperor, are so fully instructed concerning the Son of God as to be able yourself to teach others) I will not detain you longer, as you desire and claim to be told something more exactly [concerning Him], especially since you lately showed yourself to be so pleased by an argument of this nature, as to command the Basilica to be restored to the Church without any one urging you.

20. So, then, we have received the grace of your faith and the reward of our own; for we cannot say otherwise than that it was of the grace of the Holy Spirit, that when all were unconscious of it, you suddenly restored the Basilica. This is the gift, I say, this the work of the Holy Spirit, Who indeed was at that time preached by us, but was working in you.

21 And I do not regret the losses of the previous time, since the sequestration of that Basilica resulted in the gain of a sort of usury. For you sequestrated the Basilica, that you might give proof of your faith. And so your piety fulfilled its intention, which had sequestered that it might give proof, and so gave proof as to restore. I did not lose the fruit, and I have your judgment, and it has been made clear to all that, with a certain diversity of action, there was in you no diversity of opinion. It was made clear, I say, to all, that it was not of yourself that you sequestrated, that it was of yourself when you restored it.

22. Now let us establish by evidence what we have said. The first point in the discussion is that all things serve. Now it is clear that all things serve, since it is written: "All things serve Thee." This the Spirit said through the prophet. He did not say, We serve, but, "serve Thee," that you might believe that He Himself is excepted from serving. So, then, since all things serve, and the Spirit does not serve, the Holy Spirit is certainly not included amongst all things.

23. For if we say that the Holy Spirit is included amongst all things, certainly when we read that the Spirit searches the deep things of God, we deny that God the Father is over all. For since the Spirit is of God, and is the Spirit of His mouth, how can we say that the Holy Spirit is included amongst all things, seeing that God, Whose is the Spirit, is over all, possessing certainly fulness of perfection and perfect power.

25. But lest the objectors should think that the Apostle was in error, let them learn whom he followed as his authority for his belief. The Lord said in the Gospel: "When the Paraclete is come, Whom I will send to you from My Father, even the Spirit of Truth which proceedeth from the Father, He shall bear witness of Me." So the Holy Spirit both proceeds from the Father, and bears witness of the Son. For the witness Who is both faithful and true bears witness of the Father, than which witness nothing is more full for the expression of the Divine Majesty, nothing more clear as to the Unity of the Divine Power, since the Spirit has the same knowledge as the Son, Who is the witness and inseparable sharer of the Father's secrets.

26. He excludes, then, the fellowship and number of creatures from the knowledge of God, but by not excluding the Holy Spirit, He shows that He is not of the fellowship of creatures. So that the passage which is read in the Gospel: "For no man hath seen God at any time, save the Only-begotten Son Who is in the bosom of the Father He hath declared Him," also pertains to the exclusion of the Holy Spirit. For how has He not seen God Who searches even the deep things of God? How has He not seen God Who knows the things which are of God? How has He not seen God Who is of God? So, since it is laid down that no one has seen God at any

time, whereas the Holy Spirit has seen Him, clearly the Holy Spirit is excepted. He, then, is above all Who is excluded from all.

Chapter II.

The words, "All things were made by Him," are not a proof that the Holy Spirit is included amongst all things, since He was not made. For otherwise it could be proved by other passages that the Son, and even the Father Himself, must be numbered amongst all things, which would be similar irreverence.

27. This seems, gracious Emperor, to be a full account of our right feeling, but to the impious it does not seem so. Observe what they are striving after. For the heretics are wont to say that the Holy Spirit is to be reckoned amongst all things, because it is written of God the Son: "All things were made by Him."

28. How utterly confused is a course of argument which does not hold to the truth, and is involved in an inverted order of statements. For this argument would be of value for the statement that the Holy Spirit is amongst all things, if they proved that He was made. For Scripture says that all things which were made were made by the Son; but since we are not taught that the Holy Spirit was made, He certainly cannot be proved to be amongst all things Who was neither made as all things are, nor created. To me this testimony is of use for establishing each point; firstly, that He is proved to be above all things, because He was not made; and secondly, that because He is above all things, He is seen not to have been made, and is not to be numbered amongst those things which were made.

29. But if any one, because the Evangelist stated that all things were made by the Word, making no exception of the Holy Spirit (although the Spirit of God speaking in John said: "All things were made by Him," and said not we were all things which were made; whilst the Lord Himself distinctly showed that the Spirit of God spoke in the Evangelists, saying, "For it will not be you that speak, but the Spirit of your Father that speaketh in you"), yet if any one, as I said, does not except the Holy Spirit in this place, but numbers Him amongst all, he consequently does not except the Son of God in that passage where the Apostle says: "Yet to us there is one God the Father, of Whom are all things, and we by Him." But that he may know that the Son is not amongst all things, let him read what follows, for when he says: "And one Lord Jesus Christ, by Whom are all things," he certainly excepts the Son of God from all, who also excepted the Father.

30. But it is equal irreverence to detract from the dignity of the Father, or the Son, or the Holy Spirit. For he believes not in the Father who does not believe in the Son, nor does he believe in the Son of God who does not believe in the Spirit, nor can faith stand without the rule of truth. For he who has begun to deny the oneness of power in the Father and the Son and the Holy Spirit certainly cannot prove his divided faith in points where there is no division. So, then, since complete piety is to believe rightly, so complete impiety is to believe wrongly.

31. Therefore they who think that the Holy Spirit ought to be numbered amongst all things, because they read that all things were made by the Son, must needs also think that the Son is to be numbered amongst all things, because they read: "All things are of God." But, consequently, they also do not separate the Father from all things, who do not separate the Son from all creatures, since, as all things are of the Father, so, too, all things are by the Son. And the Apostle, because of his foresight in the Spirit, used this very expression, lest he should seem to the impious who had heard that the Son had said, "That which My Father hath given Me is greater than all," to have included the Son amongst all.

Chapter III.

The statement of the Apostle, that all things are of the Father by the Son, does not separate the Spirit from Their company, since what is referred to one Person is also attributed to each. So those baptized in the Name of Christ are held to be baptized in the Name of the Father and of the Holy Spirit, if, that is, there is belief in the

Three Persons, otherwise the baptism will be null. This also applies to baptism in the Name of the Holy Spirit. If because of one passage the Holy Spirit is separated from the Father and the Son, it will necessarily follow from other passages that the Father will be subordinated to the Son. The Son is worshipped by angels, not by the Spirit, for the latter is His witness, not His servant. Where the Son is spoken of as being before all, it is to be understood of creatures. The great dignity of the Holy Spirit is proved by the absence of forgiveness for the sin against Him. How it is that such sin cannot be forgiven, and how the Spirit is one.

32. But perhaps some one may say that there was a reason why the writer said that all things were of the Father, and all things through the Son, but made no mention of the Holy Spirit, and would obtain the foundation of an argument from this. But if he persists in his perverse interpretation, in how many passages will he find the power of the Holy Spirit asserted, in which Scripture has stated nothing concerning either the Father or the Son, but has left it to be understood?

40. Where, then, the grace of the Spirit is asserted, is that of God the Father or of the Only-begotten Son denied? By no means; for as the Father is in the Son, and the Son in the Father, so, too, "the love of God is shed abroad in our hearts by the Holy Spirit, Who hath been given us." And as he who is blessed in Christ is blessed in the Name of the Father, and of the Son, and of the Holy Spirit, because the Name is one and the Power one; so, too, when any divine operation, whether of the Father, or of the Son, or of the Holy Spirit, is treated of, it is not referred only to the Holy Spirit, but also to the Father and the Son, and not only to the Father, but also to the Son and the Spirit.

41. Then, too, the Ethiopian eunuch of Queen Candace, when baptized in Christ, obtained the fulness of the sacrament. And they who said that they knew not of any Holy Spirit, although they said that they had been baptized with John's baptism, were baptized afterwards, because John baptized for the remission of sins in the Name of the coming Jesus, not in his own. And so they knew not the Spirit, because in the form in which John baptized they had not received baptism in the Name of Christ. For John, though he did not baptize in the Spirit, nevertheless preached Christ and the Spirit. And then, when he was questioned whether he were perchance himself the Christ, he answered: "I baptize you with water, but a stronger than I shall come, Whose shoes I am not worthy to bear, He shall baptize you with the Holy Spirit and with fire." They therefore, because they had been baptized neither in the Name of Christ nor with faith in the Holy Spirit, could not receive the sacrament of baptism.

42. So they were baptized in the Name of Jesus Christ, and baptism was not repeated in their case, but administered differently, for there is but one baptism. But where there is not the complete sacrament of baptism, there is not considered to be a commencement nor any kind of baptism. But baptism is complete if one confess the Father, the Son, and the Holy Spirit. If you deny One you overthrow the whole. And just as if you mention in words One only, either the Father, or the Son, or the Holy Spirit, and in your belief do not deny either the Father, the Son, or the Holy Spirit, the mystery of the faith is complete, so, too, although you name the Father, Son, and Holy Spirit, and lessen the power of either the Father, the Son, or the Holy Spirit, the whole mystery is made empty. And, lastly, they who had said: "We have not heard if there be any Holy Spirit, were baptized afterwards in the Name of the Lord Jesus Christ." And this was an additional abundance of grace, for now through Paul's preaching they knew the Holy Spirit.

43. Nor ought it to seem opposed to this, that although subsequently mention is not made of the Spirit, He is yet believed in, and what had not been mentioned in words is expressed in belief. For when it is said, "In the Name of our Lord Jesus Christ," the mystery is complete through the oneness of the Name, and the Spirit is not separated from the baptism of Christ, since John baptized unto repentance, Christ in the Spirit.

44. Let us now consider whether as we read that the sacrament of baptism in the Name of Christ was complete, so, too, when the Holy Spirit alone is named, anything is wanting to the completeness of the mystery. Let us follow out the argument that he who has named One has signified the Trinity. If you name Christ, you imply both God the Father by Whom the Son was

anointed, and the Son Himself Who was anointed, and the Holy Spirit with Whom He was anointed. For it is written: "This Jesus of Nazareth, Whom God anointed with the Holy Spirit." And if you name the Father, you denote equally His Son and the Spirit of His mouth, if, that is, you apprehend it in your heart. And if you speak of the Spirit, you name also God the Father, from Whom the Spirit proceeds, and the Son, inasmuch as He is also the Spirit of the Son.

45. Wherefore that authority may also be joined to reason Scripture indicates that we can also be rightly baptized in the Spirit, when the Lord says: "But ye shall be baptized in the Holy Spirit." And in another place the Apostle says: "For we were all baptized in the body itself into one Spirit." The work is one, for the mystery is one; the baptism one, for there was one death on behalf of the world; there is, then, a oneness of working, a oneness of setting forth, which cannot be separated.

46. But if in this place the Spirit be separated from the operation of the Father and the Son, because it is said, All things are of God, and all things are through the Son, then, too, when the Apostle says of Christ, "Who is over all, God blessed for ever," He set Christ not only above all creatures, but (which it is impious to say) above the Father also. But God forbid, for the Father is not amongst all things, is not amongst a kind of crowd of His own creatures. The whole creation is below, over all is the Godhead of the Father, the Son, and the Holy Spirit. The former serves, the latter rules; the former is subject, the latter reigns; the former is the work. the latter the author of the work; the former, without exception, worships, the latter is worshipped by all without exception.

47. Lastly, of the Son it is written: "And let all the angels of God worship Him." You do not find, Let the Holy Spirit worship. And farther on: "To which of the angels said He at any time, Sit thou on My right hand till I make thine enemies the footstool of thy feet? Are they not all," says he, "ministering spirits who are sent to minister?" When he says All, does he include the Holy Spirit? Certainly not, because Angels and the other Powers are destined to serve in ministering and obedience to the Son of God.

48. But in truth the Holy Spirit is not a minister but a witness of the Son, as the Son Himself said of Him: "He shall bear witness of Me." The Spirit, then, is a witness of the Son. He who is a witness knows all things, as God the Father is a witness. For so you read in later passages, for our salvation was confirmed to us by God bearing witness by signs and wonders and by manifold powers and by distributions of the Holy Spirit. He who divides as he will is certainly above all, not amongst all, for to divide is the gift of the worker, not an innate part of the work itself.

49. If the Son is above all, through Whom our salvation received its commencement, so that it might be preached, certainly God the Father also, Who testifies and gives confirmation concerning our salvation by signs and wonders, is excepted from all. In like manner the Spirit, Who bears witness to our salvation by His diversities of gifts, is not to be numbered with the crowd of creatures, but to be reckoned with the Father and the Son; Who, when He divides, is not Himself divided by cutting off Himself, for being indivisible He loses nothing when He gives to all, as also the Son, when the Father receives the kingdom, loses nothing, nor does the Father, when He gives that which is His to the Son, suffer loss. We know, then, by the testimony of the Son that there is no loss in the division of spiritual grace; for He Who breathes where He wills is everywhere free from loss. Concerning which power we shall speak more fully farther on.

50. In the meanwhile, since our intention is to prove in due order that the Spirit is not to be reckoned amongst all things, let us take the Apostle, whose words they call inquestion, as an authority for this position. For what "all things" would be, whether visible or invisible, he himself declared when he said: "For in Him were all things created in the heavens and in earth." You see that "all things" is spoken of things in the heavens, and of things in earth, for in the heavens are also invisible things which were made.

51. But that no one should be ignorant of this he added those of whom he was speaking: "Whether thrones or dominions or principalities or powers, all things were created by Him and in Him, and He is before all, and in Him all things consist." Does he, then, include the Holy Spirit here amongst creatures? Or when he says that the Son of God is before all things, is he to be supposed to have said that He is before the Father? Certainly not; for as here he says that all things were created by the Son, and that all things in the heavens consist in Him, so, too, it cannot be doubted that all things in the heavens have their strength in the Holy Spirit, since we read: "By the word of the Lord were the heavens established and all the strength of them by the Spirit of His mouth." He, then, is above all, from Whom is all the strength of things in heaven and things on earth. He, then, Who is above all things certainly does not serve; He Who serves not is free; He Who is free has the prerogative of lordship.

52. If I were to say this at first it would be denied. But in the same manner as they deny the less that the greater may not be believed, so let us set forth lesser matters first that either they may show their perfidy in lesser matters, or, if they grant the lesser matters, we may infer greater from the lesser.

53. I think, most merciful Emperor, that they are most fully confuted who dare to reckon the Holy Spirit amongst all things. But that they may know that they are pressed not only by the testimony of the apostles, but also by that of our Lord; how can they dare to reckon the Holy Spirit amongst all things, since the Lord Himself said: "He who shall blaspheme against the Son of Man, it shall be forgiven him; but he who shall blaspheme against the Holy Ghost shall never be forgiven, either here or hereafter." How, then, can any one dare to reckon the Holy Spirit amongst creatures? Or who will so blind himself as to think that if he have injured any creature he cannot be forgiven in any wise? For if the Jews because they worshipped the host of heaven were deprived of divine protection, whilst he who worships and confesses the Holy Spirit is accepted of God, but he who confesses Him not is convicted of sacrilege without forgiveness: certainly it follows from this that the Holy Spirit cannot be reckoned amongst all things, but that He is above all things, an offence against Whom is avenged by eternal punishment.

54. But observe carefully why the Lord said: "He who shall blaspheme against the Son of Man it shall be forgiven him, but he who shall blaspheme against the Holy Ghost shall never be forgiven, either here or hereafter." Is an offence against the Son different from one against the Holy Spirit? For as their dignity is one, and common to both, so too is the offence. But if any one, led astray by the visible human body, should think somewhat more remissly than is fitting concerning the Body of Christ (for it ought not to appear of little worth to us, seeing it is the palace of chastity, and the fruit of the Virgin), he incurs guilt, but he is not shut out from pardon, which he may attain to by faith. But if any one should deny the dignity, majesty, and eternal power of the Holy Spirit, and should think that devils are cast out not in the Spirit of God, but in Beelzebub, there can be no attaining of pardon there where is the fulness of sacrilege; for he who has denied the Spirit has denied also the Father and the Son, since the same is the Spirit of God Who is the Spirit of Christ.

Chapter IV.

The Holy Spirit is one and the same Who spake in the prophets and apostles, Who is the Spirit of God and of Christ; Whom, further, Scripture designates the Paraclete, and the Spirit of life and truth.

55. But no one will doubt that the Spirit is one, although very many have doubted whether God be one. For many heretics have said that the God of the Old Testament is one, and the God of the New Testament is another. But as the Father is one Who both spake of old, as we read, to the fathers by the prophets, and to us in the last days by His Son; "and as the Son is one, Who according to the tenour of the Old Testament was offended by Adam, seen by Abraham, worshipped by Jacob; so, too, the Holy Spirit is one, who energized in the prophets, was breathed upon the apostles, and was joined to the Father and the Son in the sacrament of

baptism. For David says of Him: "And take not Thy Holy Spirit from me." And in another place he said of Him: "Whither shall I go from Thy Spirit?"

56. That you may know that the Spirit of God is the same as the Holy Spirit, as we read also in the Apostle: "No one speaking in the Spirit of God says Anathema to Jesus and no one can say, Lord Jesus, but in the Holy Spirit," the Apostle calls Him the Spirit of God. He called Him also the Spirit of Christ, as you read: "But ye are not in the flesh but in the Spirit, if so be that the Spirit of God dwelleth in you." And farther on: "But if the Spirit of Him Who raised Jesus from the dead dwelleth in you." The same is, then, the Spirit of God, Who is the Spirit of Christ.

57. The same is also the Spirit of Life, as the Apostle says: "For the law of the Spirit of Life in Christ Jesus hath delivered me from the law of sin and death."

58. Him, then, Whom the Apostle called the Spirit of Life, the Lord in the Gospel named the Paraclete, and the Spirit of Truth, as you find: "And I will ask the Father, and He will give you another Comforter [Paraclete], that He may be with you for ever, even the Spirit of Truth, Whom this world cannot receive; because it seeth Him not, neither knoweth Him." You have, then, the Paraclete Spirit, called also the Spirit of Truth, and the invisible Spirit. How, then, do some think that the Son is visible in His Divine Nature, when the world cannot see even the Spirit?

59. Receive now the saying of the Lord, that the same is the Holy Spirit Who is the Spirit of Truth, for you read in the end of this book: "Receive the Holy Spirit." And Peter teaches that the same is the Holy Spirit Who is the Spirit of the Lord, when he says: "Ananias, why has it seemed good to thee to tempt and to lie to the Holy Spirit?" And immediately after he says again to the wife of Ananias: "Why has it seemed good to you to tempt the Spirit of the Lord?" When he says "to you," he shows that he is speaking of the same Spirit of Whom he had spoken to Ananias. He Himself is, then, the Spirit of the Lord Who is the Holy Spirit.

60. And the Lord Himself made clear that the same Who is the Spirit of the Father is the Holy Spirit, when according to Matthew He said that we ought not to take thought in persecution what we should say: "For it is not ye that speak, but the Spirit of your Father that speaketh in you." Again He says according to St. Luke: "Be not anxious how ye shall answer or speak, for the Holy Spirit of God shall teach you in that hour what ye ought to say." So, although many are called spirits, as it is said: "Who maketh His Angels spirits," yet the Spirit of God is but one.

61. Both apostles and prophets received that one Spirit, as the vessel of election, the Doctor of the Gentiles, says: "For we have all drunk of one Spirit;" Him, as it were, Who cannot be divided, but is poured into souls, and flows into the senses, that He may quench the burning of this world's thirst.

Chapter V.

The Holy Spirit, since He sanctifies creatures, is neither a creature nor subject to change. He is always good, since He is given by the Father and the Son; neither is He to be numbered amongst such things as are said to fail. He must be acknowledged as the source of goodness. The Spirit of God's mouth, the amender of evils, and Himself good. Lastly, as He is said in Scripture to be good, and is joined to the Father and the Son in baptism, He cannot possibly be denied to be good. He is not, however, said to progress, but to be made perfect in goodness, which distinguishes Him from all creatures.

62. The Holy Spirit is not, then, of the substance of things corporeal, for He sheds incorporeal grace on corporeal things; nor, again, is He of the substance of invisible creatures, for they receive His sanctification, and through Him are superior to the other works of the universe. Whether you speak of Angels, or Dominions, or Powers, every creature waits for the grace of the Holy Spirit. For as we are children through the Spirit, because "God sent the Spirit of His Son into our hearts crying, Abba, Father; so that thou art now not a servant but a son;" in like manner, also, every creature is waiting for the revelation of the sons of God, whom in

truth the grace of the Holy Spirit made sons of God. Therefore, also, every creature itself shall be changed by the revelation of the grace of the Spirit, "and shall be delivered from the bondage of corruption into the liberty of the glory of the children of God."

63. Every creature, then, is subject to change, not only such as has been changed by some sin or condition of the outward elements, but also such as can be liable to corruption by a hull of nature, though by careful discipline it be not yet so; for, as we have shown in a former treatise, the nature of Angels evidently can be changed. It is certainly fitting to judge that such as is the nature of one, such also is that of others. The nature of the rest, then, is capable of change, but the discipline is better.

64. Every creature, therefore, is capable of change, but the Holy Spirit is good and not capable of change, nor can He be changed by any fault, Who does away the faults of all and pardons their sins. How, then, is He capable of change, Who by sanctifying works in others a change to grace, but is not changed Himself.

65. How is He capable of change Who is always good? For the Holy Spirit, through Whom the things that are good are ministered to us, is never evil. Whence two evangelists in one and the same place, in words in differing from each other, have made the same statement, for you read in Matthew: "If you, being evil, know how to give good gifts to your children; how much more shall your Father, Who is in heaven, give good things to them that ask Him." But according to Luke you will find it thus written: "How much more shall your heavenly Father give the Holy Spirit to them that ask Him?" We observe, then, that the Holy Spirit is good in the Lord's judgment by the testimony of the evangelists, since the one has put good things in the place of the Holy Spirit, the other has named the Holy Spirit in the place of good things. If, then, the Holy Spirit is that which is good, how is He not good?

66. Nor does it escape our notice that some copies have likewise, according to St. Luke: "How much more shall your heavenly Father give a good gift to them that ask Him." This good gift is the grace of the Spirit, which the Lord Jesus shed forth from heaven, after having been fixed to the gibbet of the cross, returning with the triumphal spoils of death deprived of its power, as you find it written: "Ascending up on high He led captivity captive, and gave good gifts to men." And well does he say "gifts," for as the Son was given, of Whom it is written: "Unto us a Child is born, unto us a Son is given;" so, too, is the grace of the Spirit given. But why should I hesitate to say that the Holy Spirit also is given to us, since. it is written: "The love of God is shed forth in our hearts by the Holy Spirit, Who is given to us." And since captive breasts certainly could not receive Him, the Lord Jesus first led captivity captive, that our affections being set free, He might pour forth the gift of divine grace.

67. And He said well "led captivity captive." For the victory of Christ is the victory of liberty, which won grace for all, and inflicted wrong on none. So in the setting free of all no one is captive. And because in the time of the Lord's passion wrong alone had no part, which had made captive all of whom it had gained possession, captivity itself turning back upon itself was made captive, not now attached to Belial but to Christ, to serve Whom is liberty. "For he who is called in the Lord as a servant is the Lord's freedman."

68. But to return to the point. "All," says He, "have gone aside, all together are become unprofitable. There is none that doeth good, not even one." If they except the Holy Spirit, even they themselves confess that He is not amongst all; if they do not except Him, then they, too, acknowledge that He has gone aside amongst all.

69. But let us consider whether He has goodness in Himself, since He is the Source and Principle of goodness. For as the Father and the Son have, so too the Holy Spirit also has goodness. And the Apostle also taught this when he said: "Now the fruit of the Spirit is peace, love, joy, patience, goodness." For who doubts that He is good Whose fruit is goodness. For "a good tree brings forth good fruit."

70. And so if God be good, how shall He Who is the Spirit of His mouth not be good, Who searcheth even the deep things of God? Can the infection of evil enter into the deep things of

God? And from this it is seen how foolish they are who deny that the Son of God is good, when they cannot deny that the Spirit of Christ is good, of Whom the Son of God says: "Therefore said I that He shall receive of Mine."

71. Or is the Spirit not good, Who of the worst makes good men, does away sin, destroys evil, shuts out crime, pours in good gifts, makes apostles of persecutors, and priests of sinners? "Ye were," it is said, "sometime darkness, but now are ye light in the Lord."

72. But why do we put them off? And if they ask for statements since they do not deny facts, let them hear that the Holy Spirit is good, for David said: "Let Thy good Spirit. lead me forth in the right way." For what is the Spirit but full of goodness? Who though because of His nature He cannot be attained to, yet because of His goodness can be received by us, filling all things His power, but only partaken of by the just, simple in substance, rich in virtues, present to each, dividing of His own to every one, and Himself whole everywhere.

73. And with good cause did the Son of God say: "Go and baptize all nations in the Name of the Father, and of the Son, and of the Holy Spirit," not disdaining association with the Holy Spirit. Why, then, do some take it ill that He Whom the Lord disdained not in the sacrament of baptism, should be joined in our devotion with the Father and the Son?

74. Good, then, is the Spirit, but good, not as though acquiring but as imparting goodness. For the Holy Spirit does not receive from creatures but is received; as also He is not sanctified but sanctifies; for the creature is sanctified, but the Holy Spirit sanctifies. In which matter, though the word is used in common, there is a difference in the nature. For both the man who receives and God Who gives sanctity are called holy, as we read: "Be ye holy, for I am holy." Now sanctification and corruption cannot share the same nature, and therefore the grace of the Holy Spirit and the creature cannot be of one substance.

75. Since, then, the whole invisible creation (whose substance some rightly believe to be reasonable and incorporeal), with the exception of the Trinity, does not impart but acquires the grace of the Spirit, and does not share in it but receives it, the whole commonalty of creation is to be separated from association with the Holy Spirit. Let them then believe that the Holy Spirit is not a creature; or, if they think Him a creature, why do they associate Him with the Father? If they think Him a creature, why do they join Him with the Son of God? But if they do not think that He should be separated from the Father and the Son, they do not consider Him to be a creature, for where the sanctification is one the nature is one.

Chapter VI.

Although we are baptized with water and the Spirit, the latter is much superior to the former, and is not therefore to be separated from the Father and the Son.

76. There are, however, many who, because we are baptized with water and the Spirit, think that there is no difference in the offices of water and the Spirit, and therefore think that they do not differ in nature. Nor do they observe that we are buried in the element of water that we may rise again renewed by the Spirit. For in the water is the representation of death, in the Spirit is the pledge of life, that the body of sin may die through the water, which encloses the body as it were in a kind of tomb, that we, by the power of the Spirit, may be renewed from the death of sin, being born again in God.

77. And so these three witnesses are one, as John said: "The water, the blood, and the Spirit." One in the mystery, not in nature. The water, then, is a witness of burial, the blood is a witness of death, the Spirit is a witness of life. If, then, there be any grace in the water, it is not from the nature of water, but from the presence of the Holy Spirit.

78. Do we live in the water or in the Spirit? Are we sealed in the water or in the Spirit. For in Him we live and He Himself is the earnest of our inheritance, as the Apostle says, writing to the Ephesians I "In Whom believing ye were sealed with the Holy Spirit of promise, Who is an earnest of our inheritance." So we were sealed by the Holy Spirit, not by nature, but by God, for

it is written: "He Who anointed us is God, Who also sealed us, and gave the earnest of the Spirit in our hearts."

79. We were then sealed with the Spirit by God. For as we die in Christ, in order to be born again, so, too, we are sealed with the Spirit, that we may possess His brightness and image and grace, which is undoubtedly our spiritual seal. For although we were visibly sealed in our bodies, we are in truth sealed in our hearts, that the Holy Spirit may portray in us the likeness of the heavenly image.

80. Who, then, can dare to say that the Holy Spirit is separated from the Father and the Son, since through Him we attain to the image and likeness of God, and through Him, as the Apostle Peter says, are partakers of the divine nature? In which there is certainly not the inheritance of carnal succession, but the spiritual connection of the grace of adoption. And in order that we may know that this seal is rather on our hearts than on our bodies, the prophet says: "The light of Thy countenance has been impressed upon us, O Lord, Thou hast put gladness in my heart."

Chapter VII.

The Holy Spirit is not a creature, seeing that He is infinite, and was shed upon the apostles dispersed through all countries, and moreover sanctifies the Angers also, to whom He makes us equal. Mary was full of the same likewise, so too, Christ the Lord, and so far all things high and low. And all benediction has its origin from His operation, as was signified in the moving of the water at Bethesda.

81. Since then, every creature is confined within certain limits of its own nature, and inasmuch as those invisible operations, which cannot be circumscribed by place and bounds, yet are closed in by the property of their own substance; how can any one dare to call the Holy Spirit a creature, Who has not a limited and circumscribed power? because He is always in all things and everywhere, which assuredly is the property of Divinity and Lordship, for: "The earth is the Lord's and the fulness thereof."

81. And so, when the Lord appointed His servants the apostles, that we might recognize that the creature was one thing and the grace of the Spirit another, He appointed them to different places, because all could not be everywhere at once. But He gave the Holy Spirit to all, to shed upon the apostles though separated the gift of indivisible grace. The persons, then, were different, but the accomplishment of the working was in all one, because the Holy Spirit is one of Whom it is said: "Ye shall receive power, even the Holy Spirit coming upon you, and ye shall be witnesses to Me in Jerusalem and in all Judea and Samaria, and unto the ends of the earth."

82. The Holy Spirit, then, is uncircumscribed and infinite, Who infused Himself into the minds of the disciples throughout the separate divisions of distant regions, and the remote bounds of the whole world, Whom nothing is able to escape or to deceive. And therefore holy David says: "Whither shall I go from Thy Spirit, or whither shall I flee from Thy face." Of what Angel does the Scripture say this? of what Dominion? of what Power? of what Angel do we find the power diffused over many? For Angels were sent to few, but the Holy Spirit was poured upon whole peoples. Who, then, can doubt that that is divine which is shed upon many at once and is not seen; but that that is corporeal which is seen and held by individuals?

83. But in like manner as the Spirit sanctifying the apostles is not a partaker of human nature; so, too, He sanctifying Angels, Dominions, and Powers, has no partnership with creatures. But if any think that the holiness of the Angels is not spiritual, but some other kind of grace belonging to the property of their nature, they will forsooth judge Angels to be inferior to men. For since themselves also confess that they would not dare to compare Angels to the Holy Spirit, and they cannot deny that the Holy Spirit is shed upon men; but the sanctification of the Spirit is a divine gift and favour, men who possess a better kind of sanctification will certainly be found to be preferred to the Angels. But since Angels come down to men to assist them, it must be understood that the nature of Angels is higher as it receives more of the grace of the Spirit, and that the favour awarded to us and to them comes from the same author.

84. But how great is that grace which makes even the lower nature of the lot of men equal to the gifts received by Angels, as the Lord Himself promised, saying: "Ye shall be as the Angels in heaven." Nor is it difficult, for He Who made those Angels in the Spirit will by the same grace make men also equal to the Angels.

85. But of what creature can it be said that it fills all things, as is written of the Holy Spirit: "I will pour My Spirit upon all flesh." This cannot be said of an Angel. Lastly, Gabriel himself, when sent to Mary, said: "Hail, full of grace," plainly declaring the grace of the Spirit which was in her, because the Holy Spirit had come upon her, and she was about to have her womb full of grace with the heavenly Word.

86. For it is of the Lord to fill all things, Who says: "I fill heaven and earth." If, then, it is the Lord Who fills heaven and earth, Who can judge the Holy Spirit to be without a share in the dominion and divine power, seeing that He has filled the world, and what is beyond the whole world, filled Jesus the Redeemer of the whole world? For it is written: "But Jesus, full of the Holy Spirit, departed from Jordan," Who, then, except one who possessed the same fulness could fill Him Who fills all things?

87. But test they should object that this was said according to the flesh, though He alone from Whose flesh went forth virtue to heal all, was more than all; yet, as the Lord fills all things, so, too, we read of the Spirit: "For the Spirit of the Lord filled the whole world." And you find it said of all who had consorted with the Apostles that, "filled with the Holy Spirit they spoke the word of God with boldness." You see that the Spirit gives both fulness and boldness, Whose operation the archangel announces to Mary, saying: "The Holy Spirit shall come on thee."

88. You read, too, in the Gospel that the Angel descended at the appointed time into the pool and troubled the water, and he who first went down into the pool was made whole, What did the Angel declare in this type but the descent of the Holy Spirit, which was to come to pass in our day, and should consecrate the waters when invoked by the prayers of the priest? That Angel, then, was a herald of the Holy Spirit, inasmuch as by means of the grace of the Spirit medicine was to be applied to our infirmities of soul and mind. The Spirit, then, has the same ministers as God the Father and Christ. He fills all things, possesses all things, works all and in all in the same manner as God the Father and the Son work.

89. What, then, is more divine than the working of the Holy Spirit, since God Himself testifies that the Holy Spirit presides over His blessings, saying: "I will put My Spirit upon thy seed and My blessings upon thy children." For no blessing can be full except through the inspiration of the Holy Spirit. Wherefore, too, the Apostle found nothing better to wish us than this, as He himself said: "We cease not to pray and make request for you that ye may be filled with the knowledge of His will, in all wisdom and spiritual understanding walking worthily of God." He taught, then, that this was the will of God, that rather by walking in good works and words and affections, we should be filled with the will of God, Who puts His Holy Spirit in our hearts. Therefore if he who has the Holy Spirit is filled with the will of God, there is certainly no difference of will between the Father and the Son.

Chapter VIII.

The Holy Spirit is given by God alone, yet not wholly to each person, since there is no one besides Christ capable of receiving Him wholly. Charity is shed abroad by the Holy Spirit, Who, prefigured by the mystical ointment, is shown to have nothing common with creatures; and He, inasmuch as He is said to proceed from the mouth of God, must not be classed with creatures, nor with things divisible, seeing He is eternal.

90. Observe at the same time that God gives the Holy Spirit. For this is no work of man, nor girl of man; but He Who is invoked by the priest is given by God, wherein is the gift of God and the ministry of the priest. For if the Apostle Paul judged that he was not able to give the Holy Spirit himself by his own authority, and considered himself so far unequal to this office that he wished us to be filled by God with the Spirit, who is sufficient to dare to arrogate to himself the conferring of this gift? So the Apostle uttered this wish in prayer, and did not claim a

fight by any authority of his own; he desired to obtain, he did not presume to command. Peter, too, says that he is not capable of compelling or restraining the Holy Spirit. For he spoke thus: "Wherefore if God has granted them the same grace as to us, who was I that I could resist God?"

91. But perchance they would not be moved by the example of apostles, and so let us use divine utterances; for it is written: "Jacob is My servant, I will uphold him; Israel is My elect, My soul hath upheld him, I put My Spirit upon him." The Lord also said by Isaiah: "The Spirit of the Lord is upon Me, because He hath anointed Me."

92. Who, then, can dare to say that the substance of the Holy Spirit is created, at Whose shining in our hearts we behold the beauty of divine truth, and the distance between the creature and the Godhead, that the work may be distinguished from its Author? Or of what creature has God so spoken as to say: "I will pour out of My Spirit"? He said not Spirit, but "of My Spirit," for we are not able to receive the fulness of the Holy Spirit, but we receive as much as our Master divides to us of His own according to His will. For as the Son of God thought it not robbery that He should be equal to God, but emptied Himself, that we might be able to receive Him in our minds; but He emptied Himself not that He was void of His own fulness, but in order that He, Whose fulness I could not endure, might infuse Himself into me according to the measure of my capacity, in like manner also the Father says that He pours out of the Spirit upon all flesh; for He did not pour Him forth wholly, but that which He poured forth abounded for all.

93. There was therefore a pouring out upon us of the Spirit, but upon the Lord Jesus, when He was in the form of man, the Spirit abode, as it is written: "Upon Whom thou shall see the Spirit descending from heaven, and abiding upon Him, He it is Who baptizeth in the Holy Spirit." Around us is the liberality of the Giver in abundant provision, in Him abides for ever the fulness of the Spirit. He shed forth then what He deemed to be sufficient for us, and what was shed forth is not separated nor divided; but He has a unity of fulness wherewith He may enlighten the sight of our hearts according to what our strength is capable of. Lastly, we receive so much as the advancing of our mind acquires, for the fulness of the grace of the Spirit is indivisible, but is Shared in by us according to the capacity of our own nature.

94. God, then, sheds forth of the Spirit, and the love of God is also shed abroad through the Spirit; in which point we ought to recognize the unity of the operation and of the grace. For as God shed forth of the Holy Spirit, so also "the love of God is shed abroad in our hearts through the Holy Spirit;" in order that we may understand that the Holy Spirit is not a work, Who is the dispenser and plenteous Fount of the divine love.

95. In like manner that you may believe that that which is shed abroad cannot be common to the creatures but peculiar to the Godhead, the name of the Son is also poured forth, as you read: "Thy Name is as ointment poured forth." Of which saying nothing can surpass the force. For as ointment closed up in a vase keeps in its perfume, so long as it is confined in the narrow space of that vase, though it cannot reach many, it yet preserves its strength. But when the ointment has been poured out of that vase wherein it was enclosed, it spreads far and wide; so, too, the Name of Christ before His coming amongst the people of Israel was enclosed in the minds of the Jews as in some vase. For "God is known in Judah, His Name is great in Israel;" that is, the Name which the vases of the Jews held confined in their narrow limits.

96. Even then that Name was indeed great, when it remained in the narrow limits of the weak and few, but it had not yet poured forth its greatness throughout the hearts of the Gentiles, and to the ends of the whole world. But after that He by His coming had shone throughout the whole world, He spread abroad that divine Name of His throughout all creatures, not filled up by any addition (for fulness admits not of increase), but filling up the empty spaces, that His Name might be wonderful in all the world. The pouring forth, then, of His Name signifies a kind of abundant exuberance of graces and copiousness of heavenly goods, for whatever is poured forth flows over from abundance.

97. So as wisdom which proceeds from the mouth of God cannot be said to be created, nor the Word Which is uttered from His heart, nor the power in which is the fulness of the eternal Majesty; so, too, the Spirit which is poured forth from the mouth of God cannot be considered to be created, since God Himself has shown their unity to be such that He speaks of His pouring forth of His Spirit. By which we understand that the grace of God the Father is the same as that of the Holy Spirit, and that without an y division or loss it is divided to the hearts of each. That, then, which is shed abroad of the Holy Spirit is neither severed, nor comprehended in any corporeal parts, nor divided.

98. For how can it be credible that the Spirit should be divided. by any parcelling out? John says of God: "Hereby know we that He abides in us by the Spirit which He hath given us." But that which abides always is certainly not changed, therefore if it suffers no change it is eternal. And so the Holy Spirit is eternal, but the creature is liable to fault, and therefore subject to change. But that which is subject to change cannot be eternal, and there cannot therefore be anything in common between the Spirit and the creature, because the Spirit is eternal, but every creature is temporal.

99. But the Apostle also shows that the Holy Spirit is eternal, for: "If the blood of bulls and of goats, and the sprinkling the ashes of an heifer sanctifieth to the purifying of the flesh, how much more the blood of Christ, Who through the eternal Spirit offered Himself without spot to God?" Therefore the Spirit is eternal.

Chapter IX.

The Holy Spirit is rightly called the ointment of Christ, and the oil of gladness; and why. Christ Himself is not the ointment, since He was anointed with the Holy Spirit. It is not strange that the Spirit should be called Ointment, since the Father and the Son are also called Spirit. And there is no confusion between them, since Christ alone suffered death, Whose saving cross is then spoken of.

100. Now many have thought that the Holy Spirit is the ointment of Christ, And well it is said ointment, because He is called the oil of gladness, the joining together of many graces giving a sweet fragrance. But God the Almighty Father anointed Him the Prince of priests, Who was, not like others anointed in a type under the Law, but was both according to the Law anointed in the body, and in truth was full with the virtue of the Holy Spirit from the Father above the Law.

101. This is the oil of gladness, of which the prophet says: "God, even Thy God, hath anointed Thee with the oil of gladness above Thy fellows." Lastly, Peter says that Jesus was anointed with the Spirit, as you read: "Ye know that word which went through all Judea beginning from Galilee after the baptism which John preached, even Jesus of Nazareth, how God anointed Him with the Holy Spirit." The Holy Spirit is, then, the oil of gladness.

102. And well did he say oil of gladness, lest you should think Him a creature; for it is the nature of this sort of oil that it will by no means mingle with moisture of another kind. Gladness, too, does not anoint the body, but brightens the inmost heart, as the prophet said: "Thou hast put gladness in my heart." So as he loses his pains who wishes to mix oil with moister matter, because since the nature of oil is lighter than others, when the others settle, it rises and is separated. How do those wretched pedlars think that the oil of gladness can by their tricks be mingled with other creatures, since of a truth corporeal things cannot be mingled with in corporeal, nor things created with uncreated?

102. And well is that called oil of gladness wherewith Christ was anointed; for neither was usual nor common oil to be sought for Him, wherewith either wounds are dressed or heat assuaged; since the salvation of the world did not seek alleviation for His wounds, nor the eternal might of His wearied Body demand refreshment.

103. Nor is it wonderful if He have the oil of gladness, Who made those about to die rejoice, put off sadness from the world, destroyed the odour of sorrowful death. And so the Apostle says: "For we are the good odour of Christ to God;" certainly showing that he is speaking of

spiritual things. But when the Son of God Himself says: "The Spirit of the Lord is upon Me, because He hath anointed Me," He points out the ointment of the Spirit. Therefore the Spirit is the ointment of Christ.

104. Or since the Name of Jesus is as ointment poured out, if they wish to understand Christ Himself, and not the Spirit of Christ to be expressed under the name of ointment, certainly when the Apostle Peter says that the Lord Jesus was anointed with the Holy Spirit, it is without doubt plain that the Spirit also is called ointment.

105. But what wonder, since both the Father and the Son are said to be Spirit. Of which we shall speak more fully when we begin to speak of the Unity of the Name. Yet since most suitable place occurs here, that we may not seem to have passed on without a conclusion, let them read that both the Father is called Spirit, as the Lord said in the Gospel, "for God is Spirit;" and Christ is called Spirit, for Jeremiah said: "The Spirit before our face, Christ the Lord."

106. So, then, both the Father is Spirit and Christ is Spirit, for that which is not a created body is spirit, but the Holy Spirit is not commingled with the Father and the Son, but is distinct from the Father and from the Son. For the Holy Spirit did not die, Who could not die because He had not taken flesh upon Him, and the eternal Godhead was incapable of dying, but Christ died according to the flesh.

107. For of a truth He died in that which He took of the Virgin, not in that which He had of the Father, for Christ died in that nature in which He was crucified. But the Holy Spirit could not be crucified, Who had not flesh and bones, but the Son of God was crucified, Who took flesh and bones, that on that cross the temptations of our flesh might die. For He took on Him that which He was not that He might hide that which He was; He hid that which He was that He might be tempted in it, and that which He was not might be redeemed, in order that He might call us by means of that which He was not to that which He was.

108. O the divine mystery of that cross, on which weakness hangs, might is free, vices are nailed, and triumphal trophies raised. So that a certain saint said: "Pierce my flesh with nails for fear of Thee;" he says not with nails of iron, but of fear and faith. For the bonds of virtue are stronger than those of punishment. Lastly, his faith bound Peter, when he had followed the Lord as far as the hall of the high priest, whom no one had bound, and punishment loosened not him, whom faith bound. Again, when he was bound by the Jews, prayer loosed him, punishment did not hold him, because he had not gone back from Christ.

109. Therefore do you also crucify sin, that you may die to sin; he who dies to sin lives to God; do you live to Him Who spared not His own Son, that in His body He might crucify our passions. For Christ died for us, that we might live in His revived Body. Therefore not our life but our guilt died in Him, "Who," it is said, "bare our sins in His own Body on the tree; that being set free from our sins we might live in righteousness, by the wound of Whose stripes we are healed."

110. That wood of the cross is, then, as it were a kind of ship of our salvation, our passage, not a punishment, for there is no other salvation but the passage of eternal salvation. Whilst expecting death I do not feel it; whilst thinking little of punishment I do not suffer; whilst careless of fear I know it not.

111. Who, then, is He by the wound of Whose stripes we are healed but Christ the Lord? of Whom the same Isaiah prophesied His stripes were our healing, of Whom Paul the Apostle wrote in his epistle: "Who knew no sin, but was made sin for us." This. indeed, was divine in Him, that His Flesh did no sin, nor did the creature of the body take in Him sin. For what wonder would it be if the Godhead alone sinned not, seeing It had no incentives to sin? But if God alone is free from sin, certainly every creature by its own nature can be, as we have said, liable to sin.

Chapter X.

That the Spirit forgives sin is common to Him with the Father and the Son, but not with the Angels.

112. Tell me, then, whoever you are who deny the Godhead of the Holy Spirit. The Spirit could not be liable to sin, Who rather forgives sin. Does an Angel forgive? Does an Archangel? Certainly not, but the Father alone, the Son alone, and the Holy Spirit alone. Now no one is unable to avoid that which he has power to forgive.

113. But perhaps some one will say that the Seraph said to Isaiah: "Behold, this hath touched thy lips, and shall take away thine iniquities, and purge away thy sins." Shall take away, he says, and shall purge, not I will take away, but that fire from the altar of God, that is, the grace of the Spirit. For what else can we piously understand to be on the altar of God but the grace of the Spirit? Certainly not the wood of the forests, nor the soot and coals. Or what is so in accordance with piety as to understand according to the mystery that it was revealed by the mouth of Isaiah that all men should be cleansed by the passion of Christ, Who as a coal according to the flesh burnt up our sins, as you read in Zechariah: "Is not this a brand cast forth from the fire? And that was Joshua clothed in filthy garments."

114. Lastly, that we may know that this mystery of the common redemption was most clearly revealed by the prophets, you have also in this place: "Lo, it hath taken away thy sins;" not that Christ put aside His sins Who did no sin, but that in the flesh of Christ the whole human race should be loosed from their sins.

115. But even if the Seraph had taken away sin, it would have been as one of the ministers of God appointed to this mystery. For thus said Isaiah: "For one of the Seraphim was sent to me."

Chapter XI.

The Spirit is sent to all, and passes not from place to place, for He is not limited either by time or space. He goes forth from the Son, as the Son from the Father, in Whom He ever abides: and also comes to us when we receive. He comes also after the same manner as the Father Himself, from Whom He can by no means be separated.

116. The Spirit, also, is indeed said to be sent, but the Seraph to one, the Spirit to all. The Seraph is sent to minister, the Spirit works a mystery. The Seraph performs what is commanded, the Spirit divides as He wills. The Seraph passes from place to place, for he does not fill all things, but is himself filled by the Spirit. The Seraph comes down with a certain mode of passage according to his nature, but we cannot think this of the Spirit, of Whom the Son of God says: "When the Paraclete shall come, even the Spirit of Truth, Whom I send unto you, Who proceedeth from the Father."

117. For if the Spirit proceeds from a place and passes to a place, both the Father Himself will be found in a place, and the Son likewise. If He goes forth from a place, Whom the Father or the Son sends, certainly the Spirit passing from a place, and making progress, seems to leave, according to those impious interpretations, both the Father and the Son like some material body.

118. I am saying this with reference to those who say that the Spirit comes down by movement. But neither the Father, Who is above all not only of corporeal nature, but also of the invisible creation, is circumscribed in any place; nor is the Son, Who, as the Worker of all creation, is above every creature, enclosed by the places or times of His own works; nor is the Spirit of Truth as being the Spirit of God, circumscribed by any corporeal limits, Who since He is incorporeal is far above the whole rational creation through the ineffable fulness of His Godhead, having over all things the power of breathing where He wills, and of inspiring as He wills.

119. The Spirit is not, then, sent as it were from a place, nor does He proceed as from a place, when He proceeds from the Son, as the Son Himself, when He says, "I came forth from the Father, and am come into the world," destroys all fancies, which can be reckoned as from place to place. In like manner, also, when we read that God is within or without, we certainly do

not either enclose God within anybody or separate Him from anybody, but weighing these things in a deep and ineffable estimation, we comprehend the hiddenness of the divine nature.

120. Lastly, Wisdom so says that she came forth from the mouth of the Most High, as not to be external to the Father, but with the Father; for "the Word was with God;" and not only with God but also in God; for He says: "I am in the Father and the Father is in Me." But neither when He goes forth from the Father does He retire from a place, nor is He separated as a body from a body; nor when He is in the Father is He as if a body enclosed as it were in a body. The Holy Spirit also, when He proceeds from the Father and the Son, is not separated from the Father nor separated from the Son. For how could He be separated from the Father Who is the Spirit of His mouth? Which is certainly both a proof of His eternity, and expresses the Unity of this Godhead.

121. He exists then, and abides always, Who is the Spirit of His mouth, but He seems to come down when we receive Him, that He may dwell in us, that we may not be alien from His grace. To us He seems to come down, not that He does come down, but that our mind ascends to Him. Of which we would speak more fully did we not remember that in the former treatise there was set forth that the Father said: "Let us go down and confound their language," and that the Son said: "He that loveth Me will keep My saying, and My Father will love him, and We will come to Him and make Our abode with Him."

122. The Spirit, then, so comes as does the Father, for where the Father is there is also the Son, and where the Son is there is the Holy Spirit. The Holy Spirit, therefore, is not to be supposed to come separately. But He comes not from place to place, but from the disposition of the order to the safety of redemption, from the grace of giving life to that of sanctification, to translate us from earth to heaven, from wretchedness to glory, from slavery to a kingdom.

123. The Spirit comes, then, as the Father comes. For the Son said, "I and the Father will come, and will make Our abode with Him." Does the Father come in a bodily fashion? Thus, then, comes the Spirit in Whom, when He comes, is the full presence of the Father and the Son.

124. But who can separate the Spirit from the Father and the Son, since we cannot even name the Father and the Son without the Spirit? "For no one saith Lord Jesus, except in the Holy Spirit?" If, then, we cannot call Jesus Lord except in the Holy Spirit, we certainly cannot proclaim Him without the Spirit. But if the Angels also proclaim Jesus to be Lord, Whom no one can proclaim except in the Spirit, then in them also the office of the Holy Spirit operates.

125. We have proved, then, that the presence and the grace of the Father, the Son, and the Holy Spirit are one, which is so heavenly and divine that the Son gives thanks therefore to the Father, saying, "I give thanks to Thee, O Father, Lord of heaven and earth, because Thou hast hidden these things from the wise and prudent, and hast revealed them unto babes."

Chapter XII.

The peace and grace of the Father, the Son, and the Holy Spirit are one, so also is Their charity one, which showed itself chiefly in the redemption of man. Their communion with man is also one.

126. Therefore since the calling is one, the grace is also one. Lastly, it is written: "Grace unto you and peace from God our Father, and from the Lord Jesus Christ." You see, then, that we are told that the grace of the Father and the Son is one, and the peace of the Father and the Son is one, but this grace and peace is the fruit of the Spirit, as the Apostle taught us himself, saying: "But the fruit of the Spirit is love, joy, peace, patience." And peace is good and necessary that no one be troubled with doubtful disputations, nor be shaken by the storm of bodily passions, but that his affections may remain quietly disposed as to the worship of God, with simplicity of faith and tranquillity of mind.

127. As to peace we have proved the point; but as to grace the prophet Zechariah says, that God promised to pour upon Jerusalem the spirit of grace and mercy, and the Apostle Peter says: "Repent and be baptized every one of you in the Name of the Lord Jesus Christ for the remission of sins, and ye shall receive the grace of the Holy Spirit." So grace comes also of the

Holy Spirit as of the Father and the Son. For how can there be grace without the Spirit, since all divine grace is in the Spirit?

128. Nor do we read only of the peace and grace of the Father, the Son, and the Holy Spirit, but also, faithful Emperor, of the love and communion. For of love it has been said: "The grace of our Lord Jesus Christ, and the love of God." We have heard of the love of the Father. The same love which is the Father's is also the Son's. For He Himself said: "He that loveth Me shall be loved of My Father, and I will love him," And what is the love of the Son, but that He offered Himself for us, and redeemed us with His own blood. But the same love is in the Father, for it is written: "God so loved the world, that He gave His Only-begotten Son."

129. So, then, the Father gave the Son, and the Son gave Himself. Love is preserved and due affection is not wronged, for affection is not wronged where there is no distress in the giving up. He gave one Who was willing, He gave One Who offered Himself, the Father did not give the Son to punishment but to grace. If you enquire into the merit of the deed, enquire into the description of the affection. The vessel of election shows plainly the unity of this divine love, because both the Father gave the Son and the Son gave Himself. The Father gave, Who "spared not His own Son, but gave Him up for us all." And of the Son he also says: "Who gave Himself for me." "Gave Himself," he says. If it be of grace, what do I find fault with. If it be that He suffered wrong, I owe the more.

130. But learn that in like manner as the Father gave the Son, and the Son gave Himself, so, too, the Holy Spirit gave Him. For it is written: "Then was Jesus led by the Spirit into the wilderness to be tempted by the devil." So, too, the loving Spirit gave the Son of God. For as the love of the Father and the Son is one, so, too, we have shown that this love of God is shed abroad by the Holy Spirit, and is the fruit of the Holy Spirit, because "the fruit of the Spirit is love, joy, peace, patience."

131. And that there is communion between the Father and the Son is plain, for it is written: "And our communion is with the Father and with His Son Jesus Christ." And in another place: "The communion of the Holy Spirit be with you all." If, then, the peace of the Father, the Son, and the Holy Spirit is one, the grace one, the love one, and the communion one, the working is certainly one, and where the working is one, certainly the power cannot be divided nor the substance separated. For, if so, how could the grace of the same working agree?

Chapter XIII.

St. Ambrose shows from the Scriptures that the Name of the Three Divine Persons is one, and first the unity of the Name of the Son and of the Holy Spirit, inasmuch as each is called Paraclete and Truth.

132. Who, then, would dare to deny the oneness of Name, when he sees the oneness of the working. But why should I maintain the unity of the Name by arguments, when there is the plain testimony of the Divine Voice that the Name of the Father, the Son, and the Holy Spirit is one? For it is written: "Go, baptize all nations in the Name of the Father, and of the Son, and of the Holy Spirit." He said, "in the Name," not "in the Names." So, then, the Name of the Father is not one, that of the Son another, and that of the Holy Spirit another, for God is one; the Names are not more than one, for there are not two Gods, or three Gods.

132. And that He might reveal that the Godhead is one and the Majesty one, because the Name of the Father, the Son, and the Holy Spirit is one, and the Son did not come in one Name and the Holy Spirit in another, the Lord Himself said: "I am come in My Father's Name, and ye did not receive Me, if another shall come in his own name ye will receive him."

133. And Scripture makes clear that that which is the Father's Name, the same is also that of the Son, for the Lord said in Exodus: "I will go before thee in My Name, and will call by My Name the Lord before thee." So, then, the Lord said that He would call the Lord by His Name. The Lord, then, is the Name of the Father and of the Son.

134. But since the Name of the Father and of the Son is one, learn that the same is the Name of the Holy Spirit also, since the Holy Spirit came in the Name of the Son, as it is written:

"But the Paraclete, even the Holy Spirit, Whom the Father will send in My Name, He shall teach you all things." But He Who came in the Name of the Son came also certainly in the Name of the Father, for the Name of the Father and of the Son is one. Thus it comes to pass that the Name of the Father and of the Son is also that of the Holy Spirit. For there is no other Name given under heaven wherein we must be saved.

155. At the same time He showed that the oneness of the Divine Name must be taught, not the difference, since Christ came in the oneness of the Name, but Antichrist will come in his own name, as it is written: "I am come in My Father's Name, and ye did not receive Me, if another shall come in his own name, ye will receive him."

156. We are, then, clearly taught by these passages that there is no difference of Name in the Father, the Son, and the Holy Spirit; and that that which is the Name of the Father is also the Name of the Son, and likewise that which is the Name of the Son is also that of the Holy Spirit, when the Son also is called Paraclete, as is the Holy Spirit. And therefore does the Lord Jesus say in the Gospel: "I will ask My Father, and He shall give you another Paraclete, to be with you for ever, even the Spirit of Truth." And He said well "another," that you might not suppose that the Son is also the Spirit, for oneness is of the Name, not a Sabellian confusion of the Son and of the Spirit.

157. So, then, the Son is one Paraclete, the Holy Spirit another Paraclete; for John called the Son a Paraclete, as you find: "If any man sin, we have a Paraclete [Advocate] with the Father, Jesus Christ." So in like manner as there is a oneness of name, so, too, is there a oneness of power, for where the Paraclete Spirit is, there is also the Son.

158. For as the Lord says in this place that the Spirit will be forever with the faithful, so, too, does He elsewhere show that He will Himself be forever with the apostles, saying: "Lo, I am with you always, even to the end of the world." Therefore the Son and the Spirit are one, the Name of the Trinity is one, and the Presence one and indivisible.

159. But as we show that the Son is called the Paraclete, so, too, do we show that the Spirit is called the Truth. Christ is the Truth, the Spirit is the Truth, for you find in John's epistle: "For the Spirit is Truth." Not only, then, is the Spirit called the Spirit of Truth. but also the Truth, as the Son is also declared to be the Truth, Who says: "I am the Way, the Truth, and the Life."

Chapter XIV.

Each Person of the Trinity is said in the sacred writings to be Light. The Spirit is designated Fire by Isaiah, a figure of which Fire was seen in the bush by Moses, in the tongues of fire, and in Gideon's pitchers. And the Godhead of the same Spirit cannot be denied, since His operation is the same as that of the Father and of the Son, and He is also called the light and fire of the Lord's countenance.

160. But why should I argue that as the Father is light, so, too, the Son is light, and the Holy Spirit is light? Which certainly pertains to the power of God. For God is Light, as John said: "For God is Light, and in Him is no darkness."

161. But the Son, too, is Light, because "the Life was the Light of men." And the Evangelist, that he might show that he was speaking of the Son of God, says of John the Baptist: "He was not light, but [was sent] to be a witness of the Light. That was the true Light, which lighteth every man that cometh into this world." 2 So, then, since God is Light, and the Son of God the true Light, without doubt the Son of God is true God.

162. And you find elsewhere that the Son of God is Light: "The people that sat in darkness and in the shadow of death have seen a great light." But, which is still more clear, it is said: "For with Thee is the fount of Life, and in Thy light we shall see light," which means that with Thee, O God the Father Almighty, Who art the Fount of Life, in Thy Son Who is the Light, we shall see the light of the Holy Spirit. As the Lord Himself shows, saying: "Receive ye the Holy Spirit," and elsewhere: "Virtue went out from Him."

163. But who can doubt that the Father is Light, when we read of His Son that He is the Brightness of eternal Light? For of Whom but of the Father is the Son the Brightness, Who both is always with the Father, and always shines, not with unlike but with the same radiance.

164. And Isaiah shows that the Holy Spirit is not only Light but also Fire, saying: "And the light of Israel shall be for a fire." So the prophets called Him a burning Fire, because in those three points we see more intensely the majesty of the Godhead; since to sanctify is of the Godhead, to illuminate is the property of fire and light, and the Godhead is wont to be pointed out or seen in the appearance of fire: "For our God is a consuming Fire," as Moses said.

165. For he himself saw the fire in the bush, and had heard God when the voice from the flame of fire came to him saying: "I am the God of Abraham, and the God of Isaac, and the God of Jacob." The voice came from the fire, and the voice was in the bush, and the fire did no harm. For the bush was burning but was not consumed, because in that mystery the Lord was showing that He would come to illuminate the thorns of our body, and not to consume those who were in misery, but to alleviate their misery; Who would baptize with the Holy Spirit and with fire, that He might give grace and destroy sin. So in the symbol of fire God keeps His intention.

166. In the Acts of the Apostles, also, when the Holy Spirit had descended upon the faithful, the appearance of fire was seen, for you read thus: "And suddenly there was a sound from heaven, as though the Spirit were borne with great vehemence, and it filled all the house where they were sitting, and there appeared unto them cloven tongues like as of fire."

167. For the same reason was it that when Gideon was about to overcome the Midianites, he commanded three hundred men to take pitchers, and to hold lighted torches inside the pitchers, and trumpets in their right hands. Our predecessors have preserved the explanation received from the apostles, that the pitchers are our bodies, fashioned of clay, which know not fear if they burn with the fervour of the grace of the Spirit, and bear witness to the passion of the Lord Jesus with a loud confession of the Voice.

168. Who, then, can doubt of the Godhead of the Holy Spirit, since where the grace of the Spirit is, there the manifestation of the Godhead appears. By which evidence we infer not a diversity but the unity of the divine power. For how can there be a severance of power, where the effect of the working in all is one?

169. What, then, is that fire? Not certainly one made up of common twigs, or roaring with the burning of the reeds of the woods, but that fire which improves good deeds like gold, and consumes sins like stubble. This is undoubtedly the Holy Spirit, Who is called both the fire and light of the countenance of God; light as we said above: "The light of Thy countenance has been sealed upon us, O Lord." What is, then, the light that is sealed, but that of the seal of the Spirit, believing in Whom, "ye were sealed," he says, "with the Holy Spirit of promise."

170. And as there is a light of the divine countenance, so, too, does fire shine forth from the countenance of God, for it is written: "A fire shall burn in His sight." For the grace of the day of judgment shines beforehand, that forgiveness may follow to reward the service of the saints. O the great fulness of the Scriptures, which no one can comprehend with human genius! O greatest proof of the Divine Unity For how many things are pointed out in these two verses!

Chapter XV.

The Holy Spirit is Life equally with the Father and the Son, in truth whether the Father be mentioned, with Whom is the Fount of Life, or the Son, that Fount can be none other than the Holy Spirit.

171. We have said that the Father is Light, the Son is Light, and the Holy Spirit is Light; let us also learn that the Father is Life, the Son Life, and the Holy Spirit Life. For John said: "That which was from the beginning, that which we have heard, and which we have seen, and have beheld with our eyes, and our hands have handled concerning the Word of Life; and the Life appeared, and we saw and testify, and declare to you of that Life which was with the Father." He said both Word of Life and Life that he might signify both the Father and the Son to be

Life. For what is the Word of Life but the Word of God? And by this phrase both God and the Word of God are shown to be Life. And as it is said the Word of Life, so, too, the Spirit of Life. Therefore, as the Word of Life is Life, so, too, the Spirit of Life is Life.

172. Learn now that as the Father is the Fount of Life, so, too, many have stated that the Son is signified as the Fount of Life; so that, he says, with Thee, Almighty God, Thy Son is the Fount of Life. That is the Fount of the Holy Spirit, for the Spirit is Life, as the Lord says: "The words which I speak unto you are Spirit and Life," for where the Spirit is, there also is Life; and where Life is, is also the Holy Spirit.

173. Many, however, consider that in this passage the Father only is signified by the Fount. Let them, however, notice what the Scripture relates: "With Thee is the Well of Life." That is, the Son is with the Father; since the Word was with God, Who was in the beginning, and was with God.

174. But whether in this place one understands the Fount to be the Father or the Son, we certainly do not understand a fount of that water which is created, but the Fount of that divine grace, that is, of the Holy Spirit, for He is the living water. Wherefore the Lord said: "If thou knowest the gift of God, and Who He is that saith to thee, Give me to drink, thou wouldst have asked Him, and He would have given thee living water."

175. This was the water for which the soul of David thirsted. The hart desires the fountain of these waters, not thirsting for the poison of serpents. For the water of the grace of the Spirit is living, that it may purify the inner parts of the mind, and wash away every sin of the soul, and purify the transgression of hidden faults.

Chapter XVI.

The Holy Spirit is that large river by which the mystical Jerusalem is watered. It is equal to its Fount, that is, the Father and the Son, as is signified in holy Scripture. St. Ambrose himself thirsts for that water, and warns us that in order to preserve it within us, we must avoid the devil, lust, and heresy, since our vessels are frail, and that broken cisterns must be forsaken, that after the example of the Samaritan woman and of the patriarchs we may find the water of the Lord.

176. But lest perchance any one should speak against as it were the littleness of the Spirit, and from this should endeavour to establish a difference in greatness, arguing that water seems to be but a small part of a Fount, although examples taken from creatures seem by no means suitable for application to the Godhead; yet lest they should judge anything injuriously from this comparison taken from creatures, let them learn that not only is the Holy Spirit called Water, but also a River, as we read: "From his belly shall flow rivers of living water. But this He said of the Spirit, Whom they were beginning to receive, who were about to believe in Him."

177. So, then, the Holy Spirit is the River, and the abundant River, which according to the Hebrews flowed from Jesus in the lands, as we have received it prophesied by the mouth of Isaiah. This is the great River which flows always and never fails. And not only a river, but also one of copious stream and overflowing greatness, as also David said: "The stream of the river makes glad the city of God."

178. For neither is that city, the heavenly Jerusalem, watered by the channel of any earthly river, but that Holy Spirit, proceeding from the Fount of Life, by a short draught of Whom we are satiated, seems to flow more abundantly among those celestial Thrones, Dominions and Powers, Angels and Archangels, rushing in the full course of the seven virtues of the Spirit. For if a river rising above its banks overflows, how much more does the Spirit, rising above every creature, when He touches the as it were low-lying fields of our minds, make glad that heavenly nature of the creatures with the larger fertility of His sanctification.

179, And let it not trouble you that either here it is said "rivers," or elsewhere "seven Spirits," for by the sanctification of these seven gifts of the Spirit, as Isaiah said, is signified the fulness of all virtue; the Spirit of wisdom and understanding, the Spirit of counsel and strength, the Spirit of knowledge and godliness, and the Spirit of the fear of God. One, then, is the River, but many the channels of the gifts of the Spirit. This River, then, goes forth from the Fount of Life.

180. And here, again, you must not turn aside your thoughts to lower things, because there seems to be some difference between a Fount and a River, and yet the divine Scripture has provided that the weakness of human understanding should not be injured by the lowliness of the language. Set before yourself any river, it springs from its fount, but is of one nature, of one brightness and beauty. And do you assert rightly that the Holy Spirit is of one substance, brightness, and glory with the Son of God and with God the Father. I will sum up all in the oneness of the qualities, and shall not be afraid of any question as to difference of greatness. For in this point also Scripture has provided for us; for the Son of God says: "He that shall drink of the water which I will give him, it shall become in him a well of water springing up unto everlasting life." This well is clearly the grace of the Spirit, a stream proceeding from the living Fount. The Holy Spirit, then, is also the Fount of eternal life.

181. You observe, then, from His words that the unity of the divine greatness is pointed out, and that Christ cannot be denied to be a Fount even by heretics, since the Spirit, too, is called a Fount. And as the Spirit is called a river, so, too, the Father said: "Behold, I come down upon you like a river of peace, and like a stream overflowing the glory of the Gentiles." And who can doubt that the Son of God is the River of life, from Whom the streams of eternal life flowed forth?

182. Good, then, is this water, even the grace of the Spirit. Who will give this Fount to my breast? Let it spring up in me, let that which gives eternal life flow upon me. Let that Fount overflow upon us, and not flow away. For Wisdom says: "Drink water out of thine own vessels, and from the founts of thine own wells, and let thy waters flow abroad in thy streets." How shall I keep this water that it flow not forth, that it glide not away? How shall I preserve my vessel, lest any crack of sin penetrating it, should let the water of eternal life exude? Teach us, Lord Jesus, teach us as Thou didst teach Thine apostles, saying: "Lay not up for yourselves treasures upon the earth, where rust and moth destroy, and where thieves break through and steal."

182. For He intimates that the thief is the unclean spirit, who cannot find entrance into those who walk in the light of good works, but if he has caught any one in the darkness of earthly desires, and in the midst of the enjoyment of earthly pleasures, he spoils them of all the flower of eternal virtue. And therefore the Lord says: "Lay up for yourselves treasures in heaven, where neither rust nor moth destroy, and where thieves do not break through and steal. For where thy treasure is, there will thy heart be also."

183. Our rust is wantonness, our rust is lust, our rust is luxury, which dim the keen vision of the mind with the filth of vices. Again, our moth is Arius, our moth is Photinus, who rend the holy vesture of the Church with their impiety, and desiring to separate the indivisible unity of the divine power, gnaw the precious veil of faith with sacrilegious tooth. The water is spilt if Arius has imprinted his tooth, it flows away if Photinus has planted his sting in any one's vessel. We are but of common clay, we quickly feel vices. But no one says to the potter, "Why hast Thou made me thus?" For though our vessel be but common, yet one is in honour, another in dishonour. Do not then lay open thy pool, dig not with vices and crimes, lest any one say: "He hath opened a pool and digged it, and is fallen into the pit which he made."

184. If you seek Jesus, forsake the broken cisterns, for Christ was wont to sit not by a pool but by a well. There that Samaritan roman found Him, she who believed, she who wished to draw water. Although you ought to have come in early morning, nevertheless if you come later, even at the sixth hour, you will find Jesus wearied with His journey. He is weary, but it is through thee, because He has long sought thee, thy unbelief has long wearied Him. Yet He is not offended if thou only comest, He asks to drink Who is about to give. But He drinks not the water of a stream flowing by, but thy salvation; He drinks thy good dispositions, He drinks the cup, that is, the Passion which stoned for thy sins, that thou drinking of His sacred blood mightest quench the thirst of this world.

185. So Abraham gained God after he had dug the well. So Isaac, while walking by the well, received that wife who was coming to him as a type of the Church. Faithful he was at the well, unfaithful at the pool. Lastly, too, Rebecca, as we read, found him who sought her at the well, and the harlots washed themselves in the blood in the pool of Jezebel.

BOOK II.

Introduction.

The Three Persons of the Godhead were not unknown to the judges of old nor to Moses, for the equality of the Son with the Father, as well as of the Three Persons amongst Themselves, is laid down both elsewhere and by him. Samson also enjoyed the assistance of the Holy Spirit, his history is touched upon and shown to be in some points typical of the Church and her mysteries. When the Holy Spirit left Samson he fell into various calamities, and St. Ambrose explains the spiritual significance of his shorn locks.

1. Even in reading the first book of the ancient history it is made clear both that the sevenfold grace of the Spirit shone forth in the judges themselves of the Jews, and that the mysteries of the heavenly sacraments were made known by the Spirit, of Whose eternity Moses was not ignorant. Then, too, at the very beginning of the world, and indeed before its beginning, he conjoined Him with God, Whom he knew to be eternal before the beginning of the world. For if any one takes good heed he will recognize in the beginning both the Father, the Son, and the Spirit. For of the Father it is written: "In the beginning God created the heaven and the earth." Of the Spirit it is said: "The Spirit was borne upon the waters." And well in the beginning of creation is there set forth the figure of baptism whereby the creature had to be purified. And of the Son we read that He it is Who divided light from darkness, for there is one God the Father Who speaks, and one God the Son Who acts.

2. But, again, that you may not think that there was assumption in the bidding of Him Who spoke, or inferiority on the part of Him Who carried out the bidding, the Father' acknowledges the Son as equal to Himself in the execution of the work, saying: "Let Us make man after Our image and likeness." For the common image and the working and the likeness can signify nothing but the oneness of the same Majesty.

3. But that we may more fully recognize the equality of the Father and the Son, as the Father spoke, the Son made, so, too, the Father works and the Son speaks. The Father works, as it is written: "My Father worketh hitherto." You find it said to the Son: "Say the word and he shall be healed." And the Son says to the Father: "I will that where I am, they too shall be with Me." The Father did what the Son said.

4. But neither was Abraham ignorant of the Holy Spirit; he saw Three and worshipped One, for there is one God, one Lord, and one Spirit. And so there is a oneness of honour, because there is a oneness of power.

5. And why should i speak of all one by one? Samson, born by the divine promise, had the Spirit accompanying him, for we read: "The Lord blessed him, and the Spirit of the Lord began to be with him in the camp." And so foreshadowing the future mystery, he demanded a wife of the aliens, which, as it is written, his father and mother knew not of, because it was from the Lord. And rightly was he esteemed stronger than others, because the Spirit of the Lord guided him, under Whose guidance he alone put to flight the people of the aliens, and at another time inaccessible to the bite of the lion, he, unconquerable in his strength, tore him asunder with his hands. Would that he had been as careful to preserve grace, as strong to overcome the beast!

6. And perhaps this was not only a prodigy of valour, but also a mystery of wisdom, an utterance of prophecy. For it does not seem to have been without a purpose that, as he was going to his marriage, a roaring lion met him, which he tore asunder with his hands, in whose body, when about to enjoy the wished-for wedlock, he found a swarm of bees, and took honey from its mouth, which he gave to his father and mother to eat. The people of the Gentiles which believed had honey, the people which was before savage is now the people of Christ.

7. Nor is the riddle without mystery, which he set forth to his companions: "Out of the eater came forth meat, and out of the strong came forth sweetness." And there was a mystery up to the point of the three days in which its answer was sought in vain, which could not be made known except by the faith of the Church, on the seventh day, the time of the Law being

completed, after the Passion of the Lord. For thus you find that the apostles did not understand, "because Jesus was not yet glorified."

8. "What," answer they, "is sweeter than honey, and what is stronger than a lion?" To which he replied: "If ye had not farmed with my heifer, you would not have found out my riddle." O divine mystery! O manifest sacrament! we have escaped from the slayer, we have overcome the strong one. The food of life is now there, where before was the hunger of a miserable death. Dangers are changed into safety, bitterness into sweetness. Grace came forth from the offence, power from weakness, and life from death.

9. There are, however, who think on the other hand that the wedlock could not have been established unless the lion of the tribe of Judah had been slain; and so in His body, that is, the Church, bees were found who store up the honey of wisdom, because after the Passion of the Lord the apostles believed more fully. This lion, then, Samson as a Jew slew, but in it he found honey, as in the figure of the heritage which was to be redeemed, that the remnant might be saved according to the election of grace.

10. "And the Spirit of the Lord," it is said, "came upon him, and he went down to Ascalon, and smote thirty men of them." For he could not fail to carry off the victory who saw the mysteries. And so in the garments they receive the reward of wisdom, the badge of intercourse, who resolve and answer the riddle.

11. Here, again, other mysteries come up, in that his wife is taken away, and for this foxes set fire to the sheaves of the aliens. For their own cunning often deceives those who contend against divine mysteries. Wherefore it is said again in the Song of Songs: "Take us the little foxes which destroy the vineyards, that our vineyards may flourish." He said well "little," because the larger could not destroy the vineyards, though to the strong even the devil is weak.

12. So, then, he (to sum up the story briefly, for the consideration of the whole passage is reserved for its own season) was unconquered so long as he kept the grace of the Spirit, as was the people of God chosen by the Lord, that Nazarite under the Law. Samson, then, was unconquered, and so invincible as to be able to smite a thousand men with the jawbone of an ass; so full of heavenly grace that when thirsty he found even water in the jawbone of an ass, whether you consider this as a miracle, or turn it to a mystery, because in the humility of the people of the Gentiles there would be both rest and triumph according to that which is written: "He that smiteth thee on the cheek, turn to him also the other." For by this endurance of injuries, which the sacrament of baptism teaches, we triumph over the stings of auger, that having passed through death we may attain to the rest of the resurrection.

13. Is that, then, Samson who broke ropes twisted with thongs, and new cords like weak threads? Is that Samson who did not feel the bonds of his hair fastened to the beam, so long as he had the grace of the Spirit? He, I say, after the Spirit of God departed from him, was greatly changed from that Samson Who returned clothed in the spoils of the aliens, but fallen from his greatness on the knees of a woman, caressed and deceived, is shorn of his hair.

14. Was, then, the hair of his head of such importance that, so long as it remained, his strength should endure unconquered, but when his head was shorn the man should suddenly lose all his strength? It is not so, nor may we think that the hair of his head has such power. There is the hair of religion and faith; the hair of the Nazarite perfect in the Law, consecrated in sparingness and abstinence, with which she (a type of the Church), who poured ointment on the feet of the Lord, wiped the feet of the heavenly Word, for then she knew Christ also after the flesh. That hair it is of which it is said: "Thy hair is as flocks of goats," growing on that head of which it is said: "The head of the man is Christ," and in another place: "His head is as fine gold, and his locks like black pine-trees."

15. And so, also, in the Gospel our Lord, pointing out that some hairs are seen and known, says: "But even the hairs of your head are all numbered," implying, indeed, acts of spiritual virtues, for God does not take care for our hair. Though, indeed, it is not absurd to believe that literally, seeing that according to His divine Majesty nothing can be hidden from Him.

137

16. But what does it profit me, if God Himself knows all my hairs? That rather abounds and profits me, if the watchful witness of good works reward me with the gift of eternal life. And, in fine, Samson himself, declaring that these hairs are not mystical, says: "If I be shorn my strength will depart from me." So much concerning the mystery, let us now consider the order of the passage.

Chapter I.
The Spirit is the Lord and Power; and in this is not inferior to the Father and the Son.

17. Above, you read that "the Lord blessed him, and the Spirit of the Lord began to go with him." Farther on it is said: "And the Spirit of the Lord came upon him." Again he says: "If I be shaven, my strength will depart from me." After he was shaven, see what the Scripture says: "The Lord," he says, "departed from him."

18. You see, then, that He Who went with him, Himself departed from him. The Same is, then, the Lord, Who is the Spirit of the Lord, that is, he called the Spirit of God, Lord, as also the Apostle says: "The Lord is the Spirit, now where the Spirit of the Lord is, there is liberty." You find, then, the Holy Spirit called the Lord; for the Holy Spirit and the Son are not one Person [*unus*] but one Substance [unum].

19. In this place he used the word Power, and implied the Spirit. For as the Father is Power, so, too, the Son is Power, and the Holy Spirit is Power. Of the Son you have read that Christ is "the Power of God and the Wisdom of God." We read, too, that the Father is Power, as it is written: "Ye shall see the Son of Man sitting at the right hand of the Power of God." He certainly named the Father Power, at Whose right hand the Son sits, as you read: "The Lord said unto My Lord, Sit Thou on My right hand." And the Lord Himself named the Holy Spirit Power, when He said: "Ye shall receive Power when the Holy Spirit cometh upon you."

Chapter II.
The Father, the Son, and the Holy Spirit are One in counsel.

20. For the Spirit Himself is Power, as you read: "The Spirit of Counsel and of Power (or might)." And as the Son is the Angel of great counsel, so, too, is the Holy Spirit the Spirit of Counsel, that you may know that the Counsel of the Father, the Son, and the Holy Spirit is One. Counsel, not concerning any doubtful matters, but concerning those foreknown and determined.

21. But that the Spirit is the Arbiter of the Divine Counsel, you may know even from this. For when above we showed that the Holy Spirit was the Lord of baptism, and read that baptism is the counsel of God, as you read, "But the Pharisees despised the counsel of God, not being baptized of Him," it is quite clear that as there can be no baptism without the Spirit, so, too, the counsel of God is not without the Spirit.

22. And that we may know more completely that the Spirit is Power, we ought to know that He was promised when the Lord said: "I will pour out of ivy Spirit upon all flesh." He, then, Who was promised to us is Himself Power, as in the Gospel the same Son of God declared when He said: "And I will send the promise of the Father upon you, but do you remain in the city until ye be endued with power from on high."

23. And the Evangelist so far shows that the Spirit is Power, that St. Luke relates that He came down with great power, when he says: "And suddenly there was a sound from heaven, as though the Spirit were borne with great power."

24. But, again, that you may not suppose that this is to be referred to bodily things and perceptible to the senses, learn that the Spirit so descended as Christ is to descend, as you find: "They shall see the Son of Man coming in the clouds with great power and majesty."

25. For how should not the power and might be one, when the work. is one, the judgment one, the temple one, the life-giving one, the sanctification one, and the kingdom also of the Father, Son, and Holy Spirit one?

Chapter III.

As to know the Father and the Son is life, so is it life to know the Holy Spirit; and therefore in the Godhead He is not to be separated from the Father.

26. Let them say, then, wherein they think that there is an unlikeness in the divine operation. Since as to know the Father and the Son is life, as the Lord Himself declared, saying: "This is life eternal to know Thee the only true God, and Jesus Christ, Whom Thou hast sent," so, too, to know the Holy Spirit is life. For the Lord said: "If ye love Me, keep My commandments, and I will ask the Father and He shall give you another Paraclete, that He may abide with you for ever, even the Spirit of Truth, Whom the world cannot receive, because it seeth Him not, neither knoweth Him, but ye know Him, for He is with you, and in you."

27. So, then, the world had not eternal life, because it had not received the Spirit; for where the Spirit is, there is eternal life; for the Spirit Himself it is Who effects eternal life. Wherefore I wonder why the Arians stir the question as to the only true God. For as it is eternal life to know the only true God, so, too, is it eternal life to know Jesus Christ; so, again, it is eternal life to know the Holy Spirit, Whom, as also the Father, the world does not see, and, as also the Son, does not know. But he who is not of this world has eternal life, and the Spirit, Who is the Light of eternal life, remains with him for ever.

28. If the knowledge of the only true God confers the same benefit as the knowledge of the Son and of the Spirit, why do you sever the Son and the Spirit from the honour of the true God, when you do not sever Him from conferring the benefit? For of necessity you must either believe that this is the greatest gift of the only true Godhead, and will confess the only true Godhead as of the Father, so also of the Son and of the Holy Spirit; or if you say that he, too, can give life eternal who is not true God, it will happen that you derogate rather from the Father, Whose work you do not consider to be the chief work of the only true Godhead, but one to be compared to the work of a creature.

Chapter IV.

The Holy Spirit gives life, not in a different way from the Father and the Son, nor by a different working.

29. And what wonder is it the Spirit works Life, Who quickens as does the Father and as does the Son? And who can deny that quickening is the work of the Eternal Majesty? For it is written: "Quicken Thy servant." He, then, is quickened who is a servant, that is, man, who before had not life, but received the privilege of having it.

30. Let us then see whether the Spirit is quickened, or Himself quickens. Now it is written: "The letter killeth, but the Spirit giveth life." So, then, the Spirit quickens.

31. But that you may understand that the quickening of the Father, Son, and Holy Spirit is no separate work, read how there is a oneness of quickening also, since God Himself quickens through the Spirit, for Paul said: "He Who raised up Christ from the dead shall also quicken your mortal bodies because of His Spirit Who dwelleth in you."

Chapter V.

The Holy Spirit, as well as the Father and the Son, is pointed out in holy Scripture as Creator, and the same truth was shadowed forth even by heathen writers, but it was shown most plainly in the Mystery of the Incarnation, after touching upon which, the writer maintains his argument from the fact that worship which is due to the Creator alone is paid to the Holy Spirit.

32. But who can doubt that the Holy Spirit gives life to all things; since both He, as the Father and the Son, is the Creator of all things; and the Almighty Father is understood to have done nothing without the Holy Spirit; and since also in the beginning of the creation the Spirit moved upon the water.

33. So when the Spirit was moving upon the water, the creation was without grace; but after this world being created underwent the operation of the Spirit, it gained all the beauty of that grace, wherewith the world is illuminated. And that the grace of the universe cannot abide

without the Holy Spirit the prophet declared when he said "Thou wilt take away Thy Spirit, and they will fail and be turned again into their dust. Send forth Thy Spirit, and they shall be made, and Thou wilt renew all the face of the earth." Not only, then, did he teach that no creature can stand without the Holy Spirit, but also that the Spirit is the Creator of the whole creation.

34. And who can deny that the creation of the earth is the work of the Holy Spirit, Whose work it is that it is renewed? For if they desire to deny that it was created by the Spirit, since they cannot deny that it must be renewed by the Spirit, they who desire to sever the Persons must maintain that the operation of the Holy Spirit is superior to that of the Father and the Son, which is far from the truth; for there is no doubt that the restored earth is better than it was created. Or if at first, without the operation of the Holy Spirit, the Father and the Son made the earth, but the operation of the Holy Spirit was joined on afterwards, it will seem that that which was made required His aid, which was then added. But far be it from any one to think this, namely, that the divine work should be believed to have a change in the Creator, an error brought in by Manicheus.

35. But do we suppose that the substance of the earth exists without the operation of the Holy Spirit, without Whose work not even the expanse of the sky endures? For it is written: "By the Word of the Lord were the heavens established, and all the strength of them by the Spirit of His Mouth." Observe what he says, that all the strength of the heavens is to be referred to the Spirit. For how should He Who was moving before the earth was made, be resting when it was being made?

36. Gentile writers, following ours as it were through shadows, because they could not imbibe the truth of the Spirit, have pointed out in their verses that the Spirit within nourishes heaven and earth, and the glittering orbs of moon and stars. So they deny not that the strength of creatures exists through the Spirit, are we who read this to deny it? But you think that they refer to a Spirit produced of the air. If they declared a Spirit of the air to be the Author of all things, do we doubt that the Spirit of God is the Creator of all things?

37. But why do I delay with matters not to the purpose? Let them accept a plain proof that there can be nothing which the Holy Spirit can be said not to have made; and that it cannot be doubted that all subsists through His operation, whether Angels, Archangels, Thrones, or Dominions; since the Lord Himself, Whom the Angels serve, was begotten by the Holy Spirit coming upon the Virgin, as, according to Matthew, the Angel said to Joseph: "Joseph, thou son of David, fear not to take Mary thy wife, for that which shall be born of her is of the Holy Spirit." And according to Luke, he said to Mary: "The Holy Spirit shall come upon thee."

38. The birth from the Virgin was, then, the work of the Spirit. The fruit of the womb is the work of the Spirit, according to that which is written: "Blessed art thou among women, and blessed is the Fruit of thy womb." The flower from the root is the work of the Spirit, that flower, I say, of which it was well prophesied: "A rod shall go forth from the root of Jesse, and a flower shall rise from his root." The root of Jesse the patriarch is the family of the Jews, Mary is the rod, Christ the flower of Mary, Who, about to spread the good odour of faith throughout the whole world, budded forth from a virgin womb, as He Himself said: "I am the flower of the plain, a lily of the valley."

39. The flower, when cut, keeps its odour, and when bruised increases it, nor if torn off does it lose it; so, too, the Lord Jesus, on the gibbet of the cross, neither failed when bruised, nor fainted when torn; and when He was cut by that piercing of the spear, being made more beautiful by the cob our of the outpoured Blood, He, as it were, grew comely again, not able in Himself to die, and breathing forth upon the dead the gift of eternal life. On this flower, then, of the royal rod the Holy Spirit rested.

40. A good rod, as some think, is the Flesh of the Lord, which, raising itself from its earthly root to heaven, bore around the whole world the sweet-smelling fruits of religion, the mysteries of the divine generation, pouring grace on the altars of heaven.

41. So, then, we cannot doubt that the Spirit is Creator, Whom we know as the Author of the Lord's Incarnation. For who can doubt when you find in the commencement of the Gospel that the generation of Jesus Christ was on this wise: "When Mary was espoused to Joseph, before they came together she was found with child of [ex] the Holy Spirit."

42. For although most authorities read "de Spiritu," yet the Greek from which the Latins translated have "ec pneumato" agiou," that is, "ex Spiritu Sancto." For that which is "of" [ex] any one is either of his substance or of his power. Of his substance, as the Son, Who says: "I came forth of the Mouth of the Most High;" as the Spirit, "Who proceedeth from the Father;" of Whom the Son says: "He shall glorify Me, for He shall receive of Mine." But of the power, as in the passage: "One God the Father, of Whom are all things."

43. How, then, was Mary with child of the Holy Spirit? If as of her substance, was the Spirit, then, changed into flesh and bones? Certainly not. But if the Virgin conceived as of His operation and power, who can deny that the Holy Spirit is Creator?

44. How is it, too, that Job plainly set forth the Spirit as his Creator, saying: "The Spirit of God hath made me"? In one short verse he showed Him to be both Divine and Creator. If, then, the Spirit is Creator, He is certainly not a creature, for the Apostle has separated the Creator and the creature, saying: "They served the creature rather than the Creator."

45. He teaches that the Creator is to be served by condemning those who serve the creature, whereas we owe our service to the Creator. And since he knew the Spirit to be the Creator, he teaches that we ought to serve Him, saying: "Beware of the dogs, beware of the evil workers, beware of the concision, for we are the circumcision who serve the Spirit of God."

46. But if any one disputes because of the variations of the Latin codices, some of which heretics have falsified, let him look at the Greek codices, and observe that it is there written: "oi pneumati Qeou latreuonte"," which is, being translated, "who serve the Spirit of God."

47. So, then, when the same Apostle says that we ought to serve the Spirit, who asserts that we must not serve the creature, but the Creator; without doubt he plainly shows that the Holy Spirit is Creator, and is to be venerated with the honour due to the eternal Godhead; for it is written: "Thou shalt worship the Lord thy God, and Him only shalt thou serve."

Chapter VI.

To those who object that according to the words of Amos the Spirit is created, the answer is made that the word is there understood of the wind, which is often created, which cannot be said of the Holy Spirit, since He is eternal, and cannot be dissolved in death, or by an heretical absorption into the Father. But if they pertinaciously contend that this passage was written of the Holy Spirit, St. Ambrose points out that recourse must be had to a spiritual Interpretation, for Christ by His coming established the thunder, that is, the force of the divine utterances, and by Spirit is signified the human soul as also the flesh assumed by Christ. And since this was created by each Person of the Trinity, it is thence argued that the Spirit, Who has before been affirmed to be the Creator of all things, was the Author of the Incarnation of the Lord.

48. Nor does it escape my notice that heretics have been wont to object that the Holy Spirit appears to be a creature, because many of them use as an argument for establishing their impiety that passage of Amos, where he spoke of the blowing of the wind, as the words of the prophet made clear. For you read thus: "Behold, I am He that establish the thunders, and create the wind [spirit], and declare unto man his Christ, that make light and mist, and ascend upon high places, the Lord God Almighty is His Name."

49. If they make an argument of this, hat he said "spirit" was created, Esdras aught us that spirit is created, saying in the fourth book: "And upon the second day Thou madest the spirit of the firmament," yet, that we may keep to our point, is it not evident that in what Amos said the order of he passage shows that the prophet was speaking of the creation of this world?

50. He begins as follows: "I am the Lord that establish the thunders and create he wind [spirit]." The order of the words itself teaches us; for if he had wished to speak of the Holy Spirit, he would certainly not have put the thunders in the first place. For thunder is not more

ancient than the Holy Spirit; though they be ungodly, they still dare not say that. And then when we, see what follows concerning light and mist, is it not plain that what is said is to be understood of the creation of this world? For we know by every-day experience, that when we have storms on this earth, thunders come first, blasts of wind follow on, the sky grows black with mists, and light shines again out of the darkness. For the blasts of wind are also called "spirits," as it is written: "Fire and brimstone and the spirit of storm."

51. And that you might know that he called this "spirit," he says: "establishing thunders and creating the wind [spirit]." For these are often created, when they take place. But the Holy Spirit is eternal, and if any one dares to call Him a creature, still he cannot say that He is daily created like the blast of the wind. Then, again, Wisdom herself, speaking after the mystery of the assumed Body, says: "The Lord created Me." Although prophesying of things to come, yet, because the coming of the Lord was predestined, it is not said "creates" but "created Me;" that men might believe that the Body of Jesus was begotten of the Virgin Mary, not often, but once only.

52. And so, as to that which the prophet declared as it were of the daily working of God in the thunder and the creation of the wind, it would be impious to understand any such thing of the Holy Spirit, Whom the ungodly themselves cannot deny to exist from before the world. Whence with pious asseveration we testify that He always exists, and abides ever. For neither can He Who before the world was moving upon the waters begin to be visible after the world's creation; or else it would be allowable to suppose that there are many Holy Spirits, Who come into being by as it were a daily production. Far be it from any one to pollute himself with such impiety as to say that the Holy Spirit is frequently or ever created. For I do not understand why He should be frequently created; unless perchance they believe that He dies frequently and so is frequently created. But how can the Spirit of life die? If, then, He cannot die, there is no reason why He should be often created.

53. But they who think otherwise fall into this sacrilege, that they do not distinguish the Holy Spirit; who think that the Word Which was sent forth returns to the Father, and the Spirit Which was sent forth is reabsorbed into God, so that there should be a reabsorption and a kind of alternation of one changing himself into various forms; whereas the distinction between the Father, Son, and Holy Spirit always abiding and unchangeable, preserves the Unity of its power.

54. But if any one thinks that the word of the prophet is to be explained with reference to the Holy Spirit, because it is said, "declaring unto men His Christ," he will explain it more easily of the Lord's Incarnation. For if it troubles you that he said Spirit, and therefore you think that this cannot well be explained of the mystery of the taking of human nature, read on in the Scriptures and you will find that all agrees most excellently with Christ, of Whom it is thoroughly fitting to think that He established the thunders by His coming, that is, the force and sound of the heavenly Scriptures, by the thunder, as it were, of which our minds are struck with astonishment, so that we learn to be afraid, and pay respect to the heavenly oracles.

55. Lastly, in the Gospel the brothers of the Lord were called Sons of Thunder; and when the voice was uttered of the Father, saying, "I have both glorified it and will glorify it again," the Jews said that it thundered on Him. For although they could not receive the grace of the truth, yet they confessed unwillingly, and in their ignorance were speaking mysteries, so that there resulted a great testimony of the Father to the Son. And in the Book of Job, too, the Scripture says: "And who knows when He will make the power of His thunder?" Certainly if these words pertained to the thunders of the heavens, he would have said that their force was already made, not about to be made.

56. Therefore he referred the thunders to the words of the Lord, the sound of which went out into all the earth, and we understand the word "spirit" in this place of the soul, which He took endowed with reason and perfect; for Scripture often designates the soul of man by the word spirit, as you read: "Who creates the spirit of man within him." So, too, the Lord signified His Soul by the word Spirit, when He said: "Into Thy hands I commend My Spirit."

57. And that you might know that he spoke of the coming down of Jesus, he added that He declared His Christ to men for in His baptism He declared Him, saying: "Thou art My beloved Son, in Whom I am well pleased." He declared Him on the mount, saying: "This is My beloved Son, hear ye Him." He declared Him in His Passion, when the sun hid itself, and sea and earth trembled. He declared Him in the Centurion, who said: "Truly this was the Son of God."

58. We ought, then, to take this whole passage either to be simply to be understood of that state in which we here live and breathe, or of the mystery of the Lord's Body; for if here it had been stated that the Holy Spirit was created, undoubtedly Scripture would elsewhere have declared the same, as we often read of the Son of God, Who according to the flesh was both made and created.

59. But it is fitting that we should consider His Majesty in the very fact of His taking flesh for us, that we may see His divine power in the very taking of the Body. For as we read that the Father created the mystery of the Lord's Incarnation, the Spirit too created it; and so too we read that Christ Himself created His own Body. For the Father created it, as it is written: "The Lord created Me," and in another place, "God sent His Son, made of a woman, made under the law." And the Spirit created the whole mystery, according to that which we read, for "Mary was found with child of the Holy Spirit."

60. You find, then, that the Father created and the Spirit created; learn, too, that the Son of God also created, when Solomon says: "Wisdom hath made herself a house." How, then, can the Holy Spirit Who created the mystery of the Lord's Incarnation, which is above all created things, be Himself a creature?

61. As we have shown above generally that the Holy Spirit is our Creator according to the flesh in the outer man, let us now show that He is our Creator also according to the mystery of grace. And as the Father creates, so too does the Son create, and so too the Holy Spirit creates, as we read in the words of Paul: "For it is the gift of God, not of works, test any one should boast. For we are His workmanship created in Christ Jesus in good works."

Chapter VII.

The Holy Spirit is no less the author of spiritual creation or regeneration than the Father and the Son. The excellence of that creation, and wherein it consists. How we are to understand holy Scripture, when it attributes a body or members to God.

62. So, then, the Father creates in good works, and the Son also, for it is written: "But as many as received Him, to them gave He power to become the sons of God, even to them who believe on His Name; who were born not of blood, nor of the will of the flesh, nor of the will of man, but of God."

63. In like manner the Lord Himself also testifies that we are born again of the Spirit according to grace, saying: "That which is born of the flesh is flesh, because it is born of flesh; and that which is born of the Spirit is spirit, because God is Spirit. Marvel not that I said unto you, Ye must be born again. The Spirit breatheth where He willeth, and thou hearest His voice, but knowest not whence He cometh or whither He goeth, so is every one who is born of the Spirit."

64. It is then clear that the Holy Spirit is also the Author of the grace of the Spirit, since we are created according to God, that we may be made the sons of God. So when He has taken us into His kingdom by the adoption of holy regeneration, do we deny Him that which is His? He has made us heirs of the new birth from above, do we claim the heritage and reject its Author? But the benefit cannot remain when its Author is shut out; the Author is not without the gift, nor the gift without the Author. If you claim the grace, believe the power; if you reject the power, do not ask for the grace. He who has denied the Spirit has at the same time denied the gift. For if the Author be of no account how can His gifts be precious? Why do we grudge the gifts we ourselves receive, diminish our hopes, repudiate our dignity, and deny our Comforter?

65. But we cannot deny Him. Far be it from us to deny that which is so great, since the Apostle says: "But ye brethren, like Isaac, are the children of promise, but as then, he that is born after the flesh persecutes him that is after the Spirit." Again certainly is understood from what has gone before, is born after the Spirit. He then who is born after the Spirit is born after God. Now we are born again when we are renewed in our inward affections and lay aside the oldness or the outer man. And so the Apostle says again: "But be ye renewed in the spirit of your mind, and put on the new man which is created according to God in truth and righteousness and holiness." Let them hear how the Scripture has signified the unity of the divine operation. He who is renewed in the spirit of his mind has put on the new man, which is created according to God.

66. That more excellent regeneration is then the work of the Holy Spirit; and the Spirit is the Author of that new man which is created after the image of God, which no one will doubt to be better than this outer man of ours. Since the Apostle has pointed out that the one is heavenly, the other earthly, when he says: "As is the heavenly, such also are the heavenly."

67. Since, then, the grace of the Spirit makes that to be heavenly which it can create earthy, we ought to observe by reason though we be without instances. For in a certain place holy Job says: "As the Lord liveth, Who thus judgeth me, and the Almighty, Who hath brought my soul to bitterness (for the Spirit of God which is in my nostrils)." He certainly did not here signify by His Spirit the vital breath and bodily breathing passages, but signifies the nostrils of the inner man within him, wherewith he gathered in the fragrance of eternal life, and drew in the grace of the heavenly ointment as with a kind of twofold sense.

68. For there are spiritual nostrils, as we read, which the spouse of the Word has, to whom it is said: "And the smell of thy nostrils;" and in another place: "The Lord smelled a smell of sweetness." There are, then, as it were, inward members of a man, whose hands are considered to be in action, his ears in hearing, his feet in a kind of progress in a good work. And so from what is done we gather as it were figures of the members, for it is not suitable for us to imagine anything in the inner man after a fleshly manner.

69. And there are some who suppose that God is fashioned after a bodily manner, when they read of His hand or finger, and they do not observe that these things are written not because of any fashion of a body, since in the Godhead are neither members nor parts, but are expressions of the oneness of the Godhead, that we may believe that it is impossible for either the Son or the Holy Spirit to be separated from God the Father; since the fulness of the Godhead dwells as it were bodily in the substance of the Trinity. For this reason, then, is the Son also called the Right Hand of the Father, as we read: "The Right Hand of the Lord hath done mighty things, the Right Hand of the Lord hath exalted me."

Chapter VIII.

St. Ambrose examines and refutes the heretical argument that because God is said to be glorified in the Spirit, and not with the Spirit, the Holy Spirit is therefore inferior to the Father. He shows that the particle in can be also used of the Son and even of the Father, and that on the other hand with may be said of creatures without any infringement on the prerogatives of the Godhead; and that in reality these prepositions simply imply the connection of the Three Divine Persons.

70. But what wonder is it if foolish men question about words, when they do so even about syllables? For some think that a distinction should be made and that God should be praised *in* the Spirit, but not *with* the Spirit, and consider that the greatness of the Godhead is to be estimated from one syllable or some custom, arguing that if they consider that God should be glorified *in* the Spirit, they point to some office of the Holy Spirit, but that if they say that God receives glory or power *with* the Spirit, they seem to imply some association and communion of the Father, the Son, and the Holy Spirit. 71. But who can separate what is in- capable of separation? who can divide that association which Christ shows to be inseparable? "Go," says He, "baptize all nations in the Name of the Father and of the Son and of the Holy Spirit." Has

He changed either a word or a syllable here concerning the Father or the Son or the Holy Spirit? Certainly not. But He says, in the Name of the Father and of the Son and of the Holy Spirit. The expression is the same for the Spirit as for the Father and for Himself. From which is inferred not any office of the Holy Spirit, but rather a sharing of honour or of working when we say "in the Spirit."

72. Consider, too, that this opinion of yours tends to the injury of the Father and the Son, for the latter did not say, "with the Name of the Father and of the Son, and of the Holy Spirit," but in the Name, and yet not any office but the power of the Trinity is expressed in this syllable,

73. Lastly, that you may know that it is not a syllable which prejudices faith, but faith which commends a syllable, Paul also speaks in Christ. Christ is not less, because Paul spoke in Christ, as you find: "We speak before God in Christ." As, then, the Apostle says that we speak in Christ, so, too, is that which we speak in the Spirit; as the Apostle himself said: "No man saith Lord Jesus, except in the Holy Spirit." So, then, in this place not any subjection of the Holy Spirit, but a connection of grace is signified.

74. And that you may know that distinction does not depend upon a syllable, he says also in another place: "And these indeed were you, but ye are washed, but ye are sanctified, but ye are justified in the Name of the Lord Jesus Christ, and in the Spirit of our God." How many instances of this I can bring forward. For it is written: "Ye are all one in Christ Jesus," and elsewhere: "To those sanctified in Christ Jesus," and again: "That we might be the righteousness of God in Him," and in another place: "Should fall from the chastity which is in Christ Jesus."

75. But what am I doing? For while I say that like things are written of the Son as of the Spirit, I am rather leading on to this, not that because it is written of the Son, therefore it would appear to be reverently written of the Holy Spirit, but that because the same is written of the Spirit, therefore men allege that the Son's honour is lessened because of the Spirit. For say they, Is it written of God the Father?

76. But let them learn that it is also said of God the Father: "In the Lord I will praise the word;" and elsewhere: "In God we will do mighty deeds;" and "My remembrance shall be ever in Thee;" and "In Thy Name will we rejoice;" and again in another place: "That his deeds may be manifested, that they are wrought in God;" and Paul: "In God Who created all things;" and again: "Paul and Silvanus and Timotheus to the Church of the Thessalonians in God the Father and the Lord Jesus Christ;" and in the Gospel: "I in the Father and the Father in Me," and "the Father that dwelleth in Me." It is also written: "He that glorieth let him glory in the Lord;" and in another place: "Our life is hid with Christ in God." Did he here ascribe more to the Son than to the Father in saying that we are with Christ in God? or does our state avail more than the grace of the Spirit, so that we can be with Christ and the Holy Spirit cannot? And when Christ wills to be with us, as He Himself said: "Father, I will that they whom Thou hast given Me be with Me where I am," would He disdain to be with the Spirit? For it is written: "Ye coming together and my spirit with the power of the Lord Jesus." Do we then come together in the power of the Lord, and dare to say that the Lord Jesus would not be willing to come together with the Spirit Who does not disdain to come together with us?

77. So the Apostle thinks that it makes no difference which particle you use. For each is a conjunctive particle, and conjunction does not cause separation, for if it divided it would not be called a conjunction.

78. What, then, moves you to say that to God the Father or to His Christ there is glory, life, greatness, or power, *in* the Holy Spirit, and to refuse to say *with* the Holy Spirit? Is it that you are afraid of seeming to join the Spirit with the Father and the Son? But hear what is written of the Spirit: "For the law of the Spirit is life in Christ Jesus." And in another place God the Father says: "They shall worship Thee, and in Thee they shall make supplication." God the Father says that we ought to pray in Christ; and do you think that it is any derogation to the Spirit if the glory of Christ is said to be in Him?

79. Hear that what you are afraid to acknowledge of the Spirit, the Apostle did not fear to claim for himself; for he says: "To be dissolved and to be with Christ is much better." Do you deny that the Spirit, through Whom the Apostle was made worthy of being with Christ, is with Christ?

80. What, then, is the reason that you prefer saying that God or Christ is glorified in the Spirit rather than with the Spirit? Is it because if you say in the Spirit, the Spirit is declared to be less than Christ? Although your making the Lord greater or less is a matter which can be refuted, yet since we read, "For Christ was made sin for us, that we might be the righteousness of God in Him," He is found chiefest in Whom we are found most low. So, too, elsewhere you read, "For in Him all things consist," that is, in His power. And the things which consist in Him cannot be compared to Him, because they receive from His power the substance whereby they consist.

81. Do you then understand that God so reigns in the Spirit that the power of the Spirit, as a kind of source of substance, imparts to God the origin of His rule? But this is impious. And so our predecessors spoke of the unity of power of the Father, the Son, and the Holy Spirit, when they said that the glory of Christ was with the Spirit, that they might declare their inseparable connection.

82. For how is the Holy Spirit separated from the Son, since "the Spirit Himself beareth witness with our spirit that we are sons of God, and if sons, also heirs, heirs, indeed, of God and joint-heirs with Christ." Who, then, is so foolish as to wish to dissever the eternal conjunction of the Spirit and Christ, when the Spirit by Whom we are made joint-heirs with Christ conjoins even what is severed.

83. "If so be," he says, "we suffer with Him, that we may be also glorified together." If we then shall be glorified together with Christ through the Spirit, how do we refuse to admit that the Spirit Himself is glorified together with Christ? Do we dissociate the life of Christ and of the Holy Spirit when the Spirit says that we shall live together with the Son of God? For the Apostle says: "If we be dead with Christ we believe that we shall also live with Him;" and then again: "For if we suffer with Him we shall also live with Him, and not only shall we live with Him, but shall be also glorified with Him, and not only be glorified but shall also reign with Him."

84. No division, then, is implied in those particles, for each is a particle of conjunction. And lastly, we often find in holy Scripture the one inserted and the other understood, as it is written: "I will enter into Thy house in whole burnt-offerings," that is, "with whole burnt-offerings;" and in another place: "He brought them forth in silver and gold," that is, "with silver and gold." And elsewhere the Psalmist says: "Wilt Thou not go forth with us in our hosts?" for that which is really meant, "with our hosts." So, then, in the use of the expression no lessening of honour can be implied, and nothing ought to be deduced derogatory to the honour of the Godhead, it is necessary that with the heart man should believe unto righteousness, and that out of the faith of the heart confession should be made in the mouth unto salvation. But they who believe not with the heart spread what is derogatory with their mouth.

Chapter IX.

A passage of St. Paul abused by heretics, to prove a distinction between the Divine Persons, is explained, and it is proved that the whole passage can be rightly said of each Person, though it refers specially to the Son. It is then proved that each member of the passage is applicable to each Person, and as to say, of Him are all things is applicable to the Father, so may all things are through Him and in Him also be said of Him.

85. Another similar passage is that which they say implies difference, where it is written: "But to us there is one Father, of Whom are all things and we unto Him, and one Lord Jesus Christ, through Whom are all things, and we through Him." For they pretend that when it is said "of Him," the matter is signified, when "through Him," either the instrument of the work or some office, but when it is said "in Him," either the place or the time in which all things that are made are seen.

86. So, then, their desire is to prove that there is some difference of substance, being anxious to make a distinction between as it were the instrument, and the proper worker or author, and also between time or place and the instrument. But is the Son, then, alien as regards His Nature from the Father, because an instrument is alien from the worker or author? or is the Son alien from the Spirit, because either time or place is not of the same class as an instrument?

87. Compare now our assertions. They will have it that matter is of God as though of the nature of God, as when you say that a chest is made of wood or a statue of stone; that after this fashion matter has come forth from God, and that the same matter has been made by the Son as if by some sort of instrument; so that they declare that the Son is not so much the Artificer as the instrument of the work; and that all things have been made in the Spirit, as if in some place or time; they attribute each part severally to each Person severally and deny that all are in common.

88. But we show that all things are so of God the Father, that God the Father has suffered no loss because all things are either through Him or in Him, and yet all things are not of Him as if of matter; then, too, that all things are through the Lord the Son, so that He is not deprived of the attribute that all things are of the Son and in Him; and that all things are in the Spirit, so that we may teach that all things are through the Spirit, and all things from the Spirit.

89. For these particles, like those of which we have spoken before, imply each other. For the Apostle did not so say, All things are of God, and all things are through the Son, as to signify that the substance of the Father and the Son could be severed, but that he might teach that by a distinction without confusion the Father is one, the Son another. Those particles, then, are not as it were in opposition to each other, but are as it were allied and agreed, so as often to suit even one Person, as it is written: "For of Him, and through Him, and in Him are all things."

90. But if you really consider whence the passage is taken you will have no doubt that it is said of the Son. For the Apostle says, according to the prophecy of Isaiah, "Who hath known the mind of the Lord, or who hath been His counsellor?" And he adds: "For of Him and in Him are all things." Which Isaiah had said of the Artificer of all, as you read: "Who hath measured out the water with his hand, and the heaven with a span, and all the earth with his closed hand? Who hath placed the mountains in scales and the hills in a balance? Who hath known the mind of the Lord, or who hath been His counsellor?"

91. And the Apostle added: "For of Him, and through Him, and in Him are all things." What is "of Him"? That the nature of everything is of His will, and He is the Author of all things which have come into being. "Through Him" means what? That the establishment and continuance of all things is His girl. What is "in Him"? That all things by a wonderful kind of longing and unspeakable love look upon the Author of their life, and the Giver of their graces and functions, according to that which is written: "The eyes of all look unto Thee," and "Thou openest Thine hand and fillest every living creature with Thy good pleasure."

92. And of the Father, too, you may rightly say "of Him," for of Him was the operative Wisdom, Which of His own and the Father's will gave being to all things which were not. "Through Him," because all things were made through His Wisdom. "In Him," because He is the Fount of substantial Life, in Whom we live and move and have our being.

93. Of the Spirit also, as being formed by Him, strengthened by Him, established in Him, we receive the gift of eternal life.

94. Since, then, these expressions seem suitable either to the Father or the Son or the Holy Spirit, it is certain that nothing derogatory is spoken of in them, since we both say that many things are of the Son, and many through the Father, as you find it said of the Son: "That we may be increased through all things in Him, Who is Christ the Head, from Whom," says he, "the whole body, flamed and knit together through every joint of the supply for the measure of every part, maketh increase of the body unto the building up of itself in love." And again, writing to the Colossians of those who have not the knowledge of the Son of God, he says: "Because they hold not the Head, from Whom all the body being supplied and joined together through joints

and bands, increaseth to the increase of God." For we said above that Christ is the Head of the Church. And in another place you read: "Of His fulness have all we received." And the Lord Himself said: "He shall take of Mine and show it unto you." And before, He said: "I perceive that virtue is gone out of Me."

95. In like manner that you may recognize the Unity, it is also said of the Spirit: "For he that soweth in the Spirit shall of the Spirit reap eternal life." And John says: "Hereby we know that He is in us because He hath given us of His Spirit." And the Angel says: "That Which shall be born of her is of the Holy Spirit." And the Lord says: "That which is born of the Spirit is Spirit."

96. So, then, as we read that all things are of the Father, so, too, that all things can be said to be of the Son, through Whom are all things; and we are taught by proof that all things are of the Spirit in Whom are all things.

97. Now let us consider whether we can teach that anything is through the Father. But it is written: "Paul the servant of Christ through the will of God;" and elsewhere: "Wherefore thou art now not a servant but a son, and if a son an heir also through God;" and again: "As Christ rose from the dead by the glory of God." And elsewhere God the Father says to the Son: "Behold proselytes shall come to Thee through Me."

98. You will find many other passages, if you look for things done through the Father. Is, then, the Father less because we read that many things are in the Son and of the Son, and find in the heavenly Scriptures very many things done or given through the Father?

99. But in like manner we also read of many things done through the Spirit, as you find: "But God hath revealed them to us through His Spirit;" and in another place: "Keep the good deposit through the Holy Spirit;" and to the Ephesians: "to be strengthened through His Spirit;" and to the Corinthians: "To another is given through the Spirit the word of wisdom;" and in another place: "But if through the Spirit ye mortify the deeds of the flesh, ye shall live;" and above: "He Who raised Christ from the dead shall also quicken your mortal bodies through the indwelling of His Spirit in you."

100. But perhaps some one may say, Show me that we can read expressly that all things are of the Son, or that all things are of the Spirit. But I reply, Let them also show that it is written that all things are through the Father. But since we have proved that these expressions suit either the Father or the Son or the Holy Spirit, and that no distinction of the divine power can arise from particles of this kind, there is no doubt but that all things are of Him through Whom all things are; and that all things are through Him through Whom all are; and that we must understand that all things are through Him or of Him in Whom all are. For every creature exists both of the will. and through the operation and in the power of the Trinity, as it is written: "Let Us make man after Our image and likeness;" and elsewhere: "By the word of the Lord were the heavens established, and all their power by the Spirit of His mouth."

Chapter X.

Being about to prove that the will, the calling, and the commandment of the Trinity is one, St. Ambrose shows that the Spirit called the Church exactly as the Father and the Son did, and proves this by the selection of SS. Paul and Barnabas, and especially by the mission of St. Peter to Cornelius. And by the way he points out how in the Apostle's vision the calling of the Gentiles was shadowed forth, who having been before like wild beasts, now by the operation of the Spirit lay aside that wildness. Then having quoted other passages in support of this view, he shows that in the case of Jeremiah cast into a pit by Jews, and rescued by Abdemelech, is a type of the slighting of the Holy Spirit by the Jews, and of His being honoured by the Gentiles.

101. And not only is the operation of the Father, Son, and Holy Spirit everywhere one but also there is one and the same will, calling, and giving of commands, which one may see in the great and saving mystery of the Church. For as the Father called the Gentiles to the Church, saying: "I will call her My people which was not My people, and her beloved who was not beloved;" and elsewhere: "My house shall be called a house of prayer for all nations," so, too, the Lord Jesus said that Paul was chosen by Him to call forth and gather together the Church, as

148

you find it said by the Lord Jesus to Ananias: "Go, for he is a chosen vessel unto Me to bear My name before all nations."

102. As, then, God the Father called the Church, so, too, Christ called it, and so, too, the Spirit called it, saying: "Separate Me Paul and Barnabas for the work to which I have called them." "So," it is added, "having fasted and prayed, they laid hands on them and sent them forth. And they, being sent forth by the Holy Spirit, went down to Seleucia." So Paul received the apostleship by the will not only of Christ, but also of the Holy Spirit, and hastened to gather together the Gentiles.

103. And not only Paul, but also, as we read in the Acts of the Apostles, Peter. For when he had seen in his prayer heaven opened and a certain vessel tied at the four corners, as it were a sheet in which were all kinds of four-footed beasts and wild beasts and fowls of the air, "a voice came to him saying, Arise, Peter, kill and eat. And Peter said, Be it far from me, Lord, I have never eaten anything common or unclean. And again a voice came to him, saying, What God hath cleansed call not thou common. And this was done three times, and the vessel was received back into heaven." And so when Peter was silently thinking over this with himself, and the servants of Cornelius appointed by the Angel had come to him, the Spirit said to him, "Lo, men are seeking thee, rise therefore, and go down and go with them; doubt not, for I have sent thee."

104. How clearly did the Holy Spirit express His own power ! First of all in that He inspired him who was praying, and was present to him who was entreating; then when Peter, being called, answered"Lord," and so was found worthy of a second message, because he acknowledged the Lord. But the Scripture declares Who that Lord was, for He Whom he had answered spoke to him when he answered. And the following words show the Spirit clearly revealed, for He Who formed the mystery made known the mystery.

105. Notice, also, that the appearance of the mystery three times repeated expressed the operation of the Trinity. And so in the mysteries the threefold question is put, and the threefold answer made, and no one can be cleansed but by a threefold confession. For which reason, also, Peter in the Gospel is asked three times whether he loves the Lord, that by the threefold answer the bonds of the guilt he had contracted by denying the Lord might be loosed.

106. Then, again, because the Angel is sent to Cornelius, the Holy Spirit speaks to Peter: "For the eyes of the Lord are over the faithful of the earth." Nor is it without a purpose that when He had said before, "What God hath cleansed call not thou common," the Holy Spirit came upon the Gentiles to purify them, when it is manifest that the operation of the Spirit is a divine operation. But Peter, when sent by the Spirit, did not wait for the command of God the Father, but acknowledged that that message was from the Spirit Himself, and the grace that of the Spirit Himself, when he said: "If, then, God has granted them the same grace as to us, who was I that I should resist God?"

107. It is, then, the Holy Spirit Who has delivered us from that Gentile impurity. For in those kinds of four-fooled creatures and wild beasts and birds there was a figure of the condition of man, which appears clothed with the bestial ferocity of wild beasts unless it grows gentle by the sanctification of the Spirit. Excellent, then, is that grace which changes the rage of beasts into the simplicity of the Spirit: "For we also were aforetime foolish, unbelieving, erring, serving divers lusts and pleasures. But now by the renewing of the Spirit we begin to be heirs of Christ, and joint-heirs with the Angels."

108. Therefore the holy prophet David, seeing in the Spirit that we should from wild beasts become like the dwellers in heaven, says, "Rebuke the wild beasts of the wood," evidently signifying, not the wood disturbed by the running of wild beasts, and shaken with the roaring of animals, but that wood of which it is written: "We found it in the fields of the wood." In which, as the prophet said: "The righteous shall flourish as the palm-tree, and shall be multipled as the cedar which is in Libanus." That wood which, shaken in the tops of the trees spoken of in prophecy, shed forth the nourishment of the heavenly Word. That wood into which Paul

entered indeed as a ravening wolf, but went forth as a shepherd, for "their sound is gone out into all the earth."

109. We then were wild beasts, and therefore the Lord said: "Beware of false prophets, which come in sheep's clothing, but inwardly are ravening wolves." But now, through the Holy Spirit, the rage of lions, the spots of leopards, the craft of foxes, the rapacity of wolves, have passed away from our feelings; great, then, is the grace which has changed earth to heaven, that the conversation of us, who once were wandering as wild beasts in the woods, might be in heaven.

110. And not only in this place, but also elsewhere in the same book, the Apostle Peter declared that the Church was built by the Holy Spirit. For you read that he said: "God, Which knoweth the hearts of men, bare witness, giving them the Holy Spirit, even as also to us; and He made no distinction between us and them, purifying their hearts by faith." In which is to be considered, that as Christ is the Cornerstone, Who joined together both peoples into one, so, too, the Holy Spirit made no distinction between the hearts of each people, but united them.

111. Do not, then, like a Jew, despise the Son, Whom the prophets foretold; for you would despise also the Holy Spirit, you would despise Isaiah, you would despise Jeremiah, whom he who was chosen of the Lord raised with rags and cords from the pit of that Jewish abode. For the people of the Jews, despising the word of prophecy, had cast him into the pit. Nor was there found any one of the Jews to draw the prophet out, but one Ethiopian Abdemelech, as the Scripture testifies.

112. In which account is a very beautiful figure, that is to say, that we, sinners of the Gentiles, black beforehand through our transgressions, and aforetime fruitless, raised from the depth the word of prophecy which the Jews had thrust down, as it were, into the mire of their mind and carnality. And therefore it is written: "Ethiopia shall stretch out her hand unto God." In which is signified the appearance of holy Church, who says in the Song of Songs: "I am black and comely, O daughters of Jerusalem;" black through sin, comely through grace; black by natural condition, comely through redemption, or certainly, black with the dust of her labours. So she is black while fighting, is comely when she is crowned with the ornaments of victory.

113. And fittingly is the prophet raised by cords, for the faithful writer said: "The lines are fallen unto me in pleasant places." And fittingly with rags; for the Lord Himself, when those who had been first invited to the marriage made excuse, sent to the partings of the highways, that as many as were found, both bad and good, should be invited to the marriage. With these rags, then, He lifted the word of prophecy from the mire.

Chapter XI.

We shall follow the example of Abdemelech, if we believe that the Son and Holy Spirit know all things. This knowledge is attributed in Scripture to the Spirit, and also to the Son. The Son is glorified by the Spirit, as also the Spirit by the Son. Also, inasmuch as we read that the Father, the Son, and the Spirit say and reveal the same things, we must acknowledge in Them a oneness of nature and knowledge. Lastly, that the Spirit searcheth the deep things of God is not a mark of ignorance, since the Father and the Son are likewise said to search, and Paul, although chosen by Christ, yet was taught by the Spirit.

114. And you, too, shall be Abdemelech, that is, chosen by the Lord, if you raise the Word of God from the depth of Gentile ignorance; if you believe that the Son of God is not deceived, that nothing escapes His knowledge, that He is not ignorant of what is going to be. And the Holy Spirit also is not deceived, of Whom the Lord says: "But when He, the Spirit of Truth, shall come, He shall lead you into all truth." He Who says all passes by nothing, neither the day nor the hour, neither things past nor things to come.

115. And that you may know that He both knows all things, and foretells things to come, and that His knowledge is one with that of the Father and the Son, hear what the Truth of God says concerning Him: "For He shall not speak from Himself, but what things He shall hear shall He speak, and He shall declare unto you the things that are to come."

116. Therefore, that you may observe that He knows all things, when the Son said: "But of that day and hour knoweth no one, not even the Angels of heaven," He excepted the Holy Spirit. But if the Holy Spirit is excepted from ignorance, how is the Son of God not excepted?

117. But you say that He numbered the Son of God also with the Angels. He numbered the Son indeed, but He did not number the Spirit also. Confess, then, either that the Holy Spirit is greater than the Son of God, so as to speak now not only as an Arian, but even as a Photinian, or acknowledge to what you ought to refer it that He said that the Son knew not. For as man He could [in His human nature] be numbered with creatures Who were created.

118. But if you are willing to learn that the Son of God knows all things, and has foreknowledge of all, see that those very things which you think to be unknown to the Son, the Holy Spirit received from the Son. He received them, however, through Unity of Substance, as the Son received from the Father. "He," says He, "shall glorify Me, for He shall receive of Mine and shall declare it unto you. All things whatsoever the Father hath are Mine, therefore said I, He shall receive of Mine, and shall declare it unto you." What, then, is more clear than this Unity? What things the Father hath pertain to the Son; what things the Son hath the Holy Spirit also has received.

119. Yet learn that the Son knows the day of judgment. We read in Zechariah: "And the Lord my God shall come, and all the saints with Him. In that day there shall not be light, but cold and frost, and it shall be one day, and that day is known unto the Lord." This day, then, was known unto the Lord, Who shall come with His saints, to enlighten us by His second Advent.

120. But let us continue the point which we have commenced concerning the Spirit. For in the passage we have brought forward you find that the Son says of the Spirit: "He shall glorify Me." So, then, the Spirit glorifies the Son, as the Father also glorifies Him, but the Son of God also glorifies the Spirit, as we said above. He, then, is not weak who is the cause of the mutual glory through the Unity of the Eternal Light, nor is He inferior to the Spirit, of Whom this is true that He is glorified by the Spirit.

122. And you too shall be chosen, if you believe that the Spirit spoke that which the Father spoke, and which the Son spoke. Paul, in fine, was therefore chosen because he so believed and so taught, since, as it is written, God "hath revealed to us by His Spirit that which eye hath not seen, nor ear heard, nor hath entered into the heart of man, the things which God hath prepared for them that love Him." And therefore is He called the Spirit of revelation, as you read: "For God giveth to those who thus prepare themselves the Spirit of wisdom and revelation, that He may be known."

123. There is, then, a Unity of knowledge, since, as the Father, Who gives the Spirit of revelation, reveals, so also the Son reveals, for it is written: "No one knoweth the Son save the Father, neither doth any one know the Father save the Son, and he to whom the Son shall will to reveal Him." He said more concerning the Son, not because He has more than the Father, but lest He should be supposed to have less. And not unfittingly is the Father thus revealed by the Son, for the Son knows the Father even as the Father knows the Son.

124. Learn now that the Spirit too knows God the Father, for it is written that, "As no one knoweth the things of a man, save the spirit which is in him, so too the things of God no one knoweth save the Spirit of God." "No one," he says, "knoweth save the Spirit of God." Is, then, the Son of God excluded? Certainly not, since neither is the Spirit excluded, when it is said: "And none knoweth the Father, save the Son."

125. Therefore the Father, Son, and Holy Spirit are of one nature and of one knowledge. And the Spirit is not to be numbered with all things which were made by the Son, since He knew the Father, Whom (as it is written) who can know save the Son? But the Holy Spirit knows also. What then? When the totality of created things is spoken of, it follows that the Holy Spirit is not included.

126. Now I should like them to answer what it is in man which knows the things of a man. Certainly that must be reasonable which surpasses the other powers of the soul, and by which the highest nature of man is estimated. What, then, is the Spirit, Who knows the deep things of God, and through Whom Almighty God is revealed? Is He inferior in the fulness of the Godhead Who is proved even by this instance to be of one substance with the Father? Or is He ignorant of anything Who knows the counsels of God, and His mysteries which have been hidden from the beginning? What is there that He knows not Who knows all things that are of God? For "the Spirit searcheth even the deep things of God."

127. But lest you should think that He searches things unknown, and so searches that He may learn that which He knows not, it is stated first that God revealed them to us through His Spirit, and at the same time in order that you may learn that the Spirit knows the things which are revealed to us through the Spirit Himself, it is said subsequently: "For who among men knoweth the things of a man, save the spirit of the man which is in him? so, too, the things of God knoweth no one save the Spirit of God." If, then, the spirit of a man knows the things of a man, and knows them before it searches, can there be anything of God which the Spirit of God knows not? Of Whom the Apostle said not without a purpose, "The things of God knoweth no one, save the Spirit of God;" not that He knows by searching, but knows by nature; not that the knowledge of divine things is an accident in Him, but is His natural knowledge.

128. But if this moves you that He said "searcheth," learn that this is also said of God, inasmuch as He is the searcher of hearts and reins. For Himself said: "I am He that searcheth the heart and reins." And of the Son of God you have also in the Epistle to the Hebrews: "Who is the Searcher of the mind and thoughts." Whence it is clear that no inferior searches the inward things of his superior, for to know hidden things is of the divine power alone. The Holy Spirit, then, is a searcher in like manner as the Father, and the Son is a searcher in like manner, by the proper signification of which expression this is implied, that evidently there is nothing which He knows not, Whom nothing escapes.

129. Lastly, he was chosen by Christ, and taught by the Spirit. For as he himself witnesses, having obtained through the Spirit knowledge of the divine secrets, he shows both that the Holy Spirit knows God, and has revealed to us the things which are of God, as the Son also has revealed them. And he adds: "But we received, not the spirit of this world, but the Spirit which is of God, that we might know the things that are given to us by God, which we also speak, not in persuasive words of man's wisdom, but in manifestation of the Spirit and in the power of God."

Chapter XII.

After proof that the Spirit is the Giver of revelation equally with the Father and the Son, it is explained how the same Spirit does not speak of Himself; and it is shown that no bodily organs are to be thought of in Him, and that no inferiority is to be supposed from the fact of our reading that He hears, since the same would have to be attributed to the Son, and indeed even to the Father, since He hears the Son. The Spirit then hears and glorifies the Son in the sense that He revealed Him to the prophets and apostles, by which the Unity of operation of the Three Persons is inferred; and, since the Spirit does the same works as the Father, the substance of each is also declared to be the same.

130. It has then been proved that like as God has revealed to us the things which are His, so too the Son, and so too the Spirit, has revealed the things of God. For our knowledge proceeds from one Spirit, through one Son to one Father; and from one Father through one Son to one Holy Spirit is delivered goodness and sanctification and the sovereign right of eternal power. Where, then, there is a manifestation of the Spirit, there is the power of God, nor can there be any distinction where the work is one. And therefore that which the Son says the Father also says, and that which the Father says the Son also says, and that which the Father and the Son say the Holy Spirit also says.

131. Whence also the Son of God said concerning the Holy Spirit: "He shall not speak from Himself," that is, not without the participation of the Father and Myself. For the Spirit is not divided and separated, but speaks what He hears. He hears, that is to say, by unity of substance and by the property of knowledge. For He receives not hearing by any orifices of the body, nor does the divine voice resound with any carnal measures, nor does He hear what He knows not; since commonly in human matters hearing produces knowledge, and yet not even in men themselves is there always bodily speech or fleshly hearing. For "he that speaketh in tongues," it is said, "speaketh not to men but to God, for no one heareth, but in the Spirit he speaketh mysteries."

132. Therefore if in men hearing is not always of the body, do you require in God the voices of man's weakness, and certain organs of fleshly hearing, when He is said to hear in order that we may believe that He knows? For we know that which we have heard, and we hear beforehand that we may be able to know; but in God Who knows all things knowledge goes before hearing. So in order to state that the Son is not ignorant of what the Father wills, we say that He has heard; but in God there is no sound nor syllable, such as usually signify the indication of the will; but oneness of will is comprehended in hidden ways in God, but in us is shown by signs.

133. What means, then, "He shall not speak from Himself"? This is, He shall not speak without Me; for He speaks the truth, He breathes wisdom. He speaks not without the Father, for He is the Spirit of God; He hears not from Himself, for all things are of God.

134. The Son received all things from the Father, for He Himself said: "All things have been delivered unto Me from My Father." All that is the Father's the Son also has, for He says again: "All things which the Father hath are Mine." And those things which He Himself received by Unity of nature, the Spirit by the same Unity of nature received also from Him, as the Lord Jesus Himself declares, when speaking of His Spirit: "Therefore said I, He shall receive of Mine and shall declare it unto you." Therefore what the Spirit says is the Son's, what the Son hath given is the Father's. So neither the Son nor the Spirit speaks anything of Himself. For the Trinity speaks nothing external to Itself.

135. But if you contend that this is an argument for the weakness of the Holy Spirit, and for a kind of likeness to the lowliness of the body, you will also make it an argument to the injury of the Son, because the Son said of Himself: "As I hear I judge," and "The Son can do nothing else than what He seeth the Father doing." For if that be true, as it is, which the Son said: "All things which the Father hath are Mine," and the Son according to the Godhead is One with the Father, One by natural substance, not according to the Sabellian falsehood; that which is one by the property of substance certainly cannot be separated, and so the Son cannot do anything except what He has heard of the Father, for the Word of God endures forever, nor is the Father ever separated from the operation of the Son; and that which the Son works He knows that the Father wills, and what the Father wills the Son knows how to work.

136. Lastly, that one may not think that there is any difference of work either in time or in order between the Father and the Son, but may believe the oneness of the same operation, He says: "The works which I do He doeth." And again, that one may not think that there is any difference in the distinction of the works, but may judge that the will, the working, and the power of the Father and the Son are the same, Wisdom says concerning the Father: "For whatsoever things He doeth, the Son likewise doeth the same." So that the action of neither Person is before or after that of the Other, but the same result of one operation. And for this reason the Son says that He can do nothing of Himself, because His operation cannot be separated from that of the Father. In like manner the operation of the Holy Spirit is not separated. Whence also the things which He speaks, He is said to hear from the Father.

137. What if I demonstrate that the Father also hears the Son, as the Son too hears the Father? For you have it written in the Gospel that the Son says: "Father, I thank Thee that Thou heardest Me." How did the Father hear the Son, since in the previous passage concerning

153

Lazarus the Son spoke nothing to the Father? And that we might not think that the Son was heard once by the Father, He added: "And I knew that Thou hearest Me always." Therefore the hearing is not that of subject obedience, but of eternal Unity.

138. In like manner, then, the Spirit is said to hear from the Father, and to glorify the Son. To glorify, because the Holy Spirit taught us that the Son is the Image of the invisible God, and the brightness of His glory, and the impress of His substance. The Spirit also spoke in the patriarchs and the prophets, and, lastly, the apostles began then to be more perfect after that they had received the Holy Spirit. There is therefore no separation of the divine power and grace, for although "there are diversities of gifts, yet it is the same Spirit; and diversities of ministrations, yet the same Lord; and diversities of operations, yet the same God Who worketh all in all." There are diversities of offices, not severances of the Trinity.

139. Lastly, it is the same God Who worketh all in all, that you may know that there is no diversity of operation between God the Father and the Holy Spirit; since those things which the Spirit works, God the Father also works, "Who worketh all in all." For while God the Father worketh all in all, yet "to one is given through the Spirit the word of wisdom; to another the word of knowledge, according to the same Spirit; to another faith, in the same Spirit; to another the gift of healings, in the one Spirit; to another the working of miracles; to another prophecy; to another discerning of spirits; to another divers kinds of tongues; to another the interpretation of sayings; but all these worketh one and the same Spirit, dividing to each one as He will."

140. There is then no doubt but that those things which the Father worketh, the Spirit worketh also. Nor does He work in accordance with a command, as he who hears in bodily fashion, but voluntarily, as being free in His own will, not the servant of the power of another. For He does not obey as being bidden, but as the giver He is the controller of His own gifts.

141. Consider meanwhile whether you can say that the Spirit effects all things which the Father effects; for you cannot deny that the Father effects those things which the Holy Spirit effects; otherwise the Father does not effect all things, if He effects not those things which the Spirit also effects. But if the Father also effects those things which the Spirit effects, since the Spirit divides His operations, according to His own will, you must of necessity say, either that what the Spirit divides He divides according to His own will, against the will of God the Father; or if you say that the Father wills the same that the Holy Spirit wills, you must of necessity confess the oneness of the divine will and operation, even if you do it unwillingly, and, if not with the heart, at least with the mouth.

142. But if the Holy Spirit is of one will and operation with God the Father, He is also of one substance, since the Creator is known by His works. So, then, it is the same Spirit, he says, the same Lord, the same God. And if you say Spirit. He is the same; and if you say Lord, He is the same; and if you say God, He is the same. Not the same, so that Himself is Father, Himself Son, Himself Spirit [one and the selfsame Person]; but because both the Father and the Son are the same Power. He is, then, the same in substance and in power, for there is not in the Godhead either the confusion of Sabellius nor the division of Arius, nor any earthly and bodily change.

Chapter XIII.

Prophecy was not only from the Father and the Son but also from the Spirit; the authority and operation of the latter on the apostles is signified to be the same as Theirs; and so we are to understand that them is unity in the three points of authority, rule, and bounty; yet need no disadvantage be feared from that participation, since such does not arise in human friendship. Lastly, it is established that this is the inheritance of the apostolic faith from the fact that the apostles are described as having obeyed the Holy Spirit.

143. Take, O sacred Emperor, another strong instance in this question, and one known to you: "In many ways and in divers manners, God spake to the fathers in the prophets." And the Wisdom of God said: "I will send prophets and apostles." And "To one is given," as it is written, "through the Spirit, the word of wisdom; to another, the word of knowledge, according to the same Spirit; to another faith, in the same Spirit; to another, the gift of healings, in the one

Spirit; to another, the working of miracles; to another, prophecy." Therefore, according to the Apostle, prophecy is not only through the Father and the Son, but also through the Holy Spirit, and therefore the office is one, and the grace one. So you find that the Spirit also is the author of prophecies.

144. The apostles also said: "It seemed good to the Holy Spirit and to us." And when they say, "It seemed good," they point out not only the Worker of the grace, but also the Author of the carrying out of that which was commanded. For as we read of God: "It pleased God;" so, too, when it is said that, "It seemed good to the Holy Spirit," one who is master of his own power is portrayed.

145. And how should He not be a master Who speaks what He wills, and commands what He wills, as the Father commands and the Son commands? For as Paul heard the voice saying to him, "I am Jesus, Whom thou persecutest," so, too, the Spirit forbade Paul and Silas to go into Bithynia. And as the Father spake through the prophets, so, too, Agabus says concerning the Spirit: "Thus saith the Holy Spirit, Thus shall the Jews in Jerusalem bind the man, whose is this girdle." And as Wisdom sent the apostles, saying, "Go ye into all the world and preach the Gospel," so, too, the Holy Spirit says: "Separate Me Barnabas and Saul for the work whereunto I have called them." And so being sent forth by the Holy Spirit, as the Scripture points out farther on, they were distinguished in nothing from the other apostles, as though they were sent in one way by God the Father, in another way by Spirit.

146. Lastly, Paul having been sent by the Spirit, was both a vessel of election on Christ's part, and himself relates that God wrought in him, saying: "For He that wrought for Peter unto the apostleship of the circumcision, wrought for me also unto the Gentiles." Since, then, the Same wrought in Paul Who wrought in Peter, it is certainly evident that, since the Spirit wrought in Paul, the Holy Spirit wrought also in Peter. But Peter himself testifies that God the Father wrought in him, as it is stated in the Acts of the Apostles that Peter rose up and said to them: "Men and brethren, ye know that a good while ago God made choice amongst us that the Gentiles should hear the word of the Gospel from my mouth." See, then, in Peter God wrought the grace of preaching. And who would dare to deny the operation of Christ in him, since he was certainly elected and chosen by Christ, when the Lord said: "Feed My lambs."

147. The operation, then, of the Father, the Son, and the Holy Spirit is one, unless perchance you, who deny the oneness of the same operation upon the Apostle, think this; that the Father and the Spirit wrought in Peter, in whom the Son had wrought, as if the operation of the Son by no means sufficed for him to the attainment of the grace. And so the strength of the Father, of the Son, and of the Holy Spirit being as it were joined and brought together, the work was manifold, lest the operation of Christ alone should be too weak to establish Peter.

148. And not only in Peter is there found to be one operation of the Father, the Son, and the Holy Spirit, but also in all the apostles the unity of the divine operation, and a certain authority over the dispensations of heaven. For the divine operation works by the power of a command, not in the execution of a ministry; for God, when He works, does not fashion anything by toil or art, but "He spake and they were made." He said, "Let there be light, and there was light," for the effecting of the work is comprised in the commandment of God.

149. We can, then, easily find, if we will consider, that this royal power is by the witness of the Scriptures attributed to the Holy Spirit; and it will be made clear that all the apostles were not only disciples of Christ, but also ministers of the Father, the Son, and the Holy Spirit. As also the teacher of the Gentiles tells us, when he says: "God hath set some in the Church, first apostles, secondarily prophets, thirdly teachers; then miracles, the gift of healings, helps, governments, divers kinds of tongues."

150. See, God set apostles, and set prophets and teachers, gave the gift of healings, which you find above to be given by the Holy Spirit; gave divers kinds of tongues. But yet all are not apostles, all are not prophets, all are not teachers. Not all, says he, have the gift of healings, nor do all, says he, speak with tongues. For the whole of the divine gifts cannot exist in each several

man; each, according to his capacity, receives that which he either desires or deserves. But the power of the Trinity, which is lavish of all graces, is not like this weakness.

151. Lastly, God set apostles. Those whom God set in the Church, Christ chose and ordained to be apostles, and sent them into the world, saying: "Go ye into all the world, and preach the Gospel to the whole creation. He that shall believe and be baptized shall be saved, but he that believeth not shall be damned. And these signs shall follow them that believe. In My Name shall they cast out devils, they shall speak with new tongues, they shall take up serpents, and if they shall drink any deadly thing, it shall not hurt them, they shall lay hands on the sick, and they shall recover." You see the Father and Christ also set teachers in the Churches; and as the Father gives the gift of healings, so, too, does the Son give; as the Father gives the gift of tongues, so, too, has the Son also granted it.

152. In like manner we have heard also above concerning the Holy Spirit, that He too grants the same kinds of graces. For it is said: "To one is given through the Spirit the gift of healings, to another divers kinds of tongues, to another prophecy." So, then, the Spirit gives the same gifts as the Father, and the Son also gives them. Let us now learn more expressly what we have touched upon above, that the Holy Spirit entrusts the same office as the Father and the Son, and appoints the same persons; since Paul said: "Take heed to yourselves, and to all the flock in the which the Holy Spirit has made you overseers to rule the Church of God."

153. There is, then, unity of authority, unity of appointment, unity of giving. For if you separate appointment and power, what cause was there [for maintaining] that those whom Christ appointed as apostles, God the Father appointed, and the Holy Spirit appointed? unless, perhaps, as if sharing a possession or a right, They, like men, were afraid of legal prejudice, and therefore the operation was divided, and the authority distributed.

154. These things are narrow and paltry, even between men, who for the most part, although they do not agree in action, yet agree in will. So that a certain person being asked what a friend is, answered, "A second self." If, then, a man so defined a friend as to say, he was a second self, that is to say, through a oneness of love and good-will, how much more ought we to esteem the oneness of Majesty, in the Father, the Son, and the Holy Ghost, when by the same operation and divine power, either the unity, or certainly that which is more, the tautoth", as it is called in Greek, is expressed, for tauto signifies "the same," so that the Father, the Son, and the Holy Spirit have the same; so that to have the same will and the same power does not arise from the affection of the will, but inheres in the substance of the Trinity.

155. This is the inheritance of apostolic faith and devotion, which one may observe also in the Acts of the Apostles. Therefore Paul and Barnabas obeyed the commands of the Holy Spirit. And all the apostles obeyed, and forthwith ordained those whom the Spirit had ordered to be separated: "Separate Me," said He, "Barnabas and Saul." Do you see the authority of Him Who commands? Consider the merit of those who obey.

156. Paul believed, and because he believed he cast off the zeal of a persecutor, and gained a crown of righteousness. He believed who used to make havoc of the Churches; but being converted to the faith, he preached in the Spirit that which the Spirit commanded. The Spirit anointed His champion, and having shaken off the dust of unbelief, presented him as an insuperable conqueror of the unbelievers to various assemblies of the ungodly, and trained him by many sufferings for the prize of his high calling in Christ Jesus.

157. Barnabas also believed, and obeyed because he believed. Therefore, being chosen by the authority of the Holy Spirit, Which came on him abundantly, as a special sign of his merits, he was not unworthy of so great a fellowship. For one grace shone in these whom one Spirit had chosen.

158. Nor was Paul inferior to Peter, though the latter was the foundation of the Church, and the former a wise builder knowing how to make firm the footsteps of the nations who believed; Paul was not, I say, unworthy of the fellowship of the apostles, but is easily comparable with the first, and second to none. For he who knows not that he is inferior makes himself equal.

BOOK III.

Chapter I.

Not only were the prophets and apostles sent by the Spirit, but also the Son of God. This is proved from Isaiah and the evangelists, and it is explained why St. Luke wrote that the same Spirit descended like a dove upon Christ and abode upon Him. N:ext, after establishing this mission of Christ, the writer infers that the Son is sent by the Father and the Spirit, as the Spirit is by the Father and the Son.

1. In the former book we have shown by the clear evidence of the Scriptures that the apostles and prophets were appointed, the latter to prophesy, the former to preach the Gospel, by the Holy Spirit in the same way as by the Father and the Son; now we add what all will rightly wonder at, and not be able to doubt, that the Spirit was upon Christ; and that as He sent the Spirit, so the Spirit sent the Son of God. For the Son of God says: "The Spirit of the Lord is upon Me, because He hath anointed Me, He hath sent Me to preach the Gospel to the poor, to proclaim liberty to the captives, and sight to the blind." And having read this from the Book of Isaiah, He says in the Gospel: "To-day hath this Scripture been fulfilled in your ears;" that He might point out that it was said of Himself.

2. Can we, then, wonder if the Spirit sent both the prophets and the apostles, since Christ said: "The Spirit of the Lord is upon Me"? And rightly did He say "upon Me," because He was speaking as the Son of Man. For as the Son of Man He was anointed and sent to preach the Gospel.

3. But if they believe not the Son, let them hear the Father also saying that the Spirit of the Lord is upon Christ. For He says to John: "Upon whomsoever thou shalt see the Spirit descending from heaven and abiding upon Him, He it is Who baptizeth with the Holy Spirit." God the Father said this to John, and John heard and saw and believed. He heard from God, he saw in the Lord, he believed that it was the Spirit Who was coming down from heaven. For it was not a dove that descended, but the Holy Spirit as a dove; for thus it is written: "I saw the Spirit descending from heaven as a dove."

4. As John says that he saw, so, too, wrote Mark; Luke, however, added that the Holy Spirit descended in a bodily form as a dove; you must not think that this was an incarnation, but an appearance. He, then, brought the appearance before him, that by means of the appearance he might believe who did not see the Spirit, and that by the appearance He might manifest that He had a share of the one honour in authority, the one operation in the mystery, the one gift in the bath, together with the Father and the Son; unless perchance we consider Him in Whom the Lord was baptized too weak for the servant to be baptized in Him.

5. And he said fittingly, "abiding upon Him," because the Spirit inspired a saying or acted upon the prophets as often as He would, but abode always in Christ.

6. Nor, again, let it move you that he said "upon Him," for he was speaking of the Son of Man, because he was baptized as the Son of Man. For the Spirit is not upon Christ, according to the Godhead, but in Christ; for, as the Father is in the Son, and the Son in the Father, so the Spirit of God and the Spirit of Christ is both in the Father and in the Son, for He is the Spirit of His mouth. For He Who is of God abides in God, as it is written: "But we received not the spirit of this world, but the Spirit which is of God." And He abides in Christ, Who has received from Christ; for it is written again: "He shall take of Mine:" and elsewhere: "The law of the Spirit of life in Christ Jesus made me free from the law of sin and death." He is, then, not over Christ according to the Godhead of Christ, for the Trinity is not over Itself, but over all things: It is not over Itself but in Itself.

7. Who, then, can doubt that the Spirit sent the prophets and apostles, since the Son of God says: "The Spirit of the Lord is. upon Me." And elsewhere: "I am the First, and I am also for ever, and Mine hand hath rounded the earth, and My right hand hath established the heaven; I will call them and they shall stand up together, and shall all be gathered together and shall hear. Who hath declared these things to them? Because I loved thee I performed thy pleasure against

Babylon, that the seed of the Chaldaeans might be taken away. I have spoken, and I have called, I have brought him and have made his way prosperous. Come unto Me and hear ye this. From the beginning I have not spoken in secret, I was there when those things were done; and now the Lord God hath sent Me and His Spirit." Who is it Who says: The Lord God hath sent Me and His Spirit, except He Who came from the Father that He might save sinners? And, as you hear, the Spirit sent Him, lest when you hear that the Son sends the Spirit, you should believe the Spirit to be of inferior power.

8. So both the Father and the Spirit sent the Son; the Father sent Him, for it is written: "But the Paraclete, the Holy Spirit, Whom the Father will send in My Name." The Son sent Him, for He said: "But when the Paraclete is come, Whom I will send unto you from the Father, even the Spirit of Truth." If, then, the Son and the Spirit send each other, as the Father sends, there is no inferiority of subjection, but a community of power.

Chapter II.

The Son and the Spirit are alike given; whence not subjection but one Godhead is shown by Its working.

9. And not only did the Father send the Son, but also gave Him, as the Son Himself gave Himself. For we read: "Grace to you from God our Father and the Lord Jesus Christ, Who gave Himself for our sins." If they think that He was subject in that He was sent, they cannot deny that it was of grace that He was given. But He was given by the Father, as Isaiah said: "Unto us a Child is born, unto us a Son is given;" but He was given, I dare to say it, by the Spirit also, Who was sent by the Spirit. For since the prophet has not defined by whom He was given, he shows that He was given by the grace of the Trinity; and inasmuch as the Son Himself gave Himself, He could not be subject to Himself according to His Godhead. Therefore that He was given could not be a sign of subjection in the God-head.

10. But the Holy Spirit also was given, for it is written: "I will ask the Father, and He shall give you another Paraclete." And the Apostle says: "Wherefore he that despiseth these things despiseth not man but God, Who hath given us His Holy Spirit." Isaiah, too, shows that both the Spirit and the Son are given: "Thus," says he, "saith the Lord God, Who made the heaven and fashioned it, Who stablished the earth, and the things which are in it, and giveth breath to the people upon it, and the Spirit to them that walk upon it." And to the Son: "I am the Lord God, Who have called Thee in righteousness, and will hold Thine hand, and will strengthen Thee; and I have given Thee for a covenant of My people, for a light of the Gentiles, to open the eyes of the blind, to bring out of their fetters those that are bound." Since, then, the Son is both sent and given, and the Spirit also is both sent and given, They have assuredly a oneness of Godhead Who have a oneness of action.

Chapter III.

The same Unity may also be recognized from the fact that the Spirit is called Finger, and the Son Right Hand; for the understanding of divine things is assisted by the usage of human language. The tables of the law were written by this Finger, and they were afterwards broken, and the reason. Lastly, Christ wrote with the same Finger; yet we must not admit any inferiority in the Spirit from this bodily comparison.

11. So, too, the Spirit is also called the Finger of God, because there is an indivisible and inseparable communion between the Father, the Son, and the Holy Spirit. For as the Scripture called the Son of God the Right Hand of God, as it is said: "Thy Right Hand, O Lord, is made glorious in power. Thy Right Hand, O Lord, hath dashed in pieces the enemy;" so the Holy Spirit is called the Finger of God, as the Lord Himself says: "But if I by the Finger of God cast out devils." For in the same place in another book of the Gospel He named the Spirit of God, as you find: "But if I by the Spirit of God cast out devils."

12. What, then, could have been said to signify more expressly the unity of the Godhead, or of Its working, which Unity is according to the Godhead of the Father, or of the Son, or of the Holy Spirit, than that we should understand that the fulness of the eternal Godhead would seem

to be divided far more than this body of ours, if any one were to sever the unity of Substance, and multiply Its powers, whereas the eternity of the same Godhead is one?

13. For oftentimes it is convenient to estimate from our own words those things which are above us, and because we cannot see those things we draw inferences from those which we can see. "For the invisible things of Him," says the Apostle, "from the creation of the world are clearly seen, being understood by those things which are made." And he adds: "His eternal power also and Godhead." Of which one thing seems to be said of the Son, and another of the Holy Spirit; that in the same manner as the Son is called the eternal Power of the Father, so, also, the Spirit, because He is divine, should be believed to be His eternal Godhead. For the Son, too, because He ever lives, is eternal life. This Finger, then, of God is both eternal and divine. For what is there belonging to God which is not eternal and divine?

14. With this Finger, as we read, God wrote on those tables of stone which Moses received. For God did not with a finger of flesh write the forms and portions of those letters which we read, but gave the law by His Spirit. And so the Apostle says: "For the Law is spiritual, which, indeed, is written not with ink, but with the Spirit of the living God; not in tables of stone, but on fleshy tables of the heart." For if the letter of the Apostle is written in the Spirit, what hinders us from believing that the Law of God was written not with ink, but with the Spirit of God, which certainly does not stain but enlightens the secret places of our heart and mind?

14. Now it was written on tables of stone, because it was written in a type, but the tables were first broken and cast out of the hands of Moses, because the Jews fell away from the works of the prophet. And fitly were the tables broken, not the writing erased. And do you see that your table be not broken, that your mind and soul be not divided. Is Christ divided? He is not divided, but is one with the Father; and let no one separate you. from Him. If your faith fails, the table of your heart is broken. The coherence of your soul is lessened if you do not believe the unity of Godhead in the Trinity. Your faith is written, and your sin is written, as Jeremiah said: "Thy sin, O Judah, is written with a pen of iron and the point of a diamond. And it is written," he says, "on thy breast and on thy heart." The sin, therefore, is there where grace is, but the sin is written with a pen, grace is denoted by the Spirit.

15. With this Finger, also, the Lord Jesus, with bowed head, mystically wrote on the ground, when the adulteress was brought before Him by the Jews, signifying in a figure that, when we judge of the sins of another, we ought to remember our own.

16. And lest, again, because God wrote the Law by His Spirit, we should believe any inferiority, as it were, concerning the ministry of the Spirit, or from the consideration of our own body should think the Spirit to be a small part of God, the Apostle says, elsewhere, that he does not speak with words of human wisdom, but in words taught by the Spirit, and that he compares spiritual things with spiritual; but that the natural man receiveth not the things which pertain to the Spirit of God. For he knew that he who compared divine with carnal things was amongst natural things, and not to be reckoned amongst spiritual men; "for they are foolishness," he says, "unto him." And so, because he knew that these questions would arise amongst natural men, foreseeing the future he says: "For who hath known the mind of the Lord, that he may instruct Him? But we have the mind of Christ."

Chapter IV.
To those who contend that the Spirit because He is called the Finger is less than the Father, St. Ambrose replies that this would also tend to the lessening of the Son, Who is called the Right Hand. That these names are to be referred only to the Unity, for which reason Moses proclaimed that the whole Trinity worked in the passage of the Red Sea. And, indeed, it is no wonder that the operation of the Spirit found place there, where there was a figure of baptism, since the Scripture teaches that the Three Persons equally sanctify and are operative in that sacrament.

17. But if any one is still entangled in carnal doubts, and hesitates because of bodily figures, let him consider that he cannot think rightly of the Son who can think wrongly of the Spirit. For

if some think that the Spirit is a certain small portion of God, because He is called the Finger of God, the same persons must certainly maintain that a small portion only is in the Son of God, because He is called the Right Hand of God.

18. But the Son is called both the Right Hand and the Power of God; if, then, we consider our words, there can be no perfection without power; let them therefore take care lest they think that which it is impious to say, namely, that the Father being but half perfect in His own Substance received perfection through the Son, and let them cease to deny that the Son is co-eternal with the Father. For when did the Power of God not exist? But if they think that at any time the Power of God existed not, they will say that at some time Perfection existed not in God the Father, to Whom they think that Power was at some time wanting.

19. But, as I said, these things are written that we may refer them to the Unity of the Godhead, and believe that which the Apostle said, that the fulness of the Godhead dwells bodily in Christ, which dwells also in the Father, and dwells in the Holy Spirit; and that, as there is a unity of the Godhead, so also is there a unity of operation.

20. And this may also be gathered from the Song of Moses, for he, after leading the people of the Jews through the sea, acknowledged the operation of the Father, the Son, and the Holy Spirit, saying: "Thy Right Hand, O Lord, is glorious in power, Thy Right Hand, O Lord, hath dashed in pieces the enemy." Here you have his confession of the Son and of the Father, Whose Right Hand He is. And farther on, not to pass by the Holy Spirit, He added: "Thou didst send Thy Spirit and the sea covered them, and the water was divided by the Spirit of Thine anger." By which is signified the unity of the Godhead, not an inequality of the Trinity.

21. You see, then, that the Holy Spirit also co-operated with the Father and the Son, so that just as if the waves were congealed in the midst of the sea, a wall as it were of water rose up for the passage of the Jews, and then, poured back again by the Spirit, overwhelmed the people of the Egyptians. And many think that from the same origin the pillar of cloud went before the people of the Jews by day, and the pillar of fire by night, that the grace of the Spirit might protect His people.

22. Now that this operation of God, which the whole world rightly wonders at, did not take place without the work of the Holy Spirit, the Apostle also declared when he said that the truth of a spiritual mystery was prefigured in it, for we read as follows: "For our fathers were all under the cloud, and all passed through the sea, and were all baptized in Moses in the cloud and in the sea, and did all eat the same spiritual meat, and did all drink the same spiritual drink."

23. For how without the operation of the Holy Spirit could there be the type of a sacrament, the whole truth of which is in the Spirit? As the Apostle also set forth, saying: "But ye were washed, but ye were sanctified, but ye were justified in the Name of our Lord Jesus Christ, and in the Spirit of our God."

24. You see, then, that the Father works in the Son, and that the Son works in the Spirit. And therefore do not doubt that, according to the order of Scripture, there was in the figure that which the Truth Himself declared to be in the truth. For who can deny His operation in the Font, in which we feel His operation and grace?

25. For as the Father sanctifies, so, too, the Son sanctifies, and the Holy Spirit sanctifies. The Father sanctifies according to that which is written: "The God of peace sanctify you, and may your spirit, soul, and body be preserved entire without blame in the day of our Lord Jesus Christ." And elsewhere the Son says: "Father, sanctify them in the truth."

26. But of the Son the same Apostle said: "Who was made unto us wisdom from God, and righteousness, and sanctification, and redemption." Do you see that He was made sanctification? But He was made so unto us, not that He should change that which He was, but that He might sanctify us in the flesh.

27. And the Apostle also teaches that the Holy Spirit sanctifies. For he speaks thus: "We are bound to give thanks to God always for you, brethren dearly beloved of the Lord; because God chose you as first-fruits unto salvation, in sanctification of the Spirit, and belief of the truth."

28. So, then, the Father sanctifies, the Son also sanctifies, and the Holy Spirit sanctifies; but the sanctification is one, for baptism is one, and the grace of the sacrament is one.

Chapter V.

The writer sums up the argument he had commenced, and confirms the statement that unity is signified by the terms finger and right hand, from the fact that the works of God are the same as are the works of hands; and that those of hands are the same as those of fingers; and lastly, that the term hand applies equally to the Son and the Spirit, and that of finger applies to the Spirit and the Son.

29. But what wonder is it if He Who Himself needs no sanctification, but abounds therewith, sanctifies each man; since, as I said, we have been taught that His Majesty is so great, that the Holy Spirit seems to be as inseparable from God the Father as the finger is from the body?

30. But if any one thinks that this should be referred not to the oneness of power, but to its lessening, he indeed will fall into such madness as to appear to fashion the Father, Son, and Holy Spirit as it were into one bodily form, and to picture to himself certain distinctions of its members.

31. But let them learn, as I have often said, that not inequality but unity of power is signified by this testimony; inasmuch as things which are the works of God are also the works of hands, and we read that the same are the works of fingers. For it is written: "The heavens declare the glory of God, and the firmament showeth the work of His hands;" and elsewhere: "In the beginning Thou didst found the earth, O Lord; and the heavens are the works of Thy hands." So, then, the works of the hands are the same as the works of God. There is not therefore any distinction of the work according to the kind of bodily members, but a oneness of power.

32. But those which are the works of the hands are also the works of the fingers, for it is equally written: "For I will behold Thy heavens, the works of Thy fingers, the moon, and the stars, which Thou hast established." What less are the fingers here said to have made than the hands, since they made the same as the hands, as it is written: "For Thou, Lord, hast made me glad through Thy work, and in the works of Thy hands will I rejoice,"

33. And yet since we read that the Son is the hand(for it is written: "Hath not My Hand made all these things?" and elsewhere: "I will place thee in the cleft of the rock, and I will cover thee with Mine hand, I have placed My hand under the covering of the rock," which refers to the mystery of the Incarnation, because the eternal Power of God took on Itself the covering of a body), it is certainly clear that Scripture used the term hand both of the Son and of the Holy Spirit.

34. And again, since we read that the Spirit is the finger of God, we think that fingers [in the plural] are spoken of to signify the Son and Spirit. Lastly, that he may state that he received the sanctification both of the Son and of the Spirit, a certain saint says: "Thy hands have made me and fashioned me."

Chapter VI.

The Spirit rebukes just as do the Father and the Son; and indeed judges could not judge without Him, as is shown by the judgments of Solomon and Daniel, which are explained in a few words, by the way; and no other than the Holy Spirit inspired Daniel.

35. Why do we reject like words when we assert the oneness of power, since the oneness of power extends so far that the Spirit rebukes, as the Father rebukes, and as the Son rebukes. For so it is written: "O Lord, rebuke me not in Thine anger, neither chasten me in Thy displeasure." Then in the forty-ninth [fiftieth] Psalm, the Lord speaks thus: "I will rebuke thee, and will set thy sins before thy face" And in like manner the Son said of the Holy Spirit: "When I go away, I will send the Paraclete to you. And He, when He is come, will rebuke the world, concerning sin, and concerning righteousness, and concerning judgment"

36. But whither is the madness of faithless men leading us, so that we appear to be proving, as if it were a matter of doubt, that the Holy Spirit rebukes, whereas judges themselves are unable to judge, except through the Spirit. Lastly, that famous judgment of Solomon, when, amongst the difficulties arising from those who were contending, as one, having overlain the child which she had borne, wished to claim the child of another, and the other was protecting her own son, he both discovered deceit in the very hidden thoughts. and affection in the mother's heart, was certainly so admirable only by the gift of the Holy Spirit For no other sword would have penetrated the hidden feeling of those women, except the sword of the Spirit, of which the Lord says: "I am not come to send peace but a sword." For the inmost mind cannot be penetrated by steel, but by the Spirit: "For the Spirit of understanding is holy, one only, manifold, subtle, lively," and, farther on, "overseeing all things."

37. Consider what the prophet says, that He oversees all things. And so Solomon also oversaw, so that he ordered that sword to be brought, because while pretending that he intended to divide the infant, he reflected that the true mother would have more regard for her son than for her comfort, and would set kindness before right, not right before kindness. But that she who feigned the feelings of a mother, blinded by the desire of gaining her end, would think little of the destruction of him in regard to whom she felt no outgoing of tenderness. And so that spiritual man, that he might judge all things (for he that is spiritual judgeth all things), sought in the feelings the natural disposition which was concealed in the language, and questioned tenderness that he might set forth the truth. So the mother overcame by the affection of love, which is a fruit of the Spirit.

38. He judges in a prophet, for the word of wisdom is given by the Spirit; how, then, do men deny that the Spirit can rebuke the world concerning judgment, Who removes doubt from judgment, and grants the successful issue?

39. Daniel also, unless he had received the Spirit of God, would never have been able to discover that lustful adultery, that fraudulent lie. For when Susanna, assailed by the conspiracy of the elders, saw that the mind of the people was moved by consideration for the old men, and destitute of all help, alone amongst men, conscious of her chastity she prayed God to judge; it is written: "The Lord heard her voice, when she was being led to be put to death, and the Lord raised up the Holy Spirit of a young youth, whose name was Daniel." And so according to the grace of the Holy Spirit received by him, he discovered the varying evidence of the treacherous, for it was none other than the operation of divine power, that his voice should make them whose inward feelings were concealed to be known.

41. Understand, then, the sacred and heavenly miracle of the Holy Spirit She who preferred to be chaste in herself, rather than in the opinion of the people, she who preferred to hazard [the reputation of] her innocence, rather than her modesty, who when she was accused was silent, when she was condemned held her peace, content with the judgment of her own conscience, who preserved regard for her modesty even in peril, that they who were not able to force her chastity might not seem to have forced her to petulance; when she called upon the Lord, she obtained the Spirit, Who made known the hidden consciousness of the elders.

42. Let the chaste learn not to dread calumny. For she who preferred chastity to life did not suffer the loss of life, and retained the glory of chastity. So, too, Abraham, once bidden to go to foreign lands, and not being held back either by the danger to his wife's modesty, nor by the fear of death before him, preserved both his own life and his wife's chastity. So no one has ever repented of trusting God, and chastity increased devotion in Sarah, and devotion chastity.

43. And lest any one should perhaps think that, as the Scripture says, "God raised up the Holy Spirit of a young youth," the Spirit in him was that of a man, not the Holy Spirit, let him read farther on, and he will find that Daniel received the Holy Spirit, and therefore prophesied. Lastly, too, the king advanced him because he had the grace of the Spirit For he speaks thus: "Thou, O Daniel, art able, forasmuch as the Holy Spirit of God is in thee." And farther on it is

written: "And Daniel was set over them, because an excellent Spirit was in him." And the Spirit of Moses also was distributed to those who were to be judges.

Chapter VII.

The Son Himself does not judge or punish without the Spirit, so that the same Spirit is called the Sword of the Word. But inasmuch as the Word is in turn called the Sword of the Spirit, the highest unity of power is thereby recognized in each.

44. But what should we say of the other points? We have heard that the Lord Jesus not only judges in the Spirit but punishes also. For neither would He punish Antichrist, whom, as we read, "the Lord Jesus shall slay with the Spirit of His mouth," unless He had before judged of his deserts. Yet here is not a grace received, but the unity remains undivided, since neither can Christ be without the Spirit, nor the Spirit without Christ. For the unity of the divine nature cannot be divided.

45. And since that instance comes before us. that the Lord Jesus shall slay with the Spirit of His mouth, the Spirit is understood to be as it were the Sword of the Word. Lastly, in the Gospel also the Lord Jesus Himself says: "I came not to send peace but a sword." For He came that He might give the Spirit; and so there is in His mouth a two-edged sword, which is in truth the grace of the Spirit So the Spirit is the Sword of the Word.

46. And that you may know that there is no inequality but unity of nature, the Word also is the Sword of the Holy Spirit, for it is written: "Taking the shield of faith, wherewith ye may be able to quench all the fiery darts of the wicked one. And take the helmet of Salvation, and the sword of the Spirit, which is the Word of God."

47. Since, then, the Sword of the Word is the Holy Spirit, and the Sword of the Holy Spirit is the Word of God, there is certainly in Them oneness of power.

Chapter VIII.

The aforesaid unity is proved hereby, that as the Father is said to be grieved and tempted, so too the Son. The Son was also tempted in the wilderness, where a figure of the cross was set up in the brazen serpent: but the Apostle says that the Spirit also was there tempted. St. Ambrose infers from this that the Israelites were guided into the promised land by the same Spirit, and that His will and power are one with those of the Father and the Son.

48. And we may behold this unity also in other passages of the Scriptures. For whereas Ezekiel says to the people of the Jews: "And thou hast grieved Me in all these things, saith the Lord;" Paul says to the new people in his Epistle: "Grieve not the Holy Spirit of God, in Whom ye were sealed." Again, whereas Isaiah says of the Jews themselves: "But they believed not, but grieved the Holy Spirit;" David says of God: "They grieved the Most High in the desert, and tempted God in their hearts."

49. Understand also that whereas Scripture in other places says that the Spirit was tempted, and that God was tempted, it says also that Christ was tempted; for you have the Apostle saying to the Corinthians: "Neither let us tempt Christ, as some of them tempted, and perished by serpents." Just was the punishment that the adversaries should feel the venom, who had not venerated the Maker.

50. And well did the Lord ordain that by the lifting up of the brazen serpent the wounds of those who were bitten should be healed; for the brazen serpent is a type of the Cross; for although in His flesh Christ was lifted up, yet in Him was the Apostle crucified to the world and the world to him; for he says: "The world hath been crucified unto me, and I unto the world." "So the world was crucified in its allurements, and therefore not a real but a brazen serpent was hanged; because the Lord took on Him the likeness of a sinner, in the truth. indeed, of His Body, but without the truth of sin, that imitating a serpent through the deceitful appearance of human weakness, having laid aside the slough of the flesh, He might destroy the cunning of the true serpent. And therefore in the Cross of the Lord, which came to man's help in avenging

temptation, I, who accept the medicine of the Trinity, recognize in the wicked the offence against the Trinity.

51. Therefore when you find in the book of Moses, that the Lord being tempted sent serpents on the people of the Jews, it is necessary that you either confess the Unity of the Father, Son, and Holy Spirit in the Divine Majesty, or certainly when the writing of the Apostle says that the Spirit was tempted, it undoubtedly pointed out the Spirit by the name of Lord. But the Apostle writing to the Hebrews says that the Spirit was tempted, for you find this: "Wherefore the Holy Ghost saith this: Today if ye shall hear His voice, harden not your hearts, like as in the provocation in the day of temptation in the wilderness, where your fathers tempted Me, proved Me, and saw My works. Forty years was I near to this generation and said: They do alway err in their heart; but they did not know My ways, as I sware in My wrath, If they shall enter into My rest."

52. Therefore, according to the Apostle, the Spirit was tempted. If He was tempted, He also certainly was guiding the people of the Jews into the land of promise, as it is written: "For He led them through the deep, as a horse through the wilderness, and they laboured not, and like the cattle through the plain. The Spirit came down from the Lord and guided them." And He certainly ministered to them the calm rain of heavenly food, He with fertile shower made fruitful that daily harvest which earth had not brought forth, and husbandman had not sown.

53. Now let us look at these points one by one. God had promised rest to the Jews; the Spirit calls that rest His. God the Father relates that He was tempted by the unbelieving, and the Spirit says that He was tempted by the same, for the temptation is one wherewith the one Godhead of the Trinity was tempted by the unbelieving. God condemns the people of the Jews, so that they cannot attain to the land flowing with milk and honey, that is, to the rest of the resurrection; and the Spirit condemns them by the same decree: "If they shall enter into My rest." It is, then, the decree of one Will, the excellency of one Power.

Chapter IX.

That the Holy Spirit is provoked is proved by the words of St. Peter, in which it is shown that the Spirit of God is one and the same as the Spirit of the Lord, both by other passages and by reference to the sentence of the same Apostle on Ananias and Sapphira, whence it is argued that the union of the Holy Spirit with the Father and the Son, as well as His own Godhead, is proved.

54. Perhaps, however, some one might say that this passage cannot be specially applied to the Holy Spirit, had not the same Apostle Peter taught us in another place that the Holy Ghost can be tempted by our sins, for you find that the wife of Ananias is thus addressed: "Why have ye agreed together to tempt the Spirit of the Lord?" For the Spirit of the Lord is the very Spirit of God; for there is one Holy Spirit, as also the Apostle Paul taught, saying: "But ye are not in the flesh, but in the Spirit, if so be that the Spirit of God dwelleth in you. But if any man hath not the Spirit of Christ, he is none of His." He first mentioned the Spirit of God and immediately adds that the Same is the Spirit of Christ. And having spoken of the Spirit, that we might understand that where the Holy Spirit is there is Christ, he added: "But if Christ be in you."

55. Then, in the same way as we here understand that where the Spirit is there also is Christ; so also, elsewhere, he shows that where Christ is, there also is the Holy Spirit. For having said: "Do ye seek a proof of Christ Who speaketh in me?" he says elsewhere: "For I think that I also have the Spirit of God." The Unity, then, is inseparable, for by the testimony of Scripture where either the Father or the Son or the Holy Spirit is designated, there is all the fulness of the Trinity.

56. But Peter himself in the instance we have brought forward spoke first of the Holy Spirit, and then called Him the Spirit of the Lord, for you read as follows: "Ananias, why hath Satan filled thine heart to lie to the Holy Spirit, and to deal fraudulently concerning the price of the field? While it remained did it not continue thine own, and when sold was it not in thy power?

Why hast thou conceived this wickedness in thy heart? Thou hast not lied unto men but unto God." And below he says to the wife: "Why have ye agreed together to tempt the Spirit of the Lord?"

57. First, we understand that he called the Holy Spirit the Spirit of the Lord. Then, since he mentioned first the Holy Spirit and added: "Thou hast not lied unto men but unto God," you must necessarily either understand the oneness of the Godhead in the Holy Spirit, since when the Holy Spirit is tempted a lie is told to God; or, if you endeavour to exclude the oneness of the Godhead, you yourself according to the words of Scripture certainly believe Him to be God.

58. For if we understand that these expressions are used both of the Spirit and of the Father, we certainly observe the unity of truth and knowledge in God the Father and the Holy Spirit, for falsehood is discovered alike by the Holy Spirit and by God the Father. But if we have received each truth concerning the Spirit, why do you, faithless man, attempt to deny what you read? Confess, then, either the oneness of the Godhead of the Father, of the Son, and of the Holy Spirit, or the Godhead of the Holy Spirit. Whichever you say, you will have said each in God, for both the Unity upholds the Godhead and the Godhead the Unity.

Chapter X.

The Divinity of the Holy Spirit is supported by a passage of St. John. This passage was, indeed, erased by heretics, but it is a vain attempt, since their faithlessness could thereby more easily be convicted. The order of the context is considered in order that this passage may be shown to refer to the Spirit. He is born of the Spirit who is born again of the same Spirit, of Whom Christ Himself is believed to have been born and born again. Again, the Godhead of the Spirit is inferred from two testimonies of St. John; and lastly, it is explained how the Spirit, the water, and the blood are called witnesses.

59. Nor does the Scripture in this place alone bear witness to the Qeoth", that is, the Godhead of the Holy Spirit; but also the Lord Himself said in the Gospel: "The Spirit is God." Which passage you, Arians, so expressly testify to be said concerning the Spirit, that you remove it from your copies, and would that it were from yours and not also from those of the Church! For at the time when Auxentius had seized the Church of Milan with the arms and forces of impious unbelief, the Church of Sirmium was attacked by Valens and Ursatius, when their priests [i.e. bishops] failed in faith; this falsehood and sacrilege of yours was found in the ecclesiastical books. And it may chance that you did the same in the past.

60. And you have indeed been able to blot out the letters, but could not remove the faith. That erasure betrayed you more. that erasure condemned you more; and you were not able to obliterate the truth, but that erasure blotted out your names from the book of life. Why was the passage removed, "For God is a Spirit," if it did not pertain to the Spirit? For if you will have it that the expression is used of God the Father, you, who think it should be erased, deny, in consequence, God the Father. Choose which you will, in each the snare of your own impiety will bind you if you confess yourselves to be heathen by denying either the Father or the Spirit to be God. Therefore your confession wherein you have blotted out the Word of God remains, while you fear the original.

61. You have blotted it out, indeed, in your breasts and minds, but the Word of God is not blotted out, the Holy Spirit is not blotted out, but turns away from impious minds; not grace but iniquity is blotted out; for it is written: "I am He, I am He that blot out thine iniquities." Lastly, Moses, making request for the people, says: "Blot me out of Thy book, if Thou sparest not this people." And yet he was not blotted out, because he had no iniquity, but grace flowed forth.

62. You are, then, convicted by your own confession that you cannot say it was done with wisdom but with cunning. For by cunning you know that you are convicted by the evidence of that passage, and that your arguments cannot apply against that testimony. For whence else could the meaning of that place be derived, since the whole tenour of the passage is concerning the Spirit?

63. Nicodemus enquires about regeneration, and the Lord replies: "Verily, verily, I say unto thee, except a man be born again by water and the Spirit, he cannot enter into the kingdom of God." And that He might show that there is one birth according to the flesh, and another according to the Spirit, He added: "That which is born of the flesh is flesh, because it is born of the flesh; and that which is born of the Spirit is Spirit, because the Spirit is God." Follow out the whole course of the passage, and you will find that God has shut out your impiety by the fulness of His statement: "Marvel not," says He, "that I said, Ye must be born again. The Spirit breatheth where He listeth, and thou hearest His voice, but knowest not whence He cometh or whither He goeth, so is every one who is born of the Spirit."

64. Who is he who is born of the Spirit, and is made Spirit, but he who is renewed in the Spirit of his mind? This certainly is he who is regenerated by water and the Holy Spirit, since we receive the hope of eternal life through the layer of regeneration and renewing of the Holy Spirit. And elsewhere the Apostle Peter says: "Ye shall be baptized with the Holy Spirit." For who is he that is baptized with the Holy Spirit but he who is born again through water and the Holy Spirit? Therefore the Lord said of the Holy Spirit, Verily, verily, I say unto thee, except a man be born again by water and the Spirit, he cannot enter into the kingdom of God. And therefore He declared that we are born of Him in the latter case, through Whom He said that we were born in the former. This is the sentence of the Lord; I rest on what is written, not on argument.

65. I ask, however, why, if there be no doubt that we are born again by the Holy Spirit, there should be any doubt that we are born of the Holy Spirit, since the Lord Jesus Himself was both born and born again of the Holy Spirit. And if you confess that He was born of the Holy Spirit, because you are not able to deny it, but deny that He was born again, it is great folly to confess what is peculiar to God, and deny what is common to men. And therefore that is well said to you which was said to the Jews: "If I told you earthly things and ye believe not, how shall ye believe if I tell you heavenly things?"

66. And yet we find each passage so written in Greek, that He said not, through the Spirit, but of the Spirit. For it stands thus: ajmhvn, ajmhvn, levgw soi eja;n mhv ti" genneqh`/ ejx u}dato" kai Pneuvmato", that is, *of water and the Spirit*. Therefore, since one ought not to doubt that "that which is born of the Spirit" is written of the Holy Spirit; there is no doubt but that the Holy Spirit also is God, according to that which is written, "the Spirit is God."

67. But the same Evangelist, that he might make it plain that he wrote this concerning the Holy Spirit, says elsewhere: "Jesus Christ came by water and blood, not in the water only, but by water and blood. And the Spirit beareth witness, because the Spirit is truth; for there are three witnesses, the Spirit, the water, and the blood; and these three are one."

68. Hear how they are witnesses: The Spirit renews the mind, the water is serviceable for the layer, and the blood refers to the price. For the Spirit made us children by adoption, the water of the sacred Font washed us, the blood of the Lord redeemed us. So we obtain one invisible and one visible testimony in a spiritual sacrament, for "the Spirit Himself beareth witness to our spirit." Though the fulness of the sacrament be in each, yet there is a distinction of office; so where there is distinction of office, there certainly is not equality of witness.

Chapter XI.

The objection has been made, that the words of St. John, "The Spirit is God," are to be referred to God the Father; since Christ afterwards declares that God is to be worshipped in Spirit and in truth. The answer is, first, that by the word Spirit is sometimes meant spiritual grace; next, it is shown that, if they insist that the Person of the Holy Spirit is signified by the words "in Spirit," and therefore deny that adoration is due to Him, the argument tells equally against the Son; and since numberless passages prove that He is to be worshipped, we understand from this that the same rule is to be laid down as regards the Spirit. Why are we commanded to fall down before His footstool? Because by this is signified the Lord's Body, and as the Spirit was the Maker of this, it follows that He is to be worshipped, and yet it does not accordingly follow that Mary is to be worshipped.

166

Therefore the worship of the Spirit is not done away with, but His union with the Father is expressed, when it is said that the Father is to be worshipped in Spirit, and this point is supported by similar expressions.

69. But perhaps reference may be made to the fact that in a later passage of the same book, the Lord again said that God is Spirit, but spoke of God the Father. For you have this passage in the Gospel: "The hour now is, when the true worshippers shall worship the Father in Spirit and truth, for such also doth the Father seek. God is Spirit, and they that worship Him must worship in Spirit and truth." By this passage you wish not only to deny the divinity of the Holy Spirit, but also, from God being worshipped in Spirit, deduce a subjection of the Spirit.

70. To which point I will briefly answer that Spirit is often put for the grace of the Spirit, as the Apostle also said: "For the Spirit Himself intercedeth for us with groanings which cannot be uttered;" that is, the grace of the Spirit, unless perchance you have been able to hear the groanings of the Holy Spirit. Therefore here too God is worshipped, not in the wickedness of the heart, but in the grace of the Spirit. "For into a malicious soul wisdom does not enter," because "no one can call Jesus Lord but in the Holy Spirit." And immediately he adds: "Now there are diversities of gifts."

71. Now this cannot pertain to the fulness, nor to the dividing of the Spirit; for neither does the mind of man grasp His fulness, nor is He divided into any portions of Himself; but He pours into [the soul] the gift of spiritual grace, in which God is worshipped as He is also worshipped in truth, for no one worships Him except he who drinks in the truth of His Godhead with pious affection. And he certainly does not apprehend Christ as it were personally, nor the Holy Spirit personally.

72. Or if you think that this is said as it were personally of Christ and of the Spirit, then God is worshipped in truth in like manner as He is worshipped in Spirit. There is therefore either a like subjection, which God forbid that you should believe, and the Son is not worshipped; or, which is true, there is a like grace of Unity, and the Spirit is worshipped.

73. Let us then here draw our inferences and put an end to the impious questionings of the Arians. For if they say that the Spirit is therefore not to be worshipped because God is worshipped in Spirit, let them then say that the Truth is not to be worshipped, because God is worshipped in truth. For although there be many truths, since it is written: "Truths are minished from the sons of men;" yet they are given by the Divine Truth, which is Christ, Who says: "I am the Way, the Truth, and the Life." If therefore they understand the truth in this passage from custom, let them also understand the grace of the Spirit, and there is no stumbling; or if they receive Christ as the Truth, let them deny that He is to be worshipped.

74. But they are refuted by the acts of the pious, and by the course of the Scriptures. For Mary worshipped Christ, and therefore is appointed to be the messenger of the Resurrection to the apostles, loosening the hereditary bond, and the huge offence of womankind. For this the Lord wrought mystically, "that where sin had exceedingly abounded, grace might more exceedingly abound." And rightly is a woman appointed [as messenger] to men; that she who first had brought the message of sin to man should first bring the message of the grace of the Lord.

75. And the apostles worshipped; and therefore they who bore the testimony of the faith received authority as to the faith. And the angels worshipped, of whom it is written: "And let all His angels worship Him."

76. But they worship not only His Godhead but also His Footstool, as it is written: "And worship His footstool, for it is holy," Or if they deny that in Christ the mysteries also of His Incarnation are to be worshipped, in which we observe as it were certain express traces of His Godhead, and certain ways of the Heavenly Word; let them read that even the apostles worshipped Him when He rose again in the glory of His Flesh.

77. Therefore if it do not at all detract from Christ, that God is worshipped in Christ, for Christ too is worshipped; it certainly also detracts nothing from the Spirit that God is worshipped in the Spirit, for the Spirit also is worshipped, as the Apostle has said: "We serve the

Spirit of God," for he who serves worships also, as it is said in an earlier passage: "Thou shalt worship the Lord thy God, and Him only shalt thou serve."

78. But lest any one should perchance seem to elude the instance we have adduced, let us consider in what manner that which the prophet says, "Worship His Footstool," appears to refer to the mystery of the divine Incarnation, for we must not estimate the footstool from the custom of men. For neither has God a body, neither is He other than beyond measure, that we should think a footstool was laid down as a support for His feet. And we read that nothing besides God is to be worshipped, for it is written: "Thou shalt worship the Lord thy God, and Him only shalt thou serve." How, then, should the prophet, brought up under the Law, and instructed in the Law, give a precept against the Law? The question, then, is not unimportant, and so let us more diligently consider what the footstool is. For we read elsewhere: "The heaven is My throne, and the earth the footstool of My feet." But the earth is not to be worshipped by us, for it is a creature of God.

79. Let us, however, see whether the prophet does not say that that earth is to be worshipped which the Lord Jesus took upon Him in assuming flesh. And so, by foot-stool is understood earth, but by the earth the Flesh of Christ, which we this day also adore in the mysteries, and which the apostles, as we said above, adored in the Lord Jesus; for Christ is not divided but is one; nor, when He is adored as the Son of God, is He denied to have been born of the Virgin. Since, then, the mystery of the Incarnation is to be adored, and the Incarnation is the work of the Spirit, as it is written, "The Holy Spirit shall come upon thee, and the power of the Most High shall overshadow thee, and that Holy Thing Which shall be born of thee shall be called the Son of God," without doubt the Holy Spirit also is to be adored, since He Who according to the flesh was born of the Holy Spirit is adored.

80. And let no one divert this to the Virgin Mary; Mary was the temple of God, not the God of the temple. And therefore He alone is to be worshipped Who was working in His temple.

81. It makes, then, nothing against our argument that God is worshipped in Spirit, for the Spirit also is worshipped. Although if we consider the words themselves, what else ought we to understand in the Father, the Son, and the Holy Spirit, but the unity of the same power. For what is "must worship in Spirit and in truth"? If, however, you do not refer this to the grace of the Spirit, nor the true faith of conscience; but, as we said, personally (if indeed this word person is fit to express the Divine Majesty), you must take it of Christ and of the Spirit.

82. What means, then, the Father is worshipped in Christ, except that the Father is in Christ, and the Father speaks in Christ, and the Father abides in Christ. Not, indeed, as a body in a body, for God is not a body; nor as a confused mixture [*confusus in confuso*], but as the true in the true, God in God, Light in Light; as the eternal Father in the co-eternal Son. So not an ingrafting of a body is meant, but unity of power. Therefore, by unity of power, Christ is jointly worshipped in the Father when God the Father is worshipped in Christ. In like manner, then, by unity of the same power the Spirit is jointly worshipped in God, when God is worshipped in the Spirit.

83. Let us investigate the force of that word and expression more diligently, and deduce its proper meaning from other passages. "Thou hast," it is said, "made them all in wisdom." Do we here understand that Wisdom was without a share in the things that were made? But "all things were made by Him." And David says: "By the Word of the Lord were theheavens established." So, then, he himself who calls the Son of God the maker even of heavenly things, has also plainly said that all things were made in the Son, that in the renewal of His works He might by no means separate the Son from the Father, but unite Him to the Father.

84. Paul, too, says: "For in Him were all things created in the heavens and in the earth, Visible and invisible." Does he, then, when he says, "in Him," deny that they were made through Him? Certainly he did not deny but affirmed it. And further he says in another place: "One Lord Jesus, through Whom are all things." In saying, then, "through Him," has he denied that all things were made in Him, through Whom he says that all things exist? These words, "in

Him" and "with Him," have this force, that by them is understood one and like in all respects, not contrary. Which he also made clear farther on, saying: "All things have been created through Him and in Him;" for, as we said above, Scripture witnesses that these three expressions, "with Him," and "through Him," and "in Him," are equivalent in Christ. For you read that all things were made through Him and in Him.

85. Learn also that the Father was with Him, and He with the Father, when all things were being made. Wisdom says: "When He was preparing the heavens I was with Him, when He was making the fountains of waters." And in the Old Testament the Father, by saying, "Let Us make," showed that the Son was to be worshipped with Himself as the Maker of all things. As, then, those things are said to have been created in the Son, of which the Son is received as the Creator; so, too, when God is said to be worshipped in truth by the proper meaning of the word itself often expressed after the same manner it ought to be understood, that the Son too is worshipped. So in like manner is the Spirit also worshipped because God is worshipped in Spirit, Therefore the Father is worshipped both with the Son and with the Spirit, because the Trinity is worshipped.

Chapter XII.

From the fact that St. Paul has shown that the light of the Godhead which the three apostles worshipped in Christ is in the Trinity, it is made clear that the Spirit also is to be worshipped. It is shown from the words themselves that the Spirit is intended by the apostles. The Godhead of the same Spirit is proved from the fact that He has a temple wherein He dwells not as a priest, but as God: and is worshipped with the Father and the Son; whence is understood the oneness of nature in Them.

86. But does any one deny that the Godhead of the eternal Trinity is to be worshipped? whereas the Scriptures also express the inexplicable Majesty of the Divine Trinity, as the Apostle says elsewhere: "Since God, Who said that light should shine out of darkness, shined in our hearts to give the light of the knowledge of the glory of God in the face of Jesus Christ."

87. The apostles truly saw this glory, when the Lord Jesus on the mount shone with the light of His Godhead: "The apostles," it says, "saw it and fell on their face." Do not you think that they even, as they fell, worshipped, when they could not with their bodily eyes endure the brightness of the divine splendour, and the glory of eternal light dulled the keenness of mortal sight? Or what else did they who saw His glory say at that time, except, "O come let us worship and fall down before Him"? For "God shined in our hearts to give the light of the knowledge of the glory of God in the face of Jesus Christ."

88. Who is He, then, Who shined that we might know God in the face of Jesus Christ? For he said, "God shined," that the glory of God might be known in the face of Jesus Christ. Whom else do we think but the manifested Spirit? Or who else is there besides the Holy Spirit to Whom the power of the Godhead may be referred? For they who exclude the Spirit must necessarily bring in another, who may with the Father and the Son receive the glory of the Godhead.

89. Let us then go back to the same words: "It is God Who shined in our hearts to give the light of the knowledge of the glory of God in the face of Jesus Christ." You have Christ plainly set forth. For Whose glory is said to give light but that of the Spirit? So, then, he set forth God Himself, since he spoke of the glory of God; if of the Father, it remains that "He who said that light should shine out of darkness, and shine in our hearts," be understood to be the Holy Spirit, for we cannot venerate any other with the Father and the Son. If, then, you understand the Spirit, Him also has the Apostle called God; it is necessary, then, that you also confess the Godhead of the Spirit, who now deny it.

90. But how shamelessly do you deny this, since you have read that the Holy Spirit has a temple. For it is written: "Ye are the temple of God, and the Holy Spirit dwelleth in you." Now God has a temple, a creature has no true temple. But the Spirit, Who dwelleth in us, has a temple. For it is written: "Your members are temples of the Holy Spirit."

91. But He does not dwell in the temple as a priest, nor as a minister, but as God, since the Lord Jesus Himself said: "I will dwell in them, and will walk among them, and will be their God, and they shall be My people." And David says: "The Lord is in His holy temple." Therefore the Spirit dwells in His holy temple, as the Father dwells and as the Son dwells, Who says: "I and the Father will come, and will make Our abode with him."

92. But the Father abides in us through the Spirit, Whom He has given us. How, then, can different natures abide together? Certainly it is impossible. But the Spirit abides with the Father and the Son. Whence, too, the Apostle joined the Communion of the Holy Spirit with the grace of Jesus Christ and the love of God, saying: "The grace of our Lord Jesus Christ, and the love of God, and the Communion of the Holy Spirit be with you all."

91. We observe, then, that the Father, the Son, and the Holy Spirit abide in one and the same [subject] through the oneness of the same nature. Therefore, He Who dwells in the temple has divine power, for as of the Father and of the Son, so are we also the temple of the Holy Spirit; not many temples, but one temple, for it is the temple of one Power.

Chapter XIII.

To those who object that Catholics, when they ascribe Godhead to the Holy Spirit, introduce three Gods, it is answered, that by the same argument they themselves bring in two Gods, unless they deny Godhead to the Son; after which the orthodox doctrine is set forth.

92. But what do you fear? Is it that which you have been accustomed to carp at? lest you should make three Gods. God forbid; for where the Godhead is understood as one, one God is spoken of. For neither when we call the Son God do we say there are two Gods. For if, when you confess the Godhead of the Spirit, you think that three Gods are spoken of, then, too, when you speak of the Godhead of the Son because you are not able to deny it, you bring in two Gods. For it is necessary according to your opinion, if you think that God is the name of one person, not of one nature, that you either say that there are two Gods, or deny that the Son is God.

93. But let us free you from the charge of ignorance, though we do not excuse you from fault For according to our opinion, because there is one God, one Godhead and oneness of power is understood. For as we say that there is one God, confessing the Father, and not denying the Son under the true Name of the Godhead; so, too, we exclude not the Holy Spirit from the Unity of the Godhead, and do not assert but deny that there are three Gods, because it is not unity but a division of power which makes plurality. For how can the Unity of the Godhead admit of plurality, seeing that plurality is of numbers, but the Divine Nature does not admit numbers?

Chapter XIV.

Besides the evidence adduced above, other passages can be brought to prove the sovereignty of the Three Persons. Two are quoted from the Epistles to the Thessalonians, and by collating other testimonies of the Scriptures it is shown that in them dominion is claimed for the Spirit as for the other Persons. Then, by quotation of another still more express passage in the second Epistle to the Corinthians, it is inferred both that the Spirit is Lord, and that where the Lord is, there is the Spirit.

94. God, then, is One, without violation of the majesty of the eternal Trinity, as is declared in the instance set before us. And not in that place alone do we see the Trinity expressed in the Name of the Godhead; but both in many places, as we have said also above, and especially in the epistles which the Apostle wrote to the Thessalonians, he most clearly set forth the Godhead and sovereignty of the Father, the Son, and the Holy Spirit. For you read as follows: "The Lord make you to increase and abound In love one toward another, and toward all men, as we also do toward you, to the stablishing of your hearts without blame in holiness before God and our Father at the coming of the Lord Jesus."

95. Who, then, is the Lord Who makes us to increase and abound before God and our Father at the coming of the Lord Jesus? He has named the Father and has named the Son; Whom, then, has he joined with the Father and the Son except the Spirit? Who is the Lord Who establishes our hearts in holiness. For holiness is a grace of the Spirit, as, too, is said farther on: "In holiness of the Spirit and belief of the truth."

96. Who, then, do you think is here named Lord, except the Spirit? And has not God the Father been able to teach you, Who says: "Upon Whomsoever thou shalt see the Spirit descending and abiding upon Him, this is He Who baptizeth in the Holy Spirit"? For the Spirit descended in the likeness of a dove, that He might both bear witness to His wisdom, and perfect the sacrament of the spiritual layer, and show that His working is one with that of the Father and the Son.

97. And that you should not suppose that anything had fallen from the Apostle by oversight, but that he knowingly and designedly and inspired by the Spirit designated Him Lord, Whom he felt to be God, he repeated the same in the second Epistle to the Thessalonians, saying: "But the Lord direct your hearts in the love of God and in the patience of Christ." If love be of God and patience of Christ, it ought to be shown Who is the Lord Who directs, if we deny that the direction is of the Holy Spirit.

98. But we cannot deny it, since the Lord said of Him: "I have yet many things to say unto you, but ye cannot bear them now. But when He, the Spirit of Truth, shall come, He will lead you into all truth." And David says of Him: "Thy good Spirit shall lead me into the right way."

99. See what the voice of the Lord uttered concerning the Holy Spirit. The Son of God came, and because He had not yet shed forth the Spirit, He declared that we were living like little children without the Spirit. He said that the Spirit was to come Who should make of these little children stronger men, by an increase, namely, of spiritual age. And this He laid down not that He might set the power of the Spirit in the first place, but that He might show that the fulness of strength consists in the knowledge of the Trinity.

100. It is therefore necessary either that you mention some fourth person besides the Spirit of whom you ought to be conscious, or assuredly that you do not consider another to be Lord, except the Spirit Who has been pointed out.

101. But if you require the plain statement of the words in which Scripture has spoken of the Spirit as Lord, it cannot have escaped you that it is written: "Now the Lord is the Spirit." Which the course of the whole passage shows to have been certainly said of the Holy Spirit. And so let us consider the apostolic statement: "As often as Moses is read," says he, "a veil is laid over their heart; but when they shall be turned to the Lord, the veil shall be taken away. Now the Lord is the Spirit; but where the Spirit of the Lord is, there is liberty."

102. So he not only called the Spirit Lord, but also added: "But where the Spirit of the Lord is, there is liberty. So we all with unveiled face, reflecting the glory of the Lord, are formed anew into the same image from glory to glory, as from the Lord the Spirit;" that is, we who have been before converted to the Lord, so as by spiritual understanding to see the glory of the Lord, as it were, in the minor of the Scriptures, are now being transformed from that glory which converted us to the Lord, to the heavenly glory. Therefore since it is · the Lord to Whom we are converted, butthe Lord is that Spirit by Whom we are formed anew, who are converted to the Lord, assuredly the Holy Ghost is pointed out, for He Who forms anew receives those who are converted. For how should He form again those whom He had not received.

103. Though why should we seek for the expression of words, where we see the expression of unity? For although you may distinguish between Lord and Spirit, you cannot deny that where the Lord is, there too is the Spirit, and he who has been converted to the Lord will have been converted to the Spirit. If you cavil at the letter, you cannot injure the Unity; if you wish to separate the Unity, you confess the Spirit Himself as the Lord of power.

Chapter XV.

Though the Spirit be called Lord, three Lords are not thereby implied; inasmuch as two Lords are not implied by the fact that the Son in the same manner as the Father is called Lord in many passages of Scripture; for Lordship exists in the Godhead, and the Godhead in Lordship, and these coincide without division in the Three Persons.

104. But perhaps, again, you may say: If I call the Spirit Lord, I shall set forth three Lords. Do you then when you call the Son Lord either deny the Son or confess two Lords? God forbid, for the Son Himself said: "Do not serve two lords." But certainly He denied not either Himself or the Father to be Lord; for He called the Father Lord, as you read: "I thank Thee, O Father, Lord of heaven and earth." And the Lord spoke of Himself, as we read in the Gospel: "Ye call Me Master and Lord, and ye do well, for so I am." But He spoke not of two Lords; indeed He shows that He did not speak of two Lords, when He warns them: "Do not serve two lords." For there are not two Lords where the Lordship is but one, for the Father is in the Son and the Son in the Father, and so there is one Lord.

105. Such, too, was the teaching of the Law: "Hear, O Israel, the Lord thy God is one Lord," that is, unchangeable, always abiding in unity of power, always the same, and not altered by any accession or diminution. Therefore Moses called Him One, and yet also relates that the Lord rained down fire from the Lord. The Apostle, too, says: "The Lord grant unto him to find mercy of the Lord." The Lord rains down from the Lord; the Lord grants mercy from the Lord. The Lord is neither divided when He rains from the Lord, nor is there a separation when He grants mercy from the Lord, but in each case the oneness of the Lordship is expressed.

106. In the Psalms, too, you find: "The Lord said unto my Lord." And he did not therefore deny that the Father was his Lord, because he spoke of the Son as his Lord; but therefore called the Son his Lord, that you might not think Him to be the Son, but the Lord of the prophet, as the Lord Himself showed in the Gospel, when He said: "If David in the Spirit called Him Lord, how is he his Son?" David, not the Spirit, calls Him Lord in the Spirit. Or if they falsely infer from this that the Spirit called Him Lord, they must necessarily by a like sacrilege seem to assert that the Son of God is also the Son of the Spirit.

107. So, as we do not say that there are two Lords, when we so style both the Father and the Son, so, too, we do not say that there are three Lords, when we confess the Spirit to be Lord. For as it is profane to say that there are three Lords or three Gods, so, too, is it utter profanity to speak of two Lords or two Gods; for there is one God, one Lord, one Holy Spirit; and He Who is God is Lord, and He Who is Lord is God, for the Godhead is in the Lordship, and the Lordship is in the Godhead.

108. Lastly, you have read that the Father is both Lord and God: "O Lord my God, I will call upon Thee, hear Thou me." You find the Son to be both Lord and God, as you have read in the Gospel, that, when Thomas had touched the side of Christ, he said, "My Lord and my God." So in like manner as the Father is God and the Son Lord, so too the Son is God and the Father Lord. The holy designation changes from one to the other, the divine nature changes not, but the dignity remains unchangeable. For they are not [as it were] contributions gathered from bounty, but free-will gifts of natural love; for both Unity has its special property, and the special properties are bound together in unity.

Chapter XVI.

The Father is holy, and likewise the Son and the Spirit, and so They are honoured in the same Trisagion: nor can we speak more worthily of God than by calling Him Holy; whence it is clear that we must not derogate from the dignity of the Holy Spirit. In Him is all which pertains to God, since in baptism He is named with the Father and the Son, and the Father has given to Him to be greater than all, nor can any one deprive Him of this. And so from the very passage of St. John which heretics used against His dignity, the equality of the Trinity and the Unity of the Godhead is established. Lastly, after explaining how the Son receives from the Father, St. Ambrose shows how various heresies are refuted by the passage cited.

109. So, then, the Father is holy, the Son is holy, and the Spirit is holy, but they are not three Holies; for there is one Holy God, one Lord. For the true holiness is one, as the true Godhead is one, as that true holiness belonging to the Divine Nature is one.

110. So everything which we esteem holy proclaims that Sole Holiness. Cherubim and Seraphim with unwearied voices praise Him and say: "Holy, Holy, Holy, is the Lord God of Sabaoth." They say it, not once, lest you should believe that there is but one; not twice, lest you should exclude the Spirit; they say not holies[in the plural], lest you should imagine that there is plurality, but they repeat thrice and say the same word, that even in a hymn you may understand the distinction of Persons in the Trinity, and the oneness of the Godhead and while they say this they proclaim God.

111. We too find nothing of more worth, whereby we are able to proclaim God, than the calling Him holy. Everything is too low for God, too low for the Lord. And therefore consider from this fact also whether one ought at all to derogate from the Holy Spirit, whose Name is the praise of God. For thus is the Father praised, thus is the Son also praised, in the same manner as the Spirit also is named and praised. The Seraphim utter praise, the whole company of the blessed utter praise, inasmuch as they call God holy, the Son holy, the Spirit holy.

112. How, then, does He not possess all that pertains to God, Who is named by priests in baptism with the Father and the Son, and is invoked in the oblations, is proclaimed by the Seraphim in heaven with the Father and the Son, dwells in the Saints with the Father and the Son, is poured upon the just, is given as the source of inspiration to the prophets? And for this reason in the divine Scripture all is called Qeopneusto", because God inspires what the Spirit has spoken.

113. Or if they are unwilling to allow that the Holy Spirit has all things which pertain to God, and can do all things, let them say what He has not, and what He cannot do. For like as the Son has all things, and the Father grudges not to give all things to the Son according to His nature, having given to Him that which is greater than all, as the Scripture bears witness, saying: "That which My Father hath given unto Me is greater than all." So too the Spirit has of Christ that which is greater than all, because righteousness knows not grudging.

114. So, then, if we attend diligently, we comprehend here also the oneness of the Divine Power. He says: "That which My Father hath given unto Me is greater than all, and no one is able to snatch them out of My Father's hand. I and the Father are One." For if we rightly showed above that the Holy Spirit is the Hand of the Father, the same is certainly the Hand of the Father which is the Hand of the Son, since the Same is the Spirit of the Father Who is the Spirit of the Son. Therefore whosoever of us receives eternal life in this Name of the Trinity, as he is not torn from the Father; so he is not torn from the Son, so too he is not torn from the Spirit.

115. Again, from the very fact that the Father is said to have given to the Son, and the Spirit to have received from the Son, as it is written: "He shall glorify Me, for He shall take of Mine, and shall declare it unto you" (which He seems to have said rather of the office of distributing, than of the prerogative of Divine Power, for those whom the Son redeemed the Spirit also, Who was to sanctify them, received), from those very words, I say, from which they construct their sophistry, the Unity of the Godhead is perceived, not the need of a gift.

116. The Father gave by begetting, not by adoption; He gave as it were that which was contained in the very prerogative of the Divine Nature, not what was lacking as it were by favour of His bounty. And so because the Son acquires persons to Himself as the Father does; so gives life as does the Father, He expressed His equality with the Father in the Unity of Power, saying: "I and the Father are One." For when He says, "I and the Father," equality is revealed; when He says, "are One," Unity is asserted. Equality excludes confusion; Unity excludes separation. Equality distinguishes between the Father and the Son; Unity does not separate the Father and the Son.

117. Therefore, when He says, "I and the Father," He rejects the Sabellian, for He says that He is one, the Father another; He rejects the Photinian, for He joins Himself with God the Father. With the former words He rejects those, for He said: "I and the Father;" with the latter words He rejects the Arians, for He says: "are One." Yet in both the former and the latter words He refutes the heretical violence (1) of the Sabellians, for He said: "We are One [Substance]," not "We are One[Person]." And (2) of the Arians, for He said: "I and the Father," not "the Father and I." Which was certainly not a sign of rudeness, but of dutifulness and foreknowledge, that we might not think wrongly from the order of the words, For unity knows no order equality knows no gradation; nor can it be laid to the Son of God that the Teacher Himself of dutifulness should offend against dutifulness by rudeness.

Chapter XVII.

St. Ambrose shows by instances that the places in which those words were spoken help to the understanding of the words of the Lord; he shows that Christ uttered the passage quoted from St. John in Solomon's porch, by which is signified the mind of a wise man, for he says that Christ would not have uttered this saying in the heart of a foolish or contentious man. He goes on to say that Christ is stoned by those who believe not these words, and as the keys of heaven were given to Peter for his confession of them, so Iscariot, because he believed not the same, perished evilly. He takes this opportunity to inveigh against the Jews who bought the Son of God and sold Joseph. He explains the price paid for each mystically; and having in the same manner expounded the murmuring of the traitor concerningMagdalene's ointment, he adds that Christ is bought in one way by heretics in another way by Catholics,and that those in vain take to themselves the name of Christians who sever the Spirit from the Father.

118. It is worth while to notice in what place the Lord held this discussion, for His utterances are often[better] estimated by the kind of places in which He conversed. When about to fast, He is led(as we read) into the wilderness to render vain the devil's temptations. For although it deserves praise to have lived temperately in the midst of abundance, yet the enticements of temptation are more frequent amongst riches and pleasures. Then the tempter, in order to try Him, promises Him abundance, and the Lord in order to overcome cherishes hunger. Now I do not deny that temperance can exist in the midst of riches; but although he who navigates the sea often escapes, yet he is more exposed to peril than he who will not go to sea.

119. Let us consider some other points. When about to promise the kingdom of heaven, Jesus went up into a mountain. At another time He leads His disciples through the corn-fields, when about to sow in their minds the crop of heavenly precepts. so that a plentiful harvest of souls should ripen. When about to consummate the work of the flesh which He had taken, having now seen perfection in His disciples, whom He had established upon the root of His words, He enters a garden, that He might plant the young olive-trees in the house of the Lord, and that He might water the just flourishing like a palm-tree, and the fruitful vine with the stream of His Blood.

120. In this passage too He was walking, as we read, in Solomon's porch on the day' of the dedication, that is, Christ was walking in the breast of the wise and prudent, to dedicate his good affection to Himself. What that porch was the prophet teaches, saying: "I will walk in the midst of Thy house in the innocency of my heart." So, then, we have in our own selves the house of God, we have the halls, we have also the porches, and we have the cents, for it is written: "Let thy waters flow abroad in thy courts." Open, then, this porch of thy heart to the Word of God, Who says to thee: "Open thy mouth wide and I will fill it."

121. Let us, therefore, hear what the Word of God, walking in the heart of the wise and peaceful, says: "I and My Father are One." He will not say this in the 'breast of the unquiet and foolish, for "the natural man receiveth not the things of the Spirit of God, for they are foolishness unto him." The narrow breasts of sinners do not take in the greatness of the faith. Lastly, the Jews hearing, "I and the Father are One, took up stones to stone Him."

122. He who cannot listen to this is a Jew; he who cannot listen to this stones Christ with the stones of his treachery, rougher than any rock, and if you believe me, he wounds Christ. For although He cannot now feel a wound: "For now henceforth we know not Christ after the flesh," yet He Who rejoices in the love of the Church is stoned by the impiety of the Arians.

123. "The law of Thy mouth, O Lord, is good unto me, I keep Thy commandments." Thou hast Thyself said that Thou art one with the Father. Because Peter believed this, he received the keys of the kingdom of heaven, and without anxiety for himself forgave sins. Judas, because he believed not this, strangled himself with the cord of his own wickedness. O the hard stones of unbelieving words! O the unseemly cord of the betrayer, and the still more hideous purchase-money of the Jews! O hateful money wherewith either the just is bought for death, or sold! Joseph was sold, Jesus Christ was bought, the one to slavery, the Other to death. O detestable inheritance, O deadly sale, which either sells a brother to suffering or sets a price on the Lord to destroy Him, the Purchaser of the salvation of all.

124. The Jews did violence to two things which are chief of all, faith and duty, and in each to Christ the Author of faith and duty. For both in the patriarch Joseph was there a type of Christ, and Christ Himself came in the truth of His Body, "Who counted it not robbery that He should be equal with God, but took on Him the form of a servant," because of our fall, that is to say, taking slavery upon Himself and not shrinking from suffering.

125. In one place the sale is for twenty pieces, in the other for thirty. For how could His true price be apprehended, Whose value cannot be limited? There is error in the price because there is error in the inquiry. The sale is for twenty pieces in the Old Testament, for thirty in the New; for the Truth is of more value than the type, Grace is more generous than training, the Presence is better than the Law, for the Law promised the Coming, the Coming fulfilled the Law.

126. The Ishmaelites made their purchase for twenty pieces, the Jews for thirty. And this is no trivial figure. The faithless are more lavish for iniquity than the faithful for salvation. It is, however, fitting to consider the quality of each agreement. Twenty pieces are the price of him sold to slavery, thirty pieces of Him delivered to the Cross. For although the Mysteries of the Incarnation and of the Passion must be in like manner matters of amazement, yet the fulfilment of faith is in the Mystery of the Passion. I do not indeed value less the birth from the holy Virgin, but I receive even more gratefully the Mystery of the sacred Body. What is more full of mercy than that He should forgive me the wrongs done to Himself? But it is even fuller measure that He gave us so great a gift, that He Who was not to die because He was God, should die by our death, that we might live by His Spirit.

127. Lastly, it was not without meaning that Judas Iscariot valued that ointment at three hundred pence, which seems certainly by the statement of the price itself to set forth the Lord's cross. Whence, too, the Lord says: "For she, pouring this ointment on My body, did it for My burial." Why, then, did Judas value this at so high a rate? Because remission of sins is of more value to sinners, and forgiveness seems to be more precious. Lastly, you find it written: "To whom much is forgiven the same loveth more." Therefore sinners themselves also confess the grace of the Lord's Passion which they have lost, and they bear witness to Christ who persecuted Him.

128. Or because, "into a malicious soul wisdom does not enter," the evil disposition of the traitor uttered this@ and he valued the suffering of the Lord's body at a dearer rate, that by the immensity of the price he might draw all away from the faith. And therefore the Lord offered Himself without price, that the necessity of poverty might hold no one hack from Christ. The patriarchs sold Him for a small price that all might buy. Isaiah said: "Ye that have no money go buy and drink; eat ye without money," that he might gain him who had no money. O traitor Judas, thou valuest the ointment of His Passion at three hundred pence, and sellest His Passion for thirty pence. Profuse in valuing, mean in selling.

129. So, then, all do not buy Christ at the same price; Photinus, who buys Him for death, buys Him at one price; the Arian, who buys Him to wrong Him, at another price; the Catholic,

who buys Him to glorify Him, at another. But he buys Him without money according to that which is written: "He that hath no money let him buy without price."

130. "Not all," says Christ, "that say unto Me, Lord, Lord, shall enter into the kingdom of heaven!" Although many call themselves Christians, and make use of the name, yet not all shall receive the reward. Both Cain offered sacrifice, and Judas received the kiss, but it was said to him, "Judas, betrayest thou the Son of Man with a kiss?" that is, thou fillest up thy wickedness with the pledge of affection, and sowest hatred with the implement of peace, and inflictest death with the outward token of love.

131. Let not, then, the Arians flatter themselves with the employment of the name, because they call themselves Christians. The Lord will answer them: You set forward My Name, and deny My Substance, but I do not recognize My Name where My eternal Godhead is not. That is not My Name which is divided from the Father, and separated from the Spirit; I do not recognize My Name where I do not recognize My doctrine; I do not recognize My Name where I do not recognize My Spirit. For he knows not that he is comparing the Spirit of the Father to those servants whom He created. Concerning which point we have already spoken at length.

Chapter XVIII.

As he purposes to establish the Godhead of the Holy Spirit by the points already discussed, St. Ambrose touches again on some of them; for instance, that He does not commit but forgives sin; that He is not a creature but the Creator; and lastly, that He does not offer but receives worship.

132. But to sum up, in order at the end more distinctly to gather up the arguments which have been used here and there, the evident glory of the Godhead is proved both by other arguments, and most especially by these four. God is known by these marks: either that He is without sin; or that He forgives sin; or that He is not a creature but the Creator; or that He does not give but receives worship.

133. So, then, no one is without sin except God alone, for no one is without sin except God. Also, no one forgives sins except God alone, for it is also written: "Who can forgive sins but God alone?" And one cannot be the Creator of all except he be not a creature, and he who is not a creature is without doubt God; for it is written: "They worshipped the creature rather than the Creator, Who is God blessed for ever." God also does not worship, but is worshipped, for it is written: "Thou shalt worship the Lord thy God, and Him only shall thou serve."

134. Let us therefore consider whether the Holy Spirit have any of these marks which may bear witness to His Godhead. And first let us treat of the point that none is without sin except God alone, and demand that they prove that the Holy Spirit has sin.

135. But they are unable to show us this, and demand our authority from us, namely, that we should show by texts that the Holy Spirit has not sinned, as it is said of the Son that He did no sin. Let them learn that we teach by authority of the Scriptures; for it is written: "For in Wisdom is a Spirit of understanding, holy, one only, manifold, subtle, easy to move, eloquent, undefiled." The Scripture says He is undefiled, has it lied concerning the Son, that you should believe it to have lied concerning the Spirit?For the prophet said in the same place concerning Wisdom, that nothing that defiles enters into her. She herself is undefiled, and her Spirit is undefiled. Therefore if the Spirit have not sin, He is God.

136. But how can He be guilty of sin Who Himself forgives sins?Therefore He has not committed sin, and if He be without sin He is not a creature. For every creature is exposed to the capability of sin, and the eternal Godhead alone is free from sin and undefiled.

137. Let us now see whether the Spirit forgives sins. But on this point there can be no doubt, since the Lord Himself said: "Receive ye the Holy Spirit. Whosoever sins ye forgive they shall be forgiven." See that sins are forgiven through the Holy Spirit. But men make use of their ministry for the forgiveness of sins, they do not exercise the right of any power of their own. For they forgive sins not in their own name but in that of the Father and of the Son and of

the Holy Spirit. They ask, the Godhead gives, the service is of man, the gift is of the Power on high.

138. And it is not doubtful that sin is forgiven by means of baptism, but in baptism the operation is that of the Father and of the Son and of the Holy Spirit. If, therefore, the Spirit forgives sin, since it is written, "Who can forgive sins except God alone?" certainly He Who cannot be separated from the oneness of the name of the Nature is also incapable of being severed from the power of God. Now if He is not severed from the power of God, how is He severed from the name of God.

139. Let us now see whether He be a creature or the Creator. But since we have above most clearly proved Him to be the Creator, as it is written: "The Spirit of God Who hath made me;" and it has been declared that the face of the earth is renewed by the Spirit, and that all things languish without the Spirit, it is clear that the Spirit is the Creator. But who can doubt this, since, as we have shown above, not even the generation of the Lord from the Virgin, which is more excellent than all creatures, is without the operation of the Spirit?

140. Therefore the Spirit is not a creature, but the Creator, and He Who is Creator is certainly not a creature. And because He is not a creature, without doubt He is the Creator Who produces all things together with the Father and the Son. But if He be the Creator, certainly the Apostle, by saying in condemnation of the Gentiles, "Who served the creature rather than the Creator, Who is God blessed for ever," and by warning men, as I said above, that the Holy Spirit is to be served, both showed Him to be the Creator, and because He is the Creator demonstrated that He ought to be called God. Which he also sums up In the Epistle written to the Hebrews, saying: "For He that created all things is God." Let them, therefore, either say what it is which has been created without the Father, Son, and Holy Spirit, or let them confess that the Spirit also is of one Godhead with the Father and the Son.

141. The writer taught also that He was to be worshipped, Whom he called Lord and God. For He Who is the God and Lord of the Universe is certainly to be worshipped by all, for it is thus written: "Thou shalt worship the Lord thy God, and Him only shall thou serve."

142. Or let them say where they have read that the Spirit worships. For it is said of the Son of God: "Let all the Angels of God worship Him;" we do not read, Let the Spirit worship Him. For how can He worship Who is not amongst servants and ministers, but, together with the Father and the Son, has the service of the just under Him, for it is written: "We serve the Spirit of God." He is, therefore, to be worshipped by us, Whom the Apostle taught that we must serve, and Whom we serve we also adore, according to that which is written, to repeat the same words again: "Thou shall worship the Lord thy God, and Him only shalt thou serve."

143. Although the Apostle has not omitted even this point, so as to omit to teach us that the Spirit is to be worshipped. For since we have demonstrated that the Spirit is in the prophets, no one can doubt that prophecy is given by the Spirit, and plainly when He Who is in the prophets is worshipped, the same Spirit is worshipped. And so you find: "If the whole Church be assembled together, and all speak with tongues, and there come in one unlearned or unbelieving, will he not say that ye are mad? But if all prophesy, and there come in one unlearned and unbelieving, he is convicted by all, he is judged by all. For the secrets of his heart are made manifest, and so falling down on his face he will worship God, declaring that God is in truth among you." It is, therefore, God Who is worshipped, God Who abides and Who speaks in the prophets; but the Spirit thus abides and speaks, therefore, also, the Spirit is worshipped.

Chapter XIX.

Having proved above that the Spirit abides and speaks in the prophets, St. Ambrose infers that He knows all things which are of God, and therefore is One with the Father and the Son. This same point he establishes again from the fact that He possesses all that God possesses, namely, Godhead, knowledge of the heart, truth, a Name above every name, and power to raise the dead, as is proved from Ezekiel, and in this He is equal to the Son.

144. And So as the Father and the Son are One, because the Son has all things which the Father has, so too the Spirit is one with the Father and the Son, because He too knows all the things of God. For He did not obtain it by force, so that there should be any injury as of one who had suffered loss; He did not seize it, lest the loss should be his from whom it might seem to have been plundered. For neither did He seize it through need, nor through superiority of greater power did He take it by force, but He possesses it by unity of power. Therefore, if He works all these things, for one and the same Spirit worketh all, how is He not God Who has all things which God has?

145. Or let us consider what God may have which the Holy Spirit has not. God the Father has Godhead, and the Son, too, in Whom dwells the fulness of the Godhead, has it, and the Spirit has it, for it is written: "The Spirit of God is in my nostrils."

146. God, again, searches the hearts and reins, for it is written: "God searcheth the hearts and reins." The Son also has this power, Who said, "Why think ye evil in your hearts?" For Jesus knew their thoughts. And the Spirit has the same power, Who manifests to the prophets also the secrets of the hearts of others, as we said above: "for the secrets of his heart are made manifest," And why do we wonder if He searches the hidden things of man Who searches even the deep things of God?

147. God has as an attribute that He is true for it is written: "Let God be true and every man a liar." Does the Spirit lie Who is the Spirit of Truth? and Whom we have shown to be called the Truth, since John called Him too the Truth, as also the Son?And David says in the psalm: "Send out Thy light and Thy truth, they have led me and brought me to Thy holy hill and to Thy tabernacles." If you consider that in this passage the Son is the light, then the Spirit is the Truth, or if you consider the Son to be the Truth, then the Spirit is the light,

148. God has a Name which is above every name, and has given a name to the Son, as we read that in the Name of Jesus knees should bow. Let us consider whether the Spirit has this Name. But it is written "Go, baptize the nations in the Name of the Father, and of the Son, and of the Holy Spirit." He has, then, a Name above every name. What, therefore, the Father and the Son have, the Holy Spirit also has through the oneness of the Name of His nature.

149. It is a prerogative of God to raise the dead. "For as the Father raiseth the dead and quickeneth them, so the Son also quickeneth whom He will." But the Spirit also(by Whom God raiseth) raiseth them, for it is written: "He shall quicken also your mortal bodies through His Spirit that dwelleth in you." But that you may not think this a trivial grace, learn that the Spirit also raises, for the prophet Ezekiel says: "Come, O Spirit, and breathe upon these dead, and they shall live. And I prophesied as He commanded me, and the Spirit of life entered into them, and they lived, and stood up on their feet an exceeding great company." And farther on God says: "Ye shall know that I am the Lord, when I shall open your graves, that I may bring My people out of their graves, and I will give you My Spirit, and ye shall live."

150. When He spoke of His Spirit, did He mention any other besides the Holy Spirit?For He would neither have spoken. of His Spirit as produced by blowing, nor could this Spirit come from the four quarters of the world, for the blowing of these winds, which we experience, is partial, not universal; and this spirit by which we live is also individual, not universal. But it is the nature of the Holy Spirit to be both over all and in all. Therefore from the words of the prophet we may see how(the flame-work of the members long since fallen asunder being scattered) the bones may come together again to the form of a revived body, when the Spirit quickens them; and the ashes may come together on the limbs belonging to them, animated by a disposition to come together before being formed anew in the appearance of living.

151. Do we not in the likeness of what is done recognize the oneness of the divine power? The Spirit raises after the same manner as the Lord raised at the time of His own Passion, when suddenly in the twinkling of an eye the graves of the dead were opened, and the bodies living again arose from the tombs, and the smell of death being removed, and the scent of life restored, the ashes of those who were dead took again the likeness of the living.

152. So, then, the Spirit has that which Christ has, and therefore what God has, for all things which the Father has the Son also has, and therefore He said: "All things which the Father hath are Mine."

Chapter XX.

The river flowing from the Throne of God is a figure of the Holy Spirit, but by the waters spoken of by David the powers of heaven are intended. The kingdom of God is the work of the Spirit; and it is no matter for wonder ff He reigns in this together with the Son, since St. Paul promises that we too shall reign with the Son.

153. And this, again, is not a trivial matter that we read that a river goes forth from the throne of God. For you read the words of the Evangelist John to this purport: "And He showed me a river of living water, bright as crystal, proceeding out of the throne of God and of the Lamb. In the midst of the street thereof, and on either side, was the tree of life, bearing twelve kinds of fruits, yielding its fruit every month, and the leaves of the tree were for the healing of all nations."

154. This is certainly the River proceeding from the throne of God, that is, the Holy Spirit, Whom he drinks who believes in Christ, as He Himself says: "If any man thirst, let him come to Me and drink. He that believeth on Me, as saith the Scripture, out of his belly shall flow rivers of living water. But this spoke He of the Spirit." Therefore the river is the Spirit.

155. This, then, is in the throne of God, for the water washes not the throne of God. Then, whatever you may understand by that water, David said not that it was above the throne of God, but above the heavens, for it is written: "Let the waters which are above the heavens praise the Name of the Lord." Let *them* praise, he says, not let *it* praise. For if he had intended us to understand the element of water, he would certainly have said, Let it praise, but by using the plural he intended the Powers to be understood.

156. And what wonder is it if the Holy Spirit is in the throne of God, since the kingdom of God itself is the work of the Holy Spirit, as it is written: "For the kingdom of God is not meat and drink, but righteousness and peace and joy in the Holy Spirit." And when the Saviour Himself says, "Every kingdom divided against itself shall be destroyed," by adding afterwards, "But if I, by the Spirit of God, cast out devils, without doubt the kingdom of God is come upon you." He shows that the kingdom of God is held undivided by Himself and by the Spirit.

157. But what is more foolish than for any one to deny that the Holy Spirit reigns together with Christ when the Apostle says that even we shall reign together with Christ in the kingdom of Christ: "If we are dead with Him, we shall also live with Him; if we endure, we shall also reign with Him." But we by adoption, He by power; we by grace, He by nature.

158. The Holy Spirit, therefore, shares in the kingdom with the Father and the Son, and He is of one nature with Them, of one Lordship, and also of one power.

Chapter XXI.

Isaiah was sent by the Spirit, and accordingly the same Spirit was seen by him. What is meant by the revolving wheels, and the divers wings, and how since the Spirit is proclaimed Lord of Sabaoth by the Seraphim, certainly none but impious men can deny Him this title.

159. Since, then, He has a share in the kingdom, what hinders us from understanding that it was the Holy Spirit by Whom Isaiah was sent? For on the authority of Paul we cannot doubt, whose judgment the Evangelist Luke so much approved in the Acts of the Apostles as to write as follows in Paul's words: "Well spake the Holy Spirit through Isaiah the prophet to our fathers, saying: Go to this people and say, Ye shall hear with the ear and shall not understand, and seeing ye shall see and shall not perceive."

160. It is, then, the Spirit Who sent Isaiah. If the Spirit sent him, it is certainly the Spirit Whom, after Uzziah's death, Isaiah saw, when he said: "I saw the Lord of Sabaoth sitting upon a throne, high and lifted up, and the house was full of His majesty. And the Seraphim stood round about Him, each one had six wings, and with two they were covering His face, and with two

they were covering His feet, and with two they were flying; and they cried out one to the other, and said, Holy, holy, holy is the Lord of Sabaoth, the whole earth is full of His majesty."

161. If the Seraphim were standing, how were they flying? If they were flying, how were they standing? If we cannot understand this, how is it that we want to understand God, Whom we have not seen?

162. But as the prophet saw a wheel running within a wheel (which certainly does not refer to any appearance to the bodily sight, but to the grace of each Testament; for the life of the saints is polished, and so consistent with itself that later portions agree with the former). The wheel, then, within a wheel is life under the Law, life undergrace; inasmuch as Jews are within the Church, the Law is included in grace. For he is within the Church who is a Jew secretly; and circumcision of the heart is a sacrament within the Church. But that Jewry is within the Church of which it is written: "In Jewry is God known;" therefore as wheel runs within wheel, so in like manner the wings were still, and the wings were flying.

163. In like manner, too, the Seraphim were veiling His face with two wings, and with two were veiling His feet, and with two were flying. For here also is a mystery of spiritual wisdom. Seasons stand, seasons fly; the past stand, the future are flying, and like the wings of the Seraphim, so they veil the face or the feet of God; inasmuch as in God, Who has neither beginning nor end, the whole course of times and seasons, from this knowledge of its beginning and its end, is at rest. So, then, times past and future stand, the present fly. Ask not after the secrets of His beginning or His end, for there is neither. You have the present, but you must praise Him, not question.

164. The Seraphim with unwearied voices praise, and do you question? And certainly when they do this they show us that we must not sometimes question about God, but always praise Him. Therefore the Holy Spirit is also the Lord of Sabaoth. Unless perchance the Teacher Whom Christ chose pleases not the impious, or they can deny that the Holy Spirit is the Lord of powers, Who gives whatever powers He Himself wills.

Chapter XXII.

In proof of the Unity in Trinity the passage of Isaiah which has been cited is considered, and it is shown that there is no difference as to its sense amongst those who expound it of the Father, or of the Son, or of the Spirit. If He Who was crucified was Lord of glory, so, too, is the Holy Spirit equal in all things to the Father and the Son, and the Arians will never be able to diminish His glory.

165. It is now possible to recognize the oneness of the majesty and rule in the Father, the Son, and the Holy Spirit. For many say that it was God the Father Who was seen at that time by Isaiah. Paul says it was the Spirit, and Luke supports him. John the Evangelist refers it to the Son. or thus has he written of the Son:"These things spake Jesus, and departed and hid Himself from them. But though He had done so great signs before them, they did not believe on Him, that the word of Isaiah might be fulfilled which he spake, Lord, who hath believed our report, and to whom hath the Arm of the Lord been revealed? Therefore, they could not believe, because Isaiah said again, He hath blinded their eyes and hardened their heart, that they might not see with their eyes and understand with their heart and be converted, and I should heal them. These things said Isaiah when he saw His glory, and spake of Him."

166. John says that Isaiah spoke these words, and revealed most clearly that the glory of the Son appeared to him. Paul, however, relates that the Spirit said these things. Whence, then, is this difference?

167. There is, indeed, a difference of words, not of meaning. For though they said different things, neither was in error, for both the Father is seen in the Son, Who said, "He that seeth Me seeth the Father also," and the Son is seen in the Spirit; for as "no man says Lord Jesus, except in the Holy Spirit," so Christ is seen not by the eye of flesh, but by the grace of the Spirit. Whence, too, the Scripture says: "Rise, thou that sleepest, and arise from the dead, and Christ shall shine upon thee." And Paul, when he had lost his eyesight, how did he see Christ except in

the Spirit? Wherefore the Lord says: "For to this end I have appeared unto thee, to appoint thee a minister and a witness of the things wherein thou hast seen Me, and of the things wherein thou shalt see Me." For the prophets also received the Spirit and saw Christ.

168. One, then, is the vision, one the right to command, one the glory. Do we deny that the Holy Spirit is also the Lord of glory when the Lord of glory was crucified who was born from the Holy Spirit of the Virgin Mary? For Christ is not one of two, but is one, and was born as Son of God of the Father before the world; and in the world born as man by taking flesh.

169. And why should I say that, as the Father and the Son, so, too, the Spirit is free from stain and Almighty, for Solomon called Him in Greek pantodunamon, panepiscopon, because He is Almighty and beholds all things, as we showed above to be, is read in the Book of Wisdom. Therefore the Spirit enjoys honour and glory.

170. Consider now lest perchance something may not beseem Him, or if this displease thee, O Arian, drag Him down from His fellowship with the Father and the Son. But if thou choose to drag Him down thou wilt see the heavens reversed above thee, for all their strength is from the Spirit. If thou choose to drag Him down, thou must first lay hands on God, for the Spirit is God. But how wilt thou drag Him down, Who searcheth the deep things of God?

THE TWO BOOKS ON THE DECEASE OF HIS BROTHER SAYTRUS.
INTRODUCTION

Besides his elder sister Marcelllina, who received the veil at the hands of Pope Liberius, at Christmas [perh. 353 a.d.], St. Ambrose had also a brother named Satyrus, to which name,in three epitaph on him ascribed to the bishop, is added Uranius. This probably, however, merely in reference to his translation from earth to heaven.

Satyrus had in his earlier years, as well as St.Ambrose, practised as an advocate, and held office. But when his brother was appointed Bishop of Milan, Saytarus at once gave up his appointment, and devoted his life to managing St. Ambrose's secular affairs, that nothing might distract him from his episcopal duties. After however, a few short years of devotion to this task, he succumbed to a severe illness October 17. a.d. 379.

The grief of St. Ambrose at the loss of his absolutely like-minded brother was intense, and to it we owe the exquisite discourse delivered at the funeral of Satyrus, and the second, on the resurrection, delivered a week later, St. Ambrose subsequently revised these two addresses, and they have come down to us as the "two books of St. Ambrose on thee decease of Satyrus," some mss. adding, "and the resurrection of the dead"

The epitaph on Satyrus, said to be by St. Ambrose, is as follows:

Uranio Satyro supremum frater honorem
Martyris ad laevam detulit Ambrosius.
Haec meriti merces, ut sacri sanguinis humor
Finitimas penetrans adluat exuvias.

BOOK I.

I. We have brought hither, dearest brethren, my sacrifice, a sacrifice undefiled, a sacrifice well pleasing to God, my lord and brother Satyrus. I did not forget that he was mortal, nor did my feelings deceive me, but grace abounded more exceedingly. And so I have nothing to complain of, but have cause for thankfulness to God, for I always desired that if any troubles should await either the Church or myself, they should rather fall on me and on my house. Thanks, therefore, be to God, that in this time of common fear, when everything is dreaded from the barbarian movements, I ended the trouble of all by my personal grief, and that I dreaded for all which was turned upon me. And may this be fully accomplished, so that my grief may be a ransom for the grief of all.

2. Nothing among things of earth, dearest brethren, was more precious to me, nothing more worthy of love, nothing more dear than such a brother, but public matters come before private. And should any one enquire what was his feeling; he would rather be slain for others than live for himself, because Christ died according to the flesh for all, that we might learn not to live for ourselves alone.

3. To this must be added that I cannot be ungrateful to God; for I must rather rejoice that I had such a brother than grieve that I had lost a brother, for the former is a gift, the latter a debt to be paid. And so, as long as I might, I enjoyed the loan entrusted to me, now He Who deposited the pledge has taken it back. There is no difference between denying that a pledge has been deposited and grieving at its being returned. In each there is untrustworthiness, and in each [eternal] life is risked. It is a fault if you refuse repayment, and piety if you refuse a sacrifice. Since, too, the lender of money can be made a fool of, but the Author of nature, the Lender of all that we need, cannot be cheated. And so the larger the amount of the loan, so much the more gratitude is due for the use of the capital.

4. Wherefore, I cannot be ungrateful concerning my brother, for he has given back that which was common to nature, and has gained what is peculiar to grace alone. For who would refuse the common lot? Who would grieve that a pledge specially entrusted to him is taken away, since the Father gave up His only Son to death for us? Who would think that he ought to be excepted from the lot of dying, who has not been excepted from the lot of being born? It is a great mystery of divine love, that not even in Christ was exception made of the death of the body; and although He was the Lord of nature, He refused not the law of the flesh which He had taken upon Him. It is necessary for me to die, for Him it was not necessary. Could not He Who said of His servant, "If I will that he tarry thus until I come, what is that to thee?" not have remained as He was, if so He willed? But by continuance of my brother's life here, he would have destroyed his reward and my sacrifice. What is a greater consolation to us than that according to the flesh Christ also died? Or why should I weep too violently for my brother, knowing as I do that that divine love could not die.

5. Why should I alone weep more than others for him for whom you all weep? I have merged my personal grief in the grief of all, especially because my tears are of no use, whereas yours strengthen faith and bring consolation. You who are rich weep, and by weeping prove that riches gathered together are of no avail for safety, since death cannot be put off by a money payment, and the last day carries off alike the rich and the poor. You that are old weep, because in him you fear that you see the lot of your own children; and for this reason, since you cannot prolong the life of the body, train your children not to bodily enjoyment but to virtuous duties. And you that are young weep too, because the end of life is not the ripeness of old age. The poor too wept, and, which is of much more worth, and much more fruitful, washed away his transgressions with their tears. Those are redeeming tears, those are groanings which hide the grief of death, that grief which through the plenteousness of eternal joy covers over the feeling of former grief. And so, though the funeral be that of a private person, yet is the mourning public; and therefore cannot the weeping last long which is hallowed by the affection of all,

6. For why should I weep for thee, my most loving brother, who wast thus torn from me that thou mightest be the brother of all? For I have not lost but changed my intercourse with thee; before we were inseparable in the body, now we are undivided in affection; for thou remainest with me, and ever wilt remain. And, indeed, whilst thou wast living with me, our country never tore thee from me, nor didst thou thyself ever prefer our country to me; and now thou art become surety for that other country, for I begin to be no stranger there where the better portion of myself already is. I was never wholly engrossed in myself, but the greater part of each of us was in the other, yet we were each of us in Christ, in Whom is the whole sum of all, and the portion of each severally. This grave is more pleasing to me than thy natal soil, in which is the fruit not of nature but of grace, for in that body which now lies lifeless lies the better work of my life, since in this body, too, which I bear is the richer portion of thyself.

7. And would that, as memory and gratitude are devoted to thee, so, too, whatever time I have still to breathe this air, I could breathe it into thy life, and that half of my time might be struck off from me and be added to thine! For it had been just that for those, whose use of hereditary property was always undivided, the period of life should not have been divided, or at least that we, who always without difference shared everything in common during life, should not have a difference in our deaths.

8. But now, brother, whither shall I advance, or whither shall I turn? The ox seeks his fellow, and conceives itself incomplete, and by frequent lowing shows its tender longing. if perchance that one is wanting with whom it has been wont to draw the plough. And shall I, my brother, not long after thee? Or can I ever forget thee, with whom I always drew the plough of this life? In work I was inferior, but in love more Closely bound; not so much fit through my strength, as endurable through thy patience, who with the care of anxious affection didst ever protect my side with thine, as a brother in thy love, as a father in thy care, as older in watchfulness, as younger in respect. So in the one degree of relationship thou didst expend on me the duties of many, so that I long after not one only but many lost in thee, in whom alone flattery was unknown, dutifulness was portrayed. For thou hadst nothing to which to add by pretence, inasmuch as all was comprised in thy dutifulness, so as neither to receive addition nor await a change.

9. But whither am I going, in my immoderate grief, forgetful of my duty, mindful of kindness received? The Apostle calls me back, and as it were puts a bit upon my sorrow, saying, as you heard just now: "We would not that ye should be ignorant, brethren, concerning them that sleep, that ye be not sorrowful, as the rest which have no hope." Pardon me, dearest brethren. For we are not all able to say: "Be ye imitators of me, as I also am of Christ." But if you seek one to imitate, you have One Whom you may imitate. All are not fitted to teach, would that all were apt to learn.

10. But we have not incurred any grievous sin by our tears. Not all weeping proceeds from unbelief or weakness. Natural grief is one thing, distrustful sadness is another, and there is a very great difference between longing for what you have lost and lamenting that you have lost it. Not only grief has tears, joy also has tears of its own. Both piety excites weeping, and prayer waters the couch, and supplication, according to the prophet's saying, washes the bed, Their friends made a great mourning when the patriarchs were buried. Tears, then, are marks of devotion, not producers of grief. I confess, then, that I too wept, but the Lord also wept. He wept for one not related to Him, I for my brother. He wept for all in weeping for one, 'I will weep for thee in all, my brother.

11. He wept for what affected us, not Himself; for the Godhead sheds no tears; but He wept in that nature in which He was sad; He wept in that in which He was crucified, in that in which He died, in that in which He was buried. He wept in that which the prophet this day brought to our minds: "Mother Sion shall say, A man, yea, a man was made in her, and the Most High Himself established her." He wept in that nature in which He called Sion Mother, born in Judaea, conceived by the Virgin. But according to His Divine Nature He could not have a

184

mother, for He is the Creator of His mother. So far as He was made, it was not by divine but by human generation, because He was made man, God was born.

12. But you read in another place: "Unto us a Child is born, unto us a Son is given." In the word Child is an indication of age, in that of Son the fulness of the Godhead. Made of His mother, born of the Father yet the Same Person was both born and given, you must not think of two but of one. For one is the Son of God, both born of the Father and sprung from the Virgin, differing in order, but in name agreeing in one, as, too, the lesson just heard teaches for "a man was made in her and the Most High Himself established her;" man indeed in the body, the Most High in power. And though He be God and man in diversity of nature, yet is He at the same time one in each nature. One property, then, is peculiar to His own nature, another He has in common with us, but in both is He one, and in both is He perfect.

13. Therefore it is no subject of wonder that God made Him to be both Lord and Christ. He made Him Jesus, Him, that is, Who received the name in His bodily nature; He made Him of Whom also the patriarch David writes: "Mother Sion shall say, A man, yea, a man is made in her." But being made man He is unlike the Father, not in Godhead but in His body; not separated from the Father, but differing in office, abiding united in power, but separated in the mystery of the Passion.

14. The treatment of this topic demands more arguments, by which to demonstrate the authority of the Father, the special property of the Son, and the Unity of the whole Trinity; but to-day I have undertaken the office of consolation, not of discussion, although it is customary in consoling to draw away the mind from its grief by application to discussion. But I would rather moderate the grief than alter the affection, that the longing may rather be assuaged than lulled to sleep. For I have no wish to turn away too far from my brother, and to be led off by other thoughts, seeing that this discourse has been undertaken, as it were, for the sake of accompanying him, that I might follow in affection him departing, and embrace in mind him whom I see with my eyes. For it gives me pleasure to fix the whole gaze of my eyes on him, to encompass him with kindly endearments; whilst my mind is stupefied, and I feel as though he were not lost whom I am able still to see present; and I think him not dead, my services to whom I do not as yet perceive to be wanting, services to which I had devoted the whole of my life and the drawing of every breath.

15. What, then, can I pay back in return for such kindness and such pains? I had made thee, my brother, my heir; thou hast left me as the heir; I hoped to leave thee as survivor, and thou hast left me. I, in return for thy kindnesses, that I might repay thy benefits, gave wishes; now I have lost my wishes yet not thy benefits. What shall I, succeeding to my own heir, do? What shall I do who outlive my own life? What shall I do, no longer sharing this light which yet shines on me? What thanks, what good offices, can I repay to thee? Thou hast nothing from me but tears. And perchance, secure of thy reward, thou desirest not those tears which are all that I have left. For even when thou wast yet alive, thou didst forbid me to weep, and didst show that our grief was more pain to thee than thine own death. Tears are bidden to flow no longer, and weeping is repressed. And gratitude to thee forbids them too, lest whilst we weep for our loss we seem to despair concerning thy merits.

16. But for myself at least thou lessenest the bitterness of that grief; I have nothing to fear who used to fear for thee. I have nothing which the world can now snatch from me. Although our holy sister still survives, venerable for her blameless life, thy equal in character, and not falling short in kindly offices; yet we both used to fear more for thee, we felt that all the sweetness of this life was stored up in thee. To live for thy sake was a delight, to die for thee were no cause of sorrow, for we both used to pray that thou mightest survive, it was no pleasure that we should survive thee. When did not our very soul shudder when a dread of this kind touched us? How were our minds dismayed by the tidings of thy sickness!

17. Alas for our wretched hopes! We thought that he was restored to us whom we see carried off, and we now recognize that thy departure hence was obtained by thy vows to the

holy martyr Lawrence! And indeed I would that thou hadst obtained not only a safe passage hence, but also a longer time of life! Thou couldst have obtained many years of life, since thou wast able to obtain thy departure hence. And I indeed thank Thee, Almighty Everlasting God, that Thou hast not denied us at least this last comfort, that Thou hast granted us the longed-for return of our much loved brother from the regions of Sicily and Africa; for he was snatched away so soon after his return as though his death were delayed for this alone, that he might return to his brethren.

18. Now, I clearly have my pledge which no change can any more tear from me; I have the relics which I may embrace, I have the tomb which I may cover with my body, I have the grave on which I may lie, and I shall believe that I am more acceptable to God, because I shall rest upon the bones of that holy body. Would that I had been able in like manner to place my body in the way of thy death! Hadst thou been attacked with the sword, I would have rather offered myself to be pierced for thee; had I been able to recall thy life as it was passing away, I would have rather offered my own.

19. It profited me nothing to receive thy last breath, nor to have breathed into the mouth of thee dying, for I thought that either I myself should receive thy death, or should transfer my life to thee. O that sad, yet sweet pledge of the last kiss! O the misery of that embrace, in which the lifeless body began to stiffen, the last breath vanished! I tightened my arms indeed, but had already lost him whom I was holding; I drew in thy last breath with my mouth, that I might share thy death. But in some way that breath became lifegiving to me, and even in death diffused an odour of greater love. And if I was unable to lengthen thy life by my breath, would that at least the strength of thy last breath might have been transfused into my mind, and that our affection might have inspired me with that purity and innocence of thine. Thou wouldst have left me, dearest brother, this inheritance, which would not smite the affections with tears of grief, but commend thine heir by notable grace.

20. What, then, shall I now do, since all the sweetness, all the solace, in fine, all the charms of that life are lost to me? For thou wast alone my solace at home, my charm abroad; thou, I say, my adviser in counsel, the sharer in my cares, the averter of anxiety, the driver away of sorrow; thou wast the protector of my acts and the defender of my thoughts; thou, lastly, the only one on whom rested care of home and of public matters. I call thy holy soul to witness that, in the building of the church, I often feared lest I might displease thee. Lastly, when thou camest back thou didst chide thy delay. So wast thou, at home and abroad, the instructor and teacher of the priest, that thou didst not suffer him to think of domestic matters, and didst take thought to care for public matters. But I may not fear to seem to speak boastingly, for this is thy meed of praise, that thou, without displeasing any, both didst manage thy brother's house and recommend his priesthood.

21. I feel, indeed, that my mind is touched by the repetition of thy services and the enumeration of thy virtues, and yet in being thus affected I find my rest, and although these memories renew my grief, they nevertheless bring pleasure. Am I able either not to think of thee, or ever to think of thee without tears? And shall I ever be able either not to remember such a brother, or to remember him without tearful gratitude? For what has ever been pleasant to me that has not had its source in thee? What, I say, has ever been a pleasure to me without thee, or to thee without me? Had we not every practice in common, almost to our very eyesight and our sleep? Were our wills ever at variance? And what step did we not take in common? So that we almost seemed in raising our feet to move each others body.

22. But if ever either had to go forth without the other, one would think that his side was unprotected, one could see his countenance troubled, one would suppose that his soul was sad, the accustomed grace, the usual vigour did not shine forth, the loneliness was a subject of dread to all, and made them fearful of some sickness. Such a strange thing it seemed to all that we were separated. I certainly, impatient at my brother's absence, and having it constantly in mind, kept on turning my head seeking him, as it were, present, and seemed to myself then to see him

and speak to him. But if I was disappointed in my hope, I seemed to myself, as it were, to be dragging a yoke on my bowed down neck, to advance with difficulty, to meet others with diffidence, and to return home hurriedly, since it gave me no pleasure to go farther without thee.

23. But when we both had to go forth, there were not more steps on the way than words, nor was our pace quicker than our talk, and it was less for the sake of walking than for the pleasure of conversing, for each of us hung on the lips of the other. We thought not of gazing intently on the view as we passed along, but listened to each other's anxious talk, drank in the kindly expression of the eyes, and inhaled the delight of the brother's appearance. How I used silently to admire within myself thy virtues, how I congratulated myself that God had given me such a brother, so modest, so capable, so innocent, so simple, so that when I thought of thy innocence I began to doubt thy capability, when I saw thy capability I could hardly imagine thy innocence! But thou didst combine both with wonderful perfection.

24. Lastly, what we both had been unable to effect, thou didst accomplish alone. Prosper, as I hear, congratulated himself because he thought that on account of my priesthood he need not restore what he had purloined, but he found thy power alone to be greater than that of us both together. And so he paid all, and was not ungrateful for thy moderation, and did not scoff at thy modesty. But for whom, brother, didst thou seek to gain that? We wished that should be the reward of thy labours which was the proof of them. Thou didst accomplish everything, and when having done all thou didst return, thou alone, who art to be preferred to all, art torn from us; as if thou hadst put off death for this end, that thou mightest fulfil the office of affection, and then carry off the palm for capability.

25. How little, dearest brother, did the honours of this world delight us, because they separated us from one another! And we accepted them, not because the acquisition of them was to be desired, but that there might be no appearance of paltry dissimulation. Or perhaps they were therefore granted to us, that, inasmuch as by thy early death thou wast about to shatter our pleasure, we might learn to live without each other.

26. And indeed I recognize the foreboding dread of my mind, when I often go again through what I have written. I endeavoured to restrain thee, brother, from visiting Africa thyself, and wished thee rather to send some one. I was afraid to let thee go that journey, to trust thee to the waves, and a greater fear than usual came over my mind; but thou didst arrange the journey, and order the business, and, as I hear, didst entrust thyself again to the waves in an old and leaky vessel For since thou wast aiming at speed, thou didst set caution aside; eager to do me a kindness, thou madest nothing of thy danger.

27. O deceitful joy! O the uncertain course of earthly affairs! We thought that he who was returned from Africa, restored from the sea, preserved after shipwreck, could not now be snatched from us; but,though on land, we suffered a more grievous shipwreck, for the death of him whom shipwreck at sea owing to strong swimming could not kill is shipwreck to us. For whatenjoyment remains to us, from whom so sweet an ornament has been taken, so bright a light in this world's darkness has beenextinguished? For in him an ornament not only of our family but of the wholefatherland has perished.

28. I feel, indeed, the deepest gratitude to you, dearest brethren, holy people, that you esteem my grief as no other than your own, that you feel this bereavement as having happened to yourselves, that you offer me the tears of the whole city, of every age, andthe good wishes of every rank, with unusual affection. For this is not the grief of private sympathy, but as it were a service and offering of public good-will. And should any sympathy with me because of the loss of such a brother touch you, I have abundant fruit from it, I have the pledge of your affection. I might prefer that my brother were living, but yet public kindness is in prosperity very pleasant, and in adversity very grateful.

29. And, indeed, so great kindness seems to me to merit no ordinary gratitude. For not without a purpose are the widows in the Acts of the Apostles described as weeping when Tabitha was dead, or the crowd in the Gospel, moved by the widow's tears and accompanying

the funeral of the young man who was to be raised again. There is, then, no doubt that by your tears the protection of the apostles is obtained; no doubt, I say, that Christ is moved to mercy, seeing you weeping. Though He has not now touched the bier, yet He has received the spirit commended to Him, and if He have not called the dead by the bodily voice, yet He has by the authority of His divine power delivered my brother's soul from the pains of death and from the attacks of wicked spirits. And though he that was dead has not sat up on the bier, yet he has found rest in Christ; and if he have not spoken to us, yet he sees those things which are above us, and rejoices in that he now sees higher things than we. For by the things which we read in the Gospels we understand what shall be, and what we see at present is a sign of what is to be.

30. He had no need of being raised again for time, for whom the raising again for eternity is waiting. For why should he fall back into this wretched and miserable state of corruption, and return to this mournful life, for whose rescue from such imminent evils and threatening dangers we ought rather to rejoice? For if no one mourns for Enoch, who was translated when the world was at peace and wars were not raging, but the people rather congratulated him, as Scripture says concerning him: "He was taken away, lest that wickedness should alter his understanding," with how much greater justice must this now be said, when to the dangers of the world is added the uncertainty of life. He was taken away that he might not fall into the hands of the barbarians; he was taken away that he might not see the ruin of the whole earth, the end of the world, the burial of his relatives, the death of fellow-citizens; lest, lastly, which is more bitter than any death, he should see the pollution of the holy virgins and widows.

31. So then, brother, I esteem thee happy both in the beauty of thy life and in the opportuneness of thy death. For thou wast snatched away not from us but from dangers; thou didst not lose life but didst escape the fear of threatening troubles. For with the pity of thy holy mind for those near to thee, if thou knewest that Italy was now oppressed by the nearness of the enemy, how wouldst thou groan, how wouldst thou grieve that our safety wholly depended on the barrier of the Alps, and that the protection of purity consisted in barricades of trees! With what sorrow wouldst thou mourn that thy friends were separated from the enemy by so slight a division, from an enemy, too, both impure and cruel, who spares neither chastity nor life.

32. How, I say, couldst thou bear these things which we are compelled to endure, and perchance (which is more grievous) to behold virgins ravished, little children torn from the embrace of their parents and tossed on javelins, the bodies consecrated to God defiled, and even aged widows polluted? How, I say, couldst thou endure these things, who even with thy last breath, forgetful of thyself, yet not without thought for us, didst warn us concerning the invasion of the barbarians, saying that not in vain hadst thou said that we ought to flee. Perchance was it because thou didst see that we were left destitute by thy death, and thou didst it, not out of weakness of spirit, but from affection, and wast weak with respect to us, but strong with respect to thyself. For when thou wast summoned home by the noble man Symmachus thy parent, because Italy was said to be blazing with war, because thou wast going into danger, because thou wast likely to fall amongst enemies, thou didst answer that this was the cause of thy coming, that thou mightest not fail us in danger, that thou mightest show thyself a sharer in thy brother's peril.

33. Happy, then, was he in so opportune a death, because he has not been preserved for this sorrow. Certainly thou art happier than thy holy sister, deprived of thy comfort, anxious for her own modesty, lately blessed with two brothers, now wretched because of both, being able neither to follow the one nor to leave the other; for whom thy tomb is a lodging, and the burying-place of thy body a home. And would that even this resting-place were safe! Our food is mingled with weeping and our drink with tears, for thou hast given us the bread of tears as food, and tears to drink in large measure, nay, even beyond measure.

34. What now shall I say of myself, who may not die lest I leave my sister, and desire not to live lest I be separated from thee? For what can ever be pleasant to me without thee, in whom was always my whole pleasure? or what satisfaction is it to remain longer in this life, and to

linger on the earth where we lived with pleasure so long as we lived together? If there were anything which could delight us here, it could not delight without thee; and if ever we had earnestly desired to prolong our life, now at any rate we would not exist without thee.

35. This is indeed unendurable. For what can be endured without thee, such a companion of my life, such a sharer of my toil and partaker of my duties? And I could not even make his loss more endurable by dwelling on it beforehand, so much did my mind fear to think of any such thing concerning him! Not that I was ignorant of his condition, but a certain kind of prayers and vows had so clouded the sense of common frailty, that I knew not how to think anything concerning him except entire prosperity.

36. And then lately, when I was oppressed by a severe attack (would that it had been fatal), I grieved only that thou wast not sitting by my couch, and sharing the kindly duty with my holy sister mightest with thy fingers close my eyes when dead. What had I wished? What am I now pondering? What vows are wanting? What services are to succeed? I was preparing one thing, I am compelled to set forth another; not being the subject of the funeral rites but the minister. O hard eyes, which could behold my brother dying! O cruel and unkind hands, which closed those eyes in which I used to see so much! O still harder neck, which could bear so sad a burden, though it were in a service full of consolation.

37. Thou, my brother, hadst more justly done these things for me. I used to expect these services at thy hands, I used to long for them. But now, having survived my own life, what comfort can I find without thee, who alone usedst to comfort me when mourning, to excite my happiness and drive away my sorrow? How do I now behold thee, my brother, who now addressest no words to me, offerest me no kiss? Though, indeed, our mutual love was so deeply seated in each of us, that it was cherished rather by inward affection than made public by open caresses, for we who professed such mutual trust and love did not seek the testimony of others. The strong spirit of our brotherhood had so infused itself into each of us, that there was no need to prove our love by caresses; but our minds being conscious of our affection, we, satisfied with our inward love, did not seem to require the show of caresses, whom the very appearance of each other fashioned for mutual love; for we seemed, I know not by what spiritual stamp or bodily likeness, to be the one in the other.

38. Who saw thee, and did not think that he had seen me? How often have I saluted those who, because they had previously saluted thee, said that they had been already saluted by me? How many said something to thee, and related that they had said it to me? What pleasure, what amusement often was given me by this, because I saw that they were mistaken in us? What an agreeable mistake, what a pleasant slip, how innocent a deceit, how sweet a trick! For there was nothing for me to fear in thy words or acts, and I rejoiced when they were ascribed to me.

39. But if they insisted all too vehemently that they had given me some information, I used to smile and answer with delight: Take care that it was not my brother whom you told. For since we had everything in common, one spirit and one disposition, yet the secrets of friends alone were not common property, not that we were afraid of danger in the communication, but that we might keep faith by withholding it. Yet if we had a matter to be consulted about, our counsel was always in common, though the secret was not always made common. For although our friends spoke to either of us, so that what they said might reach the other; yet I know that secrets were for the most part kept with such good faith that they were not imparted even to the other brother. For this is a convincing proof that was not betrayed without which had not been imparted to the brother.

40. I confess, then, that being raised by these so great and excellent benefits to a kind of mental ecstasy, I had ceased to fear that I might be the survivor, because I thought him more worthy to live, and therefore received the blow which I am unable to endure, for the wounds of such pain are more easily borne when dwelt upon beforehand than when unexpected. Who will now console me full of sorrows? Who will raise up him that is smitten down? With whom shall I share my cares? Who will set me free from the business of this world? For thou wast the

manager of our affairs, the censor of the servants, the decider between brother and sister, the decider not in matters of strife but of affection.

41. For if at any time there was a discussion between me and my holy sister on any matter, as to which was the preferable opinion, we used to take thee as judge, who wouldst hurt no one, and anxious to satisfy each, didst keep to thy loving affection and the right measure in deciding, so as to let each depart satisfied, and gain for thyself the thanks of each. Or if thou thyself broughtest anything for discussion, how pleasantly didst thou argue! and thy very indignation, how free from bitterness it was! how was thy discipline not unpleasant to the servants themselves! since thou didst strive rather to blame thyself before thy brethren than to punish through excitement! For our profession restrained in us the zeal for correction, and, indeed, thou, my brother, didst remove from us every inclination to correct, when thou didst promise to punish and desire to alleviate.

42. That is, then, evidence of no ordinary prudence, which virtue is thus defined by the wise. The first of good things is to know God, and with a pious mind to reverence Him as true and divine, and to delight in that loveable and desirable beauty of the eternal Truth with the whole affection of the mind. And the second consists in deriving from that divine and heavenly source of nature, love towards our neighbours, since even the wise of this world have borrowed from our laws. For they never could have obtained those points for the discipline of men, except from that heavenly fount of the divine law.

43. What, then, shall I say of his reverence in regard to the worship of God? He, before being initiated in the more perfect mysteries, being in danger of shipwreck when the ship that bore him, dashed upon rocky shallows, was being broken up by the waves tossing it hither and thither, fearing not death but lest he should depart this life without the Mystery, asked of those whom he knew to be initiated the divine Sacrament of the faithful; not that he might gaze on secret things with curious eyes, but to obtain aid for his faith. For he caused it to be bound in a napkin, and the napkin round his neck, and so cast himself into the sea, not seeking a plank loosened from the framework of the ship, by floating on which he might be rescued, for he sought the means of faith alone. And so believing that he was sufficiently protected and defended by this, he sought no other aid.

44. One may consider his courage at the same time, for he, when the vessel was breaking up, did not as a shipwrecked man seize a plank, but as a brave man found in himself the support of his courage, nor did his hope fail nor his expectation deceive him. And then, when preserved from the waves and brought safe to land in the port, he first recognized his Leader, to Whom he had committed himself, and at once after either himself rescuing the servants, or seeing that they were rescued, disregarding his goods, and not longing for what was lost, he sought the Church of God, that he might return thanks for his deliverance, and acknowledge the eternal mysteries, declaring that there was no greater duty than thanksgiving. But if not to be grateful to man has been judged like to murder, how enormous a crime is it not to be grateful to God!

45. Now it is the mark of a prudent man to know himself, and, as it has been defined by the wise, to live in accordance with nature. What, then, is so much in accordance with nature as to be grateful to the Creator? Behold this heaven, does it not render thanks to its Creator when He is seen? For "the heavens declare the glory of God, and the firmament proclaims His handywork." The sea itself when it is quiet and at rest sets forth a representation of the Divine Quiet; when it is stirred up, it shows that the wrath on high is terrible. Do we not all rightly admire the grace of God, when we observe that senseless nature restrains its waves as it were with sense and reason, and that the waves know their own limit? And what shall I say of the earth, which in obedience to the divine command freely supplies food to all living things; and the fields restore what they have received multiplied as it were by accumulating interest, and heaped up.

46. So he who by the guidance of nature had grasped the methods of the divine work in the ardent vigour of his mind, knew that thanks should be paid first of all to the Preserver of all; but

inasmuch as he could not repay, he could at least feel grateful. For the essence of this thankfulness is that when it is offered it is felt, and by being felt is offered. So he offered thanks and brought away faith. For he who had felt such protection on the part of the heavenly Mystery wrapped in a napkin, how much did he expect if he received it with his mouth and drew it to the very depth of his bosom? How much more must he have been expecting of that, when received into his breast, which had so benefited him when covered with a napkin?

47. But he was not so eager as to lay aside caution. He called the bishop to him, and esteeming that there can be no true thankfulness except it spring from true faith, he enquired whether he agreed with the Catholic bishops, that is, with the Roman Church? And possibly at that place the Church of the district was in schism. For at that time Lucifer had withdrawn from our communion, and although he had been an exile for the faith, and had left inheritors of his own faith, yet my brother did not think that there could be true faith in schism. For though schismatics kept the faith towards God, yet they kept it not towards the Church of God, certain of whose limbs they suffered as it were to be divided, and her members to be torn. For since Christ suffered for the Church, and the Church is the body of Christ, it does not seem that faith in Christ is shown by those by whom His Passion is made of none effect, and His body divided.

48. And so though he retained the deposit of faith, and feared to voyage as debtor of so vast an amount, yet he preferred to cross over to a place where he could make his payment in safety, for he was convinced that the payment of thankfulness to God consists in dispositions and faith, which payment, so soon as he had free access to the Church, he delayed not to make. And he both received the grace of God which he longed for, and preserved it when received. Nothing, then, can be wiser than that prudence which distinguishes between divine and human matters.

49. Why should I speak of his well-known eloquence in his forensic duties? What incredible admiration did he excite in the hall of justice of the high prefecture! But I prefer to speak of those things which he esteemed, through consideration of the mysteries of God, to be preferable to human matters.

50. And should any one wish more fully to regard his fortitude, let him consider how often after his shipwreck with invincible disregard of this life he crossed the sea and travelled through widespread regions in his journeys, and at last that at this very time he did not shrink from danger, but met it. Patient under injustice, regardless of cold, would that he had been equally thoughtful in taking precautions. But exactly herein was he blessed, that he, so long as his bodily strength allowed, spent his life fulfilling the work of youth, uninterruptedly carrying out what he wished to do, and paid no attention to his weakness.

51. But in what words can I set forth his simplicity? By this I mean a certain moderation of character and soberness of mind. Pardon me, I beseech you, and attribute it to my grief, if I allow myself to speak somewhat fully about him with whom I am no longer permitted to converse. And certainly it is an advantage for you to see that you have performed this kindly office not led by weak feelings, but by sound judgment; not as impelled by pity for his death, but moved by desire to do honour to his virtues; for every simple soul is blessed. And so great was his simplicity, that, converted as it were into a child, he was conspicuous for the simplicity belonging to that guileless age, for the likeness of perfect virtue, and for reflecting as in a mirror innocence of character. Therefore he entered into the kingdom of heaven, because he believed the word of God, because he, like a child, rejected the artifices of flattery, and chose rather to accept with gentleness the pain of injustice than to avenge himself sharply; he was more ready to listen to complaints than to guile, ready for conciliation, inaccessible to ambition, holy in modesty, so that in him one would rather speak of excess of bashfulness than have to seek for such as is needful.

52. But the foundations of virtue are never in excess, for modesty does not hinder but rather commends the discharge of duty. And so was his face suffused with a certain virginal modesty, showing forth his inward feeling in his countenance, if perchance he had, coming on a sudden,

met some female relative, he was as it were bowed down and sunk to the earth, though he was not different in company with men, he seldom lifted up his face, raised his eyes, or spoke; when he did one of these things, it was with a kind of bashful modesty of heart, with which, too, the chastity of his body agreed. For he preserved the gifts of holy baptism inviolate, being pure in body and still more pure in heart; fearing not less the shame of impurity in conversation than in his body; and thinking that no less regard was to be paid to modesty in purity of words than in chastity of body.

53. In fine, he so loved chastity as never to seek a wife, although in him it was not merely the desire of chastity, but also the grace of his love for us. But in a wonderful manner he concealed his feeling as to marriage, and avoided all boastfulness; and so carefully did he conceal his feeling, that even when we pressed it on him, he appeared rather to postpone wedlock than to avoid it. So this was the one point with which he did not trust his brother and sister, not through any doubtful hesitation, but simply through virtuous modesty.

54. Who, then, could refrain from wondering that a man in age between a brother and a sister, the one a virgin, the other a priest, yet in greatness of soul not below either, should so excel in two great gifts, as to reflect the chastity of one vocation and the sanctity of the other, being bound not by profession but by the exercise of virtue. If, then, lust and anger bring forth other vices, I may rightly call chastity and gentleness as it were the parents of virtues; although, as it is the origin of all good things, so too is piety the seed-plot of other virtues.

55. What, then, shall I say of his economy, a kind of continence regarding possessions? For he who takes care of his own does not seek other men's goods, nor is he puffed up by abundance who is contented with his own. For he did not wish to recover anything except his own, and that rather that he might not be cheated than that he might be richer. For he rightly called those who seek other men's goods hawks of money. But if avarice be the root of all evils, he who does not seek for money has certainly stripped himself of vices.

56. Nor did he ever delight in more carefully prepared feasts or many dishes, except when he invited friends, wishing for what was sufficient for nature, not for superabundance for pleasure's sake. And, indeed, he was not poor in means, but was so in spirit. Certainly we ought by no means to doubt of his happiness, who neither as a wealthy man delighted in riches, nor as a poor man thought that what he had was scanty.

57. It remains that, to come to the end of the cardinal virtues, we should notice in him the constituents of justice. For although virtues are related to each other and connected, still as it were a more distinct sketch of each is wanted, and especially of justice. For it being somewhat niggardly towards itself is wholly devoted to what is without, and whatever it has through a certain rigour towards self, being carried away by love for all, it pours forth on its neighbours.

58. But there are many kinds of this virtue. One towards friends, another towards all men, another with respect to the worship of God or the relief of the poor. So what he was towards all, the affection of the people of the province over which he was set shows; who used to say that he was rather their parent than a judge, a kind umpire for loving clients, a steadfast awarder of just law.

59. But what he was with his brother and sister, though all men were embraced in his good-will, our undivided patrimony testifies, and the inheritance neither distributed nor diminished, but preserved. For he said that love was no reason for making a will. This, too, he signified with his last words, when commending those whom he had loved, saying that it was his choice never to marry a wife, that he might not be separated from his brother and sister, and that he would not make a will, lest our feelings should in any point be hurt. Lastly, though begged and entreated by us, he thought that nothing ought to be determined by himself, not, however, forgetting the poor, but only asking that so much should be given to them as should seem just to us.

60. By this alone he gave a sufficient proof of his fear of God, and set an example of religious feeling as regards men. For what he gave to the poor he offered to God, since "he that

distributeth to the poor lendeth unto God;" and by requiring what was just, he left them not a little, but the whole. For this is the total sum of justice, to sell what one has and give to the pool For he who "hath dispersed, and hath given to the poor, his righteousness endureth for ever." So he left us as stewards, not heirs; for the inheritance is to the heirs a matter of question, the stewardship is a duty to the poor.

61. So that one may rightly say that the Holy Spirit has this day told us by the voice of the boy reader: "He that is innocent in his hands and of a clean heart, who hath not lifted up his soul to vanity, nor used deceit unto his neighbour, this is the generation of them that seek the Lord." He, then, shall both ascend into the hill of the Lord and dwell in the tabernacle of God; because "he hath walked without spot, he hath worked righteousness, he hath spoken truth, he hath not deceived his neighbour;" nor did he lend his money for usury, who always wished [no more than] to retain that which was inherited.

62. Why should I relate that in his piety he went beyond mere justice, when he, having thought that in consideration of my office something ought to be given to the unlawful possessor of our property, declared that I was the author of the bounty, but made over the receipts of his own share to the common fund.

63. These and other matters, which were then a pleasure to me, now sharpen the remembrance of my grief. They abide, however, and always will do so, nor do they ever pass away like a shadow; for the grace of virtue dies not with the body, nor do natural life and merits come to an end at the same time, although the use of natural life does not perish for ever, but rests in a kind of exemption for a time.

64. For one, then, who has performed such good deeds, and is rescued from perils, I shall weep rather from longing for him than for the loss. For the very opportuneness of his death bids us bear in mind that we must follow him rather with grateful veneration than grieve for him, for it is written that private grief should cease in public sorrow. This is said in the prophetical language, not only to that one woman, who is figured there, but to each, since it seems to be said to the Church.

65. To me, then, does this message come, and Holy Scripture says: "Dost thou teach this, is it thus that thou instructest the people of God? Knowest thou not that thy example is a danger to others? save that perchance thou complainest that thy prayer is not heard. First of all this is shameless arrogance, to desire to obtain for thyself what thou knowest to have been denied to many, even saints, when thou art aware that God is no respecter of persons?" For although God is merciful, yet if He always heard all, He would appear to act no longer of His own free will, but by a kind of necessity. Then, since all ask, if He were to hear all, no one would die. For how much dost thou daily pray? Is, then, God's appointment to be made void in consideration of thee? Why, then, dost thou lament that is sometimes not obtained, which thou knowest cannot always be obtained?

66. "Thou fool," it says, "above all women, seest thou not our mourning, and what hath happened to us, how that Sion our mother is saddened with all sadness, and humbled with humbling. Mourn now also very sore, since we all mourn, and be sad since we all are sad, and thou art grieved for a brother. Ask the earth and she shall tell thee that it is she which ought to mourn, outliving so many that grow upon her. And out of her," it says, "were all born in the beginning, and out of her shall others come, and, behold, they walk almost all into destruction, and a multitude of them is utterly rooted out. Who, then, ought to make more mourning than she that hath lost so great a multitude, and not thou, which art sorry but for one?"

67. Let, then, the common mourning swallow up ours and cut off the bitterness of our private sorrow. For we ought not to grieve for those whom we see to be set free, and we bear in mind that so many holy souls are not without a purpose at this time loosed from the chains of the body. For we see, as if by God's decree, such reverend widows dying so closely at one time, that it seems to be a sort of setting out on a journey, not a sinking in death, lest their chastity in which they have served God their full time should be exposed to peril. What groans, what

mourning, does so bitter a recollection stir up in me! And if I had no leisure for mourning, yet in my own personal grief, in the loss of the very flower of so much merit, the common lot of nature consoled me; and my grief in consideration of one alone veiled the bitterness of the public funeral by the show of piety at home.

68. I seek again, then, O sacred Scripture, thy consolations, for it delights me to dwell on thy precepts and on thy sentences. How far more easy is it for heaven and earth to pass away, than for one tittle of the law to fail! But let us now listen to what is written: "Now," it says, "keep thy sorrow to thyself, and bear with a good courage the things which have befallen thee. For if thou shalt acknowledge the determination of God to be just, thou shalt both receive thy son in time, and shalt be praised among women." If this is said to a woman, how much more to a priest! If such words are said of a son it is certainly not unfitting that they should be uttered also concerning the loss of a brother; though if he had been my son I could never have loved him more. For as in the death of children, the lost labour and the pain borne to no purpose seem to increase the sorrow; so, too, in the case of brothers the habits of intercourse and joint occupations inflame the bitterness of grief.

69. But, lo! I hear the Scripture saying: "Do not continue this discourse, but allow thyself to be persuaded. For how great are the misfortunes of Sion! Be comforted in regard of the sorrow of Jerusalem. For thou seest that our holy places are polluted and the name that was called upon us is almost profaned, they that are ours have suffered shame, our priests are burnt, our Levites gone into captivity, our wives are polluted, our virgins suffer violence, our righteous men are carried away, our little ones given up, our young men brought in bondage, and our strong men become weak. And, which is the greatest of all, the seal of Sion hast lost her glory, since now she is delivered into the hands of them that hate us. Do thou, then, shake off thy great heaviness, and put from thee the multitude of sorrows, that the Mighty may be merciful to thee again, and the Highest shall give thee rest by easing thy labours."

70. So, then, my tears shall cease, for one must yield to healthful remedies, since there ought to be some difference between believers and unbelievers. Let them, therefore, weep who cannot have the hope of the resurrection, of which not the sentence of God but the strictness of the faith deprives them. Let there be this difference between the servants of Christ and the worshippers of idols, that the latter weep for their friends, whom they suppose to have perished for ever; that they should never cease from tears, and gain no rest from sorrow, who think that the dead have no rest. But from us, for whom death is the end not of our nature but of this life only, since our nature itself is restored to a better state, let the advent of death wipe away all tears.

71. And certainly if they have ever found any consolation who have thought that death is the end of sensation and the failing of our nature, how much more must we find it so to whom the consciousness of good done brings the promise of better rewards! The heathen have their consolation, because they think that death is a cessation of all evils, and as they are without the fruit of life, so, too, they think that they have escaped all the feeling and pain of those severe and constant sufferings which we have to endure in this life. We, however, as we are better supported by our rewards, so, too, ought we to he more patient through our consolation, for they seem to be not lost but sent before, whom death is not going to swallow up, but eternity to receive.

72. My tears shall therefore cease, or if they cannot cease, I will weep for thee, my brother, in the common sorrow, and will hide my private groaning in the public grief. For how can my tears wholly cease, since they break forth at every utterance of thy name, or when my very habitual actions arouse thy memory, or when my affection pictures thy likeness, or when recollection renews my grief. For how canst thou be absent who art again made present in so many occupations? Thou art present, I say, and art always brought before me, and with my whole mind and soul do I embrace thee, gaze upon thee, address thee, kiss thee; I grasp thee whether in the gloomy night or in the clear light, when thou vouch-safest to revisit and console me

sorrowing. And now the very nights which used to seem irksome in thy lifetime, because they denied us the power of looking on each other; and sleep itself, lately, the odious interrupter of our converse, have commenced to be sweet, because they restore thee to me. They, then, are not wretched but blessed whose mutual presence fails not, whose care for each other is not lessened, whose mutual esteem is increased. For sleep is a likeness and image of death.

73. But if, in the quiet of night, our souls still cleaving to the chains of the body, and as it were bound within the prison bars of the limbs, yet are able to see higher and separate things, how much more do they see these, when in their pure and heavenly senses they suffer from no hindrances of bodily weakness. And so when, as a certain evening was drawing on, I was complaining that thou didst not revisit me when at rest, thou wast wholly present always. So that, as I lay with my limbs bathed in sleep, while I was [in mind] awake for thee, thou wast alive to me, I could say, "What is death, my brother?" For certainly thou wast not separated from me for a single moment, for thou wast so present with me everywhere, that enjoyment of each other, which we were unable to have in the intercourse of this life, is now always and everywhere with us. For at that time certainly all things could not be present, for neither did our physical constitution allow it, nor could the sight of each other, nor the sweetness of our bodily embraces at all times and in all places be enjoyed. But the pictures in our souls were always present with us, even when we were not together, and these have not come to an end, but constantly come back to us, and the greater the longing the greater abundance have we of them.

74. So, then, I hold thee, my brother, and neither death nor time shall tear thee from me. Tears themselves are sweet, and weeping itself a pleasure, for by these the eagerness of the soul is assuaged, and affection being eased is quieted. For neither can I be without thee, nor ever forget thee, or think of thee without tears. O bitter days, which show that our union is broken! O nights worthy of tears, which have lost for me so good a sharer of my rest, so inseparable a companion! What sufferings would ye cause me, unless the likeness of him present offered itself to me, unless the visions of my soul represented him whom my bodily sight shows me no more!

75. Now, now, O brother, dearest to my soul, although thou art gone by too early a death, happy at least art thou, who dost not endure these sorrows, and art not compelled to mourn the loss of a brother, separation from whom thou couldst not long endure, but didst quickly return and visit him again. But if then thou didst hasten to banish the weariness of my loneliness, to lighten the sadness of thy brother's mind, how much more often oughtest thou now to revisit my afflicted soul, and thyself lighten the sorrow which has its origin from thee!

76. But the exercise of my office now bids me rest awhile, and attention to my priestly duties draws my mind away; but what will happen to my holy sister, who though she moderates her affection by the fear of God, yet again kindles the grief itself of the affection by the zeal of her devotion? Prostrate on the ground, embracing her brother's tomb, wearied with toilsome walking, sad in spirit, day and night she renews her grief. For though she often breaks off her weeping by speech, she renews it in prayer; and although in her knowledge of her Scriptures she excels those who bring consolation, she makes up for her desire of weeping by the constancy of her prayers, renewing the abundance of her tears then chiefly, when no one can interrupt her. So thou hast that which thou mayest pity, not what thou mayest blame, for to weep in prayer is a sign of virtue. And although that be a common thing with virgins, whose softer sex and more tender affection abound in tears at the sight of the common weakness, even without the feeling of family grief, yet when there is a greater cause for sorrowing, no limit is set to that sorrow.

77. The means of consolation, then, are wanting since excuses abound. For thou canst not forbid that which thou teachest, especially when she attributes her tears to devotion, not to sorrow, and conceals the course of the common grief for fear of shame. Console her, therefore, thou who canst approach her soul, and penetrate her mind. Let her perceive that thou art present, feel that thou art not departed, that having enjoyed his consolation of whose merit she is assured, she may learn not to grieve heavily for him, who warned her that he was not to be mourned for.

78. But why should I delay thee, brother, why should I wait that my address should die and as it were be buried with thee? Although the sight and form of thy lifeless body, and its remaining comeliness and figure abiding here, comfort the eyes, I delay no longer, let us go on to the tomb. But first, before the people I utter the last farewell, declare peace to thee, and pay the last kiss. Go before us to that home, common and waiting for all, and certainly now longed for by me beyond others. Prepare a common dwelling for him with whom thou hast dwelt, and as here we have had all things in common, so there, too, let us know no divided rights.

79. Do not, I pray thee, long put off him who is desirous of thee, expect him who is hastening after thee, help him who is hurrying, and if I seem to thee to delay too long, summon me. For we have not ever been long separated from each other, but thou wast always wont to return. Nor since thou canst not return again, I will go to thee; it is just that I should repay the kindness and take my turn. Never was there much difference in the condition of our life; whether health or sickness, it was common to both, so that if one sickened the other fell ill, and when one began to recover, the other, too, was convalescent. How have we lost our rights? This time, too, we had our sickness in common, how is it that death was not ours in common?

80. And now to Thee, Almighty God, I commend this guileless soul, to Thee I offer my sacrifice; accept favourably and mercifully the gift of a brother, the offering of a priest. I offer beforehand these first libations of myself. I come to Thee with this pledge, a pledge not of money but of life, cause me not to remain too long a debtor of such an amount. It is not the ordinary interest of a brother's love, nor the common course of nature, which is increased by such an amount of virtue. I can bear it, if I shall be soon compelled to pay it.

BOOK II.

On the Belief in the Resurrection.

1. In the former book I indulged my longing to some extent, lest too sharp remedies applied to a burning wound might rather increase than assuage the pain. And as at the same time I often addressed my brother, and had him before my eyes, it was not out of place to let natural feelings have a little play, since they are somewhat satisfied by tears, soothed by weeping, and numbed by a shock. For the outward expression of affection is of a soft and tender nature, it loves nothing extravagant, nothing stern, nothing hard; and patience is proved by enduring rather than by resisting.

2. So, since the death-day might well, lately, by the sad spectacle draw aside the mind of a brother, because it occupied him wholly, now, inasmuch as on the seventh day, the symbol of the future rest, we return to the grave, it is profitable to turn our thoughts somewhat from my brother to a general exhortation addressed to all, and to give our attention to this; so as neither to cling to my brother with all our minds, lest our feelings overcome us, nor forgetting such devotion and desert, to turn wholly away from him; and in truth we should but increase the suffering of our intense grief, if his death were again the subject of to-day's address.

3. Wherefore we propose, dearest brethren, to console ourselves with the common course of nature, and not to think anything hard which awaits all. And therefore we deem that death is not to be mourned over; firstly, because it is common and due to all; next, because it frees us from the miseries of this lie and, lastly, because when in the likeness of sleep we are at rest from the toils of this world, a more lively vigour is shed upon us. What grief is there which the grace of the Resurrection does not console? What sorrow is not excluded by the belief that nothing perishes in death? nay, indeed, that by the hastening of death it comes to pass that much is preserved from perishing. So it will happen, dearest brethren, that in our general exhortation we shall turn our affections to my brother, and shall not seem to have wandered too far from him, if through hope of the Resurrection and the sweetness of future glory even in our discourse he should live again for us.

4. Let us then begin at this point, that we show that the departure of our loved ones should not be mourned by us. For what is more absurd than to deplore as though it were a special misfortune, what one knows is appointed unto all? This were to lift up the mind above the condition of men, not to accept the common law, to reject the fellowship of nature, to be puffed up in a fleshly mind, and not to recognize the measure of the flesh itself. What is more absurd than not to recognize what one is, to pretend to be what one is not? Or what can be a sign of less forethought than to be unable to bear, when it has happened, what one knew was going to happen? Nature herself calls us back, and draws us aside froth sorrow of this sort by a kind of consolation of her own. For what so deep mourning is there, or so bitter grief, in which the mind is not at times relieved? For human nature has this peculiarity, that although men may be in sad circumstances, yet if only they be men, they sometimes turn their thoughts a little away from sadness.

5. It is said, indeed, that there have been certain tribes who mourned at the birth of human beings, and kept festival at their deaths, and this not without reason, for they thought that those who had entered upon this ocean of life should be mourned over, but that they who had escaped from the waves and storms of this world should be accompanied by rejoicing not without good reason. And we too forget the birthdays of the departed, and commemorate with festal solemnity the day on which they died.

6. Therefore, in accordance with nature, excessive grief must not be yielded to, test we should seem either to claim for ourselves either an exceptional superiority of nature, or to reject the common lot. For death is alike to all, without difference for the poor, without exception for the rich. And so although through the sin of one alone, yet it passed upon all; that we may not refuse to acknowledge Him to be also the Author of death, Whom we do not refuse to

acknowledge as the Author of our race; and that, as through one death is ours, so should be also the resurrection; and that we should not refuse the misery, that we may attain to the gift. For, as we read, Christ "is come to save that which was lost," and "to be Lord both of the dead and living." In Adam I fell, in Adam I was cast out of Paradise, in Adam I died; how shall the Lord call me back, except He find me in Adam; guilty as I was in him, so now justified in Christ. If, then, death be the debt of all, we must be able to endure the payment. But this topic must be reserved for later treatment.

7. It is now our purpose to demonstrate that death ought not to cause too heavy grief, because nature itself rejects this. And so they say that there was a law among the Lycians, commanding that men who gave way to grief should be clothed in female apparel, inasmuch as they judged mourning to be soft and effeminate in a man. And it is inconsistent that those who ought to offer their breast to death for the faith, for religion, for their country, for righteous judgment, and the endeavour after virtue, should grieve too bitterly for that in the case of others which, if a fitting cause required, they would seek for themselves. For how can one help shrinking from that in ourselves which one mourns with too little patience when it has happened to others? Put aside your grief, if you can; if you cannot, keep it to yourself.

8. Is, then, all sorrow to be kept within or repressed? Why should not reason rather than time lighten one's sadness? Shall not wisdom better assuage that which the passage of time will obliterate? Further, it seems to me that it is a want of due feeling with regard to the memory of those whose loss we mourn, when we prefer to forget them rather than that our sorrow should be lessened by consolation; and to shrink from the recollection of them, rather than remember them with thankfulness; that we fear the calling to mind of those whose image in our hearts ought to be a delight; that we are rather distrustful than hopeful regarding the acceptance of the departed, and think of those we loved rather as liable to punishment than as heirs of immortality.

9. But you may say: We have lost those whom we used to love. Is not this the common lot of ourselves and the earth and elements, that we cannot keep for ever what has been entrusted to us for a time? The earth groans under the plough, is lashed by rains, struck by tempests, bound by cold, burnt by the sun, that it may bring forth its yearly fruits; and when it has clothed itself with a variety of flowers, it is stripped and spoiled of its own adornment. How many plunderers it has! And it does not complain of the loss of its fruits, to which it gave birth that it might lose them, nor thereafter does it refuse to produce what it remembers will be taken from it.

10. The heavens themselves do not always shine with the globes of twinkling stars, wherewith as with coronets they are adorned. They are not always growing bright with the dawn of light, or ruddy with the rays of the sun; but in constant succession that most pleasing appearance of the world grows dark with the damp chill of night. What is more grateful than the light? what more pleasant than the sun? each of which daily comes to an end; yet we do not take it ill that these have passed away from us, because we expect them to return. Thou art taught in these things what patience thou oughtest to manifest with regard to those who belong to thee. If things above pass away from thee, and cause no grief, why should the passing away of man be mourned?

11. Let, then, grief be patient, let there be that moderation in adversity which is required in prosperity. If it be not seemly to rejoice immoderately, is it seemly so to mourn? For want of moderation in grief or fear of death is no small evil. How many has it driven to the halter, in how many hands has it placed the sword, that they might by that very means demonstrate their madness in not enduring death, and yet seeking it; in adopting that as a remedy which they flee from as an evil. And because they were unable to endure and to suffer what is in agreement with their nature, they fall into that which is contrary to their desire, being separated for ever from those whom they desired to follow. But this is not common, since nature herself restrains although madness drives men on.

12. But it is common with women to make public wailing, as though they feared that their misery might not be known. They affect soiled clothing, as though the feeling of sorrow consisted therein; they moisten their unkempt hair with filth; and lastly, which is done habitually in many places, with their clothing torn and their dress rent in two, they prostitute their modesty in nakedness, as if they were ready to sacrifice that modesty because they have lost that which was its reward. And so wanton eyes are excited, and lust after those naked limbs, which were they not made bare they would not desire. Would that those filthy garments covered the mind rather than the bodily form. Lasciviousness of mind is often hidden under sad clothing, and the unseemly rudeness of dress is used as a covering to hide the secrets of wanton spirits.

13. She mourns for her husband with sufficient devotion who preserves her modesty and does not give up her constancy. The best duties to discharge to the departed are that they live in our memories and continue in our affection. She has not lost her husband who manifests her chastity, nor is she widowed as regards her union who has not changed her husband's name. Nor hast thou lost the heir when thou assistest the joint-heir, but in exchange for a successor in perishable things thou hast a sharer in things eternal. Thou hast one to represent thine heir, pay to the poor what was due to the heir, that there may remain one to survive, not only the old age of father or mother, but thine own life. Thou leavest thy successor all the more, if his share conduce not to luxury in things present, but to the purchasing of things to come.

14. But we long for those whom we have lost. For two things specially pain us: either the longing for those we have lost, which I experience in my own case; or that we think them deprived of the sweetness of life, and snatched away from the fruits of their toil. For there is a tender movement of love, which suddenly kindles the affection, so as to have the effect rather of soothing than of hindering the pain; inasmuch as it seems a dutiful thing to longfor what one has lost, and so under an appearance of virtue weakness increases.

15. But why dost thou think that she who has sent her beloved to foreign parts, and because of military service, or of undertaking some office, or has discovered that for the purpose of commerce he has crossed the sea, ought to be more patient than thou who art left, not because of some chance decision or desire of money, but by the law of nature? But, you say, the hope of regaining him is shut out. As though the return of any one were certain! And oftentimes doubt wearies the mind more where the fear of danger is strong; and it is more burdensome to fear lest something should happen than to bear what one already knows has happened. For the one increases the amount of fear, the other looks forward to the end of its grief.

16. But masters have the right to transfer their slaves whithersoever they determine. Has not God this right? It is not granted to us to look for their return, but it is granted us to follow those gone before. And certainly the usual shortness of life seems neither to have deprived them of much who have gone before, nor to delay very long him who remains.

17. But if one cannot mitigate one's grief, does it not seem unbecoming to wish that because of our longing the whole course of things should be upset? The longings of lovers are certainly more intense, and yet they are tempered by regard to what is necessary; and though they grieve at being forsaken they are not wont to mourn, rather being deserted they blush at loving too hastily. And so patience in regret is all the more manifested.

18. But what shall I say of those who think that the departed are deprived of the sweetness of life? There can be no real sweetness in the midst of the bitternesses and pains of this life, which are caused either by the infirmity of the body itself, or by the discomfort of things happening from without. For we are always anxious and in suspense as to our wishes for happier circumstances; we waver in uncertainty, our hope setting before us doubtful things for certain, inconvenient for satisfactory, things that will fail for what is firm, and we have neither any strength in our will nor certainty in our wishes. But if anything happens against our wish, we think we are lost, and are rather broken down by pain at adversity than cheered by the enjoyment of prosperity. What good, then, are they deprived of who are rather freed from troubles?

19. Good health, I doubt not, is more beneficial to us than bad health is hurtful. Riches bring more delights than poverty annoyance, the satisfaction in children's love is greater than the sorrow at their loss, and youth is more pleasant than old age is sad. How often is the attainment of one's wishes a weariness, and what one has longed for a regret; so that one grieves at having obtained what one was not afraid of obtaining. But what fatherland, what pleasures, can compensate for exile and the bitterness of other penalties? For even when we have these, the pleasure is weakened either by the disinclination to use or by the fear of losing them.

20. But suppose that some one remains unharmed, free from grief, in uninterrupted enjoyment of the pleasures of the whole course of man's life, what comfort can the soul attain to, enclosed in the bonds of a body of such a kind, and restrained by the narrow limits of the limbs? If our flesh shrinks from prison, if it abhors everything which denies it the power of roaming about; when it seems, indeed, to be always going forth, with its little powers of hearing or seeing what is beyond itself, how much more does our soul desire to escape from that prison-house of the body, which, being free with movement like the air, goes whither we know not, and comes whence we know not.

21. We know, however, that it survives the body, and that being set free from the bars of the body, it sees with clear gaze those things which before, dwelling in the body, it could not see. And we are able to judge of this by the instance of those who have visions of things absent and even heavenly in sleep (whose minds, when the body is as it were buried in sleep, rise to higher things and relate them to the body). So, then, if death frees us from the miseries of this world, it is certainly no evil, inasmuch as it restores liberty and excludes suffering.

22. At this point the right place occurs for arguing that death is not an evil, because it is the refuge from all miseries and all evils, a safe harbour of security, and a haven of rest. For what adversity is there which we do not experience in this life? What storms and tempests do we not suffer? by what discomforts are we not harassed? whose merits are spared?

23. The holy patriarch Israel fled from his country, was exiled from his father, relatives, and home, he mourned over the shame of his daughter and the death of his son, he endured famine, when dead he lost his own grave, for he entreated that his bones should be translated, a lest even in death he should find rest.

24. Holy Joseph experienced the hatred of his brethren, the guile of those who envied him, the service of slavery, the mastership of merchantmen, the wantonness of his mistress, the ignorance of her husband, and the misery of prison.

25. Holy David lost two sons; the one incestuous, the other a parricide. To have had them was a disgrace, to have lost them a grief. And he lost a third, the infant whom he loved. Him he wept for while still alive, but did not long for when dead. For so we read, that, while the child was sick, David entreated the Lord for him, and fasted and lay in sackcloth, and when the elders came near to raise him from the earth, he would neither rise nor eat. But when he heard that the child was dead, he changed his clothes, worshipped God, and took food. When this seemed strange to his servants, he answered that he had rightly fasted and wept while the child was alive, because he justly thought that God might have mercy, and it could not be doubted that He could preserve the life of one alive Who could give life to the departed, but now, when death had taken place, why should he fast, for he could not now bring back him that was dead, and recall him who was lifeless. "I," said he, "shall go to him, but he shall not return to me."

26. O greatest consolation for him who mourns! O true judgment of a wise man! O wonderful wisdom of one who is a bond-man! that none should take it ill that anything adverse has happened to him, or complain that he is afflicted contrary to his deserts. For who art thou who beforehand proclaimest thy deserts? Why desirest thou to anticipate Him Who takes cognizance of all? Why dost thou snatch away the verdict from Him Who is going to judge? This is permitted not even to the saints, nor has it ever been done by the saints with impunity. David confesses that he was scourged for this in his psalm: "Behold, these are the ungodly, who prosper in the world, they have obtained riches. Therefore I have cleansed my heart in vain, and

washed my hands among the innocent; and I was scourged all the day long, and my accusation came every morning."

27. Peter also, though full of faith and devotion, yet because, not yet conscious of our common weakness, he had presumptuously said to the Lord, "I will lay down my life for Thy sake," fell into the trial of his presumption before the cock crowed thrice. Although, indeed, that trial was a lesson for our salvation, that we might learn not to think little of the weakness of the flesh, lest through thus thinking little of it we should be tempted. If Peter was tempted, who can presume? who can maintain that he cannot be tempted? And without doubt for our sakes was Peter tempted, so that, the proving of the temptation did not take place in a stronger than he, but that in him we should learn how, resisting in temptations, although tried even by care for our lives, we might yet overcome the sting of the temptation with tears of patience.

28. But that same David, that the difference of his actions may not perhaps disturb those who cling to the words of Scripture; that same David, I say, who had not wept for the innocent infant, wept for the parricide when dead. For at the last, when he was wailing and mourning, he said, "O my son Absalom, my son Absalom! Who will grant me to die for thee!" But not only is Absalom the parricide wept over, Amnon is wept over; not only is the incestuous wept over, but is even avenged; the one by the scorn of the kingdom, the other by the exile of his brothers. The wicked is wept over, not the innocent. What is the cause? What is the reason? There is no little deliberation with the prudent and confirmation of results with the wise; for there is great consistency of prudence in so great a difference of actions, but the belief is one. He wept for those who were dead, but did not think that he ought to weep for the dead infant, for he thought that they were lost to him, but hoped that the latter would rise again.

29. But concerning the Resurrection more will be said later on; let us now return to our immediate subject. We have set forth that even holy men have without any consideration for their merits, suffered many and heavy things in this world, together with toil and misery. So David, entering into himself, says: "Remember; Lord, that we are dust; as for man, his days are but as grass;" and in another place: "Man is like to vanity, his days pass away as a shadow." For what is more wretched than we, who are sent into this life as it were plundered and naked, with frail bodies, deceitful hearts, weak minds, anxious in respect of cares, slothful as to labour, prone to pleasures.

30. Not to be born is then by far the best, according to Solomon's sentence. For they also who have seemed to themselves to excel most in philosophy have followed him. For he, before these philosophers in time, but later than many of our writers, spoke thus in Ecclesiastes: "And I praised all the departed, which are already dead, more than the living, who are yet alive. And better than both they is he who hath not yet been born, and who hath not seen this evil work which hath been done under the sun. And I saw all travail, and all the good of this labour, that for this a man is envied of his neighbour. And, indeed, this is vanity and vexation of spirit."

31. And who said this but he who asked for and obtained wisdom, to know how the world was made, and the power of the elements, the course of the year, and the dispositions of stars, to be acquainted with the natures of living creatures, the furies of wild beasts, and the violence of winds, and to understand the thoughts of man! How, then, should mortal matters be hidden from him, from whom heavenly things were not hidden? He who penetrated the thoughts of the woman who was claiming the child of another, who by the inspiration of divine grace knew the natures of living creatures which he did not share; could he err or say what was untrue with regard to the circumstances of that nature, which he found in his own personal experience?

32. But Solomon was not the only person who felt this, though he alone gave expression to it. He had read the words of holy Job: "Let the day perish wherein I was born." Job had recognized that to be born is the beginning of all woes, and therefore wished that the day on which he was born might perish, so that the origin of all troubles might be removed, and wished that the day of his birth might perish that he might receive the day of resurrection. For Solomon had heard his father's saying: "Lord, make me to know mine end, and the number of my days,

that I may know what is lacking unto me." For David knew that what is perfect cannot be grasped here, and therefore hastened on to those things which are to come. For now we know in part, and understand in part, but then it will be possible for that which is perfect to be grasped, when not the shadow but the reality of the Divine Majesty and eternity shall begin to shine so as to be gazed upon by us with unveiled face.

33. But no one would hasten to the end, except he were fleeing from the discomfort of this life. And so David also explained why he hastened to the end, when he said: "Behold Thou hast made my days old, and my being is as nothing before Thee, surely all things are vanity, even every man that liveth." Why, then, do we hesitate to flee from vanity? Or why does it please us to be troubled to no purpose in this world, to lay up treasures, and not know for what heir we are gathering them? Let us pray that troubles be removed from us, that we be taken out of this foolish world, that we may be free from our daily pilgrimage, and return to that country and our natural home. For on this earth we are strangers and foreigners; we have to return thither whence we have come down, we must strive and pray not perfunctorily but earnestly to be delivered from the guile and wickedness of men full of words. And he who knew the remedy groaned that his sojourn was prolonged, and that he must dwell with the unjust and sinners. What shall I do, who both am sinful and know not the remedy?

34. Jeremiah also bewails his birth in these words: "Woe is me, my mother! Why hast thou borne me a man of contention in all the earth? I have not benefited others, nor has any one benefited me, my strength hath failed." If, then, holy men shrink from life whose life, though profitable to us, is esteemed unprofitable to themselves; what ought we to do who am not able to profit others, and who feel that it, like money borrowed at interest, grows more heavily weighted every day with an increasing mass of sins?

35. "I die daily," says the Apostle. Better certainly is this saying than theirs who said that meditation on death was true philosophy, for they praised the study, he exercised the practice of death. And they acted for themselves only, but Paul, himself perfect, died not for his own weakness but for ours. But what is meditation on death but a kind of separation of body and soul, for death itself is defined as nothing else than the separation of body and soul? But this is in accordance with common opinion.

36. But according to the Scriptures we have been taught that death is threefold. One death is when we die to sin, but live to God. Blessed, then, is that death which, escaping from sin, and devoted to God, separates us from what is mortal and consecrates us to Him Who is immortal. Another death is the departure from this life, as the patriarch Abraham died, and the patriarch David, and were buried with their fathers; when the soul is set free from the bonds of the body. The third death is that of which it is said: "Leave the dead to bury their own dead." In that death not only the flesh but also the soul dies, for "the soul that sinneth, it shall die." For it dies to the Lord, through the weakness not of nature but of guilt. But this death is not the discharge from this life, but a fall through error.

37. Spiritual death, then, is one thing, natural death another, a third the death of punishment. But that which is natural is not also penal, for the Lord did not inflict death as a penalty, but as a remedy. And to Adam when he sinned, one thing was appointed as a penalty, another for a remedy, when it was said: "Because thou hast hearkened unto the voice of thy wife, and hast eaten of the tree of which I had commanded thee that of it alone thou shouldst not eat, cursed is the ground in thy labor; in sorrow shalt thou eat its fruit all the days of thy life. Thorns and thistles shall it bring forth to thee, and thou shalt eat the herb of the field. In the sweat of thy face shalt thou eat thy bread, till thou return to the earth from which thou wast taken."

38. Here you have the days of rest from penalties, for they contain the punishment decreed against the thorns of tiffs life, the cares of the world, and the pleasures of riches which shut out the Word. Death is given for a remedy, because it is the end of evils. For God said not, "Because thou hast hearkened to the voice of the woman thou shalt return to the earth," for this would have been a penal sentence, as this one is, "The earth under curse shall bring forth thorns

and thistles to thee;" but He said: "In sweat shall thou eat thy bread until thou return to the earth." You see that death is rather the goal of our penalties, by which an end is put to the course of this life.

39. So, then, death is not only not an evil, but is even a good thing. So that it is sought as a good, as it is written: "Men shall seek death and shall not find it." They will seek it who shall say to the mountains: "Fall on us, and to the hills, Cover us." That soul, too, shall seek it which has sinned. That rich man lying in hell shall seek it, who wishes that his tongue should be cooled with the finger of Lazarus.

40. We see, then, that this death is a gain and life a penalty, so that Paul says: "To me to live is Christ and to die is gain." What is Christ but the death of the body, the breath of life? And so let us die with Him, that we may live with Him. Let there then be in us as it were a daily practice and inclination to dying, that by this separation from bodily desires, of which we have spoken, our soul may learn to withdraw itself, and, as it were placed on high, when earthly lusts cannot approach and attach it to themselves, may take upon herself the likeness of death, that she incur not the penalty of death. For the law of the flesh wars against the law of the mind, and makes it over to the law of error, as the Apostle has made known to us, saying: "For I see a law of the flesh in my members warring against the law of my mind, and bringing me into captivity in the law of sin." We are all attached, we all feel this; but we are not all delivered. And so a miserable man am I, unless I seek the remedy.

41. But what remedy? "Who shall deliver me out of the body of this death? Thanks be to God through Jesus Christ our Lord." We have a physician, let us use the remedy. Our remedy is the grace of Christ, and the body of death is our body. Let us therefore be as strangers to our body, lest we be strangers to Christ. Though we are in the body, let us not follow the things which are of the body, let us not reject the rightful claims of nature, but desire before all the gifts of grace: "For to be dissolved and to be with Christ is far better; yet to abide in the flesh is more needful for your sakes."

42. But this need is not the case of all, Lord Jesus; it is not so with me, who am profitable to none; for to me death is a gain, that I may sin no more. To die is gain to me, who, in the very treatise in which I comfort others, am incited as it were by an intense impulse to the longing for my lost brother, since it suffers me not to forget him. Now I love him more, and long for him more intensely. I long for him when I speak, I long for him when I read again what I have written, and I think that I am more impelled to write this, that I may not ever be without the recollection of him. And in this I am not acting contrary to Scripture, but I am of the same mind with Scripture, that I may grieve with more patience, and long with greater intensity.

43. Thou hast caused me, my brother, not to fear death, and I only would that my life might die with thine! This Balaam wished for as the greatest good for himself, when, inspired by the spirit of prophecy, he said: "Let my soul die in the souls of the righteous, and let my seed be like the seed of them." And in truth he wished this according to the spirit of prophecy, for as he saw the rising of Christ, so also he saw His triumph, he saw His death, but saw also in Him the everlasting resurrection of men, and therefore feared not to die as he was to rise again. Let not then my soul die in sin, nor admit sin into itself, but let it die in the soul of the righteous, that it may receive his righteousness. Then, too, he who dies in Christ. is made a partaker of His grace in the Font.

44. Death is not, then, an object of dread, nor bitter to those in need, nor too bitter to the rich, nor unkind to the old, nor a mark of cowardice to the brave, nor everlasting to the faithful nor unexpected to the wise. For how many have consecrated their life by the renown of their death alone, how many have been ashamed to live, and have found death a gain! We have read how often by the death of one great nations have been delivered; the armies of the enemy have been put to flight by the death of the general, who had been unable to conquer them when alive.

45. By the death of martyrs religion has been defended, faith increased, the Church strengthened; the dead have conquered, the persecutors have been overcome. And so we

celebrate the death of those of whose lives we are ignorant. So, too, David rejoiced in prophecy at the departure of his own soul, saying: "Precious in the sight of the Lord is the death of His saints." He esteemed death better than life. The death itself of the martyrs is the prize of their life. And again, by the death of those at variance hatred is put an end to.

46. Why should more be said? By the death of One the world was redeemed. For Christ, had He Willed, need not have died, but He neither thought that death should be shunned as though there were any cowardice in it, nor could He have saved us better than by dying. And so His death is the life of all. We are signed with the sign of His death, we show forth His death when we pray; when we offer the Sacrifice we declare His death, for His death is victory, His death is our mystery, His death is the yearly recurring solemnity of the world. What now should we say concerning His death, since we prove by this Divine Example that death alone found immortality, and that death itself redeemed itself. Death, then, is not to be mourned over, for it is the cause of salvation for all; death is not to be shunned, for the Son of God did not think it unworthy of Him, and did not shun it. The order of nature is not to be loosed, for what is common to all cannot admit of exception in individuals.

47. And, indeed, death was no part of man's nature, but became natural; for God did not institute death at first, but gave it as a remedy. Let us then take heed that it do not seem to be the opposite. For if death is a good, why is it written that "God made not death, but by the malice of men death entered into the world"? For of a truth death was no necessary part of the divine operation, since for those who were placed in paradise a continual succession of all good things streamed forth; but because of transgression the life of man, condemned to lengthened labour, began to be wretched with intolerable groaning; so that it was fitting that an end should be set to the evils, and that death should restore what life had lost. For immortality, unless grace breathed upon it, would be rather a burden than an advantage.

48. And if one consider accurately, it is not the death of our being, but of evil, for being continues, it is evil that perishes. That which has been rises again; would that as it is now free from sinning, so it were without former guilt! But this very thing is a proof that it is not the death of being, that we shall be the same persons as we were. And so we shall either pay the penalty of our sins, or attain to the reward of our good deeds. For the same being will rise again, now more honourable for having paid the tax of death. And then "the dead who are in Christ shall rise first; then, too, we who are alive," it is said, "shall together with them be caught up in the clouds into the air to meet the Lord, and so we shall always be with the Lord." They first, but those that are alive second. They with Jesus, those that are alive through Jesus. To them life will be sweeter after rest, and though the living will have a delightful gain, yet they will be without experience of the remedy.

49. There is, then, nothing for us to fear in death, nothing for us to mourn, whether life which was received from nature be rendered up to her again, or whether it be sacrificed to some duty which claims it, and this will be either an act of religion or the exercise of some virtue. And no one ever wished to remain as at present. This has been supposed to have been promised to John, but it is not the truth. We hold fast to the words, and deduce the meaning from them. He himself in his own writing denies that there was a promise that he should not die, that no one from that instance might yield to an empty hope. But if to wish for this would be an extravagant hope, how much more extravagant were it to grieve without rule for what has happened according to rule!

50. The heathen mostly console themselves with the thought, either of the common misery, or of the law of nature, or of the immortality of the soul. And would that their utterances were consistent, and that they did not transmit the wretched soul into a number of ludicrous monstrosities and figures! But what ought we to do, whose reward is the resurrection, though many, not being able to deny the greatness of this gift, refuse to believe in it? And for this reason will we maintain it, not by one casual argument only, but by as many as we are able.

51. All things, indeed, are believed to be, either because of experience, or on grounds of reason, or from similar instances, or because it is fitting that they be, and each of these supports our belief. Experience teaches us that we are moved; reason, that which moves us must be considered the property of another power; similar instances show that the field has borne crops, and therefore we expect that it will continue to bear them. Fitness, because even where we do not think that there will be results, yet we believe that it is by no means fitting to give up the works of virtue.

52. Each, then, is supported by each. But belief in the resurrection is inferred most clearly on three grounds, in which all are included. These are reason, analogy from universal example, and the evidence of what has happened, since many have risen. Reason is clear. For since the whole course of our life consists in the union of body and soul, and the resurrection brings with it either the reward of good works, or the punishment of wicked ones, it is necessary that the body, whose actions are weighed, rise again. For how shall the soul be summoned to judgment without the body, when account has to be rendered of the companionship of itself and the body?

53. Rising again is the lot of all, but there is a difficulty in believing this, because it is not due to our deserts, but is the gift of God. The first argument for the resurrection is the course of the world, and the condition of all things, the series of generations, the changes in the way of succession, the setting and rising of constellations, the ending of day and night, and their daily succession coming as it were again to life. And no other reason can exist for the fertile temperament of this earth, but that the divine order restores by the dews of night as much of that moisture from which all earthly things are produced, as the heat of the sun dries up by day. Why should I speak of the fruits of the earth? Do they not seem to die when they fall, to rise again when they grow green once more? That which is sown rises again, that which is dead rises again, and they are formed once more into the same classes and kinds as before. The earth first gave back these fruits, in these first our nature found the pattern of the resurrection.

54. Why doubt that body shall rise again from body? Grain is sown, grain comes up again: fruit is sown, fruit comes up again; but the grain is clothed with blossom and husk. "And this mortal must put on immortality, and this corruptible must put on incorruption." The blossom of the resurrection is immortality, the blossom of the resurrection is incorruption. For what is more fruitful than perpetual rest? what supplied with richer store than everlasting security? Here is that abundant fruit, by whose increase man's nature shoots forth more abundantly after death.

55. But you wonder how what has yielded to putrefaction can again become solid, how scattered particles can come together, those that are consumed be made good: you do not wonder how seeds broken up under the moist pressure of the earth grow green. For certainly they too, rotting under contact with the earth, are broken up, and when the fertilising moisture of the soil gives life to the dead and hidden seeds, and, by the vital warmth, as it were breathes out a kind of soul of the green herb. Then by little and little nature raises from the ground the tender stalk of the growing ear, and as a careful mother folds it in certain sheaths, lest the sharp ice should hurt it as it grows, and to protect it from too great heat of the sun; and lest after this the rain should break down the fruit itself escaping as it were from its first cradle and just grown up, or lest the wind should scatter it, or small birds destroy it, she usually hedges it around with a fence of bristling awn.

56. Why should one, then, be surprised if the earth give back those bodies of men which it has received, seeing that it gives life to, raises, clothes, protects, and defends whatsoever bodies of seeds it has received? Cease then to doubt that the trustworthy earth, which restores multiplied as it were by usury the seeds committed to it, will also restore the entrusted deposit of the race of man. And why should I speak of the kinds of trees, which spring up from seed sown, and with revivified fruitfulness bear again their opening fruits, and repeat the old shape and likeness, and certain trees being renewed continue through many generations, and in their endurance overpass the very centuries? We see the grape rot, and the vine come up again: a graft

is inserted and the tree is born again. Is there this divine foresight for restoring trees, and no care for men? And He Who has not suffered to perish that which He gave for man's use, shall He suffer man to perish, whom he made after His own image?

57. But it appears incredible to you that the dead rise again? "Thou foolish one, that which thou thyself sowest, does it not first die that it may be quickened?" Sow any dry seed you please, it is raised up. But, you answer, it has the life-juice in itself. And our body has its blood, has its own moisture. This is the life-juice of our body. So that I think that the objection is exploded which some allege that a dry twig does not revive, and then endeavour to argue from this to the prejudice of the flesh. For the flesh is not dry, since all flesh is of clay, clay comes from moisture—moisture from the earth. Then, again, many growing plants, though always fresh, spring from dry and sandy soil, since the earth itself supplies sufficient moisture for itself. Does the earth then, which continually restores all things, fail with regard to man? From what has been said it is clear that we must not doubt that it is rather in accordance with than contrary to nature; for it is natural that all things living should rise again, but contrary to nature that they should perish.

58. We come now to a point which much troubles the heathen, how it can be that the earth should restore those whom the sea has swallowed up, wild beasts have torn to pieces or have devoured. So, then, at last we necessarily come to the conclusion that the doubt is not as to belief in resurrection in general, but as to a part. For, granted that the bodies of those torn in pieces do not rise again, the others do so, and the resurrection is not disproved, but a certain class is an exception. Yet I wonder why they think there is any doubt even concerning these, as though not all things which are of the earth return to the earth, and crumble again into earth. And the sea itself for the most part casts up on neighbouring shores whatever human bodies it has swallowed. And if this were not so, I suppose we are to believe that it would not be difficult for God to join together what was dispersed, to unite what was scattered; God, Whom the universe obeys, to Whom the dumb elements submit and nature serves; as though it were not a greater wonder to give life to clay than to join it together.

59. That bird in the country of Arabia, which is called the Phoenix, restored by the renovating juices of its flesh, after being dead comes to life again: shall we believe that men alone are not raised up again? Yet we know this by common report and the authority of writings, namely, that the bird referred to has a fixed period of life of five hundred years, and when by some warning of nature it knows that the end of its life is at hand, it furnishes for itself a casket of frankincense and myrrh and other perfumes, and its work and the time being together ended, it enters the casket and dies. Then from its juices a worm comes forth, and grows by degrees into the fashion of the same bird, and its former habits are restored, and borne up by the oarage of its wings it commences once more the course of its renewed life, and discharges a debt of gratitude. For it conveys that casket, whether the tomb of its body or the cradle of its resurrection, in which quitting life it died, and dying it rose again, from Ethiopia to Lycaonia; and so by the resurrection of this bird the people of those regions understand that a period of five hundred years is accomplished. So to that bird the five hundredth is the year of resurrection, but to us the thousandth: it has its resurrection in this world, we have ours at the end of the world. Many think also that this bird kindles its own funeral pile, and comes to life again from its own ashes.

60. But perhaps nature if more deeply investigated will seem to give a deeper reason for our belief: let our thoughts turn back to the origin and commencement of the creation of man. You are men and women, you are not ignorant of the things which have to do with human nature, and if any of you have not this knowledge, you know that we are born of nothing. But how small an origin for being so great as we are! And if I do not speak more plainly, yet you understand. what I mean, or rather what I will not say. Whence, then, is this head, and that wonderful countenance, whose maker we see not? We see the work, it is fashioned for various purposes and uses. Whence is this upright figure, this lofty stature, this power of action, this

quickness of perception, this capacity for walking upright? Doubtless the organs of nature are not known to us, but that which they effect is known. Thou too wast once seed, and thy body is the seed of that which shall rise again. Listen to Paul and learn that thou art this seed: "It is sown in corruption, it shall rise in incorruption; it is sown in dishonour, it shall rise in glory; it is sown in weakness, it shall rise in power; it is sown a natural body, it shall rise a spiritual body." Thou also, then, art sown as are other things, why wonderest thou if thou shall rise again as shall others? But thou believest as to them, because thou seest; thou believest not this, because thou seest it not: "Blessed are they that have not seen, and yet have believed."

61. However, before the season comes, those things also are not believed, for every season is not suited for the raising of seeds. Wheat is sown at one time, and comes up at another; at one time the vine is planted, at another the budding twigs begin to shoot, the foliage grows luxuriant, and the grape is formed; at one time the olive is planted, at another time, as though pregnant and loaded with its offspring of berries, it is bent down by the abundance of its fruit. But before its own period arrives for each, the produce is restricted, and that which bears has not the age of bearing in its own power. One may see the mother of all at one time disfigured with mould, at another bare of produce, at another green and full of flowers, at another dried up. Any spot which might wish to be always clothed and never to lay aside the golden dress of its seeds, or the green dress of the meadows, would be barren in itself and unendowed with the gain of its own produce which it would have transferred to others.

62. So, then, even if thou wilt not believe in our resurrection by faith nor by example, thou wilt believe by experience. For many products, as the vine, the olive, and different fruits, the end of the year is the fit time for ripening; and for us also the consummation of the world, as though the end of the year has set the fitting time for rising again. And fitly is the resurrection of the dead at the consummation of the world, lest after the resurrection we should have to fall back into this evil age. For this cause Christ suffered that He might deliver us from this evil world; lest the temptations of this world should overthrow us again, and it should be an injury to us to come again to life, if we came to life again for sin.

63. So then we have both a reason and a time for the resurrection: a reason because nature in all its produce remains consistent with itself, and does not fail in the generation of men alone; a time because all things are produced at the end of the year. For the seasons of the world consist of one year. What wonder if the year be one since the day is one. For on one day the Lord hired the labourers to work in the vineyard, when He said, "Why stand ye here all the day idle?"

64. The causes of the beginnings of all things are seeds. And the Apostle of the Gentiles has said that the human body is a seed. And so in succession after sowing there is the substance needful for the resurrection. But even if there were no substance and no cause, who could think it difficult for God to create man anew whence He will and as He wills. Who commanded the world to come into being out of no matter and no substance? Look at the heaven, behold the earth. Whence are the fires of the stars? Whence the orb and rays of the sun? Whence the globe of the moon? Whence the mountain heights, the hard rocks, the woody groves? Whence are the air diffused around, and the waters, whether enclosed or poured abroad? But if God made all these things out of nothing (for "He spake and they were made, He commanded and they were created"), why should we wonder that which has been should be brought to life again, since we see produced that which had not been?

65. It is a cause for wonder that though they do not believe in the resurrection, yet in their kindly care they make provision that the human race should not perish, and so say that souls pass and migrate into other bodies that the world may not pass away. But let them say which is the most difficult, for souls to migrate, or to return; come back to that which is their own, or seek for fresh dwelling places.

66. But let those who have not been taught doubt. For us who have read the Law, the Prophets, the Apostles, and the Gospel it is not lawful to doubt. For who can doubt when he

reads: "And in that time shall all thy people be saved which is written in the book; and many of them that sleep in the graves of the earth shall arise with one opening, these to everlasting life, and those to shame and everlasting confusion. And they that have understanding shall shine as the brightness of the firmament, and of the just many shall be as the stars for ever." Well, then, did he speak of the rest of those that sleep, that one may understand that death lasts not for ever, which like sleep is undergone for a time, and is put off at its time; and he shows that the progress of that life which shall be after death is better than that which is passed in sorrow and pain before death, inasmuch as the former is compared to the stars, the latter is assigned to trouble.

67. And why should I bring together what is written elsewhere: "Thou shalt raise me up and I will praise Thee." Or that other passage in which holy Job, after experiencing the miseries of this life, and overcoming all adversity by his virtuous patience, promised himself a recompense for present evils in the resurrection, saying: "Thou shall raise up this body of mine which has suffered many evils." Isaiah also, proclaiming the resurrection to the people, says that he is the announcer of the Lord's message, for we read thus: "For the mouth of the Lord hath spoken, and they shall say in that day." And what the mouth of the Lord declared that the people should say is set forth later on, where it is written: "Because of Thy fear, O Lord, we have been with child and have brought forth the Spirit of Thy Salvation, which Thou hast poured forth upon the earth. They that inhabit the earth shall fall, they shall rise that are in the graves. For the dew which is from Thee is health for them but the land of the wicked shall perish. Go O my people, and enter into thy chambers; hide thyself for a little until the Lord's wrath pass by."

68. How well did he by the chambers point out the tombs of the dead, in which for a brief space we are hidden, that we may be better able to pass to the judgment of God, which shall try us with the indignation due for our wickednesses. He, then, is alive who is hidden and at rest, as though withdrawing himself from our midst and retiring, lest the misery of this world should entangle him with closer snares, for whom the heavenly oracles affirm by the voices of the prophets that the joy of the resurrection is reserved, and the soundness of their freed bodies procured by the divine deed. And dew is well used as a sign, since by it all vital seeds of the earth are raised to growth. What wonder is it, then, if the dust and ashes also of our failing body grow vigorous by the richness of the heavenly dew, and by the reception of this vital moistening the shapes of our limbs are refashioned and connected again with each other?

69. And the holy prophet Ezekiel teaches and describes with a full exposition how vigour is restored to the dry bones, the senses return, motion is added, and the sinews coming back, the joints of the human body grow strong; how the bones which were very dry are clothed with restored flesh, and the course of the veins and the flow of the blood is covered by the veil of the skin drawn over them. As we read, the reviving multitude of human bodies seems to spring up under the very words of the prophet, and one can see on the widespread plain the new seed shoot forth.

70. But if the wise men of old believed that a crop of armed men sprang up in the district of Thebes from the sowing of the hydra's teeth, whereas it is certainly established that seeds of one kind cannot be changed into another kind of plant, nor bring forth produce differing from its own seeds, so that men should spring from serpents and flesh from teeth; how much more, indeed, is it to be believed that whatever has been sown rises again in its own nature, and that crops do not differ from their seed, that soft things do not spring from hard, nor hard from soft, nor is poison changed into blood; but that flesh is restored from flesh, bone from bone, blood from blood, the humours of the body from humours. Can ye then, ye heathen, who are able to assert a change, deny a restoration of the nature? Can you refuse to believe the oracles of God, the Gospel, and the prophets, who believe empty fables?

71. But let us now hear the prophet himself, who speaks thus: "The hand of the Lord was upon me, and the Lord led me forth in the Spirit, and placed me in the midst of the plain, and it was full of men's bones; and He led me through them round about, and, lo, there were very

many bones on the face of the plain, and they were very dry. And He said unto me: Son of man, can these bones live? And I said: Lord, Thou knowest; and He said to me: Prophesy over these bones, and thou shalt say unto them: O ye dry bones, hear the word of the Lord. Thus saith the Lord to these bones: Behold I bring upon you the Spirit of life, and I will lay sinews upon you, and will bring up flesh upon you, and will stretch skin over you, and will put My Spirit into you, and ye shall live, and know that I am the Lord. And I prophesied as He commanded me. And it came to pass when I was prophesying all these things, lo, there was a great earthquake."

72. Note how the prophet shows that there was hearing and movement in the bones before the Spirit of life was poured upon them. For, above, both the dry bones are bidden to hear, as if they had the sense of hearing, and that upon this each of them came to its own joint is pointed out by the words of the prophet, for we read as follows: "And the bones came together, each one to its joint. And I beheld, and, lo, sinews and flesh were forming upon them, and skin came upon them from above, and there was no Spirit in them."

73. Great is the lovingkindness of the Lord, that the prophet is taken as a witness of the future resurrection, that we, too might see it with his eyes. For all could not be taken as witnesses, but in that one all we are witnesses, for neither does lying come upon a holy man, nor error upon so great a prophet.

74. Nor ought it to appear at all improbable, that at the command of God the bones were fitted again to their joints, since we have numberless instances in which nature has obeyed the commands of heaven; as the earth was bidden to bring forth the green herb, and did bring it forth; as the rock at the touch of the rod gave forth water for the thirsting people; and the hard stone poured forth streams by the mercy of God for those parched with heat. What else did the rod changed into a serpent signify, than that at the will of God living things can be produced from those that are without life? Do you think it more incredible that bones should come together when bidden, than that streams should be turned back or the sea flee? For thus does the prophet testify: "The sea saw it and fled, Jordan was driven back." Nor can there be any doubt about this fact, which was proved by the rescue of one and the destruction of the other of two peoples, that the waves of the sea stood restrained, and at the same time surrounded one people, and poured back upon the other for their death, that they might overwhelm the one, but preserve the other. And what do we find in the Gospel itself? Did not the Lord Himself prove there that the sea grew calm at a word, the clouds were driven away, the blasts of the winds yielded, and that on the quieted shores the dumb elements obeyed God?

75. But let us go on with the other points, that we may observe how by the Spirit of life the dead are quickened, they that lie in the graves arise, and the tombs are opened: "And He said unto me: Prophesy, son of man, and say to the Spirit, Come from the four winds of heaven, O Spirit, and breathe upon these dead, that they may live. And I prophesied as He commanded me, and the Spirit of life entered into them, and they lived, and stood up on their feet, an exceeding great company. And the Lord spake unto me, saying: Son of man, these bones are the whole house of Israel. For they say, Our bones are become dry, our hope is lost, we shall perish. Therefore, prophesy and say: Thus saith the Lord: Behold I will open your graves, and will bring you up out of your graves into the land of Israel, and ye shall know that I am the Lord, when I shall open your graves, and bring forth My people out of the graves, and shall put My Spirit in you, and place you in your own land, and ye shall know that I am the Lord; I have spoken, and I will perform it, saith the Lord."

76. We notice here how the operations of the Spirit of life are again resumed; we know after what manner the dead are raised from the opening tombs. And is it in truth a matter of wonder that the sepulchres of the dead are unclosed at the bidding of the Lord, when the whole earth from its utmost limits is shaken by one thunderclap, the sea overflows its bounds, and again checks the course of its waves? And finally, he who has believed that the dead shall rise again "in a moment, in the twinkling of an eye, at the last trump (for the trumpet shall sound)," "shall be

caught up amongst the first in the clouds to meet Christ in the air;" he who has not believed shall be left, and subject himself to the sentence by his own unbelief.

77. The Lord also shows us in the Gospel, to come now to instances, after what manner we shall rise again. "For He raised not Lazarus alone, but the faith of all; and if thou believest, as thou readest, thy spirit also, which was dead, revives with Lazarus." For what does it mean, that the Lord went to the sepulchre and cried with a loud voice, "Lazarus, come forth," except that He would give us a visible proof, would set forth an example of the future resurrection? Why did He cry with a loud voice, as though He were not wont to work in the Spirit, tO command in silence, but only that He might show that which is written: "In a moment, in the twinkling of an eye, at the last trump the dead shall rise again incorruptible"? For the raising of the voice answers to the peal of trumpets. And He cried, "Lazarus, come forth." Why is the name added, except perchance lest one might seem to be raised instead of another, or that the resurrection were rather accidental than commanded.

78. So, then, the dead man heard, and came forth from the tomb, bound hand and foot with grave cloths, and his face was bound with a napkin. Conceive, if thou canst, how he makes his way with closed eyes, directs his steps with bound feet, and moves as though free with fastened limbs. The bands remained on him but did not restrain him, his eyes were covered yet they saw. So, then, he saw who was rising again, who was walking, who was leaving the sepulchre. For when the power of the divine command was working, nature did not require its own functions, and brought, as it were, into extremity, obeyed no longer its own course, but the divine will. The bands of death were burst before those of the grave. The power of moving was exercised before the means of moving were supplied.

79. If thou marvellest at this, consider Who gave the command, that thou mayest cease to wonder; Jesus Christ. the Power of God, the Life, the Light, the Resurrection of the dead. The Power raised up him that was lying prostrate, the Life produced his steps, the Light drove away the darkness and restored his sight, the Resurrection renewed the gift of life.

80. Perchance it may trouble thee that the Jews took away the stone and loosened the grave cloths, and thou mayest haply be anxious as to who shall move the stone from thy tomb. As though He Who could restore the Spirit could not remove the stone; or He Who made the bound to walk could not burst the bonds; or He Who had shed light upon the covered eyes could not uncover the face; or He Who could renew the course of nature could not cleave the stone! But, in order that they may believe their eyes who will not believe with their heart, they remove the stone, they see the corpse, they smell the stench, they loose the grave cloths. They cannot deny that he is dead whom they behold rising again; they see the signs of death and the proofs of life. What if, whilst they are busied, they are converted by the very toil itself? What if, while they hear, they believe their own ears? What if, while they behold, they are instructed by their own eyes? What if, while they loose the bonds, they free their own minds? What if, while Lazarus is being unbound, the people is set free, while they let Lazarus go, themselves return to the Lord? For, lastly, many who had come to Mary, seeing what had taken place, believed.

81. And this was not the only instance which our Lord Jesus Christ set forth, but He raised others also, that we might at any rate believe more numerous instances. He raised the young man again, moved by the tears of his widowed mother, when He came and touched the bier, and said: "Young man, I say unto thee, arise, and he that was dead sat up and began to speak." As soon as he heard he forthwith sat up, he forthwith spake. The working of power, then, is one thing, the order of nature is another.

82. And what shall I say of the daughter of the ruler of the synagogue, at whose death multitudes were weeping and the flute-players piping? For the funeral solemnities were being performed because of the conviction of death. How quickly at the word of the Lord does the spirit return, the reviving body rise up, and food is taken, that the evidence of life may be believed!

83. And why should we wonder that the soul is restored at the word of God, that flesh returns to the bones, when we remember the dead raised by the touch of the prophet's body? Elijah prayed, an d raised the dead child. Peter in the name of Christ bade Tabitha rise and walk, and the poor rejoicing believed for the food's sake which she ministered to them, and shall we not believe for our salvation's sake? They purchased the resurrection of another by their tears, shall we not believe in the purchase of ours by the Passion of Christ? Who when He gave up the ghost, in order to show that He died for our resurrection, worked out the course of the resurrection; for so soon as "He cried again with a loud voice and gave up the ghost, the earth did quake, and the rocks were rent, and the tombs were opened, and many bodies of the saints which slept arose, and, going forth out of the tombs after His resurrection, came into the holy city and appeared unto many."

84. If these things happened when He gave up the ghost, why should we think them incredible when He shall return to judgment? especially since this earlier resurrection is a pledge of that future resurrection, and a pattern of that reality Which is to come; indeed, it is rather itself truth than a pattern. Who, then, at the Lord's resurrection opened the graves, gave a hand to those who were rising, showed them the road to find the holy city? If there was no one, it was certainly the Divine Power which was working in the bodies of the dead. Shall one seek for the aid of man where one sees the work of God?

85. Divine action has no need of human assistance. God commanded that the heavens should come into existence, and it was done; He determined that the earth should be created, and it was created. Who carried together the stones on his shoulders? who supplied the expenses? who furnished assistance to God as He toiled? These things were made in a moment. Would you know how quickly? "He spake and they were made." If the elements spring up at a word. why should the dead not rise at a word? For though they be dead, yet they once lived, once had the breath of life for feeling, and strength for acting; and there is a very great difference between not having been capable of life, and having remained lifeless. The devil said: "Command this stone that it become bread." He confesses that at the command of God nature can be transformed, dost thou not believe that at the command of God nature can be remade?

86. Philosophers dispute about the course of the sun and the system of the heavens, and there are those who think that these should be believed when they are ignorant of what they are talking about. For neither have they climbed up into the heavens, nor measured the sky, nor examined the universe with their eyes; for none of them was with God in the beginning, none of them has said of God: "When He was preparing the heavens I was with Him, I was with Him as a master workman, I was he in whom He delighted." If, then, they are believed, is God not believed, Who says: "As the new heavens and the new earth, which I make to remain before Me, saith the Lord; so shall your name and your seed abide; and month shall be after month, and sabbath after sabbath, and all flesh shall come in My sight to worship in Jerusalem, saith the Lord God; and they shall go forth, and shall see the limbs of men who have transgressed against Me. For their worm shall not die and their fire shall not be quenched and they shall be a sight to all flesh."

87. If the earth and heaven are renewed, why should we doubt that man, on account of whom heaven and earth were made, can be renewed? If the transgressor be reserved for punishment, why should not the just be kept for glory? If the worm of sins does not die, how shall the flesh of the just perish? For the resurrection, as the very form of the word shows, is this, that what has fallen should rise again, that which has died should come to life again.

88. And this is the course and ground of justice, that since the action of body and soul is common to both(for what the soul has conceived the body has carried out), each should come into judgment, and each should be either given over to punishment or reserved for glory. For it would seem almost inconsistent that, since the law of the mind fights against the law of the flesh, and the mind often, when sin dwelling in man acts, does that which it hates; the mind guilty of a fault shared by another should be subjected to penalty, and the flesh, the author of

the evil, should enjoy rest: and that should alone suffer which had not sinned alone, or should alone attain to glory, not having fought alone with the help of grace.

89. The reason, unless I am mistaken, is complete and just, but I do not require a reason from Christ. If I am convinced by reason I reject faith. Abraham believed God, let us also believe Him, that we who are heirs of his race may also be heirs of his faith. David likewise believed, and therefore did he speak; let us also believe that we may be able to speak, knowing that "He Who raised up the Lord Jesus shall raise up us also with Jesus." For God, Who never lies, promised this; the Truth promised this in His Gospel, when He said: "This is the will of Him that sent Me, that of all that which He hath given Me I should lose nothing, but should raise it up at the last day." And He thought it not sufficient to have said this once, but marked it by express repetition, for this follows: "For this is the will of My Father, Who sent Me, that every one that seeth the Son and believeth on Him should have eternal life, and I will raise him up at the last day."

90. Who was He that said this? He in truth Who when dead raised up many bodies of the departed. If we believe not God, shall we not believe evidence? Do we not believe what He promised, since He did even that which He did not promise? And what reason would He have had for dying, had He not also had a reason for rising again? For, seeing that God could not die, Wisdom could not die; and inasmuch as that could not rise again which had not died, flesh is assumed, which can die, that whilst that, whose nature it is, dies, that which had died should rise again. For the resurrection could not be effected except by man; since, "as by man came death, so too by man came the resurrection of the dead."

91. So, then, man rose because man died; man was raised again, but God raised him. Then it was man according to the Flesh, now God is all in all. For now we know not Christ according to the flesh, but we possess the grace of that Flesh, so that we know Him the firstfruits of them that rest, the firstborn of the dead. Now the first-fruits are undoubtedly of the same nature and kind as the remaining fruits, the first of which are offered to God as a petition for a richer increase, as a holy thank-offering for all gifts, and as a kind of libation of that nature which has been restored. Christ, then, is the firstfruits of them that rest. But is this of His own who are at rest, who, as it were, freed from death, are holden by a kind of sweet slumber, or of all those who are dead? "As in Christ all die, so too in Christ shall all be made alive." So, then, as the firstfruits of death were in Adam, so also the firstfruits of the resurrection are in Christ.

92. All men rise again, but let no one lose heart, and let not the just grieve at the common lot of rising again, since he awaits the chief fruit of his virtue. All indeed shall rise again, but, as says the Apostle, "each in his own order." The fruit of the Divine Mercy is common to all, but the order of merit differs. The day gives light to all, the sun warms all, the rain fertilises the possessions of all with genial showers.

93. We are all born, and we shall all rise again, but in each state, whether of living or of living again, grace differs and the condition differs. For, "in a moment, in the twinkling of an eye, at the last trump, the dead shall rise incorruptible and we shall be changed." Moreover, in death itself some rest, and some live. Rest is good, but life is better. And so the Apostle rouses him that is resting to life, saying: "Rise, thou that sleepest, and arise from the dead, and Christ shall give thee light." Therefore he is aroused that he may live, that he may be like to Paul, that he may be able to say: "For we that are alive shall not prevent those that are asleep." He speaks not here of the common manner of life, and the breath which we all alike enjoy, but of the merit of the resurrection. For, having said, "And the dead which are in Christ shall rise first," he adds further; "And we that are alive shall together with them be caught up in the clouds, to meet Christ in the air."

94. Paul certainly is dead, and by his honourable passion exchanged the life of the body for everlasting glory; did he then deceive himself when he wrote that he should be caught up alive in the clouds to meet Christ? We read the same too of Enoch and of Elijah, and thou too shalt be caught up in the Spirit. Lo the chariot of Elijah, lo the fire, though not seen are prepared, that

the just may ascend, the innocent be borne forth, and thy life may not know death. For indeed the apostles knew not death, according to that which was said: "Verily, verily, I say unto you, many of those standing here shall not taste death until they see the Son of man coming in His kingdom." For he lives, who has nothing in him which can die, who has not from Egypt any shoe or bond, but has put it off before laying aside the service of this body. And so not Enoch alone is alive, for not he alone was caught up; Paul also was caught up to meet Christ.

95. The patriarchs also live, for God could not be called the God of Abraham, of Isaac, and of Jacob, except the dead were living; for He is not the God of the dead but of the living. And we, too, shall live if we be willing to copy the deeds and habits of our predecessors. We are astonished at the rewards of the patriarchs, let us copy their faithfulness; we tell of their grace, let us follow their obedience; let us not, enticed by appetite, fall into the snares of the world. Let us lay hold of the opportunity, of the commandment of the Law, the mercy of our vocation, the desire of suffering. The patriarchs went forth from their own land, let us go forth in purpose from the power of the body; let us go forth in purpose as they in exile; but they esteemed that not to be exile which the fear of God caused, necessity did not enforce. They changed their land for another soil, let us change earth for heaven; they changed in earthly habitation, let us change in spirit. To them Wisdom showed the heaven illuminated with stars, let it enlighten the eyes of our heart. Thus does the type agree with the truth, and the truth with the type.

96. Abraham, ready to receive strangers, faithful towards God, devoted in ministering, quick in his service, saw the Trinity in a type; he added religious duty to hospitality, when beholding Three he worshipped One, and preserving the distinction of the Persons, yet addressed one Lord, he offered to Three the honour of his gift, while acknowledging one Power. It was not learning but grace which spoke in him, and he believed better what he had not learnt than we who have learnt. No one had falsified the representation of the truth, and so he sees Three, but worships the Unity. He brings forth three measures of fine meal, and slays one victim, considering that one sacrifice is sufficient, but a triple gift; one victim, an offering of three. And in the four kings, who does not understand that he subjected to himself the elements of the material creation, and all earthly things in a sign whereby the Lord's Passion was prefigured? Faithful in war, moderate in his triumph, in that he preferred not to become richer by the gifts of men, but by those of God.

97. He believed that he when old could beget a son, and judged himself when a father able to sacrifice his son; nor did his fatherly affection tremble when duty aided the right hand of the old man, for he knew that his son would be more acceptable to God when sacrificed than when whole. Therefore he brings his well-beloved son to be sacrificed, and offered promptly him whom he had received late; nor is he restrained by being called by the name of father, when his son called him "Father," and he replied, "My son." Dear pledges of love are these names, but the commands of God are loved still more. And so although their hearts felt for each other, their purpose remained firm. The father's hand stretched out the knife over his son, and the father's heart struck the blow that the sentence might not fail of being carried out; he feared lest the stroke should miss, lest his right hand should fail. He felt the movings of fatherly affection, but did not shrink from the work of submission, and hastened his obedience, even when he heard the voice from heaven. Let us then set God before all those whom we love, father, brother, mother, that He may preserve for us those whom we love, as in the case of Abraham we behold rather the liberal Rewarder than the servant.

98. The father offered indeed his son, but God is appeased not by blood but by dutiful obedience. He showed the ram in the thicket in the stead of the lad, that He might restore the son to his father, and yet the victim not fail the priest. And so Abraham was not stained with his son's blood, nor was God deprived of the sacrifice. The prophet spoke, and neither yielded to boastfulness nor continued obstinate, but took the ram in exchange for the lad. And by this is shown the more how piously he offered him whom he now so gladly received back. And thou, if thou offer thy gift to God, dost not lose it. But we are tenacious of our own; God gave His

only Son for us, we refuse ours. Abraham saw this and recognized the mystery, that salvation should be to us from the Tree, nor did it escape his notice that in one and the same sacrifice it was One that seemed to be offered, Another which could be slain.

99. Let us, then, imitate the devotion of Abraham, let us imitate the goodness of Isaac, let us imitate his purity. The man was plainly good and chaste, full of devotion towards God, chaste towards his wife. He returned not evil for evil, yielded to those who would thrust him out, received them again on their repentance, neither violent towards insolence, nor stubborn towards kindness. Fleeing from strife when he went away from others, ready to forgive when he received them again, and still more lavish of goodness when he forgave them. The fellowship of his company was sought, he gave in addition a feast of pleasure.

100. In Jacob, too, let us imitate the type of Christ, let there be some likeness of his actions in ourselves. We shall have our share with him, if we imitate him. He was obedient to his mother, he yielded to his brother, he served his father-in-law, he sought his wages from the increase, not from a division of the flocks. There was no covetous division, where his portion brought such gain. Nor was that sign without a purpose, the ladder from earth to heaven, wherein was seen the future fellowship between men and angels through the cross of Christ, whose thigh was paralyzed, that in his thigh he might recognize the Heir of his body, and foretell by the paralyzing of his thigh the Passion of his Heir.

101. We see, then, that heaven is open to virtue, and that this is the privilege not only of a few: "For many shall come from the east dud from the west, and the north and the south, and shall sit down in the kingdom of God," giving expression to the enjoyment of perpetual rest since the motions of their souls are stilled. Let us follow Abraham in our habits, that he may receive us into his bosom, and cherish us with loving embrace, like Lazarus the inheritor of his humility surrounded by his own special virtues. The followers of the holy patriarch, approved of God, cherish us not in a bodily bosom, but in a clothing as it were of good works. "Be not deceived," says the Apostle, "God is not mocked."

102. We have seen, then, how grave an offence it is not to believe the resurrection; for if we rise not again, then Christ died in vain, then Christ rose not again. For if He rose not for us, He certainly rose not at all, for He had no need to rise for Himself. The universe rose again in Him, the heaven rose again in Him, the earth rose again in Him, for there shall be a new heaven and a new earth. But where was the necessity of a resurrection for Him Whom the claims of death held not? For though He died as man, yet was He free in hell itself.

103. Wilt thou know how free? "I am become as a man that hath no help, free among the dead." And well is He called free, Who had power to raise Himself, according to that which is written: "Destroy this temple, and in three days I will raise it up." And well is He called free, Who had descended to rescue others. For He was made as a man, not, indeed, in appearance only, but so fashioned in truth, for He is man, and who shall know Him? For, "being made in the likeness of men, and being found in fashion as a man, He humbled Himself, becoming obedient even unto death," in order that through that obedience we might see His glory, "the glory as of the Only-begotten of the Father," according to Saint John. For thus is the statement of Scripture preserved, if both the glory of the Only-begotten and the nature of perfect man are preserved in Christ.

104. And so He needed no helper. For He needed none when He made the world, so as to need none when He would redeem it. No legate, no messenger, but the Lord Himself made it whole. "He spake and it was done." The Lord Himself made it whole, Himself in every part, because all things were by Him. For who should help Him in Whom all things were created and by Whom all things consist? Who should help Him Who makes all things in a moment, and raises the dead at the last trump? The "last," not as though He could not raise them at the first, or the second, or the third, but an order is observed, not that a difficulty may be at last overcome, but that the prescribed number be accomplished.

214

105. But it is now time, I think, to speak of the trumpets since my discourse is nearing its end, that the trumpet may also be the sign of the finishing of my address. We read of seven trumpets in the Revelation of John, which seven angels received. And there you read that when the seventh angel sounded his trumpet, there was a great voice from heaven, saying: "The kingdom of this world is become the kingdom of our God and of His Christ, and He shall reign for ever and ever." The word trumpet is also used for a voice, as you read: "Behold a door opened in heaven, and the first voice which I heard, as of a trumpet speaking with me and saying, Come up hither, and I will show thee the things which must come to pass." We read also: "Blow up the trumpet at the beginning of the month [the new moon]; and again elsewhere: "Praise Him with the sound of the trumpet."

106. Therefore we ought with all our power to observe what is the signification of the trumpets, lest, accepting them, like old women, as part of the story, we should be in danger if we were to think things unworthy of spiritual teaching, or not befitting the dignity of the Scriptures. For when we read that our warfare is not against flesh and blood, but against spiritual hosts of wickedness, which are in high places, we ought not to think of weapons of the flesh, but of such as are mighty before God. It is not enough that one see the trumpet or hear its sound, unless one understands the signification of the sound. For if the trumpet give an uncertain sound, how shall one prepare himself for war? Wherefore it is important that we understand the meaning of the voice of the trumpet, lest we seem barbarians, when we either hear or utter trumpet-sounds of this sort. And therefore when we speak, let us pray that the Holy Spirit would interpret them to us.

107. Let us, then, investigate what we read in the Old Testament concerning the kinds of trumpets, considering that those festivals which were enjoined on the Jews by the Law are the shadow of joys above and of heavenly festivals. For here is the shadow, there the truth. Let us endeavour to attain to the truth by means of the shadow. Of which truth the figure is expressed in this manner, where we read that the Lord said to Moses: "Speak unto the children of Israel, saying, In the seventh month, on the first day of the month, shall be a rest unto you, a memorial of blowing of trumpets, it shall be called holy unto you. Ye shall not do any servile work, and ye shall kindle a whole burnt-offering unto the Lord." And in the Book of Numbers: "The Lord spake unto Moses, saying: Make thee two trumpets of beaten work, of silver shalt thou make them, and they shall be to thee for calling the assembly and for the journeying of the camp. And thou shalt blow with them, and all the congregation shall be gathered together at the door of the tabernacle of witness. But if thou blow with one trumpet, all the princes and leaders of Israel shall come to thee; and ye shall blow a signal with the trumpet the first time, and they shall move the camp forward, and place it on the east. And ye shall blow a signal with the trumpet the second time, and they shall move the camp forward, and place it towards Libanus. And ye shall blow a signal with the trumpet the third time, and they shall move the camp forward, which shall be placed towards the north [Boream]. And ye shall blow a signal with the trumpet the fourth time, and they shall move the camp forward, which shall be placed towards the north [Aquilonem]. They shall blow a signal with the trumpet when they move forward. And when ye shall gather together the assembly, blow with the trumpet, but not the signal. And the sons of Aaron, the priests, shall blow with the trumpets, and it shall be for you a statute for ever throughout your generations. But if ye shall go out to war into your own land, against the adversaries who resist you, ye shall sound a signal with the trumpets and ye shall be remembered before the Lord. and have deliverance from your dead. Also in the days of your gladness, and on your feast days, and on your new moons, ye shall blow with the trumpets, and at your whole burnt sacrifices and at your peace-offerings, and it shall be for you for your memorial before the Lord, saith the Lord."

108. What then? shall we esteem festival days by eating and drinking? But let no man judge us in respect of eating; "for we know that the Law is spiritual." "Let no man therefore judge us in any meats or in drink, or in respect of a feast day or new moons, or a sabbath day, which are a

shadow of the things to come, but the body is of Christ." Let us, then, seek the body of Christ which the voice of the Father, from heaven, as it were the last trumpet, has shown to you at the time when the Jews said that it thundered; the body of Christ, which again the last trump shall reveal; for "the Lord Himself shall descend from heaven at the voice of the Archangel, and at the trump of God, and they that are dead in Christ shall rise again;" for "where the body is, there too are the eagles," where the body of Christ is, there is the truth.

108. The seventh trumpet, then, seems to signify the sabbath of the week, which is reckoned not only in days and years and periods (for which reason the number of the jubilee is sacred), but includes also the seventieth year, when the people returned to Jerusalem, who had remained seventy years in captivity. In hundreds also and in thousands the observation of the sacred number is by no means passed over, for not without a meaning did the Lord say: "I have left the seven thousand men, who have not bent their knees before Baal." Therefore the shadow of the future rest is figured in time in the days, months, and years of this world, and therefore the children of Israel are commanded by Moses, that in the seventh month, on the first day of the month, a rest should be established for all at the "memorial of the trumpets;" and that no servile work should be done, but a sacrifice be offered to God, because that at the end of the week, as it were the sabbath of the world, spiritual and not bodily work is required of us. For that which is bodily is servile, for the body serves the soul, but innocence makes free, guilt reduces to slavery.

109. It was necessary, then, that spiritual things should be made known as in a mirror and in a riddle; "For now we see by means of a mirror, but then face to face." Now we war after the flesh, then in the Spirit we shall see the divine mysteries. Let, then, the character of the true law be expressed in our manner of life, who walk in the image of God, for the shadow of the Law has now passed away. The carnal Jews had the shadow, the likeness is ours, the reality theirs who shall rise again. For we know that according to the Law there are these three, the shadow, the image or likeness, and the reality; the shadow in the Law, the image in the Gospel, the truth in the judgment. But all is Christ's, and all is in Christ, Whom now we cannot see according to the reality, but we see Him, as it were, in a kind of likeness of future things, of which we have seen the shadow in the Law. So, then, Christ is not the shadow but the likeness of God, not an empty likeness but the reality. And so the Law was by Moses, for the shadow was through man, the likeness was through the Law, the reality through Jesus. For reality cannot proceed from any other source than from reality.

110. If, then, any one desires to see this Image of God, he must love God, that he may be loved by God; and be no longer a servant but a friend, because he has kept the commandments of God, that he may enter into the cloud where God is. Let him make to himself two reasonable trumpets of beaten work of proved silver, that is, composed of precious words and adorned, from which not a harsh shrill sound with dread-inspiring voice may be uttered, but high thanks to God may be poured forth with continuous exultation. For by the voice of such trumpets the dead are raised, not indeed by the sound of the metal, but aroused by the word of truth. And perchance it is those two trumpets by which Paul, through the Divine Spirit, spake when he said: "I will pray with the Spirit, and I will pray with the understanding, I will sing with the Spirit, and I will sing with the understanding;" for the one without the other seems by no means to have perfect utterance.

111. Yet it is not every one's business to sound each trumpet, nor every one's business to call together the whole assembly, but that prerogative is granted to the priests alone, and the ministers of God who sound the trumpets, so that whosoever shall hear and follow thither where the glory of the Lord is, and shall with early determination come to the tabernacle of witness, may be able also to see the divine works, and merit that appointed and eternal home for the entire succession of his posterity. For then is the war finished and the enemy put to flight, when the grace of the Spirit and the energy of the soul act together.

216

112. And these are salutary trumpets also, if one believe with the heart, and confess with the mouth; "For with the heart man believeth unto righteousness, and with the mouth confession is made unto salvation." For with this twofold trumpet man arrives at that holy land, namely, the grace of the resurrection. Let them, then, ever sound to thee, that thou mayest ever hear the voice of God; may the utterances of the Angels and Prophets ever incite and move thee, that thou mayest hasten to things above.

113. David was thinking of this purpose in his breast when he said: "For I will pass into the place of the marvellous tabernacle, even to the house of God, with the voice of exultation and thanksgiving, the sound of one that feasts." For not only are enemies overcome by the sound of these trumpets; but without them there could not be rejoicings, and festivals or new moons. For no one, unless he have received the promises of the Divine Word, and believes the message derived therefrom, can keep festivals or new moons, in which he desires to fill himself, freed from bodily pleasure and secular occupation, with the light of Christ. And sacrifices themselves cannot be pleasing to Christ unless confession of the mouth accompanies them, which according to custom stirs up the people to implore the grace of God at the priestly oblation.

114. Let us therefore be preachers of the Lord, and praise Him in the sound of the trumpet, not thinking little or lightly of its power, but such things as can fill the ear of the mind, and enter into the depths of our inmost consciousness, so that we think not that what suits to the body is to be applied to the Godhead, nor measure the greatness of Divine Power by human might, so as to enquire how any one can rise again, or with what kind of body he will come, or how that which has been dissolved can again coalesce, and what is lost be restored, for all these things are accomplished as soon as they are determined by the Divine Will. And it is not a sound of a trumpet distinguishable by the bodily senses which is expected, but the invisible power of the Majesty of heaven operates; for with God to will is to do; nor need we enquire into the force required for the resurrection, but seek its fruit for ourselves. Which will be accomplished all the more easily, if freed from faults we attain to the fulness of the spiritual mystery, and the renewed flesh receives grace from the Spirit, and the soul obtains from Christ the brightness of eternal light.

115. But those mysteries pertain not to individuals only, but to the whole human race. For observe the order of grace according to the type of the Law. When the first trumpet sounds, it collects those towards the east, as the chief and elect; when the second sounds, those nearly equal in merit, who, being placed towards Libanus, have abandoned the follies of the nations; when the third, those who as it were, tossed on the sea of this world, have been driven hither and thither by the waves of this life; when the fourth, those who have by no means been able sufficiently to soften the hardness of their hearts by the commandments of spiritual utterance, and therefore are said to be towards the north—for, according to Solomon, the north is a hard wind.

116. And so although all are raised again in a moment, yet all are raised in the order of their merits. And therefore they rise first, who yielding early to the impulses of devotion, and as it were going forth before the rising dawn of faith, received the rays of the eternal Sun. This one may rightly say either of the patriarchs in the course of the Old Testament, or of the apostles under the Gospel. And the second are they who, forsaking the rites of the Gentiles, passed from unholy error under the training of the Church. So, then, those first were of the fathers, those second of the Gentiles, for the light of faith took its beginning from those, among these it will remain to the end of the world. In the third place and in the fourth, those are raised who are in the south and in the north. The earth is divided into these four, of these four is the year made up, in these four is the earth completed, and from these four is the Church collected. For all who are considered to be joined to holy Church, by being called by the Divine Name, shall obtain the privilege of the resurrection and he grace of eternal bliss, for "they shall come from the east and west, and from the north and south, and shall sit down in the kingdom of God."

117. For it is no small light wherewith Christ encompasses His world: since "His going forth is from the height of heaven, and His progress to the height thereof, nor is there any who can hide himself from His heat." For with His Goodness He enlightens all, and wills not to reject but to amend the foolish, and desires not to exclude the hard-hearted from the Church, but to soften them. And so the Church in the Song of Songs and Christ in the Gospel invites them, saying: "Come unto Me, all ye who labour and are heavy laden, and I will refresh you; take My yoke upon you and learn of Me, for I am meek and lowly in heart."

118. And you may recognize also the voice of the invitation of the Church, for she says: "Awake, O north wind, and come, thou south, blow upon my garden, and let my ointment flow forth. Let my brother come down into his garden and eat the fruit of his precious trees." For knowing even then, O holy Church, that from those also there would be fruitful works for thee, thou didst promise to thy Christ fruit from such as they, thou who didst first say that thou wast brought into the King's chamber. loving His breast above wine, since thou lovedst Him Who loved thee, soughtest Him Who fed thee, and didst despise dangers for religion's sake.

119. And then, O Bride, thou art called to come from Libanus, being in the Lord's judgment all fair and without fault. For thus it is written: "Thou art all fair, my love, and there is no fault in thee. Come hither from Libanus, my bride, come hither from Libanus."

120. Afterwards, thou, fearing no rushing waters, no torrents coming down from Libanus, callest the north and south winds, wishing them to blow upon thy garden, that thy ointment may flow forth upon others, and that thou mayest offer to Christ in others the manifold fruits of thy productiveness.

121. And therefore "blessed is he who keepeth the words of this prophecy," which has revealed the resurrection to us by clearer testimony, saying: "And I saw the dead, great and small, standing before the throne, and they opened the books; and another book was opened, which is the book of life; and the dead were judged out of the things which were written in the books, according to their works. And the sea gave up the dead which were in it, and hell gave up the dead which were in it." We must, then, not question how they shall rise again, whom hell gives up and the sea restores.

122. Hear also when the future grace of the just is promised: "And I heard," he says, "a great voice from the throne saying: Behold, the tabernacle of God is with men, and He shall dwell with them, and they shall be His people, and God Himself shall be their God with them: and He shall wipe away every tear from their eyes; and death shall be no more, nor mourning, nor crying, nor pain, any more."

123. Compare now, if you will, and contrast this life with that; and choose, if you then can, unending bodily existence in toil, and in the wretched misery of such changes as we endure, in satiety when we have our wishes, in that disgust which attends our pleasures. If God were willing to let these last for ever, would you choose them? For if on its own account life is to be escaped from, that there may be an avoidance of troubles and rest from miseries, how much more is that rest to be sought for, which shall be followed by the eternal pleasure of the resurrection to come, where there is no succession of faults, no enticement to sin?

124. Who is so patient in suffering as not to pray for death? who has such endurance in weakness as not to wish rather to die than to live in debility? Who is so brave in sorrow as not to desire to escape from it even by death? But if we ourselves are dissatisfied while life lasts, although we know that a limit is fixed for it, how much more weary should we become of this life if we saw that the troubles of the body would be with us without end! For who is there who would wish to be excepted from death? Or what would be more unendurable than a miserable immortality? "If in this life only," he says, "we hope in Christ, we are more miserable than all men;" not because to hope in Christ is miserable, but because Christ has prepared another life for those who hope in Him. For this life is liable to sin, that life is reserved for the reward.

124. And how much weariness do we find that the short stages of our lives bring us! The boy longs to be a young man; the youth counts the years leading to riper age; the young man,

unthankful for the advantage of his vigorous time of life, desires the honour of old age. And so to all there comes naturally the desire of change, because we are dissatisfied with that which we now are. And lastly, even the things we have desired are wearisome to us; and what we have wished to obtain, when we have obtained it, we dislike.

125. Wherefore holy men have not without reason often lamented their lengthy dwelling here: David lamented it, Jeremiah lamented it, and Elijah lamented it. If we believe wise men, and those in whom the Divine Spirit dwelt, they were hastening to better things; and if we enquire as to the judgment of others, that we may ascertain that all agree in one opinion, what great men have preferred death to sorrow, what great men have preferred it to fear! esteeming forsooth the fear of death to be worse than death itself. So death is not feared on account of evils which belong to it, but is preferred to the miseries of life, since the departure of the dying is desired and the dread of the living is avoided.

126. So be it, then. Granted that the Resurrection is preferable to this life. What! have philosophers themselves found anything with which we should have a greater delight to continue than to rise again? Even those indeed who say that souls are immortal do not satisfy me, seeing they only allow me a partial redemption. What grace can that be by which I am not wholly benefited? What life is that if the operation of God dies out in me? What righteousness is that which, if death is the end of natural existence. is common to the sinner and the just? What is that truth, that the soul should be considered immortal, because it moves itself and is always in motion? As regards that which in the body is common to us with beasts, it is perhaps uncertain what happens before the body exists, and the truth is not to be gathered from these differences but destroyed.

127. But is their opinion preferable, who say that our souls, when they have passed out of these bodies, migrate into the bodies of beasts, or of various other living creatures? Philosophers, indeed, themselves are wont to argue that these are ridiculous fancies of poets, such as might be produced by draughts of the drugs of Circe; and they say that not so much they who are represented to have undergone such things, as the senses of those who have invented such tales are changed into the forms of various beasts as it were by Circe's cup. For what is so like a marvel as to believe that men could have been changed into the forms of beasts? How much greater a marvel, however, would it be that the soul which rules man should take on itself the nature of a beast so opposed to that of man, and being capable of reason should be able to pass over to an irrational animal, than that the form of the body should have been changed? You yourselves, who teach these things, destroy what you teach. For you have given up the production of these portentous conversions by means of magic incantations.

128. Poets say these things in sport, and philosophers blame them and at the same time they imagine that those very things are true of the dead which they consider fictitious as regards the living. For they who invented such tales did not intend to assert the truth of their own fable, but to deride the errors of philosophers, who think that that same soul which was accustomed to overcome anger by gentle and lowly purpose, can now, inflamed by the raging impulses of a lion, impatient with anger and with unbridled rage, thirst for blood and seek for slaughter. Or again, that that soul, which as it were by royal counsel used to moderate the various storms of the people, and to calm them with the voice of reason, can now endure to howl in pathless and desert places after the fashion of a wolf; or that that soul which, groaning under a heavy burden, used to low in sad complaint over the labours of the plough, now changed into the fashion of a man, seeks for horns on his smooth brow; or that another, which used of old to be borne aloft on rapid wing to the heights of heaven, now thinks of flight no longer in its power, and mourns that it grows sluggish in the weight of a human body.

129. Perchance you destroyed Icarus through some such teaching, because the youth, led on by your persuasion, imagined, it may be, that he had been a bird. By such means too have many old men been deceived so as to submit to grievous pain, having unhappily believed the fables

about swans, and thought that they, whilst soothing their pain with mournful strains, would be able to transmute their gray hair into downy feathers.

130. How incredible are these things! how odious! How much more fitting is it to believe in accordance with nature, in accordance with what takes place in every kind of fruit; to believe in accordance with the pattern of what has happened, in accordance with the utterances of prophets, and the heavenly promise of Christ 2 For what is better than to be sure that the work of God does not perish, and that those who are made in the image and likeness of God cannot be transformed into the shapes of beasts; since in truth it is not the form of the body but of the spirit which is made after the likeness of God. For in what manner could man, to whom are subjected the other kinds of living creatures, migrate with the better part of himself into an animal subjected to himself? Nature does not suffer this, and if nature did grace would not.

131. But I have seen what you, Gentiles, think of each other, and indeed it ought not to seem strange that you who worship beasts should believe that you can be changed into beasts. But I had rather that you judged better concerning what is due to you, that you may believe that you will be not in the company of wild beasts, but in the companionship of angels.

132. The soul has to depart from the surroundings of this life, and the pollutions of the earthly body, and to press on to those heavenly companies, though it is for the saints alone, to attain to them, and to sing praise to God (as in the prophet's words we hear of those who are harping and saying: "For great are Thy marvellous works, O Lord God Almighty, just and true are Thy ways, Thou King of the nations; who shall not fear and magnify Thy Name, for Thou only art holy, for all nations shall come and worship before Thee"), and to see Thy marriage feast, O Lord Jesus, in which the Bride is led from earthly to heavenly things, while all rejoice in harmony, for "to Thee shall all flesh come," now no longer subject to transitory things, but joined to the Spirit, to see the chambers adorned with linen, roses, lilies, and garlands. Of whom else is the marriage so adorned? For it is adorned with the purple stripes of confessors, the blood of martyrs, the lilies of virgins, and the crowns of priests.

133. Holy David desired beyond all else for himself that he might behold and gaze upon this, for he says: "One thing have I asked of the Lord, that will I seek after; that I may dwell in the house of the Lord all the days of my life, and see the pleasure of the Lord."

134. It is a pleasure to believe this, a joy to hope for it; and certainly, not to have believed it is a pain, to have lived in this hope a grace. But if I am mistaken in this, that I prefer to be associated after death with angels rather than with beasts, I am gladly mistaken, and so long as I live will never suffer myself to be cheated of this hope.

135. For what comfort have I left but that I hope to come quickly to thee, my brother, and that thy departure will not cause a longseverance between us, and that it may be granted me, through thy intercessions, that thou mayest quickly call me who long for thee. For who is there who ought not to wish for himself beyond all else that "this corruptible should put on incorruption, and this mortal put on immortality"? that we who succumb to death through the frailty of the body, being raised above nature, may no longer have to fear death.

EXPOSITION OF THE CHRISTIAN FAITH
PREFACE.

On the eve of setting out for the East, to aid his uncle Valens in repelling a Gothic invasion, Gratian, the Emperor of the West, requested St. Ambrose to write him a treatise in proof of the Divinity of Jesus Christ. Gratian's object in making this request was to secure some sort of preservative against the corrupting influence of Arianism, which at that time (a.d. 378) had gained the upper hand of Orthodoxy in the Eastern provinces of the Empire, owing to its establishment at the Imperial Court. In compliance with Gratian's wish, the Bishop of Milan composed a treatise, which now forms the first two Books of the *De Fide*. With this work the Emperor was so much pleased that on his return from the East, after the death of Valens at Hadrianople, he wrote to St. Ambrose, begging for a fresh copy of the treatise, and further, for its enlargement by the addition of a discourse on the Divinity of the Holy Spirit. The original treatise was, indeed, enlarged by St. Ambrose in 379, but the additional Books dealt, not with the Divinity of the Holy Spirit, but rather with new objections raised by the Arian teachers, and points which had either been passed over or not fully discussed already. In this way St. Ambrose's Exposition was brought into its present form.

The object of the Exposition is, as has already been indicated, to prove the Divinity of Jesus Christ, and His co-eternity, co-equality, and consubstantiality, as God the Son, with God the Father. This the author does by constant appeal to the Scriptures, both of the Old and of the New Testament, which the Arians had in many cases forced into the mould of false interpretation to make them fit their doctrine.

Besides the title of *De Fide*, that of *De Trinitate* was one by which this treatise was largely known in after ages; it is certain, though, that the former was that assigned by St. Ambrose himself.

PREFATORY NOTE.

The notes to the first four books of the *De Fide* have in some instances been taken over from those in Father Hurter's Edition of the treatise (Innsbruck: Wagner), which has been used in preparing the translation of these books. These notes are distinguished by the letter "H." placed at the end.

The citations from Scripture embodied in the text have been translated as they stood in the original. This will account for any divergence from the renderings in the English Bible and Prayer-book, whilst any agreement may be set down to reminiscences of the more familiar versions. It was thought best to adopt this treatment of St. Ambrose's citations, inasmuch as the divergences are worth noticing, and indeed, in some cases, the argument rather turns upon them. The references are, throughout, made to chapters and verses in the English Bible, and not to the Vulgate, unless especially stated so to be.

The Prefaces and Summaries of Contents are based on those in Father Hurter's Edition.

BOOK I.

Prologue.

The author praises Gratian's zeal for instruction in the Faith, and speaks lowly of his own merits. Taught of God Himself, the Emperor stands in no need of human instruction; yet this his devoutness prepares the way to victory. The task appointed to the author is difficult: in the accomplishment whereof he will be guided not so much by reason and argument as by authority, especially that of the Nicene Council.

1. The Queen of the South, as we read in the Book of the Kings, came to hear the wisdom of Solomon. Likewise King Hiram sent to Solomon that he might prove him. So also your sacred Majesty, following these examples of old time, has decreed to hear my confession of faith. But I am no Solomon, that you should wonder at my wisdom, and your Majesty is not the sovereign of a single people; it is the Augustus, ruler of the whole world, that has commanded the setting forth of the Faith in a book, not for your instruction, but for your approval.

2. For why, august Emperor, should your Majesty learn that Faith which, from your earliest childhood, you have ever devoutly and lovingly kept? "Before I formed thee in thy mother's belly I knew thee," saith the Scripture, "and before thou camest forth out of the womb I sanctified thee." Sanctification, therefore, cometh not of tradition, but of inspiration; therefore keep watch over the gifts of God. For that which no man hath taught you, God hath surely given and inspired.

3. Your sacred Majesty, being about to go forth to war, requires of me a book, expounding the Faith, since your Majesty knows that victories are gained more by faith in the commander, than by valour in the soldiers. For Abraham led into battle three hundred and eighteen men, and brought home the spoils of countless foes; and having, by the power of that which was the sign of our Lord's Cross and Name, overcome the might of five kings and conquering hosts, he both avenged his neighbour and gained victory and the ransom of his brother's son. So also Joshua the son of Nun, when he could not prevail against the enemy with the might of all his army, overcame by sound of seven sacred trumpets, in the place where he saw and knew the Captain of the heavenly host. For victory, then, your Majesty makes ready, being Christ's loyal servant and defender of the Faith, which you would have me set forth in writing.

4. Truly, I would rather take upon me the duty of exhortation to keep the Faith, than that of disputing thereon; for the former means devout confession, whereas the latter is liable to rash presumption. Howbeit, forasmuch as your Majesty has no need of exhortation, whilst I may not pray to be excused from the duty of loyalty, I will take in hand a bold enterprise, yet modestly withal, not so much reasoning and disputing concerning the Faith as gathering together a multitude of witness.

5. Of the Acts of Councils, I shall let that one be my chief guide which three hundred and eighteen priests, appointed, as it were, after the judgment of Abraham, made (so to speak) a trophy raised to proclaim their victory over the infidel throughout the world, prevailing by that courage of the Faith, wherein all agreed. Verily, as it seems to me, one may herein see the hand of God, forasmuch as the same number is our authority in the Councils of the Faith, and an example of loyalty in the records of old.

Chapter I.

The author distinguishes the faith from the errors of Pagans, Jews, and Heretics, and after explaining the significance of the names "God" and "Lord," shows clearly the difference of Persons in Unity of Essence. In dividing the Essence, the Arians not only bring in the doctrine of three Gods, but even overthrow the dominion of the Trinity.

6. Now this is the declaration of our Faith, that we say that God is One, neither dividing His Son from Him, as do the heathen, nor denying, with the Jews, that He was begotten of the Father before all worlds, and afterwards born of the Virgin; nor yet, like Sabellius, confounding the Father with the Word, and so maintaining that Father and Son are one and the same Person;

nor again, as doth Photinus, holding that the Son first came into existence in the Virgin's womb: nor believing, with Arius, in a number of diverse Powers, and so, like the benighted heathen, making out more than one God. For it is written: "Hear, O Israel: the Lord thy God is one God."

7. For God and Lord is a name of majesty, a name of power, even as God Himself saith: "The Lord is My name," and as in another place the prophet declareth: "The Lord Almighty is His name." God is He, therefore, and Lord, either because His rule is over all, or because He beholdeth all things, and is feared by all, without difference.

8. If, then, God is One, one is the name, one is the power, of the Trinity. Christ Himself, indeed, saith: "Go ye, baptize the nations in the name of the Father, and of the Son, and of the Holy Spirit." In the *name*, mark you, not in the *names*."

9. Moreover, Christ Himself saith: "I and the Father are One." "One," said He, that there be no separation of power and nature; but again, "*We are*," that you may recognize Father and Son, forasmuch as the perfect Father is believed to have begotten the perfect Son, and the Father and the Son are One, not by confusion of Person, but by unity of nature.

10. We say, then, that there is one God, not two or three Gods, this being the error into which the impious heresy of the Arians doth run with its blasphemies. For it says that there are three Gods, in that it divides the Godhead of the Trinity; whereas the Lord, in saying, "Go, baptize the nations in the name of the Father and of the Son and of the Holy Spirit," hath shown that the Trinity is of one power. We confess Father, Son, and Spirit, understanding in a perfect Trinity both fulness of Divinity and unity of power.

11. "Every kingdom divided against itself shall quickly be overthrown," saith the Lord. Now the kingdom of the Trinity is not divided. If, therefore, it is not divided, it is one; for that which is not one is divided. The Arians, however, would have the kingdom of the Trinity to be such as may easily be overthrown, by division against itself. But truly, seeing that it cannot be overthrown, it is plainly undivided. For no unity is divided or rent asunder, and therefore neither age nor corruption has any power over it.

Chapter II.

The Emperor is exhorted to display zeal in the Faith. Christ's perfect Godhead is shown from the unity of will and working which He has with the Father. The attributes of Divinity are shown to be proper to Christ, Whose various titles prove His essential unity, with distinction of Person. In no other way can the unity of God be maintained.

12. "Not every one that saith unto Me Lord, Lord, shall enter into the kingdom of heaven," saith the Scripture. Faith, therefore, august Sovereign, must not be a mere matter of performance, for it is written, "The zeal of thine house hath devoured me." Let us then with faithful spirit and devout mind call upon Jesus our Lord, let us believe that He is God, to the end that whatever we ask of the Father, we may obtain in His name. For the Father's will is, that He be entreated through the Son, the Son's that the Father be entreated.

13. The grace of His submission makes for agreement [with our teaching], and the acts of His power are not at variance therewith. For whatsoever things the Father doeth, the same also doeth the Son, in like manner. The Son both doeth the same things, and doeth them in like manner, but it is the Father's will that He be entreated in the matter of what He Himself proposeth to do, that you may understand, not that He cannot do it otherwise, but that there is one power displayed. Truly, then, is the Son of God to be adored and worshipped, Who by the power of His Godhead hath laid the foundations of the world, and by His submission informed our affections.

14. Therefore we ought to believe that God is good, eternal, perfect, almighty, and true, such as we find Him in the Law and the Prophets, and the rest of the holy Scriptures, for otherwise there is no God. For He Who is God cannot but be good, seeing that fulness of goodness is of the nature of God: nor can God, Who made time, be in time; nor, again, can God be imperfect,

for a lesser being is plainly imperfect, seeing that it lacks somewhat whereby it could be made equal to a greater. This, then, is the teaching of our faith—that God is not evil, that with God nothing is impossible, that God exists not in time, that God is beneath no being. If I am in error, let my adversaries prove it.

15. Seeing, then, that Christ is God, He is, by consequence, good and almighty and eternal and perfect and true; for these attributes belong to the essential nature of the Godhead. Let our adversaries, therefore, deny the Divine Nature in Christ,—otherwise they cannot refuse to God what is proper to the Divine Nature.

16. Further, that none may fall into error, let a man attend to those signs vouchsafed us by holy Scripture, whereby we may know the Son. He is called the Word, the Son, the Power of God, the Wisdom of God. The Word, because He is without blemish; the Power, because He is perfect; the Son, because He is begotten of the Father; the Wisdom, because He is one with the Father, one in eternity, one in Divinity. Not that the Father is one Person with the Son; between Father and Son is the plain distinction that comes of generation; so that Christ is God of God, Everlasting of Everlasting, Fulness of Fulness.

17. Now these are not mere names, but signs of power manifesting itself in works for while there is fulness of Godhead in the Father, there is also fulness of Godhead in the Son, not diverse, but one. The Godhead is nothing confused, for it is an unity: nothing manifold, for in it there is no difference.

18. Moreover, if in all them that believed there was, as it is written, one soul and one heart: if every one that cleaveth to the Lord is one spirit, as the Apostle hath said: if a man and his wife are one flesh: if all we mortal men are, so far as regards our general nature, of one substance: if this is what the Scripture saith of created men, that, being many, they are one, who can in no way be compared to Divine Persons, how much more are the Father and the Son one in Divinity, with Whom there is no difference either of substance or of will!

19. For how else shall we say that God is One? Divinity maketh plurality, but unity of power debarreth quantity of number, seeing that unity is not number, but itself is the principle of all numbers.

Chapter III.

By evidence gathered from Scripture the unity of Father and Son is proved, and firstly, a passage, taken from the Book of Isaiah, is compared with others and expounded in such sort as to show that in the Son there is no diversity from the Father's nature, save only as regards the flesh; whence it follows that the Godhead of both Persons is One. This conclusion is confirmed by the authority of Baruch.

20. Now the oracles of the prophets bear witness what close unity holy Scripture declares to subsist between the Father and the Son as regards their Godhead. For thus saith the Lord of Sabaoth: "Egypt hath laboured, and the commerce of the Ethiopians and Sabeans: mighty men shall come over to thee, and shall be thy servants, and in thy train shall they follow, bound in fetters, and they shall fall down before thee, and to thee shall they make supplication: for God is in thee, and there is no God beside thee. For thou art God, and we knew it not, O God of Israel."

21. Hear the voice of the prophet: "In Thee," he saith, "is God, and there is no God beside Thee." How agreeth this with the Arians' teaching? They must deny either the Father's or the Son's Divinity, unless they believe, once for all, unity of the same Divinity.

22. "In Thee," saith he, "is God"—forasmuch as the Father is in the Son. For it is written, "The Father, Who abideth in Me, Himself speaketh," and "The works that I do, He Himself also doeth." And yet again we read that the Son is in the Father, saying, "I am in the Father, and the Father in Me." Let the Arians, if they can, make away with this kinship in nature and unity in work.

23. There is, therefore, God in God, but not two Gods; for it is written that there is one God, and there is Lord in Lord, but not two Lords, forasmuch as it is likewise written: "Serve

not two lords." And the Law saith: "Hear, O Israel! The Lord thy God is one God;" moreover, in the same Testament it is written: "The Lord rained from the Lord." The Lord, it is said, sent rain "from the Lord." So also you may read in Genesis: "And God said,—and God made," and, lower down, "And God made man in the image of God;" yet it was not two gods, but one God, that made [man]. In the one place, then, as in the other, the unity of operation and of name is maintained. For surely, when we read "God of God," we do not speak of two Gods.

24. Again, you may read in the forty-fourth psalm how the prophet not only calls the Father "God" but also proclaims the Son as God, saying: "Thy throne, O God, is for ever and ever." And further on: "God, even thy God, hath anointed thee with the oil of gladness above thy fellows." This God Who anoints, and God Who in the flesh is anointed, is the Son of God. For what fellows in His anointing hath Christ, except such as are in the flesh? You see, then, that God is by God anointed, but being anointed in taking upon Him the nature of mankind, He is proclaimed the Son of God; yet is the principle of the Law not broken.

25. So again, when you read, "The Lord rained from the Lord," acknowledge the unity of Godhead, for unity in operation doth not allow of more than one individual God, even as the Lord Himself has shown, saying: "Believe Me, that I am in the Father, and the Father in Me: or believe Me for the very works' sake." Here, too, we see that unity of Godhead is signified by unity in operation.

26. The Apostle, careful to prove that there is one Godhead of both Father and Son, and one Lordship, lest we should run into any error, whether of heathen or of Jewish ungodliness, showed us the rule we ought to follow, saying: "One God, the Father, from Whom are all things, and we in Him, and one Lord, Jesus Christ, by Whom are all things, and we by Him." For just as, in calling Jesus Christ "Lord," he did not deny that the Father was Lord, even so, in saying, "One God, the Father," he did not deny true Godhead to the Son, and thus he taught, not that there was more than one God, but that the source of power was one, forasmuch as Godhead consists in Lordship, and Lordship in Godhead, as it is written: "Be ye sure that the Lord, He is God. It is He that hath made us, and not we ourselves."

27. "In thee," therefore, "is God," by unity of nature, and "there is no God beside Thee," by reason of personal possession of the Substance, without any reserve or difference.

28. Again, Scripture speaks, in the Book of Jeremiah, of One God, and yet acknowledges both Father and Son. Thus we read: "He is our God, and in comparison with Him none other shall be accounted of. He hath discovered all the way of teaching, and given it to Jacob, His servant, and to Israel, His beloved. After these things He appeared upon earth, and conversed with men."

29. The prophet speaks of the Son, for it was the Son Himself Who conversed with men, and this is what he says: "He is our God, and in comparison with Him none other shall be accounted of." Why do we call Him in question, of Whom so great a prophet saith that no other can be compared with Him? What comparison of another *can* be made, when the Godhead is One? This was the confession of a people set in the midst of dangers; reverencing religion, and therefore unskilled in strife of argument.

30. Come, Holy Spirit, and help Thy prophets, in whom Thou art wont to dwell, in whom we believe. Shall we believe the wise of this world, if we believe not the prophets? But where is the wise man, where is the scribe? When our peasant planted figs, he found that whereof the philosopher knew nothing, for God hath chosen the foolish things of this world to confound the strong. Are we to believe the Jews? for God was once known in Jewry. Nay, but they deny that very thing, which is the foundation of our belief, seeing that they know not the Father, who have denied the Son.

Chapter IV.

The Unity of God is necessarily implied in the order of Nature, in the Faith, and in Baptism. The gifts of the Magi declare (1) the Unity of the Godhead; (2) Christ's Godhead and Manhood. The truth of the doctrine of the Trinity in Unity is shown in the Angel walking in the midst of the furnace with Shadrach, Meshach, and Abednego.

31. All nature testifies to the Unity of God, inasmuch as the universe is one. The Faith declares that there is one God, seeing that there is one belief in both the Old and the New Testament. That there is one Spirit, all holy, grace witnesseth, because there is one Baptism, in the Name of the Trinity. The prophets proclaim, the apostles hear, the voice of one God. In one God did the Magi believe, and they brought, in adoration, gold, frankincense, and myrrh to Christ's cradle, confessing, by the gift of gold, His Royalty, and with the incense worshipping Him as God. For gold is the sign of kingdom, incense of God, myrrh of burial.

32. What, then, was the meaning of the mystic offerings in the lowly cattle-stalls, save that we should discern in Christ the difference between the Godhead and the flesh? He is seen as man, He is adored as Lord. He lies in swaddling-clothes, but shines amid the stars; the cradle shows His birth, the stars His dominion; it is the flesh that is wrapped in clothes, the Godhead that receives the ministry of angels. Thus the dignity of His natural majesty is not lost, and His true assumption of the flesh is proved.

33. This is our Faith. Thus did God will that He should be known by all, thus believed the three children, and felt not the fire into the midst whereof they were cast, which destroyed and burnt up unbelievers, whilst it fell harmless as dew upon the faithful, for whom the flames kindled by others became cold, seeing that the torment had justly lost its power in conflict with faith. For with them there was One in the form of an angel, comforting them, to the end that in the number of the Trinity one Supreme Power might be praised. God was praised, the Son of God was seen in God's angel, holy and spiritual grace spake in the children.

Chapter V.

The various blasphemies uttered by the Arians against Christ are cited. Before these are replied to, the orthodox are admonished to beware of the captious arguments of philosophers, forasmuch as in these especially did the heretics put their trust.

34. Now let us consider the disputings of the Arians concerning the Son of God.

35. They say that the Son of God is unlike His Father. To say this of a man would be an insult.

36. They say that the Son of God had a beginning in time, whereas He Himself is the source and ordainer of time and all that therein is. We are men, and we would not be limited to time. We began to exist once, and we believe that we shall have a timeless existence. We desire after immortality—how, then, can we deny the eternity of God's Son, Whom God declares to be eternal by nature, not by grace?

37. They say that He was created. But who would reckon an author with his works, and have him seem to be what he has himself made?

38. They deny His goodness. Their blaspheming is its own condemnation, and so cannot hope for pardon.

39. They deny that He is truly Son of God, they deny His omnipotence, in that whilst they admit that all things are made by the ministry of the Son, they attribute the original source of their being to the power of God. But what is power, save perfection of nature?

40. Furthermore, the Arians deny that in Godhead He is One with the Father. Let them annul the Gospel, then, and silence the voice of Christ. For Christ Himself has said: "I and the Father are one." It is not I who say this: Christ has said it. Is He a deceiver, that He should lie? Is He unrighteous, that He should claim to be what He never was." But of these matters we will deal severally, at greater length, in their proper place.

41. Seeing, then, that the heretic says that Christ is unlike His Father, and seeks to maintain this by force of subtle disputation, we must cite the Scripture: "Take heed that no man make spoil of you by philosophy and vain deceit, according to the tradition of men, and after the rudiments of this world, not according to Christ; for in Him dwelleth all the fulness of Godhead in bodily shape."

42. For they store up all the strength of their poisons in dialetical disputation, which by the judgment of philosophers is defined as having no power to establish aught, and aiming only at destruction. But it was not by dialectic that it pleased God to save His people; "for the kingdom of God consisteth in simplicity of faith, not in wordy contention."

Chapter VI.

By way of leading up to his proof that Christ is not different from the Father, St. Ambrose cites the more famous leaders of the Arian party, and explains how little their witness agrees, and shows what defence the Scriptures provide against them.

43. The Arians, then, say that Christ is unlike the Father; we deny it. Nay, indeed, we shrink in dread from the word. Nevertheless I would not that your sacred Majesty should trust to argument and our disputation. Let us enquire of the Scriptures, of apostles, of prophets, of Christ. In a word, let us enquire of the Father, Whose honour these men say they uphold, if the Son be judged inferior to Him. But insult to the Son brings no honour to the good Father. It cannot please the good Father, if the Son be judged inferior, rather than equal, to His Father.

44. I pray your sacred Majesty to suffer me, if for a little while I address myself particularly to these men. But whom shall I choose out to cite? Eunomius? or Arius and Aetius, his instructors? For there are many names, but one unbelief, constant in wickedness, but in conversation divided against itself; without difference in respect of deceit, but in common enterprise breeding dissent. But wherefore they will not agree together I understand not.

45. The Arians reject the person of Eunomius, but they maintain his unbelief and walk in the ways of his iniquity. They say that he has too generously published the writings of Arius. Truly, a plentiful lavishing of error! They praise him who gave the command, and deny him who executed it! Wherefore they have now fallen apart into several sects. Some follow after Eunomius or Aëtius, others after Palladius or Demophilus and Auxentius, or the inheritors of this form of unbelief. Others, again, follow different teachers. Is Christ, then, divided? Nay; but those who divide Him from the Father do with their own hands cut themselves asunder.

46. Seeing, therefore, that men who agree not amongst themselves have all alike conspired against the Church of God, I shall call those whom I have to answer by the common name of heretics. For heresy, like some hydra of fable, hath waxed great from its wounds, and, being ofttimes lopped short, hath grown afresh, being appointed to find meet destruction in flames of fire. Or, like some dread and monstrous Scylla, divided into many shapes of unbelief, she displays, as a mask to her guile, the pretence of being a Christian sect, but those wretched men whom she finds tossed to and fro in the waves of her unhallowed strait, amid the wreckage of their faith, she, girt with beastly monsters, rends with the cruel fang of her blasphemous doctrine.

47. This monster's cavern, your sacred Majesty, thick laid, as seafaring men do say it is, with hidden lairs, and all the neighbourhood thereof, where the rocks of unbelief echo to the howling of her black dogs, we must pass by with ears in a manner stopped. For it is written: "Hedge thine ears about with thorns;" and again: "Beware of dogs, beware of evil workers;" and yet again: "A man that is an heretic, avoid after the first reproof, knowing that such an one is fallen, and is in sin, being condemned of his own judgment." So then, like prudent pilots, let us set the sails of our faith for the course wherein we may pass by most safely, and again follow the coasts of the Scriptures.

Chapter VII.

The likeness of Christ to the Father is asserted on the authority of St. Paul, the prophets, and the Gospel, and especially in reliance upon the creation of man in God's image.

48. The Apostle saith that Christ is the image of the Father—for he calls Him the image of the invisible God, the first-begotten of all creation. First-begotten, mark you, not first-created, in order that He may be believed to be both begotten, in virtue of His nature, and first in virtue of His eternity. In another place also the Apostle has declared that God made the Son "heir of all things, by Whom also He made the worlds, Who is the brightness of His glory, and the express image of His substance." The Apostle calls Christ the image of the Father, and Arius says that He is unlike the Father. Why, then, is He called an image, if He hath no likeness? Men will not have their portraits unlike them, and Arius contends that the Father is unlike the Son, and would have it that the Father has begotten one unlike Himself, as though unable to generate His like.

49. The prophets say: "In Thy light we shall see light;" and again: "Wisdom is the brightness of everlasting light, and the spotless mirror of God's majesty, the image of His goodness." See what great names are declared! "Brightness," because in the Son the Father's glory shines clearly: "spotless minor," because the Father is seen in the Son: "image of goodness," because it is not one body seen reflected in another, but the whole power [of the Godhead] in the Son. The word "image" teaches us that there is no difference; "expression," that He is the counterpart of the Father's form; and "brightness" declares His eternity. The "image" in truth is not that of a bodily countenance, not one made up of colours, nor modelled in wax, but simply derived from God, coming out from the Father, drawn from the fountainhead.

50. By means of this image the Lord showed Philip the Father, saying, "Philip, he that sees Me, sees the Father also. How then dost thou say, Show us the Father? Believest thou not that I am in the Father, and the Father in Me?" Yes, he who looks upon the Son sees, in portrait, the Father. Mark what manner of portrait is spoken of. It is Truth, Righteousness, the Power of God: not dumb, for it is the Word; not insensible, for it is Wisdom; not vain and foolish, for it is Power; not soulless, for it is the Life; not dead, for it is the Resurrection. You see, then, that whilst an image is spoken of, the meaning is that it is the Father, Whose image the Son is, seeing that no one can be his own image.

51. More might I set down from the Son's testimony; howbeit, lest He perchance appear to have asserted Himself overmuch, let us enquire of the Father. For the Father said, "Let us make man in Our image and likeness." The Father saith to the Son "in *Our* image and likeness," and thou sayest that the Son of God is unlike the Father.

52. John saith, "Beloved, we are sons of God, and it doth not yet appear what we shall be: we know that if He be revealed, we shall be like Him." O blind madness! O shameless obstinacy! We are men, and, so far as we may, we shall be in the likeness of God: dare we deny that the Son is like God?

53. Therefore the Father hath said: "Let us make man in Our image and likeness." At the beginning of the universe itself, as I read, the Father and the Son existed, and I see one creation. I hear Him that speaketh. I acknowledge Him that doeth: but it is of one image, one likeness, that I read. This likeness belongs not to diversity but to unity. What, therefore, thou claimest for thyself, thou takest from the Son of God, seeing, indeed, that thou canst not be in the image of God, save by help of the image of God.

Chapter VIII.

The likeness of the Son to the Father being proved, it is not hard to prove the Son's eternity, though, indeed, this may be established on the authority of the Prophet Isaiah and St. John the Evangelist, by which authority the heretical leaders are shown to be refuted.

54. It is plain, therefore, that the Son is not unlike the Father, and so we may confess the more readily that He is also eternal, seeing that He Who is like the Eternal must needs be eternal. But if we say that the Father is eternal, and yet deny this of the Son, we say that the Son

is unlike the Father, for the temporal differeth from the eternal. The Prophet proclaims Him eternal, and the Apostle proclaims Him eternal; the Testaments, Old and New alike, are full of witness to the Son's eternity.

55. Let us take them, then, in their order. In the Old Testament—to cite one out of a multitude of testimonies—it is written: "Before Me hath there been no other God, and after Me shall there be none." I will not comment on this place, but ask thee straight: "Who speaks these words,—the Father or the Son?" Whichever of the two thou sayest, thou wilt find thyself convinced, or, if a believer, instructed. Who, then, speaks these words, the Father or the Son? If it is the Son, He says, "Before Me hath there been no other God;" if the Father, He says, "After Me shall there be none." The One hath none before Him, the Other none that comes after; as the Father is known in the Son, so also is the Son known in the Father, for whensoever you speak of the Father, you speak also by implication of His Son, seeing that none is his own father; and when you name the Son, you do also acknowledge His Father, inasmuch as none can be his own son. And so neither can the Son exist without the Father, nor the Father without the Son. The Father, therefore, is eternal, and the Son also eternal.

56. "In the beginning was the Word, and the Word was with God, and the Word was God. The same was in the beginning with God." "Was," mark you, "with God." "Was"—see, we have "was" four times over. Where did the blasphemer find it written that He "was not." Again, John, in another passage—in his Epistle—speaketh of "That which was in the beginning." The extension of the "was" is infinite. Conceive any length of time you will, yet still the Son "was."

57. Now in this short passage our fisherman hath barred the way of all heresy. For that which was "in the beginning" is not comprehended in time, is not preceded by any beginning. Let Arius, therefore, hold his peace. Moreover, that which was "with God" is not confounded and mingled with Him, but is distinguished by the perfection unblemished which it hath as the Word abiding with God; and so let Sabellius keep silence. And "the Word was God," This Word, therefore, consisteth not in uttered speech, but in the designation of celestial excellence, so that Photinus' teaching is refuted. Furthermore, by the fact that in the beginning He was with God is proven the indivisible unity of eternal Godhead in Father and Son, to the shame and confusion of Eunomius. Lastly, seeing that all things are said to have been made by Him, He is plainly shown to be author of the Old and of the New Testament alike; so that the Manichaean can find no ground for his assaults. Thus hath the good fisherman caught them all in one net, to make them powerless to deceive, albeit unprofitable fish to take.

Chapter IX.

St. Ambrose questions the heretics and exhibits their answer, which is, that the Son existed, indeed, before all time, yet was not co-eternal with the Father, whereat the Saint shows that they represent the Godhead as changeable, and further, that each Person must be believed to be eternal.

58. Tell me, thou heretic,—for the surpassing clemency of the Emperor grants me this indulgence of addressing thee for a short space, not that I desire to confer with thee, or am greedy to hear thy arguments, but because I am willing to exhibit them,—tell me, I say, whether there was ever a time when God Almighty was not the Father, and yet was God. "I say nothing about time," is thy answer. Well and subtly objected! For if thou bringest time into the dispute, thou wilt condemn thyself, seeing that thou must acknowledge that there was a time when the Son was not, whereas the Son is the ruler and creator of time. He cannot have begun to exist after His own work. Thou, therefore, must needs allow Him to be the ruler and maker of His work.

59. "I do not say," answerest thou, "that the Son existed not before time;" but when I call Him "Son," I declare that His Father existed before Him, for, as you say, father exists before son." But what means this? Thou deniest that time was before the Son, and yet thou wilt have it that something preceded the existence of the Son—some creature of time,—and thou showest certain stages of generation intervening, whereby thou dost give us to understand that the

generation from the Father was a process in time. For if He began to be a Father, then, in the first instance, He was God, and afterwards He became a Father. How, then, is God unchangeable? For if He was first God, and then the Father, surely He has undergone change by reason of the added and later act of generation.

60. But may God preserve us from this madness; for it was but to confute the impiety of the heretics that we brought in this question. The devout spirit affirms a generation that is not in time, and so declares Father and Son to be co-eternal, and does not maintain that God has ever suffered change.

61. Let Father and Son, therefore, be associated in worship, even as They are associated in Godhead; let not blasphemy put asunder those whom the close bond of generation hath joined together. Let us honour the Son, that we may honour the Father also, as it is written in the Gospel. The Son's eternity is the adornment of the Father's majesty. If the Son hath not been from everlasting, then the Father hath suffered change; but the Son is from all eternity, therefore hath the Father never changed, for He is always unchangeable. And thus we see that they who would deny the Son's eternity would teach that the Father is mutable.

Chapter X.

Christ's eternity being proved from the Apostle's teaching, St. Ambrose admonishes us that the Divine Generation is not to be thought of after the fashion of human procreation, nor to be too curiously pried into. With the difficulties thence arising he refuses to deal, saying that whats ever terms, taken from our knowledge of body, are used in speaking of this Divine Generation, must be understood with a spiritual meaning.

65. Hear now another argument, showing clearly the eternity of the Son. The Apostle says that God's Power and Godhead are eternal, and that Christ is the Power of God—for it is written that Christ is "the Power of God and the Wisdom of God." If, then, Christ is the Power of God, it follows that, forasmuch as God's Power is eternal, Christ also is eternal.

63. Thou canst not, then, heretic, build up a false doctrine from the custom of human procreation, nor yet gather the wherewithal for such work from our discourse, for we cannot compass the greatness of infinite Godhead, "of Whose greatness there is no end," in our straitened speech. If thou shouldst seek to give an account of a man's birth, thou must needs point to a time. But the Divine Generation is above all things; it reaches far and wide, it rises high above all thought and feeling. For it is written: "No man cometh to the Father, save by Me." Whatsoever, therefore, thou dost conceive concerning the Father—yea, be it even His eternity—thou canst not conceive aught concerning Him save by the Son's aid, nor can any understanding ascend to the Father save through the Son. "This is My dearly-beloved Son," the Father saith. "Is" mark you—He Who is, what He is, forever. Hence also David is moved to say: "O Lord, Thy Word abideth for ever in heaven," —for what abideth fails neither in existence nor in eternity.

64. Dost thou ask me how He is a Son, if He have not a Father existing before Him? I ask of thee, in turn, when, or how, thinkest thou that the Son was begotten. For me the knowledge of the mystery of His generation is more than I can attain to, —the mind fails, the voice is dumb—ay, and not mine alone, but the angels' also. It is above Powers, above Angels, above Cherubim, Seraphim, and all that has feeling and thought, for it is written: "The peace of Christ, which passeth all understanding." If the peace of Christ passes all understanding, how can so wondrous a generation but be above all understanding?

65. Do thou, then (like the angels), cover thy face with thy hands, for it is not given thee to look into surpassing mysteries! We are suffered to know that the Son is begotten, not to dispute upon the manner of His begetting. I cannot deny the one; the other I fear to search into, for if Paul says that the words which he heard when caught up into the third heaven might not be uttered, how can we explain the secret of this generation from and of the Father, which we can neither hear nor attain to with our understanding?

66. But if you will constrain me to the rule of human generation, that you may be allowed to say that the Father existed before the Son, then consider whether instances, taken from the generation of earthly creatures, are suitable to show forth the Divine Generation. If we speak according to what is customary amongst men, you cannot deny that, in man, the changes in the father's existence happen before those in the son's. The father is the first to grow, to enter old age, to grieve, to weep. If, then, the son is after him in time, he is older in experience than the son. If the child comes to be born, the parent escapes not the shame of begetting.

67. Why take such delight in that rack of questioning? You hear the name of the Son of God; abolish it, then, or acknowledge His true nature. You hear speak of the womb—acknowledge the truth of undoubted begetting. Of His heart—know that here is God's word. Of H is right hand—confess His power. Of His face—acknowledge His wisdom. These words are not to be understood, when we speak of God, as when we speak of bodies. The generation of the Son is incomprehensible, the Father begets impassibly, and yet of Himself and in ages inconceivably remote hath very God begotten very God. The Father loves the Son, and you anxiously examine His Person; the Father is well. pleased in Him, you, joining the Jews, look upon Him with an evil eye; the Father knows the Son, and you join the heathen in reviling Him.

Chapter XI.

It cannot be proved from Scripture that the Father existed before the Son, nor yet can arguments taken from human reproduction avail to this end, since they bring in absurdities without end. To dare to affirm that Christ began to exist in the course of time is the height of blasphemy.

68. You ask me whether it is possible that He Who is the Father should not be prior in existence. I ask you to tell me when the Father existed, the Son as yet being not; prove this, gather it from argument or evidence of Scripture. If you lean upon arguments, you have doubtless been taught that God's power is eternal. Again, you have read the Scripture that saith: "O Israel, if thou wilt hearken unto Me, there shall be no new God in thee, neither shalt thou worship a strange God." The first of these commands betokens [the Son's] eternity, the second His possession of an identical nature, so that we can neither believe Him to have come into existence after the Father, nor suppose Him the Son of another Divinity. For if He existed not always with the Father, He is a "new" [God]; if He is not of one Divinity with the Father, He is a "strange" [God]. But He is not after the Father, for He is not "a new God;" nor is He "a strange God," for He is begotten of the Father, and because, as it is written, He is "God above all, blessed for ever."

69. But if the Arians believe Him to be a strange God, why do they worship Him, when it is written: "Thou shalt worship no strange God"? Else, if they do not worship the Son, let them confess thereto, and the case is at an end,—that they deceive no one by their professions of religion. This, then, we see, is the witness of the Scriptures. If you have any others to produce, it will be your business to do so.

70. Let us now go further, and gather the truth in conclusion from arguments. For although arguments usually give place, even to human evidence, still, heretic, argue as thou wilt. "Experience teaches us," you say, "that the being which generates is prior to that which is generated." I answer: Follow our customary experience through all its departments, and if the rest agree herewith, I oppose not your claim that your point be granted; but if there be no such agreement, how can you claim assent on this one point, when in all the rest you lack support? Seeing, then, that you call for what is customary, it comes about that the Son, when He was begotten of the Father, was a little child. You have seen Him an infant, crying in the cradle. As the years passed, He has gone forward from strength to strength—for if He was weak with the weakness of things begotten, He must also have fallen under the weakness, not only of birth, but of life also.

71. But perchance you run to such a pitch of folly as not to flinch from asserting these things of the Son of God, measuring Him, as you do, by the rule of human infirmity. What,

then, if, while you cannot refuse Him the name of God, you are bent to prove Him, by reason of weakness, to be a man? What if, whilst you examine the Person of the Son, you are calling the Father in question, and whilst you hastily pass sentence upon the Former, you include the Latter in the same condemnation!

72. If the Divine Generation has been subject to the limits of time,—if we suppose this, borrowing from the custom of human generation, then it follows, further, that the Father bare the Son in a bodily womb, and laboured under the burden whilst ten months sped their courses. But how can generation, as it commonly takes place, be brought about without the help of the other sex? You see that the common order of generation was not the commencement, and you think that the courses of generation, which are ruled by certain necessities whereunto bodies are subject, have always prevailed. You require the customary course, I ask for difference of sex: you demand the supposition of time, I that of order: you enquire into the end, I into the beginning. Now surely it is the end that depends on the beginning, not the beginning on the end.

73. "Everything," say you, "that is begotten has a beginning, and therefore because the Son is the Son, He has a beginning, and came first into existence within limits of time. Let this be taken as the word of their own mouth; as for myself, I confess that the Son is begotten, but the rest of their declaration makes me shudder. Man, dost thou confess God, and diminish His honour by such slander? From this madness may God deliver us.

Chapter XII.

Further objections to the Godhead of the Son are met by the same answer—to wit, that they may equally be urged against the Father also. The Father, then, being in no way confined by time, place, or anything else created, no such limitation is to be imposed upon the Son, Whose marvellous generation is not only of the Father, but of the Virgin also, and therefore, since in His generation of the Father no distinction of sex, or the like, was involved, neither was it in His generation of the Virgin.

74. The next objection is this: "If the Son has not those properties which all sons have, He is no Son." May Father, Son, and Holy Spirit pardon me, for I would propound the question in all devoutness. Surely the Father is, and abides for ever: created things, too, are as God hath ordained them. Is there any one, then, amongst these creatures which is not subject to the limitations of place, time, or the fact of having been created, or to some originating cause or creator, Surely, none. What, then?Is there any one of them whereof the Father stands in need? So to say were blasphemy. Cease, then, to apply to the Godhead what is proper only to created existences, or, if you insist upon forcing the comparison, bethink you whither your wickedness leads. God forbid that we should even behold the end thereof.

75. We maintain the answer given by piety. God is Almighty, and therefore God the Father needs none of those things, for in Him there is no changing, nor any place for such help as we need, we whose weakness is supported by means of things of this kind. But He Who is Almighty, plainly He is uncreate, and not confined to any place, and surpasses time. Before God was not anything—nay, even to speak about anything being before God is a grave sin. If, then, you grant that in the nature of God the Father there is nought that implies a being sustained, because He is God, it follows that nothing of this sort can be supposed to exist in the Son of God, nothing that connotes a beginning, or growth, forasmuch as He is "very God of very God."

76. Seeing, then, that we find not the customary order prevailing, be content, Arian, to believe in a miraculous generation of the Son. Be content, I say, and if you believe me not, at least have respect unto the voice of God saying, "To whom have ye esteemed Me to be like?" and again: "God is not like a man that He should repent." If, indeed, God works mysteriously, seeing that He doth not work any work, or fashion anything, or bring it to completion, by labor of hands, or in any course of days, "for He spake, and they were made; He gave the word and they were created," why should we not believe that He Whom we acknowledge as a Creator, mysteriously working, discerning it in His works, also begat His Son in a mysterious manner?

Surely it is fitting that He should be regarded as having begotten the Son in a special and mysterious way. Let Him Who hath the grace of majesty unrivalled likewise have the glory of mysterious generation.

77. Not only Christ's generation of the Father, but His birth also of the Virgin, demands our wonder. You say that the former is like unto the manner wherein we men are conceived. I will show—nay more, I will compel you yourself to confess, that the latter also hath no likeness to the manner of our birth. Tell me how it was that He was born of Mary, with what law did His conception in a Virgin's womb agree, how there could be any birth without the seed of a man, how a maiden could become great with child, how she became a mother before experience of such intercourse as is between wives and husbands. There was no [visible] cause,—and yet a son was begotten. How, then, came about this birth, under a new law?

78. If, then, the common order of human generation was not found in the case of the Virgin Mary, how can you demand that God the Father should beget in such wise as you were begotten in? Surely the common order is determined by difference of sex; for this is implanted in the nature of our flesh, but where flesh is not, how can you expect to find the infirmity of flesh? No man calls in question one who is better than he is: to believe is enjoined upon you, without permission to question. For it is written, "Abraham believed God, and it was accounted to him for righteousness." Language is vain to set forth, not only the generation of the Son, but even the works of God, for it is written: "All His works are executed in faithfulness;" His works, then, are done in faithfulness, but not His generation? Ay, we call in question that which we see not, we who are bidden to believe rather than enquire of that we see.

Chapter XIII.

Discussion of the Divine Generation is continued. St. Ambrose illustrates its method by the same example as that employed by the author of the Epistle to the Hebrews. The duty of believing what is revealed is shown by the example of Nebuchadnezzar and St. Peter. By the vision granted to St. Peter was shown the Son's Eternity and Godhead—the Apostle, then, must be believed in preference to the teachers of philosophy, whose authority was everywhere falling into discredit. The Arians, on the other hand, are shown to be like unto the heathen.

79. It will be asked: "In what sort was the Son begotten?" As one who is for ever, as the Word, as the brightness of eternal light, for brightness takes effect in the instant of its coming into existence. Which example is the Apostle's, not mine. Think not, then, that there was ever a moment of time when God was without wisdom, any more than that there was ever a time when light was without radiance. Judge not, Arian, divine things by human, but believe the divine where thou findest not the human.

80. The heathen king saw in the fire, together with the three Hebrew children, the form of a fourth, like as of an angel, and because he thought that this angel excelled all angels, he judged Him to be the Son of God, Whom he had not read of, but in Whom he believed. Abraham, also, saw Three, and adored One.

81. Peter, when he saw Moses and Elias on the mountain, with the Son of God, was not deceived as to their nature and glory. For he enquired, not of them, but of Christ, what he ought to do, inasmuch as though he prepared to do homage to all three, yet he waited for the command of one. But since he ignorantly thought that for three persons three tabernacles should be set up, he was corrected by the sovereign voice of God the Father, saying, "This is My dearly beloved Son: hear ye Him." That is to say: "Why dost thou join thy fellow-servants in equality with thy Lord?" "This is My Son." Not "Moses is My Son," nor "Elias is My Son," but "This is My Son." The Apostle was not dull to understand the rebuke; he fell on his face, brought low by the Father's voice and the glorious beauty of the Son, but he was raised up by the Son, Whose wont it is to raise up them that are fallen. Then he saw one only, the Son of God alone, for the servants had withdrawn, that He might be seen to be Lord alone, Who alone was entitled Son.

82. What, then, was the purpose of that vision, which signified not that Christ and His servants were equal, but betokened a mystery, save that it should be made plain to us that the Law and the Prophets, in agreement with the Gospel, revealed as eternal the Son of God, Whom they had heralded. When we, therefore, hear of the Son coming forth of the womb, the Word from the heart, let us believe that the Son was not fashioned with hands but begotten of the Father, not the work of a craftsman but the offspring of a parent.

83. He, therefore, Who said, "This is My Son," said not, "This is a creature of time," nor "This being is of My creation, My making, My servant," but "This is My Son, Whom ye see glorified." This is the God of Abraham, the God of Isaac, the God of Jacob, Who appeared to Moses in the bush, concerning Whom Moses saith, "He Who is hath sent me." It was not the Father Who spake to Moses in the bush or in the desert, but the Son. It was of this Moses that Stephen said, "This is He Who was in the church, in the wilderness, with the Angel." This, then, is He Who gave the Law, Who spake with Moses, saying, "I am the God of Abraham, the God of Isaac, the God of Jacob." This, then, is the God of the patriarchs, this is the God of the prophets.

84. It is of the Son, therefore, that we read, thy mind understandeth the reading, let thy tongue make confession. Away with arguments, where faith is required; now let dialectic hold her peace, even in the midst of her schools. I ask not what it is that philosophers say, but I would know what they do. They sit desolate in their schools. See the victory of faith over argument. They who dispute subtly are forsaken daily by their fellows; they who with simplicity believe are daily increased. Not philosophers but fishermen, not masters of dialectic but tax-gatherers, now find credence. The one sort, through pleasures and luxuries, have bound the world's burden upon themselves; the other, by fasting and mortification, have cast it off, and so doth sorrow now begin to win over more followers than pleasure.

85. Let us now see how far Arians and pagans do differ. The latter call upon gods, who are different in sex and unequal in power; the former affirm a Trinity where there is likewise inequality of power and diversity of Godhead. The pagans assert that their Gods began to exist once upon a time; the Arians lyingly declare that Christ began to exist in the course of time. Have they not all dyed their impiety in the vats of philosophy? But indeed the pagans do extol that which they worship, the Arians maintain that the Son of God, Who is God, is a creature.

Chapter XIV.

That the Son of God is not a created being is proved by the following arguments: (1) That He commanded not that the Gospel should be preached to Himself; (2) that a created being is given over unto vanity; (3) that the Son has created all things; (4) that we read of Him as begotten; and (5) that the difference of generation and adoption has always been understood in those places where both natures—the divine and the human—are declared to co-exist in Him. All of which testimony is confirmed by the Apostle's interpretation.

86. It is now made plain, as I believe, your sacred Majesty, that the Lord Jesus is neither unlike the Father, nor one that began to exist in course of time. We have yet to confute another blasphemy, and to show that the Son of God is not a created being. Herein is the quickening word that we read as our help, for we have heard the passage read where the Lord saith: "Go ye into all the world, and preach the Gospel to all creation." He Who saith "all creation" excepts nothing. How, then, do they stand who call Christ a "creature"? If He were a creature, could He have commanded that the Gospel should be preached to Himself? It is not, therefore, a creature, but the Creator, Who commits to His disciples the work of teaching created beings.

87. Christ, then, is no created being; for "created beings are," as the Apostle hath said, "given over to vanity." Is Christ given over unto vanity? Again, "creation"—according to the same Apostle—"groans and travails together even until now." What, then? Doth Christ take any part in this groaning and travailing—He Who hath set us miserable mourners free from death? "Creation," saith the Apostle, "shall be set free from the slavery of corruption." We see, then,

that between creation and its Lord there is a vast difference, for creation is enslaved, but "the Lord is the Spirit, and where the Spirit of the Lord is, there is freedom."

88. Who was it that led first into this error, of declaring Him Who created and made all things to be a creature? Did the Lord, I would ask, create Himself? We read that "all things were made by Him, and without Him was nothing made." This being so, did He make Himself? We reaD—and who shall deny?—that in wisdom hath God made all things. If so, how can we suppose that wisdom was made in itself?

89. We read that the Son is begotten, inasmuch as the Father saith: "I brought thee forth from the womb before the morning star" We read of the "first-born" Son, of the "only-begotten" —first-born, because there is none before Him; only-begotten, because there is none after Him. Again, we read: "Who shall declare His generation?" "Generation," mark you, not "creation." What argument can be brought to meet testimonies so great and mighty as these?

90. Moreover, God's Son discovers the difference between generation and grace when He says: "I go up to My Father and your Father, to My God and your God." He did not say, "I go up to our Father," but "I go up to My Father and your Father." This distinction is the sign of a difference, inasmuch as He Who is Christ's Father is our Creator.

91. Furthermore He said, "to My God and your God," because although He and the Father are One, and the Father is His Father by possession of the same nature, whilst God began to be our Father through the office of the Son, not by virtue of nature, but of grace—still He seems to point us here to the existence in Christ of both natures, Godhead and Manhood,—Godhead of His Father, Manhood of His Mother, the former being before all things, the latter derived from the Virgin. For the first, speaking as the Son, He called God His Father, and afterward, speaking as man, named Him as God.

92. Everywhere, indeed, we have witness in the Scriptures to show that Christ, in naming God as His God, does so as man. "My God, My God, why hast Thou forsaken Me?" And again: "From My mother's womb Thou art My God." In the former place He suffers as a man; in the latter it is a man who is brought forth from his mother's womb. And so when He says, "From My mother's womb Thou art My God," He means that He Who was always His Father is His God from the moment when He was brought forth from His Mother's womb.

93. Seeing, then, that we read in the Gospel, in the Apostle, in the Prophets, of Christ as begotten, how dare the Arians to say that He was created or made? But, indeed, they ought to have bethought them, where they have read of Him as created, where as made. For it has been plainly shown that the Son of God is begotten of God, born of God—let them, then, consider with care where they have read that He was made, seeing that He was not made God, but born as God, the Son of God; afterward, however, He was, according to the flesh, made man of Mary.

94. "But when the fulness of time was come, God sent His Son, *made* of a woman, made under the Law." "*His* Son," observe, not as one of many, not as His in common with another, but His own, and in saying "His Son," the Apostle showed that it is of the Son's nature that His generation is eternal. Him the Apostle has affirmed to have been afterwards "made" of a woman, in order that the making might be understood not of the Godhead, but of the putting on of a body—"made of a woman," then, by taking on of flesh; "made under the Law" through observance of the Law. Howbeit, the former, the spiritual generation is before the Law was, the latter is after the Law.

Chapter XV.

An explanation of Acts ii. 36 and Proverbs viii. 22, which are shown to refer properly to Christ's manhood alone.

95. To no purpose, then, is the heretics' customary citation of the Scripture, that "God made Him both Lord and Christ." Let these ignorant persons read the whole passage, and understand it. For thus it is written. "God made this Jesus, Whom ye crucified, both Lord and Christ." It

was not the Godhead, but the flesh, that was crucified. This, indeed, was possible, because the flesh allowed of being crucified. It follows not, then, that the Son of God is a created being.

96. Let us despatch, then, that passage also, which they do use to misrepresent,—let them learn what is the sense of the words, "The Lord created Me." It is not "the Father created," but "the Lord created Me." The flesh acknowledgeth its Lord, praise declareth the Father: our created nature confesseth the first, loveth, knoweth the latter. Who, then, cannot but perceive that these words announce the Incarnation? Thus the Son speaketh of Himself as created in respect of that wherein he witnesseth to Himself as being man, when He says, "Why seek ye to kill Me, a *man*, Who have told you the truth?" He speaketh of His Manhood, wherein He was crucified, and died, and was buried.

97. Furthermore, there is no doubt but that the writer set down as past that which was to come; for this is the usage of prophecy, that things to come are spoken of as though they were already present or past. For example, in the twenty-first psalm you have read: "Fat bulls (of Bashan) have beset me," and again: "They parted My garments among them." This the Evangelist showeth to have been spoken prophetically of the time of the Passion, for to God the things that are to come are present, and for Him Who foreknoweth all things, they are as though they were past and over; as it is written, "Who hath made the things that are to be."

98. It is no wonder that He should declare His place to have been set fast before all worlds, seeing that the Scripture tells us that He was foreordained before the times and ages. The following passage discovers how the words in question present themselves as a true prophecy of the Incarnation: "Wisdom hath built her an house, and set up seven pillars to support it, and she hath slain her victims. She hath mingled her wine in the bowl, and made ready her table, and sent her servants, calling men together with a mighty voice of proclamation, saying: 'He who is simple, let him turn in to me.'" Do we not see, in the Gospel, that all these things were fulfilled after the Incarnation, in that Christ disclosed the mysteries of the Holy Supper, sent forth His apostles, and cried with a loud voice, saying, "If any man thirst, let him come to Me and drink." That which followeth, then, answereth to that which went before, and we behold the whole story of the Incarnation set forth in brief by prophecy.

99. Many other passages might readily be seen to be prophecies of this sort concerning the Incarnation, but I will not delay over books, lest the treatise appear too wordy.

Chapter XVI.
The Arians blaspheme Christ, if by the words "created" and "begotten" they mean and understand one and the same thing. If, however, they regard the words as distinct in meaning, they must not speak of Him, of Whom they have read that He was begotten, as if He were a created being. This rule is upheld by the witness of St. Paul, who, professing himself a servant of Christ, forbade worship of a created being. God being a substance pure and uncompounded, there is no created nature in Him; furthermore, the Son is not to be degraded to the level of things created, seeing that in Him the Father is well pleased.

100. Now will I enquire particularly of the Arians, whether they think that begotten and created are one and the same. If they call them the same, then is there no difference betwixt generation and creation. It follows, then, that forasmuch as we also are created, there is between us and Christ and the elements no difference. Thus much, however, great as their madness is, they will not venture to say.

101. Furthermore—to concede that which is no truth, to their folly—I ask them, if there is, as they think, no difference in the words, why do they not call upon Him Whom they worship by the better title? Why do they not avail themselves of the Father's word? Why do they reject the title of honour, and use a dishonouring name?

102. If, however, there is—as I think there is—a distinction between "created" and "begotten," then, when we have read that He is begotten, we shall surely not understand the same by the terms "begotten" and "created." Let them therefore confess Him to be begotten of

the Father, born of the Virgin, or let them say how the Son of God can be both begotten and created. A single nature, above all, the Divine Being, rejects strife (within itself).

103. But in any case let our private judgment pass: let us enquire of Paul, who, filled with the Spirit of God, and so foreseeing these questionings, hath given sentence against pagans in general and Arians in particular, saying that they were by God's judgment condemned, who served the creature rather than the Creator. Thus, in fact, you may read: "God gave them over to the lusts of their own heart, that they might one with another dishonour their bodies, they who changed God's truth into a lie, and worshipped and served the thing created rather than the Creator, Who is God, blessed for ever."

104. Thus Paul forbids me to worship a creature, and admonishes me of my duty to serve Christ. It follows, then, that Christ is not a created being. The Apostle calls himself "Paul, a servant of Jesus Christ," and this good servant, who acknowledges his Lord, will likewise have us not worship that which is created. How, then, could he have been himself a servant of Christ, if he thought that Christ was a created person? Let these heretics, then, cease either to worship Him Whom they call a created being, or to call Him a creature, Whom they feign to worship, lest under colour of being worshippers they fall into worse impiety. For a domestic is worse than a foreign foe, and that these men should use the Name of Christ to Christ's dishonour increaseth their guilt.

105. What better expounder of the Scriptures do we indeed look for than that teacher of the Gentiles, that chosen vessel—chosen from the number of the persecutors? He who had been the persecutor of Christ confesses Him. He had read Solomon more, in any case, than Arius hath, and he was well learned in the Law, and so, because he had read, he said not that Christ was created, but that He was begotten. For he had read, "He spake, and they were made: He commanded, and they were created." Was Christ, I ask, made at a word? Was He created at a command?

106. Moreover, *how* can there be any created nature in God? In truth, God is of an uncompounded nature; nothing can be added to Him, and that alone which is Divine hath He in His nature; filling all things, yet nowhere Himself confounded with aught; penetrating all things, yet Himself nowhere to be penetrated; present in all His fulness at one and the same moment, in heaven, in earth, in the deepest depth of the sea, to sight invisible, by speech not to be declared, by feeling not to be measured; to be followed by faith, to be adored with devotion; so that whatsoever title excels in depth of spiritual import, in setting forth glory and honour, in exalting power, this you may know to belong of right to God.

107. Since, then, the Father is well pleased in the Son; believe that the Son is worthy of the Father, that He came out from God, as He Himself bears witness, saying: "I went out from God, and am come;" and again: "I went out from God." He Who proceeded and came forth from God can have no attributes but such as are proper to God.

Chapter XVII.

That Christ is very God is proved from the fact that He is God's own Son, also from His having been begotten and having come forth from God, and further, from the unity of will and operation subsisting in Father and Son. The witness of the apostles and of the centurion—which St. Ambrose sets over against the Arian teaching—is adduced, together with that of Isaiah and St. John.

108. Hence it is that Christ is not only God, but very God indeed—very God of very God, insomuch that He Himself is the Truth, If, then, we enquire His Name, it is "the Truth;" if we seek to know His natural rank and dignity, He is so truly the very Son of God, that He is indeed God's *own* Son; as it is written, "Who spared not His own Son, but gave Him up for our sakes," gave Him up, that is, so far as the flesh was concerned. That He is God's own Son declares His Godhead; that He is very God shows that He is God's own Son; His pitifulness is the earnest of His submission, His sacrifice, of our salvation.

109. Lest, however, men should wrest the Scripture, that "God gave Him up," the Apostle himself has said in another place, "Peace from God the Father, and our Lord Jesus Christ, Who gave Himself for our sins;" and again: "Even as Christ hath loved us, and given Himself for us." If, then, He both was given up by the Father, and gave Himself up of His own accord, it is plain that the working and the will of Father and Son is one.

110. If, then, we enquire into His natural pre-eminence, we find it to consist in being begotten. To deny that the Son of God is begotten [of God] is to deny that He is God's *own* Son, and to deny Christ to be God's own Son is to class Him with the rest of mankind, as no more a Son than any of the rest. If, however, we enquire into the distinctive property of His generation, it is this, that He came forth from God. For whilst, in our experience, to come out implies something already existent, and that which is said to come out seems to proceed forth from hidden and inward places, we, though it be presented but in short passages, observe the peculiar attribute of the Divine Generation, that the Son doth not seem to have come forth out of any place, but as God from God, a Son from a Father, nor to have had a beginning in the course of time, having come forth from the Father by being born, as He Himself Who was born said: "I came forth from the mouth of the Most High."

111. But if the Arians acknowledge not the Son's nature, if they believe not the Scriptures, let them at least believe the mighty works. To whom doth the Father say, "Let *us* make man?" save to Him Whom He knew to be His true Son? In Whom, save in one who was true, could He recognize His Image? The son by adoption is not the same as the true Son; nor would the Son say, "I and the Father are one," if He, being Himself not true, were measuring Himself with One Who is true. The Father, therefore, says, "Let us make." He Who spake is true; can He, then, Who made be not true? Shall the honour rendered to Him Who speaks be withheld from Him Who makes?

112. But how, unless the Father knew Him to be His true Son, should He commend to Him His will, for perfect co-operation, and His works, for perfect bringing in out in actuality? Seeing that the Son worketh the works which the Father doeth, and that the Son quickens whom He will, as it is written, He is then equal in power and free in respect of His will. And thus is the Unity maintained, forasmuch as God's power consists in that the Godhead is proper to each Person, and freedom lies not in any difference, but in unity of will.

113. The apostles, being storm-tossed in the sea, as soon as they saw the waters leaping up round their Lord's feet, and beheld His fearless footsteps on the water, as He walked amid the raging waves of the sea, and the ship, which was beaten upon by the waves, had rest as soon as Christ entered it, and they saw the waves and the winds obeying Him,—then, though as yet they did not believe in their hearts they believed Him to be God's true Son, saying, "Truly Thou art the Son of God."

114. To the same effect the confession of the centurion, and others who were with him, when the foundations of the world were shaken at the Lord's Passion,—and this, heretic, thou deniest! The centurion said, "Truly this was the Son of God." "Was" said the centurion—"Was *not*" says the Arian. The centurion, then, with bloodstained hands, but devout mind, declares both the truth and the eternity of Christ's generation; and thou, O heretic deniest its truth, and makest it matter of time! Would that thou hadst imbued thy hands rather than thy soul! But thou, unclean even of hand, and murderous of intent, seekest Christ's death, so far as in thee lies, seeing that thou thinkest of Him as mean and weak; nay, and this is a worse sin, thou, albeit the Godhead can feel no wound, still wouldst do thy diligence to slay in Christ, not His Body, but His Glory.

115. We cannot then doubt that He is very God, Whose true Godhead even executioners believed in and devils confessed. Their testimony we require not now, but it is withal greater than your blasphemies. We have called them in to witness, to put you to the blush, whilst we have also cited the oracles of God, to the end that you should believe.

116. The Lord proclaimeth by the mouth of Isaiah: "In the mouth of them that serve Me shall a new name be called upon, which shall be blessed over all the earth, and they shall bless the true God, and they who swear upon earth shall swear by the true God." These words, I say, Isaiah spake when he saw God's Glory, and thus in the Gospel it is plainly said that he saw the Glory of Christ and spoke of Him.

117. But hear again what John the Evangelist hath written in his Epistle, saying: "We know that the Son of God hath appeared, and hath given us discernment, to know the Father, and to be in His true Son Jesus Christ, our Lord. He is very God, and Life Eternal." John calls Him true Son of God and very God. If, then, He be very God, He is surely uncreate, without spot of lying or deceit, having in Himself no confusion, nor unlikeness to His Father.

Chapter XVIII.

The errors of the Arians are mentioned in the Nicene Definition of the Faith, to prevent their deceiving anybody. These errors are recited, together with the anathema pronounced against them, which is said to have been not only pronounced at Nicaea, but also twice renewed at Ariminum.

118. Christ, therefore, is "God of God, Light of Light, very God of very God; begotten of the Father, not made; of one substance with the Father."119. So, indeed, following the guidance of the Scriptures, our fathers declared, holding, moreover, that impious doctrines should be included in the record of their decrees, in order that the unbelief of Arius should discover itself, and not, as it were, mask itself with dye or face-paint. For they give a false colour to their thoughts who dare not unfold them openly. After the manner of the censor's rolls, then, the Arian heresy is not discovered by name, but marked out by the condemnation pronounced, in order that he who is curious and eager to hear it should be preserved from falling by knowing that it is condemned already, before he hears, it set forth to the end that he should believe.

120. "Those," runs the decree, "who say that there was a time when the Son of God was not, and that before He was born He was not, and who say that he was made out of nothing, or is of another substance or ousia, or that He is capable of changing, or that with Him is any shadow of turning,—them the Catholic and Apostolic Church declares accursed."

121. Your sacred Majesty has agreed that they who utter such doctrines are rightly condemned. It was of no determination by man, of no human counsel, that three hundred and eighteen bishops met, as I showed above more at length, in Council, but that in their number the Lord Jesus might prove, by the sign of His Name and Passion, that He was in the midst, where His own were gathered together. In the number of three hundred was the sign of His Cross, in that of eighteen was the sign of the Name Jesus.

122. This also was the teaching of the First Confession in the Council of Ariminum, and of the Second Correction, after that Council. Of the Confession, the letter sent to the Emperor Constantine beareth witness, and the Council that followed declares the Correction.

Chapter XIX.

Arius is charged with the first of the above-mentioned errors, and refuted by the testimony of St. John. The miserable death of the Heresiarch is described, and the rest of his blasphemous errors are one by one examined and disproved.

123. Arius, then, says: "There was a time when the Son of God existed not," but Scripture saith: "He was," not that "He was not." Furthermore, St. John has written: "In the beginning was the Word, and the Word was with God, and the Word was God. The same was in the beginning with God." Observe how often the verb "was" appears, whereas "was not" is nowhere found. Whom, then, are we to believe?—St. John, who lay on Christ's bosom, or Arius, wallowing amid the outgush of his very bowels?—so wallowing that we might understand how Arius in his teaching showed himself like unto Judas, being visited with like punishment.

124. For Arius' bowels also gushed out—decency forbids to say where—and so he burst asunder in the midst, falling headlong, and besmirching those foul lips wherewith he had denied

Christ. He was rent, even as the Apostle Peter said of Judas, because he bought a field with the price of evil-doing, and falling headlong he burst asunder in the midst, and all his bowels gushed out." It was no chance manner of death, seeing that like wickedness was visited with like punishment, to the end that those who denied and betrayed the same Lord might likewise undergo the same torment.

125. Let us pass on to further points. Arius says: "Before He was born, the Son of God was not," but the Scripture saith that all things are maintained in existence by the Son's office. How, then, could He, Who existed not, bestow existence upon others? Again, when the blasphemer uses the words "when" and "before," he certainly uses words which are marks of time. How, then, do the Arians deny that time was ere the Son was, and yet will have things created in time to exist before the Son, seeing that the very words, "when," "before," and "did not exist once," announce the idea of time?

126. Arius says that the Son of God came into being out of nought. How, then, is He Son of God—how was He begotten from the womb of the Father—how do we read of Him as the Word spoken of the heart's abundance, save to the end that we should believe that He came forth, as it is written, from the Father's inmost, unapproachable sanctuary? Now a son is so called either by means of adoption or by nature, as we are called sons by means of adoption. Christ is the Son of God by virtue of His real and abiding nature. How, then, can He, Who out of nothing fashioned all things, be Himself created out of nothing?

127. He who knows not whence the Son is hath not the Son. The Jews therefore had not the Son, for they knew not whence He was. Wherefore the Lord said to them: "Ye know not whence I came;" and again: "Ye neither have found out Who I am, nor know My Father," for he who denies that the Son is of the Father knows not the Father, of Whom the Son is; and again, he knows not the Son, because he knows not the Father.

128. Arius says: "[The Son is] of another Substance." But what other substance is exalted to equality with the Son of God, so that simply in virtue thereof He is Son of God? Or what right have the Arians for censuring us because we speak, in Greek, of the ousia, or in Latin, of the *Substantia* of God, when they themselves, in saying that the Son of God is of another "Substance," assert a divine *Substantia*.

129. Howbeit, should they desire to dispute the use of the words "divine Substance" or "divine Nature," they shall easily be refuted, for Holy Writ oft-times hath spoken of ousia in Greek, or *Substantia* in Latin, and St. Peter, as we read, would have us become partakers in the divine Nature. But if they will have it that the Son is of another "Substance," they with their own lips confute themselves, in that they both acknowledge the term "Substance," whereof they are so afraid, and rank the Son on a level with the creatures above which they feign to exalt Him.

130. Arius calls the Son of God a creature, but "not as the rest of the creatures." Yet what created being is not different from another? Man is not as angel, earth is not as heaven, the sun is not as water, nor light as darkness. Arius' preference, therefore, is empty—he hath but disguised with a sorry dye his deceitful blasphemies, in order to take the foolish.

131. Arius declares that the Son of God may change and swerve. How, then, is He God if He is changeable, seeing that He Himself hath said: "I am, I am, and I change not"?

Chapter XX.
St. Ambrose declares his desire that some angel would fly to him to purify him, as once the Seraph did to Isaiah—nay more, that Christ Himself would come to him, to the Emperor, and to his readers, and finally prays that Gratian and the rest of the faithful may be exalted by the power and spell of the Lord's Cup, which he describes in mystic language.

132. Howbeit, now must I needs confess the Prophet Isaiah's confession, which he makes before declaring the word of the Lord: "Woe is me, my heart is smitten, for I, a man of unclean lips, and living in the midst of a people of unclean lips, have seen the Lord of Sabaoth." Now if

Isaiah said "Woe is me," who looked upon the Lord of Sabaoth, what shall I say of myself, who, being "a man of unclean lips," am constrained to treat of the divine generation? How shall I break forth into speech of things whereof I am afraid, when David prays that a watch may be set over his mouth in the matter of things whereof he has knowledge? O that to me also one of the Seraphim would bring the burning coal from the celestial altar, taking it in the tongs of the two testaments, and with the fire thereof purge my unclean lips!

133. But forasmuch as then the Seraph came down in a vision to the Prophet, whilst Thou, O Lord, in revelation of the mystery hast come to us in the flesh, do Thou, not by any deputy, nor by any messenger, but Thou Thyself cleanse my conscience from my secret sins, that I too, erstwhile unclean, but now by Thy mercy made clean through faith, may sing in the words of David: "I will make music to Thee upon a harp, O God of Israel, my lips shall rejoice, in all my song to Thee, and so, too, shall my soul, whom Thou hast redeemed."

134. And so, O Lord, leaving them that slander and hate Thee, come unto us, sanctify the ears of our sovereign ruler, Gratian, and all besides into whose hands this little book shall come—and purge my ears, that no stains of the infidelity they have heard remain anywhere. Cleanse thoroughly, then, our ears, not with water of well, river, or rippling and purling brook, but with words cleansing like water, clearer than any water, and purer than any snow—even the words Thou hast spoken—"Though your sins be as scarlet, I will make them white as snow."

135. Moreover, there is a Cup, wherewith Thou dost use to purify the hidden chambers of the soul, a Cup not of the old order, nor filled from a common Vine,—a new Cup, brought down from heaven to earth, filled with wine pressed from the wondrous cluster, which hung in fleshly form upon the tree of the Cross, even as the grape hangs upon the Vine. From this Cluster, then, is the Wine that maketh glad the heart of man, uplifts the sorrowful, is fragrant with, pours into us, the ecstasy of faith, true devotion, and purity.

136. With this Wine, therefore, O Lord my God, cleanse the spiritual ears of our sovereign Emperor, to the end that, just as men, being uplifted with common wine, love rest and quietness, cast out the fear of death, have no feeling of injuries, seek not that which belongs to others, and forget their own; and so he, too, intoxicated with thy wine, may love peace, and, confident in the exultation of faith, may never know the death of unbelief, and may display loving patience, have no part in other men's profanities, and hold the faith of more account even than kindred and children, as it is written: "Leave all that thou hast, and come, follow Me."

137. With this Wine, also, Lord Jesus, purify our senses, that we may adore Thee, and worship Thee, the Creator of things visible and invisible. Truly, Thou canst not fail of being Thyself invisible and good, Who hast given invisibility and goodness to the works of Thy Hands.

BOOK II.

Introduction.

Twelve names of the Son of God are recounted, being distributed into three classes. These names are so many proofs of the eternity not only of the Son, but of the Father also. Furthermore, they are compared with the twelve stones in the High Priest's breastplate, and their inseparability is shown by a new distribution of them. Returning to the comparison with the High Priest's breastplate, the writer sets forth the beauty of the woven-work and the precious stones of the mystic raiment, and the hidden meaning of that division into woven-work and precious stones, which being done, he expounds the comparison drawn by him, showing that faith must be woven in with works, and adds a short summary of the same faith, as concerning the Son.

1. Enough hath been said, as I think, your sacred Majesty, in the book preceding to show that the Son of God is an eternal being, not diverse from the Father, begotten, not created: we have also proved, from passages of the Scriptures, that God's true Son is God, and is declared so to be by the evident tokens of His Majesty.

2. Wherefore, albeit what hath already been set forth is plentiful even to overflowing for maintaining the Faith—seeing that the greatness of a river is mostly judged of from the manner in which its springs rise and flow forth—still, to the end that our belief may be the plainer to sight, the waters of our spring ought, methinks, to be parted off into three channels. There are, then, firstly, plain tokens declaring essential inherence in the Godhead; secondly, the expressions of the likeness of the Father and the Son; and lastly, those of the undoubtable unity of the Divine Majesty. Now of the first sort are the names "begetting," "God," "Son," "The Word;" of the second, "brightness," "expression," "mirror," "image;" and of the third, "wisdom," "power," "truth," "life."

3. These tokens so declare the nature of the Son, that by them you may know both that the Father is eternal, and that the Son is not diverse from Him; for the source of generation is He Who is, and as begotten of the Eternal, He is God; coming forth from the Father, He is the Son; from God, He is the Word; He is the radiance of the Father's glory, the expression of His substance, the counterpart of God, the image of His majesty; the Bounty of Him Who is bountiful, the Wisdom of Him Who is wise, the Power of the Mighty One, the Truth of Him Who is true, the Life of the Living One. In agreement, therefore, stand the attributes of Father and Son, that none may suppose any diversity, or doubt but that they are of one Majesty. For each and all of these names would we furnish examples of their use were we not constrained by a desire to maintain our discourse within bounds.

4. Of these twelve, as of twelve precious stones, is the pillar of our faith built up. For these are the precious stones—sardius, jasper, smaragd, chrysolite, and the rest,—woven into the robe of holy Aaron, even of him who bears the likeness of Christ, that is, of the true Priest; stones set in gold, and inscribed with the names of the sons of Israel, twelve stones close joined and fitting one into another, for if any should sunder or separate them, the whole fabric of the faith falls in ruins.

5. This, then, is the foundation of our faith—to know that the Son of God is begotten; if He be not begotten, neither is He the Son. Nor yet is it sufficient to call Him Son, unless you shall also distinguish Him as the Only-begotten Son. If He is a creature, He is not God; if He is not God, He is not the Life; if He is not the Life, then is He not the Truth.

6. The first three tokens, therefore, that is to say, the names "generation," "Son," "Only-begotten," do show that the Son is of God originally and by virtue of His own nature.

7. The three that follow—to wit, the names "God," "Life," "Truth," reveal His Power, whereby He hath laid the foundations of, and upheld, the created world. "For," as Paul said, "in Him we live and move and have our being;" and therefore, in the first three the Son's natural right, in the other three the unity of action subsisting between Father and Son is made manifest.

8. The Son of God is also called the "image" and "effulgence" and "expression" [of God], for these names have disclosed the Father's incomprehensible and unsearchable Majesty

dwelling in the Son, and the expression of His likeness in Him. These three names, then, as we see, refer to [the Son's] likeness [to the Father].

9. We have yet the operations of Power, Wisdom, and Justice left, wherewith, severally, to prove [the Son's] eternity.

10. This, then, is that robe, adorned with precious stones; this is the amice of the true Priest; this the bridal garment; here is the inspired weaver, who well knew how to weave that work. No common woven work is it, whereof the Lord spake by His Prophet: "Who gave to women their skill in weaving?' No common stones again, are they—stones, as we find them called, "of filling;" for all perfection depends on this condition, that there be nought lacking. They are stones joined together and set in gold—that is, of a spiritual kind; the joining of them by our minds and their setting in convincing argument. Finally Scripture teaches us how far from common are these stones, inasmuch as, whilst some brought one kind, and others another, of less precious offerings, these the devout princes brought, wearing them upon their shoulders, and made of them the "breastplate of judgment," that is, a piece of woven work. Now we have a woven work, when faith and action go together.

11. Let none suppose me to be misguided, in that I made at first a threefold division, each part containing four, and afterwards a fourfold division, each part containing three terms. The beauty of a good thing pleases the more, if it be shown under various aspects. For those are good things, whereof the texture of the priestly robe was the token, that is to say, either the Law, or the Church, which latter hath made two garments for her spouse, as it is written —the one of action, the other of spirit, weaving together the threads of faith and works. Thus, in one place, as we read, she makes a groundwork of gold, and afterwards weaves thereon blue, and purple, with scarlet, and white. Again, [as we read] elsewhere, she first makes little flowerets of blue and other colours, and attaches gold, and there is made a single priestly robe, to the end that adornments of diverse grace and beauty, made up of the same bright colours, may gain fresh glory by diversity of arrangement.

12. Moreover (to complete our interpretation of these types), it is certain that by refined gold and silver are designated the oracles of the Lord, whereby our faith stands firm. "The oracles of the Lord are pure oracles, silver tried in the fire, refined of dross, purified seven times." Now blue is like the air we breathe and draw in; purple, again, represents the appearance of water; scarlet signifies fire; and white linen, earth, for its origin is in the earth. Of these four elements, again, the human body is composed.

13. Whether, then, you join to faith already present in the soul, bodily acts agreeing thereto; or acts come first, and faith be joined as their companion, presenting them to God—here is the robe of the minister of religion, here the priestly vestment.

14. Faith is profitable, therefore, when her brow is bright with a fair crown of good works. This faith—that I may set the matter forth shortly—is contained in the following principles, which cannot be overthrown. If the Son had His origin in nothing, He is not Son; if He is a creature, He is not the Creator; if He was made, He did not make all things; if He needs to learn, He hath no foreknowledge; if He is a receiver, He is not perfect; if He progress, He is not God. If He is unlike (the Father) He is not the (Father's) image; if He is Son by grace, He is not such by nature; if He have no part in the Godhead, He hath it in Him to sin. "There is none good, but Godhead."

Chapter I.

The Arian argument from S. Mark x. 18, "There is none good but one, that is, God," refuted by explanation of these words of Christ.

15. The objection I have now to face, your sacred Majesty, fills me with bewilderment, my soul and body faint at the thought that there should be men, or rather not men, but beings with the outward appearance of men, but inwardly full of brutish folly—who can, after receiving at

the hands of the Lord benefits so many and so great, say that the Author of all good things is Himself not good.

16. It is written, say they, that "There is none good but God alone." I acknowledge the Scripture—but there is no falsehood in the letter; would that there were none in the Arians' exposition thereof. The written signs are guiltless, it is the meaning in which they are taken that is to blame. I acknowledge the words as the words of our Lord and Saviour—but let us bethink ourselves when, to whom, and with what comprehension He speaks.

17. The Son of God is certainly speaking as man, and speaking to a scribe,—to him, that is, who called the Son of God "Good Master," but would not acknowledge Him as God. What he believes not, Christ further gives him to understand, to the end that he may believe in God's Son not as a good master, but as the good God, for if, wheresoever the "One God" is named, the Son of God is never sundered from the fulness of that unity, how, when God alone is said to be good, can the Only-begotten be excluded from the fulness of Divine Goodness? The Arians must therefore either deny that the Son of God is God, or confess that God is good.

18. With divinely inspired comprehension, then, our Lord said, *not* "There is none good but the Father alone," but "There is none good but God alone," and "Father" is the proper name of Him Who begets. But the unity of God by no means excludes the Godhead of the Three Persons, and therefore it is His Nature that is extolled. Goodness, therefore, is of the nature of God, and in the nature of God, again, exists the Son of God—wherefore that which the predicate expresses belongs not to one single Person, but to the [complete] unity [of the Godhead].

19. The Lord, then, doth not deny His goodness—He rebukes this sort of disciple. For when the scribe said, "Good Master," the Lord answered, "Why callest thou Me good?"—which is to say, "It is not enough to call Him good, Whom thou believest not to be God." Not such do I seek to be My disciples—men who rather consider My manhood and reckon Me a good master, than look to My Godhead and believe Me to be the good God."

Chapter II.

The goodness of the Son of God is proved from His works, namely, His benefits that He showed towards the people of Israel under the Old Covenant, and to Christians under the New. It is to one's own interest to believe in the goodness of Him Who is one's Lord and Judge. The Father's testimony to the Son. No small number of the Jewish people bear witness to the Son; the Arians therefore are plainly worse than the Jews. The words of the Bride, declaring the same goodness of Christ.

20. Howbeit, I would not that the Son should rely on the mere prerogative of His nature and the claims of peculiar rights of His Majesty. Let us not call Him good, if He merit not the title; and if He merit not this by works, by acts of lovingkindness, let Him waive the right He enjoys by virtue of His nature, and be submitted to our judgment. He Who is to judge us disdains not to be brought to judgment, that He may be "justified in His saying, and clear when He is judged."

21. Is He then not good, Who hath shown me good things? Is He not good, Who when six hundred thousand of the people of the Jews fled before their pursuers, suddenly opened the tide of the Red Sea, an unbroken mass of waters?—so that the waves flowed round the faithful, and were walls to them, but poured back and overwhelmed the unbelievers.

22. Is He not good, at Whose command the seas became firm ground for the feet of them that fled, and the rocks gave forth water for the thirsty? so that the handiwork of the true Creator might be known, when the fluid became solid, and the rock streamed with water? That we might acknowledge this as the handiwork of Christ, the Apostle said: "And that rock was Christ."

23. Is He not good, Who in the wilderness fed with bread from heaven such countless thousands of the people, lest any famine should assail them, without need of toil, in the enjoyment of rest?—so that, for the space of forty years, their raiment grew not old, nor were

their shoes worn, a figure to the faithful of the Resurrection that was to come, showing that neither the glory of great deeds, nor the beauty of the power wherewith He hath clothed us, nor the stream of human life is made for nought?

24. Is He not good, Who exalted earth to heaven, so that, just as the bright companies of stars reflect His glory in the sky, as in a glass, so the choirs of apostles, martyrs, and priests, shining like glorious stars, might give light throughout the world.

25. Not only, then, is He good, but He is more. He is a good Shepherd, not only for Himself, but to His sheep also, "for the good shepherd layeth down his life for his sheep." Aye, He laid down His life to exalt ours—but it was in the power of His Godhead that He laid it down and took it again: "I have power to lay down My life, and I have power to take it. No man taketh it from Me, but I lay it down of Myself."

26. Thou seest His goodness, in that He laid it down of His own accord: thou seest His power, in that He took it again—dost thou deny His goodness, when He has said of Himself in the Gospel, "If I am good, why is thine eye evil"? Ungrateful wretch what doest thou? Dost thou deny His goodness, in Whom is thy hope of good things—if, indeed, thou believest this? Dost thou deny His goodness, Who hath given us what "eye hath not seen, nor ear heard?"

27. It concerns my interest to believe Him to be good, for "It is a good thing to trust in the Lord." It is to my interest to confess Him Lord, for it is written: "Give thanks unto the Lord, for He is good."

28. It is to my interest to esteem my Judge to be good, for the Lord is a righteous Judge to the house of Israel. If, then, the Son of God is Judge, surely, seeing that the Judge is the righteous God and the Son of God is Judge, [it follows that] He who is Judge and Son of God is the righteous God.

29. But perchance thou believest not others, nor the Son. Hear, then, the Father saying: "My heart hath brought forth out of its depth the good Word." The Word, then, is good—the Word, of Whom it is written: "And the Word was with God, and the Word was God." If, therefore, the Word is good, and the Son is the Word of God, surely, though it displease the Arians, the Son of God is God. Let them now at least blush for shame.

30. The Jews used to say: "He is good." Though some said: "He is not," yet others said: "He is good,"—and ye do *all* deny His goodness.

31. He is good who forgives the sin of one man; is He not good Who has taken away the sin of the world? For it was of Him that it was said: "Behold the Lamb of God, behold Him Who taketh away the sin of the world."

32. But why do we doubt? The Church hath believed in His goodness all these ages, and hath confessed its faith in the saying: "Let Him kiss me with the kisses of His mouth; for thy breasts are better than wine;" and again: "And thy throat is like the goodliest wine." Of His goodness, therefore. He nourisheth us with the breasts of the Law and Grace, soothing men's sorrows with telling them of heavenly things; and do we, then, deny His goodness, when He is the manifestation of goodness, expressing in His Person the likeness of the Eternal Bounty, even as we showed above that it was written, that He is the spotless reflection and counterpart of that Bounty?

Chapter III.

Forasmuch as God is One, the Son of God is God, good and true.

33. Yet what think ye, who deny the goodness and true Godhead of the Son of God, though it is written that there is no God but One? For although there be gods so-called, would you reckon Christ amongst them which are called gods, but are not, seeing that eternity is of His Essence, and that beside Him there is none other that is good and true God, forasmuch as God is in Him; whilst it follows from the very nature of the Father, that after Him there is no other true God, because God is One, neither confounding [the Persons of] the Father and Son, as the

Sabellians do, nor, like the Arians, severing the Father and the Son. For the Father and the Son, as Father and Son, are distinct persons, but they admit no division of their Godhead.

Chapter IV.
The omnipotence of the Son of God, demonstrated on the authority of the Old and the New Testament.

34. Seeing, then, that the Son of God is true and good, surely He is Almighty God. Can there be yet any doubt on this point? We have already cited the place where it is read that "the Lord Almighty is His Name." Because, then, the Son is Lord, and the Lord is Almighty, the Son of God is Almighty.

35. But hear also such a passage as you can build no doubts upon: "Behold, He cometh," saith the Scripture, "with the clouds, and every eye shall see Him, and they which pierced Him, and all the tribes of the earth shall mourn because of Him. Yea, amen. I am Alpha and Omega, saith the Lord God, Who is, and Who was, and Who is to come, the Almighty." Whom, I ask, did they pierce? For Whose coming hope we but the Son's? Therefore, Christ is Almighty Lord, and God.

36. Hear another passage, your sacred Majesty,—hear the voice of Christ. "Thus saith the Lord Almighty: After His glory hath He sent me against the nations which have made spoil of you, forasmuch as he that toucheth you is as he that toucheth the pupil of His eye. For lo, I lay my hand upon them which despoiled you, and I will save you, and they shall be for a spoil, which made spoil of you, and they shall know that the Lord Almighty hath sent Me." Plainly, He Who speaks is the Lord Almighty, and He Who hath sent is the Lord Almighty. By consequence, then, almighty power appertains both to the Father and to the Son; nevertheless, it is One Almighty God, for there is oneness of Majesty.

37. Moreover, that your most excellent Majesty may know that it is Christ which hath spoken as in the Gospel, so also in the prophet, He saith by the mouth of Isaiah, as though foreordaining the Gospel: "I Myself, Who spake, am come," that is to say, I, Who spake in the Law, am present in the Gospel.

38. Elsewhere, again, He saith: "All things that the Father hath are Mine." What meaneth He by "all things"? Clearly, not things created, for all these were made by the Son, but the things that the Father hath—that is to say, Eternity, Sovereignty, Godhead, which are His possession, as begotten of the Father. We cannot, then, doubt that He is Almighty, Who hath all things that the Father hath (for it is written: "All things that the Father hath are Mine").

Chapter V.
Certain passages from Scripture, urged against the Omnipotence of Christ, are resolved; the writer is also at especial pains to show that Christ not seldom spoke in accordance with the affections of human nature.

39. Although it is written concerning God, "Blessed and only Potentate," yet I have no misgiving that the Son of God is thereby severed from Him, seeing that the Scripture entitled God, not the Father by Himself, the "only Potentate." The Father Himself also declares by the prophet, concerning Christ, that "I have set help upon one that is mighty." It is not the Father alone, then, Who is the only Potentate; God the Son also is Potentate, for in the Father's praise the Son is praised too.

40. Aye, let some one show what there is that the Son of God cannot do. Who was His helper, when He made the heavens,—Who, when He laid the foundations of the world? Had He any need of a helper to set men free, Who needed none in constituting angels and principalities?

41. "It is written," say they: "'My Father, if it be possible, take away this cup from Me.' If, then, He is Almighty, how comes He to doubt of the possibility?" Which means that, because I have proved Him to be Almighty, I have proved Him unable to doubt of possibility.

42. The words, you say, are the words of Christ. True—consider, though, the occasion of His speaking them, and in what character He speaks. He hath taken upon Him the substance of

man, and therewith its affections. Again, you find in the place above cited, that "He went forward a little further, and fell on His face, praying, and saying: Father, if it be possible." Not as God, then, but as man, speaketh He, for could God be ignorant of the possibility or impossibility of aught? Or is anything impossible for God, when the Scripture saith: "For Thee nothing is impossible"?

43. Of Whom, howbeit, does He doubt—of Himself, or of the Father? Of Him, surely, Who saith: "Take away from Me,"—being moved as man is moved to doubt. The prophet reckons nothing impossible with God. The prophet doubts not; think you that the Son doubts? Wilt thou put God lower than man? What—God hath doubts of His Father, and is fearful at the thought of death! Christ, then, is afraid—afraid, whilst Peter fears nothing. Peter saith: "I will lay down my life for Thy sake." Christ saith: "My soul is troubled."

44. Both records are true, and it is equally natural that the person who is the less should not fear, as that He Who is the greater should endure this feeling, for the one has all a man's ignorance of the might of death, whilst the other, as being God inhabiting a body, displays the weakness of the flesh, that the wickedness of those who deny the mystery of the Incarnation might have no excuse. Thus, then, hath He spoken, yet the Manichaean believed not; Valentinus denied, and Marcion judged Him to be a ghost.

45. But indeed He so far put Himself on a level with man, such as He showed Himself to be in the reality of His bodily frame, as to say, "Nevertheless, not as I will, but as Thou wilt," though truly it is Christ's especial power to will what the Father wills, even as it is His to do what the Father doeth.

46. Here, then, let there be an end of the objection which it is your custom to oppose to us, on the ground that the Lord said, "Not as I will, but as Thou wilt;" and again, "For this cause I came down from heaven, not to do My own will, but the will of Him that sent Me."

Chapter VI.

The passages of Scripture above cited are taken as an occasion for a digression, wherein our Lord's freedom of action is proved from the ascription to the Spirit of such freedom, and from places where it is attributed to the Son.

47. Let us now, for the present, explain more fully why our Lord said, "If it be possible," and so call a truce, as it were, while we show that He possessed freedom of will. Ye deny—so far are ye gone in the way of iniquity—that the Son of God had a free will. Moreover, it is your wont to detract from the Holy Spirit, though you cannot deny that it is written: "The Spirit doth breathe, where He will." "Where He will," saith the Scripture, not "where He is ordered." If, then, the Spirit doth breathe where He will, cannot the Son do what He will? Why, it is the very same Son of God Who in His Gospel saith that the Spirit has power to breathe where He will. Doth the Son, therefore, confess the Spirit to be greater, in that He has power to do what is not permitted to Himself?

48. The Apostle also saith that "all is the work of one and the same Spirit, distributing to each according to His will." "According to His will," mark you—that is, according to the judgment of a free will, not in obedience to compulsion. Furthermore, the gifts distributed by the Spirit are no mean gifts, but such works as God is wont to do,—the gift of healing and of working deeds of power. While the Spirit, then, distributes as He will, the Son of God cannot set free whom He will. But hear Him speak when He does even as He will: "I have willed to do Thy will, O my God;" and again: "I will offer Thee a freewill offering."

49. The holy Apostle later knew that Jesus had it in His power to do as He would, and therefore, seeing Him walk upon the sea, said: "Lord, if it be Thou, bid me come to Thee over the waters." Peter believed that if Christ commanded, the natural conditions could be changed, so that water might support human footsteps, and things discrepant be reduced to harmony and agreement. Peter asks of Christ to command, not to request: Christ requested not, but commanded, and it was done—and Arius denies it!

50. What indeed is there that the Father will have, but the Son will not, or that the Son will have, but the Father will not? "The Father quickeneth whom He will," and the Son quickeneth whom He will, even as it is written. Tell me now whom the Son hath quickened, and the Father would not quicken. Since, however, the Son quickeneth whom He will, and the action [of Father and Son] is one, you see that not only doeth the Son the Father's will, but the Father also doeth the Son's. For what is quickening but quickening through the passion of Christ? But the passion of Christ is the Father's will. Whom, therefore, the Son quickeneth, He quickeneth by the will of the Father; therefore their will is one.

51. Again, what was the will of the Father, but that Jesus should come into the world and cleanse us from our sins? Hear the words of the leper: "If Thou wilt, Thou canst make me clean." Christ answered, "I will," and straightway health, the effect, followed. See you not that the Son is master of His own will, and Christ's will is the same as the Father's. Indeed, seeing that He hath said, "All things that the Father hath are Mine," nothing of a certainty being excepted, the Son hath the same will that the Father hath.

Chapter VII.
The resolution of the difficulty set forth for consideration is again taken in hand. Christ truly and really took upon Him a human will and affections, the source of whatsoever was not in agreement with His Godhead, and which must be therefore referred to the fact that He was at the same time both God and an.

52. There is, therefore, unity of will where there is unity of working; for in God His will issues straightway in actual effect. But the will of God is one, and the human will another. Further, to show that life is the object of human will, because we fear death, whilst the passion of Christ depended on the Divine Will, that He should suffer for us, the Lord said, when Peter would have detained Him from suffering: "Thou savourest not of the things which be of God, but the things which be of men."

53. My will, therefore, He took to Himself, my grief. In confidence I call it grief, because I preach His Cross. Mine is the will which He called His own, for as man He bore my grief, as man He spake, and therefore said, "Not as I will, but as Thou wilt." Mine was the grief, and mine the heaviness with which He bore it, for no man exults when at the point to die. With me and for me He suffers, for me He is sad, for me He is heavy. In my stead, therefore, and in me He grieved Who had no cause to grieve for Himself.

54. Not Thy wounds, but mine, hurt Thee, Lord Jesus; not Thy death, but our weakness, even as the Prophet saith: "For He is afflicted for our sakes" —and we, Lord, esteemed Thee afflicted, when Thou grievedst not for Thyself, but for me.

55. And what wonder if He grieved for all, Who wept for one? What wonder if, in the hour of death, He is heavy for all, Who wept when at the point to raise Lazarus from the dead? *Then,* indeed, He was moved by a loving sister's tears, for they touched His human heart,—here by secret grief He brought it to pass that, even as His death made an end of death, and His stripes healed our scars, so also His sorrow took away our sorrow.

56. As being man, therefore, He doubts; as man He is amazed. Neither His power nor His Godhead is amazed, but His soul; He is amazed by consequence of having taken human infirmity upon Him. Seeing, then, that He took upon Himself a soul He also took the affections of a soul, for God could not have been distressed or have died in respect of His being God. Finally, He cried: "My God, My God, why hast Thou forsaken Me?" As being man, therefore, He speaks, bearing with Him my terrors, for when we are in the midst of dangers we think ourself abandoned by God. As man, therefore, He is distressed, as man He weeps, as man He is crucified.

57. For so hath the Apostle Paul likewise said: "Because they have crucified the flesh of Christ." And again the Apostle Peter saith: "Christ having suffered according to the flesh." It was the flesh, therefore, that suffered; the Godhead above secure from death; to suffering His body yielded, after the law of human nature; can the Godhead die, then, if the soul cannot?"

"Fear not them," said our Lord, "which can kill the body, but cannot kill the soul." If the soul, then, cannot be killed, how can the Godhead?

58. When we read, then, that the Lord of glory was crucified, let us not suppose that He was crucified as in His glory. It is because He Who is God is also man, God by virtue of His Divinity, and by taking upon Him of the flesh, the man Christ Jesus, that the Lord of glory is said to have been crucified; for, possessing both natures, that is, the human and the divine, He endured the Passion in His humanity, in order that without distinction He Who suffered should be called both Lord of glory and Son of man, even as it is written: "Who descended from heaven."

Chapter VIII.
Christ's saying, "The Father is greater than I," is explained in accordance with the principle just established. Other like sayings are expounded in like fashion. Our Lord cannot, as touching His Godhead, be called inferior to the Father.

59. It was due to His humanity, therefore, that our Lord doubted and was sore distressed, and rose from the dead, for that which fell doth also rise again. Again, it was by reason of His humanity that He said those words, which our adversaries use to maliciously turn against Him: "Because the Father is greater than I."

60. But when in another passage we read: "I came out from the Father, and am come into the world; again, I leave the world, and go to the Father," how doth He go, except through death, and how comes He, save by rising again? Furthermore, He added, in order to show that He spake concerning His Ascension: "Therefore have I told you before it come to pass, in order that, when it shall have come to pass, ye may believe." For He was speaking of the sufferings and resurrection of His body, and by that resurrection they who before doubted were led to believe—for, indeed, God, Who is always present in every place, passes not from place to place. As it is a man who goes, so it is He Himself Who comes. Furthermore, He says in another place: "Rise, let us go hence." In that, therefore, doth He go and come, which is common to Him and to us.

61. How, indeed, can He be a lesser God when He is perfect and true God? Yet in respect of His humanity He is less—and still you wonder that speaking in the person of a man He called the Father greater than Himself, when in the person of a man He called Himself a worm, and not a man, saying: "But I am a worm, and no man;" and again: "He was led as a sheep to the slaughter."

62. If you pronounce Him less than the Father in this respect, I cannot deny it; nevertheless, to speak in the words of Scripture, He was not begotten inferior, but "made lower," that is, *made* inferior. And how was He "made lower," except that, "being in the form of God, He thought it not a prey that He should be equal with God, but emptied Himself;" not, indeed, parting with what He was, but taking up what He was not, for "He took the form of a servant."

63. Moreover, to the end that we might know Him to have been "made lower," by taking upon Him a body, David has shown that he is prophesying of a man, saying: "What is man, that Thou art mindful of him, or the son of man, but that Thou visitest him? Thou hast made him a little lower than the angels." And in interpreting this same passage the Apostle says: "For we see Jesus, made a little lower than the angels, crowned with glory and honour because that He suffered death. in order that apart from God He might taste death for all."

64. Thus, the Son of God was made lower than, not only the Father, but angels also. And if you will turn this to His dishonour; [I ask] is then the Son, in respect of His Godhead, less than His angels who serve Him and minister to Him? Thus, in your purpose to diminish His honour, you run into the blasphemy of exalting the nature of angels above the Son of God. But "the servant is not above his master." Again, angels ministered to Him even after His Incarnation, to the end that you should acknowledge Him to have suffered no loss of majesty by reason of His

bodily nature, for God could not submit to any loss of Himself, whilst that which He has taken of the Virgin neither adds to nor takes away from His divine power.

65. He, therefore, possessing the fulness of Divinity and glory, is not, in respect of His Divinity, inferior. Greater and less are distinctions proper to corporeal existences; one who is greater is so in respect of rank, or qualities, or at any rate of age. These terms lose their meaning when we come to treat of the things of God. He is commonly entitled the greater who instructs and informs another, but it is not the case with God's Wisdom that it has been built up by teaching received from another, forasmuch as Itself hath laid the foundation of all teaching. But how wisely wrote the Apostle: "In order that apart from God He might taste death for all,"— lest we should suppose the Godhead, not the flesh, to have endured that Passion!

66. If our opponents, then, have found no means to prove [the Father] greater [than the Son], let them not pervert words unto false reports, but seek out their meaning. I ask them, therefore, as touching what do they esteem the Father the greater? If it is because He is the Father, then [I answer] here we have no question of age or of time—the Father is not distinguished by white hairs, nor the Son by youthfulness—and it is on these conditions that the greater dignity of a father depends." But "father" and "son" are names, the one of the parent, the other of the child—names which seem to join rather than separate; for dutifulness inspires no loss of personal worth, inasmuch as kinship binds men together, and does not rend them asunder.

67. If, then, they cannot make the order of nature a support for any questioning, let them now believe the witness [of Scripture]. Now the Evangelist testifies that the Son is not lower [than the Father] by reason of being the Son; nay, he even declares that, in being the Son, He is equal, saying, "For the Jews sought to kill Him for this cause, that not only did He break the Sabbath, but even called God His own Father, making Himself equal to God."

68. This is not what the Jews said—it is the Evangelist who testifies that, in calling Himself God's own Son, He made Himself equal to God, for the Jews are not presented as saying, "For this cause we sought to kill Him;" the Evangelist, speaking for himself, says, "For the Jews sought to kill Him for this cause." Moreover, he has discovered the cause, [in saying] that the Jews were stirred with desire to slay Him because, when as God He broke the Sabbath, and also claimed God as His own Father, He ascribed to Himself not only the majesty of divine authority in breaking the Sabbath, but also, in speaking of His Father, the right appertaining to eternal equality.

69. Most fitting was the answer which the Son of God made to these Jews, proving Himself the Son and equal of God. "Whatsoever things," He said, "the Father hath done, the Son doeth also in like wise." The Son, therefore, is both entitled and proved the equal of the Father—a true equality, which both excludes difference of Godhead, and discovers, together with the Son, the Father also, to Whom the Son is equal; for there is no equality where there is difference, nor again where there is but one person, inasmuch as none is by himself equal to himself. Thus hath the Evangelist shown why it is fitting that Christ should call Himself the Son of God, that is, make Himself equal with God.

70. Hence the Apostle, following this revelation, hath said: "He thought it not a prey that He should be equal with God." For that which a man has not he seeks to carry off as a prey. Equality with the Father, therefore, which, as God and Lord, He possessed in His own substance, He had not as a spoil wrongfully seized. Wherefore the Apostle added [the words]: "He took the form of a servant." Now surely a servant is the opposite of an equal. Equal, therefore, is the Son, in the form of God, but inferior in taking upon Him of the flesh and in His sufferings as a man. For how could *the same* nature be both lower and equal? And how, if [the Son] be inferior, can He do the same things, in like manner, as the Father doeth? How, indeed, can there be sameness of operation with diversity of power? Can the inferior ever work such effects as the greater, or can there be unity of operation where there is diversity of substance?

71. Admit, therefore, that Christ, as touching His Godhead, cannot be called inferior [to the Father]. Christ speaks to Abraham: "By Myself have I sworn." Now the Apostle shows that He Who swears by Himself cannot be lower than any. Thus he saith, "When God rewarded Abraham with His promise, He swore by Himself, forasmuch as He had none other that was greater, saying, Surely with blessing will I bless thee, and with multiplying will I multiply thee." Christ had, therefore, none greater, and for that cause sware He by Himself. Moreover, the Apostle has rightly added, "for men swear by one greater than themselves," forasmuch as men have one who is greater than themselves, but God hath none.

72. Otherwise, if our adversaries will understand this passage as referred to the Father, then the rest of the record does not agree with it. For the Father did not appear to Abraham, nor did Abraham wash the feet of God the Father, but the feet of Him in Whom is the image of the man that shall be. Moreover, the Son of God saith, "Abraham saw My day, and rejoiced." It is He, therefore, Who sware by Himself, [and] Whom Abraham saw.

73. And how, indeed, hath He any greater than Himself Who is one with the Father in Godhead? Where there is unity, there is no dissimilarity, whereas between greater and less there is a distinction. The teaching, therefore, of the instance from Scripture before us, with regard to the Father and the Son, is that neither is the Father greater, nor hath the Son any that is above Him, inasmuch as in Father and Son there is no difference of Godhead parting them, but one majesty.

Chapter IX.

The objection that the Son, being sent by the Father, is, in that regard at least, inferior, is met by the answer that He was also sent by the Spirit, Who is yet not considered greater than the Son. Furthermore, the Spirit, in His turn, is sent by the Father to the Son, in order that Their unity in action might be shown forth. It is our duty, therefore, carefully to distinguish what utterances are to be fitly ascribed to Christ as God, and what to be ascribed to Him as man.

74. I Have no fears in the matter of that commonly advanced objection, that Christ is inferior because He was sent. For even if He be inferior, yet this is not so proved; on the other hand, His equal title to honour is in truth proved. Since all honour the Son as they honour the Father, it is certain that the Son is not, in so far as being sent, inferior.

75. Regard not, therefore, the narrow bounds of human language, but the plain meaning of the words, and believe facts accomplished. Bethink you that our Lord Jesus Christ said in Isaiah that He had been sent by the Spirit. Is the Son, therefore, less than the Spirit because He was sent by the Spirit? Thus you have the record, that the Son declares Himself sent by the Father and His Spirit. "I am the beginning," He saith, "and I live for ever, and My hand hath laid the foundations of the earth, My right hand hath made the heaven to stand abidingly;" and further on: "I have spoken, and I have called; I have brought him, and have made his way to prosper. Draw ye near to Me, and hear these things: not in secret have I spoken from the beginning. When they were made, I was there: and now hath the Lord and His Spirit sent Me." Here, indeed, He Who made the heaven and the earth Himself saith that He is sent by the Lord and His Spirit. Ye see, then, that the poverty of language takes not from the honour of His mission. He, then, is sent by the Father; by the Spirit also is He sent.

76. And that you may gather that there is no separating difference of majesty, the Son in turn sends the Spirit, even as He Himself hath said: "But when the Comforter is come, whom I will send you from My Father—the Spirit of truth, who cometh forth from My Father." That this same Comforter is also to be sent by the Father He has already taught, saying, "But the Comforter, that Holy Spirit, whom the Father will send in My name." Behold their unity, inasmuch as whom God the Father sends, the Son sends also, and Whom the Father sends, the Spirit sends also. Else, if the Arians will not admit that the Son was sent, because we read that the Son is the right hand of the Father, then they themselves will confess with respect to the

Father, what they deny concerning the Son, unless perchance they discover for themselves either another Father or another Son.

77. A truce, then, to vain wranglings over words, for the kingdom of God, as it is written, consisteth not in persuasive words, but in power plainly shown forth. Let us take heed to the distinction of the Godhead from the flesh. In each there speaks one and the same Son of God, for each nature is present in Him; yet while it is the same Person Who speaks, He speaks not always in the same manner. Behold in Him, now the glory of God, now the affections of man. As God He speaks the things of God, because He is the Word; as man He speaks the things of man, because He speaks in my nature.

78. "This is the living bread, which came down from heaven." This bread is His flesh, even as He Himself said: "This bread which I will give is My flesh." This is He Who came down from heaven, this is He Whom the Father hath sanctified and sent into this world. Even the letter itself teaches us that not the Godhead but the flesh needed sanctification, for the Lord Himself said, "And I sanctify Myself for them," in order that thou mayest acknowledge that He is both sanctified in the flesh for us, and sanctifies by virtue of His Divinity.

79. This is the same One Whom the Father sent, but "born of a woman, born under the law," as the Apostle hath said. This is He Who saith: "The Spirit of the Lord is upon Me; wherefore He hath anointed Me, to bring good tidings to the poor hath He sent Me:" This is He Who saith: My doctrine is not Mine, but His, Who sent Me. If any man will do His will, he shall know of the doctrine, whether it be of God, or whether I speak of Myself." Doctrine that is of God, then, is one thing; doctrine that is of man, another; and so when the Jews, regarding Him as man, called in question His teaching, and said, "How knoweth this man letters, having never learnt?" Jesus answered and said, "My doctrine is not Mine," for, in teaching without elegance of letters, He seems to teach not as man, but rather as God, having not learned, but devised His doctrine.

80. For He hath found and devised all the way of discipline, as we read above, inasmuch as of the Son of God it hath been said: "This is our God, and none other shall be accounted of in comparison with Him, Who hath found all the way of discipline. After these things He was seen on earth, and conversed with men." How, then, could He, as divine, not have His own doctrine—He Who hath found all the way of discipline before He was seen on earth? Or how is He inferior, of Whom it is said, "None shall be accounted of in comparison with Him"? Surely He is entitled incomparable, in comparison of Whom none other can be accounted of—yet so that He cannot be accounted of before the Father. Now if men suppose that the Father is spoken of, they shall not escape running into the blasphemy of Sabellius, of ascribing the assumption of human nature to the Father.

81. Let us proceed with what follows. "He who speaketh of himself, seeketh his own glory." See the unity wherein Father and Son are plainly revealed. He who speaks cannot but be; yet that which He speaks cannot be solely from Him, for in Him all that is, is naturally derived from the Father.

82. What now is the meaning of the words "seeketh his own glory"? That is, not a glory in which the Father has no part—for indeed the Word of God is His glory. Again, our Lord saith: "that they may see My glory." But that glory of the Word is also the glory of the Father, even as it is written: "The Lord Jesus Christ is in the glory of God the Father." In regard of His Godhead, therefore, the Son of God so hath His own glory, that the glory of Father and Son is one: He is not, therefore, inferior in splendour, for the glory is one, nor lower in Godhead, for the fulness of the Godhead is in Christ.

83. How, then, you ask, is it written, "Father, the hour is come; glorify Thy Son?" He Who saith these words needs to be glorified, say you. Thus far you have eyes to see; the remainder of the Scripture you have not read, for it proceeds: "that Thy Son may glorify Thee." Hath ever the Father need of any, in that He is to be glorified by the Son?

Chapter X.

The objection taken on the ground of the Son's obedience is disproved, and the unity of power, Godhead, and operation in the Trinity set forth, Christ's obedience to His mother, to whom He certainly cannot be called inferior, is noticed.

84. In like manner our adversaries commonly make a difficulty of the Son's obedience, forasmuch as it is written: "And being found in appearance as a man, He humbled Himself, and became obedient even unto death." The writer has not only told us that the Son was obedient even unto death, but also first shown that He was man, in order that we might understand that obedience unto death was the part not of His Godhead but of His Incarnation, whereby He took upon Himself both the functions and the names belonging to our nature.

85. Thus we have learnt that the power of the Trinity is one, as we are taught both in and after the Passion itself: for the Son suffers through His body, which is the earnest of it; the Holy Spirit is poured upon the apostles: into the Father's hands the spirit is commended; furthermore, God is with a mighty voice proclaimed the Father. We have learnt that there is one form, one likeness, one sanctification, of the Father and of the Son, one activity, one glory, finally, one Godhead.

86. There is, therefore, but one only God, for it is written: "Thou shall worship the Lord thy God, and Him only shalt thou serve." One God, not in the sense that the Father and the Son are the same Person, as the ungodly Sabellius affirms—but forasmuch as there is one Godhead of the Father and of the Son and of the Holy Ghost. But where there is one Godhead, there is one will, one purpose.

87. Again, that thou mayest know that the Father is, and the Son is, and that the work of the Father and of the Son is one, follow the saying of the Apostle: "Now may God Himself, and our Father, and our Lord Jesus Christ direct our way unto you." Both Father and Son are named, but there is unity of direction, because unity of power. So also in another place we read: "Now may our Lord Himself, Jesus Christ, and God and our Father, Who hath loved us, and given us eternal consolation, and good hope in grace, console and strengthen your hearts." How perfect a unity it is that the Apostle presents to us, insomuch that the fount of consolation is not many, but one. Let doubt be dumb, then, or, if it will not be overcome by reason, let the thought of our Lord's gracious kindliness bend it.

88. Let us call to mind how kindly our Lord hath dealt with us, in that He taught us not only faith but manners also. For, having taken His place in the form of man, He was subject to Joseph and Mary. Was He less than all mankind, then, because He was subject? The part of dutifulness is one, that of sovereignty is another, but dutifulness doth not exclude sovereignty. Wherein, then, was He subject to the Father's law? In His body, surely, wherein He was subject to His mother.

Chapter XI.

The purpose and healing effects of the Incarnation. The profitableness of faith, whereby we know that Christ bore all infirmities for our sakes,—Christ, Whose Godhead revealed Itself in His Passion; whence we understand that the mission of the Son of God entailed no subservience, which belief we need not fear lest it displease the Father, Who declares Himself to be well pleased in His Son.

89. Let us likewise deal kindly, let us persuade our adversaries of that which is to their profit, "let us worship and lament before the Lord our Maker." For we would not overthrow, but rather heal; we lay no ambush for them, but warn them as in duty bound. Kindliness often bends those whom neither force nor argument will avail to overcome. Again, our Lord cured with oil and wine the man who, going down from Jerusalem to Jericho, fell among thieves; having forborne to treat him with the harsh remedies of the Law or the sternness of Prophecy.

90. To Him, therefore, let all come who would be made whole. Let them receive the medicine which He hath brought down from His Father and made in heaven, preparing it of the juices of those celestial fruits that wither not. This is of no earthly growth, for nature nowhere

possesseth this compound. Of wondrous purpose took He our flesh, to the end that He might show that the law of the flesh had been subjected to the law of the mind. He was incarnate, that He, the Teacher of men, might overcome as man.

91. Of what profit would it have been to me, had He, as God, bared the arm of His power, and only displayed His Godhead inviolate? Why should He take human nature upon Him, but to suffer Himself to be tempted under the conditions of my nature and my weakness? It was right that He should be tempted, that He should suffer with me, to the end that I might know how to conquer when tempted, how to escape when hard pressed. He overcame by force of continence, of contempt of riches, of faith; He trampled upon ambition, fled from intemperance, bade wantonness be far from Him.

93. This medicine Peter beheld, and left His nets, that is to say, the instruments and security of gain, renouncing the lust of the flesh as a leaky ship, that receives the bilge, as it were, of multitudinous passions. Truly a mighty remedy, that not only removed the scar of an old wound, but even cut the root and source of passion. O Faith, richer than all treasure-houses; O excellent remedy, healing our wounds and sins!

93. Let us bethink ourselves of the profitableness of right belief. It is profitable to me to know that for my sake Christ bore my infirmities, submitted to the affections of my body, that for me, that is to say, for every man, He was made sin, and a curse, that for me and in me was He humbled and made subject, that for me He is the Lamb, the Vine, the Rock, the Servant, the Son of an handmaid, knowing not the day of judgment, for my sake ignorant of the day and the hour.

94. For how could He, Who hath made days and times, be ignorant of the day? How could He not know the day, Who hath declared both the season of Judgment to come, and the cause? A curse, then, He was made not in respect of His Godhead, but of His flesh; for it is written: "Cursed is every one that hangeth on a tree." In and after the flesh, therefore, He hung, and for this cause He, Who bore our curses, became a curse. He wept that thou, man, mightest not weep long. He endured insult, that thou mightest not grieve over the wrong done to thee.

95. A glorious remedy—to have consolation of Christ! For He bore these things with surpassing patience for our sakes—and we forsooth cannot bear them with common patience for the glory of His Name! Who may not learn to forgive, when assailed, seeing that Christ, even on the Cross, prayed,—yea, for them that persecuted Him? See you not that those weaknesses, as you please to call them, of Christ's are your *strength?* Why question Him in the matter of remedies for us? His tears wash us, His weeping cleanses us,—and there is strength in *this* doubt, at least, that if you begin to doubt, you will despair. The greater the insult, the greater is the gratitude due.

96. Even in the very hour of mockery and insult, acknowledge His Godhead. He hung upon the Cross, and all the elements did Him homage. The sun withdrew his rays, the daylight vanished, darkness came down and covered the land, the earth trembled; yet He Who hung there trembled not. What was it that these signs betokened, but reverence for the Creator? That He hangs upon the Cross—this, thou Arian, thou regardest; that He gives the kingdom of God—this, thou regardest not. That He tasted of death, thou readest, but that He also invited the robber into paradise, to this thou givest no heed. Thou dost gaze at the women weeping by the tomb, but not upon the angels keeping watch by it. What He *said,* thou readest: what He *did,* thou dost not read. Thou sayest that the Lord said to the Canaanitish woman: "I am not sent, but to the lost sheep of the house of Israel," thou dost not say that He did what He was besought by her to do.

97. Thou shouldst hereby understand that His being "sent" means not that He was compelled, at the command of another, but that He acted, of free will, according to His own judgment, otherwise thou dost accuse Him of despising His Father. For if, according to thine expounding, Christ had come into Jewry, as one executing the Father's commands, to relieve the inhabitants of Jewry, and none besides, and yet before that was accomplished, set free the

Canaanitish woman's daughter from her complaint, surely He was not only the executor of another's instruction, but was free to exercise His own judgment. But where there is freedom to act as one will, there can be no transgressing the terms of one's mission.

98. Fear not that the Son's act displeased the Father, seeing that the Son Himself saith: "Whatsoever things are His good pleasure, I do always," and "The works that I do, He Himself doeth." How, then, could the Father be displeased with that which He Himself did through the Son? For it is One God, Who, as it is written, "hath justified circumcision in consequence of faith, and uncircumcision through faith."

99. Read all the Scriptures, mark all diligently, you will then find that Christ so manifested Himself that God might be discerned in man. Misunderstand not maliciously the Son's exultation in the Father, when you hear the Father declaring His pleasure in the Son.

Chapter XII.

Do the Catholics or the Arians take the better course to assure themselves of the favour of Christ as their Judge? An objection grounded on Ps. cx. 1 is disposed of, it being shown that when the Son is invited by the Father to sit at His right hand, no subjection is intended to be signified—nor yet any preferment, in that the Son sits at the Father's right hand. The truth of the Trinity of Persons in God, and of the Unity of their Nature, is shown to be proved by the angelic Trisagion.

100. Howbeit, if our adversaries cannot be turned by kindness, let us summon them before the Judge. To what Judge, then, shall we go? Surely to Him Who hath the Judgment. To the Father, then? Nay, but "the Father judgeth no man, for He hath given all judgment to the Son." He hath given, that is to say, not as of largess, but in the act of generation. See, then, how unwilling He was that thou shouldst dishonour His Son—even so that He gave Him to be thy Judge.

101. Let us see, then, before the judgment which hath the better cause, thou or I? Surely it is the care of a prudent party to a suit to gain first the favourable regard of the judge. Thou dost honour man,—dost thou not honour God? Which of the two, I ask, wins the favour of the magistrate—respect or contempt? Suppose that I am in error—as I certainly am not: is Christ displeased with the honour shown Him? We are all sinners—who, then, will deserve forgiveness, he who renders worship, or he who displays insolence?

102. If reasoning move thee not, at least let the plain aspect of the judgment move thee! Raise thine eyes to the Judge, see Who it is that is seated, with Whom He is seated, and where. Christ sitteth at the right hand of the Father. If with thine eyes thou canst not perceive this, hear the words of the prophet: "The Lord said unto my Lord, Sit Thou on My right hand." The Son, therefore, sitteth at the right hand of the Father. Tell me now, thou who holdest that the things of God are to be judged of from the things of this world—say whether thou thinkest Him Who sits at the right hand to be lower? Is it any dishonour to the Father that He sits at the Son's left hand? The Father honours the Son, and thou makest it to be insult! The Father would have this invitation to be a sign of love and esteem, and thou wouldst make it an overlord's command! Christ hath risen from the dead, and sitteth at the right hand of God.

103. "But," you object, "the Father *said*." Good, hear now a passage where the Father doth not speak, and the Son prophesies: "Hereafter ye shall see the Son of Man sitting at the right hand of power." This He said with regard to taking back to Himself His body—to Him the Father said: "Sit Thou at My right hand." If indeed you ask of the eternal abode of the Godhead, He said—when Pilate asked Him whether He were the King of the Jews—"For this I was born." And so indeed the Apostle shows that it is good for us to believe that Christ sitteth at the right hand of God, not by command, nor of any boon, but as God's most dearly beloved Son. For it is written for you: "Seek the things that are above, where Christ is, sitting at the right hand of God; savour the things that are above." This is to savour the things that be above—to believe that Christ, in His sitting, does not obey as one who receives a command, but is

honoured as the well-beloved Son. It is with regard, then, to Christ's Body that the Father saith: "Sit Thou at My right hand, until I make Thine enemies Thy footstool."

104. If, again, you seek to pervert the sense of these words, "I will make Thine enemies Thy footstool," I answer that the Father also bringeth to the Son such as the Son raiseth up and quickeneth. For "No man," saith Christ, "can come to Me, except the Father, Which hath sent Me, draw him, and I will raise him up at the last day." And you say that the Son of God is subject by reason of weakness—the Son, to Whom the Father bringeth men that He may raise them up in the last day. Seemeth this in your eyes to be subjection, I pray you, where the kingdom is prepared for the Father, and the Father bringeth to the Son and there is no place for perversion of words, since the Son giveth the kingdom to the Father, and none is preferred before Him? For inasmuch as the Father rendereth to the Son, and the Son, again, to the Father, here are plain proofs of love and regard: seeing that They so render, the One to the Other, that neither He Who receiveth obtaineth as it were what was another's, nor He That rendereth loseth.

105. Moreover, the sitting at the right hand is no preferment, nor doth that at the left hand betoken dishonour, for there are no degrees in the Godhead, Which is bound by no limits of space or time, which are the weights and measures of our puny human minds. There is no difference of love, nothing that divideth the Unity.

106. But wherefore roam so far afield? Thou hast looked upon all around thee, thou hast seen the Judge, thou hast remarked the angels proclaiming Him. *They* praise, and *thou* revilest Him! Dominations and powers fall down before Him—thou speakest evil of His Name! All His Saints adore Him, but the Son of God adores not, nor the Holy Spirit. The seraphim say: "Holy, Holy, Holy!"

107. What meaneth this threefold utterance of the same name "Holy"? If thrice repeated, why is it but one act of praise? If one act of praise, why a threefold repetition? Why the threefold repetition, unless that the Father and the Son and the Holy Spirit are one in holiness? The seraph spake the name, not once, lest he should exclude the Son; not twice, lest he should pass by the Holy Spirit; not four times, lest he should conjoin created beings [in the praise of the Creator]. Furthermore, to show that the Godhead of the Trinity is One, he, after the threefold "Holy," added in the singular number "the Lord God of Sabaoth." Holy, therefore, is the Father, holy the Son, holy likewise the Spirit of God, and therefore is the Trinity adored, but adores not, and is praised, but praises not. As for me, I will rather believe as the seraphim, and adore after the manner of all the principalities and powers of heaven.

Chapter XIII.

The wicked and dishonourable opinions held by Arians, Sabellians, and Manichaeans as concerning their Judge are shortly refuted. Christ's remonstrances regarding the rest of His adversaries being set forth, St. Ambrose expresses a hope of milder judgment for himself.

108. Let us proceed, then, with your accusations, and see how you gain the favour of your Judge. Speak now, speak, I say, and tell Him: "I consider Thee, O Christ, to be unlike Thy Father;" and He will answer: "Mark, if thou canst, mark, I say, and tell Me wherein thou holdest Me to differ."

109. Say again: "I judge Thee to be a created being;" and Christ will reply: "If the witness of two men is true, oughtest thou not to have believed both Me and My Father, Who hath called Me His Son?"

110. Then you will say: "I deny Thy [perfect] goodness;" and He will answer: "Be it unto thee according to thy faith; so will I not be good to thee."

111. "That Thou art Almighty, I hold not;" and He will answer, in turn: "Then can I not forgive thee thy sins."

112. "Thou art a subject being." Whereto He will reply: "Why, then, dost thou seek freedom and pardon of Him Whom thou thinkest to be subject as a slave?"

113. I see your accusation halt here. I press you not, forasmuch as I myself know my own sins. I grudge you not pardon, for I myself would obtain indulgence, but I would know the object of your prayers. Look, then, whilst I recite before the Judge your desires. I betray not your sins, but look to behold your prayers and wishes set forth in their order.

114. Speak, therefore, those desires, which all alike would have granted to them. "Lord, make me in the image of God." Whereto He will answer: "In what image? The image which thou hast denied?"

115. "Make me incorruptible." Surely His reply will be: "How can I make thee incorruptible, I, Whom thou callest a created being, and so wouldst make out to be corruptible? The dead shall rise purified from corruption—dost thou call Him corruptible Whom thou seest to be God?"

116. "Be good to me." "Why dost thou ask what thou hast denied [to Me]? I would have had thee to be good, and I said 'Be ye holy, for I Myself am holy,' and thou settest thyself to deny that I am good? Dost *thou* then look for forgiveness of sins? Nay, none can forgive sins, but God alone. Seeing, then, that to thee I am not the true and only God, I cannot by any means forgive thee thy sins."

117. Thus let the followers of Arius and Photinus speak. "I deny Thy Godhead." To whom the Lord will make answer: "'The fool hath said in his heart: There is no God' Of whom, think you, is this said?—of Jew or Gentile, or of the devil. Whosoever he be of whom it is said, O disciple of Photinus, he is more to be borne with, who held his peace; thou, nevertheless, hast dared to lift up thy voice to utter it, that thou mightest be proved more foolish than the fool. Thou deniest My Godhead, whereas I said, 'Ye are gods, and ye are all the children of the Most Highest?' And thou deniest Him to be God, Whose godlike works thou seest around thee."

118. Let the Sabellian speak in his turn. "I consider Thee, by Thyself, to be at once Father and Son and Holy Spirit." To whom the Lord: "Thou hearest neither the Father nor the Son. Is there any doubt on this matter? The Scripture itself teaches thee that it is the Father Who giveth over the judgment, and the Son Who judges. Thou hast not given ear to My words: 'I am not alone, but I and the Father, Who sent Me.'"

119. Now let the Manichaean have his word. "I hold that the devil is the creator of our flesh." The Lord will answer him: "What, then, doest thou in the heavenly places? Depart, go thy way to thy creator. 'My will is that they be with Me, whom my Father hath given Me.' Thou, Manichaean, holdest thyself for a creature of the devil; hasten, then, to his abode, the place of fire and brimstone, where the fire thereof is not quenched, lest ever the punishment have an end."

120. I set aside other heretical—not persons, but portents. What manner of judgment awaits them, what shall be the form of their sentence? To all these He will, indeed, reply, rather in sorrow than in anger: "O My people, what have I done unto thee, wherein have I vexed thee? Did I not bring thee up out of Egypt, and lead thee out of the house of bondage into liberty?"

121. But it is not enough to have brought us out of Egypt into freedom, and to have saved us from the house of bondage: a greater boon than this, Thou hast given Thyself for us. Thou wilt say then: "Have I not borne all your sufferings? Have I not given My Body for you? Have I not sought death, which had no part in My Godhead, but was necessary for your redemption? Are *these* the thanks I am to receive? Is it this that My Blood hath gained, even as I spake in times past by the mouth of the prophet: 'What profit is there in My Blood, for that I have gone down to corruption?' Is this the profit, that you should wickedly deny Me—you, for whom I endured those things?"

122. As for me, Lord Jesu, though I am conscious within myself of great sin, yet will I say: "I have not denied Thee; Thou mayest pardon the infirmity of my flesh. My transgression I confess; my sin I deny not. If Thou wilt Thou canst make me clean. For this saying, the leper obtained his request. Enter not, I pray, into judgment with Thy servant. I ask, not that Thou mayest judge, but that Thou mayest forgive."

Chapter XIV.

The sentence of the Judge is set forth, the counterpleas of the opposers are considered, and the finality of the sentence, from which there is no appeal, proved.

123. What verdict do we look for from Christ? That do I know. Do I say, what verdict *will* He give? Nay, He hath already pronounced sentence. We have it in our hands. "Let all," saith He, "honour the Son, even as they honour the Father. He that honoureth not the Son, honoureth not the Father, Who hath sent Him."

124. If the sentence please you not, appeal to the Father, cancel the judgment that the Father hath given. Say that He hath a Son Who is unlike Him. He will reply: "Then have I lied, I, Who said to the Son, 'Let us make man in Our image and likeness.'"

125. Tell the Father that He hath created the Son, and He will answer: "Why, then, hast thou worshipped One Whom thou thoughtest to be a created being?"

126. Tell Him that He hath begotten a Son Who is inferior to Himself, and He will reply: "Compare Us, and let Us see."

127. Tell Him that you owed no credence to the Son, whereto He will answer: "Did I not say to thee, 'This is My well-beloved Son, in Whom I am well pleased: hear ye Him'?" What mean these words "hear ye Him," if not "Hear Him when He saith: 'All things that the Father hath are Mine'"? This did the apostles hear, even as it is written: "And they fell upon their faces, and were greatly afraid." If they who confessed Him fell to the earth, what shall they do who have denied Him? But Jesus laid His hand upon His apostles, and raised them up—you He will suffer to lie prone, that ye may see not the glory ye have denied.

128. Let us look to it, then, forasmuch as whom the Son condemneth, the Father condemneth also, and therefore let us honour the Son, even as we honour the Father, that by the Son we may be able to come to the Father.

Chapter XV.

St. Ambrose deprecates any praise of his own merits: in any case, the Faith is sufficiently defended by the authoritative support of holy Scripture, to whose voice the Arians, stubborn as the Jews, are deaf. He prays that they may be moved to love the truth; meanwhile, they are to be avoided, as heretics and enemies of Christ.

129. These arguments, your Majesty, I have set forth, briefly and summarily, in the rough, rather than in any form of full explanation and exact order. If indeed the Arians regard them as imperfect and unfinished, I indeed confess that they are scarce even begun; if they think that there be any still to be brought forward, I allow that there be well-nigh all; for whereas the unbelievers are in uttermost need of arguments, the faithful have enough and to spare. Indeed, Peter's single confession was abundant to warrant faith in Christ: "Thou art the Christ, the Son of the living God;" for it is enough to know His Divine Generation, without division or diminution, being neither derivation nor creation.

130. This, indeed, is declared in the books of Holy Writ, one and all, and yet is still doubted by misbelievers: "For," as it is written, "the heart of this people is become gross, and with their ears they have been dull of hearing, and their eyes have they darkened, lest ever they should see with their eyes, and hear with their ears, and understand in their heart." For, like the Jews, the Arians' wont is to stop their ears, or make an uproar, as often as the Word of salvation is heard.

131. And what wonder, if unbelievers doubt the word of man, when they refuse to believe the Word of God? The Son of God, as you will find it written in the Gospel, said: "Father, glorify Thy Name," and from heaven was heard the voice of the Father, saying: "I have both glorified it, and again will glorify." These words the unbelievers heard, but believed not. The Son spake, the Father answered, and the Jews said: "A peal of thunder answered Him;" others said: "An angel spake to Him."

132. Paul, moreover, as it is written in the Acts of the Apostles, when by the Voice of Christ he received the call of grace, several companions journeying with him at the same time, alone said that he had heard Christ's Voice. Thus, your sacred Majesty, he who believes, hears—and

he hears, that he may believe, whilst he who believes not, hears not, nay, he will not, he cannot hear, lest he should believe!

133. As for me, indeed, would that they might have a will to hear, that they might believe—to hear with true love and meekness, as men seeking what is true, and not assailing all truth. For it is written that we pay no heed to "endless fables and genealogies, which do rather raise disputes than set forward the godly edification, which is in faith. But the aim of the charge is love from a pure heart, and a good conscience, and faith unfeigned, whence some have erred and betaken themselves to empty babbling, desirous of being teachers of the law, without understanding the words they say, nor the things whereof they speak with assurance." In another place also the same Apostle saith: "But foolish and ignorant questionings do thou avoid."

134. Such men, who sow disputes—that is to say, heretics—the Apostle bids us leave alone. Of them he says in yet another place, that "certain shall depart from the faith, giving heed to deceitful spirits, and the doctrines of devils."

135. John, likewise, saith that heretics are Antichrists, plainly marking out the Arians. For this [Arian] heresy began to be after all other heresies, and hath gathered the poisons of all. As it is written of theAntichrist, that "he opened his mouth to blasphemy against God, to blaspheme His Name, and to make war with His saints," so do they also dishonour the Son of God, and His martyrs have they not spared. Moreover, that which perchance Antichrist will not do, they have falsified the holy Scriptures. And thus he who saith that Jesus is not the Christ, the same is Antichrist; he who denies the Saviour of the world, denies Jesus; he who denies the Son, denies the Father also, for it is written; "Every one which denieth the Son, denieth the Father likewise."

Chapter XVI.

St. Ambrose assures Gratian of victory, declaring that it has been foretold in the prophecies of Ezekiel. This hope is further stayed upon the emperor's piety, the former disasters being the punishment of Eastern heresy. The book closes with a prayer to God, that He will now show His mercy, and save the army, the land, and the sovereign of the faithful.

136. I Must no further detain your Majesty, in this season of preparation for war, and the achievement of victory over the Barbarians. Go forth, sheltered, indeed, under the shield of faith, and girt with the sword of the Spirit; go forth to the victory, promised of old time, and foretold in oracles given by God.

137. For Ezekiel, in those far-off days, already prophesied the minishing of our people, and the Gothic wars, saying: "Prophesy, therefore, Son of Man, and say: O Gog, thus saith the Lord—Shalt thou not, in that day when My people Israel shall be established to dwell in peace, rise up and come forth from thy place, from the far north, and many nations with thee, all riders upon horses, a great and mighty gathering, and the valour of many hosts? Yea, go up against my people Israel, as clouds to cover the land, in the last days."

138. That Gog is the Goth, whose coming forth we have already seen, and over whom victory in days to come is promised, according to the word of the Lord: "And they shall spoil them, who had been their despoilers, and plunder them, who had carried off their goods for a prey, saith the Lord. And it shall be in that day, that I will give to Gog"—that is, to the Goths—"a place that is famous, for Israel an high-heaped tomb of many men, of men who have made their way to the sea, and it shall reach round about, and close the mouth of the valley, and there [the house of Israel shall] overthrow Gog and all his multitude, and it shall be called the valley of the multitude of Gog: and the house of Israel shall overwhelm them, that the land may be cleansed."

139. Nor, furthermore, may we doubt, your sacred Majesty, that we, who have undertaken the contest with alien unbelief, shall enjoy the aid of the Catholic Faith that is strong in you. Plainly indeed the reason of God's wrath has been already made manifest, so that belief in the Roman Empire was first overthrown, where faith in God gave way.

140. No desire have I to recount the deaths, tortures, and banishments of confessors, the offices of the faithful made into presents for traitors. Have we not heard, from all along the border,—from Thrace, and through Dacia by the river, Moesia, and all Valeria of the Pannonians,—a mingled tumult of blasphemers preaching and barbarians invading? What profit could neighbours so bloodthirsty bring us, or how could the Roman State be safe with such defenders?

141. Enough, yea, more than enough, Almighty God, have we now atoned for the deaths of confessors, the banishment of priests, and the guilt of wickedness so overweening, by our own blood, our own banishment—sufficiently plain is it that they, who have broken faith, cannot be safe. Turn again, O Lord, and set up the banners of Thy faith.

142. No military eagles, no flight of birds, here lead the van of our army, but Thy Name, Lord Jesus, and Thy worship. This is no land of unbelievers, but the land whose custom it is to send forth confessors—Italy; Italy, ofttimes tempted, but never drawn away; Italy, which your Majesty hath long defended, and now again rescued from the barbarian. No wavering mind in our emperor, but faith firm fixed.

143. Show forth now a plain sign of Thy Majesty, that he who believes Thee to be the true Lord of Hosts, and Captain of the armies of heaven; he who believes that Thou art the true Power and Wisdom of God, no being of time nor of creation, but even as it is written, the eternal Power and Divinity of God, may, upheld by the aid of thy Might Supreme, win the prize of victory for his Faith.

BOOK III.

Chapter I.

Statement of the reasons wherefore the matters, treated of shortly in the two former, are dealt with more at length in the three later books. Defence of the employment of fables, which is supported by the example of Holy Writ, wherein are found various figures of poetic fable, in particular the Sirens, which are figures of sensual pleasures, and which Christians ought to be taught to avoid, by the words of Paul and the deeds of Christ.

1. Forasmuch as your most gracious Majesty had laid command upon me to write for your own instruction some treatise concerning the Faith, and had yourself called me to your presence and encouraged my timidity, I, being as one on the eve of battle, composed but two books only, for the pointing out of certain ways and paths by which our faith progresses.

2. Seeing, however, that certain malicious minds, bent on sowing disputes, have not yet exhausted the force of their assaults, whilst your gracious Majesty's pious anxiety calls me to further labours, inasmuch as you desire to try in more things him whom you have proved in a few, I am resolved to deal somewhat more particularly with the matters whereof I have already treated in a few words, lest it should be thought, not that I have advanced those propositions in quietness and confidence, but that I, having asserted them, doubted and so abandoned their defence.

3. Again, seeing that we spoke of the Hydra and Scylla (I. vi. 46), and brought them in by way of comparison, to show how we must beware, whether of the ever-renewed outgrowths of infidelity, or the ill-omened shipwrecks made upon its shallows, if any one holds that such embellishments of an argument, borrowed from the romances of poets, are unlawful, and, from lack of opportunity to speak evil of my faith, assails something in my language, then let him know that not only phrases but complete verses of poetry have been woven into the text of Holy Writ.

4. Whence, for instance, came that verse, "His offspring truly are we," whereof Paul, by prophetic experience, taught, makes use? The course of prophetic speech avoids neither the Giants nor the Valley of the Titans, and Isaiah spake of sirens and the daughters of ostriches. Jeremiah also hath prophesied concerning Babylon, that the daughters of sirens shall dwell therein, in order to show that the snares of Babylon, that is, of the tumult of this world, are to be likened to stories of old-time lust, that seemed upon this life's rocky shores to sing some tuneful song, but deadly withal, to catch the souls of youth,—which the Greek poet himself tells us that the wise man escaped through being bound, as it were, in the chains of his own prudence. So hard a thing, before Christ's coming, was it esteemed, even for the stronger, to save themselves from the deceitful shows and allurements of pleasure.

5. But if the poet judged the enticement of worldly pleasure and licence destructive of men's minds and a sure cause of shipwreck, what ought we to think, for whom it hath been written: "Train not the flesh in concupiscence"? And again: "I chastise my body and bring it into servitude, lest whilst I preach to others, I myself become a castaway."

6. Truly, Christ won salvation for us, not by luxury but by fasting. Moreover, it was not to obtain favour for Himself, but to instruct us, that He fasted. Nor yet did He hunger because He was overcome by the weakness of the body, but by His hunger He proved that He had verily taken upon Himself a body; that so He might teach us that He had taken not only our body, but also the weaknesses of that body, even as it is written: "Surely He hath taken our infirmities and borne our sicknesses."

Chapter II.

The incidents properly affecting the body which Christ for our sake took upon Him are not to be accounted to His Godhead, in respect whereof He is the Most Highest. To deny which is to say that the Father was incarnate. When we read that God is one, and that there is none other beside Him, or that He alone has immortality, this must be understood as true of Christ also, not only to avoid the sinful heresy above-mentioned (Patripassianism), but also because the activity of the Father and the Son is declared to be one and the same.

7. It was a bodily weakness, then, that is to say, a weakness of ours, that He hungered; when He wept, and was sorrowful even unto death, it was of our nature. Why ascribe the properties and incidents of our nature to the Godhead? That He was even, as we are told, "made," is a property of a body. Thus, indeed, we read: "Sion our mother shall say: 'He is a man,' and in her He was made man, and the Most High Himself laid her foundations." "He was made man," mark you, not "He was made God."

8. But what is He Who is at once the Most High and man, what but "the Mediator between God and man, the man Christ Jesus Who gave Himself as a ransom for us"? This place indeed refers properly to His Incarnation, for our redemption was made by His Blood, our pardon comes through His Power, our life is secured through His Grace. He gives as the Most High, He prays as man. The one is the office of the Creator, the other of a Redeemer. Be the gifts as distinct as they may, yet the Giver is one, for it was fitting that our Maker should be our Redeemer.

9. Who indeed can deny that we have plain evidence that Christ is the Most High? He who knows otherwise makes the sacrament of Incarnation to be the work of God the Father. But that Christ is the Most High is removed beyond doubt by what Scripture hath said in another place, concerning the mystery of the Passion: "The Most High sent forth His Voice, and the earth was shaken." And in the Gospel you may read: "And thou, child, shalt be called the Prophet of the Highest; for thou shalt go before the face of the Lord, to prepare His ways." Who is "the Highest"? The Son of God. He, then, Who is the Most High God is Christ.

10. Again, whilst God is everywhere said to be One God, the Son of God is not separated from this Unity. For He Who is the Most High is alone, as it is written: "And let them know that Thy Name is the Lord: Thou alone art Most High over all the earth."

11. And so the adversaries' injurious conclusion is rejected with contempt and disgrace, which they drew from the Scripture speaking of God: "Who alone hath immortality and dwelleth in light unapproachable; for these words are written of God which Name belongs equally to Father and to Son.

12. If, indeed, wheresoever they read the Name of God, they deny that there is any thought of the Son [as well as the Father], they blaspheme, inasmuch as they deny the Son's Divine Sovereignty, and they shall appear as though they shared the sinful error of the Sabellians in teaching the Incarnation of the Father. Let them, indeed explain how they can fail to interpret in a sense blasphemous to the Father the words of the Apostle: "In Whom ye did also rise again, by faith in the working of God, Who raised Him from the dead." Let them also take warning from what follows of what they are running upon—for this is what comes after: "And though ye were dead in your sins and the uncircumcision of your flesh, He quickened us with Him, pardoning us all our offences, blotting out the handwriting of the Ordinance, which was opposed to us, and removed it from our midst, nailing it to His Cross, divesting Himself of the flesh."

13. We are not, then, to suppose that the Father Who raised the flesh is alone [God]; nor, again, are we to suppose the like of the Son, Whose Body was raised again. He Who raised, did surely also quicken; and He who quickened, also pardoned sins; He who pardoned sins, also blotted out the handwriting; He Who blotted out the handwriting, also nailed it to the Cross: He who nailed it to the Cross, divested Himself of the flesh. But it was not the Father Who divested Himself of the flesh; for *not* the Father, but, as we read, the Word was made flesh. You see,

then, that the Arians, in dividing the Father from the Son, run into danger of saying that the Father endured the Passion.

14. We, however, can easily show that the words treat of the Son's action, for the Son Himself indeed raised His own Body again, as He Himself said: "Destroy this Temple, and in three days I will raise it again." And He Himself quickens us together with His Body: "For as the Father raiseth the dead and quickeneth them, so also the Son quickeneth Whom He will." And He Himself hath granted forgiveness for sins, saying, "Thy sins be forgiven thee." He too hath nailed the handwriting of the record to His Cross, in that He was crucified, and suffered in the body. Nor did any divest Himself of the flesh, save the Son of God, Who invested Himself therewith. He, therefore, Who hath achieved the work of our resurrection is plainly pointed out to be very God.

Chapter III.

That the Father and the Son must not be divided is proved by the words of the Apostle, seeing that it is befitting to the Son that He should be blessed, only Potentate, and immortal, by nature, that is, and not by grace, as even the angels themselves are immortal, and that He should dwell in the unapproachable light. How it is that the Father and the Son are alike and equally said to be "alone."

15. When, therefore, you read the Name "God," separate neither Father nor Son, for the Godhead of the Father and the Son is one and the same, and therefore separate them not, when you read the words "blessed and only Potentate," for the words are spoken of God, even as you may read: "I charge thee before God, Who quickeneth all things." Christ also indeed doth quicken, and therefore the Name of God is meetly given both to the Father and to the Son, inasmuch as the effect of their activity is in agreement. Let us go on to the words following: "I Charge thee," he says, "before God, Who quickeneth all things, and Jesus Christ."

16. The Word is in God, even as it is written: "In God will I praise His Word." In God is His Eternal Power, even Jesus; in [speaking of] God, therefore, the Apostle hath witnessed to the unity of the Godhead, whilst by the Name of Christ he hath witnessed to the sacrament of the Incarnation.

17. Furthermore, to show that he hath spoken of the Incarnation of Christ, he added: "Who bore witness under Pontius Pilate with the good confession," [I charge thee] "keep undefiled the commandment, until the coming of our Lord Jesus Christ, Which in His own good time the blessed and only Potentate shall manifest, the King of kings and Lord of lords, Who alone hath immortality, and dwelleth in light unapproachable, Whom no man hath seen, nor can see." Those words, then, are written with regard to God, of which Name the dignity and truth are common to [both the Father and] the Son.

18. Why, then, should there be no thought of the Son in this place, seeing that all these things hold good of the Son also? If they do not so, then deny His Godhead, and so mayest thou deny what is proper to be said of God. His Blessedness cannot be denied, Who bestows blessings, for "Blessed are they whose iniquities are forgiven." He cannot but be called "Blessed," Who hath given us wholesome teaching, even as it is written: "Which is according to the Gospel of the beauty of the Blessed God." His Power cannot be denied, of Whom the Father saith: "I have laid help upon One that is mighty." And who dare refuse to acknowledge Him to be immortal, when He Himself bath made others also immortal, as it is written of the Wisdom of God: "By her shall I possess immortality."

19. But the immortality of His Nature is one thing, that of ours is another. Things perishable are not to be compared to things divine. The Godhead is the one only Substance that death cannot touch, and therefore it is that the Apostle, though knowing both the [human] soul and angels to be immortal, declared that God only had immortality. In truth, even the soul may die: "The soul that sinneth, it shall die," and an angel is not absolutely immortal, his immortality depending on the will of the Creator.

20. Do not hastily reject this, because Gabriel dies not, nor Raphaël, nor Uriel. Even in their nature there is a capacity of sin, though not one of improvement by discipline, for every reasonable creature is exposed to influences from without itself, and liable to judgment. It is on the influences which work upon us that the award of judgment, and corruption, or advance to perfection, do depend, and therefore Ecclesiastes saith: "For God shall bring all His work to judgment." Every creature, then, has within it the possibility of corruption and death, even though it do not [at present] die or commit sin; nor, if in anything it deliver not itself over to sin, hath it this boon of its immortal nature, but of discipline or of grace. Immortality, then, that is of a gift is one thing: immortality without the possibility of change is another.

21. Do we deny the immortality of Christ's Godhead, because He tasted death for all in the flesh? Then is Gabriel better than Christ, for Gabriel never died, but Christ gave up the ghost. But the servant is not above his lord, and we must discern the weakness of flesh from the eternity of Godhead. Christ's Death had its source in the flesh, immortality is of the nature of Christ's sovereignty. But if the Godhead brought it to pass that the flesh saw not corruption, the flesh being surely by nature liable to corruption, how could the Godhead itself have died?

22. And how is it that the Son dwelleth not in light unapproachable, if He is in the bosom of the Father, if the Father is Light, and the Son also is Light, because God is Light? Or, if we suppose some other light, beside the Light of the Godhead, to be the unapproachable Light, is, then, this Light better than the Father, so that He is not in that Light, Who, as it is written, is both with the Father and in the Father? Let men, therefore, not exclude the thought of the Son, when they read only of "God"—and let them not exclude that of the Father, when they read of "the *Son*" only.

23. On earth, the Son is not without the Father, and thou thinkest that the Father is without the Son in heaven? The Son is in the flesh—(when I say "He is in the flesh" or "He is on earth," I speak as though we lived in the days whose story is in the Gospel, for now we no longer know Christ "after the flesh")—He is in the flesh, and He is not alone, as it is written: "And I am not alone, because the Father is with Me," and think you that the Father dwells alone in the Light?

24. Lest you should regard this argument as mere speculation take this sentence of authority. "No man," saith the Scripture, "hath seen God at any time, save the Only-begotten Son, Who is in the bosom of the Father; He hath revealed Him." How can the Father be in solitude, if the Son be in the bosom of the Father? How doth the Son reveal Him, Whom He seeth not? The Father, then, exists not alone.

25. Observe now what the "solitude" of the Father and of the Son is. The Father is alone, because there is no other Father; the Son is alone, because there is no other Son; God is alone, because the Godhead of the Trinity is One.

Chapter IV.
We are told that Christ was only "made" so far as regards the flesh. For the redemption of mankind He needed no means of aid, even as He needed none in order to His Resurrection, whereas others, in order to raise the dead, had need of recourse to prayer. Even when Christ prayed, the prayer was offered by Him in His capacity as human; whilst He must be accounted divine from the fact that He commanded (that such and such things should be done). On this point the devil's testimony is truer than the Arians' arguments. The discussion concludes with an explanation of the reason why the title of "mighty" is given to the Son of Man.

26. It is now sufficiently made plain that the Father is not God in solitude, without the Son, and that the Son cannot be thought of as God alone, without the Father, for it is in respect of His flesh that we read that the Son of God was "made," not in respect of His generation from God the Father.

27. Indeed, in what sense He was "made" He has declared by the mouth of the holy patriarch, saying: "For My soul is filled with sorrow to overflowing, and My life hath drawn near unto hell. I have been counted with them that go down into the pit; I have been made as a man

free, without help, amongst the dead." Here, then, we read: "I have been made as a man," not "I have been made as God;" and again: "My soul overfloweth with sorrows." "My soul," mark you, not "My Godhead." He was "made" in so far as that was concerned wherein He was due to hell, wherein He was reckoned with others, for the Godhead admits of no likeness which may be ground for classing it with others. Yet mark how the majesty of Godhead shows itself in Christ, even in that flesh which was appointed to death. Although He was "made" as a man, and "made" as flesh, yet He was made free amongst the dead, "free, without help."

28. But how can the Son say here that He was without help, when it has already been said: "I have laid help upon One that is mighty"? Distinguish here also the two natures present. The flesh hath need of help, the Godhead hath no need. He is free, then, because the chains of death had no hold upon Him. He was not made prisoner by the powers of darkness, it is He Who exerted power amongst them. He is "without help," because He Himself, the Lord, hath by no office of messenger or ambassador, but by His own might, saved His people. How could He, Who raised others to life, require any help in order to raise His own body?

29. And though men also have raised the dead, still they did this not of their own power, but in the Name of Christ. To ask is one thing, to command is another; to obtain is different from bestowing.

30. Elijah, then, raised the dead, but he prayed—he did not command. Elisha raised one to life after laying himself upon the dead body, in accordance with its posture; and, again, the very contact of Elisha's corpse gave life to the dead, that the prophet might foreshow the coming of Him, Who, being sent in the likeness of sinful flesh, should, even after His burial, raise the dead to life.

31. Peter, again, when he healed Aeneas, said: "In the Name of Jesus of Nazareth, rise and walk." Not in his own name, but in the Name of Christ. But "rise" is a command; on the other hand, it is an instance of confidence in one's right, not an arrogant claim to power, and the authority of the command stood in the effective influence of the Name, not in its own might. What answer, then, make the Arians? Peter commands in the Name of Christ,—this on the one hand: on the other, they will have it that the Son of God did not command, but requested.

32. We read, they objected, of His uttering a prayer. But take note of the difference. He prays as Son of *Man*, He commands as Son of *God*. Will you not ascribe unto the Son of God what even the devil has ascribed? Will you accuse yourselves of greater wickedness than Satan's? The devil saith: "If Thou be the Son of God, command this stone that it become bread." Satan saith "command," you say "entreat." The devil believes that, at the word of God's Son, the nature of an elementary substance may be exchanged for that of a composite one; you think that, unless the Son of God prefers a request, even His Will cannot be done. Again, the devil thinks that the Son of God is to be esteemed from His power, you that He is to be esteemed from His infirmity. The devil's temptations are more tolerable than the Arians' disputings.

33. Let us not, then, be troubled if we find the Son of Man entitled "mighty" in one place, and yet in another, that the Lord of glory was crucified. What might is greater than sovereignty over the powers of heaven? But this was in the hands of Him Who ruled over thrones, principalities, angels; for, although He was amongst the wild beasts, as it is written, yet angels ministered to Him, that you may perceive the difference between what is proper to the Incarnation, and what is proper to Sovereignty. So far as His flesh is concerned, then, He endures the assault of wild beasts; in regard of His Godhead, He is adored by angels.

34. We have learnt, then, that He was made man, and that His being made must be referred to His manhood. Furthermore, in another passage of Scripture, you may read: "Who was made for Him of the seed of David," that is to say, in respect of the flesh He was "made" of the seed of David, but He was God begotten of God before the worlds.

Chapter V.

Passages brought forward from Scripture to show that "made" does not always mean the same as "created;" whence it is concluded that the letter of Holy Writ should not be made the ground of captious arguments, after the manner of the Jews, who, however, are shown to be not so bad as the heretics, and thus the principle already set forth is confirmed anew.

35. At the same time, becoming does not always imply *creation;* for we read: "Lord, Thou art become our refuge," and "Thou hast become my salvation." Plainly, here is no statement of the fact or purpose of a *creation*, but God is said to have become my "refuge" and have turned to my "salvation," even as the Apostle hath said: "Who became for us Wisdom from God, and Righteousness, and Sanctification, and Redemption," that is, that Christ was "made" for us, of the Father, not *created*. Again, the writer has explained in the sequel in what sense he says that Christ was made Wisdom for us: "But we preach the Wisdom of God in doctrine of mystery, which Wisdom is hidden, foreordained by God before the existence of the world for our glory, and which none of the princes of this world knew, for had they known they would never have crucified the Lord of glory." When the mystery of the Passion is set forth, surely there is no speaking of an eternal process of generation.

36. The Lord's Cross, then, is my wisdom; the Lord's Death my redemption; for we are redeemed with His precious blood, as the Apostle Peter bath said. With His blood, then, as man, the Lord redeemed us, Who also, as God, hath forgiven sins.

37. Let us not, therefore, lay snares as it were in words, and eagerly seek out entanglements therein; let us not, because misbelievers make out the written word to mean that it means not, set forth only what this letter bears on the face of it, instead of the underlying sense. This way went the Jews to destruction, despising the deep-hidden meaning, and following only after the bare form of the word, for "the letter killeth, but the Spirit maketh alive."

38. And yet, of these two grievous impieties, to ascribe to the Godhead what is true only of manhood is perchance more detestable than to attribute to spirit what belongs only to letter. The Jews feared to believe in manhood taken up into God, and therefore have lost the grace of redemption, because they reject that on which salvation depends; the Arians degrade the majesty of Godhead to the weakness of humanity. Detestable as are the Jews, who crucified the Lord's flesh, more detestable still do I hold them who have believed that the Godhead of Christ was nailed to the Cross. So one who ofttimes had dealings with Jews said: "An heretic avoid, after once reproving him"

39. Nor, again, are these men careful to avoid doing dishonour to the Father, in their impious application of the fact, that Christ was "made" Wisdom for us, to His incomprehensible generation, that transcends all limits and divisions of time; for, leaving it out of account that dishonour done to the Son is an insult to the Father, they do even carry their blasphemy in assault upon the Father, of Whom it is written: "Let God be made truthful, but every man a liar." If indeed they think that the Son is spoken of, they do not foreclose against His generation, but in that they rest on the authority of this text they do confess that which they reject, namely, that Christ is God, and true God.

40. It would be a lengthy matter were I to pass in review each several place where we read of His being "made," not indeed by nature, but by way of gracious dispensation. Moses, for example, saith: "Thou art made my Helper and Protector, to save me;" and David: "Be unto me for a God of salvation, and an house of refuge, that Thou mayest save me;" and Isaiah: "He is become an Helper for every city that is lowly." Of a surety the holy men say not to God: "Thou hast been created," but "By Thy grace Thou art made a Protector and Helper unto us."

Chapter VI.

In order to dispose of an objection grounded on a text in St. John, St. Ambrose first shows that the Arian interpretation lends countenance to the Manichaeans; then, after setting forth the different ways of dividing the words in this same passage, he shows plainly that it cannot, without dishonour to the Father, be understood with such reference to the Godhead as the Arians give it, and expounds the true meaning thereon.

41. We have no reason, therefore, to fear the argument which the Arians, in their reckless manner of expounding, use to construct, showing that the Word of God was "made," for, say they, it is written: "That which has been made in Him is life."

42. First of all, let them understand that if they make the words "That which has been made" to refer to the Godhead, they entangle themselves in the difficulties raised by the Manichaeans, for these people argue: "If that which has been made in Him is life, then there is something which has not been made in Him, and is death," so that they may impiously bring in two principles. But this teaching the Church condemns.

43. Again, how can the Arians prove that the Evangelist actually said this? The most part of those who are learned in the Faith read the passage as follows: "All things were made by Him, and without Him was not anything made that has been made." Others read thus: "All things were made by Him, and without Him was nothing made." Then they proceed: "What has been made," and to this they join the words "in Him;" that is to say, "But whatsover is has been made in Him." But what mean the words "in Him"? The Apostle tells us, when he says: "In Him we have our being, and live, and move."

44. Howbeit, let them read the passage as they will, they cannot diminish the majesty of God the Word, in referring to His Person, as subject, the words "That which was made," without also doing dishonour to God the Father, of Whom it is written: "But he who doeth the truth cometh to the light, that his works may be made manifest that they are wrought in God." See then—here we read of man's works being wrought in God, and yet for all that we cannot understand the Godhead as the subject of them. We must either recognize the works as wrought through Him, as the Apostle's affirmation showeth that "all things are through Him, and were created in Him, and He is before all, and all things *exist together* in Him," or, as the witness of the text here cited teaches us, we ought to regard the virtues whereby the fruit of life eternal is gained, as wrought in God—chastity, piety, devoutness, faith, and others of this kind, whereby the will of God is expressed.

45. Just as the works, then, are the expression of the will and power of God the Father, so are they of Christ's, even as we read: "Created in Christ in good works;" and in the psalm: "Peace be made in Thy power;" and again: "In wisdom hast Thou made them all." "In wisdom hast Thou made," mark you—not "Thou hast made wisdom;" for since all things have been made in wisdom, and Christ is the Wisdom of God, then this Wisdom is plainly not an accident, but a substance, and an everlasting one, but if the Wisdom hath been made, then is it made in a worse condition than all things, forasmuch as it could not, by itself, be made Wisdom. If, then, being made is oftentimes referred to something accidental, not to the essence of a thing, so may creation also be referred to some end had in view.

Chapter VII.

Solomon's words, "The Lord created Me," etc., mean that Christ's Incarnation was done for the redemption of the Father's creation, as is shown by the Son's own words. That He is the "beginning" may be understood from the visible proofs of His virtuousness, and it is shown how the Lord opened the ways of all virtues, and was their true beginning.

46. Hereby we are brought to understand that the prophecy of the Incarnation, "The Lord created me the beginning of His ways for His works," means that the Lord Jesus was created of the Virgin for the redeeming of the Father's works. Truly, we cannot doubt that this is spoken of the mystery of the Incarnation, forasmuch as the Lord took upon Him our flesh, in order to save the works of His hands from the slavery of corruption, so that He might, by the sufferings of His own body, overthrow him who had the power of death. For Christ's flesh is for the sake of things created, but His Godhead existed before them, seeing that He is before all things, whilst all things exist together in Him.

47. His Godhead, then, is not by reason of creation, but creation exists because of the Godhead; even as the Apostle showed, saying that all things exist because of the Son of God, for we read as follows: "But it was fitting that He, through Whom and because of Whom are all things, after bringing many sons to glory, should, as Captain of their salvation, be made perfect through suffering." Has he not plainly declared that the Son of God, Who, by reason of His Godhead, was the Creator of all, did in after time, for the salvation of His people, submit to the taking on of the flesh and the suffering of death?

48. Now for the sake of what works the Lord was "created" of a virgin, He Himself, whilst healing the blind man, has shown, saying: "In Him must I work the works of Him that sent Me." Furthermore He said in the same Scripture, that we might believe Him to speak of the Incarnation: "As long as I am in this world, I am the Light of this world," for, so far as He is man, He is in this world for a season, but as God He exists at all times. In another place, too, He says: "Lo, I am with you even unto the end of the world."

49. Nor is there any room for questioning with respect to "the beginning," seeing that when, during His earthly life, He was asked, "Who art Thou?" He answered: "The beginning, even as I tell you." This refers not only to the essential nature of the eternal Godhead, but also to the visible proofs of virtues, for hereby hath He proved Himself the eternal God, in that He is the beginning of all things, and the Author of each several virtue, in that He is the Head of the Church, as it is written: "Because He is the Head of the Body, of the Church; Who is the beginning, first-begotten from the dead."

50. It is clear, then, that the words "beginning of His ways," which, as it seems, we must refer to the mystery of the putting on of His body, are a prophecy of the Incarnation. For Christ's purpose in the Incarnation was to pave for us the road to heaven. Mark how He says: "I go up to My Father and your Father, to My God and your God." Then, to give you to know that the Almighty Father appointed His ways to the Son, after the Incarnation, you have in Zechariah the words of the angel speaking to Joshua clothed in filthy garments: "Thus saith the Lord Almighty: If thou wilt walk in My ways and observe My precepts." What is the meaning of that filthy garb save the putting on of the flesh?

51. Now the ways of the Lord are, we may say, certain courses taken in a good life, guided by Christ, Who says, "I am the Way, and the Truth, and the Life." The way, then, is the surpassing power of God, for Christ, is our way, and a good way, too, is He, a way which hath opened the kingdom of heaven to believers. Moreover, the ways of the Lord are straight, as it is written: "Make Thy ways known unto me, O Lord." Chastity is a way, faith is a way, abstinence is a way. There is, indeed, a way of virtue, and there is a way of wickedness; for it is written: "And see if there be any way of wickedness in me."

52. Christ, then, is the beginning of our virtue. He is the beginning of purity, Who taught maidens not to look for the embraces of men, but to yield the purity of their bodies and minds to the service of the Holy Spirit rather than to a husband. Christ is the beginning of frugality, for He became poor, though He was rich. Christ is the beginning of patience, for when He was reviled, He reviled not again, when He was struck, He did not strike back. Christ is the beginning of humility, for He took the form of a servant, though in the majesty of His power He was equal with God the Father. From Him each several virtue has taken its origin.

53. For this cause, then, that we might learn these divers virtues, "a Son was given us, Whose beginning was upon His shoulder." That "beginning" is the Lord's Cross—the beginning of strong courage, wherewith a way has been opened for the holy martyrs to enter the sufferings of the Holy War.

Chapter VIII.

The prophecy of Christ's Godhead and Manhood, contained in the verse of Isaiah just now cited, is unfolded, and its force in refuting various heresies demonstrated.

54. This beginning did Isaiah see, and therefore he says: "A Child is born, a Son is given to us," as also did the Magi, and therefore worshipped they, when they saw the little One in the stable, and said: "A Child is born," and, when they saw the star, declared, "A Son is given to us." On the one hand, a gift from earth—on the other, a gift from heaven—and both are One Person, perfect in respect of each, without any changeableness in the Godhead, as without any taking away from the fulness of the Manhood. One Person did the Magi adore, to one and the same they offered their gifts, to show that He Who was seen in the stall was the very Lord of heaven.

55. Mark how the two verbs differ in their import: "A Child is born, a Son is given." Though born of the Father, yet is He not born, but given to us, forasmuch as the Son is not for our sakes, but we for the Son's. For indeed He was not born to us, being born before us, and the maker of all things created: nor is He now brought to life for the first time, Who was always, and was in the beginning; on the other hand, that which before-time was not is born to us. Again we find it thus recorded, how that the angel, when he spoke to the shepherds, said that He had been born: "Who is this day born to us a Saviour, Who is Christ the Lord, in the city of David." To us, then, was born that which was not before—that is, a child of the Virgin, a body from Mary—for this was made after man had been created, whereas [the Godhead] was before us.

56. Some manuscripts read as follows: "A Child is born to us a Son is given to us;" that is to say, He, Who is Son of God, is born as Mary's child for us, and given to us. As for the fact that He is "given," listen to the prophet's words: "And grant us Thy salvation." But that which is above us is given: what is from heaven is given: even as indeed we read concerning the Spirit, that "the love of God is shed abroad in our hearts by the Holy Spirit, Who is given unto us."

57. But note how this passage is as water upon fire to a crowd of heresies. "A Child is born to *us*," not to the Jews; "to *us*," not to the Manichaeans; "to *us*," not to the Marcionites. The prophet says "to *us*," that is, to those who believe, not to unbelievers. And He indeed, in His pitifulness, was born for all, but it is the disloyalty of heretics that hath brought it to pass that the birth of Him Who was born for all should not profit all. For the sun is bidden to rise upon the good and the bad, but to them that see not there is no appearance of sunrise.

58. Even as the Child, then, is born not unto all, but unto the faithful: so the Son is given to the faithful and not to the unbelieving. He is given to us, not to the Photinians; for they affirm that the Son of God was not given unto us, but was born and first began to exist amongst us. To us is He given, not to the Sabellians, who will not hear of a Son being given, maintaining that Father and Son are one and the same. Unto us is He given, not unto the Arians, in whose judgment the Son was not given for salvation, but sent over subject and inferior, to whom, moreover, He is no "Counsellor," inasmuch as they hold that He knows nought of the future, no Son, since they believe not in His eternity, though of the Word of God it is written: "That which was in the beginning;" and again: "In the beginning was the Word." To return to the passage we set before us to discuss. "In the beginning," saith the Scripture, "before He made the earth, before He made the deeps, before He brought forth the springs of water, before all the hills He begat Me."

Chapter IX.

The preceding quotation from Solomon's Proverbs receives further explanation.

59. Perchance you will ask how I came to cite, as referring to the Incarnation of Christ, the place, "The Lord created Me," seeing that the creation of the universe took place before the Incarnation of Christ? But consider that the use of holy Scripture is to speak of things to come

as though already past, and to make intimation of the union of two natures, Godhead and Manhood, in Christ, lest any should deny either His Godhead or His Manhood.

60. In Isaiah, for example, you may read: "A Child is born unto us, and a Son is given unto us;" so here also [in the Proverbs] the prophet sets forth first the creation of the flesh, and joined thereto the declaration of the Godhead, that you might know that Christ is not two, but One, being both begotten of the Father before the worlds, and in the last times created of the Virgin. And thus the meaning is: I, Who am begotten before the worlds, am He Who was created of mortal woman, created for a set purpose.

61. Again, immediately before the declaration, "The Lord created Me," He says, "I will tell of the things which are from eternity," and before saying, "He begat," He premised, "In the beginning, before He made the earth, before all hills." In its extent, the preposition "before" reaches back into the past without end or limit, and so "Before Abraham was, I am," clearly need not mean "after Adam," just as "before the Morning Star" need not mean "after the angels." But when He said "before," He intended, not that He was included in any one's existence, but that all things are included in His, for thus it is the custom of Holy Writ to show the eternity of God. Finally, in another passage you may read: "Before the mountains were brought forth, or ever the earth and the world were made, Thou art from everlasting to everlasting."

62. Before all created things, then, is the Son begotten; within all and for the good of all is He made; begotten of the Father, above the Law, brought forth of Mary, under the Law.

Chapter X.

Observations on the words of John the Baptist (John i. 30), which may be referred to divine fore-ordinance, but at any rate, as explained by the foregoing considerations, must be understood of the Incarnation. The precedence of Christ is mystically expounded, with reference to the history of Ruth.

63. But [say they] it is written: "After me cometh a Man, Who is made before me, because He was before me;" and so they argue: "See, He Who was aforetime is 'made.'" Let us take the words by themselves. "After me cometh a Man." He, then, Who came is a Man, and this is the Man Who "was made." But the word "man" connotes sex, and sex is attributed to human nature, but never to the Godhead.

64. I might argue: The Man [Christ Jesus] was in pre-existence so far as His body was foreknown, though His power is from everlasting—for both the Church and the Saints were foreordained before the worlds began. But here I lay aside this argument, and urge that the being made concerns not the Godhead, but the nature of the Incarnation, even as John himself said: "This is He of Whom I said: After me cometh a Man, Who was made before me."

65. The Scripture, then, having, as I showed above, discovered the twofold nature in Christ, that you might understand the presence of both Godhead and Manhood, here begins with the flesh; for it is the cutsom of Holy Writ to begin without fixed rule sometimes with the Godhead of Christ, and descend to the visible tokens of Incarnation; sometimes, on the other hand, to start from its humility, and rise to the glory of the Godhead, as oftentimes in the Prophets and Evangelists, and in St. Paul. Here, then, after this use, the writer begins with the Incarnation of our Lord, and then proclaims His Divinity, not to confound, but to distinguish, the human and the divine. But Arians, like Jew vintners, mix water with the wine, confounding the divine generation with the human, and ascribing to the majesty of God what is properly said only of the lowliness of the flesh.

66. I have no fears of a certain objection they are likely to put forward, namely, that in the words cited we have "a *man*"—for some have, "Who cometh after me." But here, too, let them observe what precedes. "The Word," it is said, "was made flesh." Having said that the Word was made *flesh*, the Evangelist added no mention of *man*. We understand "man" there in the mention of "flesh," and "flesh" by the mention of "man." After the statement made, then, that

"the Word was made *flesh*," there was no need here to particularly mention "man," whom he already intended by using the name "flesh."

67. Later on, St. John uses the lamb, that "taketh away the sins of the world," as an example; and to teach you plainly the Incarnation of Him, of Whom he had spoken before, he says: "This is He of Whom I said before: After me cometh a Man, Who is made before me," to wit, of Whom I said that He was "made" as being man, not as being God. However, to show that it was He Who was before the worlds, and none other, that became flesh, lest we should suppose two Sons of God, he adds: "because He was before me." If the words "was made" had referred to the divine generation, what need was there that the writer should add this, and repeat himself? But, having first said, with regard to the Incarnation only, "After me cometh a Man, Who is made before me," he added: "because He was before me," because it was needful to teach the eternity of [Christ's] Godhead; and this is the reason why St. John acknowledged Christ's priority, that He, Who is His own Father's eternal Power, may be presented as on that account duly preferred.

68. But the abounding activity of the spiritual understanding makes it a pleasing exercise to sally forth and drive into a corner the Arians, who will understand the term "made" in this passage, not of the manhood, but of the Godhead [of Christ]. What ground, indeed, is left for them to take their stand upon, when the Baptist has declared that "after me cometh One Who is made before me," that is, Who, though in the course of earthly life He comes after me, yet is placed above the degree of my worth and grace, and Who has title to be worshipped as God. For the words "cometh after me" belong to an event in time, but "was before me" signify Christ's eternity; and "is made before me" refer to His pre-eminence, forasmuch as, indeed, the mystery of the Incarnation is above human deserving.

69. Again, St. John Baptist also taught in less weighty language what ideas they were he had combined, saying: "After me cometh a Man, Whose shoes I am not worthy to bear," setting forth at least the more excellent dignity [of Christ], though not the eternity of His Divine Generation. Now these words are so fully intended of the Incarnation, that Scripture hath given us, in an earlier book, a human counterpart of the mystic sandal. For, by the Law, when a man died, the marriage bond with his wife was passed on to his brother, or other man next of kin, in order that the seed of the brother or next of kin might renew the life of the house, and thus it was that Ruth, though she was foreign-born, but yet had possessed a husband of the Jewish people, who had left a kinsman of near relation, being seen and loved of Boaz whilst gleaning and maintaining herself and her mother-in-law with that she gleaned, was yet not taken of Boaz to wife, until she had first loosed the shoe from [the foot of] him whose wife she ought, by the Law, to have become.

70. The story is a simple one, but deep are its hidden meanings, for that which was done was the outward betokening of somewhat further. If indeed we should rack the sense so as to fit the letter exactly, we should almost find the words an occasion of a certain shame and horror, that we should regard them as intending and conveying the thought of common bodily intercourse; but it was the foreshadowing of One Who was to arise from Jewry—whence Christ was, after the flesh—Who should, with the seed of heavenly teaching, revive the seed of his dead kinsman, that is to say, the people, and to Whom the precepts of the Law, in their spiritual significance, assigned the sandal of marriage, for the espousals of the Church.

71. Moses was not the Bridegroom, for to him cometh the word, "Loose thy shoe from off thy foot," that he might give place to his Lord. Nor was Joshua, the son of Nun, the Bridegroom, for to him also it was told, saying, "Loose thy shoe from off thy foot," lest, by reason of the likeness of his name, he should be thought the spouse of the Church. None other is the Bridegroom but Christ alone, of Whom St. John said: "He Who hath the bride is the Bridegroom." They, therefore, loose their shoes, but His shoe cannot be loosed, even as St. John said: "I am not worthy to loose the latchet of His shoe."

72. Christ alone, then, is the Bridegroom to Whom the Church, His bride, comes from the nations, and gives herself in wedlock; aforetime poor and starving, but now rich with Christ's harvest; gathering in the hidden bosom of her mind handfuls of the rich crop and gleanings of the Word, that so she may nourish with fresh food her who is worn out, bereaved by the death of her son, and starving, even the mother of the dead people,—leaving not the widow and destitute, whilst she seeks new children.

73. Christ, then, alone is the Bridegroom, grudging not even to the synagogue the sheaves of His harvest. Would that the synagogue had not of her own will shut herself out! She had sheaves that she might herself have gathered, but, her people being dead, she, like one bereaved by the death of her son, began to gather sheaves, whereby she might live, by the hand of the Church— the which sheaves they who come in joyfulness shall carry, even as it is written: "Yet surely shall they come with joy, bringing their sheaves with them."

74. Who, indeed, but Christ could dare to claim the Church as His bride, whom He alone, and none other, hath called from Libanus, saying: "Come hither from Libanus, my bride; come hither from Libanus"? Or of Whom else could the Church have said: "His throat is sweetness, and He is altogether desirable"? And seeing that we entered upon this discussion from speaking of the shoes of His feet,—to Whom else but the Word of God incarnate can those words apply? "His legs are pillars of marble, set upon bases of gold." For Christ alone walks in the souls and makes His path in the minds of His saints, in which, as upon bases of gold and foundations of precious stone the heavenly Word has left His footprints ineffaceably impressed.

75. Clearly we see, then, that both the man and the type point to the mystery of the Incarnation.

Chapter XI.

St. Ambrose returns to the main question, and shows that whenever Christ is said to have "been made" (or "become"), this must be understood with reference to His Incarnation, or to certain limitations. In this sense several passages of Scripture—especially of St. Paul—are expounded. The eternal Priesthood of Christ, prefigured in Melchizedek. Christ possesses not only likeness, but oneness with the Father.

76. When, therefore, Christ is said to have been "made," to have "become," the phrase relates, not to the substance of the Godhead, but often to the Incarnation—sometimes indeed to a particular office; for if you understand it of His Godhead, then God was made into an object of insult and derision inasmuch as it is written: "But thou hast rejected thy Christ, and brought Him to nought; thou hast driven Him to wander;" and again: "And He was made the derision of His neighbours." Of His neighbours, mark you—not of them of His household, not of them who clave to Him, for "he who cleaveth to the Lord is one Spirit;" he who is neighbour doth not cleave to Him. Again, "He was made a derision," because the Lord's Cross is to Jews a stumbling-block, and to Greeks is foolishness: for to them that are wise He is, by that same Cross, *made* higher than the heavens, higher than angels, and is made the Mediator of the better covenant, even as He was Mediator of the former.

77. Mark how I repeat the phrase; so far am I from seeking to avoid it. Yet take notice in what sense He is "made."

78. In the first place, "having made purification, He sitteth on the right hand of Majesty on high, being made so much better than the angels." Now where purification is, there is a victim; where there is a victim, there is also a body; where a body is, there is oblation; where there is the office of oblation, there also is sacrifice made with suffering.

79. In the next place, He is the Mediator of a better covenant. But where there is testamentary disposition, the death of the testator must first come to pass, as it is written a little further on. Howbeit, the death is not the death of His eternal Godhead, but of His weak human frame.

80. Furthermore, we are taught how He is made "higher than the heavens." "Unspotted," saith the Scripture, "separate from sinners, and made higher than the heavens; not having daily

need, as the priests have need, to offer a victim first for his own sins, and then for those of the people. For this He did by sacrificing Himself once and for all." None is said to be made higher, save he who has in some respect been lower; Christ, then, is, by His sitting at the right hand of the Father, made higher in regard of that wherein, being made lower than the angels, He offered Himself to suffer.

81. Finally, the Apostle himself saith to the Philippians, that "being made in the likeness of man, and found in outward appearance as a man, He humbled Himself, being made obedient even unto death." Mark that, in regard whereof He is "made," He is made, the Apostle saith, in the likeness of man, not in respect of Divine Sovereignty, and He was made obedient unto death, so that He displayed the obedience proper to man, and obtained the kingdom appertaining of right to Godhead.

82. How many passages need we cite further in evidence that His "being made" must be understood with reference to His Incarnation, or to some particular dispensation? Now whatsoever is made, the same is also created, for "He spake and they were made; He gave also the word, and they were created." "The Lord created me." These words are spoken with regard to His Manhood; and we have also shown, in our First Book, that the word "created" appears to have reference to the Incarnation.

83. Again, the Apostle himself, by declaring that no worship is to be rendered to a created existence, has shown that the Son has not been created, but begotten, of God. At the same time he shows in other places what there was in Christ that was created, in order to make plain in what sense he has read in Solomon's book: "The Lord created Me."

84. Let us now review a whole passage in order. "Seeing, then, that the sons have parts of flesh and blood, He too likewise was made to have part in the same, to the end that by death He might overthrow him who had the power of death." Who, then, is He Who would have us to be partakers in His own flesh and blood? Surely the Son of God. How, save by means of the flesh, was He made partaker with us, or by what, save by bodily death, brake He the chains of death? For Christ's endurance of death was made the death of Death. This text, then, speaks of the Incarnation.

85. Let us see what follows: "For He did not indeed [straightway] put on Him the nature of angels, but that of Abraham's seed. And thus was He able to be made like to His brethren in all things throughout, that He might become a compassionate and faithful Prince, a Priest unto God, to make propitiation for the sins of the people; for in that He Himself suffered He is able also to help them that are tempted. Wherefore, brethren most holy, ye who have each his share in a heavenly calling, look upon the Apostle and High Priest of our confession, Jesus, regard His faithfulness to His Creator, even as Moses was in his house." These, then, are the Apostle's words.

86. You see what it is in respect whereof the writer calls Him created.: "In so far as He took upon Him the seed of Abraham;" plainly asserting the begetting of a body. How, indeed, but in His body did He expiate the sins of the people? In what did He suffer, save in His body—even as we said above: "Christ having suffered in the flesh"? In what is He a priest, save in that which He took to Himself from the priestly nation?

67. It is a priest's duty to offer something, and, according to the Law, to enter into the holy places by means of blood; seeing, then, that God had rejected the blood of bulls and goats, this High Priest was indeed bound to make passage and entry into the holy of holies in heaven through His own blood, in order that He might be the everlasting propitiation for our sins. Priest and victim, then, are one; the priesthood and sacrifice are, however, exercised under the conditions of humanity, for He was led as a lamb to the slaughter, and He is a priest after the order of Melchizedek.

88. Let no man, therefore, when he beholds an order of human establishment, contend that in it resides the claim of Divinity; for even that Melchizedek, by whose office Abraham offered sacrifice, the Church doth certainly not hold to be an angel (as some Jewish triflers do), but a

holy man and priest of God, who, *prefiguring* our Lord, is described as "without father or mother, without history of his descent, without beginning and without end," in order to show beforehand the coming into this world of the eternal Son of God, Who likewise was incarnate and then brought forth without any father, begotten as God without mother, and was without history of descent, for it is written: "His generation who shall declare?"

89. This Melchizedek, then, have we received as a priest of God made upon the model of Christ, but the one we regard as the type, the other as the original. Now a type is a shadow of the truth, and we have accepted the royalty of the one in the name of a single city, but that of the other as shown in the reconciliation of the whole world; for it is written: "God was in Christ, reconciling the world to Himself;" that is to say, [in Christ was] eternal Godhead: or, if the Father is in the Son, even as the Son is in the Father, then Their unity in both nature and operation is plainly not denied.

90. But how, indeed, could our adversaries justly deny this, even if they would, when the Scripture saith: "But the Father, Who abideth in Me, even He doeth the works;" and "The works that I do, He Himself worketh"? Not "He *also* doeth the works," but one should regard it as similarity rather than unity of work; in saying, "The things that I do, He Himself doeth," the Apostle has left it clear that we ought to believe that the work of the Father and the work of the Son is one.

91. On the other hand, when He would have similarity, not unity, of works, to be understood, He said: "He that believeth in Me, the works which I do, shall he do also." Skilfully inserting here the word "also," He hath allowed us similarity, and yet hath not ascribed natural unity. One, therefore, is the work of the Father and the work of the Son, whether the Arians please so to think or not.

Chapter XII.

The kingdom of the Father and of the Son is one and undivided, so likewise is the Godhead of each.

92. I Would now ask how they suppose the kingdom of the Father and the Son to be divided, when the Lord hath said, as we showed above: "Every kingdom divided against itself shall be speedily overthrown."

93. Indeed, it was to debar the impious teaching of Arian enmity that Saint Peter himself asserted the dominion of the Father and the Son to be one, saying: "Wherefore, my brethren, labour to make your calling and election sure, for so doing you shall not go astray, for thus your entrance into the eternal realm of God and our Lord and Saviour Jesus Christ shall be granted with the greater abundance of grace.

94. Now, if it be thought that Christ's dominion alone is spoken of, and the place be therefore understood in such sense that the Father and the Son are regarded as divided in authority—yet it will be still acknowledged that it is the dominion of the Son, and that an eternal one, and thus not only will two kingdoms, separate, and so liable to fail, be brought in, but, furthermore, inasmuch as no kingdom is to be compared with God's kingdom, which they cannot, however greatly they may desire to, deny to be the kingdom of the Son, they must either turn back upon their opinion, and acknowledge the kingdom of the Father and the Son to be one and the same; or they must ascribe to the Father the government of a lesser kingdom— which is blasphemy; or they must acknowledge Him, Whom they wickedly declare to be inferior in respect of Godhead, to possess an equal kingdom, which is inconsistent.

95. But this [their teaching] squares not, agrees not, holds not [with its premises]. Let them confess, then, that the kingdom is one, even as we confess and prove, not indeed on our own evidence, but upon testimony vouchsafed from heaven.

96. To begin with, learn, from further testimonies [of Scripture], how that the kingdom of heaven is also the kingdom of the Son: "Verily, verily, I say unto you, that there are some amongst those which stand here with us, who shall not taste death, until they see the Son of

Man coming into His kingdom." There is therefore no room for doubt that the kingdom appertaineth to the Son of God.

97. Now learn that the kingdom of the Son is the very same as the kingdom of the Father: "Verily, I say unto you that there be some of those which stand around us, who shall not taste death until they see the kingdom of God coming in power." So far, indeed, is it one kingdom, that the reward is one, the inheritor is one and the same, and so also the merit, and He Who promises [the reward].

98. How can it but be one kingdom, above all when the Son Himself hath said of Himself: "Then shall the righteous shine like the sun in the kingdom of My Father"? For that which is the Father's, by fitness to His majesty, is also the Son's, by unity in the same glory." The Scripture, therefore, hath declared the kingdom to be the kingdom both of the Father and of the Son.

99. Now learn that where the kingdom of God is named, there is no putting aside of the authority either of the Father or of the Son, because both the kingdom of the Father and the kingdom of the Son is included under the single name of God, saying: "When ye shall see Abraham, Isaac, and Jacob, and all the prophets, in the kingdom of God." Do we deny that the prophets are in the kingdom of the Son, when even to a dying robber who said, "Remember me, when Thou comest into Thy kingdom," the Lord made answer: "Verily, I say unto thee, to-day shalt thou be with Me in paradise." What, indeed, do we understand by being in the kingdom of God, if not the having escaped eternal death? But they who have escaped eternal death see the Son of Man coming into His kingdom.

100. How, then, can He not have in His power that which He gives, saying: "To thee will I give the keys of the kingdom of heaven"? See the gulf between [the one and the other]. The servant opens, the Lord bestows; the One through Himself, the other through Christ; the minister receives the keys, the Lord appoints powers: the one is the right of a giver, the other the duty of a steward.

101. See now yet another proof that the kingdom, the government, of the Father and the Son is one. It is written in the Epistle to Timothy: "Paul, an apostle of Jesus Christ, according to the government of God, our Saviour, and Christ Jesus, our Hope." One, therefore, the kingdom of the Father and the Son is plainly declared to be, even as Paul the Apostle also asserted, saying: "For know this, that no shameless person, none that is impure, or covetous (which meaneth idolatry), hath inheritance in the kingdom of Christ and of God." It is, therefore, one kingdom, one Godhead.

102. Oneness in Godhead the Law hath proved, which speaks of one God, as also the Apostle, by saying of Christ; "In Whom dwelleth all the fulness of the Godhead bodily." For if, as the Apostle saith, all the fulness of the Godhead, bodily, is in Christ, then must the Father and the Son be confessed to be of one Godhead; or if it is desired to sunder the Godhead of the Son from the Godhead of the Father, whilst the Son possesses all the fulness of the Godhead bodily, what is supposed to be further reserved, seeing that nothing remains over and above the fulness of perfection? Therefore the Godhead is one.

Chapter XIII.

The majesty of the Son is His own, and equal to that of the Father, and the angels are not partakers, but beholders thereof.

103. Now, we having already laid down that the Father and the Son are of one image and likeness, it remains for us to show that They are also of one majesty. And we need not go far afield for proof, inasmuch as the Son Himself has said of Himself: "When the Son of Man shall come in His majesty, and all the angels with Him, then shall He sit upon the throne of His majesty." Behold, then, the majesty of the Son declared! What lacketh He yet, Whose uncreated majesty cannot be denied? Majesty, then, belongeth to the Son.

104. Let our adversaries now hold it proved beyond doubt that the majesty of the Father and of the Son is one, forasmuch as the Lord Himself hath said: "For he who shall be ashamed of

Me and of My words, of Him shall the Son of Man be ashamed, when He cometh in His majesty and His Father's, and the majesty of the holy angels." What is the force of the words "and the majesty of the holy angels," but that the servants derive honour from the worship of their Lord?

105. The Son, therefore, ascribed His majesty to His Father as well as to Himself, not, indeed, in such sort that the angels should share in that majesty on equal terms with the Father and the Son, but that they should behold the surpassing glory of God; for truly not even angels possess a majesty of their own, after the manner in which Scripture speaks of the Son: "When He shall sit upon the throne of His majesty," but they stand in the presence, that they may see the glory of the Father and the Son, in such degrees of vision as they are either worthy of or able to bear.

106. Furthermore, the God-given words themselves declare their own meaning, that you may understand that glory of the Father and the Son not to be held in common with them by angels, for thus they run: "But when the Son of Man shall come in His majesty, and all the angels with Him." Again, to show that His Father's majesty and glory and His own majesty and glory are one and the same, our Lord Himself saith in another book: "And the Son of Man shall confound him, when He shall come in the glory of His Father, with the holy angels." The angels come in obedience, He comes in glory: they are His retainers, He sits upon His throne: they stand, He is seated—to borrow terms of the daily dealings of human life, He is the Judge: they are the officers of the court. Note that He did not place first His Father's divine majesty, and then, in the second place, His own and the angels', lest He should seem to have made out a sort of descending order, from the highest to lower natures. He placed His own majesty first, and then spoke of His Father's, and the majesty of the angels (because the Father could not appear lower than they), in order that He might not, by placing mention of Himself between that of His Father and that of the angels, seem to have made out some ascending scale, leading from angels to the Father through increase of His own dignity; nor, again, be believed to have, contrariwise, shown a descent from the Father to angels, entailing diminution of that dignity. Now we who confess one Godhead of the Father and the Son suppose no such order of distinction as the Arians do.

Chapter XIV.
The Son is of one substance with the Father.

108. And now, your Majesty, with regard to the question of the substance, why need I tell you that the Son is of one substance with the Father, when we have read that the Son is the image of the Father's substance, that you may understand that there is nothing wherein, so far as Godhead is regarded, the Son differs from the Father.

109. In virtue of this likeness Christ said: "All things that the Father hath are Mine." We cannot, then, deny substance to God, for indeed He is not unsubstantial, Who hath given to others the ground of their being, though this be different in God from what it is in the creature. The Son of God, by Whose agency all things endure, could not be unsubstantial.

110. And therefore, the Psalmist saith: "My bones are not hidden, which Thou didst make in secret, and my substance in the underworld." For to His power and Godhead, the things that before the foundation of the world were done, though their magnificence was [as yet] invisible, could not be hidden. Here, then, we find mention of "substance."

111. But it may be objected that the mention of His substance is the consequence of His Incarnation. I have shown that the word "substance" is used more than once, and that not in the sense of inherited possessions, as you would construe it. Now, if it please you, let us grant that, in accordance with the mystic prophecy, the substance of Christ was present in the underworld—for truly He did exert His power in the lower world to set free, in the soul which animated His own body, the souls of the dead, to loose the bands of death, to remit sins.

112. And, indeed, what hinders you from understanding, by that substance, His divine substance, seeing that God is everywhere, so that it hath been said to Him: "If I go up into heaven, Thou art there; if I go down into hell, Thou art present."

113. Furthermore, the Psalmist hath in the words following made it plain that we must understand the divine substance to be mentioned when he saith: "Thine eyes did see My being, [as] not the effect of working;" inasmuch as the Son is not made, nor one of God's works, but the begotten Word of eternal power. He called Him "acatergston," meaning that the Word neither made nor created, is begotten of the Father without the witnessing presence of any created being. Howbeit, we have abundance of testimony besides this. Let us grant that the substance here spoken of is the bodily substance, provided you also yourself say not that the Son of God is something effected by working, but confess His uncreated Godhead.

114. Now I know that some assert that the mystic incarnate form was uncreated, forasmuch as nothing was done therein through intercourse with a man, because our Lord was the offspring of a virgin. If, then, many have, on the strength of this passage, asserted that neither that which was brought forth of Mary was produced by creative operation, dare you, disciple of Arius, think that the Word of God is something so produced?

115. But is this the only place where we read of "substance"? Hath it not also been said in another passage: "The gates of the cities are broken down, the mountains are fallen, and His substance is revealed"? What, does the word mean something created here also? Some, I know, are accustomed to say that the substance is substance in money. Then, if you give this meaning to the word, the mountains fell, in order that some one's possessions of money might be seen.

116. But let us remember *what* mountains fell, those, namely, of which it hath been said: "If ye shall have faith as a grain of mustard seed ye shall say to this mountain: Be thou removed, and be thou cast into the sea!" By mountains, then, are meant high things that exalt themselves.

117. Moreover, in the Greek, the rendering is this: "The palaces are fallen." What palaces, save the palace of Satan, of whom the Lord said: "How shall His kingdom stand?" We are reading, therefore, of the things which are the devil's palaces as being very mountains, and therefore in the fall of those palaces from the hearts of the faithful, the truth stands revealed, that Christ, the Son of God, is of the Father's eternal substance. What, again, are those mountains of bronze, from the midst of which four chariots come forth?

118. We behold that height, lifting up itself against the knowledge of God, cast down by the word of the Lord, when the Son of God said: "Hold thy peace, and come forth, thou foul spirit." Concerning whom the prophet also said: "Behold, I am come to thee, thou mount of corruption!"

119. *Those* mountains, then, are fallen, and it is revealed that in Christ was the substance of God, in the words of those who had seen Him: "Truly Thou art the Son of God," for it was in virtue of divine, not human power, that He commanded devils. Jeremiah also saith: "Make mourning upon the mountains, and beat your breasts upon the desert tracks, for they have failed; forasmuch as there are no men, they have not heard the word of substance: from flying fowl to beasts of burden, they trembled, they have failed."

120. Nor has it escaped us, that in another place also, setting forth the frailties of man's estate, in order to show that He had taken upon Himself the infirmity of the flesh, and the affections of our minds, the Lord said, by the mouth of His prophet: "Remember, O Lord, what My substance is," because it was the Son of God speaking in the nature of human frailty.

121. Of Him the Scripture saith, in the passage cited, in order to discover the mysteries of the Incarnation: "But Thou hast rejected, O Lord, and counted for nought—Thou hast cast out Thy Christ. Thou hast overthrown the covenant made with Thy Servant, and trampled His holiness in the earth." What was it, in regard whereof the Scripture called Him "Servant," but His flesh?—seeing that "He did not hold equality with God as a prey, but emptied Himself, taking the form of a servant, being made into the likeness of men, and found in fashion as a

man." So, then, in that He took upon Himself My nature, He was a servant, but by virtue of His own power He is the Lord.

122. Furthermore, what meaneth it that thou readest: "Who hath stood in the *truth* (*substantia*) of the Lord?" and again: "Now if they had stood in My *truth*, and had given ear to My words, and had taught My people, I would have turned them from their follies and transgressions"?

Chapter XV.

The Arians, inasmuch as they assert the Son to be "of another substance," plainly acknowledge substance in God. The only reason why they avoid the use of this term is that they will not, as Eusebius of Nicomedia has made it evident, confess Christ to be the true Son of God.

123. How can the Arians deny the substance of God? How can they suppose that the word "substance" which is found in many places of Scripture ought to be debarred from use, when they themselves do yet, by saying that the Son is "eteroousio"," that is, of another substance, admit substance in God?

124. It is not the term itself, then, but its force and consequences, that they shun, because they will not confess the Son of God to be true [God]. For though the process of the divine generation cannot be comprehended in human language, still the Fathers judged that their faith might be fitly distinguished by the use of such a term, as against that of "eteroousio"," following the authority of the prophet, who saith: "Who hath stood in the truth (*substantia*) of the Lord, and seen His Word?" Arians, therefore, admit the term "substance" when it is used so as to square with their blasphemy; contrariwise, when it is adopted in accordance with the pious devotion of the faithful, they reject and dispute against it.

125. What other reason can there be for their unwillingness to have the Son spoken of as "omoousio"," of the same substance, with the Father, but that they are unwilling to confess Him the true Son of God? This is betrayed in the letter of Eusebius of Nicomedia. "If," writes he, "we say that the Son is true God and uncreate, then we are in the way to confess Him to be of one substance (omoousio") with the Father." When this letter had been read before the Council assembled at Nicaea, the Fathers put this word in their exposition of the Faith, because they saw that it daunted their adversaries; in order that they might take the sword, which their opponents had drawn, to smite off the head of those opponents' own blasphemous heresy.

126. Vain, however, is their plea, that they avoid the use of the term, because of the Sabellians; whereby they betray their own ignorance, for a being is of the same substance (omoousion) with another, not with itself. Rightly, then, do we call the Son "omoousio"" (of the same substance), with the Father, forasmuch as that term expresses both the distinction of Persons and the unity of nature.

127. Can they deny that the term "ousia" is met with in Scripture, when the Lord has spoken of bread, that is, "epiousio"," and Moses has written "umei" esesqe moi lao" periousio""? What does "ousia" mean, whence comes the name, but from "ousaaei," "that which endures for ever? For He Who *is*, and *is* for ever, is God; and therefore the Divine Substance, abiding everlastingly, is called ousia. Bread is epiousio", because, taking the substance of abiding power from the substance of the Word, it supplies this to heart and soul, for it is written: "And bread strengtheneth man's heart."

128. Let us, then, keep the precepts of our forefathers, nor with rude and reckless daring profane the symbols bequeathed to us. That sealed book of prophecy, whereof we have heard, neither elders, nor powers, nor angels, nor archangels, ventured to open; for Christ alone is reserved the peculiar right of opening it. Who amongst us dare unseal the book of the priesthood, sealed by confessors, and long hallowed by the testimony of many? They who have been constrained to unseal, nevertheless have since, respecting the deceit put upon them, sealed again; they who dared not lay sacrilegious hands upon it, have stood forth as martyrs and confessors. How can we deny the Faith held by those whose victory we proclaim?

Chapter XVI.

In order to forearm the orthodox against the stratagems of the Arians, St. Ambrose discloses some of the deceitful confessions used by the latter, and shows by various arguments, that though they sometimes call the Son "God," it is not enough, unless they also admit His equality with the Father.

129. Let none fear, let none tremble; he who threatens gives the advantage to the faithful. The soothing balms of deceitful men are poisoned—then must we be on our guard against them, when they pretend to preach that they do deny. Thus were those aforetime, who lightly trusted to them, deceived, so that they fell into the snares of treachery, when they thought all was good faith.

130. "Let him be accursed," say they, "who says that Christ is a creature, after the manner of the rest of created beings." Plain folks have heard this, and put faith in it, for, as it is written, "the simple man believes every word." Thus have they heard and believed, being taken in by the first sound thereof, and, like birds, eager for the bait of faith, have not noted the net spread for them, and so, pursuing after faith, have caught the hook of ungodly deceit. Wherefore "be ye wise as serpents," saith the Lord, "and harmless as doves." Wisdom is put foremost, in order that harmlessness may be unharmed.

131. For those are serpents, such as the Gospel intends, who put off old habits, in order to put on new manners: "Putting off the old man, together with his acts, and putting on the new man, made in the image of Him Who created him." Let us learn then, the ways of those whom the Gospel calls the serpents, throwing off the slough of the old man, that so, like serpents, we may know how to preserve our life and beware of fraud.

132. It would have been sufficient to say, "Accursed be he who saith that Christ is a created being." Why, then, Arian, dost thou mingle poison with the good that is in thy confession, and so defile the whole body of it? For by addition of "after the manner of the rest of created beings," you deny not that Christ is a being created, but that He is a created being like [all] others—for created being you do entitle Him, albeit you assign to Him dignity transcending the rest of creation. Furthermore, Arius, the first teacher of this ungodly doctrine, said that the Son of God was a perfect created being, and not as the rest of created beings. See you, then, how that you have adopted language bequeathed you from your father. To deny that Christ is a being created is enough: why add "but not as the rest of beings created"? Cut away the gangrened part, lest the contagion spread—it is poisonous, deadly.

133. Again, you say sometimes that Christ is God. Nay, but so call Him true God, as meaning, that you acknowledge Him to possess the fulness of the Father's Godhead—for there are gods, so called, alike in heaven or upon earth. The name "God," then, is not to be used as a mere manner of address and mention, but with the understanding that you affirm, of the Son, that same Godhead which the Father hath, as it is written: "For as the Father hath life in Himself, so hath He given to the Son also to have life in Himself;" that is to say, He hath given it to Him, as to His Son, through begetting Him—not by grace, as to one indigent.

134. "And He hath given Him power to execute judgment, because He is the Son of Man." Note well this addition, that you may not take occasion, upon a word, to preach falsehood. You read that He is the Son of Man; do you therefore deny that He accepts [the power given]? Deny God, then, if all things proper to God are not given to the Son, for whereas He has said, "All things that the Father hath are Mine," why not acknowledge that all the properties and attributes of Divinity are in the Son [as they are in the Father]? For He who saith, "All things that the Father hath are Mine," what does He except as having not?

135. Why is it that you recount "with insistence" and in such sincere language, Christ's raising the dead to life, walking upon the waters, healing the sicknesses of men? These powers, indeed, He has given to His bondmen to display as well as Himself. They do the more arouse my wonder when seen present in men, forasmuch as God hath given them power sogreat. I would hear somewhat concerning Christ that is His distinctly and peculiarly, and cannot be held

in common with Him by created beings, now that He is begotten, the only Son of God, very God of very God, sitting at the Father's right hand.

136. Wheresoever I read of the Father and Son sitting side by side, I find the Son always upon the right hand. Is that because the Son is above the Father? Nay, we say not so; but He Whom God's love honours is dishonoured by man's ungodliness. The Father knew that doubts as concerning the Son must needs be sown, and He hath given us an example of reverence for us to follow after, lest we dis-honour the Son.

Chapter XVII.

An objection based on St. Stephen's vision of the Lord standing is disposed of, and from the prayers of the same saint, addressed to the Son of God, the equality of the Son with the Father is shown.

137. There is just one place, in which Stephen hath said that he saw the Lord Jesus *standing* at the right hand of God. Learn now the import of these words, that you may not use them to raise a question upon. Why (you would ask) do we read every where else of the Son as sitting at the right hand of God, but in one place of His standing? He sits as Judge of quick and dead; He stands as His people's Advocate. He stood, then, as a Priest, whilst He was offering to His Father the sacrifice of a good martyr; He stood, as the Umpire, to bestow, as it were, upon a good wrestler the prize of so mighty a contest.

138. Receive thou also the Spirit of God, that thou mayest discern those things, even as Stephen received the Spirit; and thou mayest say, as the martyr said: "Behold, I see the heavens opened, and the Son of Man standing at the right hand of God." He who hath the heavens opened to him, seeth Jesus at the right hand of God: he whose soul's eye is closed, seeth not Jesus at the right hand of God. Let us, then, confess Jesus at God's right hand, that to us also the heavens may be opened. They who confess otherwise close the gates of heaven against themselves.

139. But if any urge in objection that the *Son* was standing, let them show upon this passage that the Father was seated, for though Stephen said that the Son of Man was standing, still he did not further say here that the Father was sitting.

140. Howbeit, to make it more abundantly clear and known that the standing implied no dishonour, but rather sovereignty, Stephen prayed to the Son, being desirous to commend himself the more to the Father, saying: "Lord Jesu, receive my spirit." Again, to show that the sovereignty of the Father and of the Son is one and the same, he prayed again, saying, "Lord, lay not this sin to their charge." These are the words that the Lord, in His own Passion, speaks to the Father, as the Son of Man—these the words of Stephen's prayer, in his own martyrdom to the Son of God. When the same grace is sought of both the Father and the Son, the same power is affirmed of each.

141. Otherwise, if our opponents will have it that Stephen addressed himself to the Father, let them consider what, on their own showing, they affirm. We indeed are unmoved by their arguments; howbeit, let them, to whom the letter and sequence is all important, take notice that the *first* petition is addressed to the Son. Now we, even on their understanding of the passage, prove from it the unity of the Father's and the Son's majesty; for when the Son is addressed in prayer as well as the Father, the equality which the prayer assigns points to unity in action. But if they will not allow that the Son was addressed with the title "Lord," we see that they do indeed seek to deny that He is Lord.

142. Seeing, however, that so great a martyr's crown has been brought forth, let us abate the eagerness of disputation, and bring to-day's discourse to a close. Let us sing the praises of the holy martyr, as is fitting always after a mighty conflict—the martyr bleeding indeed from the enemy's blows, but rewarded with the crown bestowed by Christ.

BOOK IV.

Chapter I.

The marvel is, not that men have failed to know Christ, but that they have not listened to the words of the Scriptures. Christ, indeed, was not known, even of angels, save by revelation, nor again, by His forerunner. Follows a description of Christ's triumphal ascent into heaven, and the excellence of its glory over the assumption of certain prophets. Lastly, from exposition of the conversation with angels upon this occasion, the omnipotence of the Son is proved, as against the Arians.

1. On consideration, your Majesty, of the reason wherefore men have so far gone astray, or that many—alas!—should follow diverse ways of belief concerning the Son of God, the marvel seems to be, not at all that human knowledge has been baffled in dealing with superhuman things, but that it has not submitted to the authority of the Scriptures.

2. What reason, indeed, is there to wonder, if by their worldly wisdom men failed to comprehend the mystery of God the Father and the Lord Jesus Christ, in Whom all the treasures of wisdom and knowledge are hidden, that mystery of which not even angels have been able to take knowledge, save by revelation?

3. For who could by force of imagination, and not by faith, follow the Lord Jesus, now descending from the highest heaven to the shades below, now rising again from Hades to the heavenly places; in a moment self-emptied, that He might dwell amongst us, and yet never made less than He was, the Son being ever in the Father and the Father in the Son?

4. Even Christ's forerunner, though only in so far as representing the synagogue, doubted concerning Him, even he who was appointed to go before the face of the Lord, and at last sending messengers, enquired: "Art Thou He that should come, or do we look for another?"

5. Angels, too, stood spellbound in wonder at the heavenly mystery. And so, when the Lord rose again, and the heights of heaven could not bear the glory of His rising from the dead, Who of late, so far as regarded His flesh, had been confined in the narrow bounds of a sepulchre, even the heavenly hosts doubted and were amazed.

6. For a Conqueror came, adorned with wondrous spoils, the Lord was in His holy Temple, before Him went angels and archangels, marvelling at the prey wrested from death, and though they knew that nothing can be added to God from the flesh, because all things are lower than God, nevertheless, beholding the trophy of the Cross, whereof "the government was upon His shoulder," and the spoils borne by the everlasting Conqueror, they, as if the gates could not afford passage for Him Who had gone forth from them, though indeed they can never o'erspan His greatness—they sought some broader and more lofty passage for Him on His return—so entirely had He remained undiminished by His self-emptying.

7. However, it was meet that a new way should be prepared before the face of the new Conqueror—for a Conqueror is always, as it were, taller and greater in person than others; but, forasmuch as the Gates of Righteousness, which are the Gates of the Old and the New Testament, wherewith heaven is opened, are eternal, they are not indeed changed, but raised, for it was not merely one man but the whole world that entered, in the person of the All-Redeemer.

8. Enoch had been translated, Elias caught up, but the servant is not above his Master. For "No man hath ascended into heaven, but He Who came down from heaven;" and even of Moses, though his corpse was never seen on earth, we do nowhere read as of one abiding in celestial glory, unless it was after that the Lord, by the earnest of His own Resurrection, burst the bonds of hell and exalted the souls of the godly. Enoch, then, was translated, and Elias caught up; both as servants, both in the body, but not after resurrection from the dead, nor with the spoils of death and the triumphal train of the Cross, had they been seen of angels.

9. And therefore [the angels] descrying the approach of the Lord of all, first and only Vanquisher of Death, bade their princes that the gates should be lifted up, saying in adoration, "Lift up the gates, such as are princes amongst you, and be ye lifted Up, O everlasting doors, and the King of glory shall come in."

10. Yet there were still, even amongst the hosts of heaven, some that were amazed, overcome with astonishment at such pomp and glory as they had never yet beheld, and therefore they asked: "Who is the King of glory?" Howbeit, seeing that the angels (as well as ourselves) acquire their knowledge step by step, and are capable of advancement, they certainly must display differences of power and understanding, for God alone is above and beyond the limits imposed by gradual advance, possessing, as He does, every perfection from everlasting.

11. Others, again,—those, to wit, who had been present at His rising again, those who had seen or who already recognized Him,—made reply: "It is the Lord, strong and mighty, the Lord mighty in battle."

12. Then, again, sang the multitude of angels, in triumphal chorus: "Lift up the gates, O ye that are their princes, and be ye lift up, ye everlasting doors, and the King of glory shall come in."

13. And back again came the challenge of them that stood astonished: "Who is that King of glory? For we saw Him having neither form nor comeliness; if then it be not He, *who* is that King of glory?"

14. Whereto answer they which know: "The Lord of Hosts, He is the King of glory." Therefore, the Lord of Hosts, He is the Son. How then do the Arians call Him fallible, Whom we believe to be Lord of Hosts, even as we believe of the Father? How can they draw distinctions between the sovereign powers of Each, when we have found the Son, even as also the Father, entitled "Lord of Saboath"? For, in this very passage, the reading in many copies is: "The Lord of Sabaoth, He is the King of glory." Now the translators have, for the "Lord of Sabaoth," rendered in some places "the Lord of Hosts," in others "the Lord the King," and in others "the Lord Omnipotent." Therefore, since He Who ascended is the Son, and, again, He Who ascended is the Lord of Sabaoth, it surely follows that the Son of God is omnipotent!

Chapter II.

None can ascend to heaven without faith; in any case, he who hath so ascended thither will be cast out wherefore, faith must be zealously preserved. We ourselves each have a heaven within, the gates whereof must be opened and be raised by confession of the Godhead of Christ, which gates are not raised by Arians, nor by those who seek the Son amongst earthly things, and who must therefore, like the Magdalene, be sent back to the apostles, against whom the gates of hell shall not prevail. Scriptures are cited to show that the servant of the Lord must not diminish aught of his Master's honour.

15. What shall we do, then? How shall we ascend unto heaven? There, powers are stationed, principalities drawn up in order, who keep the doors of heaven, and challenge him who ascends. Who shall give me passage, unless I proclaim that Christ is Almighty? The gates are shut,—they are not opened to any and every one; not every one who will shall enter, unless he also believes according to the true Faith. The Sovereign's court is kept under guard.

16. Suppose, however, that one who is unworthy hath crept up, hath stolen past the principalities who keep the gates of heaven, hath sat down at the supper of the Lord; when the Lord of the banquet enters, and sees one not clad in the wedding garment of the Faith, He will cast him into outer darkness, where is weeping and gnashing of teeth, if he keep not the Faith and peace.

17. Let us, therefore, keep the wedding garment which we have received, and not deny Christ that which is His own, Whose omnipotence angels announce, prophets foretel, apostles witness to, even as we have already shown above.

18. Perchance, indeed, the prophet hath spoken of His entering in not only with regard to the gates of the universal heaven; for there be other heavens also where-into the Word of God passeth, whereof it is said: "We have a great Priest, a High Priest, Who hath passed through the heavens, Jesus, the Son of God." What are those heavens, but even the heavens whereof the prophet sayeth that "the heavens declare the glory of God"?

19. For Christ standeth at the door of thy soul. Hear Him speaking. "Behold, I stand at the door, and knock: if any man open to Me, I will come in to him, and I will sup with him, and he with Me." And the Church saith, speaking of Him: "The voice of my brother soundeth at the door."

20. He stands, then—but not alone, for before Him go angels, saying: "Lift up the gates, O ye the princes." What gates? Even those of the which the Psalmist sings in another place also: "Open to me the gates of righteousness." Open, then, thy gates to Christ, that He may come into thee—open the gates of righteousness, the gates of chastity, the gates of courage and wisdom.

21. Believe the message of the angels: "Be ye lift up, ye everlasting doors, and the King of glory shall come in, the Lord of Sabaoth." Thy gate is the loud confession made with faithful voice; it is the door of the Lord, which the Apostle desires to have opened for him, as he says: "That a door of the word may be opened for me, to proclaim the mystery of Christ."

22. Let thy gate, then, be opened to Christ, and let it be not only opened, but lifted up, if, indeed, it be eternal and not condemned to ruin; for it is written: "And be ye lift up, ye *everlasting* doors." The lintel was lift up for Isaiah, when the seraph touched his lips and he saw the Lord of Sabaoth.

23. Thy gates shall be lifted up, then, if thou believest the Son of God to be eternal, omnipotent, above and beyond all praise and understanding, knowing all things, both past an d to come, whilst if thou judgest Him to be of limited power and knowledge, and subordinate, thou liftest not up the everlasting doors.

24. Be thy gates lifted up, then, that Christ may come in unto thee, not such a Christ as the Arians take Him to be—petty, and weak, and menial—but Christ in the form of God, Christ with the Father; that He may enter such as He is, exalted above the heaven and all things; and that He may send forth upon thee His holy Spirit. It is expedient for thee that thou shouldst believe that He hath ascended and is sitting at the right hand of the Father, for if in impious thought thou detain Him amongst things created and earthly, if He depart not for thee, ascend not for thee, then to thee the Comforter shall not come, even as Christ Himself hath told us: "For if I go not away, the Comforter will not come unto you, but if I depart, I will send Him unto you."

25. But if thou shouldst seek Him amongst earthly beings, even as Mary of Magdala sought Him, take heed lest He say to thee, as unto her: "Touch Me not, for I am not yet ascended unto My Father." For thy gates are narrow—they give me no passage—they cannot be lifted up, and therefore I cannot come in.

26. Go thy way, therefore, to my brethren—that is, to those everlasting doors, which, as soon as they see Jesus, are lifted up. Peter is an "everlasting door," against whom the gates of hell shall not prevail. John and James, the sons of thunder, to wit, are "everlasting doom." Everlasting are the doors of the Church, where the prophet, desirous to proclaim the praises of Christ, says: "That I may tell all thy praises in the gates of the daughter of Sion."

27. Great, therefore, is the mystery of Christ, before which even angels stood amazed and bewildered. For this cause, then, it is thy duty to worship Him, and, being a servant, thou oughtest not to detract from thy Lord. Ignorance thou mayest not plead, for to this end He came down, that thou mayest believe; if thou believest not, He has not come down for thee, has not suffered for thee. "If I had not come," saith the Scripture, "and spoken with them, they would have no sin: but now have they no excuse for their sin. He that hateth Me, hateth My Father also." Who, then, hates Christ, if not he who speaks to His dishonour?—for as it is love's part to render, so it is hate's to withdraw honour. He who hates, calls in question; he who loves, pays reverence.

Chapter III.

The words, "The head of every man is Christ …and the head of Christ is God" misused by the Arians, are now turned back against them, to their confutation. Next, another passage of Scripture, commonly taken by the same heretics as a ground of objection, is called in to show that God is the Head of Christ, in so far as Christ is human, in regard of His Manhood, and the unwisdom of their opposition upon the text, "He who planteth He who watereth are one," is displayed. After which explanations, the meaning of the doctrine that the Father is in the Son, and the Son in the Father, and that the faithful are in Both, is expounded.

28. Now let us examine some other objections raised by the Arians. It is written, say they, that "the head of every man is Christ, and the head of woman is man, and the head of Christ is God." Let them, if they please, tell me what they mean by this objection—whether to join together, or to dissociate, these four terms. Suppose they mean to join them, and say that God is the Head of Christ in the same sense and manner as man is the head of woman. Mark what a conclusion they fall into. For if this comparison proceeds on the supposed equality of the terms of it, and these four—woman, man, Christ, and God—are viewed together as in virtue of a likeness resulting from their being of one and the same nature, then woman and God will begin to come under one definition.

29. But if this conclusion be not satisfactory, by reason of its impiety, let them divide, on what principle they will. Thus, if they will have it that Christ stands to God the Father in the same relation as woman to man, then surely they pronounce Christ and God to be of one substance, inasmuch as woman and man are of one nature in respect of the flesh, for their difference is in respect of sex. But, seeing that there is no difference of sex between Christ and His Father, they will acknowledge then that which is one, and common to the Son and the Father, in respect of nature, whereas they will deny the difference lying in sex.

30. Does this conclusion content them? Or will they have woman, man, and Christ to be of one substance, and distinguish the Father from them? Will this, then, serve their turn? Suppose that it will, then observe what they are brought to. They must either confess themselves not merely Arians, but very Photinians, because they acknowledge only the Manhood of Christ, Whom they judge fit only to be placed on the same scale with human beings. Or else they must, however contrary to their leanings, subscribe to our belief, by which we dutifully and in godly fashion maintain that which they have come at by an impious course of thought, that Christ is indeed, after His divine generation, the power of God, whilst after His putting on of the flesh, He is of one substance with all men in regard of His flesh, excepting indeed the proper glory of His Incarnation, because He took upon Himself the reality, not a phantom likeness, of flesh.

31. Let God, then, be the Head of Christ, with regard to the conditions of Manhood. Observe that the Scripture says not that the *Father* is the Head of Christ; but that *God* is the Head of Christ, because the Godhead, as the creating power, is the Head of the being created. And well said [the Apostle] "the Head of Christ is God;" to bring before our thoughts both the Godhead of Christ and His flesh, implying, that is to say, the Incarnation in the mention of the name of Christ, and, in that of the name of God, oneness of Godhead and grandeur of sovereignty.

32. But the saying, that in respect of the Incarnation God is the Head of Christ, leads on to the principle that Christ, as Incarnate, is the Head of man, as the Apostle has clearly expressed in another passage, where he says: "Since man is the head of woman, even as Christ is the Head of the Church;" whilst in the words following he has added: "Who gave Himself for her." After His Incarnation, then, is Christ the head of man, for His self-surrender issued from His Incarnation.

33. The Head of Christ, then, is God, in so far as His form of a servant, that is, of man, not of God, is considered, But it is nothing against the Son of God, if, in accordance with the reality of His flesh, He is like unto men, whilst in regard of His Godhead He is one with the Father, for by this account of Him we do not take aught from His sovereignty, but attribute compassion to Him.

34. But who can with a good conscience deny the one Godhead of the Father and the Son, when our Lord, to complete His teaching for His disciples, said: "That they may be one, even as we also are one." The record stands for witness to the Faith, though Arians turn it aside to suit their heresy; for, inasmuch as they cannot deny the Unity so often spoken of, they endeavour to diminish it, in order that the Unity of Godhead subsisting between the Father and the Son may seem to De such as is unity of devotion and faith amongst men, though even amongst men themselves community of nature makes unity thereof.

35. Thus with abundant clearness we disprove the objection commonly raised by Arians, in order to loosen the Divine Unity, on the ground that it is written: "But he who planteth and he who watereth are one." This passage the Arians, if they were wise, would not quote against us; for how can they deny that the Father and the Son are One, if Paul and Apollos are one, both in nature and in faith? At the same time, we do grant that these cannot be one throughout, in all relations, because things human cannot bear comparison with things divine.

36. No separation, then, is to be made of the Word from God the Father, no separation in power, no separation in wisdom, by reason of the Unity of the Divine Substance. Again, God the Father is in the Son, as we ofttimes find it written, yet [He dwells in the Son] not as sanctifying one who lacks sanctification, nor as filling a void, for the power of God knows no void. Nor, again, is the power of the one increased by the power of the other, for there are not two powers, but one Power; nor does Godhead entertain Godhead, for there are not two Godheads, but one Godhead. We, contrariwise, shall be One in Christ through Power received [from another] and dwelling in us.

37. The letter [of the unity] is common, but the Substance of God and the substance of man are different. We shall be, the Father and the Son. [already] are, one; we shall be one by grace, the Son is so by substance. Again, unity by conjunction is one thing, unity by nature another. Finally, observe what it is that Scripture hath already recorded: "That they may all be one, as Thou, Father, art in Me, and I in Thee."

38. Mark now that He said not "Thou in us, and we in Thee," but "Thou in Me, and I in Thee," to place Himself apart from His creatures. Further He added: "that they also may be in Us," in order to separate here His dignity and His Father's from us, that our union in the Father and the Son may appear the issue, not of nature, but of grace, whilst with regard to the unity of the Father and the Son it may be believed that the Son has not received this by grace, but possesses by natural right of His Sonship.

Chapter IV.

The passage quoted adversely by heretics, namely, "The Son can do nothing of Himself," is first explained from the words which follow; then, the text being examined, word by word, their acceptation in the Arian sense is shown to be impossible without incurring the charge of impiety or absurdity, the proof resting chiefly on the creation of the world and certain miracles of Christ.

39. Again, another objection that the Arians bring up, denying that the Power of the Father and the Son can be one and the same, is rested on His saying: "Verily, verily, I say unto you; the Son can do nothing of Himself, but what He hath seen the Father doing." And therefore they affirm that the Son has done nothing of Himself, and can do nothing, save what He hath seen the Father doing.

40. O wise foreknowledge of the arguments of unbelievers, which made further provision of means whereby to answer questions, by adding the words that follow: "For whatsoever the Father doeth, the same doeth the Son also, in like fashion," for this indeed is the sequel. Why, then, is it written: "The Son doeth the same things," and not "such like things," but that thou mightest judge that in the Son there is unity in the Father's works, not imitation of them?

41. But to put their proofs in turn upon trial: I would have them answer the question, whether the Son sees the works of the Father. Does He see, I ask, or not? If He sees them, then

He also does them; if He does them, let heretics cease to deny the omnipotence of Him Whom they confess able to do all things that He has seen the Father doing.

42. But what are we to understand by "hath seen"? Has the Son any need of bodily eyes? Nay, if they will affirm this of the Son, they will make out in the Father also a need of bodily activity, in order that the Son may see that which He Himself is to do.

43. Furthermore, what mean the words: "The Son can do nothing of Himself"? Let us put this question, and debate it. Now is there anything impossible to God's Power and Wisdom? These, observe, are names of the Son of God, Whose Might is certainly not a gift received from another, but just as He is the Life, not depending upon another's quickening action, but Himself quickening others, because He is the Life; so also He is Wisdom, not as one that is ignorant acquiring wisdom, but making others wise from His own store; so, too, He is Power, not as having through weakness obtained increase of strength, but being Himself Power, and bestowing power upon the strong.

44. How, then, does Power assert, as it were, under oath: "Verily, verily I say unto you," which means: "Of a truth, of a truth, I tell you"? Truly, then, Thou speakest, Lord Jesus, and dost affirm, repeating indeed thy solemn declaration, that Thou canst do nothing, save what Thou hast seen the Father doing. Thou didst make the universe. Did Thy Father then make another universe, for Thee to take as a model? So must Thy blasphemers confess that there are two, or a multitude of universes, as philosophers affirm, and thus also entangle themselves in this heathen error, or, if they will follow the truth, let them say that what Thou hast made, Thou didst make, without any pattern.

45. Tell me, Lord, when Thou sawest Thy Father incarnate, and walking upon the sea, for I know not, I hold it impious to believe this thing of the Father, knowing that Thou only hast taken our flesh upon Thee. When sawest Thou the Father at a marriage-feast, turning water into wine? Nay, but I have read that Thou alone art the only Son, begotten of the Father. I have been taught that Thou alone, in the mystery of the Incarnation, wast born of the Holy Ghost and the Virgin. The things, then, which we have cited as Thy doings, the Father did not, but Thou alone, without guidance of any work done by Thy Father, for the purchase of the world's salvation with Thy Blood, didst come forth spotless from the Virgin's womb.

46. When they say, "The Son can do nothing of Himself," they indeed except nothing, so that one blasphemer has even said: "He cannot make even a gnat," mocking with so headstrong profanity and with insolence so overweening the majesty of Supreme Power; yet perhaps they may think the mystery of Thine Incarnate Life a needful exception. But say, Lord Jesu, what earth the Father made without Thee. For without Thee He made no heaven, seeing that it is written: "By the Word of the Lord were the heavens established."

47. But neither did the Father make the earth without Thee, for it is written: "All things were made by Him, and without Him was not anything made." For if the Father made aught without Thee, God the Word, then not all things were made by the Word, and the Evangelist lies. Whereas if all things were made by the Word, and if by Thee all things begin to be, which before were not, then surely Thou Thyself, of Thyself, hast made what Thou didst not see made by the Father; though perchance our adversaries may have recourse to that theory of Plato, and place before Thee the ideas supposed by philosophers, which, indeed, we know have been exploded by philosophers themselves. On the other hand, if Thou Thyself hast of Thyself made all things, vain are the assertions of the unbelieving, which ascribe progress in learning to the Maker of all, Who of Himself supplies the teaching of His craft.

48. But if heretics deny that either the heavens or the earth were made by Thee, let them take heed into what a gulf they are by their own madness hurling themselves, seeing that it is written: "Perish the gods, which have not made heaven and earth." Shall He then perish, O Arian, Who has found and saved that which had perished? But to purpose.

Chapter V.

Continuing the exposition of the disputed passage, which he had begun, Ambrose brings forward four reasons why we affirm that something cannot be, and shows that the first three fail to apply to Christ, and infers that the only reason why the Son can do nothing of Himself is His Unity in Power with the Father.

49. In what sense can the Son do nothing of Himself? Let us ask what it is that He cannot do. There are many different sorts of impossibilities. One thing is naturally impossible, another is naturally possible, but impossible by reason of some weakness. Again, there are things which are rendered possible by strength, impossible by unskilfulness or weakness, of body and mind. Further, there are things which it is impossible to change, by reason of the law of an unchangeable purpose, the endurance of a firm will, and, again, faithfulness in friendship.

50. To make this clearer, let us consider the matter in the light of examples. It is impossible for a bird to pursue a course of learning in any science or become trained to any art: it is impossible for a stone to move in any direction, inasmuch as it can only be moved by the motion of another body. Of itself, then, a stone is incapable of moving, and passing from its place. Again, an eagle cannot be taught in the ways of human learning.

51. It is, to take another example, impossible for a sick man to do a strong man's work; but in this case the reason of the impossibility is of a different kind, for the man is rendered unable, by sickness, to do what he is naturally capable of doing. In this case, then, the cause of the impossibility is sickness, and this kind of impossibility is different from the first, since the man is hindered by bodily weakness from the possibility of doing.

52. Again, there is a third cause of impossibility. A man may be naturally capable, and his bodily health may allow of his doing some work, which he is yet unable to do by reason of want of skill, or because his rank in life disqualifies him; because, that is, he lacks the required learning or is a slave.

53. Which of these three different causes of impossibility, think you, which we have enumerated (setting aside the fourth) can we meetly assign to the case of the Son of God? Is He naturally insensible and immovable, like a stone? He is indeed a stone of stumbling to the wicked, a cornerstone for the faithful; but He is not insensible, upon Whom the faithful affection of sentient peoples are stayed. He is not an immovable rock, "for they drank of a Rock that followed them, and that Rock was Christ." The work of the Father, then, is not rendered impossible to Christ by diversity of nature.

54. Perchance we may suppose some things were made impossible for Him by reason of weakness. But He was not weakly Who could heal the weaknesses of others by His word of authority. Seemed He weak when bidding the paralytic take up his bed and walk? He charged the man to perform an action of which health was the necessary condition, even whilst the patient was yet praying a remedy for his disease. Not weak was the Lord of hosts when He gave sight to the blind, made the crooked to stand upright, raised the dead to life, anticipated the effects of medicine at our prayers, and cured them that besought Him, and when to touch the fringe of His robe was to be purified.

55. Unless, peradventure, you thought it was weakness, you wretches, when you saw His wounds. Truly, they were wounds piercing His Body, but there was no weakness betokened by that wound, whence flowed the Life of all, and therefore was it that the prophet said: "By His stripes we are healed." Was He, then, Who was not weak in the hour when He was wounded, weak in regard of His Sovereignty? How, then, I ask? When He commanded the devils, and forgave the offences of sinners? Or when He made entreaty to the Father?

56. Here, indeed, our adversaries may perchance enquire: "How can the Father and the Son be One, if the Son at one time commands, at another entreats?" True, They are One; true also, He both commands and prays: yet whilst in the hour when He commands He is not alone, so also in the hour of prayer He is not weak. He is not alone, for whatsoever things the Father doeth, the same things doeth the Son also, in like manner. He is not weak, for though in the

flesh He suffered weakness for our sins yet that was the chastisement of our peace upon Him, not lack of sovereign Power in Himself.

57. Moreover, that thou mayest know that it is after His Manhood that He entreats, and in virtue of His Godhead that He commands, it is written for thee in the Gospel that He said to Peter: "I have prayed for thee, that thy faith fail not." To the same Apostle, again, when on a former occasion he said, "Thou art the Christ, the Son of the living God," He made answer: "Thou art Peter, and upon this Rock will I build My Church, and I will give thee the keys of the kingdom of heaven." Could He not, then, strengthen the faith of the man to whom, acting on His own authority, He gave the kingdom, whom He called the Rock, thereby declaring him to be the foundation of the Church? Consider, then, the manner of His entreaty, the occasions of His commanding. He entreats, when He is shown to us as on the eve of suffering: He commands, when He is believed to he the Son of God.

58. We see, then, that two sorts of impossibility furnish no explanation, inasmuch as the Power of God can be neither insensible nor weakly. Will you then proffer the third kind [as an account of the matter], namely, that He can do nothing, just as an unskilled apprentice can do nothing without his master's instructions, or a slave can do nothing without his lord. Then didst Thou speak falsely, Lord Jesu, in calling Thyself Master and Lord, and Thou didst deceive Thy disciples by Thy words: "Ye call Me Master and Lord, and ye say well, for so I am." Nay, but Thou, O Truth, wouldst never have deceived men, least of all them whom Thou didst call friends.

59. Yet if our enemies sunder Thee from the Creator, as being unskilled, let them see how they affirm that skill was lacking to Thee, that is to say, to the Divine Wisdom; for all that, however, they cannot divide the unity of substance that Thou hast with the Father. It is not, indeed, by nature, but by reason of ignorance, that the difference exists between the craftsman and the unskilled; but neither is handicraft attributable to the Father, nor ignorance to Thee, for there is no such thing as ignorant wisdom.

60. Therefore, if insensibility is no attribute of the Son, and if neither weakness, nor ignorance, nor servility, let unbelievers put it to their minds for meditation that both by nature and sovereignty the Son is One with the Father, and by its working His power is not at cross-purpose with the Father, inasmuch as "all things that the Father hath done, the Son doeth likewise," for no one can do in like fashion the same work that another has done, unless he shares in the unity of the same nature, whilst he is also not inferior in method of working.

61. Yet I would still enquire *what* it is that the Son cannot do, unless He see the Father doing it. I will take the fool's line, and propound some examples drawn from things of a lower world. "I am become a fool; ye have compelled me." What indeed is more foolish than to debate over the majesty of God, which rather occasions questionings, than godly instruction which is in faith. But to arguments let arguments reply; let words make answer to them, but love to us, the love which is in God, issuing of a pure heart and good conscience and faith unfeigned. And so I stickle not to introduce even the ludicrous for the confutation of so vain a thesis.

62. How, then, does the Son see the Father? A horse sees a painting, which naturally it is unable to imitate. Not thus does the Son behold the Father. A child sees the work of a grown man, but he cannot reproduce it; certainly not thus, again, does the Son see the Father.

63. If, then, the Son can, by virtue of a common hidden power of the same nature which He has with the Father, both see and act in an invisible manner, and by the fulness of His Godhead execute every decree of His Will, what remains for us but to believe that the Son, by reason of indivisible unity of power, does nothing, save what He has seen the Father doing, forasmuch as because of His incomparable love the Son does nothing of Himself, since He wills nothing that is against His Father's Will? Which truly is the proof not of weakness but of unity.

Chapter VI.

The fourth kind of impossibility (§49) is now taken into consideration, and it is shown that the Son does nothing that the Father approves not, there being between Them perfect unity of will and power.

64. The Son, moreover,—to consider now our fourth premiss,—is not self-assertive, for He, the Divine Assessor, hath done nought that is not in agreement with His Father's Will. Further, the Father hath seen the things that the Son made, and pronounced them very good; for so it is written in Genesis: "And God said, Let there be light; and there was light. And God saw the light that it was good."

65. Now, did the Father say on that occasion, "Let there be such light as I Myself have made," or "Let there be light"—light having as yet not existed; or did the Son ask what sort of light the Father made? Nay, the Son made light, according to His own Will, and so far in accordance with the Father's good pleasure, that He approved. It is of new, original work by the Son that the place speaks.

66. Again, if, as Arian, expositions of the Scriptures make out, it is a discredit to the Son to have made what He saw, whereas the Scriptures present Him as having made what He [before] saw not, and to have given being to things which as yet were not, what should they say of the Father, Who praised that He had seen, as though He could not have foreseen the things that were to be made?

67. The Son, therefore, sees the Father's work in like manner as the Father sees the Son's, and the Father praises not the work as one would praise work of another's doing, but recognizes it as His own, for "whatsoever things the Father hath done, the same doeth the Son, in like manner." [So was it written, that] you might understand one and the same work to be the work both of the Father and of the Son. And thus the Son does nothing save what is approved of by the Father, praised by the Father, willed by the Father, because His whole Being is of the Father; and He is not as the created being, which commits many faults, ofttimes offending the Will of its Creator, in lusting after and falling into sin. Nought, then, is of the Son's doing, save what is pleasing to the Father, forasmuch as one Will, one Purpose, is Theirs, one true Love, one effect of action.

68. Furthermore, to prove to you that it comes of Love, that the Son can do nothing of Himself save what He hath seen the Father doing, the Apostle has added to the words, "Whatsoever the Father hath done, the same things doeth the Son also, in like manner," this reason: "For the Father loveth the Son," and thus Scripture refers the Son's inability to do, whereof it testifies, to unity in Love that suffers no separation or disagreement.

69. But if the inseparableness of the Persons in Love rest, as it truly does, upon [identity of] nature, thou surely they are also inseparable, for the same reason, in action, and it is impossible that the work of the Son should not be in agreement with the Father's Will, when what the Son works, the Father works also, and what the Father works, the Son works also, and what the Son speaks, the Father speaks also, as it is written: "My Father, Who dwelleth in Me, He it is that speaketh, and the works that I do He Himself doeth." For the Father appointed nought save by the exercise of His Power and Wisdom, forasmuch as He made all things wisely, as it is written: "In wisdom hast Thou made them all" and likewise, God the Word made nought without the Father's participation.

70. Not without the Father does He work; not without His Father's Will did He offer Himself for that most holy Passion, the Victim slain for the salvation of the whole world; not without His Father's Will concurring did He raise the dead to life. For example, when He was at the point to raise Lazarus to life, He lifted up His eyes and said, "Father, I thank Thee, for that Thou hast heard Me. And I knew that Thou dost always hear Me, but for the sake of the multitude that standeth round I spake, that they may believe that Thou hast sent Me," in order that, though speaking agreeably to His assumed character of man, in the flesh, He might still express His oneness with the Father in will and operation, in that the Father hears all and sees

all that the Son wills, and therefore also the Father sees the Son's doings, hears the utterances of His Will, for the Son made no request, and yet said that He had been heard.

71. Again, we cannot suppose that the Father hears not all, whatsoever the Son's will resolves; and to show that He is always heard by the Father, not as a servant, not as a prophet, but as Son, He said: "And I knew that Thou dost always hear Me, but for the sake of the multitude which standeth round I spake, that they may believe that Thou hast sent Me."

72. It is for our sakes, therefore, that He renders thanks, lest we should suppose that the Father and the Son are one and the same Person, when we hear of one and the same work being wrought by the Father and the Son. Further, to show us that His rendering of thanks had not been the tribute due from one wanting in power, that, on the contrary, He, as Son of God, ever claimed for Himself the possession of divine authority, He cried, "Lazarus, come forth." Here, surely, is the voice of command, not of prayer.

Chapter VII.
The doctrine had in view for enforcement is corroborated by the truth that the Son is the Word of the Father—the Word, not in the sense in which we understand the term, but a living and active Word. This being so, we cannot deny Him to be of the same Will, Power, and Substance with the Father.

73. To return, however, to what we had in hand before, and finish the task set before us. The Son, as the Word. carries out His Father's Will. Now, a word, as we understand and use it, is an *utterance*. There are syllables and sounds, which, however, are not at variance with the thought of our mind, and what we apprehend and are affected by inwardly we give token of by the testimony of the spoken word, which, as it were, works [for us]. But the words we speak have no direct efficacy in themselves, it is the Word of God alone, which is neither an utterance, nor an "inward concept," as they call it, but works efficaciously, is living, and has healing power.

74. Wouldst thou know what is the nature of the Word—hear the Scriptures. "For the Word of God is living and mighty, yea, working effectually, sharp and keener than any the sharpest sword, piercing even to the sundering of soul and spirit, of limbs and marrow."

75. Hearest thou, then, the Word of God, and wilt separate Him from the Father's Will and Power? Thou hearest Him called the living Word, the healing Word—seek not then to compare Him with the word of our mouth; for if the word we utter, through it have not eyes to see, nor ears to hear, yet speaks, and still the knowledge of what it speaks is wrought by virtue of hidden mysteries of man's nature, how can he escape the charge of blasphemy, who requires that some sort of bodily vision and hearing shall go along with the Godhead in the Word of God, and thinks that the Son can do nothing of Himself, save what He shall have seen the Father doing, though (as we have said) there is in the Father, Son, and Holy Spirit the same Will, both to do and not to do, and the same Power, by reason of unity in the same substance.

76. But if, though men are, as a rule, different in respect of their thoughts and feelings, they yet agree as to the meaning of a single proposition, what ought we to think as concerning the Father and the Son of God, seeing that in the Substance of the Godhead there is that is imitated by human love?

77. Let us, however, suppose—as our adversaries would have it—that the Son does, as it were, copy the pattern of that which He has seen His Father doing. But even this, we must confess, means that He is of the same substance, for none can completely imitate the working of another, unless he be one with him in the same nature.

Chapter VIII.
The heretical objection, that the Son cannot be equal to the Father, because He cannot beget a Son, is turned back upon the authors of it. From the case of human nature it is shown that whether a person begets offspring or not, has nothing to do with his power. Most of all must this be true since, otherwise, the Father Himself would have to be pronounced wanting in power. Whence it

follows that we have no right to judge of divine things by human, and must take our stand upon the authority of Holy Writ, otherwise we must deny all power either to the Father or to the Son.

78. There is a fool's demurrer, your Majesty, which certain persons are given to raising, in order to show the Father and the Son to be not equal together, saying that the Father is Almighty, because He hath begotten the Son, but that the Son is not Almighty, because He hath not been able to beget.

79. But see how wild is their blasphemy, how their philosophers' logic confutes itself. For the raising of this question must lead either to their confessing with their own mouths that the Son is co-eternal with the Father, or, if they impose a beginning upon the Son's existence, to their assigning of necessity a beginning to the Father's power. When, therefore, they deny that the Son is Almighty, they are on the road to assert—which is impious—that the Father began to be Almighty by help of the Son.

80. For if the Father is Almighty by reason of begetting the Son, then, certainly, either the Son is co-eternal with the Father, because if the Father is eternally Almighty, then the Son also is eternal, or, if there was a time when there was not an eternal Son, there was by consequence a time when there was not an Almighty Father. For when they would make out that there was a time when the Son began to be, they are sliding back into [the error of] saying that the Father's Power also has not been from everlasting, but began to be in consequence of the generation of the Son. So, in their desire to do dishonour to the Son of God, they do so increase His honour as to seem to make Him, contrary to all right belief, the source of His Father's Power, though the Son saith, "All things that the Father hath are Mine" —that is to say, not the things which He has bestowed upon the Father, but which He has received from the Father, by right as the Son Whom the Father has begotten.

81. And therefore we do declare the Son to be Eternal Power; if, then, His Power and Godhead be eternal, surely His Sovereignty is eternal also. He, then, who dishonours the Son dishonours the Father, and is an enemy and offender against duty and love. Let us honour the Son, in Whom the Father is well pleased, for it is the Father's pleasure that praise be given to the Son, in Whom He Himself is well pleased.

82. Let us, however, make answer to the conclusion they strive to establish; but we seem to have sought, in pursuit of a personal appeal, to escape from the difficulty of treating the question before us. The Father, they say, has begotten a Son; the Son has not. What proof is this that they are not equal? To beget is the Father's natural function, as a Father, and no necessary outcome of His Sovereign Power. Furthermore, dutiful regard places persons on an equality with each other, and does not sunder them. Again, our own experience of what holds good amongst us frail mortals teaches us that it may frequently happen that weak men have sons, whilst stronger men have not; that slaves have children, whilst their masters are childless; and that the poor beget offspring, whilst rich men are unblessed with any.

83. But if our adversaries say that this too may be the result of infirmity, inasmuch as men may desire to beget children, but be unable to do so; then, though things divine are not to be judged of and determined by things human, yet let them understand that with men also, as with God, whether one has children or no, is not dependent upon or derived of his authoritative power, but upon the personal attributes of a father, and that begetting lies not in the power of our will, but is contingent upon our qualities of body; for if it were a matter of sovereign authority, then the mightier king would have the greater number of sons. To have sons, then, or to be childless, therefore, is not in necessary connection or relation to sovereign authority. Is it, then, so with nature?

84. If you [my Arian adversaries] regard what you object as natural weakness, and rely upon examples taken from the nature of mankind, remember that the Father's nature is the same as the Son's, and therefore you do either confess the Son to be a true Son, and dishonour the Father in the Person of the Son, by reason of Their unity in one and the same Nature (for as the Father is by Nature God, so also is the Son; whereas the Apostle says that the "gods many" are

not so by nature, but are only so called); or, if you deny Him to be a true Son, that is to say, possessing the same Nature, then He is not begotten, and if the Son is not begotten, the Father did not beget Him.

85. The conclusion we come at, therefore, on the line of your persuasion, is that God the Father is not Almighty, because He could not beget, if He did not beget the Son, but created Him. But forasmuch as the Father is Almighty, He being, as you hold, the Almighty in so far as He is the only Author of Being, then surely He has begotten His Son, and not created Him. Howbeit, we ought to believe His word before yours. He says: "I have begotten," and that more than once, witnessing to Himself as begetting.

86. It is no sign, then, of infirmity, whether of nature or authority, in Christ, that He has not begotten, for to beget, as we have already said ofttimes, bears no relation to supremacy of authority, but to a personal property in a nature. For if the Omnipotence of the Father is thereby constituted, that He hath a Son, then He might have been more Almighty had He begotten more Sons.

87. Then is His power exhausted in the begetting of One? Nay, but I will show that Christ also hath sons, whom He begets every day, but with that generation, or rather regeneration, which is related to personal authority rather than nature, for adoption is the exercise and bestowal of authority, and generation the manifestation of a property, as Scripture itself hath taught us: for John saith that "He was in this world, and the world was made by Him, and the world knew Him not. He came to His own, and His own received Him not. But as many as received Him, to them gave He power to become sons of God, to them which believe in His Name."

88. We say, therefore, that it is the function and exercise of His Authority that He has made us sons of God, whereas the oracles of God discover that His generation is in relation to personal attribute, for the Wisdom of God saith: "I came forth out of the mouth of the Most High," that is to say not of compulsion, but free, not under bond of authority, but born in a hidden birth, according to personal powers of Supreme Sovereignty and rightfulness of authority. Again, concerning the same Wisdom, Which is the Lord Jesus, the Father saith in another place: "Out of the womb I begat Thee, before the morning star."

89. Now this He said, not to make us think of a bodily womb, but to show that true generation is His proper activity, for if we understand the words as speaking of generation from a body, then [we imply] the Father Almighty conceived and brought forth in travail. But far be it from us that we should make this weak bodily frame the measure of God's greatness. The word "womb" represents the hidden mystery, the inner sanctuary of the Father's being, into which neither angels nor archangels nor powers nor dominations, nor any created nature, hath been able to enter. For the Son is always with the Father, and in the Father—with the Father, by virtue of the distinction, without division, proper to the Eternal Trinity; in the Father, by reason of the essential unity of the Divine Nature.

90. What room here, then, for one to sit in judgment upon the Godhead, to call in question the Father and the Son,—the One for begetting, the Other for not begetting. No man condemns his servant or handmaid for begetting (or bearing) offspring; but those Arians condemn Christ for not begetting—they do condemn Him, for they privately pass sentence of condemnation upon Him, when they take from His glory and dignity. The question, why they have not begotten offspring, does not lead those who are joined in marriage into loss of their love, or denial of each other's merits, but the Arians, because Christ hath not begotten a Son, make light of His sovereignty.

91. Why, ask they, is the Son not a Father? Because, on the other side, the Father is not a Son. Why has not Christ begotten? Even because the Father is not begotten. Yet the Son stands none the lower, because He is not a Father; nor the Father, because He is not a Son, for the Son said: "All things that the Father hath are Mine" —so truly is generation involved in the Father's personal attributes, and comes not by mere right of sovereignty.

92. The Substance of the Trinity is, so to say, a common Essence in that which is distinct, an incomprehensible, ineffable Substance. We hold the distinction, not the confusion of Father, Son, and Holy Spirit; a distinction without separation; a distinction without plurality; and thus we believe in Father, Son, and Holy Spirit as each existing from and to eternity in this divine and wonderful Mystery: not in twoFathers, nor in two Sons, nor in two Spirits. For "there is one God, the Father, of Whom are all things, and we in Him; and one Lord, Jesus Christ, by Whom are all things, and we by Him." There is One born ofthe Father, the Lord Jesus, and therefore He is the Only-begotten."There is also One Holy Spirit," as the same Apostle hath said. So we believe,so we read, so we hold. We know the fact of distinction, we know nothing of the hidden mysteries; we pry not into the causes, but keep the outward signs vouchsafed unto us.

93. O monstrous wickedness, that they who have no power over their own procreation should claim and usurp power to enquire into the Divine Generation! Let them deny, them, that the Son is equal to the Father, forasmuch as He hath not begotten; let them deny that the Son is equal to the Father, because He hath a Father! But if they talked after this fashion about men, who sometimes desire to beget sons, yet cannot, we should call it an insult, just as we should so call it, if of two men, one having sons and the other childless, the latter were said to be inferior to the former on that ground. So monstrous also, I say, does it seem, in regard simply to men, that one should therefore be esteemed the more lightly because he hath a father. Peradventure, indeed, the Arians suppose that Christ is in the position of one in a family, and frets because He is not set free and independent of His Father's authority, and is not empowered to administer the estate. But Christ is not under tutelage; nay, rather has He abolished all tutelage.

94. How then, let them tell us, would they have these things to be?—a true generation, the true Son begotten of God the Father, that is, of the Substance of the Father, or of another substance? If they say "begotten of the Father, that is, of the Substance of God," well and good, for then they acknowledge the Son as begotten of the Substance of the Father. If, then, they are of one Substance, surely they are also of one sovereign Power. Whereas, if the Son is begotten of another substance, how can the Father be Almighty, and the Son not Almighty? For what advantage hath God, if He have made His Son of another substance, when confessedly the Son, on His part, hath of another substance made us sons of God? The Son, therefore, is either of one Substance with the Father, or of one sovereign Power.

95. Our adversaries' question, then, falls flat, because they cannot judge Christ—or rather, because He is clear, when He is judged. They are worthy, however, to be condemned upon their own sentence, who raise this question against us, for if the Son be therefore not equal to the Father, because He hath not begotten a Son, then by all means let them who sow discussions of this kind confess, if they have not children, that their very servants are to be preferred before themselves, inasmuch as they cannot be the equals of those who have children—whereas, if they have children, let them regard the merit thereof as due not to themselves, but of right to their sons.

96. The objection, then, holds not together, that the Son cannot be equal to the Father, by reason of the Father having begotten the Son, whilst the Son has begotten no Son of Himself, for the spring: begets the stream, though the stream begets no spring out of itself, and light begets radiance, and not radiance light, yet the nature of radiance and light is one.

Chapter IX.

Various quibbling arguments, advanced by the Arians to show that the Son had a beginning of existence, are considered and refuted, on the ground that whilst the Arians plainly prove nothing, or if they prove anything, prove it against themselves, (inasmuch as He Who is the beginning of all cannot Himself have a beginning), their reasonings do not even hold true with regard to facts of human existence. Time could not be before He was, Who is the Author of time—if indeed at some time He was not in existence, then the Father was without His Power and Wisdom. Again, our own human experience shows that a person is said to exist before he is born.

97. Now that our opponents have failed to maintain their objection against the truth of His Son's equality with the Father, on the ground of His Generation, let them see that their well known device of controversy, their stock misrepresentation, is frustrated. Their common use is to propound this riddle: "How can the Son be equal with the Father? If He is a Son, then before He was begotten He was not in existence. If He was in existence, why was He begotten?" And men who advance difficulties raised by Arius yet sturdily deny that they are Arians.

98. Accordingly, they demand our answer, intending, if we say, "The Son existed before He was begotten," to meet us with a subtle retort, that "If so, then, before He was begotten, He was created, and there is no difference between Him and the rest of created beings, for He began to be a creature before He began to be the Son." To which they add: "Why was He begotten, when He was already in existence? Because He was imperfect, and in order that He might afterwards be made more perfect?" Whilst if we reply that the Son did not exist before He was begotten, they will immediately reply: "Then by being begotten He was brought into existence, not having existed before He was begotten," so as to lead on from this to the conclusion that "the Son existed, when He did not exist."

99. But let those who propound this difficulty and endeavour to enwrap the truth in a cloud tell us themselves whether the Father exerts His power of begetting within or without limits of time. If they say "within limits of time," then they will attribute to the Father what they object against the Son, so as to make the Father seem to have begun to be what He was not before. If their answer is "without such limits," then what is left them but to resolve for themselves the problem they have propounded, and acknowledge that the Son is not begotten under limits and conditions of time, since they deny that the Father so begets?

100. If the Son, then, is not begotten within limits of time, we are free to judge that nothing can have existed before the Son, Whose being is not confined by time. If, indeed, there was anything in being before the Son, then it instantly follows that in Him were not created all things in heaven or in earth, and the Apostle is shown to have erred in so setting it down in his Epistle, whereas, if before He was begotten there was nothing, I see not wherefore He, before Whom none was, should be said to have been after any.

101. With the consideration whereof we must join another most blasphemous objection of theirs, which covers a subtle purpose to confuse the sense and understanding of simple folk. They ask whether everything that comes to an end had also at any time a beginning. If they are told that what has an end also had a beginning, then they return to the charge with the question whether the Father has ceased to beget His Son. This by our consent being granted them, they conclude that the generation of the Son had a beginning. The which if you allow, it seems to follow that if the Generation had a beginning, it appears to have begun in Him Who was begotten; so that one, who had not existed before, may be called "begotten"—their intent being to close the inquiry by laying down as conclusive that there was a time when the Son existed not.

102. Besides this, there are other vain objections, such as persons of their glibness of tongue would readily urge. If, say they, the Son is the Word of the Father, then He is called "begotten," inasmuch as He is the Word. But then since He is the Word, He is not a work. Now the Father has spoken "in divers manners," whence it follows that He has begotten many Sons, if He has spoken His Word, not created it as a work of His hands. O fools, talking as though they knew not the difference between the word uttered and the Divine Word, abiding eternally, born of the Father—born, I say, not uttered only—in Whom is no combination of syllables, but the fulness of the eternal Godhead and life without end!

103. Follows another blasphemy, whereby they enquire whether it was of His own free will, or on compulsion, that the Father begat [His Son], intending, if we say, "Of His own free will," that we should appear as though we acknowledged that the Father's Will preceded the [Divine] Generation, and to answer that there being something that preceded the existence of the Son, the Son is not co-eternal with the Father, or that He, like the rest of the world, is a being created, forasmuch as it is written, "He hath made all things, as many as He would," though this

is spoken, not of the Father and the Son, but of those creatures which the Son made. Whereas if we answered that the Father begat [His Son] on compulsion, we should seem to have attributed infirmity to the Father.

104. But in the eternal Generation there is no foregoing condition, neither of will, nor of unwillingness, and therefore I can neither say that the Father begat of His free Will, nor yet that He begat on compulsion, for to beget depends not upon possibility as determined by will, but rather appears to stand in a certain right and property of the hidden being of the Father. For just as the Father is not good because He wills to be so, or is compelled to be so, but is above these conditions—is good, that is, by nature,—even so the putting forth of His generative power is neither of will nor of necessity.

105. Yet let us grant their proposal, Granted that the Generation depends on the Will of Him Who generates; when do they say that this act of will took place? If it was in the beginning, then, plainly; the Son was in the beginning. If the Will is eternal, then the Son also is eternal. If the Will began to exist, then God the Father, as He was, was so displeased with Himself, that He made a change in His condition, that is to say, without His Son He was displeasing to Himself; in His Son He began to be well pleased.

106. To follow out the consequences thereof. If the Father conceived, after the manner of human nature, a desire to beget, then did He also pass through all the experiences which befal men before the birth takes place—but we find that generation is not determined merely by will, but is an object of wish.

107. Thus do they betray their own ungodliness, who would have it that Christ's generation had a beginning, in order that it may seem, not that true begetting of the Word abiding, but the utterance of words that pass and are forgotten, and that by intrusion of [the premiss of] a multitude of sons, they may [be warranted to] deny Christ's personal possession of the divine attributes, to the end that He may be regarded as neither the only-begotten nor the first-begotten Son; and lastly, that given the belief that His existence had a beginning, it may also be deemed as appointed to have an end.

108. But neither had the Son of God any beginning, seeing that He already was at the beginning, nor shall He come to an end, Who is the Beginning and the End of the Universe; for being the Beginning, how could He take and receive that which He already had, or how shall He come to an end, being Himself the End of all things, so that in that End we have an abiding-place without end? The Divine Generation is not an event occurring in the course of time, and within its limits, and therefore before it time is not, and in it time has no place.

109. Again, their aimless and futile question finds no loophole for entry, even when directed upon the creation itself; nay, indeed, temporal existences appear, in certain cases, to admit of no division of time. For instance, light generates radiance, but we can neither conceive that the radiance begins to exist after the light, nor that the light is in existence before the radiance, for where there is a light, there is radiance, and where there is radiance there is also a light; and thus we can neither have a light without radiance, nor radiance without light, because both the light is in the radiance, and the radiance in the light. Thus the Apostle was taught to call the Son "the Radiance of the Father's Glory," for the Son is the Radiance of His Father's light, co-eternal, because of eternity of Power; inseparable, by unity of brightness.

110. If then we can neither understand the mystery of, nor dissociate, these created objects in the sky above us, which we see, can we comprehend Him Whom we see not, Who is above every created existence, God, as He is in the very Holy of Holies of His own Generation? Can we make time a barrier between Him and the Son, when all time is the creation of the Son?

111. Let them cease therefore, and say no more that before He was begotten the Son was not. For the word "before" is a mark of time, whereas the Generation is before all times, and therefore that which comes after aught comes not before it, and the work cannot be before the maker, seeing that necessarily objects made take their commencement from the craftsman who makes them. How can the customary action of any created object be regarded as existing prior

to the maker of it, whilst all time is a creation, and every creation has taken its being from its creator?

112. I would, therefore, further examine our opponents, who esteem themselves so cunning, and have them make good the application of their theory to human existence, seeing that they use it to disparage the glory of God's Existence, and keep far away from any confession of an inscrutable mystery in the Divine Generation. I would have them find ground for their objection in the facts of human generation. Of God's Son they assert that before He was begotten He was not,—that is to say, they say this of the Wisdom, the Power, the Word of God, Whose Generation knows nothing prior to itself. But if, as they would have us believe, there was a time when the Son existed not (the which it is blasphemy to affirm), then there was a time when God lacked the fulness of Divine Perfection, if afterwards He passed through a process of begetting a Son.

113. To show them, however, the weakness and transparency of their objection, though it has no real relation to any truth, divine or human, I will prove to them that men have existed before they were born. Else, let them show that Jacob, who whilst yet hidden in the secret chamber of his mother's womb supplanted his brother, had not been appointed and ordained, ere ever he was born; let them show that Jeremiah had not likewise been so, before his birth, - Jeremiah, to whom the message comes: "Before I formed thee in thy mother's womb, I knew thee; and before thou camest forth from the belly, I sanctified thee, and appointed thee for a prophet amongst the nations." What testimony can we have stronger than the case of this great prophet, who was sanctified before he was born, and known before he was shaped?

114. What, again, shall I say of John, of whom his holy mother testifies that, whilst he yet lay in her womb, he perceived in spirit the presence of his Lord, and leaped for joy, as we remember it to be written, his mother saying: "For lo, as soon as the voice of the salutation entered mine ears, the babe leaped in my womb for joy." Was he, then, who prophesied, in existence or not? Nay, surely he was—surely he was in being who worshipped his Maker; he was in being who spake in his mother's womb. And so Elisabeth was filled with the spirit of her son, and Mary sanctified by the Spirit of hers, for thus you may find it recorded, that "the babe leaped in her womb, and Elisabeth was filled with the Holy Ghost."

115. Consider the proper force of each word. Elisabeth was indeed the first to hear the voice of Mary, but John was first to feel His Lord's gracious Presence. Sweet is the harmony of prophecy with prophecy, of woman with woman, of babe with babe. The women speak words of grace, the babes move hiddenly, and as their mothers approach one another, so do they engage in mysterious converse of love; and in a twofold miracle, though in diverse degrees of honour, the mothers prophesy in the spirit of their little ones. Who, I ask, was it that performed this miracle? Was it not the Son of God, Who made the unborn to be?

116. Thus your objection fails of reconcilement with the truths of human existence—can it attain thereto with divine mysteries? What mean you by your principle that "before He was begotten He was not"? Was the Father engaged for some time in conception, so that certain epochs passed away before the Son was begotten? Was He, like women, in travail of birth, so that just this travail? What would you? Why seek we to pry into divine mysteries? The Scriptures tell me the necessary effects of the Divine Generation, not how it is done.

Chapter X.

The objection that Christ, on the showing of St. John, lives because of the Father, and therefore is not to be regarded as equal with the Father, is met by the reply that for the Life of the Son, in respect of His Godhead, there has never been a time when it began; and that it is dependent upon none, whilst the passage in question must be understood as referring to the His human life, as is shown by His speaking there of His body and blood. Two expositions of the passage are given, the one of which is shown to refer to Christ's Manhood, whilst the second teaches His equality with the Father, as also His likeness with men. Rebuke is administered to the Arians for the insult which they are seeking to inflict upon the Son, and the sense in which the Son can be said to live "because of" the Father is explained, as also the union of life with our the divine Life. A further objection, based upon the Son's prayer that He may be glorified by the Father, is briefly refuted.

118. There are not a few who raise this further objection, that it is written: "As the living Father hath sent Me, and I live by the Father; so he that eateth Me, liveth also by Me." "How," ask they, "is the Son equal with the Father, when He has said that He lives by the Father?"

119. Let those who oppose us on this ground tell us first what the Life of the Son is. Is it a life bestowed by the Father upon one lacking life? But how could the Son ever fail to possess life, He Himself being the Life, as He says, "I am the Way, the Truth, and the Life." Truly, His life is eternal, even as His power is eternal. Was there a time, then, when (so to speak) Life possessed not itself?

120. Bethink you what is read this day concerning the Lord Jesus, that "He died for our sakes, to the end that whether we wake or whether we sleep, we may live with Him." He Whose Death is Life, is not His Godhead Life, seeing that the Godhead is Life eternal?

121. But is His Life truly in the Father's power? Why, He showed that even His bodily life was not in the power of any other, as we have it on record: "I lay down My life, that I may take it again. No man taketh it from Me, but I lay it down of Myself. I have power to lay it down, and again I have power to take it. This commandment have I received of My Father."

122. Is His divine Life then to be regarded as depending upon the power of another, when His bodily life was subject to no other power but His own? For it would have been the power of another, but for the Unity of power. But just as He gives us to understand that His laying down His life was done of His own power, and of His free Will, so also He teaches us, in laying it down in obedience to His Father's command, the unity of His own with the Father's Will.

123. If, then, there has neither been slime when the Life of the Son took a commencement, nor any power to which it has been subjected, let us consider what His meaning was when He said: "Even as the living Father hath sent Me, and I live by the Father"? Let us expound His meaning as best we can; nay, rather let Him expound it Himself.

124. Take notice, then, what He said in an earlier part of His discourse. "Verily, verily, I say unto you." He first teaches thee how thou oughtest to listen. "Verily, verily, I say unto you, unless ye eat the flesh of the Son of Man, and drink His blood, ye shall have no life in you." He first premised that He was speaking as Son of Man; dost thou then think that what He hath said, as Son of Man, concerning His Flesh and His Blood, is to be applied to His Godhead?

125. Then He added: "For My Flesh is meat indeed, and My Blood is drink [indeed]." Thou hearest Him speak of His Flesh and of His Blood, thou perceivest the sacred pledges, [conveying to us the merits and power] of the Lord's death, and thou dishonourest His Godhead. Hear His own words: "A spirit hath not flesh and bones." Now we, as often as we receive the Sacramental Elements, which by the mysterous efficacy of holy prayer are transformed into the Flesh and the Blood, "do show the Lord's Death."

126. Then, alter calling on us to take notice that He speaks as Son of Man, and frequent repeated mention of His Flesh and His Blood, He adds: "Even as the living Father hath sent Me, and I live by the Father, so he that eateth Me, he also liveth by Me." How then do they suppose that we are to understand these words?—for the comparison can be shown as a double one. The first comparison being after the following manner: "Even as the living Father hath sent Me, I live by the Father;" the second: "Even as the living Father hath sent Me, and I live by the Father, so also he that eateth Me, he too liveth by Me."

127. If our adversaries choose the former, the meaning is this, that, "as I am sent by the Father and am come down from the Father, so (in accordance therewith) I live by the Father." But in what character was He sent, and came down, save as Son of Man, even as He Himself said before: "No man hath ascended into heaven, save He that hath come down from heaven as Son of Man." Then, just as He was sent and came down as Son of Man, so as Son of Man He lives by the Father. Furthermore, he that eateth Him, as eating the Son of Man, doth himself

also live by the Son of Man. Thus, He has compared the effect of His Incarnation to His coming.

128. But if they choose the second method, do we not infer both the equality of the Son with the Father, and His likeness to men, together, though in clear mutual distinction? For what is the meaning of the words, "Even as He Himself liveth by the Father, so we also live by Him," but that the Son so quickeneth a man, as the Father hath in the Son quickened human nature? "For as the Father raiseth the dead and quickeneth them, so also the Son quickeneth whom He will," as the Lord Himself hath already said.

129. Thus the equality of the Son to the Father is established simply upon unity in the action of quickening, since the Son so quickeneth as the Father doth. Acknowledge therefore the eternity of His Life and Sovereignty. Again, our likeness with the Son is discovered, and a certain unity with Him in the flesh, because that, like as the Son of God was quickened in the flesh by the Father, so also is man quickened; for thus it is written, that as God raised Jesus Christ from the dead, so we also, as men, are quickened by the Son of God.

130. According to this interpretation, then, immortality is not only applied to our condition by grace of bounty, but is also proclaimed as the property of Godhead—the latter, because it is the Godhead which quickeneth; the former, because manhood is quickened in Christ.

131. But if any would apply the force of either comparison to Christ's *Godhead*, then the Son of God is put on one footing with men, so that the Son of God lives by the Father just as we live by the Son of God. But the Son of God bestows eternal life by free gift, we cannot so do. If then He be placed on a level with us, He too does not bestow this gift. Let Arius' disciples then have the due reward of their faith—which is, not to obtain eternal life of the Son.

132. I would now go further. If our opponents are pleased to apply the teaching of this passage to the principle of the eternity of the Divine Substance, let them hear a third exposition: Does not our Lord plainly appear to say that as the Father is a living Father, so too the Son also lives?-and who can but observe that here we must understand a reference to unity of Life, forasmuch as the same Life is the Life of the Father and the Life of the Son? "For as the Father hath Life in Himself, so hath He given to the Son also to have Life in Himself." He hath given—by reason of unity with Him. He hath given, not to take away, but that He may be glorified in the Son. He hath given, not that He, the Father, might keep guard over it, but that the Son might have it in possession.

133. But the Arians think that they must oppose hereto the fact that He had said, "I live by the Father." Of a certainty (suppose that they conceive the words as referring to His Godhead) the Son lives by the Father, because He is the Son begotten of the Father,—by the Father, because He is of one Substance with the Father,—by the Father, because He is the Word given forth from the heart of the Father, because He came forth from the Father, because He is begotten of the "bowels of the Father," because the Father is the Fountain and Root of the Son's being.

134. But peradventure they may urge: "If you hold that the Son, in saying, 'And I live by the Father,' spoke of the unity of life subsisting between the Father and the Son, does it not follow that He discovered the unity of life between the Son and mankind in saying that 'he that eateth Me, the same liveth by Me'?"

135. Even so. Just as I confess the unity of celestial Life subsisting in Father and Son by reason of the unity of the substance of the Godhead, so too, save as concerns the prerogatives of the Divine Nature or those which are the effect of the Incarnation of our Lord, I affirm of the Son a participation of spiritual life with us by virtue of the unity of His Manhood with ours, for "as is the heavenly, such are they also that are heavenly." Further, even as in Him we sit at the right hand of the Father, not in the sense that we share His throne, but that we rest in the Body of Christ—even as, I say, we have part in Christ's session by reason of corporal unity, so too we live in Christ by reason of unity of our bodies with His Body.

136. Not only, then, have I no fears of the text, "I live by the Father," but I should have none, even though Christ had said, "I live by help of the Father."

137. Now another objection commonly urged by them starts from the text: "This sickness is not unto death, but for the glory of God, to the end that His Son may be glorified by Him." But not only is the Son glorified through the Father and by the Father, as it is written: "Glorify Me, Father;" and again: "Now hath the Son of Man been glorified, and God hath been glorified in Him, and God glorifieth Him," but the Father also is glorified through the Son and by the Son, for Truth hath said: "I have glorified Thee upon earth."

138. Even as the Son, therefore, is glorified through the Father, so too He lives by the Father. There are some who have been led by consideration of these words to the supposition that [the Greek] "doxa" means "opinion, belief," rather than "glory," and therefore have interpreted as follows: "I have given thee a doxa upon earth, I have finished the work which Thou gavest Me to do, and now, O Father, give me a doxa;" that is to say: "I have taught men so to believe concerning Thee, as to know that Thou art the true God; do Thou also establish in them, concerning Me, the belief that I am Thy Son, and very God."

Chapter XI.

The particular distinction which the Arians endeavoured to prove upon the Apostle's teaching that all things are "of" the Father and "through" the Son, is overthrown, it being shown that in me passage cited the same Omnipotence is ascribed both to Father and to Son, as is proved from various texts, especially from the words of St. Paul himself, in which heretics foolishly find a reference to the Father only, though indeed there is no diminution or inferiority of the Son's sovereignty proved, even by such a reference. Finally, the three phrases, "of Whom," "through Whom," "in Whom," are shown to suppose or imply no difference (of power), and each and all to hold true of the Three Persons.

139. Now we come to that laughable method, attempted by some, of showing a difference of Power to subsist between Father and Son, on the strength of apostolic testimony, it being written "But for us there is One God, the Father, of Whom are all things, and we in Him, and One Lord, Jesus Christ, through Whom are all things, and we through Him." It is urged that no small difference in degree of Divine Majesty is signified in the affirmation that all things are "of" the Father, and "through" the Son. Whereas nothing is clearer than that here a plain reason is given of the Omnipotence of the Son, inasmuch as whilst all things are "of" the Father, none the less are they all "through" the Son.

140. The Father is not "amongst" all things, for to Him it is confessed that "all things serve Thee." Nor is the Son reckoned "amongst" all things, for "all things were made by Him," and "all things exist together in Him, and He is above all the heavens." The Son, therefore, exists not "amongst" but *above* all things, being, indeed, after the flesh, of the people, of the Jews, but yet at the same time God over all, blessed for ever, having a Name which is above every name, it being said of Him, "Thou hast put all things in subjection under His feet." But in making *all things* subject to Him, He left nothing that is not subject, even as the Apostle hath said. But suppose that the Apostle's words were intended with reference to the Incarnate Lord; how then can we doubt the incomparable majesty of His Divine Generation?

141. Certain it is, then, that between Father and Son there can be no difference of Power. Nay, so far is such difference from being present, that the same Apostle has said that all things are "of" Him, by Whom are all things, as followeth: "For of Him and through Him and in Him are all things."

142. Now if, as they suppose, it is the Father alone Who is spoken of, it cannot be that He is at once Omnipotent because all things are of Him, and not Omnipotent because all things are through Him. On their own showing, then, they will declare the Father lacking in Power, and not Omnipotent, or at the least they will be confessing with their own mouth, all against their will though it be, the Omnipotence of the Son as well as of the Father.

143. Howbeit, let them decide whether they will understand this affirmation as made concerning the Father. If they do so decide then all things are "through" Him also. If they decide that it is the Son Who is spoken of, then all things are "of" Him as well as "of" the Father. But if all things are "through" the Father also, then surely there is no argument for diminishing from the honour due to the Son; and if all things are "of" the Son, the Son must be honoured in like manner as the Father is.

144. In case our opponents should suspect that we are taking advantage of some intrusion of a single spurious verse into the text, let us review the whole passage. "O depth of the riches of God's wisdom and knowledge!" exclaims the Apostle, "how un-searchable are His judgments, and His ways past finding out! For Who hath known the mind of the Lord, or who hath been His counsellor? Or who hath been first to give unto Him, and shall be recompensed? For of Him and through Him and in Him are all things. To Him be glory for ever!"

145. Who, then, think they, is here spoken of—the Father or the Son? If it be the Father—then we answer that the Father is not the Wisdom of God, for the Son is. But what is there that is impossible to Wisdom, of Whom it is written: "Seeing that she is almighty and abiding, she maketh all things new in herself"? We read of Wisdom, then, not as approaching, but as abiding. Thus have you the authority of Solomon to teach you of the Omnipotence and Eternity of Wisdom, and of her Goodness as well, for it is written: "But malice overcometh not Wisdom."

146. But to purpose. "How unsearchable," saith the Apostle, "are His judgments!" Now if "the Father hath given all judgment to the Son," it seems that the Father points to the Son as Judge.

147. But now, to show us that He is speaking of the Son, not of the Father, St. Paul proceeds: "Who was first in giving to Him?" For "the Father hath given to the Son," but it was as acknowledging the rights of Him Whom He has begotten, not by way of largess. Therefore, it being undeniable that the Son has received at the hands of the Father, as it is written, "All things have been given unto Me of My Father," yet, in saying, "Who was first in giving to Him?" the Apostle has not denied that the Son has received gifts of the Father, by virtue of His Nature, but he has indeed shown that, of Father and Son, Neither can be said to be before the Other, forasmuch as, albeit the Father has given gifts unto the Son, yet He has not so bestowed them as upon one that began to be after Him; because the uncreate and incomprehensible Trinity, Which is of One Eternity and Glory, admits neither difference of time nor degree of precedence.

148. If, however, we hold ourselves more bound to observe those Greek manuscripts which show "ti" prosedwcen autw" it is clear that He to Whom nothing can be added is not unequal to Him Who is perfect and complete. Therefore, if this passage from the Apostle, in its entirety, is better understood with reference to the Son, we see that we must also believe concerning the Son, that all things are of Him, even as it is written: "For of Him and through Him and in Him are all things."

149. Be it so, nevertheless, that they suppose the passage to be intended of the Father, then let us call to mind that even as we read of all things being *of* Him, so too we read of all things being *through* Him, that is to say, the authority of the Father and of the Son is extended over the whole created universe. And, though we have already proved the Omnipotence of the Son by the Omnipotence of the Father, still—forasmuch as they are ever bent upon disparagement—let them consider that they disparage the Father as well as the Son. For if the Son be limited in might, because all things are *through* Him, do we say further, that the Father likewise is limited, because all things are through Him also?

150. But to bring them to understand that these phrases involve no difference, I will once again show that it is the same person, "of" whom anything is, and "through" whom anything is, and that we read of things being related in both these ways to the Father. For we find: "Faithful is God, through Whom ye were called into the fellowship of His Son." Let our adversaries weigh the meaning of the Apostle's words. We are called "through" the Father—they raise no

controversy: we are created "through" the Son—and this they have set down as a mark of inferiority. The Father has called us into fellowship with His Son, and this truth we, as in duty bound, devoutly receive. The Son has created all things, and Arius' followers imagine that here they have not the decree of a free Will, but a forced service, slavishly performed!

151. Again, to obtain fuller understanding that, forasmuch as we are called through the Father into fellowship with His Son, there is no difference of Power in the Father and the Son, [note that] the fellowship itself has its beginning of the Son, as it is written: "For from His fulness have we all received," though, if we follow the Greek text of the Gospel, we ought to render "*of* His fulness."

152. See, then, how there is fellowship both *through* the Father and *of* the Son, and yet not a different fellowship, but one and the same. "And that our fellowship be with the Father and with His Son Jesus Christ."

153. Observe, further, that Scripture speaks of our having one fellowship not only "of" the Father and the Son, but also "of" the Holy Spirit. "The grace of Our Lord Jesus Christ," saith the Apostle, "and the love of God, and the fellowship of the Holy Spirit be with you all."

154. Now, I ask, wherein does He, through Whom are all things, appear less than He, of Whom are all things? Is it because He is declared to be the Worker? But the Father also works, for He is true who said, "My Father worketh hitherto, and I work." Therefore, even as the Father worketh, so worketh the Son also; and so He Who worketh is not limitary in power nor abject, for the Father also worketh; which being so, that which is common to the Son with the Father, or even which the Son has by the Father, ought not to be the less esteemed, lest heretics further dishonour the Father in the Person of the Son.

155. Not to be passed over for silencing the disputings of Arian misbelief are those words of the same Saint John, which he set down in another Scripture: "If ye know that He is just, know that he which doeth righteousness is born of Him." But who is righteous, save the Lord, Who loveth righteousness? Or whom—as the foregoing texts warn us—have we to assure us of everlasting life, if we have not the Son? If, therefore, the Son of God hath promised us everlasting life, and He is righteous, surely we are born "of" Him. Else, if our adversaries deny that we are born of the Son by grace, they likewise deny His righteousness.

156. Thou must therefore believe that all things are of the Son of God [even as of God the Father, for even as God is the Father of all, so likewise is the Son the Author and Creator of all. We see, then, the vanity of this their questioning, forasmuch as it holds good of the Son [as of the Father], that "of Him and through Him and in Him are all things."

157. We have shown how all things are "of" Him, and likewise how all things are also "through" Him. Who then doubts that all things are "in" Him, when another Scripture saith: "For in Him are all things founded, that are in the heavens, and in Him they were created, and He is before all things, and all things consist in Him"? (Col. i. 16). Of Him, then, thou hast grace; Himself thou hast for thy Creator; in Him thou findest the foundation of all things.

Chapter XII.

The comparison, found in the Gospel of St. John, of the Son to a Vine and the Father to a husbandman, must be understood with reference to the Incarnation. To understand it with reference to the Divine Generation is to doubly insult the Son, making Him inferior to St. Paul, and bringing Him down to the level of the rest of mankind, as well as in like manner the Father also, by making Him not merely to be on one footing with the same Apostle, but even of no account at all. The Son, indeed, in so far as being God, is also the husbandman, and, as regards His Manhood, a grape-cluster. True statement of the Father's pre-eminence.

158. There is yet another Scripture, which our opponents commonly object against us, in order to prove their division of the Godhead of the Father from the Godhead of the Son, namely, our Lord's words in the Gospel: "I am the true Vine and My Father is the Husbandman." The vine and the husbandman, say they, are of different natures, and the vine is in the power of the husbandman.

159. Thus, then, ye would have us believe that the Son, as touching His Godhead, is like to a vine, so that without a vine-dresser He is nothing, and may be neglected or even rooted up. Thus ye juggle up a lie from the letter of the Scripture which sayeth that our Lord called Himself the Vine, intending thereby the mystery of His Incarnation. Howbeit, if ye are bent on it that we dispute upon the letter, I too confess, yea, I proclaim, that the Son called Himself the Vine. For woe be to me, if I deny the pledge of the salvation of His people!

160. How then do you purpose to understand the truth that the Son of God called Himself the Vine? If you interpret the saying with respect to the Substance of His Godhead, and if you suppose such a diversity of Godhead between the Father and the Son as there is of nature between a husbandman and a vine, you do double insult both to Father and to Son—to the Son, because if, as you affirm, He is, as touching His Godhead, beneath a husbandman, then must He on the same showing be esteemed lower than the Apostle Paul, forasmuch as Paul indeed called himself a husbandman, as we find it written: "I have planted, Apollos hath watered: but God hath given the increase." Will you have Paul, then, to be better than the Son of God?

161. Thus far the one insult. As for the other, it lies herein, that if the Son is the Vine in respect of His eternally-begotten Person, then, He having said: "I am the Vine, ye are the branches," that divinely-begotten One appears to be of one substance with us. But "who is like unto Thee among the gods, O Lord?" as it is written; and again, in the Psalms: "For who is there among the clouds that shall be equal to the Lord? Or who among the sons of God shall be like unto God."

162. Moreover, ye disparage not only the Son, but the Father also. For if the term "husbandman" is to comprehend in its designation all the prerogative of the Father's Sovereignty, then, seeing that Paul too is a husbandman, you set the Apostle, to whom you deny that the Son is equal, on an even footing with the Father.

163. Again, it being written, "But neither he which planteth is anything, nor he that watereth; but God, Who giveth the increase," you will rest the fulness of the Father's Majesty in a name which, as you see, stands for weakness. For if he that planteth is nothing, and he that watereth is nothing, but it is God, Who giveth the increase [Who is all], observe what your blasphemy intends—even to expose the Father to contempt under the title of a husbandman, and to demand another God to provide the increase of the Father's labour. Wickedly, therefore, do they think to extol the Dignity of God the Father by this use of the term "husbandman," in which God the Father is brought down to the level of man, as being designated by a common title.

164. Yet what wonder if, as ye heretics would have it, the Father is to be exalted above a Son Whose Godhead differs not a whir from the common condition of mankind? If ye suppose the Son to have been entitled the Vine with respect to His Godhead, then do ye esteem Him not only as liable to corruption and subject to changes of wind and weather, but even as partaking of manhood only, forasmuch as the Vine and its branches are of one nature, so that the Son of God appears, not to have taken upon Him our flesh, through the mystery of Incarnation, but to have altogether sprung into being from the flesh.

165. But I will indeed openly confess that His flesh, though born in a new and mysterious birth, was yet of the same nature with ours, and that this is the pledge of our salvation, not the source of the Divine Generation. He indeed is the Vine, for He bears my sufferings, whensoever manhood, hitherto frail, leans on Him and so matures with plenteous fruit of renewed devotion.

166. Yet if the husbandman's power allure thee, tell me, prithee, who it was that spake in the prophet, saying: "0 Lord, make it known to me, that I may know; then saw I their thoughts. I was led as a harmless lamb to the slaughter and knew it not: they took counsel together against me, saying, Come, let us throw wood into his bread." For if the Son here speaks of the mystery of His coming Incarnation—for it were blasphemy to suppose that the words are spoken concerning the Father—then surely it is the Son Who speaks in an earlier passage: "I have planted thee as a fruitful vine—how art Thou become bitter, and a wild vine?"

167. And thus thou seest that the Son also is the husbandman,—the Son, of one Name with the Father, one work, one dignity and Substance. If, then, the Son is both Vine and Husbandman, plainly we infer the meaning of the Vine with regard to the mystery of the Incarnation.

168. But not only has our Lord called Himself a Vine—He has also given Himself, by the voice of the prophet, the title of a Grape-cluster—even when Moses, at the command of the Lord, sent spies to the Valley of the Cluster. What is that valley but the humility of the Incarnation and the fruitfulness of the Passion? I indeed think that He is called the Cluster, because that from the Vine brought out of Egypt, that is, the people of the Jews, there grew a fruit for the world's good. No man, truly, can understand the Cluster as a token of the Divine Generation—or if there be any who so understand it, they leave no conclusion open but that we should believe that Cluster to have sprung from the Vine: And thus in their folly they attribute to the Father that which they refuse to believe of the Son.

169. But if there be now left no room for doubt that the Son of God is called the Vine with respect and intention to His Incarnation, you see what hidden truth it was to which our Lord had regard in saying, "The Father is greater than I." For after this premised, He proceeded immediately: "I am the true Vine, and My Father is the Husbandman," that you might know that the Father is greater in so far as He dresses and tends our Lord's flesh, as the husbandman dresses and tends his vines. Further, our Lord's flesh is that which could increase in stature with age, and be wounded through suffering, to the end that the whole human race might rest guarded from the pestilent heat of the pleasures of this world, under the shadow of the Cross whereon Its limbs are spread.

BOOK V.

Prologue.

Who is a faithful and wise servant? His reward is pointed out in the case of Peter, as also in the case of Paul. Ambrose, being anxious to follow Paul's guidance, wished this book to be added to the others, for it could not be included in the preceding one. The subject for discussion is then stated, and the reason for such a discussion given. He must needs be pardoned, for usury is to be demanded from every servant for the money which has been entrusted to him. Their faithfulness is the usury desired in his own case. He will be happy if he may hope for a reward; but he does not look so much for the recompense of the saints, as for exemption from punishment. He urges all to seek to merit this.

1. "Who, then, is a faithful and wise servant, whom his lord hath made ruler over his household, to give them meat in due season? Blessed is that servant, whom his lord when he cometh shall find so doing." Not worthless is this servant: some great one ought he to be. Let us think who he may be.

2. It is Peter, chosen by the Lord Himself to feed His flock, who merits thrice to hear the words: "Feed My little lambs; feed My lambs; feed My sheep." And so, by feeding well the flock of Christ with the food of faith, he effaced the sin of his former fall. For this reason is he thrice admonished to feed the flock; thrice is he asked whether he loves the Lord, in order that he may thrice confess Him, Whom he had thrice denied before His Crucifixion.

3. Blessed also is that servant who can say: "I have fed you with milk and not with meat; for hitherto ye were not able to bear it." For he knew how to feed them. Who of us can do this? Who of us can truly say: "To the weak became Ins weak, that I might gain the weak"?

4. Yet he, being so great a man, and chosen by Christ for the care of His flock, so as to strengthen the weak and to heal the sick,—he, I say, rejects forthwith after one admonition a heretic from the fold entrusted to him, for fear that the taint of one erring sheep might infect the whole flock with a spreading sore. He further bids that foolish questions and contentions be avoided.

5. How, then, shall we act, being but ignorant dwellers set amongst these fresh tares in the old-standing harvest field? If we are silent, we shall seem to be giving way; and if we contend against them, there is the fear that we too shall be held to be carnal. For it is written of matters of this sort, which beget strife: "The servant of the Lord must not strive, but be gentle unto all, apt to teach, patient, with moderation instructing those that oppose themselves." And in another place: "If any man is contentious, we have no such custom, neither the Church of God." For this reason it was our intention to write somewhat, in order that our writings might without any din answer the impiety of heretics on our behalf.

6. And so we prepare to commence this our Fifth Book, O Emperor Augustus. For it was but right that the Fourth Book should end with our discussion on the Vine, lest otherwise we should seem to have overloaded that book with a tumultuous mass of subjects, rather than to have filled it with the fruit of the spiritual vineyard. On the other hand, it was not seemly that the gathering of the vintage of the faith should be left unfinished, whilst there was still all abundance of such great matters for discussion.

7. In the Fifth Book, therefore, we speak of the indivisible Godhead of the Father, the Son, and the Holy Ghost (omitting, however, a full discussion on the Holy Ghost), being urged by the teaching of the Gospel to let out on interest to human minds the five talents of the faith entrusted to these five books being as it were the principal; lest perhaps when the Lord comes, and finds His money hidden in the earth, He may say to me: "Thou wicked and slothful servant, thou knewest that I reap where I do not sow; and gather where I have not strawed; thou oughtest therefore to have put My money to the exchangers, that at My coming I might have received Mine Own," or as it stands in another book: "And I," it says, "at My coming might have received it with usury."

8. I pray those to pardon me, whom the boldness of such a lengthy address displeases. The thought of my office compels me to entrust to others what I have received. "We are stewards of the heavenly mysteries." We are ministers, but not all alike. "But," it says, "even as the Lord gave to every man, I have planted; Apollos watered; but God gave the increase." Let each one then strive that be may be able to receive a reward according to his labour. "For we are labourers together with God," as the Apostle said; "we are God's husbandry, God's building." Blessed therefore is he who sees such usury on his principal; blessed too is he who beholds the fruit of his work; blessed again is he "who builds upon the foundation of faith, gold, silver, precious stones."

9. Ye who hear or read these words are all things to us. Ye are the usury of the money-lender,—the usury on speech, not on money; ye are the return given to the husbandman; ye are the gold, the silver, the precious stones of the builder. In your merits lie the chief results of the labours of the priest; in your souls shines forth the fruit of a bishop's work; in your progress glitters the gold of the Lord; the silver is increased if ye hold fast the divine words. "The words of the Lord are pure words, as silver tried in the fire; proved on the earth, purified seven times." Ye therefore will make the lender rich, the husbandman to abound in produce; ye will prove the master-builder to be skilful. I do not speak boastfully; for I do not desire so much my own advantage as yours.

10. Oh that I might safely say of you at that time: "Lord, Thou gavest me five talents, behold I have gained five other talents;" and that I might show the precious talents of your virtues! "For we have a treasure in earthen vessels." These are the talents which the Lord bids us spiritually to trade with, or the two coins of the New and the Old Testament, which that Samaritan in the Gospel left for the man robbed by the thieves, for the purpose of getting his wounds healed.

11. Neither do I, my brethren, with greedy desires, long for this, so that I may be set over many things; the recompense I get from the fact of your advance is enough for me. Oh that I may not be found unworthy of that which I have received! Let those things which are too great for me be assigned to better men. I demand them not! Yet mayest Thou say, O Lord: "I will give unto this last, even as unto thee." Let the man that deserves it receive authority over ten cities.

12. Let him be such an one as was Moses, who wrote the Ten Words of the Law. Let him be as Joshua, the son of Nun, who subdued five kings, and brought the Gibeonites into subjection, that he might be the figure of a Man of his own name Who was to come, by Whose power all fleshly lust should be overcome, and the Gentiles should be converted, so that they might follow the faith of Jesus Christ rather than their former pursuits and desires. Let him be as David, whom the young maidens came to meet with songs, saying: "Saul hath triumphed over thousands, David over ten thousands."

13. It is enough for me, if I am not thrust out into the outer darkness, as he was, who hid the talent entrusted to him in the earth so to speak, of his own flesh. This the ruler of the synagogue did, and the other rulers of the Jews; for they employed , the words of the Lord, which had been entrusted to them, on the ground as it were of their bodies; and, delighting in the pleasures of the flesh, sunk the heavenly trust as though into the pit of an overweening heart.

14. Let us then not keep the Lord's money buried and hidden in the flesh; nor let us hide our one talent in a napkin; but like good money-changers let us ever weigh it out with labour of mind and body, with an even and ready will, that the word may be near, even in thy mouth and in thy heart.

15. This is the word of the Lord, this is the precious talent, whereby thou art redeemed. This money must often be seen on the tables of souls, in order that by constant trading the sound of the good coins may be able to go forth into every land, by the means of which eternal life is purchased. "This is eternal life," which Thou, Almighty Father, givest freely, that we may know "Thee the only true God, and Jesus Christ Whom Thou hast sent."

Chapter I.

How impious the Arians are, in attacking that on which human happiness depends. John ever unites the Son with the Father, especially where he says: "That they may know Thee, the only true God, etc." In that place, then, we must understand the words "true God" also of the Son; for it cannot be denied that He is God, and it cannot be said He is a false god, and least of all that He is God by appellation only. This last point being proved from the Apostle's words, we rightly confess that Christ is true God.

16. Wherefore let the Arians observe, how impious they are in calling in question our hope and the object of our desires. And since they are wont to cry out on this point above all others, saying that Christ is distinct from the only and true God, let us confute their impious ideas so far as lies in our power.

17. For on this point they ought rather to understand, that this is the benefit, this the reward of perfect virtue, namely, this divine and incomparable gift, that we may know Christ together with the Father, and not separate the Son from the Father; as also the Scriptures do not separate them. For the following tells rather for the unity than for the diversity of the Divine Majesty, namely, that the knowledge of the Father and of the Son gives us the same recompense, and one and the same honour; which reward no man will have but he that has known both the Father and the Son. For as the knowledge of the Father procures eternal life, so also does the knowledge of the Son.

18. Therefore as the Evangelist forthwith at the outset joined the Word with God the Father in his devout confession of faith, saying: "And the Word was with God;" and here too, in writing the words of the Lord: "That they may know Thee, the only true God, and Jesus Christ Whom Thou hast sent," he has undoubtedly, by thus connecting Them, bound together the Father and the Son, so that no one may separate Christ as true God from the majesty of the Father, for union does not dissever.

19. Therefore in saying, "That they may know Thee, the only true God, and Jesus Christ Whom Thou hast sent," he put an end to the Sabellians, and has also put the Jews out of court,—those at any rate who heard him speak; so that the former might not suppose the Same to be the Father as the Son, which they might have done if he had not added also Christ, and that the latter might not sever the Son from the Father.

20. But, I ask, why do they not think we ought to gather and understand this from what has been already said; that as he has declared the Father to be only, true God, so we may understand Jesus Christ also to be only, true God? For it could not be expressed in any other way, for fear he might seem to be speaking of two Gods. For neither do we speak of two Gods; and yet we confess the Son to be of the same Godhead with the Father.

21. May we ask, therefore, on what grounds they think a distinction is made in the Godhead, and whether they deny Christ to be God? But they cannot deny it. Do they deny Him to be true God? But if they deny Him to be true God, let them say whether they declare Him to be a false God, or God by appellation only. For according to the Scriptures the word "God" is used either of the true God, or by appellation only, or of a false god. True God as the Father; God by appellation as the saints; a false god like the demons and idols. Let them say then how they will acknowledge and describe the Son of God. Do they suppose the name of God to have been falsely assumed; or was there in truth merely an indwelling of God within Him, as it were by appellation only?

22. I do not think they can say the name was falsely assumed, and so involve themselves in the open wickedness of blasphemy; lest they should betray themselves on the one hand to the demons and idols, and on the other to Christ, by insinuating that the name of God was falsely given to Him. But if they think He is called God because He had an indwelling of the Godhead within Him,—as many holy men were (for the Scripture calls them Gods to whom the word of God came), —they do not place Him before other men, but think He is to be compared with them; so that they consider Him to be the same as He has granted other men to be, even as He

says to Moses: "I have made thee a god unto Pharaoh." Wherefore it is also said in the Psalms: "I have said, ye are gods."

23. This idea of these blasphemers Paul puts aside; for he said: "For though there be that are called gods, whether in heaven or in earth." He said not: "There begods," but "There be that are called gods." But "Christ," as it is written, "is the same yesterday and to-day." "He is," it says; that is, not only in name but also in truth.

24. And well is it written: "He is the same yesterday and to-day," so that the impiety of Arius might find no room to pile up its profanity. For he, in reading in the second psalm of the Father saying to the Son, "Thou art My Son, this day have I begotten Thee," noted the word "to-day," not "yesterday," referring this which was spoken of the assumption of our flesh to the eternity of the divine generation; of which Paul also says in the Acts of the Apostles: "And we declare unto you the promise which was made to our fathers: for God has fulfilled the same to our children, in that He hath raised up the Lord Jesus Christ again, as it is written in the second psalm: Thou art My Son, this day have I begotten Thee." Thus the Apostle, filled with the Holy Ghost, in order that he might destroy that fierce madness of his, said: "The same, yesterday, to-day, and for ever." "Yesterday" on account of His eternity; "to-day" on account of His taking to Himself a human body.

25. Christ therefore is, and always is; for He, Who is, always is. And Christ always is, of Whom Moses says: "He that is hath sent me." Gabriel indeed was, Raphael was, the angels were; but they who sometime have not been are by no means with equal reason said always to be. But Christ, as we read, "was not it is, and, it is not, but, it is was in Him." Wherefore it is the property of God alone to be, Who ever is.

26. Therefore if they dare not say He is God by appellation, and it is a mark of deep impiety to say He is a false god, it remains that He is true God, not unlike to the true Father, but equal to Him. And as He sanctifies and justifies whom He will, not by assuming that power from without Himself, but having within Himself the power of sanctification, how is He not true God? For the Apostle called Him indeed true God, Who according to His nature was God, as it is written: "Howbeit then, when ye knew not God, ye did service unto them, who by nature were not gods;" that is, who could not be true gods, for this title by no means belonged to them by nature.

Chapter II.

Since it has been proved that the Son is true God, and in that is not interior to the Father, it is shown that by the word solus (alone) when used of the Father in the Scriptures, the Son is not excluded; nay, that this expression befits Him above all, and Him alone. The Trinity is alone, not amongst all, but above all. The Son alone does what the Father does, and alone has immortality. But we must not for this reason separate Him from the Father in our controversies. We may, however, understand that passage of the Incarnation. Lastly the Father is shut out from a share in the redemption of men by those who would have the Son to be separated from Him.

27. We have fully demonstrated by passages of Scripture, in the earlier books, that Christ is true, yea, very true God. Therefore if Christ, as it has been taught, is true God, let us enquire why they desire to separate the Son from the Father, when they read that the Father is the only true God.

28. If they say that the Father alone is true God, they cannot deny that God the Son alone is the Truth; for Christ is the Truth. Is the Truth then something inferior to Him that is true, seeing that according to the use of terms a man is called true from the word "truth," as also wise from wisdom, just from justice? We donor deem it so between the Father and the Son. For there is nothing wanting to the Father, because the Father is full of truth; and the Son, because He is the Truth, is equal to Him that is true.

29. But that they may know, when they see the word "alone," that the Son is in no wise to be separated from the Father, let them remember it was said by God in the Prophets: "I

stretched forth the heavens alone." The Father certainly did not stretch them forth without the Son. For the Son Himself, Who is the Wisdom of God, says: "When He prepared the heavens I was present with Him." And Paul declares that it was said of the Son: "Thou, Lord, in the beginning hast laid the foundation of the earth, and the heavens are the work of Thy hands." Whether therefore the Son made the heavens, as also the Apostle would have it understood, whilst He Himself certainly did not alone spread out the heavens without the Father; or as it stands in the Book of Proverbs: "The Lord in wisdom hath rounded the earth, in understanding hath He prepared the heavens;" it is proved that neither the Father made the heavens alone without the Son, nor yet the Son without the Father. And yet He who spread out the heavens is said to be alone.

30. To show indeed how plainly we must understand the expression "alone" of the Son (although we may never believe that He did anything without the knowledge of the Father), we have here also another passage, where it is written: "Which alone spreadeth out the heavens, and walketh as it were on a pavement over the sea." For the Gospel of the Lord has taught us that it was not the Father but the Son that walked upon the sea, when Peter asked Him, saying, "Lord, bid me come unto Thee." But even prophecy itself gives proof of this. For holy Job prophesied of the coming of the Lord; of Whom he said in truth that He would vanquish the great Leviathan, and it was done. For that dread Leviathan that is, the devil, He smote, and struck down, and laid low in the last times by the adorable Passion of His own Body.

31. The Son therefore is only and true God for this also is assigned to the Son as His sole right. For of no created being can it be accurately said that he is alone. How can he to whom fellowship in creation belongs be separated from the rest, as though he were alone? Thus man is seen to be a rational being amongst all earthly creatures, yet he is not the only rational being; for we know that the heavenly works of God also are rational, we confess that angels and archangels are rational beings. If then the angels are rational, man cannot be said to be the only rational being.

32. But they say that the sun can be said to be alone, because there is no second sun. But the sun himself has many things in common with the stars, for he travels across the heavens, he is of that ethereal and heavenly substance, he is a creature, and is reckoned amongst all the works of God. He serves God in union with all, blesses Him with all, praises Him with all. Therefore he cannot accurately be said to be alone, for he is not set apart from the rest.

33. Wherefore since no created being can be compared with the Godhead of the Father, the Son, and the Holy Ghost, Which is alone, not amongst all, but over all (our declaration concerning the Spirit being meanwhile held back); as the Father is said to be the only true God, because He has nothing in common with others; so also is the Son alone the Image of the true God, He alone is the Hand of the Father, He alone is the Virtue and Wisdom of God.

34. Thus the Son alone does what the Father does; for it is written: "Whatsoever things I do, He doth." And since the work of the Father and of the Son is one, it is well said of the Father and the Son, that God worked alone; wherefore also when we speak of the Creator, we own both the Father and the Son. For assuredly when Paul said, "Who served the creature more than the Creator," he neither denied the Father to be the Creator, from Whom are all these things, nor yet the Son, through Whom are all things.

35. And it does not seem out of agreement with this that it is written: "Who alone hath immortality." For how could He not have immortality Who has life in Himself? He has it in His nature; He has it in His essential Being; and He has it not as a temporal grace, but owing to His eternal Godhead. He has it not by way of a gift as a servant, but by peculiar right of His Generation, as the co-eternal Son. He has it, too, as has the Father. "For as the Father hath life in Himself, so also hath He given to the Son to have life in Himself." As He has it, it says, so He has given it. Thou hast learnt already how He gave it, that thou mayest not think it to be a free gift of grace, when it is a secret of His generation. Since, then, there is no divergence of life

between the Father and the Son, how can it be supposed that the Father alone has immortality, whilst the Son has it not?

36. Wherefore let them understand that in this passage the Son is not to be separated from the Father, Who is the only true God. For they cannot prove that the Son is not the only and true God, especially as here also it may be gathered, as I have said, that Christ too is true and only God; or the passage may at least be understood partly in reference to the Godhead of the Father and the Son, and partly to the Incarnation of Christ: for knowledge is not perfect unless it confesses Jesus Christ from eternity to be only-begotten God, true Son of God, and, according to the flesh, begotten of a Virgin. Which also this very Evangelist has taught us elsewhere, saying: "Every spirit that confesseth that Jesus Christ is come in the flesh, is of God."

37. Lastly, the whole of our passage teaches us that it is not improper in this verse to understand a reference to the sacrament of the Incarnation. For thus it is written: "Father, the hour is come, glorify Thy Son." When, therefore, He states that the hour is come, and prays to be glorified, how can one suppose Him to have spoken but only in accordance with the assumption of our flesh? For the Godhead has no fixed moments of time, nor does eternal light stand in need of glorification. Therefore in the only true God, Who is the Father, we also understand the only true Son of God to be in accordance with the unity of the Godhead. And in the name of Jesus Christ, which He received when born of the Virgin, we acknowledge the sacrament of the Incarnation.

38. But if they wish to separate the Son, when they read that the Father is the only true God, I suppose that when they read of the Incarnation of the Son: "This is the stone which was set at naught of you builders, which is become the head of the corner;" and further: "There is none other name under heaven given among men, whereby we must be saved;" then they imagine the Father is to be cut off from the benefit of imparting salvation to us. But there is neither salvation without the Father, nor eternal life without the Son.

Chapter III.

To the objection of the Arians, that two Gods are introduced by a unity of substance, the answer is that a plurality of Gods is more likely to be inferred from diversity of substance. Further, their charge recoils upon themselves. Manifold diversity is the reason why two men cannot be said to be one man, though all men are called individually man, where a unity of nature is referred to. There is one nature alone in them, but there is wholly a unity in the Divine Persons. Therefore the Son is not to be severed from the Father, especially as they dare not deny that worship is due to Him.

39. But the Arians maintain the following: If you say that, as the Father is the only true God, so also is the Son, and confess that the Father and the Son are both of one substance, you introduce not one God, but two. For they who are of one substance seem not to be one God but two Gods. Just as two men or two sheep or more are spoken of, but a man and a sheep are not spoken of as two men or two sheep, but as one man and one sheep.

40. This is what the Arians say; and by this cunning argument they attempt to catch the more simple-minded. However if we read the divine Scriptures we shall find that plurality occurs rather amongst those things which are of a diverse and different substance, that is, eterousia. We have this set forth in the books of Solomon, in that passage in which he said: "There are three things impossible to understand, yea, a fourth which I know not, the track of an eagle in the air, the way of a serpent upon a rock, the path of a ship in the sea, and the way of a man in his youth." An eagle and a ship and a serpent are not of one family and nature, but of a distinguishable and different substance, and yet they are three. On the testimony of Scripture, therefore, they learn that their arguments are against themselves.

41. Therefore, in saying that the substance of the Father and of the Son is diverse and their Godhead distinguishable, they themselves assert there are two Gods. But we, when we confess the Father and the Son, in declaring them still to be of one Godhead, say that there are not two Gods, but one God. And this we establish by the word of the Lord. For where there are several,

there is a difference either of nature or of will and work. Lastly, that they may be refuted on their own witness, two men are mentioned: But though they are of one nature by right of birth, yet in time and thought and work and place, they are apart; and so one man cannot be spoken of under the signification and number of two; for there is no unity where there is diversity. But God is said to be one, and the glory and completeness of the Father, the Son, and the Holy Spirit is thus expressed.

42. Such, indeed, is the truth of unity that, when the nature alone of human birth or of human flesh is indicated, one man is the term used for the many, as it is written "The Lord is my helper, I will not fear what man can do unto me;" that is, not the one person of a man, but the one flesh, the one frailty of human birth. It added also: "It is better to trust in the Lord than to trust in man." Here, too, it did not denote one particular man, but a universal condition. Then, immediately after it added, speaking of many: "It is better to put confidence in the Lord than to put confidence in princes." Where man is spoken of, as we have already said, there the common unity of the nature, which exists between all is indicated; but where the princes are mentioned, there is a certain distinction between their different powers.

43. Amongst men, or in men, there exists a unity in some one thing, either in love, or desire, or flesh, or devotion, or faith. But a universal unity, that embraces within itself all things agreeably to the divine glory, is the property of the Father, the Son, and the Holy Spirit alone.

44. Wherefore the Lord also, in pointing out the diversity that exists among men, who have nothing in common that can tend towards the unity of an indivisible substance, says: "In your law it is written that the testimony of two men is true." But though He had said, "The testimony of two men is true," when He came to the testimony of Himself and His Father, He said not: "Our testimony is true, for it is the testimony of two Gods;" but: "I am One that bear witness of Myself, and the Father that sent Me beareth witness of Me." Earlier He also says: "If I judge, My judgment is true; for I am not alone, but I and the Father that sent Me." Thus, both in one place and the other, He indicated both the Father and the Son, but neither implied the plurality, nor severed the unity of their divine Substance.

45. It is plain, then, that whatsoever is of one substance cannot be severed, even though it be not single, but one. By singleness I mean that which the Greeks call monoth". Singleness has to do with a person; unity with a nature. That those things which are of a different substance are Wont to be called, not one alone, but many, though already proved on the testimony of the prophet, the Apostle himself has stated in so many words, saying: "For though there be that are called gods, whether in heaven or in earth." Dost thou see, then, that those who are of different substances, and not of the verity of one nature, are called "gods"? But the Father and the Son, being of one substance, are not two Gods, but "One God, the Father, of Whom are all things, and one Lord Jesus Christ, through Whom are all things." "One God," he says, "and one Lord Jesus;" and above: "One God, not two Gods;" and then: "One Lord, not two Lords."

46. Plurality, therefore, is excluded, but the unity is not destroyed. But as, on the one hand, when we read of the Lord Jesus, we do not dissociate the Father, as I have already said, from the prerogative of ruling, because He has that in common with the Son; so, on the other hand, when we read of the only true God, the Father, we cannot sever the Son from the prerogative of the only true God, for He has that in common with the Father.

47. Let them say what they feel or what they think, when we read: "Thou shall worship the Lord thy God, and Him only shall thou serve." Do they think Christ should not be worshipped, and that He Ought not to be served? But if that woman of Canaan who worshipped Him, merited to gain what she asked for, and the Apostle Paul, who confessed himself to be the servant of Christ in the very outset of his letters, merited to be an Apostle "not of men, neither by man, but by Jesus Christ;" let them say what they think should follow. Would they prefer to join with Arius in a league of treachery, and so show, by denying Christ to be the only true God, that they consider He should neither be worshipped nor served? Or would they sooner go in

company with Paul, who in serving and worshipping Christ did not disown in word and heart the only true God, Whom he acknowledged with dutiful service?

Chapter IV.

It is objected by heretics that Christ offered worship to His Father. But instead it is shown that this must be referred to His humanity, as is clear from an examination of the passage. However, it also offers fresh witness to His Godhead, as we often see it happening in other actions that Christ did.

48. But if any one were to say that the Son worships God the Father, because it is written, "Ye worship ye know not what, we know what we worship," let him consider when it was said, and to whom, and to whose wishes it was in answer.

49. In the earlier verses of this chapter it was stated, not without reason, that Jesus, being weary with the journey, was sitting down, and that He asked a woman of Samaria to give Him drink; for He spoke as man; for as God He could neither be weary nor thirst.

50. So when this woman addressed Him as a Jew, and thought Him a prophet, He answers her, as a Jew who spiritually taught the mysteries of the Law: "Ye worship ye know not what, we know what we worship." "We," He says; for He joined Himself with men. But how is He joined with men, but according to the flesh? And to show that He answered as being incarnate, He added: "for salvation is of the Jews."

51. But immediately after this He put aside His human feelings, saying: "But the hour cometh, and now is, when the true worshippers shall worship the Father." He said not: "We shall worship." This He would certainly have said, if He had a share in our obedience.

52. And when we read that Mary worshipped Him, we ought to learn that it is not possible for Him under the same nature both to worship as a servant, and to be worshipped as Lord; but rather that as man He is said to worship among men, and that as Lord He is worshipped by His servants.

53. Many things therefore we read and believe, in the light of the sacrament of the Incarnation. But even in the very feelings of our human nature we may behold the Divine Majesty. Jesus is wearied with His journey, that He may refresh the weary; He desires to drink, when about to give spiritual drink to the thirsty; He was hungry, when about to supply the food of salvation to the hungry; He dies, to live again; He is buried, to rise again; He hangs upon the dreadful tree, to strengthen those in dread; He veils the heaven with thick darkness, that He may give light; He makes the earth to shake, that He may make it strong; He rouses the sea, that He may calm it; He opens the tombs of the dead, that He may show they are the homes of the living; He is made of a Virgin, that men may believe He is born of God; He feigns not to know, that He may make the ignorant to know; as a Jew He is said to worship, that the Son may be worshipped as true God.

Chapter V.

Ambrose answers those who press the words of the Lord to the mother of Zebedee's children, by saying that they were spoken out of kindness, because Christ was unwilling to cause her grief. Ample reason for such tenderness is brought forward. The Lord would rather leave the granting of that request to the Father, than declare it to be impossible. This answer of Christ's, however, is not to His detriment, as is shown both by His very words, and also by comparing them with other passages.

54. "How," they say, "can the Son of God be the only true God, like to the Father, when He Himself said to the sons of Zebedee: 'Ye shall drink indeed of My cup; but to sit on My right hand or on My left, is not Mine to give to you, but to those for whom it has been prepared of My Father'?" This, then, is, as you desire, your proof of divine inequality; though in it you ought rather to reverence the Lord's kindness and to adore His grace; if, that is, you could but perceive the deep secrets of the virtue and wisdom of God.

55. For think of her who, with and for her sons, makes this request. It is a mother, who in her anxiety for the honour of her sons, though somewhat unrestrained in the measure of her

desires, may for all that yet find pardon. It is a mother, old in years, devout in her zeal, deprived of consolation; who at that time, when she might have been helped and supported by the aid of her able bodied offspring, suffered her children to leave her, and preferred the reward her sons should receive in following Christ to her own pleasure. For they when called by the Lord, at the first word, as we read, left their nets and their father and followed Him.

56. She then, somewhat yielding to the devotion of a mother's zeal, besought the Saviour, saying: "Grant that these my two sons may sit the one on Thy right hand, the other on Thy left in Thy kingdom." Although it was an error, it was an error of a mother's affections; for a mother's heart knows no patience. Though eager for the object of her desires, yet her longing was pardonable, for she was not greedy for money, but for grace. Not shameless was her request, for she thought not of herself, but of her children. Contemplate the mother, reflect upon her.

57. But it is nothing wonderful if the feelings of parents for their children seem nothing to you, who think the love of the Almighty Father for His only-begotten Son a trifling matter. The Lord of heaven and earth was ashamed (to speak as accords with the assumption of our flesh and the virtues of the soul)—He was ashamed, I say, and, to use His own word, disturbed, to refuse a share even in His own seat to a mother making request for her sons. You maintain sometimes that the proper Son of the eternal God stands to give service, at other times you would have His co-session to be as that of an attendant, that is, not because there is a oneness of majesty, but because it is the order of the Father; and you deny to the Son of God, Who is true God, that which He plainly was unwilling to refuse to men.

58. For He thought of the mother's love, who solaced her old age with the thought of her sons' reward, and, though harassed with a mother's longings, endured the absence of those dearest pledges of her love.

59. Think also of the woman, that is, the weaker sex, whom the Lord had not yet strengthened by His own Passion. Think, I say, of a descendant of Eve, the first woman, sinking under the inheritance of unrestrained passion, which had been passed on to all; one, too, whom the Lord had not yet redeemed with His own Blood, and from whom He had not yet washed out in His Blood the desire implanted in the hearts of all for unbounded honour even beyond what is right. Thus the woman offended owing to an inherited tendency to wrong.

60. And what wonder if a mother should strive to win preference for her children (which is far better than if she had done it for herself), when even the Apostles themselves, as we read, strove amongst themselves, as to who should have the preference?

61. The physician, therefore, ought not to wound a mother who has been deprived of all, nor a suffering mind, with shameful reproaches, lest when the request had been made and had been proudly denied, she should grieve over the condemnation of her petition as being unreasonable.

62. Lastly, the Lord, Who knew that a mother's affection is to be honoured, answered not the woman, but her sons, saying: "Are ye able to drink of the cup that I shall drink of?" When they say: "We are able," Jesus says to them: "Ye shall drink indeed of My cup; but to sit on My right hand and on My left is not Mine to give to you, but to those for whom it is prepared of My Father."

63. How patient and kind the Lord is; how deep is His wisdom and good His love! For wishing to show that the disciples asked for no slight thing, but one they could not obtain, He reserved His own peculiar rights for His Father's honour, not fearing to detract aught from His own rights: "Who thought it not robbery to be equal with God;" and loving, too, His disciples (for "He loved them," as it is written, "unto the end"), He was unwilling to seem to refuse to those whom He loved what they desired; He, I say, the good and holy Lord, Who would rather keep some of His own prerogative secret, than lay aside aught of His love. "For charity suffereth long, and is kind; charity envieth not, and seeketh not her own."

64. Lastly, that you may learn it was no sign of weakness, but rather of tenderness, that He said: "It is not Mine to give to you;" note that when the sons of Zebedee make the request without their mother, He said nothing about the Father; for thus it is written: "It is not Mine to give to you, but those for whom it has been prepared." So the Evangelist Mark has stated it. But when the mother makes this request on her sons' behalf, as we find it in Matthew, He says: "It is not Mine to give to you, but to those for whom it has been prepared of My Father." Here He added: "of My Father," for a mother's feelings demanded greater tenderness.

65. But if they think that by saying, "For whom it hath been prepared of My Father," He assigned greater power to His Father, or detracted aught from His own; let them say whether they think there is any detraction from the Father's power, because the Son in the Gospel says of the Father: "The Father judgeth no man."

66. But if we think it impious to believe that the Father has handed over all judgment to the Son in such wise that He has it not Himself,—for He has it, and cannot lose what the Divine Majesty has by its very nature,—we ought to consider it equally impious to suppose that the Son cannot give what either men can merit, or any creature can receive; especially as He Himself has said: "I go unto My Father, and whatsoever ye shall ask of Him in My name, that will I do." For if the Son cannot give what the Father can give, the Truth has lied, and cannot do what the Father has been asked for in His name. He therefore did not say: "For whom it has been prepared of My Father," in order that requests should be made only of the Father. For all things which are asked of the Father, He has declared that He will give. Lastly, He did not say: "Whatsoever ye shall ask of Me, that will I do;" but: "Whatsoever ye shall ask of Him in My name, that will I do."

Chapter VI.

Wishing to answer the above-stated objection somewhat more fully, he maintains that this request, had it not been impossible in itself, would have been possible for Christ to grant; especially as the Father has given all judgment to Him; which gift we must understand to have been given without any feature of imperfection. However, he proves that the request must be reckoned amongst the impossibilities. To make it really possible, he teaches that Christ's answer must be taken in accordance with His human nature, and shows this next by an exposition of the passage. Lastly, he once more confirms the reply he as given on the impossibility of Christ's session.

67. I Ask now whether they think the request made by the wife and sons of Zebedee was possible or impossible to human circumstances, or to any created being? If it was possible, how is it that He Who made all things which were not had not the power of granting a seat to His apostles on His right hand and on His left? or how was it that He, to Whom the Father gave all judgment, could not judge of men's merits?

68. We know well in what way He gave it; for how did the Son, who created all things out of nothing, receive it as though in want? Had He not the judgment of those whose natures He had made? The Father gave all judgment to the Son, "that all men should honour the Son, even as they honour the Father." It is not therefore the power of the Son, but our knowledge of it, that increases; nor does what is learnt by us add aught to His being, but only to our advantage; so that by knowing the Son of God, we may have eternal life.

69. As, then, in our knowledge of the Son of God His honour, but our profit, not His, is concerned; if any one thinks that the power of God is augmented by that honour, He must also believe that God the Father can receive augmentation; for He is glorified by our knowledge of Him, as is the Son: as it is written on the word of the Son: "I have glorified Thee upon the earth." Therefore if that which was asked for was at all possible, it certainly was in the power of the Son to grant it.

70. Let them show, if they consider it possible, who of men or of other created beings sits either on the right hand or the left of God. For the Father says to the Son: "Sit Thou on My right hand." Therefore if any one sits on the right hand of the Son, the Son is found to be sitting (to speak in human wise) between Himself and the Father.

71. A thing impossible for man, then, was asked of Him. But He was unwilling to say that men could not sit with Him; seeing that He desired His divine glory should be veiled, and not revealed before He rose again. For before this, when He had appeared in glory between His attendants Moses and Elias, He had warned His disciples that they should tell no man what they had seen.

72. Therefore if it was not possible for men or other created beings to merit this, the Son ought not to seem to have less power because He gave not to His apostles, what the Father has not given to men or other created beings. Or else let them say to which of them He has given it. Certainly not to the angels; of whom Scripture says that all the angels stood round about the throne. Thus Gabriel said that he stands, as it says: "I am Gabriel that stand before God."

73. Not to the angels, then, has He given it, nor to the elders who worship Him that sitteth; for they do not sit upon the seat of majesty, but as the Scripture has said, round about the throne; for there are four and twenty other seats, as we have it in the Revelation of John: "And upon the seats four and twenty elders sitting." In the Gospel also the Lord Himself says: "When the Son of Man shall sit in the throne of His glory, ye also shall sit upon twelve thrones, judging the twelve tribes of Israel." He did not say that a share in His own throne could be given to the apostles, but that there were those other twelve thrones; which, however, we ought not to think of as referring to actual sitting down, but as showing the happy issue of spiritual grace.

74. Lastly, in the Book of the Kings, Micaiah the prophet said: "I saw the Lord God of Israel sitting on His throne, and all the host of heaven standing around Him, on His right hand and on His left." How then, when the angels stand on the right hand and on the left of the Lord God, when all the host of heaven stands, shall men sit on the right hand of God or on His left, to whom is promised as a reward for virtue likeness to the angels, as the Lord says: "Ye shall be as the angels in heaven?" "As the angels," He says, not "more than the angels."

75. If, then, the Father has given nothing more than the Son, the Son certainly has given nothing less than the Father. Therefore the Son can in no wise be less than the Father.

76. Suppose, however, that it had been possible for men to obtain what was desired; what does it mean when He says: "But to sit on My right hand and on My left is not Mine to give to you"? What is "Mine"? Above He said: "Ye shall drink indeed of My cup;" and again He added: "It is not Mine to give to you." Above He said "Mine," and again lower down He said "Mine." He made no change. And so the earlier passages tell us why He said "Mine."

77. For being asked by a woman as man to allow her sons to sit on His right hand and His left, because she asked Him as man, the Lord also as though only man answered concerning His Passion: "Are ye able to drink of the cup that I shall drink of?"

78. Therefore because He spoke according to the flesh of the Passion of His Body, He wished to show that according to the flesh He left behind Him an example and pattern to us of the endurance of suffering; but that according to His position as man He could not grant them fellowship in the throne above. This is the reason why He said: "It is not Mine;" as also in another place He says: "My doctrine is not Mine." It is not, He says, spoken after my flesh; for the words which are divine belong not to the flesh.

79. But how plainly He showed His tenderness for His disciples, whom He loved, saying first: "Will ye drink of My cup?" For as He could not grant what they sought, He offered them something else, so that He might mention what He would assign to them, before He denied them anything; in order that they might understand that the failure lay more in the equity of their request to Him, than in the wish of their Lord to show kindness.

80. "Ye shall indeed drink of My cup," He says; that is, "I will not refuse you the suffering, which My flesh will undergo. For all that I have taken on Myself as man, ye can imitate. I have granted you the victory of suffering, the inheritance of the cross. But to sit on My right hand and on My left is not Mine to give to you.'" He did not say, "It is not Mine to give," but: "It is not Mine to give to you;" meaning by this, not that He lacked the power, but that His creatures were wanting in merit.

81. Or take in another way the words: "It is not Mine to give to you," that is. "It is not Mine, for I came to teach humility; it is not Mine, for I came, not to be ministered unto, but to minister; it is not Mine, for I show justice, not favour."

82. Then, speaking of the Father, He added: "For whom it has been prepared," to show that the Father also is not wont to give heed merely to requests, but to merits; for God is not a respecter of persons. Wherefore also the Apostle says: "Whom He did foreknow, He also did predestinate." He did not predestinate them before He knew them, but He did predestinate the reward of those whose merits He foreknew.

83. Rightly then is the woman checked, who demanded what was impossible, as a special kind of privilege from Him the Lord, Who of His own free gift granted not only to two apostles, but to all the disciples, those things which He had adjudged to be given to the saints; and that too without a prayer from any one, as it is written: "Ye shall sit upon twelve thrones, judging the twelve tribes of Israel."

84. Therefore, although we may think the demand to have been possible, there is no room for false attacks. However, when I read that the seraphim stand, how can I suppose that men may sit on the right hand or the left of the Son of God? The Lord sits upon the cherubim, as it says: "Thou that sittest upon the cherubim, show myself." And how shall the apostles sit upon the cherubim?

85. And I do not come to this conclusion of my own mind, but because of the utterances of our Lord's own mouth. For the Lord Himself later on, in commending the apostles to the Father, says: "Father, I will that they also whom Thou hast given Me be with Me where I am." But if He had thought that the Father would give the divine throne to men, He would have said: "I will that where I sit, they also may sit with Me." But He says: "I will that they be with Me," not "that they may sit with Me;" and "where I am," not "as I am."

86. Then follow the words: "That they may see My glory." Here too He did not say: "that they may have My glory," but "that they may see" it. For the servant sees, the Lord possesses; as David also has taught us, saying: "That I may see the delight of the Lord." And the Lord Himself in the Gospel has revealed it, stating: "Blessed are the pure in heart, for they shall see God." "They shall see," He says; not "They shall sit with God upon the cherubim."

87. Let them therefore cease to think little of the Son of God according to His Godhead, lest they should think little also of the Father. For he who believes wrongly of the Son cannot think rightly of the Father; he who thinks wrongly of the Spirit cannot think rightly of the Son. For where there is one dignity, one glory, one love, one majesty, whatsoever thou thinkest is to be withdrawn in the case of any one of the Three Persons, is withdrawn from all alike, For that can never have completeness which thou canst separate and divide into various portions.

Chapter VII.

Objection is taken to the following passage: "Thou hast loved them, as Thou hast loved Me." To remove it, he shows first the impiety of the Arian explanation; then compares these words with others; and lastly, takes the whole passage into consideration. Hence he gathers that the mission of Christ, although it is to be received according to the flesh, is not to His detriment. When this is proved he shows how the divine mission takes place.

88. There are some, O Emperor Augustus, who in their desire to deny the unity of the divine Substance, strive to make little of the love of the Father and the Son, because it is written: "Thou hast loved them, as Thou hast loved Me." But when they say this, what else do they do but adopt a likeness of comparison between the Son of God and men?

89. Can men indeed be I loved by God as the Son is, in Whom the Father is well-pleased? He is well-pleasing in Himself; we through Him. For those in whom God sees His own Son after His own likeness, He admits through His Son into the favour of sons. So that as we go through likeness unto likeness, so through the Generation of the Son are we called unto adoption. The eternal love of God's Nature is one thing, that of grace is another.

90. And if they start a debate on the words that are written: "And Thou hast loved them, as Thou hast loved Me," and think a comparison is intended; they must think that the following also was said by way of comparison: "Be ye merciful, as your Father Which is in heaven is merciful;" and elsewhere: "Be ye perfect, as My Father Which is in heaven is perfect." But if He is perfect in the fulness of His glory, we are but perfect according to the growth of virtue within us. The Son also is loved by the Father according to the fulness of a love that ever abideth, but in us growth in grace merits the love of God.

91. Thou seest, then, how God has given grace to men, and dost thou wish to dissever the natural and indivisible love of the Father and the Son? And dost thou still strive to make nothing of words, where thou dost note the mention of a unity of majesty?

92. Consider the whole of this passage, and see from what standpoint He speaks; for thou hearest Him saying: "Father, glorify Thou Me with the glory which I had with Thee before the world was." See how He speaks from the standpoint of the first man. For He begs for us in that request those things which, as Man, He remembered were granted in paradise before the Fall, as also He spoke of it to the thief at His Passion: "Verily, verily, I say unto thee, today shalt thou be with Me in paradise." This is the glory before the world was. But He used the word "world" instead "men," as also thou hast it: "Lo! the whole world goeth after Him;" and again "That the world may know that Thou hast sent Me."

93. But that thou mightest know the great God, even the life-giving and Almighty Son of God, He has added a proof of His majesty by saying: "And all Mine are Thine, and Thine are Mine." He has all things, and dost thou turn aside the fact that He was sent, to wrong Him?

94. But if thou dost not accept the truth of His mission according to the flesh, as the Apostle spoke of it, and dost raise out of a mere word a decision against it, to enable thee to say that inferiors are wont to be sent by superiors; what answer wilt thou give to the fact that the Son was sent to men? For if thou dost think that he who is sent is inferior to him by whom he is sent, thou must learn also that an inferior has sent a superior, and that superiors have been sent to inferiors. For Tobias sent Raphael the archangel, and an angel was sent to Balsam, and the Son of God to the Jews.

95. Or was the Son of God inferior to the Jews to whom He was sent? For of Him it is written: "Last of all He sent unto them His only Son, saying, They will reverence My Son." And mark that He mentioned first the servants, then the Son, that thou mayest know that God, the only-begotten Son according to the power of His Godhead, has neither name nor lot in common with servants. He is sent forth to be reverenced, not to be compared with the household.

96. And rightly did He add the word "My," that we might believe He came, not as one of many, nor as one of a lower nature or of some inferior power, but as true from Him that is true, as the Image of the Father's Substance.

97. Suppose, however, that he who is sent is inferior to him by whom he is sent. Christ then was inferior to Pilate; for Pilate sent Him to Herod. But a word does not prejudice His power. Scripture, which says that He was sent from the Father, says that He was sent from a ruler.

98. Wherefore, if we sensibly hold to those things which be worthy of the Son of God, we ought to understand Him to have been sent in such a way that the Word of God, out of the incomprehensible and ineffable mystery of the depths of His majesty, gave Himself for comprehension to our minds, so far as we could lay hold of Him, not only when He "emptied" Himself, but also when He dwelt in us, as it is written: "I will dwell in them." Elsewhere also it stands that God said: "Go to, let us go down and confound their language." God, indeed, never descends from any place; for He says: "I fill heaven and earth." But He seems to descend when the Word of God enters our hearts, as the prophet has said: "Prepare ye the way of the Lord, make His paths straight." We are to do this, so that, as He Himself promised, He may come together with the Father and make His abode with us. It is clear, then, how He comes.

Chapter VIII.

Christ, so far as He is true Son of God, has no Lord, but only so far as He is Man; as is shown by His words in which He addressed at one time the Father, at another the Lord. How many heresies are silenced by one verse of Scripture! We must distinguish between the things that belong to Christ as Son of God or as Son of David. For under the latter title only must we ascribe it to Him that He was a servant. Lastly, he points out that many passages cannot be taken except as referring to the Incarnation.

99. Wherefore also it is plain how He calls Him Lord, Whom He knew as Father. For He says: "I confess to Thee, Father, Lord of heaven and earth." First Wisdom spoke of His own Father, and then proclaimed Him Lord of creation. For this reason the Lord shows in His Gospel that no lordship is exercised where there is a true offspring, saying: "What think ye of Christ? Whose Son is He? They say unto Him, The son of David. Jesus saith to them, How then doth David in spirit call Him Lord, saying: The Lord said unto my Lord: Sit Thou on My right hand"? Then he added: "If David in spirit then call Him Lord. how is He his son? And no man was able to answer Him a word."

100. With what care did the Lord provide for the faith in this witness because of the Arians! For He did not say: "The spirit calls Him Lord," but that "David spake in spirit;" in order that men might believe that as He is his, that is, David's son according to the flesh, so also He is his Lord and God according to His Godhead. Thou seeest, then, that there is a distinction between the titles that are used of relationship and of lordship.

101. And rightly did the Lord speak of His own Father, but of the Lord of heaven and earth; so that thou, when thou readest of the Father and the Lord, mayest understand it is the Father of the Son, and the Lord of Creation. In the one title rests the claim of nature, in the other the authority to rule. For taking on Himself the form of a servant, He calls Him Lord, because He has submitted to service; being equal to Him in the form of God, but being a servant in the form of His body: for service is the due of the flesh, but lordship is the due of the Godhead. Wherefore also the Apostle says: "The God of our Lord Jesus Christ, the Father of glory," that is, terming Him God of the adoption of humanity but the Father of glory. Did God have two Sons, Christ and Glory? Certainly not. Therefore if there is one Son of God, even Christ, Christ is Glory. Why dost thou strive to belittle Him who is the glory of the Father?

102. If then the Son is glory, and the Father is glory (for the Father of glory cannot be anything else than glory), there is no separation of glories, but glory is one. Thus glory is referred to its own proper nature, but lordship to the service of the body that was assumed. For if the flesh is subject to the soul of a just man as it is written: "I chastise my body and bring it into subjection;" how much more is it subject to the Godhead, of Which it is said: "For all things serve Thee"?

103. By one question the Lord has shut out both Sabellians and Photinians and Arians. For when He said that the Lord spoke to the Lord, Sabellius is set aside, who will have it that the same Person is both Father and Son. Photinus is set aside, who thinks of Him merely as man; for none could be Lord of David the King, but He Who is God, for it is written: "Thou shalt worship the Lord 'thy God, and Him only shalt thou serve." Would the prophet who ruled under the Law act contrary to the Law? Arius is set aside, who hears that the Son sits on the right hand of the Father; so that if he argues from human ways, he refutes himself, and makes the poison of his blasphemous arguments to flow back upon himself. For in interpreting the inequality of the Father and the Son by the analogy of human habits (wandering from the truth in either case), he puts Him first Whom he makes little of, confessing Him to be the First, Whom he hears to be at the right hand. The Manichaean also is set aside, for he does not deny that He is the Son of David according to the flesh, Who, at the cry of the blind men, "Jesus, Thou Son of David, have mercy on us," was pleased at their faith and stood and healed them. But He does deny that this refers to His eternity, if He is called Son of David alone by those who are false.

104. For "Son of God" is against Ebion, "Son of David," is against the Manichees; "Son of God" is against Photinus, "Son of David" is against Marcion; "Son of God" is against Paul of Samosata, "Son of David" is against Valentinus; "Son of God" is against Arius and Sabellius, the inheritors of heathen errors. "Lord of David" is against the Jews, who beholding the Son of God in the flesh, in impious madness believed Him to be only man.

105. But in the faith of the Church one and the same is both Son of God the Father and Son of David. For the mystery of the Incarnation of God is the salvation of the whole of creation, according to that which is written: "That without God He should taste death for every man;" that is, that every creature might be redeemed without any suffering at the price of the blood of the Lord's Divinity, as it stands elsewhere: "Every creature shall be delivered from the bondage of corruption."

106. It is one thing to be named Son according to the divine Substance, it is another thing to be so called according to the adoption of human flesh. For, according to the divine Generation, the Son is equal to God the Father; and, according to the adoption of a body, He is a servant to God the Father. "For," it says, "He took upon Him the form of a servant." The Son is, however, one and the same. On the other hand, according to His glory, He is Lord to the holy patriarch David, but his Son in the line of actual descent, not abandoning aught of His own, but acquiring for Himself the rights that go with the adoption into our race.

107. Not only does He undergo service in the character of man by reason of His descent from David, but also by reason of His name, as it is written: "I have found David My Servant;" and elsewhere: "Behold I will send unto you My Servant, the Orient is His name." And the Son Himself says: "Thus saith the Lord, that formed Me from the womb to be His servant, and said unto Me: It is a great thing for Thee to be called My Servant. Behold I have set Thee up for a witness to My people, and a light to the Gentiles, that Thou mayest be for salvation unto the ends of the earth." To whom is this said, if not to Christ? Who being in the form of God, emptied Himself and took upon Him the form of a servant. But what can be in the form of God, except that which exists in the fulness of the Godhead?

108. Learn, then, what this means: "He took upon Him the form of a servant." It means that He took upon Him all the perfections of humanity in their completeness, and obedience in its completeness. And so it says in the thirtieth Psalm: "Thou hast set my feet in a large room. I am made a reproach above all mine enemies. Make Thy face to shine upon Thy servant." "Servant" means the Man in whom He was sanctified; it means the Man in whom He was anointed; it means the Man in whom He was made under the law, made of the Virgin; and, to put it briefly, it means the Man in whose person He has a mother, as it is written: "O Lord, I am Thy Servant, I am Thy Servant, and the Son of Thy hand-maid;" and again: "I am cast down and sore humbled."

109. Who is sore humbled, but Christ, Who came to free all through His obedience? "For as by one man's disobedience many were made sinners, so by the obedience of one shall many be made righteous." Who received the cup of salvation? Christ the High Priest, or David who never held the priesthood, nor endured suffering? Who offered the sacrifice of Thanksgiving?

110. But that is insufficient; take again: "Preserve My soul, for I am holy." Did David say this of himself? Nay, He says it, Who also says: "Thou wilt not leave My soul in hell, neither wilt Thou suffer Thine Holy One to see corruption." The Same then says both of these.

111. He has added further: "Save Thy Servant;" and, further on: "Give Thy strength to Thy servant, and to the Son of Thy handmaid;" and, elsewhere, that is, in Ezekiel: "And I will set up one Shepherd over them, and He shall rule them, even My Servant David. He shall feed them, and He shall be their Shepherd. And I the Lord will be their God, and My Servant David a prince among them." Now David the Son of Jesse was already dead. Therefore he speaks of Christ, Who for our sakes was made the Son of a handmaiden in the form of man; for according to His divine Generation He has no Mother, but a Father only: nor is He the fruit of earthly desire, but the eternal Power of God.

318

112. And so, also, when we read that the Lord said: "My time is not yet full come;" and: "Yet a little while I am with you;" and: "I go unto Him that sent Me;" and: "Now is the Son of Man glorified;" we ought to refer all this to the sacrament of the Incarnation. But when we read: "And God is glorified in Him, and God hath glorified Him;" what doubt is there here, where the Son is glorified by the Father, and the Father is glorified by the Son?

113. Next, to make clear the faith of the Unity, and the Union of the Trinity, He also said that He would be glorified by the Spirit, as it stands: "He shall receive of Mine, and shall glorify Me." Therefore the Holy Spirit also glorifies the Son of God. How, then, did He say: "If I glorify Myself, My glory is nothing." Is then the glory of the Son nothing? It is blasphemy to say so, unless we apply these words to His flesh; for the Son spoke in the character of man, for by comparison with the Godhead, there is no glory of the flesh.

114. Let them cease from their wicked objections which are but thrown back upon their own falseness. For they say, it is written: "Now is the Son of Man glorified." I do not deny that it is written: "The Son of Man is glorified." But let them see what follows:

"And God is glorified in Him." I can plead some excuse for the Son of Man, but He has none for His Father; for the Father took not flesh upon Himself. I can plead an excuse, but do not use it. He has none, and is falsely attacked. I can either understand it in its plain sense, or I can apply to the flesh what concerns the flesh. A devout mind distinguishes between the things which are spoken after the flesh or after the Godhead. An impious mind turns aside to the dishonour of the Godhead, all that is said with regard to the littleness of the flesh.

Chapter IX.

The saint meets those who in Jewish wise object to the order of the words: "In the name of the Father and of the Son and of the oly Ghost," with the retort that the Son also is often placed before the Father; though he first points out that an answer to this objection has been already given by him.

115. Why is it that the Arians, after the Jewish fashion, are such false and shameless interpreters of the divine words, going indeed so far as to say that there is one power of the Father, another of the Son, and another of the Holy Ghost, since it is written: "Go ye, teach all nations, baptizing them in the name of the Father and of the Son and of the Holy Ghost"? And why do they make a distinction of divine power owing to the mere order of words?

116. Though I have already given this very witness for a unity of majesty and name in my former books, yet if they make this the ground of debate, I can maintain on the testimony of the Scriptures that the Son is mentioned first in many places, and that the Father is spoken of after Him. Is it therefore a fact that, because the name of the Son is placed first, by the mere accident of a word, as the Arians would have it, the Father comes second to the Son? God forbid, I say, God forbid. Faith knows nothing of such order as this;it knows nothing of a divided honour of the Father and the Son. I have not read of, nor heard of, nor found any varying degree in God. Never have I read of a second, never of a third God. I have read of a first God, I have heard of a first and only God.

117. If we pay such excessive regard to order, then the Son ought not to sit at the right hand of the Father, nor ought He to call Himself the First and the Beginning. The Evangelist was wrong in beginning with the Word and not with God, where he says: "In the beginning was the Word, and the Word was with God." For, according to the order of human usage, he ought to name the Father first. The Apostle also was ignorant of their order, who says: "Paul the servant of Jesus Christ, called to be an Apostle, separated unto the Gospel of Go;" and elsewhere: "The grace of our Lord Jesus Christ, and the love of God, and the communion of the Holy Ghost." If we follow the order of the words, he has placed the Son first, and the Father second. But the order of the words is often changed; and therefore thou oughtest not to question about order or degree, in the case of God the Father and His Son, for there is no severance of unity in the Godhead.

Chapter X.

The Arians openly take sides with the heathen in attacking the words: "He that believeth on Me, believeth not on Me," etc. The true meaning of the passage is unfolded; and to prevent us from believing that the Lord forbade us to have faith in Him, it is shown how He spoke at one time as God, at another as Man. After bringing forward examples of various results of that faith, he shows that certain other passages also must be taken in the same way.

118. Last of all, to show that they are not Christians, they deny that we are to believe on Christ, saying that it is written: "He that believeth on Me, believeth not on Me, but on Him that sent Me." I was awaiting this confession; why did you delude me with your quibbles? I knew I had to contend with heathens. Nay, they indeed are converted, but ye are not. If they believe, that the sacrament [of Baptism] is safe; ye have received it, and destroyed it, or perchance it has never been received, but was unreal from the first.

119. It is written, they say: "He that believeth on Me, believeth not on Me, but on Him that sent Me." But see what follows, and see how the Son of God wishes to be seen; for it continues: "And he that seeth Me, seeth Him that sent Me," for the Father is seen in the Son. Thus, He has explained what He had spoken earlier, that he who confesses the Father believes on the Son. For he who knows not the Son, neither knows the Father. For every one that denies the Son has not the Father, but he that confesses the Son has both the Father and the Son.

120. What, then, is the meaning of "Believeth not on Me"? That is, not on that which you can perceive in bodily form, nor merely on the man whom you see. For He has stated that we are to believe not merely on a man, but that thou mayest believe that Jesus Christ Himself is both God and Man. Wherefore, for both reasons He says: "I came not from Myself;" and again: "I am the beginning, of which also I speak to you." As Man He came not from Himself; as Son of God He takes not His beginning from men; but "I am," He says, "Myself 'the beginning of which also I speak to you.' Neither are the words which I speak human, but divine."

121. Nor is it right to believe that He denied we were to believe on Him, since He Himself said: "That whosoever believeth on Me should not abide in darkness;" and in another place again: "For this is the will of My Father that sent Me, that every one that seeth the Son, and believeth on Him, may have eternal life;" and again: "Ye believe in God, believe also in Me."

122. Let no one, therefore, receive the Son without the Father, because we read of the Son. The Son hath the Father, but not in a temporal sense, nor by reason of His passion, nor owing to His conception, nor by grace. I have read of His Generation, I have not read of His Conception. And the Father says: "I have begotten;" He does not say: "I have created." And the Son calls not God His Creator in the eternity of His divine Generation, but Father.

123. He represents Himself also now in the character of man, now in the majesty of God; now claiming for Himself oneness of Godhead with the Father, now taking upon Him all the frailty of human flesh; now saying that He has not His own doctrine, and now that He seeks not His own will; now pointing out that His testimony is not true, and now that it is true. For He Himself has said: "If I bear witness of Myself, My witness is not true." Later on He says: "If I bear witness of Myself, My witness is true."

124. And how is Thy testimony, Lord Jesus, not true? Did not he who believed it, though he hung upon the cross, and paid the penalty for the crime he owned to, cast aside the deserts of the robber and gain the reward of the innocent?

125. Was Paul deceived, who received his sight, because he believed; which sight he had lost, before he believed?

126. And did Joshua, the son of Nun, err in recognizing the leader of the heavenly host? But after he believed, be forthwith conquered, being found worthy to triumph in the battle of faith. Again, he did not lead forth his armed ranks into the fight, nor did he overthrow the ramparts of the enemy's walls, with battering rams or other engines of war, but with the sound of the seven trumpets of the priests. Thus the blare of the trumpet and the badge of the priest brought a cruel war to an end.

127. A harlot saw this; and she who in the destruction of the city lost all hope of any means of safety, because her faith had conquered, bound a scarlet thread in her window, and thus uplifted a sign of her faith and the banner of the Lord's Passion; so that the semblance of the mystic blood, which should redeem the world, might be in memory. So, without, the name of Joshua was a sign of victory to those who fought; within, the semblance of the Lord's Passion was a sign of salvation to those in danger. Wherefore, because Rahab understood the heavenly mystery, the Lord says in the Psalm: "I will be mindful of Rahab and Babylon that know Me."

128. How, then, is Thy testimony not true, O Lord, except it be given in accordance with the frailty of man? For "every man is a liar."

129. Lastly, to prove that He spoke as man, He says: "The Father that sent Me, He beareth witness of Me." But His testimony as God is true, as He Himself says: "My record is true: for I know whence I come, and whither I go, but ye know not whence I come, and whither I go. Ye judge after the flesh." They judge then not after the Godhead but after the manhood, who think that Christ had not the power of bearing witness.

130. Therefore, when thou hearest: "He that believeth, believeth not on Me;" or: "The Father that sent Me, He gave Me a commandment;" thou hast now learnt whither thou oughtest to refer those words. Lastly, He shows what the commandment is, saying: "I lay down My life, that I may take it again. No man taketh it from Me, but I lay it down of Myself." Thou seest, then, what is said so as to show He had full power to lay down or to take up His life; as He also said: "I have power to lay it down, and I have power again to take it up. This commandment have I received of My Father."

131. Whether, then, a command, or, as some Latin manuscripts have it, a direction was given, it was certainly not given to Him as God, but as incarnate man, with reference to the victory He should gain in undergoing His Passion.

Chapter XI.

We must refer the fact that Christ is said to speak nothing of Himself, to His human nature. After explaining how it is right to say that He hears and sees the Father as being God, He shows conclusively, by a large number of proofs, that the Son of God is not a creature.

132. Are we indeed to bring the Son of God to such a low estate that He may not know how to act or speak, except as He hears, and are we to suppose that a fixed measure of action or of speech is assigned to Him, because it is written: "I speak not of Myself," and, further on: "As the Father hath said unto Me, even so I speak"? But those words have reference to the obedience of the flesh, or else to the faith in the Unity. For many learned men allow that the Son hears, and that the Father speaks to the Son through the unity of their Nature; for that which the Son, through the unity of their will, knows that the Father wills, He seems to have heard.

133. Whereby is meant no personal duty, but an indivisible sentence of co-operation. For this does not signify any actual hearing of words, but the unity of will and of power, which exists both in the Father and in the Son. He has stated that this exists also in the Holy Spirit, in another place, saying, "For He shall not speak of Himself, but whatsoever He shall hear, that shall He speak," so that we may learn that whatsoever the Spirit says, the Son also says; and whatsoever the Son says, the Father says also; for there is one mind and one mode of working in the Trinity. For, as the Father is seen in the Son, not indeed in bodily appearance, but in the unity of the Godhead, so also the Father speaks in the Son, not with a voice of earth, not with a human sound, but in the unity of Their work. So when He had said: "The Father that dwelleth in Me, He speaketh; and the works that I do, He doeth;" He added: "Believe Me, that I am in the Father, and the Father in Me; or else believe Me for the very work's sake."

134. This is what we understand according to the whole course of the holy Scriptures; but the Arians, who will not think of God the things that be right, may be put to silence by an example just suited to their deserts; that they may not believe everything in carnal fashion, since

they themselves do not see the works of their father the devil with bodily eyes. So the Lord has declared of their fellows the Jews, saying: "Ye do what ye have seen your father doing;" though they are reproved not because they saw the work of the devil, but because they did his will, since the devil unseen works out sin in them in accordance with their own wickedness, We have written this, as the Apostle did, because of the folly of these traitors.

135. But we have sufficiently proved by examples from Scripture that it is a property of the unity of the divine majesty that the Father should abide in the Son, and that the Son should seem to have heard from the Father those things which He speaks. How else can we understand the unity of majesty than by the knowledge that the same deference is paid to the Father and the Son? For what can be better put than the Apostle's saying that the Lord of glory was crucified?

136. The Son then is the God of glory and the Lord of glory, but glory is not subject to creatures; the Son therefore is not a creature.

137. The Son is the Image of the Father's Substance; but every creature is unlike that divine Substance, but the Son of the Father is not unlike God; therefore the Son is not a creature.

138. The Son thought it not robbery to be equal with God; but no creature is equal with God, the Son, however, is equal; therefore the Son is not a creature.

139. Every creature is changeable; but the Son of God is not changeable; therefore the Son of God is not a creature.

140. Every creature meets with chance occurrences of good and evil after the powers of its nature, and also feels their passing away; but nothing can pass away from or bring addition to the Son of God in His Godhead; therefore the Son of God is not a creature.

141. Every work of His God will bring into judgment; but the Son of God is not brought into judgment; for He Himself judges; therefore the Son of God is not a creature.

142. Lastly, that thou mayest understand the unity, the Saviour in speaking of His sheep says: "No man is able to pluck them out of My hand. My Father Which gave them to Me is greater than all, and no man is able to pluck them out of My Father's hand. I and My Father are one." 143. So the Son gives life as does the Father. "For as the Father raiseth up the dead and quickeneth them, even so the Son quickeneth whom He will." So the Son raises up as does the Father: so too the Son preserves as does the Father. He Who is not unequal in grace, how is He unequal in power? So also the Son does not destroy, as neither does the Father. Therefore lest any one should believe there were two Gods, or should imagine a diversity of power, He said that He was one with His Father. How can a creature say that? Therefore the Son of God is not a creature.

144. It is not the same thing to rule as to serve; but Christ is both a King and the Son of a King. The Son of God therefore is not a servant. Every creature, however, gives service. But the Son of God, Who makes servants become the sons of God, does not give service. Therefore the Son of God is not a servant.

Chapter XII.

He confirms what has been already said, by the parable of the rich man who went into a far country to receive for himself a kingdom; and shows that when the Son delivers up the kingdom to the Father, we must not regard the fact that the Father is said to put all things in subjection under Him, in a disparaging way. Here we are the kingdom of Christ, and in Christ's kingdom. Hereafter we shall be in the kingdom of God, where the Trinity will reign together.

145. In divine fashion has He represented that parable of the rich man, who went to a far-off country to receive a kingdom, and to return, thus describing Himself in the substance of the Godhead, and of His Manhood. For He being rich in the fulness of His Godhead, Who was made poor for us though He was rich and an eternal King, and the Son of an eternal King; He, I say, went to a foreign country in taking on Him a body, for He entered upon the ways of men as though upon a strange journey, and came into this world to preparefor Himself a kingdom from amongst us.

146. Jesus therefore came to this earth to receive for Himself a kingdom from us, to whom He says: "The kingdom of God is within you." This is the kingdom which Christ has received, this the kingdom which He has delivered to the Father. For how did He receive for Himself a kingdom, Who was a King eternal? "The Son of Man therefore came to receive a kingdom and to return." The Jews were unwilling to acknowledge Him, of whom He says: "They which would not that I should reign over them, bring hither and slay them."

147. Let us follow the course of the Scriptures. He Who came will deliver up the kingdom to God the Father; and when He has delivered up the kingdom, then also shall He be subject to Him, Who has put all things in subjection under Him, that God may be all in all. If the Son of God has received the kingdom as Son of Man, surely as Son of Man also He will deliver up what He has received. If He delivers it up as Son of Man, as Son of Man He confesses His subjection indeed under the conditions of the flesh, and not in the majesty of His Godhead.

148. And dost thou make objections and contemn Him, because God has put all things in subjection under Him, when thou hearest that the Son of Man delivers up the kingdom to God, and hast read, as we said in our earlier books: "No man can come to Me, except the Father draw him; and I will raise him up at the last day"? If we follow it literally, see rather and notice the unity of honour each gives to other: The Father has put all things in subjection under the Son, and the Son delivers the kingdom to the Father. Say now which isthe greater, to deliver up, or to raise up to life? Do we not after human fashion speak of the service of delivering up, and the power of raising to life? But both the Son delivers up to the Father, and also the Father to the Son. The Son raises to life, and the Father also raises to life, Let them create the fiction of a blasphemous division where there is a unity of power.

149. Let the Son then deliver up His kingdom to the Father. The kingdom which He delivers up is not lost to Christ, hut grows. We are the kingdom, for it was said to us: "The kingdom of God is within you." And we are the kingdom, first of Christ, then of the Father; as it is written: "No man cometh to the Father, but by Me." When I am on the way, I am Christ's; when I have passed through, I am the Father's; but everywhere through Christ, and everywhere under Him.

150. It is a good thing to be in the kingdom of Christ, so that Christ may be with us; as He Himself says: "Lo I am with you always, even unto the end of the world." But it is better to be with Christ: "For to depart and be with Christ is far better." Though we are under sin in this world, Christ is with us, that "by the obedience of one man many may be made just." And if I escape the sin of this world, I shall begin to be with Christ. And so He says: "I will come again, and receive you unto Myself;" and further on: "I will that where I am, there ye may be also with Me."

151. Therefore we are now under Christ's rule, whilst we are in the body, and are not yet stripped of the form of a servant, which He put upon Him, when He "emptied Himself." But when we shall see His glory, which He had before the world was, we shall be in the kingdom of God, in which are the patriarchs and prophets, of whom it is written: "When ye shall see Abraham, Isaac, and Jacob, and all the prophets in the kingdom of God;" and shall thus acquire a deeper knowledge of God.

152. But in the kingdom of the Son the Father also reigns; and in the kingdom of the Father the Son also reigns: for the Father is in the Son, and the Son in the Father; and in whomsoever the Son dwells, in him also the Father dwells; and in whomsoever the Father dwells, in him also the Son dwells, as it is written: "Both I and My Father will come to Him, and make Our abode with Him." Thus as there is one dwelling, so also there is one kingdom. Yea, and so far is the kingdom of the Father and of the Son but one, that the Father receives what the Son delivers, and the Son does not lose what the Father receives. Thus in the one kingdom there is a unity of power. Let no one therefore sever the Godhead between the Father and the Son.

Chapter XIII.

With the desire to learn what subjection to Christ means after putting forward and rejecting various ideas of subjection, he runs through the Apostle's words; and so puts an end to the blasphemous opinions of the heretics on this matter. The subjection, which is shown to be future, cannot concern the Godhead, since there has always been the greatest harmony of wills between the Father and the Son. Also to that same Son in His Godhead all things have indeed been made subject; but they are said to be not yet subject to Him in this sense, because all men do not obey His commands. But after that they have been made subject, then shall Christ also be made subject in them, and the Father's work be perfected.

153. But if the one name and right of God belong to both the Father and the Son, since the Son of God is also true God, and a King eternal, the Son of God is not made subject in His Godhead. Let us then, Emperor Augustus, think how we ought to regard His subjection.

154. How is the Son of God made subject? As the creature to vanity? But it is blasphemous to have any such idea of the Substance of the Godhead.

155. Or as every creature is to the Son of God, for it is rightly written: "Thou hast put all things in subjection under His feet"? But Christ is not made subject to Himself.

156. Or as a woman to a man, as we read: "Let the wives be subject to their husbands;" and again: "Let the woman learn in silence in all subjection"? But it is impious to compare a man to the Father, or a woman to the Son of God.

157. Or as Peter said: "Submit yourselves to every human creature"? But Christ was certainly not so subject.

158. Or as Paul wrote: "Submitting yourselves mutually to God and the Father in the fear of Christ"? But Christ was not subject either in His own fear, nor in the fear of another Christ. For Christ is but one. But note the force of these words, that we are subject to the Father, whilst we also fear Christ.

159. How, then, do we understand His subjection? Shall we review the whole chapter which the Apostle wrote, so as to give no appearance of having falsely withheld anything, or of having weakened its force with intention to deceive? "If in this life only," he says, "we have hope in Christ, we are of all men most miserable. But if Christ is risen from the dead, He is the first-fruits of them that sleep." Ye see how he discusses the question of Christ's Resurrection.

160. "For since by one man,'" he says, "came death, by man came also the resurrection of the dead. For as in Adam all die, even so in Christ shall all be made alive. But each one in his own order: Christ the firstfruits; afterward they that are Christ's, who have believed in His coming. Then cometh the end, when He shall have delivered up the kingdom to God,even the Father, when He shall have put down all rule and authority and power. For He must reign until He hath put all enemies under His feet. The last enemy that shall be destroyed is death; for He hath put all things under His feet. But when He saith, all things are put under Him, it is manifest that He is excepted Which did put all things under Him. But when all things shall be subdued unto Him, then shall the Son also Himself be subject unto Him, that put all things under Him, that God may be all in all." Thus also the same Apostle said to the Hebrews: "But now we see not yet all things put under Him." We have heard the whole of the Apostle's discourse.

161. How, then, do we speak of His subjection? The Sabellians and Marcionites say that this subjection of Christ to God the Father will be in such wise that the Son will be re-absorbed into the Father. If, then, the subjection of the Word means that God the Word is to be absorbed into the Father; then whatsoever is made subject to the Father and the Son will be absorbed into the Father and the Son, that God may be all and in all His creatures. But it is foolish to say so. There is therefore no subjection through re-absorption. For there are other things which are made subject, those, that is to say, which are created, and there is Another, to Whom that subjection is made. Let the expounders of a cruel re-absorption keep silence.

162. Would that they too were silent, who, as they cannot prove that the Word of God and Wisdom of God can be re-absorbed, attribute the weakness of subjection to His Godhead,

saying that it is written: "But when all things shall be subdued unto Him, then shall the Son also Himself be subject unto Him."

163. We see, then, that the Scripture states that He is not yet made subject, but that this is to come: Therefore now the Son is not made subject to God the Father. In what, then, do ye say that the Son will be made subject? If in His Godhead, He is not disobedient, for He is not at variance with the Father; nor is He made subject, for He is not a servant, but the only Son of His own proper Father. Lastly, when He created heaven, and formed the earth, He exercised both power and love. There is therefore no subjection as that of a servant in the Godhead of Christ. But if there is no subjection then the will is free.

164. But if they think of this as the subjection of the Son, namely, that the Father makes all things in union with His will, let them learn that this is really a proof of inseparable power. For the unity of Their will is one that began not in time, but ever existed. But where there is a constant unity of will, there can be no weakness of temporal subjection. For if He were made subject through His nature, He would always remain in subjection; but since He is said to be made subject in time, that subjection must be part of an assumed office and not of an everlasting weakness: especially as the eternal Power of God cannot change His state for a time, neither can the right of ruling fall to the Father in time. For if the Son ever will be changed in such wise as to be made subject in His Godhead, then also must God the Father, if ever He shall gain more power, and have the Son in subjection to Himself in His Godhead, be considered now in the meantime inferior according to your explanation.

165. But what fault has the Son been guilty of, that we should believe that He could hereafter be made subject in His Godhead? Has he as man seized for Himself the right to sit at His Father's side, or has He claimed for Himself the prerogative of His Father's throne, against His Father's will? But He Himself says: "For I do always those things that please Him." Therefore if the Son pleases the Father in all things, why should He be made subject, Who was not made subject before?

166. Let us see then that there be not a subjection of the Godhead, but rather of us in the fear of Christ, a truth so full of grace, and so full of mystery. Wherefore, again, let us weigh the Apostle's words: "But when all things shall be subdued unto Him, then shall the Son also Himself be subject unto Him that put all things under Him: that God may be all in all." What then dost thou say? Are not all things now subject unto Him? Are not the choirs of the saints made subject? Are not the angels, who ministered to Him when on the earth. Are not the archangels who were sent to Mary to foretell the coming of the Lord? Are not all the heavenly hosts? Are not the cherubim and seraphim, are not thrones and dominions and powers which worship and praise Him?

167. How, then, will they be brought into subjection? In the way that the Lord Himself has said. "Take My yoke upon you." It is not the fierce that bear the yoke, but the humble and the gentle. This clearly is no base subjection for men, but a glorious one: "that in the Name of Jesus every knee should bow, of things in heaven and things beneath; and that every tongue should confess that Jesus is Lord in the glory of God the Father." But for this reason all things were not made subject before, for they had not yet received the wisdom of God, not yet did they wear the easy yoke of the Word on the neck as it were of their mind. "But as many as received Him," as it is written, "to them gave He power to become the sons of God."

168. Will any one say that Christ is now made subject, because many have believed? Certainly not. For Christ's subjection lies not in a few but in all. For just as I do not seem to be brought into subjection, if the flesh in me as yet lusts against the spirit, and the spirit against the flesh, although I am in part subdued; so because the whole Church is the one body of Christ, we divide Christ as long as the human race disagrees. Therefore Christ is not yet made subject, for His members are not yet brought into subjection. But when we have become, not many members, but one spirit, then He also will become subject, in order that through His subjection "God may be all and in all."

169. But as Christ is not yet made subject, so is the work of God not yet perfected; for the Son of God said: "My meat is to do the will of My Father that sent Me, and to finish His work." What manner of doubt is there that the subjection of the Son in me iS still in the future, in whom the work of the Father is unfinished, because I myself am not yet perfect? I, who make the work of God to be unfinished, do I make the Son of God to be in subjection? But that is not a matter of wrong, it is a matter of grace. For in so far as we are made subject, it is to our profit, not to that of the Godhead, that we are made subject to the law, that we are made subject to grace. For formerly, as the Apostle himself has said, the wisdom of the flesh was at enmity with God, for "it was not made subject to the law," but now it is made subject through the Passion of Christ.

Chapter XIV.

He continues the discussion of the difficulty he has entered upon, and teaches that Christ is not subject but only according to the flesh. Christ, however, whilst in subjection in the Flesh, still gave proofs of His Godhead. He combats the idea that Christ is made subject in This. The humanity indeed, which He adopted, has been so far made subject in us, as ours has been raised in that very humanity of His. Lastly, we are taught, when that same subjection of Christ will take place.

170. However, lest anyone should cavil, see what care Scripture takes under divineinspiration. For it shows to us in whatChrist is made subject to God, whilst it also teaches us in what He made the universesubject to Himself. And so it says: "Now we see not yet all things put under Him." For we see Jesus made a little lower than the angels for the suffering of death. It shows therefore that He was made lower in taking on Him our flesh. What then hinders Him from openly showing His subjection in taking on Him our flesh, through which He subjects all things to Himself, whilst He Himself is made subject in it to God the Father?

171. Let us then think of His subjection. "Father," He says, "if Thou be willing, remove this cup from Me; nevertheless not My will but Thine be done." Therefore that subjection will be according to the assumption of human nature; as we read: "Being found in fashion as a man, He humbled Himself, being made obedient unto death." The subjection therefore is that of obedience; the obedience is that of death; the death is that of the assumed humanity; that subjection therefore will be the subjection of the assumed humanity. Thus in no wise is there a weakness in the Godhead, but there is such a discharge of pious duty as this.

172. See how I do not fear their intentions. They allege that He must be subject to God the Father, I say He was subject to Mary His Mother. For it is written of Joseph and Mary: "He was subject unto them." But if they think so, let them say how the Deity was made subject to men.

173. Let not the fact that He is said to have been made subject work against Him, Who receives no hurt from the fact that He is called a servant, or is stated to have been crucified, or is spoken of as dead. For when He died He lived; when He was made subject He was reigning; when He was buried He revived again. He offered Himself in subjection to human power, yet at another time He declared He was the Lord of eternal glory. He was before the judge, yet claimed for Himself a throne at the right hand of God, as Judge forever. For thus it is written: "Hereafter ye shall see the Son of Man sitting on the right hand of the power of God, and coming in the clouds of heaven." He was scourged by the Jews, and commanded the angels; He was born of Mary under the law; He was before Abraham above the law. On the cross He was revered by nature; the sun fled; the earth trembled; the angels became silent. Could the elements see the Generation of Him Whose Passion they feared to see? And will they uphold the subjection of an adorable Nature in Him, in Whom they could not endure the subjection of the body?

174. But since the Father, the Son, and the Holy Spirit are of one Nature, the Father certainly will not be in subjection to Himself. And therefore the Son will not be in subjection in that in which He is one with the Father; test it should seem that through the unity of the Godhead the Father also is in subjection to the Son. Therefore, as upon that cross it was not the

fulness of the Godhead, but our weakness that was brought into subjection, so also will the Son hereafter become subject to the Father in the participation of our nature, in order that when the lusts of the flesh are brought into subjection the heart may have no care for riches, or ambition, or pleasures; but that God may be all to us, if we live after His image and likeness, as far as we can attain to it, through all.

175. The benefit has passed, then, from the individual to the community; for in His flesh He has tamed the nature of all human flesh. Thus, according to the Apostle: "As we have borne the image of the earthly, so also shall we bear the image of the heavenly." This thing certainly cannot come to pass except in the inner man. Therefore, "laying aside all these," that is those things which we read of: "anger, malice, blasphemy, filthy communication;" as he also says below: "Let us, having put off the old man with his deeds, put on the new man, which is renewed in knowledge after the image of Him that created Him."

176. And that thou mightest know that when he says: "That God may be all in all," he does not separate Christ from God the Father, he also says to the Colossians: "Where there is neither male nor female, Jew nor Greek, Barbarian nor Scythian, bond nor free, but Christ is all and in all." So also saying to the Corinthians: "That God may be all and in all," he comprehended in that the unity and equality of Christ with God the Father, for the Son is not separated from the Father. And in like manner as the Father worketh all and in all, so also Christ worketh all in all. If, then, Christ also worketh all in all, He is not made subject in the glory of the Godhead, but in us. But how is He made subject in us, except in the way in which He was made lower than the angels, I mean in the sacrament of His body? For all things which served their Creator from their first beginning seemed not as yet to be made subject to Him in that.

177. But if thou shouldst ask how He was made subject in us, He Himself shows us, saying: "I was in prison, and ye came unto Me; I was sick, and ye visited Me: Inasmuch as ye have done it unto one of the least of these ye have done it unto Me." Thou hearest of Him as sick and weak, and art not moved. Thou hearest of Him in subjection, and art moved, though He is sick and weak in Him in whom He is in subjection, in whom He was made sin and a curse for us.

178. As, then, He was made sin and a curse not on His own account but on ours, so He became subject in us not for His own sake but for ours, being not in subjection in His eternal Nature, nor accursed in His eternal Nature. "For cursed is every one that hangeth on a tree." Cursed He was, for He bore our curses; in subjection, also, for He took upon Him our subjection, but in the assumption of the form of a servant, not in the glory of God; so that whilst he makes Himself a partaker of our weakness in the flesh, He makes us partakers of the divine Nature in His power. But neither in one nor the other have we any natural fellowship with the heavenly Generation of Christ, nor is there any subjection of the Godhead in Christ. But as the Apostle has said that on Him through that flesh which is the pledge of our salvation, we sit in heavenly places, though certainly not sitting ourselves, so also He is said to be subject in us through the assumption of our nature.

179. For who is so mad as to think, as we have said already, that a seat of honour is due to Him at the right hand of God the Father, when that is granted to Christ according to the flesh by the Father of His Generation, even a seat of a heavenly and equal power? The angels worship, and dost thou attempt to overthrow the throne of God with impious presumption?

180. It is written, thou sayest, that "when we were dead in sins, He hath quickened us in Christ, by Whose grace ye are saved, and hath raised us up together, and made us sit together in heavenly places in Christ Jesus." I acknowledge that it is so written; but it is not written that God suffers men to sit on His right hand, but only to sit there in the Person of Christ. For He is the foundation of all, and is the head of the Church, in Whom our common nature according to the flesh has merited the right to the heavenly throne. For the flesh is honoured as having a share in Christ Who is God, and the nature of the whole human race is honoured as having a share in the flesh.

181. As we then sit in Him by fellowship in our fleshly nature, so also He, Who through the assumption of our flesh was made a curse for us (seeing that a curse could not fall upon the blessed Son of God), so, I say, He through the obedience of all will become subject in us; when the Gentile has believed, and the Jew has acknowledged Him Whom he crucified; when the Manichaean has worshipped Him, Whom he has not believed to have come in the flesh; when the Arian has confessed Him to be Almighty, Whom he has denied; when, lastly, the wisdom of God, His justice, peace, love, resurrection, is in all. Through His own works and through the manifold forms of virtues Christ will be in us in subjection to the Father. And when, with vice renounced and crime at an end, one spirit in the heart of all peoples has begun to cleave to God in all things, then will God be all and in all.

Chapter XV.

He briefly takes up again the same points of dispute, and shrewdly concludes from the unity of the divine power in the Father and the Son, that whatever is said of the subjection of the Son is to be referred to His humanity alone. He further confirms this on proof of the love, which exists alike in either.

182. Let us then shortly sum up our conclusion on the whole matter. A unity of power puts aside all idea of a degrading subjection. His giving up of power, and His victory as conqueror won over death, have not lessened His power. Obedience works out subjection. Christ has taken obedience upon Himself, obedience even to taking on Him our flesh, the cross even to gaining our salvation. Thus where the work lies, there too is the Author of the work. When therefore, all things have become subject to Christ, through Christ's obedience, so that all bend their knees in His name, then He Himself will be all in all. For now, since all do not believe, all do not seem to be in subjection. But when all have believed and done the will of God, then Christ will be all and in all. And when Christ is all and in all, then will God be all and in all; for the Father abides ever in the Son. How, then, is He shown to be weak, Who redeemed the weak?

183. And lest thou shouldst by chance attribute to the weakness of the Son, that it is written, that God hath put all things in subjection under Him; learn that He has Himself brought all things into subjection to Himself, for it is written: "Our conversation is in heaven, from whence also we look for the Saviour, the Lord Jesus, Who shall change our vile body that it may be fashioned like unto His glorious body according to the working, whereby He is able to subdue all things unto Himself." Thou has learnt, therefore, that He can subdue all things unto Himself according to the working of His Godhead.

184. Learn now how He receives all things in subjection according to the flesh, as it is written: "Who wrought in Christ, raising Him from the dead, and setting Him at His own right hand in the heavenly places, above principality and power and might and dominion and every name that is named not only in this world, but also in that which is to come; and hath put all things under His feet." According to the flesh then all things are given to Him in subjection; according to which also He was raised from the dead, both in His human soul and His rational subjection.

185. Many nobly interpret that which is written: "Truly my soul will be in subjection to God;" He said soul not Godhead, soul not glory. And that we might know that the Lord has spoken through the prophet of the adoption of our human nature, He added: "How long will ye cast yourselves upon a man?" As also He says in the Gospel: "Why do ye seek to kill Me, a man?" And He added again: "Nevertheless they desired to refuse My price, they ran in thirst, they blessed with their mouth, and cursed with their heart." For the Jews, when Judas brought back the price, would not receive it, running on in the thirst of madness, for they refused the grace of a spiritual draught.

186. This is the reverent interpretation of subjection, for since this is the office of the Lord's Passion, He will be subject in us in that in which He suffered. Do we ask wherefore? That "neither angels, nor powers, nor height, nor depth, nor things present, nor things to come, nor any other creature may separate us from the love of God, which is in Christ Jesus." we see then,

from what has been said, that no creature is excepted; but that every one, of whatever kind it may be, is enumerated among those he mentioned above.

187. At the same time, we must also think of the words which, after first saying "Who shall separate us from the love of Christ?" he wrote next: "Neither death, nor life, nor any other creature can separate us from the love of God, which is in Christ Jesus." we see, then, that the love of God is the same as the love of Christ. Thus it was not without reason that he wrote of the love of God, "which is in Christ Jesus," lest otherwise thou mightest imagine that the love of God and of Christ was divided. But there is nothing that love divides, nothing that the eternal Godhead cannot do, nothing that is unknown to the Truth, or deceives Justice, or escapes the notice of Wisdom.

Chapter IV.

The Arians are condemned by the Holy Spirit through the mouth of David: for they dare to limit Christ's knowledge. The passage cited by them in proof of this is by no means free from suspicion of having been corrupted. But to set this right, we must mark the word "Son." For knowledge cannot fail Christ as Son of God, since He is Wisdom; nor the recognition of any part, for He created all things. It is not possible that He, who made the ages, cannot know the future, much less the day of judgment. Such knowledge, whether it concerns anything great or small, may not be denied to the Son, nor yet to the Holy Spirit. Lastly, various proofs are given from which we can gather that this knowledge exists in Christ.

188. Wherefore we ought to know that they who make such statements are accursed and condemned by the Holy Spirit. For whom else but the Arians in chief does the prophet condemn, seeing that they say that the Son of God knows neither times nor years. For there is nothing which God is ignorant of; and Christ, yea the most high Christ, is God, for He is "God over all."

189. See how horrified holy David is at such men, in limiting the knowledge of the Son of God. For thus it is written: "They are not in the troubles of other men, neither will they be scourged with men; therefore their pride has laid hold on them; they are covered with their wickedness and blasphemy; their iniquity hath stood forth as it were with fatness; they have passed on to the thoughts of their heart." Truly he condemns those who think that divine things are to be regarded in the light of the thoughts of the heart. For God is not subject to arrangement or order; seeing that we do not perceive even those very things, which are common among men and often occur in the history of the human race, to turn out always after the arrangement of some stated rule, but often to happen suddenly in some secret and mysterious manner.

190. "They have thought," he says, "and have spoken wickedness. They have spoken wickedness against the Most High. They have set their mouth against heaven." We see then that he condemns, as guilty of wicked blasphemy, those who claim for themselves the right to arrange the heavenly secrets after the semblance of our human nature.

191. And they have said: "How hath God known? And is there knowledge in the Most High?" Do not the Arians echo this daily, saying that all knowledge cannot exist in Christ? For He, they say, stated that He knew not the day nor hour. Do they not say, how did He know, while they maintain that He could not know anything but what He heard and saw, and apply by a blasphemous interpretation that which concerns the unity of the divine Nature to weaken His power?

192. It is written, they say: "But of that day and that hour knoweth no man, no, not the angels which are in heaven, neither the Son, but the Father only." First of all the ancient Greek manuscripts do not contain the words, "neither the Son." But it is not to be wondered at if they who have corrupted the sacred Scriptures, have also falsified this passage. The reason for which it seems to have been inserted is perfectly plain, so long as it is applied to unfold such blasphemy.

193. Suppose however that the Evangelist wrote thus. The name of "Son" embraces both natures. For He is also called Son of Man, so that in the ignorance attached to the assumption of our nature, He seems not to have known the day of the judgment to come. For how could the Son of God be ignorant of the day, seeing that the treasures of the wisdom and knowledge of God are hidden in Him?

194. I ask then, whether He had this knowledge by reason of His Being, or by chance? For all knowledge comes to us either through nature, or by learning. It is supplied by nature, as for instance to a horse to enable it to run, or to a fish to enable it to swim. For they do this without learning. On the other hand, it is by learning that a man is enabled to swim. For he could not do so unless he had learnt. Since therefore nature enables dumb animals to do and to know what they have not learnt, why shouldst thou give an opinion on the Son of God, and say whether He has knowledge by instruction or by nature? If by instruction, then He was not begotten as Wisdom, and gradually began to be perfect, but was not always so. But if He has knowledge by nature, then He was perfect in the beginning, He came forth perfect from the Father; and so needed no foreknowledge of the future.

195. He therefore was not ignorant of the days; for it does not fall to the lot of the Wisdom of God to know in part and in part to be ignorant. For how can He who made all things be ignorant of a part, since it is a less thing to know than to make. For we know many things which we cannot make, neither do we all know things in the same way but we know them in part. For a countryman knows the force of the wind and the courses of the stars in one way—the inhabitant of a city knows them in another way—and a pilot in yet a third way. But although all do not know all things, they are said to know them; but He alone knows all things in full, Who made all things. The pilot knows for how many watches Arcturus continues, what sort of a rising of Orion he will discover, but he knows nothing of the connection of the Vergiliae and of the other stars, or of their number or names, as does He "Who numbers the multitude of stars, and calleth them all by their names;" Whom indeed the power of His work cannot escape.

196. How then do you wish the Son of God to have made these things? Like a signet ring which does not feel the impression it makes? But the Father made all things in wisdom, that is, He made all things through the Son, who is the Virtue and Wisdom of God. But it befits such Wisdom as that to know both the powers and the causes of His own works. Thus the Creator of all things could not be ignorant of what He did—or be without knowledge of what He had Himself given. Therefore He knew the day which He made.

197. But thou sayest that He knows the present and does not know the future. Though this is a foolish suggestion, yet that I may satisfy thee on Scriptural grounds, learn that He made not only what is past, but also what is future, as it is written: "Who made things to come." Elsewhere too Scripture says: "By whom also He made the ages, who is the brightness of His glory and the express Image of His Person." Now the ages are past and present and future· How then were those made which are future, unless it is that His active power and knowledge contains within itself the number of all the ages? For just as He calls the things that are not as though they were, so has He made things future as though they were. It cannot come to pass that they should not be. Those things which He has directed to be, necessarily will be. Therefore He who has made the things that are to be, knows them in the way in which they will be.

198. If we are to believe this about the ages, much more must we believe it about the day of judgment, on the ground that the Son of God has knowledge of it, as being already made by Him. For it is written: "According to Thine ordinance the day will continue." He did not merely say "the day continues," but even "will continue," so that the things which are to come might be governed by His ordinance· Does He not know what He ordered? "He who planted the ear, shall He not hear? He that formed the eye shall He not see?"

199. Let us however see if by chance there may be some great thing, which could be beyond the knowledge of its Creator; or at least let them choose whether they will think of something great and superior to other things, or something very little and mean. If it is very little and mean,

330

it is no loss, to speak after our fashion, to know nothing of worthless and petty things. For as it is a sign of power to know the greatest things, it seems rather to be a sign of inferior work to look upon what is worth less. Thus He is freed from fastidiousness, yet is not deprived of His power.

200. But if they think it a great and important thing to know the day of judgment: Let them say what is greater or better than God the Father. He knows God the Father, as He Himself says: "No man knoweth the Father but the Son and he to whomsoever the Son will reveal Him." I say, does He know the Father and yet not know the day? So then ye believe that He reveals the Father, and yet cannot reveal the day?

201. Next because you make certain grades, so as to put the Father before the on, and the Son before the Holy Spirit, tell me whether the Holy Spirit knew the day of judgment For no thing is written of Him in this place. You deny it entirely. But what if I show you He knew it? For it is written: "But God hath revealed them to us by His Spirit, for the Spirit searcheth all things, yea the deep things of God." Wherefore, because He searches the deep things of God, since God knows the day of judgment, the Spirit also knows it. For He knows all that God knows, as also the Apostle states, saying: "For what man knoweth the things of a man, save the spirit of man which is in him, even so the things of God knoweth no man, but the Spirit of God." Take heed therefore lest either by denying that the Holy Spirit knows, you should deny that the Father knows; (For the things of God, the Spirit of God also knows, but the things which the Spirit of God does not know, are not the things of God). Or by confessing that the Spirit of God knows, what you deny that the Son of God knows, you should put the Spirit before the Son in opposition to your own declaration. But to hesitate on this point is not only blasphemous but also foolish.

202. Now consider how knowledge is acquired, and let us show that the Son Himself proved that He knew the day. For what we know we make clear either by mention of time or place or signs or persons, or by giving their order. How then did He not know the day of judgment Who described both the hour and the place of judgment, and the signs and the cases?

203. And so thou hast it: "In that hour he which shall be on the housetop let him not come down to take his goods out of his house, and he that is in the field, let him likewise not return back." To such a point in the future did He know the issues of dangers, that He even showed the means of safety to those in danger.

204. Could the Lord be ignorant of a day Who Himself said of Himself that the Son of Man is Lord of the Sabbath?

205. He has also elsewhere marked out a place, when He said to His disciples who were showing Him the building of the temple, "Do ye see all these things? Verily I say unto you, there shall not be left one stone upon another which shall not be thrown down."

206. When questioned also about a sign by His disciples, He answered: "Take heed that ye be not deceived. For many shall come in My name, saying I am Christ;" and further on He says: "and great earthquakes shall be in divers places, and famines, and pestilences, and terrors from heaven, and there shall be great signs." Thus He has described both persons and signs.

207. In what manner He tells that the armies will surround Jerusalem, or that the times of the Gentiles are to be fulfilled, and in what order,—all this is disclosed to us by the witness of the Gospel words. Therefore He knew all things.

Chapter XVII.
Christ acted for our advantage in being unwilling to reveal the day of judgment. This is made plain by other words of our Lord and by a not dissimilar passage from Paul's writings. Other passages inwhich the same ignorance seems to be attributed to the Father are brought forward to meet those who are anxious to know why Christ answered His disciples, as though He did not know. From these Ambrose argues against them that if they admit ignorance and inability in the Father, they must admit that the same Substance exists in the Son as in the

Father; unless they prefer to accuse the Son of falsehood; since it belongs neither to Him nor to the Father to deceive, but the unity of both is pointed out in the passage named.

208. But we ask for what reason He was unwilling to state the time. If we ask it, we shall not find it is owing to ignorance, but to wisdom. For it was not to our advantage to know; in order that we being ignorant of the actual moments of judgment to come, might ever be as it were on guard, and set on the watch-tower of virtue, and so avoid the habits of sin; lest the day of the Lord should come upon us in the midst of our wickedness. For it is not to our advantage to know but rather to fear the future; for it is written: "Be not high-minded but fear."

209. For if He had distinctly stated the day, he would seem to have laid down a rule of life for that one age which was nearest to the judgment, and the just man in the earlier times would be more negligent, and the sinner more free from care. For the adulterer cannot cease from the desire of committing adultery unless he fears punishment day by day, nor can the robber forsake the hiding places in the woods where he dwells, unless he knows punishment is hanging over him day by day. For impurity generally spurs them on, but fear is irksome to the end.

210. Therefore I have said that it was not to our advantage to know; nay, it is to our advantage to be ignorant, that through ignorance we might fear, through watchfulness be corrected, as He Himself said: "Be ye ready, for ye know not at what hour the Son of Man cometh." For the soldier does not know how to watch in the camp unless he knows that war is at hand.

211. Wherefore at another time also the Lord Himself when asked by his Apostles (Yes, for they did not understand it as Arius did, but believed that the Son of God knew the future. For unless they had believed this, they would never have asked the question.)—the Lord, I say, when asked when He would restore the kingdom to Israel, did not say that He did not know, but says: "It is not for you to know the times or years, which the Father hath put in His own power." Mark what He said: It is not for you to know! Read again, "It is not for you." "For you," He said, not "for Me," for now He spoke not according to His own perfection but as was profitable to the human body and our soul. "For you" therefore He said, not "for Me."

212. Which example the Apostle also followed: "But of the times and seasons, brethren," he says, "ye have no need that I write unto you." Thus not even the Apostle himself, the servant of Christ, said that he knew not the seasons, but that there was no need for the people to be taught; for they ought ever to be armed with spiritual armour, that the virtue of Christ may stand forth in each one. But when the Lord says: "Of the times which the Father hath put in His own power, " He certainly cannot be without a share in His Father's knowledge, in whose power He is by no means without a share. For power grows out of wisdom and virtue; and Christ is both of these.

213. But you ask, why did He not refuse His disciples as one who knew, but would not say; and, why did He state instead that neither the angels nor the Son knew? I too will ask you why God says in Genesis: "I will go down now, and see whether they have done altogether according to the cry that is come unto Me. And if not, that I may know." Why does Scripture also say of God: "And the Lord came down to see the city and the tower, which the sons of men builded." Why also does the prophet say in the Book of the Psalms: "The Lord looked down upon the children of men, to see if there were any that did understand, and that did seek God"? Just as though in one place, if God had not descended, and in the other, if He had not looked down, He would have been ignorant either of men's work or of their merits.

214. But in the Gospel of Luke also thou hast the same, for the Father says: "What shall I do? I will send My beloved Son; it may be that they will reverence Him." In Matthew and in Mark thou hast: "But He sent His only Son, saying: they will reverence My Son;" In one book He says: "It may be that they will reverence My Son;" and is in doubt as though He does not know; for this is the language of one in doubt. But in the two other books He says: "They will reverence My Son;" that is, He declares that reverence will be shown.

215. But God can neither be in doubt, nor can He be deceived. For he only is in doubt, who is ignorant of the future; and he is deceived, who has predicted one thing, whilst another has happened. Yet what is plainer than the fact that Scripture states the Father to have said one thing of the Son, and that the same Scripture proves another think to have taken place? The Son was beaten, He was mocked, was crucified, and died. He suffered much worse things in the flesh than those servants who had been appointed before. Was the Father deceived, or was He ignorant of it, or was He unable to give help? But He that is true cannot make a mistake; for it is written: "God is faithful Who doth not lie." . How was He ignorant, Who knows all? What could He not do, Who could do all?

216. Yet if either He was ignorant, or had not power (for you would sooner agree to say that the Father did not know than own that the Son knows), you see from this very fact that the Son is of one Substance with the Father; seeing that the Son like the Father (to speak in accordance with your foolish ideas) does not know all things, and cannot do all things. For I am not so eager or rash in giving praise to the Son as to dare to say that the Son can do more than the Father; for I make no distinction of power between the Father and the Son.

217. But perhaps you say that the Father did not say so, but that the Son erred about the Father. So now you convict the Son not only of weakness, but also of blasphemy and lying. However if you do not believe the Son with regard to the Father, neither may you believe Him with regard to that. For if He wished to deceive us in saying that the Father was in doubt as though He knew not what would take place, He wished also to deceive us about Himself in saying that He did not know the future. It would be far more endurable for Him to stretch the veil of ignorance in front of that which He does of His own accord, than that He should seem to be deluded by a result contrary to what He had foretold in the things He had declared of His Father.

218. But neither is the Father deceived not does the Son deceive. It is the custom of the holy Scriptures to speak thus, as the examples I have already given, and many others testify, so that God feigns not to know what He does know. In this then a unity of Godhead, and a unity of character is proved to exist in the Father and in the Son; seeing that, as God the Father hides what is known to Him, so also the Son, Who is the image of God in this respect, hides what is known to Him.

Chapter XVIII.

Wishing to give a reason for the Lord's answer to the apostles, he assigns the one received to Christ's tenderness. Then when another reason is supplied by others he confesses that it is true; for the Lord spoke it by reason of His human feelings. Hence he gathers that the knowledge of the Father and the Son is equal, and that the Son is not inferior to the Father. After having set beside the text, in which He is said to be inferior, another whereby He is declared to be equal, he censures the rashness of the Arians in judging about the Son, and shows that whilst they wickedly make Him to be inferior, He is rightly called a Stone by Himself.

219. We have been taught therefore that the Son of God is not ignorant of the future. If they confess this, I too—that I may now answer why He declared that neither angels, nor the Son, but only the Father knows—call to mind His wonted love for His disciples also in this passage, and His grace, which by its very frequency ought to have been known to all. For the Lord, filled with deep love for His disciples, when they asked from Him what He thought unprofitable for them to know, prefers to seem ignorant of what He knows, rather than to refuse an answer. He loves rather to provide what is useful for us, than to show His own power.

220. There are, however, some not so faint-hearted as I. For I would rather fear the deep things of God, than be wise. There are some, however, relying on the words: "And Jesus increased in age and in wisdom and in favour with God and man," who boldly say, that according to His Godhead indeed He could not be ignorant of the future, but that in His assumption of our human state He said that He as Son of Man was in ignorance before His crucifixion. For when He speaks of the Son, He does not speak as it were of another; for He

Himself is our Lord the Son of God and the Son of a Virgin. But by a word which embraces both, He guides our mind, so that He as Son of Man according to His adoption of our ignorance and growth of knowledge, might be believed as yet not fully to have known all things. For it is not for us to know the future. Thus He seems to be ignorant in that state in which He makes progress. For how does He progress according to His Godhead, in Whom the fulness of the Godhead dwells? Or what is there which the Son of God does not know, Who said: "Why think ye evil in your hearts?" How does He not know, of Whom Scripture says: "But Jesus knew their thoughts"?

221. This is what others say, but I—to return to my former point, where I stated it was written of the Father: "It may be they will reverence My Sen,"—I think indeed this was written in order that the Father, as He was speaking of men, might also seem to have spoken with human feelings. But still more am I inclined to think that the Son Who went about with men, and lived the life of man, and took upon Him our flesh, assumed also our feelings; so that after our ignorance He might say He knew not, though there was not anything He did not know. For though He seemed to be a man in the reality of His body, yet was He Life, and Light, and virtue came out of Him, to heal the wounds of the injured by the power of His Majesty.

222. Ye see then that this matter has been solved for you, since the saying of the Son is referred to the assumption of our state in its fulness, and it was thus written concerning the Father, in order that you might cease to cavil at the Son.

223. There was nothing then of which the Son of God was ignorant, for there was nothing of which the Father was ignorant. But if the Son was ignorant of nothing, as we now conclude, let them say in what respect they wish Him to seem to be inferior. If God has begotten a Son inferior to Himself, He has granted Him less. If He has granted Him less, He either wished to give less, or could only give less. But the Father is neither weak nor envious, seeing that there was neither will nor power before the Son. For wherein is He inferior, Who has all things even as the Father has them? He has received all things from the Father by right of His Generation, and has shown forth the Father wholly by the glory of His Majesty.

224. It is written, they say: "For the Father is greater than I." It is also written: "He thought it not robbery to be equal with God" It is written again that the Jews wished to kill Him, because He said He was the Son of God, making Himself equal with God. It is written: "I and My Father are one." They read "one" they do not read "many." Can He then be both inferior and equal in the same Nature? Nay, the one refers to His Godhead, the other to His flesh.

225. They say He is inferior: I ask who has measured it, who is of so overweening a heart, as to place the Father and the Son before his judgment seat to decide upon which is the greater? "My heart is not haughty nor are mine eyes raised unto vanity," says David. King David feared to raise his heart in pride in human affairs, but we raise ours even in opposition to the divine secrets. Who shall decide about the Son of God? Thrones, dominions, angels, powers? But archangels give attendance and serve Him, cherubim and seraphim minister to Him and praise Him. Who then decides about the Son of God, on reading that the Father Himself knows the Son, but will not judge Him. "For no man knoweth the Son, but the Father." "Knoweth" it says, not "judgeth." It is one thing to know, another to judge. The Father has knowledge in Himself. The Son has no power superior to Himself. And again: "No man knoweth the Father, but the Son;" and He Himself knows the Father, as the Father knows Him.

226. But thou sayest that He said He was inferior, He said also He was a Stone. Thou sayest more and yet dost impiously attack Him. I say less and with reverence add to His honour. Thou sayest He is inferior and confessest Him to be above the angels. I say He is less than the angels, yet do not take from His honour; for I do not refute His Godhead, but I do proclaim His pity.

Chapter XIX.
The Saint having turned to God the Father, explains why he does not deride that the Son is inferior to the Father, then he declares it is not for him to measure the Son of God, since it was given to an angel—nay, perhaps

even to Christ as man—to measure merely Jerusalem. Arius, he says, has shown himself to be an imitator of Satan. It is a rash thing to hold discussions on the divine Generation. Since so great a sign of human generation has been given by Isaiah, we ought not to make comparisons in divine things. Lastly he shows how carefully we ought to avoid the pride of Arius, by putting before us various examples of Scriptures.

227. To Thee now, Almighty Father, do I direct my words with tears. I indeed have readily called Thee inapproachable, incomprehensible, inestimable; but I dared not say Thy Son was inferior to Thyself. For when I read that He is the Brightness of Thy glory, and the Image of Thy Person, I fear lest, in saying that the Image of Thy Person is inferior, I should seem to say that Thy Person is inferior, of which the Son is the Image; for the fulness of Thy Godhead is wholly in the Son. I have often read, I freely believe, that Thou and Thy Son and the Holy Spirit are boundless, unmeasurable, inestimable, ineffable. And therefore I cannot appraise Thee so as to weigh Thee.

228. But be it so, that I desired with a daring and rash spirit to measure Thee? From whence, I ask, shall I measure Thee, The prophet saw a line of flax with which the angel measured Jerusalem. An angel was measuring, not Arius. And he was measuring Jerusalem, not God. And perchance even an angel could not measure Jerusalem, for it was a man. Thus it is written: "I raised mine eyes and saw and beheld a man, and in his hand there was a line of flax." He was a man, for a type of the body that was to be assumed was thus shown. He was a man, of whom it was said: "There cometh a man after me, Whose shoe's latchet I am not worthy to unloose." Therefore Christ in a type measures Jerusalem. Arius measures God.

229. Even Satan transforms himself into an angel of light; what wonder then if Arius imitates his Author in taking upon himself what is forbidden? Though his father the devil did it not in his own case, that man with intolerable blasphemy assumes to himself the knowledge of divine secrets and the mysteries of the heavenly Generation. For the devil confessed the true Son of God, Arius denies Him.

230. If, then, I cannot measure Thee, Almighty Father, can I without blasphemy discuss the secrets of Thy Generation? Can I say there is anything more or less between Thee and Thy Son when He Himself Who was begotten of Thee, says: "All things which the Father hath are Mine." Who has made Me a judge and a divider of human affairs? This the Son says, and do we claim to make a division and to give judgment between the Father and the Son? A right feeling of duty avoids arbiters even in the division of an inheritance. And shall we become arbiters, to divide between Thee and Thy Son the glory of the uncreated Substance?

231. "This generation," it says, "is an evil generation. It seeketh a sign, and there shall no sign be given it, but the sign of Jonas the prophet." A sign of the Godhead then is not given, but only of the Incarnation. Thus when about to speak of the Incarnation the prophet says: "Ask thee a sign." And when the king had said: "I will not ask, neither will I tempt the Lord," the answer was: "Behold a Virgin shall conceive." Therefore we cannot see a sign of the Godhead, and do we seek a measure of it? Alas! woe is me! we impiously dare to discuss Him, to Whom we cannot worthily pray!

232. Let the Arians see to what they do. I have unlawfully compared Thee, O Father, with Thy works in saying that Thou art greater than all. If greater than Thy Son, as Arius maintains, I have judged wickedly. Concerning Thee first will that judgment be. For no choice can be made except by comparison, nor can anyone be put before another without a decision being first given on Himself.

233. It is not lawful for us to swear by heaven, but it is lawful to judge about God. Yet Thou hast given to Thy Son alone judgment over all.

234. John feared to baptize the flesh of the Lord, John forbade Him, saying: "I have need to be baptized of Thee, and comest Thou to me?" And shall I bring Christ under my judgment.?

235. Moses excuses himself from the Priesthood, Peter is for avoiding the obedience demanded in the Ministry; and does Arius examine even the deep things of God? But Arius is

not the Holy Spirit. Nay, it was said even to Arius and to all men: "Seek not that which is too deep for thee."

236. Moses is prevented from seeing the face of God; Arius merited to see it in secret. Moses and Aaron among His Priests. Moses who appeared with the Lord in glory, that Moses then saw only the back parts of God in appearance; Arius beholds God wholly face to face! But "no one," it says, "can see My face and live."

237. Paul also speaks of inferior beings: "We know in part and we prophesy in part." Arius says: "I know God altogether and not in part." Thus Paul is inferior to Arius, and the vessel of election knows in part, but the vessel of perdition knows wholly. "I know," he says, "a man, whether in the body or out of the body, I cannot tell, God knoweth, how he was caught up into Paradise and heard unspeakable words." Paul carried up to the third heaven, knew not himself; Arius rolling in filth, knows God. Paul says of himself: "God knows;" Arius says of God: "I know."

238. But Arius was not caught up to heaven, although he followed him who with accursed boastfulness presumed on what was divine, saying: "I will set my throne upon the clouds; I will be like the Most High." For as he said: "I will be like the Most High," so too Arius wishes the Most High Son of God to seem like himself, Whom he does not worship in the eternal glory of His Godhead, but measures by the weakness of the flesh.

On the Mysteries. Introduction.

The writer explains in the commencement of this treatise that his object was to set forth, for the benefit of those about to be baptized, the rites and meaning of that Sacrament, as well as of Confirmation and the Holy Eucharist. For all these matters were treated with the greatest reserve in the Early Church, for fear of profanation by the heathen, and it was the custom, as in the case of the well-known Catechetical Lectures of St. Cyril of Jerusalem, to explain them to the catechumens during the latter part of Lent.

Treatises of this kind possess therefore a special interest, as in them we find clearly stated the full teaching of the Church at the time when those addresses which have come down to our times were drawn up.

St. Ambrose goes through and explains the greater part, first of the rites usual at the time of solemn baptism, pointing out the deep truths and mysteries underlying these outward things. He then treats Confirmation, referring to the seven gifts of the Holy Spirit; and lastly, speaks of the Holy Eucharist, especially setting forth the doctrine of the Real Presence.

Some writers in and since the sixteenth century have endeavoured to prove that this treatise has been falsely attributed to St. Ambrose, but there can be no real doubt on the matter, as is conclusively shown by the Benedictine Editors, and now universally admitted. The treatise was composed for use during Lent, but in what year cannot be fixed, possibly, from reference made to the treatise De *Patriarchis*, about a.d. 387.

THE BOOK CONCERNING THE MYSTERIES.

Chapter I.

St. Ambrose states that after the explanations he has already given of holy living, he will now explain the Mysteries. Then after giving his reasons for not having done so before, he explains the mystery of the opening of the ears, and shows how this was of old done by Christ Himself.

1. We have spoken daily upon subjects connected with morals, when the deeds of the Patriarchs or the precepts of the Proverbs were being read, in order that being taught and instructed by these you might grow accustomed to enter the ways of the ancients and to walk in their paths, and obey the divine commands; in order that being renewed by baptism you might hold to that manner of life which beseems those who are washed.

2. The season now warns us to speak of the Mysteries, and to set forth the purport of the sacraments, which if we had thought it well to teach before baptism to those who were not yet initiated, we should be considered rather to have betrayed than to have portrayed the Mysteries. And then, too, another reason is that the light itself of the Mysteries will shed itself with more effect upon those who are expecting they know not what, than if any discourse had come beforehand.

3. Open, then, your ears, inhale the good savour of eternal life which has been breathed upon you by the grace of the sacraments; which was signified to you by us, when, celebrating the mystery of the opening, we said, "Epphatha, which is, Be opened," that whosoever was coming in quest of peace might know what he was asked, and be bound to remember what he answered.
4. Christ made use of this mystery in the Gospel, as we read, when He healed him who was deaf and dumb. But He touched the mouth, because he who was healed was dumb and was a man, as regards one point that he might open his mouth with the sound of the voice given to him; as regards the other point because that touch was seemly towards a man, but would have been unseemly towards a woman.

Chapter II.

What those who were to be initiated promised on entering the Church, of the witnesses to these promises, and wherefore they then turned themselves to the East.

5. After this the Holy of holies was opened to you, you entered the sanctuary of regeneration; recall what you were asked, and remember what you answered. You renounced the devil and his works, the world with its luxury and pleasures. That utterance of yours is preserved not in the tombs of the dead, but in the book of the living.

6. You saw there the deacon, you saw the priest, you saw the chief priest [i.e. the bishop]. Consider not the bodily forms, but the grace of the Mysteries. You spoke in the presence of the angels, as it is written: "For the priest's lips keep knowledge, and they seek the law at his mouth, for he is the angel of the Lord Almighty." There is no place for deception nor for denial. He is an angel who proclaims the kingdom of Christ and eternal life. He is to be esteemed by you not according to his appearance, but according to his office. Consider what he delivered, reflect upon the rule of life he gave you, recognize his position.

7. You entered, then, that you might discern your adversary, whom you were to renounce as it were to his face, then you turned to the east; for he who renounces the devil turns to Christ, and beholds Him face to face.

Chapter III.

St. Ambrose points out that we must consider the divine presence and working in the water and the sacred ministers, and then brings forward many Old Testament figures of baptism.

8. What did you see? Water, certainly, but not water alone; you saw the deacons ministering there, and the bishop asking questions and hallowing. First of all, the Apostle taught you that those things are not to be considered "which we see, but the things which are not seen, for the

things which are seen are temporal, but the things which are not seen are eternal." For you read elsewhere: "That the invisible things of God, since the creation of the world, are understood through those things which have been made; His eternal power also and Godhead are estimated by His works." Wherefore also the Lord Himself says: "If ye believe not Me, believe at least the works." Believe, then, that the presence of the Godhead is there. Do you believe the working, and not believe the presence? Whence should the working proceed unless the presence went before?

9. Consider, however, how ancient is the mystery prefigured even in the origin of the world itself. In the very beginning, when God made the heaven and the earth, "the Spirit," it is said, "moved upon the waters." He Who was moving upon the waters, was He not working upon the waters? But why should I say, "working"? As regards His presence He was moving. Was He not working Who was moving? Recognize that He was working in that making of the world, when the prophet says: "By the word of the Lord were the heavens made, and all their strength by the spirit of His mouth." Each statement rests upon the testimony of the prophet, both that He was moving and that He was working. Moses says that He was moving, David testifies that he was working.

10. Take another testimony. All flesh was corrupt by its iniquities. "My Spirit," says God, "shall not remain among men, because they are flesh." Whereby God shows that the grace of the Spirit is turned away by carnal impurity and the pollution of grave sin. Upon which, God, willing to restore what was lacking, sent the flood and bade just Noah go up into the ark. And he, after having, as the flood was passing off, sent forth first a raven which did not return, sent forth a dove which is said to have returned with an olive twig. You see the water, you see the wood [of the ark], you see the dove, and do you hesitate as to the mystery?

11. The water, then, is that in which the flesh is dipped, that all carnal sin may be washed away. All wickedness is there buried. The wood is that on which the Lord Jesus was fastened when He suffered for us. The dove is that in the form of which the Holy Spirit descended, as you have read in the New Testament, Who inspires in you peace of soul and tranquillity of mind. The raven is the figure of sin, which goes forth and does not return, if, in you, too, inwardly and outwardly righteousness be preserved.

12. There is also a third testimony, as the Apostle teaches us: "For all our fathers were under the cloud, and all passed through the sea, and were all baptized to Moses in the cloud and in the sea." And further, Moses himself says in his song: "Thou sentest Thy Spirit, and the sea covered them." You observe that even then holy baptism was prefigured in that passage of the Hebrews, wherein the Egyptian perished, the Hebrew escaped. For what else are we daily taught in this sacrament but that guilt is swallowed up and error done away, but that virtue and innocence remain unharmed?

13. You hear that our fathers were under the cloud, and that a kindly cloud, which cooled the heat of carnal passions. That kindly cloud overshadows those whom the Holy Spirit visits. At last it came upon the Virgin Mary, and the Power of the Highest overshadowed her, when she conceived Redemption for the race of men. And that miracle was wrought in a figure through Moses. If, then, the Spirit was in the figure, is He not present in the reality, since Scripture says to us: "For the law was given by Moses, but grace and truth came by Jesus Christ."

14. Marah was a fountain of most bitter water: Moses cast wood into it and it became sweet. For water without the preaching of the Cross of the Lord is of no avail for future salvation, but, after it has been consecrated by the mystery of the saving cross, it is made suitable for the use of the spiritual layer and of the cup of salvation. As, then, Moses, that is, the prophet, cast wood into that fountain, so, too, the priest utters over this font the proclamation of the Lord's cross, and the water is made sweet for the purpose of grace.

15. You must not trust, then, wholly to your bodily eyes; that which is not seen is more really seen, for the object of sight is temporal, but that other eternal, which is not apprehended by the eye, but is discerned by the mind and spirit.

16. Lastly, let the lessons lately gone through from the Kings teach you. Naaman was a Syrian, and suffered from leprosy, nor could he be cleansed by any. Then a maiden from among the captives said that there was a prophet in Israel, who could cleanse him from the defilement of the leprosy. And it is said that, having taken silver and gold, he went to the king of Israel. And he, when he heard the cause of his coming, rent his clothes, saying, that occasion was rather being sought against him, since things were asked of him which pertained not to the power of kings. Elisha, however, sent word to the king, that he should send the Syrian to him, that he might know there was a God in Israel. And when he had come, he bade him dip himself seven times in the river Jordan.

17. Then he began to reason with himself that he had better waters in his own country, in which he had often bathed and never been cleansed of his leprosy; and so remembering this, he did not obey the command of the prophet, yet on the advice and persuasion of his servants he yielded and dipped himself. And being forthwith cleansed, he understood that it is not of the waters but of grace that a man is cleansed.

18. Understand now who is that young maid among the captives. She is the congregation gathered out of the Gentiles, that is, the Church of God held down of old by the captivity of sin, when as yet it possessed not the liberty of grace, by whose counsel that foolish people of the Gentiles heard the word of prophecy as to which it had before been in doubt. Afterwards, however, when they believed that it ought to be obeyed, they were washed from every defilement of sin. And he indeed doubted before he was healed; you are already healed, and therefore ought not to doubt.

Chapter IV.

That water does not cleanse without the Spirit is shown by the witness of John and by the very form of the administration of the sacrament. And this is also declared to be signified by the pool in the Gospel and the man who was there healed. In the same passage, too, is shown that the Holy Spirit truly descended on Christ at His baptism, and the meaning of this mystery is explained.

19. The reason why you were told before not to believe only what you saw was that you might not say perchance, This is that great mystery "which eye hath not seen, nor ear heard, neither has it entered into the heart of man." I see water, which I have been used to see every day. Is that water to cleanse me now in which I have so often bathed without ever being cleansed? By this you may recognize that water does not cleanse without the Spirit.

20. Therefore read that the three witnesses in baptism, the water, the blood, and the Spirit, are one, for if you take away one of these, the Sacrament of Baptism does not exist. For what is water without the cross of Christ? A common element, without any sacramental effect. Nor, again, is there the Sacrament of Regeneration without water: "For except a man be born again of water and of the Spirit, he cannot enter into the kingdom of God." Now, even the catechumen believes in the cross of the Lord Jesus, wherewith he too is signed; but unless he be baptized in the Name of the Father, and of the Son, and of the Holy Spirit, he cannot receive remission of sins nor gain the gift of spiritual grace.

21. So that Syrian dipped himself seven times under the law, but you were baptized in the Name of the Trinity, you confessed the Father. Call to mind what you did: you confessed the Son, you confessed the Holy Spirit. Mark well the order of things in this faith: you died to the world, and rose again to God. And as though buried to the world in that element, being dead to sin, you rose again to eternal life. Believe, therefore, that these waters are not void of power.

22. Therefore it is said: "An angel of the Lord went down according to the season into the pool, and the water was troubled; and he who first after the troubling of the water went down into the pool was healed of whatsoever disease he was holden." This pool was at Jerusalem, in

which one was healed every year, but no one was healed before the angel had descended. Because of those who believed not the water was troubled as a sign that the angel had descended. They had a sign, you have faith; for them an angel descended, for you the Holy Spirit; for them the creature was troubled, for you Christ Himself, the Lord of the creature, works.

23. Then one was healed, now all are made whole; or more exactly, the Christian people alone, for in some even the water is deceitful. The baptism of unbelievers heals not but pollutes. The Jew washes pots and cups, as though things without sense were capable of guilt or grace. But do you wash this living cup of yours, that in it your good works may shine and the glory of your grace be bright. For that pool was as a type, that you might believe that the power of God descends upon this font.

24. Lastly, that paralytic was waiting for a man. And what man save the Lord Jesus, born of the Virgin, at Whose coming no longer the shadow should heal men one by one, but the truth should heal the whole. He it is, then, Whose coming down was being waited for, of Whom the Father said to John the Baptist: "Upon Whom thou shalt see the Spirit descending and abiding upon Him, this is He Who baptizeth with the Holy Spirit." And John bare witness of Him, and said: "I saw the Spirit descending from heaven like a dove and abiding upon Him." And why did the Spirit descend like a dove, but in order that you might see, that you might acknowledge, that that dove also which just Noah sent forth from the ark was a likeness of this dove, that you might recognize the type of the sacrament?

25. Perhaps you may object: Since that was a real dove which was sent forth, and the Spirit descended like a dove, how is it that we say that the likeness was there and the reality here, whereas in the Greek it is written that the Spirit descended in the likeness of a dove? But what is so real as the Godhead which abides for ever? Now the creature cannot be the reality, but only a likeness, which is easily destroyed and changed. So, again, because the simplicity of those who are baptized ought to be not in appearance but in reality, and the Lord says: "Be ye wise as serpents and simple as doves." Rightly, then, did He descend like a dove, in order to admonish us that we ought to have the simplicity of the dove. And further we read of the likeness being put for the reality, both as regards Christ: "And was found in likeness as a man;" and as regards God the Father: "Nor have ye seen His likeness."

Chapter V.

Christ is Himself present in Baptism, so that we need not consider the person of His ministers. A brief explanation of the confession of the Trinity as usually uttered by those about to be baptized.

26. Is there, then, here any room left for doubt, when the Father clearly calls from heaven in the Gospel narrative, and says: "This is My beloved Son, in Whom I am well pleased"? When the Son also speaks, upon Whom the Holy Spirit showed Himself in the likeness of a dove? When the Holy Spirit also speaks, Who came down in the likeness of a dove? When David, too, speaks: "The voice of the Lord is above the waters, the God of glory thundered, the Lord above many waters"? When Scripture testifies that at the prayer of Jerubbaal, fire came down from heaven, and again, when Elijah prayed, fire was sent forth and consecrated the sacrifice.

27. Do not consider the merits of individuals, but the office of the priests. Or, if you look at the merits, consider the priest as Elijah. Look upon the merits of Peter also, or of Paul, who handed down to us this mystery which they had received of the Lord Jesus. To those [of old] a visible fire was sent that they might believe; for us who believe, the Lord works invisibly; for them that happened for a figure, for us for warning. Believe, then, that the Lord Jesus is present at the invocation of the priest, Who said: "Where two or three are, there am I also." How much where the Church is, and where His Mysteries are, does He vouchsafe to impart His presence!

28. You went down, then (into the water), remember what you replied to the questions, that you believe in the Father, that you believe in the Son, that you believe in the Holy Spirit. The statement there is not: I believe in a greater and in a less and in a lowest person, but you are

bound by the same guarantee of your own voice, to believe in the Son in like manner as you believe in the Father; and to believe in the Holy Spirit in like manner as you believe in the Son, with this one exception, that you confess that you must believe in the cross of the Lord Jesus alone.

Chapter VI.

Why they who come forth from the layer of baptism are anointed on the head; why, too, after baptism, their feet are washed, and what sins are remitted in each case.

29. After this, you went up to the priest, consider what followed. Was it not that of which David speaks: "Like the ointment upon the head, which went down to the beard, even Aaron's beard"? This is the ointment of which Solomon, too, says: "Thy Name is ointment poured out, therefore have the maidens loved Thee and drawn Thee." How many souls regenerated this day have loved Thee, Lord Jesus, and have said: "Draw us after Thee, we are running after the odour of Thy garments," that they might drink in the odour of Thy resurrection.

30. Consider now why this is done, for "the eyes of a wise man are in his head;" therefore the ointment flows down to the beard, that is to say, to the beauty of youth; and therefore, Aaron's beard, that we, too, may become a chosen race, priestly and precious, for we are all anointed with spiritual grace for a share in the kingdom of God and in the priesthood.

31. You went up from the font; remember the Gospel lesson. For our Lord Jesus Christ in the Gospel washed the feet of His disciples. When He came to Simon Peter, Peter said: "Thou shalt never wash my feet." He did not perceive the mystery, and therefore he refused the service, for he thought that the humility of the servant would be injured, if he patiently allowed the Lord to minister to him. And the Lord answered him: "If I wash not thy feet, thou wilt have no part with Me." Peter, hearing this, replies: "Lord, not my feet only, but also my hands and my head." The Lord answered: "He that is washed needeth not save to wash his feet but is clean every whit."

32. Peter was clean, but he must wash his feet, for he had sin by succession from the first man, when the serpent overthrew him and persuaded him to sin. His feet were therefore washed, that hereditary sins might be done away, for our own sins are remitted through baptism.

33. Observe at the same time that the mystery consists in the very office of humility, for Christ says: "If I, your Lord and Master, have washed your feet; how much more ought you to wash one another's feet." For, since the Author of Salvation Himself redeemed us through His obedience, how much more ought we His servants to offer the service of our humility and obedience.

Chapter VII.

The washing away of sins is indicated by the white robes of the catechumens, whence the Church speaks of herself as black and comely. Angels marvel at her brightness as at that of the flesh of the Lord. Moreover, Christ Himself commended His beauty to His Spouse under many figures. The mutual affection of the one for the other is described.

34. After this white robes were given to you as a sign that you were putting off the covering of sins, and putting on the chaste veil of innocence, of which the prophet said: "Thou shalt sprinkle me with hyssop and I shall be cleansed, Thou shalt wash me and I shall be made whiter than snow." For he who is baptized is seen to be purified both according to the Law and according to the Gospel: according to the Law, because Moses sprinkled the blood of the lamb with a bunch of hyssop; according to the Gospel, because Christ's garments were white as snow, when in the Gospel He showed forth the glory of His Resurrection. He, then, whose guilt is remitted is made whiter than snow. So that God said by Isaiah: "Though your sins be as scarlet, I will make them white as snow."

35. The Church, having put on these garments through the layer of regeneration, says in the Song of Songs: "I am black and comely, O daughters of Jerusalem." Black through the frailty of her human condition, comely through the sacrament of faith. And the daughters of Jerusalem beholding these garments say in amazement "Who is this that cometh up made white?" She was black, how is she now suddenly made white?

36. The angels, too, were in doubt when Christ arose; the powers of heaven were in doubt when they saw that flesh was ascending into heaven. Then they said: "Who is this King of glory?" And whilst some said "Lift up your gates, O princes, and be ye lift up, ye everlasting doors, and the King of glory shall come in." In Isaiah, too, we find that the powers of heaven doubted and said: "Who is this that cometh up from Edom, the redness of His garments is from Bosor, He who is glorious in white apparel?"

37. But Christ, beholding His Church, for whom He Himself, as you find in the book of the prophet Zechariah, had put on filthy garments, now clothed in white raiment, seeing, that is, a soul pure and washed in the layer of regeneration, says: "Behold, thou art fair, My love, behold thou art fair, thy eyes are like a dove's," in the likeness of which the Holy Spirit descended from heaven. The eyes are beautiful like those of a dove, because in the likeness of a dove the Holy Spirit descended from heaven.

38. And farther on: "Thy teeth are like a flock of sheep that are shorn, which are come up from the pool, which all bear twins, and none is barren among them, thy lips are as a cord of scarlet." This is no slight praise. First by the pleasing comparison to those that are shorn; for we know that goats both feed in high places without risk, and securely find their food in rugged places, and then when shorn are freed from what is superfluous, The Church is likened to a flock of these, having in itself the many virtues of those souls which through the laver lay aside the superfluity of sins, and offer to Christ the mystic faith and the grace of good living, which speak of the cross of the Lord Jesus.

39. The Church is beautiful in them. So that God the Word says to her: "Thou art all fair, My love, and there is no blemish in thee," for guilt has been washed away. "Come hither from Lebanon, My spouse, come hither from Lebanon, from the beginning of faith wilt thou pass through and pass on," because, renouncing the world, she passed through things temporal and passed on to Christ. And again, God the Word says to her: "How beautiful and sweet art thou made, O love, in thy delights! Thy stature is become like that of a palm-tree, and thy breasts like bunches of grapes."

40. And the Church answers Him, "Who will give Thee to me, my Brother, that didst suck the breasts of my mother? If I find Thee without, I will kiss Thee, and indeed they will not despise me. I will take Thee, and bring Thee into the house of my mother; and into the secret chamber of her that conceived me. Thou shalt teach me." You see how, delighted with the gifts of grace, she longs to attain to the innermost mysteries, and to consecrate all her affections to Christ. She still seeks, she still stirs up His love, and asks of the daughters of Jerusalem to stir it up for her, and desires that by their beauty, which is that of faithful souls, her spouse may be incited to ever richer love for her.

41. So that the Lord Jesus Himself, invited by such eager love and by the beauty of comeliness and grace, since now no offences pollute the baptized, says to the Church: "Place Me as a seal upon thy heart, as a signet upon thine arm;" that is, thou art comely, My beloved, thou art all fair, nothing is wanting to thee. Place Me as a seal upon thine heart, that thy faith may shine forth in the fulness of the sacrament. Let thy works also shine and set forth the image of God in the Whose image thou wast made. Let no persecution lessen thy love, which many waters cannot quench, nor many rivers drown.

42. And then remember that you received the seal of the Spirit; the spirit of wisdom and understanding, the spirit of counsel and strength, the spirit of knowledge and godliness, and the spirit of holy fear, and preserved what you received. God the Father sealed you, Christ the Lord

strengthened you, and gave the earnest of the Spirit in your heart, as you have learned in the lesson from the Apostle.

Chapter VIII.

Of the mystical feast of the altar of the Lord. Lest any should think lightly of it, St. Ambrose shows that it is of higher antiquity than the sacred rites of the Jews, since it was foreshadowed in the sacrifice of Melchisedech, and far better than the manna, as being the Body of Christ.

43. The cleansed people, rich with these adornments, hastens to the altar of Christ, saying: "I will go to the altar of God, to God Who maketh glad my youth;" for having laid aside the slough of ancient error, renewed with an eagle's youth, it hastens to approach that heavenly feast. It comes, and seeing the holy altar arranged, cries out: "Thou hast prepared a table in my sight." David introduces the people as speaking, where he says: "The Lord feedeth me, and nothing shall be wanting to me, in a place of good pasture hath He placed me. He hath led me forth by the water of refreshment." And later: "For though I walk in the midst of the shadow of death, I will fear no evils, for Thou art with me. Thy rod and Thy staff have comforted me. Thou hast prepared in my sight a table against them that trouble me. Thou hast anointed my head with oil, and Thy inebriating cup, how excellent it is!"

44. We must now pay attention, lest perchance any one seeing that what is visible (for things which are invisible cannot be seen nor comprehended by human eyes), should say, "God rained down manna and rained down quails upon the Jews," but for the Church beloved of Him the things which He has prepared are those of which it is said: "That eye hath not seen, nor ear heard, neither hath it entered into the heart of man, what things God hath prepared for them that love Him." So, lest any one should say this, we will take great pains to prove that the sacraments of the Church are both more ancient than those of the synagogue, and more excellent than the manna.

45. The lesson of Genesis just read shows that they are more ancient, for the synagogue took its origin from the law of Moses. But Abraham was far earlier, who, after conquering the enemy, and recovering his own nephew, as he was enjoying his victory, was met by Melchisedech, who brought forth those things which Abraham reverently received. It was not Abraham who brought them forth, but Melchisedech, who is introduced without father, without mother, having neither beginning of days, nor ending, but like the Son of God, of Whom Paul says to the Hebrews: "that He remaineth a priest for ever," Who in the Latin version is called King of righteousness and King of peace.

46. Do you recognize Who that is? Can a man be king of righteousness, when himself he can hardly be righteous? Can he be king of peace, when he can hardly be peaceable? He it is Who is without mother according to His Godhead, for He was begotten of God the Father, of one substance with the Father; without a father according to His Incarnation, for He was born of a Virgin; having neither beginning nor end, for He is the beginning and end of all things, the first and the last. The sacrament, then, which you received is the gift not of man but of God, brought forth by Him Who blessed Abraham the father of faith, whose grace and deeds we admire.

47. We have proved the sacraments of the Church to be the more ancient, now recognize that they are superior. In very truth it is a marvellous thing that God rained manna on the fathers, and fed them with daily food from heaven; so that it is said, "So man did eat angels' food." But yet all those who ate that food died in the wilderness, but that food which you receive, that living Bread which came down from heaven, furnishes the substance of eternal life; and whosoever shall eat of this Bread shall never die, and it is the Body of Christ.

49. Now consider whether the bread of angels be more excellent or the Flesh of Christ, which is indeed the body of life. That manna came from heaven, this is above the heavens; that was of heaven, this is of the Lord of the heavens; that was liable to corruption, if kept a second day, this is far from all corruption, for whosoever shall taste it holly shall not be able to feel corruption. For them water flowed from the rock, for you Blood flowed from Christ; water

satisfied them for a time, the Blood satiates you for eternity. The Jew drinks and thirsts again, you after drinking will be beyond the power of thirsting; that was in a shadow, this is in truth.

49. If that which you so wonder at is but shadow, how great must that be whose very shadow you wonder at. See now what happened in the case of the fathers was shadow: "They drank, it is said, of that Rock that followed them, and that Rock was Christ. But with many of them God was not well pleased, for they were overthrown in the wilderness. Now these things were done in a figure concerning us." You recognize now which are the more excellent, for light is better than shadow, truth than a figure, the Body of its Giver than the manna from heaven.

Chapter IX.

In order that no one through observing the outward part should waver in faith, many instances are brought forward wherein the outward nature has been changed, and so it is proved that bread is made the true body of Christ. The treatise then is brought to a termination with certain remarks as to the effects of the sacrament, the disposition of the recipients, and such like.

50. Perhaps you will say, "I see something else, how is it that you assert that I receive the Body of Christ?" And this is the point which remains for us to prove. And what evidence shall we make use of? Let us prove that this is not what nature made, but what the blessing consecrated, and the power of blessing is greater than that of nature, because by blessing nature itself is changed.

51. Moses was holding a rod, he cast it down and it became a serpent. Again, he took hold of the tail of the serpent and it returned to the nature of a rod. You see that by virtue of the prophetic office there were two changes, of the nature both of the serpent and of the rod. The streams of Egypt were running with a pure flow of water; of a sudden from the veins of the sources blood began to burst forth, and none could drink of the river. Again, at the prophet's prayer the blood ceased, and the nature of water returned. The people of the Hebrews were shut in on every side, hemmed in on the one hand by the Egyptians, on the other by the sea; Moses lifted up his rod, the water divided and hardened like walls, and a way for the feet appeared between the waves. Jordan being turned back, returned, contrary to nature, to the source of its stream. Is it not clear that the nature of the waves of the sea and of the river stream was changed? The people of the fathers thirsted, Moses touched the rock, and water flowed out of the rock. Did not grace work a result contrary to nature, so that the rock poured forth water, which by nature it did not contain? Marah was a most bitter stream, so that the thirsting people could not drink. Moses cast wood into the water, and the water lost its bitterness, which grace of a sudden tempered. In the time of Elisha the prophet one of the sons of the prophets lost the head from his axe, which sank. He who had lost the iron asked Elisha, who cast in a piece of wood and the iron swam. This, too, we clearly recognize as having happened contrary to nature, for iron is of heavier nature than water.

52. We observe, then, that grace has more power than nature, and yet so far we have only spoken of the grace of a prophet's blessing. But if the blessing of man had such power as to change nature, what are we to say of that divine consecration where the very words of the Lord and Saviour operate? For that sacrament which you receive is made what it is by the word of Christ. But if the word of Elijah had such power as to bring down fire from heaven, shall not the word of Christ have power to change the nature of the elements? You read concerning the making of the whole world: "He spake and they were made, He commanded and they were created." Shall not the word of Christ, which was able to make out of nothing that which was not, be able to change things which already are into what they were not? For it is not less to give a new nature to things than to change them.

53. But why make use of arguments? Let us use the examples He gives, and by the example of the Incarnation prove the truth of the mystery. Did the course of nature proceed as usual when the Lord Jesus was born of Mary? If we look to the usual course, a woman ordinarily conceives after connection with a man. And this body which we make is that which was born of

344

the Virgin. Why do you seek the order of nature in the Body of Christ, seeing that the Lord Jesus Himself was born of a Virgin, not according to nature? It is the true Flesh of Christ which crucified and buried, this is then truly the Sacrament of His Body.

54. The Lord Jesus Himself proclaims: "This is My Body." Before the blessing of the heavenly words another nature is spoken of, after the consecration the Body is signified. He Himself speaks of His Blood. Before the consecration it has another name, after it is called Blood. And you say, Amen, that is, It is true. Let the heart within confess what the mouth utters, let the soul feel what the voice speaks.

55. Christ, then, feeds His Church with these sacraments, by means of which the substance of the soul is strengthened, and seeing the continual progress of her grace, He rightly says to her: "How comely are thy breasts, my sister, my spouse, how comely they are made by wine, and the smell of thy garments is above all spices. A dropping honeycomb are thy lips, my spouse, honey and milk are under thy tongue, and the smell of thy garments is as the smell of Lebanon. A garden enclosed is my sister, my spouse, a garden enclosed, a fountain sealed." By which He signifies that the mystery ought to remain sealed up with you, that it be not violated by the deeds of an evil life, and pollution of chastity, that it be not made known to thou, for whom it is not fitting, nor by garrulous talkativeness it be spread abroad amongst unbelievers. Your guardianship of the faith ought therefore to be good, that integrity of life and silence may endure unblemished.

56. For which reason, too, the Church, guarding the depth of the heavenly mysteries, repels the furious storms of wind, and calls to her the sweetness of the grace of spring, and knowing that her garden cannot displease Christ, invites the Bridegroom, saying: "Arise, O north wind, and come, thou south; blow upon my garden, and let my ointments flow down. Let my Brother come down to His garden, and eat the fruit of His trees." For it has good trees and fruitful, which have dipped their roots in the water of the sacred spring, and with fresh growth have shot forth into good fruits, so as now not to be cut with the axe of the prophet, but to abound with the fruitfulness of the Gospel.

57. Lastly, the Lord also, delighted with their fertility, answers: "I have entered into My garden, My sister, My spouse; I have gathered My myrrh with My spices, I have eaten My meat with My honey, I have drunk My drink with My milk." Understand, you faithful, why He spoke of meat and drink. And there is no doubt that He Himself eats and drinks in us, as you have read that He says that in our persons He is in prison.

58. Wherefore, too, the Church, beholding so great grace, exhorts her sons and her friends to come together to the sacraments, saying: "Eat, my friends, and drink and be inebriated, my brother." What we eat and what we drink the Holy Spirit has elsewhere made plain by the prophet, saying, "Taste and see that the Lord is good, blessed is the man that hopeth in Him." In that sacrament is Christ, because it is the Body of Christ, it is therefore not bodily food but spiritual. Whence the Apostle says of its type: "Our fathers ate spiritual food and drank spiritual drink," for the Body of God is a spiritual body; the Body of Christ is the Body of the Divine Spirit, for the Spirit is Christ, as we read: "The Spirit before our face is Christ the Lord." And in the Epistle of Peter we read: "Christ died for us." Lastly, that food strengthens our heart, and that drink "maketh glad the heart of man," as the prophet has recorded.

59. So, then, having obtained everything, let us know that we are born again, but let us not say, How are we born again? Have we entered a second time into our mother's womb and been born again? I do not recognize here the course of nature. But here there is no order of nature, where is the excellence of grace. And again, it is not always the course of nature which brings about conception, for we confess that Christ the Lord was conceived of a Virgin, and reject the order of nature. For Mary conceived not of man, but was with child of the Holy Spirit, as Matthew says: "She was found with child of the Holy Spirit." If, then, the Holy Spirit coming down upon the Virgin wrought the conception, and effected the work of generation, surely we

must not doubt but that, coming down upon the Font, or upon those who receive Baptism, He effects the reality of the new birth.

Two Books Concerning Repentance. Introduction.

These two books were written against the Novatian heresy, which took its name, and to a considerable extent its form, from Novatus, a priest of the Church of Carthage, and Novatian, schismatically consecrated bishop at Rome. It was the outcome of a struggle which had long existed in the Church upon the question of the restitution to Church privileges of those who had fallen into grievous sin, and the possibility of their repentance.

The severest ground was taken by the Novatians, who were condemned successively by many councils, which maintained the power of the Church to admit those guilty of any sin whatsoever to repentance, and prescribed various rules and penalties applicable to different cases. The heresy, however, lasted for some time, becoming weaker in the fifth century, and gradually fading away as a separate body with a distinctive name. "Novatianism, in the tests which it used, its efforts after a perfectly pure communion, its crotchetty interpretations of Scripture, and many other features, presents a striking parallel to many modern sects." [See *Dict. Chr. Biog.*, Blunt, Sects and heresies, Ceillier, II. 427, etc.]

St. Ambrose, in writing against the Novatians, seems to have had some recent publication of theirs in his mind, which is now unknown. He begins by commending gentleness, a quality singularly wanting in the sect; speaks of the power committed to the Church of forgiving the greatest sins, and points out how God is more inclined to mercy than to severity, and refutes the arguments of the Novatians based on certain passages of holy Scripture. In the second book, after urging the necessity of careful and speedy repentance, and the necessity of confessing one's sins, St. Ambrose meets the Novatian arguments based on Heb. vi. 4–6, from which they inferred the impossibility of restoration; and on St. Matt. xii. 31, Matt. xii. 32, our Lord's words concerning sin against the Holy Spirit.

As regards the date of this treatise, it must have been somewhat before the exposition of Ps. xxxvii., which refers to it, but there is nothing else which can be taken as a certain guide. Possibly the Benedictine Editors are right in assigning it to about a.d. 384.

Some few persons, probably on doctrinal grounds, have been led to question the author-ship of this treatise, but it is quoted by St. Augustine, and there has never been any real doubt on the subject.

TWO BOOKS CONCERNING REPENTANCE.
BOOK I.

Chapter I.

St. Ambrose writes in praise of gentleness, pointing out how needful that grace is for the rulers of the Church, and commended to them by the meekness of Christ. As the Novatians have fallen away from this, they cannot be considered disciples of Christ. Their pride and harshness are inveighed against.

1. If the highest end of virtue is that which aims at the advancement of most, gentleness is the most lovely of all, which does not hurt even those whom it condemns, and usually renders those whom it condemns worthy of absolution. Moreover, it is the only virtue which has led to the increase of the Church which the Lord sought at the price of His own Blood, imitating the lovingkindness of heaven, and aiming at the redemption of all, seeks this end with a gentleness which the ears of men can endure, in presence of which their hearts do not sink, nor their spirits quail.

2. For he who endeavours to amend the faults of human weakness ought to bear this very weakness on his own shoulders, let it weigh upon himself, not cast it off. For we read that the Shepherd in the Gospel carried the weary sheep, and did not cast it off. And Solomon says: "Be not overmuch righteous;" for restraint should temper righteousness. For how shall he offer himself to you for healing whom you despise, who thinks that he will be an object of contempt, not of compassion, to his physician?

3. Therefore had the Lord Jesus compassion upon us in order to call us to Himself, not frighten us away. He came in meekness, He came in humility, and so He said: "Come unto Me, all ye that labour and are heavy laden, and I will refresh you." So, then, the Lord Jesus refreshes, and does not shut out nor cast off, and fitly chose such disciples as should be interpreters of the Lord's will, as should gather together and not drive away the people of God. Whence it is clear that they are not to be counted amongst the disciples of Christ, who think that harsh and proud opinions should be followed rather than such as are gentle and meek; persons who, while they themselves seek God's mercy, deny it to others, such as are the teachers of the Novatians, who call themselves pure.

4. What can show more pride than this, since the Scripture says: "No one is free from sin, not even an infant of a day old;" and David cries out: "Cleanse me from my sin." Are they more holy than David, of whose family Christ vouchsafed to be born in the mystery of the Incarnation, whose descendant is that heavenly Hall which received the world's Redeemer in her virgin womb? For what is more harsh than to inflict a penance which they do not relax, and by refusing pardon to take away the incentive to penance and repentance? Now no one can repent to good purpose unless he hopes for mercy.

Chapter II.

The assertion of the Novatians that they refuse communion only to the lapsed agrees neither with the teaching of holy Scripture nor with their own. And whereas they allege as a pretext their reverence for the divine power, they really are contemning it, inasmuch as it is a sign of low estimation not to use the whole of a power entrusted to one. But the Church rightly claims the power of binding and loosing, which heretics have not, inasmuch as she has received it from the Holy Spirit, against Whom they act presumptuously.

5. But they say that those should not be restored to communion who have fallen into denial of the faith. If they made the crime of sacrilege the only exception to receiving forgiveness, they would be acting harshly indeed, and, as it would seem, would be in opposition to the divine utterances only, while consistent with their own assertions. For when the Lord forgave all sins, He made an exception of none. But since, as it were after the fashion of the Stoics, they think that all sins are equal in gravity, and assert that he who has stolen a common fowl, as they say, no less than he who has smothered his father, should be for ever excluded from the divine

mysteries, how can they select those guilty of one special offence, since even they themselves cannot deny that it is most unjust that the penalty of one should extend to many?

6. They affirm that they are showing great reverence for God, to Whom alone they reserve the power of forgiving sins. But in truth none do Him greater injury than they who choose to prune His commandments and reject the office entrusted to them. For inasmuch as the Lord Jesus Himself said in the Gospel: "Receive ye the Holy Spirit whosesoever sins ye forgive they are forgiven unto them, and whosoever sins ye retain, they are retained," Who is it that honours Him most, he who obeys His bidding or he who rejects it?

7. The Church holds fast its obedience on either side, by both retaining and remitting sin; heresy is on the one side cruel, and on the other disobedient; wishes to bind what it will not loosen, and will not loosen what it has bound, whereby it condemns itself by its. own sentence. For the Lord willed that the power of binding and of loosing should be alike, and sanctioned each by a similar condition. So he who has not the power to loose has not the power to bind. For as, according to the Lord's word, he who has the power to bind has also the power to loose, their teaching destroys itself, inasmuch as they who deny that they have the power of loosing ought also to deny that of binding. For how can the one be allowed and the other disallowed? It is plain and evident that either each is allowed or each is disallowed in the case of those to whom each has been given. Each is allowed to the Church, neither to heresy, for this power has been entrusted to priests alone. Rightly, therefore, does the Church claim it, which has true priests; heresy, which has not the priests of God, cannot claim it. And by not claiming this power heresy pronounces its own sentence, that not possessing priests it cannot claim priestly power. And so in their shameless obstinacy a shamefaced acknowledgment meets our view.

8. Consider, too, the point that he who has received the Holy Ghost has also received the power of forgiving and of retaining sin. For thus it is written: "Receive the Holy Spirit: whosoever sins ye forgive, they are forgiven unto them, and whosoever sins ye retain, they are retained." So, then, he who has not received power to forgive sins has not received the Holy Spirit. The office of the priest is a gift of the Holy Spirit, and His right it is specially to forgive and to retain sins. How, then, can they claim His gift who distrust His power and His right?

9. And what is to be said of their excessive arrogance? For although the Spirit of God is more inclined to mercy than to severity, their will is opposed to that which He wills, and they do that which He wills not; whereas it is the office of a judge to punish, but of mercy to forgive. It would be more endurable, Novatian, that thou shouldst forgive than that thou shouldst bind. In the one case thou wouldst assume the right as one who rarely offended; in the other thou wouldst forgive as one who had fellowfeeling with the misery of sin.

Chapter III.

To the argument of the Novatians, that they only deny forgiveness in the case of greater sins, St. Ambrose replies, that this is also an offence against God, Who gave the power to forgive all sins, but that of course a more severe penance must follow in case of graver sins. He points out likewise that this distinction as to the gravity of sins assigns, as it were, severity to God, Whose mercy in the Incarnation is overlooked by the Novatians.

10. But they say that, with the exception of graver sins, they grant forgiveness to those of less weight. This is not the teaching of your father, Novatian, who thought that no one should be admitted to penance, considering that what he was unable to loose he would not bind, lest by binding he should inspire the hope that he would loose. So that your father is condemned by your own sentence, you who make a distinction between sins, some of which you consider that you can loose, and others which you consider to be without remedy. But God does not make a distinction, Who has promised His mercy to all, and granted to His priests the power of loosing without any exception. But he who has heaped up sin must also increase his penitence. For greater sins are washed away by greater weeping. So neither is Novatian justified, who excluded all from pardon; nor are you, who imitate and, at the same time, condemn him, for you diminish

zeal for penance where it ought to be increased, since the mercy of Christ has taught us that graver sins must be made good by greater efforts.

11. And what perversity it is to claim for yourselves what can be forgiven, and, as you say, to reserve to God what cannot be forgiven. This would be to reserve to oneself the cases for mercy, to God those for severity. And what as to that saying: "Let God be true but every man a liar, as it is written, That Thou mightest be justified in Thy words, and overcome when Thou art judged"? In order, then, that we may recognize that the God of mercy is rather prone to indulgence than to severity, it is said: "I desire mercy rather than sacrifice." How, then, can your sacrifice, who refuse mercy, be acceptable to God, since He says that He wills not the death of a sinner, but his correction?

12. Interpreting which truth, the Apostle says: "For God, sending His own Son in the likeness of sinful flesh, and for sin condemned sin in the flesh, that the righteousness of the Law might be fulfilled in us." He does not say "in the likeness of flesh," for Christ took on Himself the reality not the likeness of flesh; nor does He say in the likeness of sin, for He did no sin, but was made sin for us. Yet He came "in the likeness of sinful flesh;" that is, He took on Him the likeness of sinful flesh, the *likeness,* because it is written: "He is man, and who shall know Him?" He was man in the flesh, according to His human nature, that He might be recognized, but in power was above man, that He might not be recognized, so He has our flesh, but has not the failings of this flesh.

13. For He was not begotten, as is every man, by intercourse between male and female, but born of the Holy Spirit and of the Virgin; He received a stainless body, which not only no sins polluted, but which neither the generation nor the conception had been stained by any admixture of defilement. For we men are all born under sin, and our very origin is in evil, as we read in the words of David: "For lo, I was conceived in wickedness, and in sin did my mother bring me forth." Therefore the flesh of Paul was a body of death, as he himself says: "Who shall deliver me from the body of this death?" But the flesh of Christ condemned sin, which He felt not at His birth, and crucified by His death, so that in our flesh there might be justification through grace, in which before there had been pollution by guilt.

14. What, then, shall we say to this, except that which the Apostle said: "If God is for us, who is against us? He who spared not His own Son, but gave Him up for us all, how has He not with Him also given us all things? Who shall lay a charge against the elect? It is God Who justifieth, who is he that shall condemn? It is Christ Who died, yea, Who also rose again, Who is at the right hand of God, Who also maketh intercession for us." Novatian then brings charges against those for whom Christ intercedes. Those whom Christ has redeemed unto salvation Novatian condemns to death. Those to whom Christ says: "Take My yoke upon you, and learn of Me, for I am gentle," Novatian says, I am not gentle. On those to whom Christ says: "Ye shall find rest for your souls, for My yoke is pleasant and My burden is light," Novatian lays a heavy burden and a hard yoke.

Chapter IV.

St. Ambrose proceeds with the proof of the divine mercy, and shows by the testimony of the Gospels that it prevails over severity, and he adduces the instance of athletes to show that of those who have denied Christ before men, all are not to be esteemed alike.

15. Although what has been said sufficiently shows how inclined the Lord Jesus is to mercy, let Him further instruct us with His own words, when He would arm us against the assaults of persecution. "Fear not," He says, "those who kill the body, but cannot kill the soul, but rather fear Him Who can cast both body and soul into hell." And farther on: "Every one, therefore, who shall confess Me before men, him will I also confess before My Father, Who is in heaven, but he who shall deny Me before men, him will I also deny before My Father, Who is in heaven."

16. Where He says that He will confess, He will confess "every one." Where He speaks of denying, He does not speak of denying "every one." For, whereas in the former clause He says, "Every one who shall confess Me, him will I confess," we should expect that in the following clause He would also say, "Every one who shall deny Me." But in order that He might not appear to deny every one, He concludes: "But he who shall deny Me before men, him will I also deny." He promises favour to every one, but He does not threaten the penalty to every one. He makes more of that which is merciful. He makes less of what is penal.

17. And this is written not only in that book of the Gospel of the Lord Jesus, which is written according to Matthew, but it is also to be read in that which we have according to Luke, that we might know that neither had thus related the saying by chance.

18. We have said that it is thus written. Let us now consider the meaning. "Every one," He says, "who shall confess Me," that is to say, of whatever age, of whatever condition he may be, who shall confess Me, he shall have Me as the Rewarder of his confession. Whereas the expression is, "every one," no one who shall confess is excluded from the reward. But it is not said in like manner, "Every one who shall deny shall be denied," for it is possible that a man overcome by torture may deny God in word, and yet worship Him in his heart.

19. Is the case the same with him who denies voluntarily, and with him whom torture, not his own will, has led to denial? How unfit were it, since with men credit is given for endurance in a struggle, that one should assert that it had no value with God! For often in this world's athletic contests the public crown together with the victors even the vanquished whose conduct has been approved, especially if perchance they have seen that they lost the victory by some trick or fraud. And shall Christ suffer His athletes, whom He has seen to yield for a moment to severe torments, to remain without forgiveness?

20. Shall not He take account of their toil, Who will not cast off for ever even those whom He casts off? For David says: "God will not cast off for ever," and in opposition to this shall we listen to heresy asserting, "He does cast off for ever"? David says: "God will not for ever cut off His mercy from generation to generation, nor will He forget to be merciful." This is the prophet's declaration, and there are those who would maintain a forgetfulness of mercy on God's part.

Chapter V.

The objection from the unchangeableness of God is answered from several passages of Scripture, wherein God promises forgiveness to sinners on their repentance. St. Ambrose also shows that mercy will be more readily accorded to such as have sinned, as it were, against their will, which he illustrates by the case of prisoners taken in war, and by language put into the mouth of the devil.

21. But they say that they make these assertions in order not to seem to make God liable to change, as He would be if He forgave those with whom He was angry. What then? Shall we reject the utterances of God and follow their opinions? But God is not to be judged by the statements of others, but by His own words. What mark of His mercy have we more ready at hand than that He Himself, through the prophet Hoses, is at once merciful as though reconciled to those whom in His anger He had threatened? For He says: "O Ephraim, what shall I do unto thee, or what shall I do unto thee, O Judah? Your kindness," etc. And further on: "How shall I establish thee? I will make thee as Admah, and as Zeboim." In the midst of His indignation He hesitates, as it were, with fatherly love, doubting how He can give over the wanderer to punishment; for although the Jew deserves it, God yet takes counsel with Himself. For immediately after having said, "I will make thee as Admah and as Zeboim," which cities, owing to their nearness to Sodom, suffered together in like destruction, He adds, "My heart is turned against Me, My compassion is aroused, I will not do according to the fierceness of Mine anger."

22. Is it not evident that the Lord Jesus is angry with us when we sin in order that He may convert us through fear of His indignation? His indignation, then, is not the carrying out of vengeance, but rather the working out of forgiveness, for these are His words: "If thou shalt

turn and lament, thou shall be saved." He waits for our lamentations here, that is, in time, that He may spare us those which shall be eternal. He waits for our tears, that He may pour forth His goodness. So in the Gospel, having pity on the tears of the widow, He raised her son. He waits for our conversion, that He may Himself restore us to grace, which would have continued with us had no fall overtaken us. But He is angry because we have by our sins incurred guilt, in order that we may be humbled; we are humbled, in order that we may be found worthy rather of pity than of punishment.

23. Jeremiah, too, may certainly teach when he says: "For the Lord will not cast off for ever; for after He has humbled, He will have compassion according to the multitude of His mercies, Who hath not humbled from His whole heart nor cast off the children of men." This passage we certainly find in the Lamentations of Jeremiah, and from it, and from what follows, we note that the Lord humbles all the prisoners of the earth under His feet, in order that we may escape His judgment. But He does not bring down the sinner even to the earth with His whole heart Who raises the poor even from the dust and the needy from the dunghill. For He brings not down with His whole heart Who reserves the intention of forgiving.

24. But if He brings not down every sinner with His whole heart, how much less does He bring down him with His whole heart who has not sinned with his whole heart! For as He said of the Jews: "This people honoureth Me with their lips, but their heart is far from Me," so perhaps He may say of some of the fallen: "They denied Me with their lips, but in heart they are with Me. It was pain which overcame them, not unfaithfulness which turned them aside." But some without cause refuse pardon to those whose faith the persecutor himself confessed up to the point of striving to overcome it by torture. They denied the Lord once, but confess Him daily; they denied Him in word, but confess Him with groans, with cries, and with tears; they confess Him with willing words, not under compulsion. They yielded, indeed, for a moment to the temptation of the devil, but even the devil afterwards departed from those whom he was unable to claim as his own. He yielded to their weeping, he yielded to their repentance, and after making them his own lost those whom he attached when they belonged to Another.

25. Is not the case such as when any one carries away captive the people of a conquered city? The captive is led away, but against his will. He must of necessity go to foreign lands, does not willingly make the journey; he takes his native land with him in his heart, and seeks an opportunity to return. What then? When any such return, does any one urge that they should not be received; with less honour indeed, but with readier will, that the enemy may have nothing with which to reproach them? If you pardon an armed man who was able to fight, do you not pardon him in whom faith alone waged the battle?

26. If we were to enquire what is the opinion of the devil concerning those who have fallen after this sort, would he not probably reply: "This people honours me with their lips, but their heart is far from me? For how can he be with me who does not depart from Christ? Without any cause do they appear to honour me who keep the doctrine of Jesus, and I thought that they would teach mine. They condemn me all the more when they forsake me after trial. Indeed Jesus is more glorified in these, when He receives them on their return to Him. All the angels rejoice, for in heaven there is greater joy over one sinner that repents, than over ninety and nine just persons who need not repentance. I am triumphed over in heaven and on earth. Christ loses nothing when they who came to me with weeping return with longing to the Church, and I am in danger even as regards my own, who will learn that in reality there is nothing here where men are led on by present rewards, but that there must be very much there where groans and tears and fasts are preferred to my feasts."

Chapter VI.

The Novatians, by excluding such from the banquet of Christ, imitate not indeed the good Samaritan, but the proud lawyer, the priest, and the Levite who are blamed in the Gospel, and are indeed worse than these.

27. Do you then, O Novatians, shut out these? For what is it when you refuse the hope of forgiveness but to shut out? But the Samaritan did not pass by the man who had been left half dead by the robbers; he dressed his wounds with oil and wine, first pouring in oil in order to comfort them; he set the wounded man on his own beast, on which he bore all his sins; nor did the Shepherd despise His wandering sheep.

28. But you say: "Touch me not." You who wish to justify yourselves say, "He is not our neighbour," being more proud than that lawyer who wished to tempt Christ, for he said "Who is my neighbour?" He asked, you deny, going on like that priest, like that Levite passing by him whom you ought to have taken and tended, and not receiving them into the inn for whom Christ paid the two pence, whose neighbour Christ bids you to become that you might show mercy to him. For he is our neighbour whom not only a similar condition has joined, but whom mercy has bound to us. You make yourself strange to him through pride, in vain puffing up yourself in your carnal mind, and not holding the Head. For if you held the Head you would consider that you must not forsake him for whom Christ died. If you held the Head you would consider that the whole body, by joining together rather than by separating, grows unto the increase of God by the bond of charity and the rescue of a sinner.

29. When, then, you take away all the fruits of repentance, what do you say but this: Let no one who is wounded enter our inn, let no one be healed in our Church? With us the sick are not cared for, we are whole, we have no need of a physician, for He Himself says: "They that are whole need not a physician, but they that are sick"

Chapter VII.

St. Ambrose, addressing Christ, complains of the Novatians, and shows that they have no part with Christ, Who wishes all men to be saved.

30. So, then, Lord Jesus, come wholly to Thy Church, since Novatian makes excuse. Novatian says, "I have bought a yoke of oxen," and he puts not on the light yoke of Christ, but lays upon his shoulders a heavy burden which he is not able to bear. Novatian held back Thy servants by whom he was invited, treated them contemptuously and slew them, polluting them with the stain of a reiterated baptism. Send forth, therefore, into the highways, and gather together good and bad, bring the weak, the blind, and the lame into Thy Church. Command that Thy house be filled, bring in all unto Thy supper, for Thou wilt make him whom Thou shalt call worthy, if he follow Thee. He indeed is rejected who has not the wedding garment, that is, the vestment of charity, the veil of grace. Send forth I pray Thee to all.

31. Thy Church does not excuse herself from Thy supper, Novatian makes excuse. Thy family says not, "I am whole, I need not the physician," but it says: "Heal me, O Lord, and I shall be healed; save me, and I shall be saved." The likeness of Thy Church is that woman who went behind and touched the hem of Thy garment, saying within herself: "If I do but touch His garment I shall be whole." So the Church confesses her wounds, but desires to be healed.

32. And Thou indeed, O Lord, desirest that all should be healed, but all do not wish to be healed. Novatian wishes not, who thinks that he is whole. Thou, O Lord, sayest that Thou art sick, and feelest our infirmity in the least of us, saying: "I was sick and ye visited Me." Novatian does not visit that least one in whom Thou desirest to be visited. Thou saidst to Peter when he excused himself from having his feet washed by Thee: "If I wash not thy feet, thou wilt have no part with Me." What fellowship, then, can they have with Thee, who receive not the keys of the kingdom of heaven, saying that they ought not to remit sins?

33. And this confession is indeed rightly made by them, for they have not the succession of Peter, who hold not the chair of Peter, which they rend by wicked schism; and this, too, they do, wickedly denying that sins can be forgiven even in the Church, whereas it was said to Peter: "I

will give unto thee the keys of the kingdom of heaven. and whatsoever thou shalt bind on earth shall be bound also in heaven, and whatsoever thou shall loose on earth shall be loosed also in heaven." And the vessel of divine election himself said: "If ye have forgiven anything to any one, I forgive also, for what I have forgiven I have done it for your sakes in the person of Christ." Why, then, do they read Paul's writings, if they think that he has erred so wickedly as to claim for himself the right of his Lord? But he claimed what he had received, he did not usurp that which was not due to him.

Chapter VIII.

It was the Lord's will to confer great gifts on His disciples. Further, the Novatians confute themselves by the practices of laying on of hands and of baptism, since it is by the same power that sins are remitted in penance and in baptism. Their conduct is then contrasted with that of our Lord.

34. It is the will of the Lord that His disciples should possess great powers; it is His will that the same things which He did when on earth should be done in His Name by His servants. For He said: "Ye shall do greater things than these." He gave them power to raise the dead. And whereas He could Himself have restored to Saul the use of his sight, He nevertheless sent him to His disciple Ananias, that by his blessing Saul's eyes might be restored, the sight of which he had lost. Peter also He bade walk with Himself on the sea, and because he faltered He blamed him for lessening the grace given him by the weakness of his faith. He Who Himself was the light of the world granted to His disciples to be the light of the world through grace. And because He purposed to descend from heaven and to ascend thither again, He took up Elijah into heaven to restore him again to earth at the time which should please Him. And being baptized with the Holy Spirit and with fire, He foreshadowed the Sacrament of Baptism at the hands of John.

35. And in fine He gave all gifts to His disciples, of whom He said: "In My Name they shalt cast out devils; they shall speak with new tongues; they shall take up serpents; and if they shall drink any deadly thing it shall not hurt them; they shall lay hands on the sick, and they shall do well." So, then, He gave them all things, but there is no power of man exercised in these things, in which the grace of the divine gift operates.

36. Why, then, do you lay on hands, and believe it to be the effect of the blessing, if perchance some sick person recovers? Why do you assume that any can be cleansed by you from the pollution of the devil? Why do you baptize if sins cannot be remitted by man? If baptism is certainly the remission of all sins, what difference does it make whether priests claim that this power is given to them in penance or at the font? In each the mystery is one.

37. But you say that the grace of the mysteries works in the font. What works, then, in penance? Does not the Name of God do the work? What then? Do you, when you choose, claim for yourselves the grace of God, and when you choose reject it? But this is a mark of insolent presumption, not of holy fear, when those who wish to do penance are despised by you. You cannot, forsooth, endure the tears of the weepers; your eyes cannot bear the coarse clothing, the filth of the squalid; with proud eyes and puffed-up hearts you delicate ones say with angry tones, "Touch me not, for I am pure."

38. The Lord said indeed to Mary Magdalene, "Touch Me not," but He Who was pure did not say, "because I am pure." Do you, Novatian, dare to call yourself pure, whilst, even if you were pure as regards your acts, you would be made impure by this saying alone? Isaiah says: "O wretched that I am, and pricked to the heart; for that being a man, and having unclean lips, I dwell also in the midst of a people having unclean lips," and do you say, "I am clean," when, as it is written, not even an infant of a day old is pure? David says, "And cleanse me from my sin," whom for his tender heart the grace of God often cleansed; are you pure who are so unrighteous as to have no tenderness, as to see the mote in your brother's eye, but not to consider the beam which is in your own eye? For with God no one who is unjust is pure. And what is more unjust than to desire to have your sins forgiven you, and yet yourself to think that

he who entreats you ought not to be forgiven? What is more unjust than to justify yourself in that wherein you condemn another, whilst you yourself are committing worse offences?

39. Then, too, the Lord Jesus when about to consecrate the forgiveness of our sins replied to John, who said: "I ought to be baptized of Thee, and comest Thou to me? Suffer it now, for thus it becometh us to fulfil all righteousness." And the Lord indeed came to a sinner, though indeed He had no sin, and desired to be baptized, having no need of cleansing; who, then, can tolerate you, who think there is no need for you to be cleansed by penance, because you say you are cleansed by grace, as though it were now impossible for you to sin?

Chapter IX.

By collating similar passages with 1 Sam. iii. 25, St. Ambrose shows that the meaning is not that no one shall intercede, but that the intercessor must be worthy as were Moses and Jeremiah, at whose prayers we read that God spared Israel.

40. But you Say, It is written: "If a man sin against the Lord, who shall entreat for him?" First of all, as I already said before, I might allow you to make that objection if you refused penance to those only who denied the faith. But what difficulty does that question produce? For it is not written, "No one shall entreat for him;" but, "Who shall entreat?" that is to say, the question is, Who in such a case can entreat? The entreaty is not excluded.

41. Then you have in the fifteenth Psalm "Lord, who shall dwell in Thy tabernacle, or who shall rest upon Thy holy hill?" It is not that no one, but that he who is approved shall dwell there, nor does it say that no one shall rest, but he who is chosen shall rest. And that you may know that this is true, it is said not much later in the twenty-fourth Psalm: "Who shall ascend into the hill of the Lord, or who shall stand in His holy place?" The writer implies, not any ordinary person, or one of the common sort, but only a man of excellent life and of singular merit. And that we may understand that when the question is asked, Who? it does not imply no one, but some special one is meant, after having said "Who shall ascend into the hill of the Lord?" the Psalmist adds: "He that hath clean hands and a pure heart, who hath not lift up his mind unto vanity." And elsewhere it is said: "Who is wise and he shall understand these things?" And in the Gospel: "Who is the faithful and wise steward, whom the Lord shall set over His household to give them their measure of wheat in due season?" And that we may understand that He speaks of such as really exist, the Lord added: "Blessed is that servant, whom his Lord when He cometh shall find so doing." And I am of opinion that where it is said, "Lord, who is like unto Thee?" it is not meant that none is like, for the Son is the image of the Father.

42. We must then understand in the same manner, "Who shall entreat for him?" as implying: It must be some one of excellent life who shall entreat for him who has sinned against the Lord. The greater the sin, the more worthy must be the prayers that are sought. For it was not any one of the common people who prayed for the Jewish people, but Moses, when forgetful of their covenant they worshipped the head of the calf. Was Moses wrong? Certainly he was not wrong in praying, who both merited and obtained that for which he asked. For what should such love not obtain as that of his when he offered himself for the people and said: "And now, if Thou wilt forgive their sin, forgive; but if not, blot me out of the book of life." We see that he does not think of himself, like a man full of fancies and scruples, whether he may incur the risk of some offence, as Novatian says he dreads that he might, but rather, thinking of all and forgetful of himself, he was not afraid test he should offend, so that he might rescue and free the people from danger of offence.

43. Rightly, then, is it said: "Who shall entreat for him?" It implies that it must be such an one as Moses to offer himself for those who sin, or such as Jeremiah, who, though the Lord said to him, "Pray not thou for this people," and yet he prayed and obtained their forgiveness. For at the intercession of the prophet, and the entreaty of so great a seer, the Lord was moved and said to Jerusalem, which had meanwhile repented for its sins, and had said: "O Almighty Lord God of Israel, the soul in anguish, and the troubled spirit crieth unto Thee, hear, O Lord, and have

mercy." And the Lord bids them lay aside the garments of mourning, and to cease the groanings of repentance, saying: "Put off, O Jerusalem, the garment of thy mourning and affliction. and clothe thyself in beauty, the glory which God hath given thee for ever."

Chapter X.

St. John did not absolutely forbid that prayer should be made for those who "sin unto death," since he knew that Moses, Jeremiah, and Stephen had so prayed, and he himself implies that forgiveness is not to be denied them.

44. Such intercessors, then, must be sought for after very grievous sins, for if any ordinary persons pray they are not heard.

45. So that point of yours will have no weight, which you take from the Epistle of John, where he says: "He who knows that his brother sinneth a sin not unto death, let him ask, and God will give him life, because he sinned not unto death. There is a sin unto death: not concerning it do I say, let him ask." He was not speaking to Moses and Jeremiah, but to the people, who must seek another intercessor for their sins; the people, for whom it is sufficient they entreat God for their lighter faults, and consider that pardon for weightier sins must be reserved for the prayers of the just. For how could John say that graver sins should not be prayed for, when he had read that Moses prayed and obtained his request, where there had been wilful casting off of faith, and knew that Jeremiah also had entreated?

46. How could John say that we should not pray for the sin unto death, who himself in the Apocalypse wrote the message to the angel of the Church of Pergamos? "Thou hast there those that hold the doctrine of Balaam, who taught Balac to put a stumbling-block before the children of Israel, to eat things sacrificed unto idols, and to commit fornication. So hast thou also them that hold the doctrines of the Nicolaitans. Repent likewise, or else I will come to thee quickly." Do you see that the same God Who requires repentance promises forgiveness? And then He says: "He that hath ears let him hear what the Spirit saith to the churches: To him that overcometh will I give to eat of the hidden manna."

47. Did not John himself know that Stephen prayed for his persecutors, who had not been able even to listen to the Name of Christ, when he said of those very men by whom he was being stoned: "Lord, lay not this sin to their charge"? And we see the result of this prayer in the case of the Apostle, for Paul, who kept the garments of those who were stoning Stephen, not long after became an apostle by the grace of God, having before been a persecutor.

Chapter XI.

The passage quoted from St. John's Epistle is confirmed by another in which salvation is promised to those who believe in Christ, which refutes the Novatians who try to induce the lapsed to believe, although denying them pardon. Furthermore, many who had lapsed have received the grace of martyrdom, whilst the example of the good Samaritan shows that we must not abandon those in whom even the faintest amount of faith is still alive.

48. Since, then, we have spoken of the general Epistle of St. John, let us enquire whether the writings of John in the Gospel agree with your interpretation. For he writes that the Lord said: "God so loved this world, that He gave His only-begotten Son, that every one that believeth on Him should not perish but have everlasting life." If, then, you wish to reclaim any one of the lapsed, do you exhort him to believe, or not to believe? Undoubtedly you exhort him to believe. But, according to the Lord's words, he who believes shall have everlasting life. How, then, will you forbid to pray for him, who has a claim to everlasting life? since faith is of divine grace, as the Apostle teaches where he speaks of the differences of gifts, for "to another is given faith by the same Spirit." And the disciples say to the Lord: "Increase our faith." He then who has faith has life, and he who has life is certainly not shut out from pardon; "that every one," it is said, "that believeth on Him should not perish." Since it is said, Every one, no one is shut out, no one is excepted, for He does not except him who has lapsed, if only afterwards he believes effectually.

49. We find that many have at length recovered themselves after a fall, and have suffered for the Name of God. Can we deny fellowship with the martyrs to these to whom the Lord Jesus has not denied it? Do we dare to say that life is not restored to those to whom Christ has given a crown? As, then, a crown is given to many after they have lapsed, so, too, if they believe, their faith is restored, which faith is the gift of God, as you read: "Because unto you it hath been granted by God not only to believe in Him, but also to suffer in His behalf." Is it possible that he who has the gift of God should not have His forgiveness?

50. Now it is not a single but a twofold grace that every one who believes should also suffer for the Lord Jesus. He, then, who believes receives his grace, but he receives a second, if his faith be crowned by suffering. For neither was Peter without grace before he suffered, but when he suffered he received a second gift. And many who have not had the grace to suffer for Christ have nevertheless had the grace of believing on Him.51. Therefore it is said: "That every. one that believeth in Him should not perish." Let no one, that is, of whatever condition, after whatever fall, fear that he will perish. For it may come to pass that the good Samaritan of the Gospel may find some one going down from Jerusalem to Jericho, that is, falling back from the martyr's conflict to the pleasures of this life and the comforts of the world; wounded by robbers, that is, by persecutors, and left half dead; that good Samaritan, Who is the Guardian of our souls (for the word Samaritan means Guardian), may, I say, not pass by him but tend and heal him.

52. Perchance He therefore passes him not by, because He sees in him some signs of life, so that there is hope that he may recover. Does it not seem to you that he who has fallen is half alive if faith sustains any breath of life? For he is dead who wholly casts God out of his heart. He, then, who does not wholly cast Him out, but under pressure of torments has denied Him for a time, is half dead. Or if he be dead, why do you bid him repent, seeing he cannot now be healed? If he be half dead, pour in oil and wine, not wine without oil, that may be the comfort and the smart. Place him upon thy beast, give hint over to the host, lay out two pence for his cure, be to him a neighbour. But you cannot be a neighbour unless you have compassion on him; for no one can be called a neighbour unless he have healed, not killed, another. But if you wish to be called a neighbour, Christ says to you: "Go and do likewise."

Chapter XII.

Another passage of St. John is considered. The necessity of keeping the commandments of God may be complied with by those who, having fallen, repent, as well as by those who have not fallen, as is shown in the case of David.

53. Let us consider another similar passage: "He that believeth on the Son hath eternal life, but he that believeth not the Son shall not see life, but the wrath of God abideth on him." That which abideth has certainly had a commencement, and that from some offence, viz., that first he not believe. When, then, any one believes, the wrath of God departs and life comes. To believe, then, in Christ is to gain life, for "he that believeth in Him is not judged."

54. But with reference to this passage they allege that he who believes in Christ ought to keep His sayings, and say that it is written in the Lord's own words: "I am come a light into this world, that whosoever believeth in Me may not abide in darkness. And if any man hear My word and keep it, I judge him not." He judges not, and do you judge? He says, "that whosoever believeth on Me may not abide in darkness," that is, that if he be in darkness he may not remain therein, but may amend his error, correct his fault, and keep My commandments, for I have said, "I will not the death of the wicked, but the correction." I said above that he that believeth on Me is not judged, and I keep to this: "For I am not come to judge the world, but that the world may be saved through Me." I pardon willingly, I quickly forgive, "I will have mercy rather than sacrifice," because by sacrifice the just is rendered more acceptable, by mercy the sinner is redeemed. "I come not to call the righteous but sinners." Sacrifice was under the Law, in the Gospel is mercy. "The Law was given by Moses, grace by Me."

55. And again further on He says: "He that despiseth Me, and receiveth not My words, hath one that judgeth him." Does he seem to you to have received Christ's words who has not corrected himself? Undoubtedly not. He, then, who corrects himself receives His word, for this is His word, that every one should turn back from sin. So, then, of necessity you must either reject this saying of His, or if you cannot deny it you must accept it.

56. It is also necessary that he who leaves off sinning must keep the commandments of God and renounce his sins. We ought not, then, to interpret this saying of him who has always kept the commandments, for if this had been His meaning He would have added the word *always*, but by not adding it He shows that He was speaking of him who has kept what he has heard, and what he heard has led him to correct his faults; he has then kept what he has heard.

57. But how hard it is to condemn to penance for life one who even afterwards keeps the commandments of the Lord, let Him teach us Himself Who has not refused forgiveness. Even to those who do not keep His commandments, as you read in the Psalm: "If they profane My statutes and keep not My commandments, I will visit their offences with the rod and their sins with scourges, but My mercy will I not take from them." So, then, He promises mercy to all.

58. Yet that we may not think that this mercy is without judgment, there is a distinction made between those who have paid continual obedience to God's commandments, and those who at some time, either by error or by compulsion, have fallen. And that you may not think that it is only our arguments which press you, consider the decision of Christ, Who said: "If the servant knew his Lord's will and did it not, he shall be beaten with many stripes, but if he knew it not, he shall be beaten with few stripes." Each, then, if he believes, is received, for God "chasteneth every son whom He receiveth," and him whom He chasteneth He does not give over unto death, for it is written: "The Lord hath chastened me sore, but He hath not given me over unto death."

Chapter XIII.

They who have committed a "sin unto death" are not to be abandoned, but subjected to penance, according to St. Paul. Explanation of the phrase "Deliver unto Satan." Satan can afflict the body, but these afflictions bring spiritual profit, showing the power of God, Who thus turns Satan's devices against himself.

59. Lastly, Paul teaches us that we must not abandon those who have committed a sin unto death, but that we must rather coerce them with the bread of tears and tears to drink, yet so that their sorrow itself be moderated. For this is the meaning of the passage: "Thou hast given them to drink in large measure," that their sorrow itself should have its measure, lest perchance he who is doing penance should be consumed by overmuch sorrow, as was said to the Corinthians: "What will ye? Shall I come to you with a rod, or in love and a spirit of meekness?" But even the rod is not severe, since he had read: "Thou shalt beat him indeed with the rod, but shalt deliver his soul from death."

60. What the Apostle means by the rod is shown by his invective against fornication, his denunciation of incest, his reprehension of pride, because they were puffed up who ought rather to be mourning, and lastly, his sentence on the guilty person, that he should be excluded from communion, and delivered to the adversary, not for the destruction of the soul but of the flesh. For as the Lord did not give power to Satan over the soul of holy Job, but allowed him to afflict his body, so here, too, the sinner is delivered to Satan for the destruction of the flesh, that the serpent might lick the dust of his flesh, but not hurt his soul.

61. Let, then, our flesh die to lusts, let it be captive, let it be subdued, and not war against the law of our mind, but die in subjection to a good service, as in Paul, who buffeted his body that he might bring it into subjection, in order that his preaching might become more approved, if the law of his flesh agreed and was consonant with the law of his flesh. For the flesh dies when its wisdom passes over into the spirit, so that it no longer has a taste for the things of the flesh, but for the things of the spirit. Would that I might see my flesh growing weak, would that I were

not dragged captive into the law of sin, would that I lived not in the flesh, but in the faith of Christ! And so there is greater grace in the infirmity of the body than in its soundness.

62. Having explained Paul's meaning, let us now consider the words themselves, in what sense he said that he had delivered him to Satan for the destruction of the flesh, for the devil it is who tries us. For he brings ailments on each of our limbs, and sickness on our whole bodies. And then, too, he smote holy Job with evil sores from the feet to the head, because he had received the power of destroying his flesh, when God said: "Behold, I give him up unto thee, only preserve his life." This the Apostle took up in the same words, giving up this man to Satan for the destruction of the flesh, that his spirit might be saved in the day of our Lord Jesus Christ.

63. Great is the power, great is the gift, which commands the devil to destroy himself. For he destroys himself when he makes the man whom he is seeking to overthrow by temptation stronger instead of weak, because whilst he is weakening the body he is strengthening his soul. For sickness of the body restrains sin, but luxury sets on fire the sin of the flesh.

64. The devil is then deceived so as to wound himself with his own bite, and to arm against himself him whom he thought to weaken. So he armed holy Job the more after he wounded him, who, with his whole. body covered with sores, endured indeed the bite of the devil, but felt not his poison. And so it is well said of him, "Thou shalt draw out the dragon with an hook, thou wilt play with him as with a bird, thou shall bind him as a boy doth a sparrow, thou shalt lay thine hand upon him."

65. You see how he is mocked by Paul, so that, like the child in prophecy, he lays his hand on the hole of the asp, and the serpent injures him not; he draws him out of his hiding-places, and makes of his venom a spiritual antidote, so that what is venom becomes a medicine, the venom serves to the destruction of the flesh, it becomes medicine to the healing of the spirit. For that which hurts the body benefits the spirit.

66. Let, then, the serpent bite the earthy part of me, let him drive his tooth into my flesh, and bruise my body; and may the Lord say of me: "I give him up unto thee, only preserve his life." How great is the power of Christ, that the guardianship of man is made a charge even to the devil himself, who always desires to injure him. Let us then make the Lord Jesus favourable to ourselves. At the command of Christ the devil himself becomes the guardian of his prey. Even unwillingly he carries out the commands of heaven, and, though cruel, obeys the commands of gentleness.

67. But why do I commend his obedience? Let him be ever evil that God may be ever good, Who converts his ill-will into grace for us. He wishes to injure us, but cannot if Christ resist him. He wounds the flesh but preserves the life. And then it is written: "Then shall the wolves and the lambs feed together, the lion and the ox shall eat straw, and they shall not hurt nor destroy in My holy mountain, saith the Lord." For this is the sentence of condemnation on the serpent: "Dust shall be thy food." What dust? Surely that of which it is said: "Dust thou art, and into dust shall thou return."

Chapter XIV.

St. Ambrose explains that the flesh given to Satan for destruction is eaten by the serpent when the soul is set free from carnal desires. He gives, therefore, various rules for guarding the senses, points out the snares laid for us by means of pleasures, and exhorts his hearers not to fear the destruction of the flesh by the serpent.

68. The serpent eats this dust, if the LordJesus is favourable to us, that our spirit may not sympathize with the weakness of the flesh, nor be set on fire by the vapours of the flesh and the heat of our members. "It is better to marry than to burn," for there is a flame which burns within. Let us not then suffer this fire to approach the bosom of our minds and the depths of our hearts, lest we burn up the covering of our inmost hearts, and lest the devouring fire of lust consume this outward garment of the soul and its fleshy veil, but let us pass through the fire. And should any one fall into the fire of love let him leap over it and pass forth; let him not bind

to himself adulterous lust with the bands of thoughts, let him not tie knots around himself by the fastenings of continual reflection, let him not too often turn his attention to the form of a harlot, and let not a maiden lift her eyes to the countenance of a youth. And if by chance she has looked and is caught, how much more will she be entangled if she gazes with curiosity.

69. Let custom itself teach us. A woman covers her face with a veil for this reason, that in public her modesty may be safe, That her face may not easily meet the gaze of a youth, let her be covered with the nuptial veil, so that not even in chance meetings she might be exposed to the wounding of another or of herself, though the wound of either were indeed hers. But if she cover her head with a veil that she may not accidentally see or be seen(for when the head is veiled the face is hidden), how much more ought she to cover herself with the veil of modesty, so as even in public to have her own secret place.

70. But granted that the eye has fallen upon another, at least let not the inward affection follow. For to have seen is no sin, but one must be careful that it be not the source of sin. The bodily eye sees, but let the eye of the heart be closed; let modesty of mind remain. We have a Lord Who is both strict and indulgent. The prophet indeed said: "Look not upon the beauty of a woman that is all harlot." But the Lord said: "Whoever shall look on a woman to lust after her, hath committed adultery with her already in his heart." He does not say, "Whosoever shall look hath committed adultery," but "Whosoever shall look on her to last after her." He condemned not the look but sought out the inward affection. But that modesty is praiseworthy which has so accustomed itself to close the bodily eyes as often not to see what we really behold. For we seem to behold with the bodily sight whatever meets us; but if there be not joined to this any attention of the mind, the sight also, according to what is usual in the body, fades away, so that in reality we see rather with the mind than with the body.

71. And if the flesh has seen the flame, let us not cherish that flame in our bosoms, that is, in the depths of the heart and the inward part of the mind. Let us not instil this fire into our bones, let us not bind bonds upon ourselves, let us not join in conversation with such as may be the cause to us of unholy fires. The speech of a maiden is a snare to a youth, the words of a youth are the bonds of love.

72. Joseph saw the fire when the woman eager for adultery spoke to him. She wished to catch him with her words. She set the snares of her lips, but was not able to capture the chaste man. For the voice of modesty, the voice of gravity, the rein of caution, the care for integrity, the discipline of chastity, loosed the woman's chains. So that unchaste person could not entangle him in her meshes. She laid her hand upon him; she caught his garment, that she might tighten the noose around him. The words of a lascivious woman are the snares of lust, and her hands the bonds of love; but the chaste mind could not be taken either by snares or by bonds. The garment was cast off, the bonds were loosed, and because he did not admit the fire into the bosom of his mind, his body was not burnt.

73. You see, then, that our mind is the cause of our guilt. And so the flesh is innocent, but is often the minister of sin. Let not, then, desire of beauty overcome you. Many nets and many snares are spread by the devil. The look of a harlot is the snare of him who loves her. Our own eyes are nets to us, wherefore it is written: "Be not taken with thine eyes." So, then, we spread nets for ourselves in which we are entangled and hampered. We bind chains on ourselves, as we read: "For every one is bound with the chains of his own sins."

74. Let us then pass through the fires of youth and the glow of early years; let us pass through the waters, let us not remain therein, lest the deep floods shut us in. Let us rather pass over, that we too may say: "Our soul has passed over the stream," for he who has passed over is safe. And lastly, the Lord speaks thus: "If thou pass through the water, I am with thee, the rivers shall not overflow thee." And the prophet says: "I have seen the wicked exalted above the cedars of Libanus, and I passed by, and lo, he was not." Pass by things of this world, and you will see that the high places of the wicked have fallen. Moses, too, passing by things of this

world, saw a great sight and said: "I will turn aside and see this great sight," for had he been held by the fleeting pleasures of this world he would not have seen so great a mystery.

75. Let us also pass over this fire of lust, fearing which Paul—but fearing for us, inasmuch as by buffeting his body he had come no longer to fear for himself—says to us: "Flee fornication." Let us then flee it as though following us, though indeed it follows not behind us, but within our very selves. Let us then diligently take heed lest while we are fleeing from it we carry it with ourselves. For we wish for the most part to flee, but if we do not wholly cast it out of our mind, we rather take it up than forsake it. Let us then spring over it, lest it be said to us: "Walk ye in the flame of your fire, which ye have kindled for yourselves." For as he who "takes fire into his bosom burns his clothes," so he who walks upon fiery coals must of necessity burn his feet, as it is written: "Can one walk upon coals of fire and not burn his feet?"

76. This fire is dangerous, let us then not feed it with the fuel of luxury. Lust is fed by feastings, nourished by delicacies, kindled by wine, and inflamed by drunkenness. Still more dangerous than these are the incentives of words, which intoxicate the mind as it were with a kind of wine of the vine of Sodore. Let us be on our guard against abundance of this wine, for when the flesh is intoxicated the mind totters, the heart wavers, the heart is carried to and fro. And so with regard to each that precept is useful wherein Timothy is warned: "Drink a little wine because of thy frequent infirmities." When the body is heated, it excites the glow of the mind; when the flesh is chilled with the cold of disease the spirit is chilled; when the body is in pain, the mind is sad, but the sadness shall become joy.

77. Do not then fear if your flesh be eaten away, the soul is not consumed. And so David says that he does not fear, because the enemy were eating up his flesh but not his soul, as we read: "When evil-doers come near upon me to eat up my flesh, my foes who trouble me, they were weakened and fell." So the serpent works overthrow for himself alone, therefore is he who has been injured by the serpent given over to the serpent that he may raise up again him whom he cast down, and the overthrow of the serpent may be the raising again of the man. And Scripture testifies that Satan is the author of this bodily suffering and weakness of the flesh, where Paul says: "There was given unto me a thorn in the flesh, a messenger of Satan to buffet me, that I should not be exalted." So Paul learned to heal even as he himself had been made whole.

Chapter XV.

Returning from this digression, St. Ambrose explains what is the meaning of St. Paul where he speaks of coming "with a rod or in the spirit of meekness." One who has grievously fallen is to be separated, but to be again restored to religious privileges when he has sufficiently repented. The old leaven is purged out when the hardness of the letter is tempered by the meal of a milder interpretation. All should be sprinkled with the Church's meal and fed with the food of charity, lest they become like that envious elder brother, whose example is followed by the Novatians.

78. That faithful teacher, having promised one of two things, gave each. He came with a rod, for he separated the guilty man from the holy fellowship. And well is he said to be delivered to Satan who is separated from the body of Christ. But he came in love and with the spirit of meekness, whether because he so delivered him up as to save his soul, or because he afterwards restored to the sacraments him whom he had before separated.

79. For it is needful to separate one who has grievously fallen, lest a little leaven corrupt the whole lump. And the old leaven must be purged out, or the old man in each person; that is, the outward man and his deeds, he who among the people has grown old in sin and hardened in vices. And well did he say purged, not cast forth, for what is purged is not considered wholly valueless, for to this end is it purged, that what is of value be separated from the worthless, but that which is cast forth is considered to have in itself nothing of value.

80. The Apostle then judged that the sinner should then at once be restored to the heavenly sacraments if he himself wished to be cleansed. And well is it said "Purge," for he is purged as

by certain things done by the whole people, and is washed in the tears of the multitude, and redeemed from sin by the weeping of the multitude, and is purged in the inner man. For Christ granted to His Church that one should be redeemed by means of all, as she herself was found worthy of the coming of the Lord Jesus, in order that through One all might be redeemed.

81. This is Paul's meaning which the words make more obscure. Let us consider the exact words of the Apostle: "Purge out," says he, "the old leaven, that ye may be a new lump, even as ye are unleavened." Either that the whole Church takes up the burden of the sinner, with whom she has to suffer in weeping and prayer and pain, and, as it were, covers herself with his leaven, in order that by means of all that which is to be done away in the individual doing penance may be purged by a kind of contribution and commixture of compassion and mercy offered with manly vigor. Or one may understand it as that woman in the Gospel teaches us, who is a type of the Church, when she hid the leaven in her meal, till all was leavened, and the whole could be used as pure.

82. The Lord taught me in the Gospel what leaven is when He said: "Do ye not understand that I said not concerning bread, Beware of the leaven of the Pharisees and Sadducees?" Then, it is said, they understood that He spake not of bread, but that they should beware of the doctrine of the Pharisees and Sadducees. This leaven, then—that is, the doctrine of the Pharisees and the contentiousness of the Sadducees—the Church hides in her meal, when she softened the hard letter of the Law by a spiritual interpretation, and ground it as it were in the mill of her explanations, bringing out as it were from the husks of the letter the inner secrets of the mysteries, and setting forth the belief in the Resurrection, wherein the mercy of God is proclaimed, and wherein it is believed that the life of those who are dead is restored.

83. Now this comparison seems to be not unfitly brought forward in this place, since the kingdom of heaven is redemption from sin, and therefore we all, both bad and good, are mingled with the meal of the Church that we all may be a new lump. But that no one may be afraid that an admixture of evil leaven might injure the lump, the Apostle said: "That ye may be a new lump, even as ye are unleavened;" that is to say, This mixture will render you again such, as in the pure integrity of your innocence. If we thus have compassion, we are not stained with the sins of others, but we gain the restoration of another to the increase of our own grace, so that our integrity remains as it was. And therefore he adds: "For Christ our Passover is sacrificed for us; " that is, the Passion of the Lord profited all, and gave redemption to sinners who repented of the sins they had committed.

84. Let us then keep the feast on good food, doing penance yet joyful in our redemption, for no food is sweeter than kindness and gentleness. Let no envy towards the sinner who is saved be mingled with our feasts and joy, lest that envious brother, as is set forth in the Gospel, exclude himself from the house of his Father, because he grieved at the reception of his brother, at whose lasting exile he was wont to rejoice.

85. And you Novatians cannot deny that you are like him, who, as you say, do not come together to the Church because by penance a hope of return had been given to those who had lapsed. But this is only a pretence, for Novatian contrived his schism through grief at his loss of the episcopal office.

86. But do you not understand that the Apostle also prophesied of you and says to you: "And ye are puffed up and did not rather mourn, that he who did this deed might be taken away from among you"? He is, then, wholly taken away when his sin is done away, but the Apostle does not say that the sinner is to be shut out of the Church who counsels his cleansing.

Chapter XVI.

Comparison between the apostles and Novatians. The fitness of the words, "Ye know not what spirit ye are of," when applied to them. The desire of penance is extinguished by them when they take away its fruit. And thus are sinners deprived of the promises of Christ, though, indeed, they ought not to be too soon admitted to the mysteries. Some examples of repentance.

87. Inasmuch, then, as the Apostle forgave sins, by what authority do you say that they are not to be forgiven? Who has the most reverence for Christ, Paul or Novatian? But Paul knew that the Lord was merciful. He knew that the Lord Jesus was offended more by the harshness of the disciples than by their pitifulness.

88. Furthermore, Jesus rebuked James and John when they spoke of bringing down fire from heaven to consume those who refused to receive the Lord, and said to them: "Ye know not whose spirit ye are of; for the Son of Man is not come to destroy men's lives but to save them." To them, indeed, He said, "Ye know not whose spirit ye are of," who were of His spirit; but to you He says, "Ye are not of My spirit, who hold not fast My clemency, who reject My mercy, who refuse repentance which I willed to be preached by the apostles in My Name."

89. For it is in vain that you say that you preach repentance who remove the fruits of repentance. For men are led to the pursuit of anything either by rewards or results, and every pursuit grows slack by delay. And for this reason the Lord, in order that the devotion of His disciples might be increased, said that every one who had left all that was his, and followed God, should receive sevenfold more both here and hereafter. First of all He promised the reward *here*, to do away with the tedium of delay, and again *hereafter*, that we might learn to believe that rewards will also be given to us hereafter. Present rewards are then an earnest of those hereafter.

90. If, then, any one, having committed hidden sins, shall nevertheless diligently do penance, how shall he receive those rewards if not restored to the communion of the Church? I am willing, indeed, that the guilty man should hope for pardon, should seek it with tears and groans, should seek it with the aid of the tears of all the people, should implore forgiveness; and if communion be postponed two or three times, that he should believe that his entreaties have not been urgent enough, that he must increase his tears, must come again even in greater trouble, clasp the feet of the faithful with his arms, kiss them, wash them with tears, and not let them go, so that the Lord Jesus may say of him too: "His sins which are many are forgiven, for he loved much."

91. I have known penitents whose countenance was furrowed with tears, their cheeks worn with constant weeping, who offered their body to be trodden under foot by all, who with faces ever pale and worn with fasting bore about in a yet living body the likeness of death.

Chapter XVII.

That gentleness must be added to severity, as is shown in the case of St. Paul at Corinth. The man had been baptized, though the Novatians argue against it. And by the word "destruction" is not meant annihilation but severe chastening.

92. Why do we postpone the time of pardon for those who have mortified themselves, who during life have done themselves to death? "Sufficient," says St. Paul, "to such a one is this punishment which is inflicted by the many; so that contrariwise, ye should rather forgive him and comfort him, lest by any means he should be swallowed up with overmuch sorrow." If the punishment which is inflicted by the many is sufficient for condemnation, the intercession which is made by many is also sufficient for the remission of sin. The Master of morals, Who both knows our weakness and is the interpreter of the will of God, wills that comfort should be given, lest sorrow through the weariness of long delay should swallow up the penitent.

93. The Apostle then forgave him, and not only forgave him, but desired that love to him should again grow strong. He who is loved receives not harshness but mercy. And not only did he himself forgive him only, but willed that all should forgive him, and says that he forgave for the sake of others, lest many should be longer saddened on account of one. "To whom," says he, "ye have forgiven anything, I forgive also, for I also have forgiven for your sakes in the person of Christ, for we are not ignorant of his devices." Rightly can he be on his guard against the serpent who is not ignorant of his devices, of which there are so many to our detriment. He is always desirous to do harm, always desirous to circumvent us, that he may cause death; but we ought to take heed lest our remedy become an occasion of triumph for him; for we are

circumvented by him, if any one perish through overmuch sorrow, who might be set free by pitifulness.

94. And that we may know that this person was baptized, he added: "I wrote to you in my epistle to have no company with fornicators, not altogether with fornicators of this world." And farther on he adds: "But now I write unto you not to keep company if any man that is named a brother be a fornicator, or covetous, or an idolator." Those whom he has joined together under one penalty, he willed to attain together to forgiveness. "If any be such," he says, "with him not to eat." How severe he is with the obstinate, how indulgent to those who seek. Against those rises up in arms the injury done to Christ, whilst the calling upon Christ aids these.

95. But lest any one be perplexed because it is written: "I have delivered such an one unto Satan for the destruction of the flesh," and should say: How can he attain forgiveness whose whole flesh has perished, seeing that it is evident that man was redeemed both in body and soul, and is saved in both and that neither the soul without the body, nor yet the body without the soul, since both are united by their fellowship in the deeds that have been done, can be without fellowship either in punishment or in reward? Let this suffice for an answer to him: That "destruction" does not mean the complete annihilation of the flesh, but its chastening. For as he who is dead to sin lives to God, so the allurements of the flesh perish, and the flesh dies to its lusts, in order that it may live again to purity and to other good works.

96. And what more suitable example can we take than one from our common mother? For the earth itself, from which we are all taken, when it is not worked and cultivated, seems to be desert; and the field dies to the vines or olive-trees with which it was planted, and yet it does not lose its own nutritive power, which is, as it were, its life. And then later, when cultivation begins once more, and the seed is sown for which the land seems suitable, it breaks forth again more fruitful than before with its products. It is not, then, anything so strange if our flesh is said to die, and yet is understood to be subdued rather than annihilated.

BOOK II.

Chapter I.

St. Ambrose gives additional rules concerning repentance, and shows that it must not be delayed.

1. Although in the former book we have written many things which may tend to the more perfect practice of repentance, yet inasmuch as a great deal more may be added, we will continue the repast so as not to seem to have relinquished the provisions of our teaching only half consumed.

2. For repentance must be taken in hand not only anxiously, but also quickly, lest perchance that father of the house in the Gospel who planted a fig-tree in his vineyard should come and seek fruit on it, and finding none, say to the vine-dresser: "Cut it down, why doth it cumber the ground?" And unless the vine-dresser should intercede and say: "Lord, let it alone this year also, until I dig about it and dung it, and if it bear fruit—well; but if not let it be cut down."

3. Let us then dung this field which we possess, and imitate those hard-working farmers, who are not ashamed to satiate the land with rich dung and to scatter the grimy ashes over the field, that they may gather more abundant crops.

4. And the Apostle teaches us how to dung it, saying: "I count all things but dung, that I may gain Christ," and he, through evil report and good report, attained to pleasing Christ. For he had read that Abraham, when confessing himself to be but dust and ashes, in his deep humility found favour with God. He had read how Job, sitting among the ashes, regained all that he had lost. He had heard in the utterance of David, how God "raiseth the poor out of the dust, and lifteth the needy out of the dunghill."

5. Let us then not be ashamed to confess our sins unto the Lord. Shame indeed there is when each makes known his sins, but that shame, as it were, ploughs his land, removes the ever-recurring brambles, prunes the thorns, and gives life to the fruits which he believed were dead. Follow him who, by diligently ploughing his field, sought for eternal fruit: "Being reviled we bless, being persecuted we endure, being defamed we entreat, we are made as the offscouring of the world." If you plough after this fashion you will sow spiritual seed. Plough that you may get rid of sin and gain fruit. He ploughed so as to destroy in himself the last tendency to persecution. What more could Christ give to lead us on to the pursuit of perfection, than to convert and then give us for a teacher one who was a persecutor?

Chapter II.

A passage quoted by the heretics against repentance is explained in two ways, the first being that Heb. vi. 4 refers to the impossibility of being baptized again; the second, that what is impossible with man is possible with God.

6. Being then refuted by the clear example of the Apostle and by his writings, the heretics yet endeavour to resist further, and say that their opinion is supported by apostolic authority, bringing forward the passage in the Epistle to the Hebrews: "For it is impossible that those who were once enlightened, and have tasted the heavenly gift, and have been made partakers of the Holy Spirit, and have tasted the good word of God, and the powers of the world to come, should if they fall away be again renewed unto repentance, crucifying again the Son of God, and put Him to open shame."

7. Could Paul teach in opposition to his own act? He had at Corinth forgiven sin through penance, how could he himself speak against his own decision? Since, then, he could not destroy what he had built, we must assume that what he says was different from, but not contrary to, what had gone before. For what is contrary is opposed to itself, what is different has ordinarily another meaning. Things which are contrary are not such that one can support the other. Inasmuch, then, as the Apostle spoke of remitting penance, he could not be silent as to those who thought that baptism was to be repeated. And it was right first of all to remove our anxiety,

and to let us know that even after baptism, if any sinned their sins could be forgiven them, lest a false belief in a reiterated baptism should lead astray those who were destitute of all hope of forgiveness. And secondly, it was right to set forth in a well-reasoned argument that baptism is not to be repeated.

8. And that the writer was speaking of baptism is evident from the very words in which it is stated that it is impossible to renew unto repentance those who were fallen, inasmuch as we are renewed by means of the laver of baptism, whereby we are born again, as Paul says himself: "For we are buried with Him through baptism into death, that, like as Christ rose from the dead through the glory of the Father, so we, too, should walk in newness of life." And in another place: "Be ye renewed in the spirit of your mind, and put on the new man which is created after God." And elsewhere again: "Thy youth shall be renewed like the eagle," because the eagle after death is born again from its ashes, as we being dead in sin are through the Sacrament of Baptism born again to God, and created anew. So, then, here as elsewhere, he teaches one baptism. "One faith," he says, "one baptism."

9. This, too, is plain, that in him who is baptized the Son of God is crucified, for our flesh could not do away sin unless it were crucified in Jesus Christ. And then it is written that: "All we who were baptized into Jesus Christ were baptized into His death." And farther on: "If we have been planted in the likeness of His death, we shall be also in the likeness of His resurrection, knowing that our old man was fastened with Him to His cross." And to the Colossians he says: "Buried with Him by baptism, wherein ye also rose again with Him." Which was written to the intent that we should believe that He is crucified in us, that our sins may be purged through Him, that He, Who alone can forgive sins, may nail to His cross the handwriting which was against us. In us He triumphs over principalities and powers, as it is written of Him: "He made a show of principalities and powers, triumphing over them in Himself."

10. So, then, that which he says in this Epistle to the Hebrews, that it is impossible for those who have fallen to be "renewed unto repentance, crucifying again the Son of God, and putting Him to open shame," must be considered as having reference to baptism, wherein we crucify the Son of God in ourselves, that the world may be by Him crucified for us, who triumph, as it were, when we take to ourselves the likeness of His death, who put to open shame upon His cross principalities and powers, and triumphed over them, that in the likeness of His death we, too, might triumph over the principalities whose yoke we throw off. But Christ was crucified once, and died to sin once, and so there is but one, not several baptisms.

11. But what of the passage wherein the doctrine of baptisms is spoken of? Because under the Law there were many baptisms or washings, he rightly rebukes those who forsake what is perfect and seek again the first principles of the word. He teaches us that the whole of the washings under the Law are done away with, and that there is one baptism in the sacraments of the Church. But he exhorts us that leaving the first principles of the word we should go on to perfection. "And this," he says, "we will do, if God permits," for no one can be perfect without the grace of God.

12. And indeed I might also say to any one who thought that this passage spoke of repentance, that things which are impossible with men are possible with God; and God is able whensoever He wills to forgive us our sins, even those which we think cannot be forgiven. And so it is possible for God to give us that which it seems to us impossible to obtain. For it seemed impossible that water should wash away sin, and Naaman the Syrian thought that his leprosy could not be cleansed by water. But that which was impossible God made to be possible, Who gave us so great grace. In like manner it seemed impossible that sins should be forgiven through repentance, but Christ gave this power to His apostles, which has been transmitted to the priestly office. That, then, has become possible which was impossible. But, by a true reasoning, he convinces us that the reiteration by any one of the Sacrament of Baptism is not permitted.

Chapter III.

Explanation of the parable of the Prodigal Son, in which St. Ambrose applies it to refute the teaching of the Novatians, proving that reconciliation ought not to be refused to the greatest offender upon suitable proof of repentance.

13. And the Apostle does not contradict the plain teaching of Christ, Who set forth, as a comparison of a repentant sinner, one going to a foreign country after receiving all his substance from his father, wasted it in riotous living, and later, when feeding upon husks, longed for his father's bread and then gained the robe, the ring, the shoes, and the slaying of the calf, which is a likeness of the Passion of the Lord, whereby we receive forgiveness.

14. Well is it said that he went into a foreign country who is cut off from the sacred altar, for this is to be separated from that Jerusalem which is in heaven, from the citizenship and home of the saints. For which reason the Apostle says: "Therefore now ye are no more strangers and foreigners, but fellow-citizens with the saints and of the household of God."

15. "And," it is said, "wasted his substance." Rightly, for he whose faith halts in bringing forth good works does consume it. For, "faith is the substance of things hoped for, the evidence of things not seen." And faith is a good substance, the inheritance of our hope.

16. And no wonder if he was perishing for hunger, who lacked the divine nourishment, impelled by the want of which he says: "I will arise and go to my father, and will say unto him: Father, I have sinned against heaven, and before thee." Do you not see it plainly declared to us, that we are urged to prayer for the sake of gaining the sacrament? and do you wish to take away that for the sake of which penance is undertaken? Deprive the pilot of the hope of reaching port, and he will wander uncertainly here and there on the waves. Take away the crown from the athlete, and he will fail and lie on the course. Take from the fisher the power of catching his booty, and he will cease to cast the nets. How, then, can he, who suffers hunger in his soul, pray more earnestly to God, if he has no hope of the heavenly food?

17. "I have sinned," he says, "against heaven, and before thee." He confesses what is clearly a sin unto death, that you maynot think that any one doing penance is rightly shut out from pardon. For he who has sinned against heaven has sinned either against the kingdom of heaven, or against his own soul, which is a sin unto death, and against God, to Whom alone is said: "Against Thee only have I sinned, and done evil before Thee."

18. So quickly does he gain forgiveness, that, as he is coming, and is still a great way off, his father meets him, gives him a kiss, which is the sign of sacred peace; orders the robe to be brought forth, which is the marriage garment, which if any one have not, he is shut out from the marriage feast; places the ring on his hand, which is the pledge of faith and the seal of the Holy Spirit; orders the shoes to be brought out, for he who is about to celebrate the Lord's Passover, about to feast on the Lamb, ought to have his feet protected against all attacks of spiritual wild beasts and the bite of the serpent; bids the calf to be slain, for "Christ our Passover hath been sacrificed." For as often as we receive the Blood of the Lord, we proclaim the death of the Lord. As, then, He was once slain for all, so whensoever forgiveness of sins is granted, we receive the Sacrament of His Body, that through His Blood there may be remission of sins.

19. Therefore most evidently are we bidden by the teaching of the Lord to confer again the grace of the heavenly sacrament on those guilty even of the greatest sins, if they with open confession bear the penance due to their sin.

Chapter IV.

St. Ambrose turns against the Novatians themselves another objection concerning blasphemy against the Holy Spirit, showing that it consists in an erroneous belief, proving this by St. Peter's words against Simon Magus, and other passages, exhorting the Novatians to return to the Church, affirming that such is our Lord's mercy that even Judas would have found forgiveness had he repented.

20. But we have heard that you are accustomed to bring forward as an objection that which is written: "Every sin and blasphemy shall be forgiven unto men, but blasphemies against the

Spirit shall not be forgiven unto men. And whosoever shall speak a word against the Son of Man, it shall be forgiven him, but whosoever shall speak against the Holy Spirit, it shall not be forgiven him, neither in this world, nor in that which is to come." By which quotation the whole of your assertion is destroyed and done away, for it is written: "Every sin and blasphemy shall be forgiven unto men." Why, then, do you not remit them? Why do you bind chains which you do not loose? Why do you tie knots which you do not unfasten? Forgive the others, and deal with those who you think are bound for ever by the authority of the Gospel for sinning against the Holy Spirit.

21. But let us consider the case of those whom the Lord so binds, going back to the words before the passage quoted, that we may understand it more clearly: The Jews were saying: "This man doth not cast out devils, but by Beelzebub, prince of the devils." Jesus replied: "Every kingdom divided against itself shall be destroyed, and every city or house divided against itself shall not stand; for if Satan casteth out Satan, he is divided against himself, how then shall his kingdom stand? But if I cast out devils by Beelzebub, by whom do your sons cast them out?"

22. Now we see plainly here that the words are expressly used of those who were saying that the Lord Jesus cast out devils through Beelzebub, to whom the Lord gave that answer, because they were of the heritage of Satan, who compared the Saviour of all to Satan, and attributed the grace of Christ to the kingdom of the devil. And that we might know that He was speaking of this blasphemy, He added: "O generation of vipers, how can ye speak good, being yourselves evil?" He says, then, that those who thus speak attain not to forgiveness.

23. Then, when Simon, depraved by long practice of magic, had thought he could gain by money the power of conferring the grace of Christ and the infusion of the Holy Spirit, Peter said: "Thou hast neither part nor lot in this faith, for thy heart is not right with God. Repent therefore of this thy wickedness, and pray the Lord, if per-chance this thought of thy heart may be forgiven thee, for I see that thou art in the bond of iniquity and in the bitterness of gall." We see that Peter by his apostolic authority condemns him who blasphemes against the Holy Spirit through magic vanity, and all the more because he had not the clear consciousness of faith. And yet he did not exclude him from the hope of forgiveness, for he called him to repentance.

24. The Lord then replies to the blasphemy of the Pharisees, and refuses to them the grace of His power, which consists in the remission of sins, because they asserted that His heavenly power rested on the help of the devil. And He affirms that they act with satanic spirit who divide the Church of God, so that He includes the heretics and schismatics of all times, to whom He denies forgiveness, for every other sin is concerned with single persons, this is a sin against all. For they alone wish to destroy the grace of Christ who rend asunder the members of the Church for which the Lord Jesus suffered, and the Holy Spirit was given us.

25. Lastly, that we may know that He is speaking of those who destroy the unity of the Church, we find it written: "He that is not with Me is against Me, and he that gathered not with Me, scattereth." And that we might know that He is speaking of these, He at once added: "Therefore I say unto you, every sin and blasphemy shall be forgiven unto men, but blasphemies against the Spirit shall not be forgiven unto men." When He says, "Therefore say I unto you," is it not evident that He intended the words following to be laid to heart by us beyond the others? And He rightly added: "A good tree bringeth forth good fruits, but a bad tree bringeth forth bad fruits," for an evil association cannot produce good fruits. The tree, then, is the association; the fruits of the good tree are the children of the Church.

26. Return, then, to the Church, those of you who have wickedly separated yourselves. For He promises forgiveness to all who are converted, since it is written: "Whosoever shall call on the Name of the Lord shall be saved." And lastly, the Jewish people who said of the Lord Jesus, "He hath a devil," and "He casteth out devils through Beelzebub," and who crucified the Lord Jesus, are, by the preaching of Peter, called to baptism, that they may put away the guilt of so great a wickedness.

27. But what wonder is it if you should deny salvation to others, who reject your own, though they lose nothing who seek for penance from you? For I suppose that even Judas might through the exceeding mercy of God not have been shut out from forgiveness, if he had expressed his sorrow not before the Jews but before Christ. "I have sinned," he said, "in that I have betrayed righteous blood." Their answer was: "What is that to us, see thou to that." What other reply do you give, when one guilty of a smaller sin confesses his deed to you? What do you answer but this: "What is that to us, see thou to that"? The halter followed on those words, but the punishment is all the more severe, the smaller the sin is.

28. But if they be not converted, do you at least repent, who by many a slip have fallen from the lofty pinnacle of innocence and faith. We have a good Lord, Whose will it is to forgive all, Who called you by the prophet, and said: "I, even I, am He that blotteth out transgressions, and I will not remember, but do thou remember, and let us plead together."

Chapter V.

As to the words of St. Peter to Simon Magus, from which the Novatians infer that there was no forgiveness for the latter, it is pointed out that St. Peter, knowing his evil heart, might well use words of doubt, and then by some Old Testament instances it is pointed out that "perchance" does not exclude forgiveness. The apostles transmitted to us that penitence, the fruits of which are shown in the case of David. St. Ambrose then adduces the example of the Ephraimites, whose penitence must be followed in order to gain the divine mercy and the sacraments.

29. The Novatians bring up a question from the words of the Apostle Peter. Because he said, "if perchance," they think that he did not imply that forgiveness would be granted on repentance. But let them consider concerning whom the words were spoken: of Simon, who did not believe through faith, but was meditating trickery. So too the Lord to him who said, "Lord, I will follow Thee withersoever Thou goest," replied, "Foxes have holes." For e knew that the man's sincerity was not wholly perfect. If, then, the Lord refused to him who was not baptized permission to follow Him, because He saw that he was not sincere, do you wonder that the Apostle did not absolve him who after baptism was guilty of deceit, and whom he declared to be still in the bond of iniquity?

30. But let this be my answer to them. As to myself, I say that Peter did not doubt, and I do not think that so great a question can be burked by the questionable interpretation of a single word. For if they think that Peter doubted, did God doubt, Who said to the prophet Jeremiah: "Stand in the court of the Lord's house, and thou shall give an answer to all Judah, to those who come to worship in the Lord's house, even all the words which I have appointed for thee to answer them. Keep not back a word, perchance they will hearken and be converted." Let them say, then, that God also knew not what would happen.

31. But ignorance is not implied in that word, but the common custom of holy Scripture is observed, in order to simplicity of utterance. Inasmuch as the Lord says also to Ezekiel: "Son of man, I will send thee unto the house of Israel, to those who have angered Me, both themselves and their fathers, unto this day, and thou shall say unto them, Thus saith the Lord, if perchance they will hear and be afraid." Did He not know that they could or could not be converted? So, then, that expression is not always a proof of doubt.

32 Lastly, the wise men of this world, who stake all their reputation on expressions and words, do not everywhere use the Latin word *forte*, "perchance," or its Greek equivalent taca, as an expression of doubt. And so they say that their earliest poet used the words,

… h taca chrh

… esomai,

which is, "I shall soon be a widow;" and the passage goes on:

… taca gar se katakneousin ÆAcaioi

pante" eformhqente".

But he had no doubt that when all were Joining in the attack one might well be laid low by all.

33. But let us use our own instances rather than foreign ones. You find in the Gospel that the Son Himself says of the Father (when He had sent His servants to His vineyard, and they had been slain), that the Father said, "I will send My well-beloved Son, perchance they will reverence Him." And in another place the Son says of Himself: "Ye know neither Me nor My Father; for if ye knew Me, ye would perchance know My Father also."

34. If, then, Peter used those words which were used by God without any prejudice to His knowledge, why should we not assume that Peter also used them without prejudice to his belief? For he could not doubt concerning the gift of Christ, Who had given him the power of forgiving sins; especially since he was bound not to leave any place for the craftiness of heretics who desire to deprive men of hope, in order the more easily to insinuate into the despairing their opinion as to the reiteration of baptism.

35. But the apostles, having this baptism according to the direction of Christ, taught repentance, promised forgiveness, and remitted guilt, as David taught when he said: "Blessed are they whose transgressions are forgiven, and whose sins are covered. Blessed is the man to whom the Lord hath not imputed sin." He calls each blessed both him whose sins are remitted by the font, and him whose sin is covered by good works. For he who repents ought not only to wash away his sin by his tears, but also to cover and hide his former transgressions by amended deeds, that sin may not be imputed to him.

36. Let us, then, cover our falls by our subsequent acts; let us purify ourselves by tears, that the Lord our God may hear us when we lament, as He heard Ephraim when weeping, as it is written: "I have surely heard Ephraim weeping." And He expressly repeats the very words of Ephraim: "Thou hast chastised me and I was chastised, like a calf I was not trained." For a calf disports itself, and leaves its stall, and so Ephraim was untrained like a calf far away from the stall; because he had forsaken the stall of the Lord, followed Jeroboam, and worshipped the calves, which future event was prophetically indicated through Aaron, namely, that the people of the Jews would fall after this manner. And so repenting, Ephraim says: "Turn Thou me, and I shall be turned, for Thou art the Lord my God. Surely in the end of my captivity I repented, and after I learned I mourned over the days of confusion, and subjected myself to Thee because I received reproach and made Thee known."

37. We see how to repent, with what words and with what acts, that the days of sin are called "days of confusion;" for there is confusion when Christ is denied.

38. Let us, then, submit ourselves to God, and not be subject to sin, and when we ponder the remembrance of our offences, let us blush as though at some disgrace, and not speak of them as a glory to us, as some boast of overcoming modesty, or putting down the feeling of justice. Let our conversion be such, that we who did not know God may now ourselves declare Him to others, that the Lord, moved by such a conversion on our part, may answer to us: "Ephraim is from youth a dear son, a pleasant child, for since My words are concerning him, I will verily remember him, therefore have I hastened to be over him; I will surely have mercy on him, saith the Lord."

39. And what mercy He promises us, the Lord also shows, when He says further on: "I have satiated every thirsty soul, and have satisfied every hungry soul. Therefore, I awaked and beheld, and My sleep was sweet unto Me." We observe that the Lord promises His sacraments to those who sin. Let us, then, all be converted to the Lord.

Chapter VI.

St. Ambrose teaches out of the prophet Isaiah what they must do who have fallen. Then referring to our Lord's proverbial expression respecting piping and dancing, he condemns dances. Next by the example of Jeremiah he sets forth the necessary accompaniments of repentance. And lastly, in order to show the efficacy of this medicine of penance, he enumerates the names of many who have used it for themselves or for others.

40. But if they be not converted, do you at least repent, who by many a slip have fallen from the lofty pinnacle of innocence and faith. We have a good Lord, Whose will it is to forgive all, Who called you by the prophet and said: "I, even I, am He that blotteth out thy transgressions, and I will not remember, but do thou remember that we may plead together." "I," He says, "will not remember, but do thou remember," that is to say, "I do not recall those transgressions which I have forgiven thee, which are covered, as it were, with oblivion, but do thou remember them. I will not remember them because of My grace, do thou remember them in order to correction; remember, thou mayest know that the sin is forgiven, boast not as though innocent, that thou aggravate not the sin, but thou wilt be justified, confess thy sin." For a shamefaced confession of sins looses the bands of transgression.

41. You see what God requires of you, that you remember that grace which you have received, and boast not as though you had not received it. You see by how complete a promise of remission He draws you to confession. Take heed, lest by resisting the commandments of God you fall into the offence of the Jews, to whom the Lord Jesus said: "We piped to you and ye danced not; we wailed and ye wept not."

42. The words are ordinary words, but the mystery is not ordinary. And so one must be on one's guard, lest, deceived by any common interpretation of this saying, one should suppose that the movements of wanton dances and the madness of the stage were commended; for these are full of evil in youthful age. But the dancing is commended which David practised before the ark of God. For everything is seemly which is done for religion, so that we need be ashamed of no service which tends to the worship and honouring of Christ.

43. Dancing, then, which is an accompaniment of pleasures and luxury, is not spoken of, but spiritually such as that wherewith one raises the eager body, and suffers not the limbs to lie slothfully on the ground, nor to grow stiff in their accustomed tracks. Paul danced spiritually, when for us he stretched forward, and forgetting the things which were behind, and aiming at those which were before, he pressed on to the prize of Christ. And you, too, when you come to baptism, are warned to raise the hands, and to cause your feet wherewith you ascend to things eternal to be swifter. This dancing accompanies faith, and is the companion of grace.

44. This, then, is the mystery. "We piped to you," singing in truth the song of the New Testament, "and ye danced not." That is, did not raise your souls to the spiritual grace. "We wailed, and ye wept not." That is, ye did not repent. And therefore was the Jewish people forsaken, because it did not repent, and rejected grace. Repentance came by John, grace by Christ. He, as the Lord, gives the one; the other is proclaimed, as it were, by the servant. The Church, then, keeps both that it may both attain to grace and not cast away repentance, for grace is the gift of One Who confers it; repentance is the remedy of the sinner.

45. Jeremiah knew that penitence was a great remedy, which he in his Lamentations took up for Jerusalem, and brings forward Jerusalem itself as repenting, when he says: "She wept sore in the night, and her tears are on her cheeks, nor is there one to comfort her of all who love her. The ways of Sion do mourn." And he says further: "For these things I weep, my eyes have grown dim with weeping, because he who used to comfort me is gone far from me." We notice that he thought this the bitterest addition to his woes, that he who used to comfort the mourner was gone far from him. How, then, can you take away the very comfort by refusing to repentance the hope of forgiveness?

46. But let those who repent learn how they ought to carry it out, with what zeal, with what affection, with what intention of mind, with what shaking of the inmost bowels, with what conversion of heart: "Behold," he says, "O Lord, that I am in distress, my bowels are troubled by my weeping, my heart is turned within me."

47. Here you recognize the intention of the soul, the faithfulness of the mind, the disposition of the body: "The elders of the daughters of Sion sat," he says, "upon the ground, they put dust upon their heads, they girded themselves with haircloth, the princes hung their

heads to the ground, the virgins of Jerusalem fainted with weeping, my eyes grew dim, my bowels were troubled, my glory was poured on the earth."

48. So, too, did the people of Nineveh mourn, and escaped the destruction of their city. Such is the remedial power of repentance, that God seems because of it to change His intention. To escape is, then, in your own power; the Lord wills to be entreated, He wills that men should hope in Him, He wills that supplication should be made to Him. Thou art a man, and wiliest to be asked to forgive, and dost thou think that God will pardon thee without asking Him?

49. The Lord Himself wept over Jerusalem, that, inasmuch as it would not weep itself, it might obtain forgiveness through the tears of the Lord. He wills that we should weep in order that we may escape, as you find it in the Gospel: "Daughters of Jerusalem, weep not for Me, but weep for yourselves."

50. David wept, and obtained of the divine mercy the removal of the death of the people who were perishing, when of the three things proposed for his choice he selected that in which he might have the most experience of the divine mercy. Why do you blush to weep for your sins, when God commanded even the prophets to weep for the people?

51. And, lastly, Ezekiel was bidden to weep for Jerusalem, and he took the book, at the beginning of which was written "Lamentation, and melody, and woe," two things sad and one pleasant, for he shall be saved in the future who has wept most in this age. "For the heart of the wise is in the house of mourning, and the heart of fools in the house of feasting." And the Lord Himself said: "Blessed are ye that weep now, for ye shall laugh."

Chapter VII.

An exhortation to mourning and confession of sins for Christ is moved by these and the tears of the Church. Illustration from the story of Lazarus. After showing that the Novatians are the successors of those who planned to kill Lazarus, St. Ambrose argues that the full forgiveness of every sin is signified by the odour of the ointment poured by Mary on the feet of Christ; and further, that the Novatian heretics find their likeness in Judas, who grudged and envied when others rejoiced.

52. Let us, then, mourn for a time, that we may rejoice for eternity. Let us fear the Lord, let us anticipate Him with the confession of our sins, let us correct our backslidings and amend our faults, lest of us too it be said: "Woe is me, my soul, for the godly man is perished from the earth, and there is none amongst men to correct them."

53. Why do you fear to confess your sins to our good Lord? "Set them forth," He says, "that thou mayest be justified." The rewards of justification are set before him who is still guilty of sin, for he is justified who voluntarily confesses his own sin; and lastly, "the just man is his own accuser in the beginning of his speaking." The Lord knows all things, but He waits for your words, not that He may punish, but that He may pardon. It is not His will that the devil should triumph over you and accuse you when you conceal your sins. Be beforehand with your accuser: if youaccuse yourself, you will fear no accuser; if you report yourself, though you were dead you shall live.

54. Christ will come to your grave, and if He finds there weeping for you Martha the woman of good service, and Mary who carefully heard the Word of God, like holy Church which has chosen the best part, He will be moved with compassion, when at your death He shall see the tears of many and will say: "Where have ye laid him?" that is to say, in what condition of guilt is he? in which rank of penitents? I would see him for whom ye weep, that he himself may move Me with his tears. I will see if he is already dead to that sin for which forgiveness is entreated.

55. The people will say to Him, "Come and see." What is the meaning of "Come"? It means, Let forgiveness of sins come, let the life of the departed come, the resurrection of the dead, let Thy kingdom come to this sinner also.

56. He will come and will command that the stone be taken away which his fall has laid on the shoulders of the sinner. He could have removed the stone by a word of command, for even inanimate nature is wont to obey the bidding of Christ. He could by the silent power of His

working have removed the stone of the sepulchre, at Whose Passion the stones being suddenly removed many sepulchres of the dead were opened, but He bade men remove the stone, in very truth indeed, that the unbelieving might believe what they saw, and see the dead rising again, but in a type that He might give us the power of lightening the burden of sins, the heavy pressure as it were upon the guilty. Ours it is to remove the burdens, His to raise again, His to bring forth from the tombs those set free from their bands.

57. So the Lord Jesus, seeing the heavy burden of the sinner, weeps, for the Church alone He suffers not to weep. He has compassion with His beloved, and says to him that is dead, "Come forth," that is, "Thou who liest in darkness of conscience, and in the squalor of thy sins, as in the prison-house of the guilty, come forth, declare thy sins that thou mayest be justified. "For with the mouth confession is made unto salvation."

58. If you have confessed at the call of Christ the bars will be broken, and every chain loosed, even the stench of the bodily corruption be grievous. For he had been dead four days and his flesh stank in the tomb; but He Whose flesh saw no corruption was three days in the sepulchre, for He knew no evils of the flesh, which consists of the substances of the four elements. However great, then, the stench of the dead body may be, it is all done away so soon as the sacred ointment has shed its odour; and the dead rises again, and the command is given to loose his hands who till now was in sin; the covering is taken from his face which veiled the truth of the grace which he had received. But since he has received forgiveness, the command is given to uncover his face, to lay bare his features. For he whose sin is forgiven has nothing whereof to be ashamed.

59. But in the presence of such grace given by the Lord, of such a miracle of divine bounty, when all ought to have rejoiced, the wicked were stirred up and gathered a council against Christ, and wished moreover to kill Lazarus also. Do you not recognize that you are the successors of those whose hardness you inherit? For you too are angry and gather a council against the Church, because you see the dead come to life again in the Church, and to be raised again by receiving forgiveness of their sins. And thus, so far as? you, you desire to slay again through envy those who are raised to life.

60. But Jesus does not revoke His benefits, nay, rather He amplifies them by additions of His liberality, He anxiously revisits him who was raised again, and rejoicing in the gift of the restored life, He comes to the feast which His Church has prepared for Him, at which he who had been dead is found as one amongst those sitting down with Christ.

61. Then all wonder who look upon him with the pure gaze of the mind, who are free from envy, for such children the Church has. They wonder, as I said, how he who yesterday and the day before lay in the tomb is one of those sitting with the Lord Jesus.

62. Mary herself pours ointment on the feet of the Lord Jesus. Perchance for this reason on His feet, because one of the lowliest has been snatched from death, for we are all the body of Christ, but others perchance are the more honourable members. The Apostle was the mouth of Christ, for he said, "Ye seek a proof of Christ that speaketh in me." The prophets through whom He spake of things to come were His month, would that I might be found worthy to be His foot, and may Mary pour on me her precious ointment, and anoint me and wipe away my sin.

63. What, then, we read concerning Lazarus we ought to believe of every sinner who is converted, who, though he may have been stinking, nevertheless is cleansed by the precious ointment of faith. For faith has such grace that there where the dead stank the day before, now the whole house is filled with good odour.

64. The house of Corinth stank, when it was written concerning it: "It is reported that there is fornication among you, and such fornication as is not even among the Gentiles." There was a stench, for a little leaven had corrupted the whole lump. A good odour began when it was said: "If ye forgive anything to any one I forgive also. For what I also have forgiven, for your sakes have I done it in the person of Christ." And so, the sinner being set free, there was great joy in that place, and the whole house was filled with the odour of the sweetness of grace. Wherefore

the Apostle, knowing well that he had shed upon all the ointment of apostolic forgiveness, says: "We are a sweet savour of Christ unto God in them that are saved."

65. At the pouring forth, then, of this ointment all rejoice; Judas alone speaks against it. So, too, now he who is a sinner speaks against it, he who is a traitor blames it, but he is himself blamed by Christ, as he knows not the remedy of the Lord's death, and understands not the mystery of that so great burial. For the Lord both suffered and died that He might redeem us from death. This is manifest from themost excellent value from His death, which is sufficient for the absolution of the sinner, and hisrestoration to fresh grace; so that all may come and wonder at his sitting at table with Christ, and may praise God, saying: "Let us eat and feast, for he was dead and is alive again, had perished and is found." But any one devoid of faith objects: "Why does He eat with publicans and sinners?" This is his answer: "They that are whole have no need of the physician, but they that are sick."

Chapter VIII.

In urging repentance St. Ambrose turns to his own case, expressing the wish that he could wash our Lord's feet like the woman in the Gospel, which is a great pattern of penitence, though such as cannot attain to it find acceptance. He prays for himself, especially that he may sorrow with sinners, who are better than himself. Those for whom Christ died are not to be contemned.

66. Show, then, your wound to the Physician that He may heal it. Though you show it not, He knows it, but waits to hear your voice. Do away your scars by tears. Thus did that woman in the Gospel, and wiped out the stench of her sin; thus did she wash away her fault, when washing the feet of Jesus with her tears.

67. Would that Thou, Lord Jesus, mightest reserve for me the washing off from Thy feet of the stains contracted since Thou walkest in me! O that Thou mightest offer to me to cleanse the pollution which I by my deeds have caused on Thy steps! But whence can I obtain living water, wherewith I may wash Thy feet? If I have no water I have tears, and whilst with them I wash Thy feet I trust to cleanse myself. Whence is it that Thou shouldst say to me: "His sins which are many are forgiven, because he loved much"? I confess that I owe more, and that more has been forgiven me who have been called to the priesthood from the tumult and strife of the law courts and the dread of public administration; and therefore I fear that I may be found ungrateful, if I, to whom more has been forgiven, love less.

68. But all are not able to equal that woman, who was deservedly preferred even to Simon, who was giving the feast to the Lord; who gave a lesson to all who desire to gain forgiveness, by kissing the feet of Christ, washing them with her tears, wiping them with her hair, and anointing them with ointment.

69. In a kiss is the sign of love, and therefore the Lord Jesus says: "Let her kiss Me with the kisses of her mouth." What is the meaning of the hair, but that you may learn that, having laid aside all the pomp of worldly trappings, you must implore pardon, throw yourself on the earth with tears, and prostrate on the ground move pity. In the ointment, too, is set forth the savour of a good conversation. David was a king, yet he said: "Every night will I wash my bed, I will water my couch with tears." And therefore he obtained such a favour, as that of his house the Virgin should be chosen, who by her child-bearing should bring forth Christ for us. Therefore is this woman also praised in the Gospel.

70. Nevertheless if we are unable to equal her, the Lord Jesus knows also how to aid the weak, when there is no one who can prepare the feast, or bring the ointment, or carry with her a spring of living water. He comes Himself to the sepulchre.

71. Would that Thou wouldst vouchsafe to come to this sepulchre of mine, O Lord Jesus, that Thou wouldst wash me with Thy tears, since in my hardened eyes I possess not such tears as to be able to wash away my offence. If Thou shalt weep for me I shall be saved; if I am worthy of Thy tears I shall cleanse the stench of all my offences; if I am worthy that Thou weep but a little, Thou wilt call me out of the tomb of this body and will say: "Come forth," that my

meditations may not be kept pent up in the narrow limits of this body, but may go forth to Christ, and move in the light, that I may think no more on works of darkness but on works of light. For he who thinks on sins endeavours to shut himself up within his own consciousness.

72. Call forth, then, Thy servant. Although bound with the chain of my sins I have my feet fastened and my hands tied; being now buried in dead thoughts and works, yet at Thy call I shall go forth free, and shall be found one of those sitting at Thy feast, and Thy house shall be filled with precious ointment. If Thou hast vouchsafed to redeem any one, Thou wilt preserve him. For it shall be said, "See, he was not brought up in the bosom of the Church, nor trained from childhood, but hurried from the judgment-seat, brought away from the vanities of this world, growing accustomed to the singing of the choir instead of the shout of the crier, but he continues in the priesthood not by his own strength, but by the grace of Christ, and sits among the guests at the heavenly table.

73. Preserve, O Lord, Thy work, guard the gift which Thou hast given even to him who shrank from it. For I knew that I was not worthy to be called a bishop, because I had devoted myself to this world, but by Thy grace I am what I am. And I am indeed the least of all bishops, and the lowest in merit; yet since I too have undertaken some labour for Thy holy Church, watch over this fruit, and let not him whom when lost Thou didst call to the priesthood, to be lost when a priest. And first grant that I may know how with inmost affection to mourn with those who sin; for this is a very great virtue, since it is written: "And thou shall not rejoice over the children of Judah in the day of their destruction, and speak not proudly in the day of their trouble." Grant that so often as the sin of any one who has fallen is made known to me I may suffer with him, and not chide him proudly, but mourn and weep, so that weeping over another I may mourn for myself, saying, "Tamar hath been more righteous than I."

74. Perchance a maiden may have fallen, deceived and hurried away by those occasions which are the sources of sins. Well, we who are older sin too. In us, too, the law of this flesh wars against the law of our mind, and makes us captives of sin, so that we do what we would not. Her youth is an excuse for her, I now have none, for she ought to learn, we ought to teach. So that "Tamar hath been more righteous than I."

75. We inveigh against some one's covetousness, let us call to mind whether we ourselves have never done anything covetously; and if we have, since covetousness is the root of all evils, and is working in our bodies like a serpent secretly under the earth, let each of us say: "Tamar hath been more righteous than I."

76. If we have been seriously moved against any one, a layman may act hastily for a smaller matter than a bishop. Let us ponder that with ourselves and say, He who is reproved for quick temper is more righteous than I. For if we thus speak, we guard ourselves against this, that the Lord Jesus or one of His disciples should say to us: "Thou beholdest the mote in thy brother's eye, but beholdest not the beam which is in thine own eye. Thou hypocrite, cast out first the beam out of thine own eye, and then shalt thou see to cast out the mote out of thy brother's eye."

77. Let us, then, not be ashamed to say that our fault is more serious than that of him whom we think we must reprove, for this is what Judah did who reprimanded Tamar, and remembering his own fault said: "Tamar is more righteous than I." In which saying there is a deep mystery and a moral precept; and therefore is his offence not reckoned to him, because he accused himself before he was accused by others.

78. Let us, then, not rejoice over the sin of any one, but rather let us mourn, for it is written: "Rejoice not against me, O my enemy, because I have fallen, for I shall arise; for if I sit in darkness the Lord shall be a light unto me, I will bear the indignation of the Lord, because I have sinned against Him, until He maintain my cause, and execute judgment for me, and bring me forth to the light. and I shall behold His righteousness. Mine enemy, too, shall see it and shall be covered with confusion, which said unto me, Where is the Lord thy God? Mine eyes shall behold her, and she shall be for treading down as the mire in the streets," And this not

unreservedly, for he who rejoices at the fall of another rejoices at the victory of the devil. Let us, then, rather mourn when we hear that one has perished for whom Christ died, Who despises not even the straw in time of harvest.

79. O that He may not cast away this straw at His harvest, the empty stalks of my produce; but may He gather it in, as is said by some one: "Woe is me, for I am become as one that gathereth straw in harvest, and grape gleanings in the vintage," that He may eat of the firstfruits at least of His grace in me, though He approve not the later fruit.

Chapter IX.

In what way faith is necessary for repentance. Means for paying our debts, in which work, prayer, tears, and fasting are of more value than money. Some instances are adduced, and St. Ambrose declares that generosity is profitable, but only when joined with faith; it is, moreover, liable to certain defects. He goes on to speak of some defects in repentance, such as too great haste in seeking reconciliation, considering abstinence from sacraments all that is needed, of committing sin in hope of repenting later.

80. So, then, it is fitting for us to believe both that sinners must repent and that forgiveness is to be given on repentance, yet still as hoping for forgiveness as granted upon faith, not as a debt, for it is one thing to earn, and an other presumptuously to claim a right. Faith asks for forgiveness, as it were, by covenant, but presumption is more akin to demand than to request. Pay first that which you owe, that you may be in a position to ask for what you have hoped. Come with the disposition of an honest debtor, that you may not contract a fresh liability, but may pay that which is due of the existing debt with the possessions of your faith.

81. He who owes a debt to God has more help towards payment than he whets indebted to man. Man requires money for money, and this is not always at the debtor's command. God demands the affection of the heart, which is in our own power. No one who owes a debt to God is poor, except one who has made himself poor. And even if he have nothing to sell, yet has he wherewith to pay. Prayer, fasting, and tears are the resources of an honest debtor, and much more abundant than if one from the price of his estate offered money without faith.

82. Ananias was poor, when after selling his land he brought the money to the apostles, and was not able with it to pay his debt, but involved himself the more. That widow was rich who cast her two small pieces into the treasury, of whom Christ said: "This poor widow hath cast in more than they all." For God requires not money but faith.

83. And I do not deny that sins may be l diminished by liberal gifts to the poor, but only if faith commend what is spent. For what would the giving of one's whole property benefit without charity?

84. There are some who aim at the credit of generosity for pride alone, because they wish thereby to gain the good opinion of the multitude for leaving nothing to themselves; but whilst they are seeking rewards in this life, they are laying up none for the life to come, and having received their reward here they cannot hope for it there.

85. Some again, having, through impulsive excitement and not after long consideration, given their possessions to the Church, think that they can claim them back. These gain neither the first nor the second reward, for the gift was made thoughtlessly, its recall sacrilegiously.

86. Some repent of having distributed their property to the poor. But they who are doing penance must not repent of this, lest they repent of their own repentance. For many seek for penance through fear of future punishment, being conscious of their sins, and having received their penance are held back by fear of the public entreaties. These persons seem to have sought for repentance for their evil deeds, but to exercise it for their good ones.

87. Some seek penance because they wish to be at once restored to communion. These wish not so much to loose themselves as to bind the priest, for they do not put off the guilt from their own conscience, but lay it on that of the priest, to whom the command is given: "Give not that which is holy to the dogs, neither cast your pearls before the swine;" that is to say, that partaking of the holy Communion is not to be allowed to those polluted with impurity.

88. And so one may see those walking in other attire, who ought to be weeping and groaning because they had defiled the robe of sanctification and grace; and women loading their ears with pearls, and weighing down their necks, who had better have bent to Christ than to gold, and who ought to be weeping for themselves, because they have lost the pearl from heaven.

89. There are, again, some who think that it is penitence to abstain from the heavenly sacraments. These are too cruel judges of themselves, who prescribe a penalty for themselves but refuse the remedy, who ought to be mourning over their self-imposed penalty, because it deprives them of heavenly grace.

90. Others think that licence is granted them to sin, because the hope of penitence is before them, whereas penitence is the remedy, not an incentive to sin. For the salve is necessary for the wound, not the wound for the salve, since a salve is sought because of the wound, the wound is not wished for on account of the salve. The hope which is put off to a future season is but feeble, for every season is uncertain, and hope does not outlive all time.

Chapter X.

In order to do away with the feeling of shame which holds back theguilty from public penance, St. Ambrose points out the advantage of prayers offered by the whole Church, and sets forth the example of saints who have sorrowed. Then, after reproving those who imagine that penance may be often repeated, he points on the difficulty of repentance, and how it is to be carried out.

91. Can any one endure that you should blush to entreat God, when you do not blush to entreat a man? That you should be ashamed to entreat Him Who knows you fully, when you are not ashamed to confess your sins to a man who knows you not? Do you shrink from witnesses and sympathizers in your prayers, when, if you have to satisfy a man, you must visit many and entreat them to be kind enough to intervene; when you throw yourself at a man's knees, kiss his feet, bring your children, still unconscious of guilt, to entreat also for their father's pardon? And you disdain to do this in the Church in order to entreat God, in order to gain for yourself the support of the holy congregation; where there is no cause for shame, except indeed not to confess, since we are all sinners, amongst whom he is the most praiseworthy who is the most humble; he is the most just who feels himself the lowest.

92. Let the Church, our Mother, weep for you, and wash away your guilt with her tears; let Christ see you mourning and say, "Blessed are ye that are sad, for ye shall rejoice." It pleases Him that many should entreat for one. In the Gospel, too, moved by the widow's tears, because many were weeping for her, He raised her son. He heard Peter more quickly when He raised Dorcas, because the poor were mourning over the death of the woman. He also forthwith forgave Peter, for he wept most bitterly. And if you weep bitterly Christ will look upon you and your guilt shall leave you. For the application of pain does away with the enjoyment of the wickedness and the delight of the sin. And so while mourning over our past sins we shut the door against fresh ones, and from the condemnation of our guilt there arises as it were a training in innocence.

93. Let, then, nothing call you away from penitence, for this you have in common with the saints, and would that such sorrowing for sin as that of the saints were copied by you. David, as it were, "ate ashes for bread, and mingled his drink with weeping," and therefore now rejoices the more because he wept the more: "Mine eyes ran down," he said, "with rivers of water."

94. John wept sore, and, as he tells us, the mysteries of Christ were revealed to him. But that woman who, when she was in sin and ought to have wept, nevertheless rejoiced, and covered herself with a robe of purple and scarlet, and adorned herself with much gold and precious stones, now mourns the misery of eternal weeping.

95. Deservedly are they blamed who think that they often do penance, for they are wanton against Christ. For if they went through their penance in truth, they would not think that it could be repeated again; for as there is but one baptism, so there is but one course of penance,

so far as the outward practice goes, for we must repent of our daily faults, but this latter has to do with lighter faults, the former with such as are graver.

96. But I have more easily found such as had preserved their innocence than such as had fittingly repented. Does any one think that that is penitence where there still exists the striving after earthly honours, where wine flows, and even conjugal connection takes place? The world must be renounced; less sleep must be indulged in than nature demands; it must be broken by groans, interrupted by sighs, put aside by prayers; the mode of life must be such that we die to the usual habits of life. Let the man deny himself and be wholly changed, as in the fable they relate of a certain youth, who left his home because of his love for a harlot, and, having subdued his love, returned; then one day meeting his old favourite and not speaking to her, she, being surprised and supposing that he had not recognized her, said, when they met again, "It is I." "But," was his answer, "I am not the former I."

97. Well then did the Lord say: "If any man will come after Me, let him deny himself, and take up his cross and follow Me." For they who are dead and buried in Christ ought not again to make their conclusions as though. living in the world. "Touch not," it is said, "nor attend to those things which tend to corruption by their very use, for the very customs of this life corrupt integrity."

Chapter XI.

The possibility of repentance is a reason why baptism should not be deferred to old age, a practice which is against the will of God in holy Scripture. But it is of no use to practise penance whilst still serving lusts. These must be first subdued.

98. Good, then, is penitence, and if there were no place for it, every one would defer the grace of cleansing by baptism to old age. And a sufficient reason is that it is better, to have a robe to mend, than none to put on; but as that which has been repaired once is restored, so that which is frequently mended is destroyed.

99. And the Lord has given a sufficient warning to those who put off repentance, when He says: "Repent ye, for the kingdom of heaven is at hand." We know not at what hour the thief will come, we know not whether our soul may be required of us this next night. God cast Adam out of Paradise immediately after his fault; there was no delay. At once the fallen were severed from all their enjoyments that they might do penance; at once God clothed them with garments of skins, not of silk.

100. And what reason is there for putting off is it that you may sin yet more? Then because God is good you are evil, and "despise the riches of His goodness and long-suffering." But the goodness of the Lord ought rather to draw you to repentance. Wherefore holy David says to all: "Come, let us worship and fall down beford Him, and mourn before our Lord Who made us." But for a sinner who has died without repentance, because nothing remains but to mourn grievously and to weep, you find him groaning and saying: "O my son Absalom I my son Absalom!" For him who is wholly dead mourning is without alleviation.

101. But of those who as exiles and banished from their ancestral homes, which the holy law of Moses had assigned them, will be entangled in the errors of the world, you hear him saying: "By the waters of Babylon we sat down and wept, when we remembered Zion." He sets forth the wailings of those who have fallen, and shows that they who are living in this condition of passing time and changing circumstances ought to repent, after the example of those who, as a reward for sin, had been led into miserable captivity.

102. But nothing causes such exceeding grief as when any one, lying under the captivity of sin, calls to mind whence he has fallen, because he turned aside to carnal and earthly things, instead of directing his mind in the beautiful ways of the knowledge of God.

103. So you find Adam concealing himself, when he knew that God was present, and wishing to be hidden when called by God with that voice which wounded the soul of him who was hiding: "Adam, where art thou?" That is to say, Wherefore hidest thou thyself? Why art

thou concealed? Why dost thou avoid Him, Whom thou once didst long to see? A guilty conscience is so burdensome that it punishes itself without a judge, and wishes for covering, and yet is bare before God.

104. And so no one in a state of sin ought to claim a right to or the use of the sacraments, for it is written: "Thou hast sinned, be still." As David says in the Psalm lately quoted: "We hanged our harps upon the willows in the midst thereof;" and again: "How shall we sing the Lord's song in a strange land?" For if the flesh wars against the mind, and is not subject to the guidance of the Spirit, that is a strange land which is not subdued by the toil of the cultivator, and so cannot produce the fruits of charity, patience, and peace. It is better, then, to be still when you cannot practise the works of repentance, lest in the very acts of repentance there be that which afterward will need further repentance. For if it be once entered upon and not rightly carried out, it obtains not the result of a first repentance and takes away the use of a later one.

105. When, then, the flesh resists, the soul must be intent upon God, and if results do not follow, let not faith fail. And if the enticements of the flesh come upon us, or the powers of the enemy attack us, let the soul keep in submission to God. For we are then specially oppressed when the flesh yields. And some there are who trouble heavily the wretched soul, seeking to deprive it of all protection. To which case the words apply: "Ruse it, ruse it, even to the foundations."

106. And David, pitying her,, says: "O wretched daughter of Babylon." Wretched indeed, as being the daughter of Babylon, when she ceased to be the daughter of Jerusalem. And yet he calls for a healer for her, and says: "Blessed is he who shall take thy little ones and dash them against the rock." That is to say, shall dash all corrupt and filthy thoughts against Christ, Who by His fear and His rebuke will break down all motions against reason, so as, if any one is seized by an adulterous love, to extinguish the fire, that he may by his zeal put away the love of a harlot, and deny himself that he may gain Christ.

107. We have then learned that we must do penance, and this at a time when the heat of luxury and sin is giving way; and that we, when under the dominion of sin, must show ourselves God fearing by refraining, rather than allowing ourselves in evil practices. For if it is said to Moses when he was desiring to draw nearer: "Put off thy shoes from off thy feet," how much more must we free the feet of our soul from the bonds of the body, and clear our steps from all connection with this world.

Note on the Penitential Discipline of the Early Church.

It was always believed in the Church that the power of binding and loosing had been entrusted by our Lord to His apostles, and by them handed on to their successors in the ministry. The earlier practice would seem to have been short and simple: exclusion from Communion, some outward discipline, not always continued for a long period, and reconciliation on true repentance, these matters being decided by the bishop at his discretion. Gradually the practice became more systematized, various periods of discipline were prescribed for various sins, and the time for this discipline was lengthened.

There were three parts in the discipline of Penitence as a whole:

1. Confession, exomologhsi", a term used frequently of the whole course.
2. Penance, properly so called, i.e. the mortifications, fasting, etc., prescribed.
3. Reconciliation, performed solemnly by the bishop, often at Easter.

The confession was probably in private to the bishop, who determined whether any public confession should be made or not. But as only great sins—at first, idolatry, adultery, and murder (*peccata mortalia*)—were punished by outward penance, it was clear that the sin must have been very grievous.

The Montanists taught that the Church had not power to forgive great sins, and this led to clearing the doctrine, and from the middle of the third century, even those who had lapsed into idolatry were admitted to penance.

Hermas already says: toi" douloi" touqeou metanoia esti mia *Mand.* iv. 1. And this rule seems to have been maintained as regards the formal penance and reconciliation, not as implying doubt of possible forgiveness, but as a matter of discipline, and this rule deprived those who fell a second time from communion at least till their deathbed.

For this public penance the Greek words are metanoia and exomologhsi"; the Latin, *penitentia* and frequently *exomologesis*. As the word *penitentia* includes not merely sorrow for sin and change of heart, but also penance, or the penalty inflicted by authority, and is used in such phrases as *penitentiam agere* or *facere*, it has been necessary in the translation of the *De Penitentia* to vary the English terms, and to use sometimes repentance, sometimes penance.

For further information on this subject, the reader is referred specially to the Articles, Buss-Disciplin, in the *Freiburg Kirchen-Lexikon*, by Wetzer and Welte; and to those on Exomologesis, Penitence, and Reconciliation, in the *Dict. of Christian Antiquities*, where other authorities and references will be found.

Concerning Virgins. Introduction.

The state of Virginity is undoubtedly commended in holy Scripture, both by our Lord and St. Paul, but learned men have differed in their opinions as to the original customs and rules observed by virgins in the earliest ages. Some suppose that from the very beginning it was the custom for them to make a solemn profession of the virgin life, and to live together in common. Others consider that their vows were private, and they lived sometimes together, sometimes in the homes of their parents. Others, again, believing that there was no more than a simple purpose on the part of the virgins signified by the veil, and the simplicity of their dress, attribute the first commencements of communitylife to St. Ambrose himself.

The first opinion is hardly tenable as regards any profession which was notorious. Statements in the earlier Acts of Martyrs are to be regarded with suspicion, as so much of this class of writings is spurious. The utterances also of Fathers and Councils hardly establish anything on this point more than on the second mentioned above.

There would seem to have been some who publicly, like Marcellina, the sister of St. Ambrose, made their profession, and formally received the veil at the hands of the Bishop; and others, equally steadfast in purpose, whose vow of virginity was made in private. Of the former, those living in Milan hardly seem to have led a life in common, but at Bologna [I. 60] they did. The terms, vow, taking the veil, and profession, were in use in St. Ambrose's day, as at present.

It would appear, then, that from the days of the apostles there were some who devoted themselves to God in a life of chastity, and that later on the promise or vow was made in the presence of others—the bishop, clergy, and friends. These virgins lived at home with their parents, whilst the times of persecution endured, making it practically impossible for them to live elsewhere. Common life amongst them would seem to have commenced in the East, and St. Athanasius, when, seeking refuge from the Arians, he came to Rome, introduced the custom to the Western Church.

St. Ambrose worked vigorously in this direction, not only in his own diocese, but in neighbouring provinces, and even in Africa. Early in his episcopate he addressed his flock on the subject, and at the request of his sister, Marcellina, gathered up his teachingin the following three books.

In the first book he treats of the dignity of Virginity, and states his reason for writing. As he commences his addresses on the anniversary of the martyrdom of St. Agnes, he takes her story as the subject of the earlier part of the treatise, and shows how, amongst the Jews, and even amongst the heathen, the grace of virginity was shadowed forth, and eventually proclaimed by the corning of our Lord. He then warns parents, especially widows, not to prevent their daughters from hearing addresses on this subject, and touches on the number of those who came even from great distances to receive the veil at Milan.

In the second book, speaking of the character and manner of life of virgins, he does this, as he says, by adducing examples and instances, preferably to laying down a code of rules. He speaks of Thecla, patron saint of Milan, a disciple of St. Paul, and of other virgins.

In the third book he goes through a summary of the address given by Pope Liberius, when Marcellina received the veil at his hands, before a large congregation. Some cautions are introduced by St. Ambrose against excessive austerity, and instead of some outward acts, prayer and the practice of interior virtues are recommended. The subject of certain virgins who had committed suicide rather than lose their chastity is dwelt upon in answer to a question of Marcellina.

The writer himself states that this treatise was composed in the third year of his episcopate, a.d. 377, and it is quoted with approval by St. Jerome, Ep. XXII. 22 and XLVIII. 14 [Vol. VI., pp. 31 and 75, of this series, and St. Augustine, *de doct. Christ.* IV. 48, 50.

THREE BOOKS CONCERNING VIRGINS

To Marcellina, His Sister.

BOOK I.

Chapter I.

St. Ambrose, reflecting upon the account he will have to give of his talents, determines to write, and consoles himself with certain examples of God's mercy. Then recognizing his own deficiencies desires that he may be dealt with like the fig-tree in the Gospel, and expresses a hope that words will not fail him in his endeavour to preach Christ.

1. If, according to the decree of heavenly truth, we have to give account of every idle word which we have spoken, and if every servant will incur no small blame when his lord returns, who, either like a timid money-lender or covetous owner, has hidden in the earth the talents of spiritual grace which were entrusted to him in order that they might be multiplied by increasing interest, I, who, although possessed of but moderate ability, yet have a great necessity laid on me of making increase of the sayings of God entrusted to me, must rightly fear lest an account of the profit of my words be demanded of me, especially seeing that the Lord exacts of us effort, not profit. Wherefore I determined to write something, since, too, my words are listened to with greater risk to modesty than when they are written, for a book has no feeling of modesty.

2. And so distrusting indeed my own ability, but encouraged by the instances of divine mercy, I venture to compose an address, for when God willed even the ass spoke. And I will open my mouth long dumb, that the angel may assist me also, engaged in the burdens of this world, for He can do away with the hindrances of unskilfulness. Who in the ass did away those of nature. In the ark of the Old Testament the priest's rod budded; with God it is easy that in Holy Church a flower should spring from our knots also. And why should we despair that God should speak in men, Who spoke in the thorn bush? God did not despise the bush, and would He might give light also to my thorns. Perhaps some may wonder that there is some light even in our thorns; some our thorns will not burn; there will be some whose shoes shall be put off their feet at the sound of my voice, that the steps of the mind may be freed from bodily hindrances.

3. But these things are gained by holy men. Would that Jesus would cast a glance upon me still lying under that barren fig-tree, and that my fig-tree might also after three years bear fruit. But whence should sinners have so great hope? Would that at least that Gospel dresser of the vineyard, perhaps already bidden to cut down my fig-tree, would let it alone this year also, until he dig about it and dung it, that he may perchance lift the helpless out of the dust, and lift the poor out of the mire. Blessed are they who bind their horses under the vine and olive, consecrating the course of their labours to light and joy: the fig-tree, that is, the tempting attraction of the pleasures of the world, still overshadows me, low in height, brittle for working, soft for use, and barren of fruit.

4. And perhaps some one may wonder why I, who cannot speak, venture to write. And yet if we consider what we read in the writings of the Gospel, and the deeds of the priests, and the holy prophet Zacharias is taken as an instance, he will find that there is something which the voice cannot explain, but the pen can write. And if the name John restored speech to his father, I, too, ought not to despair that although dumb I may yet receive speech, if I speak of Christ, of Whom, according to the prophet's word: "Who shall declare the generation?" And so as a servant I will announce the family of the Lord, for the Lord has consecrated to Himself a family even in this body of humanity replete with frailty.

Chapter II.

This treatise has a favourable beginning, since it is the birthday of the holy Virgin Agnes, of whose name, modesty, and martyrdom St. Ambrose speaks in commendation, but more especially of her age, seeing that she, being but twelve years old, was superior to terrors, promises, tortures, and death itself, with a courage wholly worthy of a man.

5. And my task begins favourably, that since to-day is the birthday of a virgin, I have to speak of virgins, and the treatise has its beginning from this discourse. It is the birthday of a martyr, let us offer the victim. It is the birthday of St. Agnes, let men admire, let children take courage, let the married be astounded, let the unmarried take an example. But what can I say worthy of her whose very name was not devoid of bright praise? In devotion beyond her age, in virtue above nature, she seems to me to have borne not so much a human name, as a token of martyrdom, whereby she showed what she was to be.

6. But I have that which may assist me. The name of virgin is a title of modesty. I will call upon the martyr, I will proclaim the virgin. That panegyric is long enough which needs no elaboration, but is within our grasp. Let then labour cease, eloquence be silent. One word is praise enough. This word old men and young and boys chant. No one is more praiseworthy than he who can be praised by all There are as many heralds as there are men, who when they speak proclaim the martyr.

7. She is said to have suffered martyrdom when twelve years old. The more hateful was the cruelty, which spared not so tender an age, the greater in truth was the power of faith which found evidence even in that age. Was there room for a wound in that small body? And she who had no room for the blow of the steel had that wherewith to conquer the steel. But maidens of that age are unable to bear even the angry looks of parents, and are wont to cry at the pricks of a needle as though they were wounds. She was fearless under the cruel hands of the executioners, she was unmoved by the heavy weight of the creaking chains, offering her whole body to the sword of the raging soldier, as yet ignorant of death, but ready for it. Or if she were unwillingly hurried to the altars, she was ready to stretch forth her hands to Christ at the sacrificial fires, and at the sacrilegious altars themselves, to make the sign of the Lord the Conqueror, or again to place her neck and both her hands in the iron bands, but no band could enclose such slender limbs.

8. A new kind of martyrdom! Not yet of fit age for punishment but already ripe for victory, difficult to contend with but easy to be crowned, she filled the office of teaching valour while having the disadvantage of youth. She would not as a bride so hasten to the couch, as being a virgin she joyfully went to the place of punishment with hurrying step, her head not adorned with plaited hair, but with Christ. All wept, she alone was without a tear. All wondered that she was so readily prodigal of her life, which she had not yet enjoyed, and now gave up as though she had gone through it. Every one was astounded that there was now one to bear witness to the Godhead, who as yet could not, because of her age, dispose of herself. And she brought it to pass that she should be believed concerning God, whose evidence concerning man would not be accepted. For that which is beyond nature is from the Author of nature.

9. What threats the executioner used to make her fear him, what allurements to persuade her, how many desired that she would come to them in marriage! But she answered: "It would be an injury to my spouse to look on any one as likely to please me. He who chose me first for Himself shall receive me. Why are you delaying, executioner? Let this body perish which can be loved by eyes which I would not." She stood, she prayed, she bent down her neck. You could see the executioner tremble, as though he himself had been condemned, and his right hand shake, his face grow pale, as he feared the peril of another, while the maiden feared not for her own. You have then in one victim a twofold martyrdom, of modesty and of religion. She both remained a virgin and she obtained martyrdom.

Chapter III.

Virginity is praised on many grounds, but chiefly because it brought down the Word from heaven, and hence its pursuit, which existed in but few under the old covenant, has spread to countless numbers.

10. And now the love of purity draws me on, and you, my holy sister, even though not speaking in your silent habit, to say something about virginity, test that which is a principal virtue should seem to be passed by with only a slight reference. For virginity is not praiseworthy because it is found in martyrs, but because itself makes martyrs.

11. But who can comprehend that by human understanding which not even nature has included in her laws? Or who can explain in ordinary language that which is above the course of nature? Virginity has brought from heaven that which it may imitate on earth. And not unfittingly has she sought her manner of life from heaven, who has found for herself a Spouse in heaven. She, passing beyond the clouds, air, angels, and stars, has found the Word of God in the very bosom of the Father, and has drawn Him into herself with her whole heart. For who having found so great a Good would forsake it? For "Thy Name is as ointment poured out, therefore have the maidens loved Thee, and drawn Thee." And indeed what I have said is not my own, since they who marry not nor are given in marriage are as the angels in heaven. Let us not, then, be surprised if they are compared to the angels who are joined to the Lord of angels. Who, then, can deny that this mode of life has its source in heaven, which we don't easily find on earth, except since God came down into the members of an earthly body? Then a Virgin conceived, and the Word became flesh that flesh might become God.

12. But some one will say: "But Elijah is seen to have had nothing to do with the embraces of bodily love." And therefore was he carried by a chariot into heaven, therefore he appeared glorified with the Lord, and therefore he is to come as the forerunner of the Lord's advent. And Miriam taking the timbrel led the dances with maidenly modesty. But consider whom she was then representing. Was she not a type of the Church, who as a virgin with unstained spirit joins together the religious gatherings of the people to sing divine songs? For we read that there were virgins appointed also in the temple at Jerusalem. But what says the Apostle? "These things happened to them in a figure, that they might be signs of what was to come." For the figure is shown in few, the life exists in many.

13. But in truth after that the Lord, coming in our flesh, joined together the Godhead and flesh without any confusion or mixture, then the practice of the life of heaven spreading throughout the whole world was implanted in human bodies. This is that which angels ministering on earth signified should come to pass, which ministry should be offered to the Lord with the service of an unstained body. This is that heavenly service which the host of rejoicing angels spoke of for the earth, We have, then, the authority of antiquity from of old, the fulness of the setting forth from Christ Himself.

Chapter IV.

The comeliness of virginity never existed amongst the heathen, neither with the vestal virgins, nor amongst philosophers, such as Pythagoras.

14. I Certainly have not this in common with the heathen, nor in regard to it am I associated with barbarians, nor practise it with other animals, with whom, although we breathe one and the same vital air, and have a common condition of an earthly body, and from whom we differ not in the mode of generation, in this point alone we nevertheless avoid the reproach of likeness, that virginity is aimed at by the heathen, but when consecrated it is violated, it is attacked by barbarians, and is unknown to others.

15. Who will allege to me the virgins of Vesta. and the priests of Pallas? What sort of chastity is that which is not of morals, but of years, which is appointed not for ever, but for a term! Such purity is all the more wanton of which the corruption is put off for a later age. They teach their virgins ought not to persevere, and are unable to do so, who have set a term to virginity. What sort of a religion is that in which modest maidens are bidden to be immodest old women? Nor

is she modest who is bound by law, and she immodest who is set free by law. O the mystery! O the morals! where chastity is enforced by law and authority given for lust! And so she is not chaste, who is constrained by fear; nor honourable, who is hired for a price; nor is that modesty which, exposed to the daily importunity of lascivious eyes, is attacked by disgraceful looks. Exemptions are bestowed upon them, prices are offered them, as though to sell one's chastity were not the greatest sign of wantonness. That which is promised for a price is given up for a price; is made over for a price; is considered to have its price. She who is wont to sell her chastity knows not how to redeem it.

16. What shall I say of the Phrygian rites, in which immodesty is the rule, and that too of the weaker sex? What of the orgies of Bacchus, where the mystery of the rites is an incentive to lust? Of what sort can the lives of priests be, then, where the adulteries of the gods are matters of religion. So then they have no sacred virgins.

17. Let us see whether perchance the precepts of philosophers have formed any, for they are wont to claim the teaching of all virtues. A certain Pythagorean virgin is spoken of in story, whom a tyrant was endeavouring to compel to reveal the secret, and lest it should be possible even in her torments for revelation to be extorted from her, she bit off her tongue and spat it in the tyrant's face, that he who would not make an end of questioning might not have aught to question.

18. But that same virgin, so constant in mind, was overcome by lust, though she could not be overcome by torments. And so she who could keep the secret of her mind could not conceal the shame of her body. She overcame nature, but observed not discipline. How she would desire that her speech had existed as a defence of her chastity! So she was not unconquered on every side, for although the tyrant could not find out that which he sought, yet he did find what he sought not.

19. How much stronger are our virgins, who overcome even those powers which they do not see; whose victory is not only over flesh and blood, but also over the prince of this world, and ruler of this age! In age, Agnes indeed was less, but in virtue greater, triumphing over more, more constant in her confidence; she did not destroy her tongue through fear, but kept it for a trophy. For there was nothing in her which she feared to betray, since that which she acknowledged was holy, not sinful. And so the former merely concealed her secret, the latter bore witness to the Lord, and confessed Him in her body, Whom her age did not yet suffer to confess.

Chapter V.

Heaven is the home of virginity, and the Son of God its Author, Who though He was a Virgin before the Virgin, yet bein of the Virgin took the Virgin Church as His bride. Of her we have

all been born. Some of her gifts are enumerated. Her daughters have a special excellence in that virginity is not a matter of precept, and that it is a most powerful help in the pursuit of piety.

20. It is the custom in encomiums to speak of country and parentage of the subject, that the greatness of the offspring may be enhanced by mention of the father. Now I, who have not undertaken to praise but to set forth virginity, yet think it to the purpose to make known its country and its parent. First, let us settle where is its country. Now, if one's country be there where is the home of one's birth, without doubt heaven is the native country of chastity. And so she is a stranger here, but a denizen there.

21. And what is virginal chastity but purity free from stain? And whom can we judge to be its author but the immaculate Son of God, Whose flesh saw no corruption, Whose Godhead experienced no infection?. Consider, then, how great are the merits of virginity. Christ was before the Virgin, Christ was of the Virgin. Begotten indeed of the Father before the ages, but born of the Virgin for the ages. The former was of His own nature, the latter is for our benefit. The former always was, the latter He willed.

22. Consider, too, another merit of virginity. Christ is the spouse of the Virgin, and if one may so say of virginal chastity, for virginity is of Christ, not Christ of virginity. He is, then, the Virgin Who was espoused, the Virgin Who bare us, Who fed us with her own milk, of whom we read: "How great things hath the virgin of Jerusalem done! The teats shall not fail from the rock, nor snow from Lebanon, nor the water which is borne by the strong wind." Who is this virgin that is watered with the streams of the Trinity, from whose rock waters flow, whose teats fail not, and whose honey is poured forth? Now, according to the Apostle, the rock is Christ. Therefore, from Christ the teats fail not, nor brightness from God, nor the river from the Spirit. This is the Trinity which waters their Church, the Father, Christ, and the Spirit.

23. But let us now come down from the mother to the daughters. "Concerning virgins," says the Apostle, "I have no commandment of the Lord." If the teacher of the Gentiles had none, who could have one? And in truth he had no commandment, but he had an example. For virginity cannot be commanded, but must be wished for, for things which are above us are matters for prayer rather than under mastery. "But I would have you," he says, "be without carefulness. For he who is without a wife is careful for the things which are the Lord's, how he may please God.... And the virgin taketh thought for the things of the Lord, that she may be holy in body and in spirit. For she that is married taketh thought for the things of the world, how she may please her husband."

Chapter VI.

St. Ambrose explains that he is not speaking against marriage, and proceeds to compare the advantages and disadvantages of the single and married state.

24. I Am not indeed discouraging marriage, but am enlarging upon the benefits of virginity. "He who is weak," says the Apostle, "eateth herbs." I consider one thing necessary, I admire another. "Art thou bound to a wife? Seek not to be loosed. Art thou free from a wife? Seek not a wife." This is the command to those who are. But what does he say concerning virgins? "He who giveth his virgin in marriage doeth well, and he who giveth her not doeth better." The one sins not if she marries, the other, if she marries not, it is for eternity. In the former is the remedy for weakness, in the latter the glory of chastity. The former is not reproved, the latter is praised.

25. Let us compare, if it pleases you, the advantages of married women with that which awaits virgins. Though the noble woman boasts of her abundant offspring, yet the more she bears the more she endures. Let her count up the comforts of her children, but let her likewise count up the troubles. She marries and weeps. How many vows does she make with tears. She conceives, and her fruitfulness brings her trouble before offspring. She brings forth and is ill. How sweet a pledge which begins with danger and ends in danger. which will cause pain before pleasure! It is purchased by perils, and is not possessed at her own will.

26. Why speak of the troubles of nursing, training, and marrying? These are the miseries of those who are fortunate. A mother has heirs, but it increases her sorrows. For we must not speak of adversity, lest the minds of the holiest parents tremble. Consider, my sister, how hard it must be to bear what one must not speak of. And this is in this present age. But the days shall come when they shall say: "Blessed are the barren, and the wombs that never bare." For the daughters of this age are conceived, and conceive; but the daughter of the kingdom refrains from wedded pleasure, and the pleasure of the flesh, that she may be holy in body and in spirit.

27. Why should I further speak of the painful ministrations and services due to their husbands from wives, to whom before slaves God gave the command to serve? And I mention these things that they may comply more willingly, whose reward, if approved, is love; if not approved, punishment for the fault.

28. And in this position spring up those incentives to vice, in that they paint their faces with various colours, fearing not to please their husbands; and from staining their faces, come to think of staining their chastity. What madness is here, to change the fashion of nature and seek a painting, and while fearing a husband's judgment to give up their own. For she is the first to

speak against herself who wishes to change that which is natural to her. So, while studying to please others, she displeases herself. What truer witness to thy unsightliness do we require, O woman, than thyself who art afraid to be seen? If thou art beautiful, why hidest thou thyself? If unsightly, why dost thou falsely pretend to beauty, so as to have neither the satisfaction of thy own conscience, nor of the error of another? For he loves another, thou desirest to please another. And art thou angry if he love another, who is taught to do so in thy own person? Thou art an evil teacher of thy own injury.

29. And next, what expense is necessary that even a beautiful wife may not fail to please? Costly necklaces on the one hand hang on her neck, on the other a robe woven with gold is dragged along the ground. Is this display purchased, or is it a real possession? And what varied enticements of perfumes are made use of! The ears are weighed down with gems, a different colour from nature is dropped into the eyes. What is there left which is her own, when so much is changed? The married woman loves her own perceptions, and does she think that this is to live?

30. But you, O happy virgins, who know not such torments, rather than ornaments, whose holy modesty, beaming in your bashful cheeks, and sweet chastity are a beauty, ye do not, intent upon the eyes of men, consider as merits what is gained by the errors of others. You, too, have indeed your own beauty, furnished by the comeliness of virtue, not of the body, to which age puts not an end, which death cannot take away, nor any sickness injure. Let God alone be sought as the judge of loveliness, Who loves even in less beautiful bodies the more beautiful souls. You know nothing of the burden and pain of childbearing, but more are the offspring of a pious soul, which esteems all as its children, which is rich in successors, barren of all bereavements, which knows no deaths, but has many heirs.

31. So the holy Church, ignorant of wedlock, but fertile in bearing, is in chastity a virgin, yet a mother in offspring. She, a virgin, bears us her children, not by a human father, but by the Spirit. She bears us not with pain, but with the rejoicings of the angels. She, a virgin, feeds us, not with the milk of the body, but with that of the Apostle, wherewith he fed the tender age of the people who were still children. For what bride has more children than holy Church, who is a virgin in her sacraments and a mother to her people, whose fertility even holy Scripture attests, saying, "For many more are the children of the desolate than of her that hath an husband"? She has not an husband, but she has a Bridegroom, inasmuch as she, whether as the Church amongst nations, or as the soul in individuals, without any loss of modesty, she weds the Word of God as her eternal Spouse, free from all injury, full of reason.

Chapter VII.

St. Ambrose exhorts parents to train their children to virginity, and sets before them the troubles arising from their desire to have grandchildren. He says however that he does not forbid marriage, but rather defends it against heretics who oppose it. Still setting virginity before marriage, he speaks of the beauty of their spouse, and of the gifts wherewith He adorns them, and applies to these points certain vetoes of the Song of Songs.

32. You have heard, O parents, in what virtues and pursuits you ought to train your daughters, that you may possess those by whose merits your faults may be redeemed. The virgin is an offering for her mother, by whose daily sacrifice the divine power is appeased. A virgin is the inseparable pledge of her parents, who neither troubles them for a dowry, nor forsakes them, nor injures them in word or deed.

33. But some one perhaps wishes to have grandchildren, and to be called grandfather. In the first place, such a one gives up what is his own, while seeking what is another's, and is already losing what is certain, while hoping to gain what is uncertain; he gives away his own riches, and still more is asked for; if he does not pay the dowry, it is exacted; if he lives long, he becomes a burden. This is to buy a son-in-law, not to gain one who would sell a sight of their daughter to her parents. Was she borne so long in her mother's womb in order that she might pass under

the power of another? And so the parents take the charge of setting off their virgin that she may so be the sooner removed from them.

34. Some one may say, Do you, then, discourage marriage? Nay, I encourage it, and condemn those who are wont to discourage it, so much so, that indeed I am wont to speak of the marriages of Sarah, Rebecca, and Rachel, and other women of old time, as instances of singular virtues. For he who condemns marriage, condemns the birth of children, and condemns the fellowship of the human race, continued by a series of successive generations. For how could generation succeed generation in a continual order, unless the gift of marriage stirred up the desire of offspring? Or how could one set forth that Isaac went to the altar of God as a victim of his father's piety, or that Israel, when yet in the body, saw God, and gave a holy name to the people while speaking against that whereby they came into being? Those men, though wicked, have one point at any rate, wherein they are up-proved even by the wise persons, that in speaking against marriage they declare that they ought not to have been born.

35. I do not then discourage marriage, but recapitulate the advantages of holy virginity. This is the gift of few only, that is of all. And virginity itself cannot exist, unless it have some mode of coming into existence. I am comparing good things with good things, that it may be clear which is the more excellent. Nor do I allege any opinion of my own, but I repeat that which the Holy Spirit spake by the prophet: "Blessed is the barren that is undefiled."

36. First of all, in that which those who purpose to marry desire above all things, that they may boast of the beauty of their husband, they must of necessity confess that they are inferior to virgins, to Whom alone it is suitable to say: "Thou art fairer than the children of men, grace is poured on Thy lips." Who is that Spouse? One not given to common indulgences, not proud of possessing riches, but He Whose throne is for ever and ever. The king's daughters share in His honour: "At Thy right hand stood the queen in a vesture of gold, clothed with variety of virtues. Hearken, then, O daughter, and consider, and incline thine ear, and forget thine own people and thy father's house; for the king hath desired thy beauty, for He is thy God."

37. And observe what a kingdom the Holy Spirit by the witness of the divine Scriptures has assigned to thee—gold, and beauty; gold, either because thou art the bride of the Eternal King, or because having an unconquered mind, thou art not taken captive by the allurements of pleasures, but rulest over them like a queen. Gold again, because as that metal is more precious when tried by fire, so the appearance of the virginal body, consecrated to the Divine Spirit, gains an increase of its own comeliness, for who can imagine a loveliness greater than the beauty of her who is loved by the King, approved by the judge, dedicated to the Lord, consecrated to God; ever a bride, ever unmarried, so that neither does love suffer an ending, nor modesty loss.

38. This is indeed true beauty, to which nothing is wanting, which alone is worthy to hear the Lord saying: "Thou art all fair, My love, and no blemish is in thee. Come hither from Lebanon, My spouse, come hither from Lebanon. Thou shalt pass and pass through from the beginning of faith, from the top of Sanir and Hermon, from the dens of the lions, from the mountains of the leopards." By which references is set forth the perfect and irreproachable beauty of a virgin soul, consecrated to the altars of God, not moved by perishable things amidst the haunts and dens of spiritual wild beasts, but intent, by the mysteries of God, on being found worthy of the Beloved, Whose breasts are full of joy. For "wine maketh glad the heart of man."

39. "The smell of thy garments," says He, "is above all spices." And again: "And the smell of thy garments is like the smell of Lebanon." See what progress thou settest forth, O Virgin. Thy first odour is above all spices, which were used upon the burying of the Saviour, and the fragrance arises from the mortified motions of the body, and the perishing of the delights of the members. Thy second odour, like the odour of Lebanon, exhales the incorruption of the Lord's body, the flower of virginal chastity.

Chapter VIII.

Taking the passage concerning the honeycomb in the Song of Songs, he expounds it, comparing the sacred virgins to bees.

40. Let, then, your work be as it were a honeycomb, for virginity is fit to be compared to bees, so laborious is it, so modest, so continent. The bee feeds on dew, it knows no marriage couch, it makes honey. The virgin's dew is the divine word, for the words of God descend like the dew. The virgin's modesty is unstained nature. The virgin's produce is the fruit of the lips, without bitterness, abounding in sweetness. They work in common, and their fruit is in common.

41. How I wish you, my daughter, to be an imitator of these bees, whose food is flowers, whose offspring is collected and brought together by the mouth. Do imitate her, my daughter. Let no veil of deceit be spread over your words; let them have no covering of guile, that they may be pure, and full of gravity.

42. And let an eternal succession of merits be brought forth by your mouth. Gather not for yourself alone (for how do you know when your soul shall be required of you?), lest leaving your granaries heaped full with corn, which will be a help neither to your life nor to your merits, you be hurried thither where you cannot take your treasure with you. Be rich then, but towards the poor, that as they share in your nature they may also share your goods.

43. And I also point out to you what flower is to be culled, that one it is Who said: "I am the Flower of the field, and the Lily of the valleys, as a lily among thorns," which is a plain declaration that virtues are surrounded by the thorns of spiritual wickedness, so that no one can gather the fruit who does not approach with caution.

Chapter IX.

Other passages from the Song of Songs are considered with relation to the present subject, and St. Ambrose exhorting the virgin to seek for Christ, points out where He may be found. A description of His perfections follows, and a comparison is made between virgins and the angels.

44. Take, then, O Virgin, the wings of the Spirit, that you may fly far above all vices, if you wish to attain to Christ: "He dwelleth on high, but beholdeth lowly things;" and His appearance is as that of a cedar of Lebanon, which has its foliage in the clouds, its roots in the earth. For its beginning is from heaven, its ending on earth, and it produces fruit very close to heaven. Search diligently for so precious a flower, if perchance you may find it in the recesses of your breast, for it is most often to be enjoyed in lowly places.

45. It loves to grow in gardens, in which Susanna, while walking, found it, and was ready to die rather than it should be violated. But what is meant by the gardens He Himself points out, saying: "A garden enclosed is My sister, My spouse, a garden enclosed, a fountain sealed;" because in gardens of this kind the water of the pure fountain shines, reflecting the features of the image of God, test its streams mingled with mud from the wallowing places of spiritual wild beasts should be polluted. For this reason, too, that modesty of virgins fenced in by the wall of the Spirit is enclosed lest it should lie open to be plundered. And so as a garden inaccessible from without smells of the violet is scented with the olive, and is resplendent with the rose, that religion may increase in the vine, peace in the olive, and the modesty of consecrated virginity in the rose. This is the odour of which the patriarch Jacob smelt when he heard his father say: "See the smell of my son is as the smell of a field which is full." For although the field of the holy patriarch was full of almost all fruits, the other brought forth its crops with greater labour, the latter flowers.

46. To work, then, O Virgin, and if you wish your garden to be sweet after this sort, enclose it with the precepts of the prophets: "Set a watch before thy mouth, and a door to thy lips," that you, too, may be able to say: "As the apple-tree among the trees of the wood, so is my Beloved among the sons. In His shadow I delighted and sat down, and His fruit was sweet to my palate. I found Him Whom my soul loved, I held Him and would not let him go. My beloved came

down into His garden to eat the fruit of His trees. Come, my Beloved, let us go forth into the field. Set me as a signet upon Thine heart, and as a seal upon Thine arm. My Beloved is white and ruddy." For it is fitting, O Virgin, that you should fully know Him Whom you love, and should recognize in Him all the mystery of His Divine Nature and the Body which He has assumed. He is white fittingly, for He is the brightness of the Father; and ruddy, for He was born of a Virgin. The colour of each nature shines and glows in Him. But remember that the marks of His Godhead are more ancient in Him than the mysteries of His body, for He did not take His origin from the Virgin, but, He Who already existed came into the Virgin.

47. He Who was spoiled by the soldiers, Who was wounded by the spear, that He might heal us by the blood of His sacred wounds, will assuredly answer you (for He is meek and lowly of heart, and gentle in aspect): "Arise, O north wind, and come, O south, and blow upon My garden, that My spices may flow out." For from all parts of the world has the perfume of holy religion increased, and the limbs of the consecrated Virgin have glowed. "Thou art beautiful, O my love, as Tirzah, comely as Jerusalem." So it is not the beauty of the perishable body, which will come to an end with sickness or old age, but the reputation for good deserts, subject to no accidents and never to perish, which is the beauty of virgins.

48. And since you are worthy to be compared not now with men but with heavenly beings, whose life you are living on earth, receive from the Lord the precepts you are to observe: "Set Me as a signet upon thine heart, and as a seal upon thine arm;" that clearer proofs of your prudence and actions may be set forth, in which Christ the Figure of God may shine, Who, equalling fully the nature of the Father, has expressed the whole which He took of the Father's Godhead. Whence also the Apostle Paul says that we are sealed in the Spirit; since we have in the Son the image of the Father, and in the Spirit the seal of the Son. Let us, then, sealed by this Trinity, take more diligent heed, lest either levity of character or the deceit of any unfaithfulness unseal the pledge which we have received in our hearts.

49. But let fear secure this for the holy virgins, for whom the Church first provided such protection, who, anxious for the prosperity of her tender offspring, herself as a wall with breasts as many towers, increases her care for them, until, the fear of hostile attack being at an end, she obtains by the care of a mother's love peace for her vigorous children. Wherefore the prophet says: "Peace be on thy virtue, and abundance in thy towers."

50. Then the Lord of peace Himself, after having embraced in His strong arms the vineyards committed to Him, and beholding their shoots putting forth buds, with glad looks, tempers the breezes to the young fruits, as Himself testifies, saying: "My vineyard is in My sight, a thousand for Solomon, and two hundred who keep the fruit thereof."

51. Above it is said: "Sixty strong men round about its offspring, armed with drawn swords, and expert in warlike discipline," here there are a thousand and two hundred. The number has increased, where the fruit has increased, for the more holy each is, the more is he guarded. So Elisha the prophet showed the hosts of angels who were present to guard him; so Joshua the son of Nun recognized the Captain of the heavenly host. They, then, who are able also to fight for us are able to guard the fruit that is in us. And for you, holy virgins, there is a special guardianship, for you who with unspotted chastity keep the couch of the Lord holy. And no wonder if the angels fight for you who war with the mode of life of angels. Virginal chastity merits their guardianship whose life it attains to.

52. Why should I continue the praise of chastity in more words? For chastity has made even angels. He who has preserved it is an angel; he who has lost it a devil. And hence has religion also gained its name. She is a virgin who is the bride of God, a harlot who makes gods for herself. What shall I say of the resurrection of which you already hold the rewards: "For in the resurrection they will neither be given in marriage, nor marry, but shall be," He says, "as the angels in heaven." That which is promised to us is already present with you, and the object of your prayers is with you; ye are of this world, and yet not in this world. This age has held you, but has not been able to retain you.

389

53. But what a great thing it is that angels because of incontinence fell from heaven into this world, that virgins because of chastity passed from the world into heaven. Blessed virgins, whom the delights of the flesh do not allure, nor the defilement of pleasures cast down. Sparing food and abstinence in drink train them in ignorance of vices, seeing they keep them from knowing the causes of vices. That which causes sin has often deceived even the just. In this way the people of God after they sat down to eat and drink denied God. In this way, too, Lot knew not, and so endured his daughters' wickedness. So, too, the sons of Noah going backward covered their father's nakedness, which he who was wanton saw, he who was modest blushed at and dutifully hid, fearful of offending if he too saw it. How great is the power of wine, so that wine made him naked which the waters of the deluge could not.

Chapter X.

Finally, another glory of virginity is mentioned, that it is free from avarice. St. Ambrose, addressing his sister, reminds her of the great happiness of those who are free from those troubles as to luxury and vanity which come upon those who are about to marry. What then? What happiness it is that no desire of possessions inflames you! The poor man demands what you have, he does not ask for what you have not. The fruit of your labour is a treasure for the needy, and two mites, if they be all one has, are wealth on the part of the giver.

54. Listen, then, my sister, from what you escape. For it is not for me to teach nor for you to learn what you ought to guard against, for the practice of perfect virtue does not require teaching, but instructs others. You see how like she is to the litters at processions, who lays herself out to please, attracting to herself the look and gaze of all; less beautiful is she because she strives to please, for she displeases the people before she pleases her husband. But in you the rejection of all care for spendour is far more becoming, and the very fact that you do not adorn yourselves is an ornament.

55. Look at the ears pierced with wounds, and pity the neck weighed down with burdens. That the metals are different does not lighten the suffering. In one case a chain binds the neck, in another a fetter encloses the foot. It makes no difference whether the body be loaded with gold or with iron. Thus the neck is weighed down and the steps are hindered. The price makes it no better, except that you women are afraid lest that which causes you suffering be lost. What is the difference whether the sentence of another or your own condemn you? Nay, you, even more wretched than those, are condemned by public justice, since they desire to be set free, you to be bound.

56. But how wretched a position, that she who is marriageable is in a species of sale put up as it were to auction to be bid for, so that he who offers the highest price purchases her. Slaves are sold on more tolerable conditions, for they often choose their masters; if a maiden chooses it is an offence, if not it is an insult. And she, though she be beautiful and comely, both fears and wishes to be seen; she wishes it that she may sell herself for a better price; she fears lest the fact of her being seen should itself be unbecoming. But what absurdities of wishes and fears and suspicions are there as to how the suitors will turn out, lest a poor man may beguile her, or a rich one contemn her, lest a handsome suitor mock her, lest a noble one despise her.

Chapter XI.

St. Ambrose answers objections made to the uselessness of his exhortations in favour of virginity, and brings forward instances of virgins especially in various places he mentions, and speaks of their zeal in the cause.

57. Some one may say, you are always singing the praises of virgins. What shall I do who am always singing them and have no success? But this is not my fault. Then, too, virgins come from Placentia to be consecrated, or from Bononia, and Mauritania, in order to receive the veil here. You see a striking thing here. I treat the matter here, and persuade those who are elsewhere. If this be so, let me treat the subject elsewhere, that I may persuade you.

58. What is it, then, that even they who hear me not follow my teaching, and those who hear me follow me not? For I have known many virgins who had the desire, but were prevented

from going forward by their mothers, and, which is more serious, mothers who were widows, to whom I will now address myself. For if your daughters desired to love a man, they could, by law, choose whom they would. Are they, then, who are allowed to choose a man not allowed to choose God?

59. Behold how sweet is the fruit of modesty, which has sprung up even in the affections of barbarians. Virgins coming from the most distant on this and that side of Mauritania desire to be consecrated here; and though all the families be in bonds, yet modesty cannot be bound. She who mourns over the hardship of slavery avows an eternal kingdom.

60. And what shall I say of the virgins of Bononia, a fertile band of chastity, who, forsaking worldly delights, inhabit the sanctuary of virginity? Not being of the sex which lives in common, attaining in their common chastity to the number of twenty, and fruit to an hundredfold, leaving their parents' dwelling they press into the houses of Christ, as soldiers of unwearied chastity; at one time singing spiritual songs, they provide their sustenance by labour, and seek with their hands supplies for their liberality.

61. But if the attraction of searching for virgins has grown strong (for they beyond others follow up the search and watch for purity), they follow up their hidden prey with the greatest perseverance to its very chambers; or, if the flight of any one shall have seemed more free, one may see them rise on the wing, hear the rustling of their feathers, and the bursting of applause; so as to surround the one on wing with a chaste band of modesty, until rejoicing in that fair companionship, forgetful of her father's house, she enters the regions of modesty and the fenced-in home of chastity.

Chapter XII.

It is very desirable that parents should encourage the desire for the virgin life, but more praiseworthy when the love of God draws a maiden even against their will. The violence of parents and the loss of property are not to be feared, and an instance of this is related by St. Ambrose.

62. It is a good thing, then, that the zeal of parents, like favouring gales, should aid a virgin; but it is more glorious if the fire of tender age even without the incitement of those older of its own self burst forth into the flame of chastity. Parents will refuse a dowry, but you have a wealthy Spouse, satisfied with Whose treasures you will not miss the revenues of a father's inheritance. How much is poverty to chastity superior to bridal gifts!

63. And yet of whom have you heard as ever, because of her desire for chastity, having been deprived of her lawful inheritance? Parents speak against her, but are willing to be overcome. They resist at first because they are afraid to believe; they often are angry that one may learn to overcome; they threaten to disinherit to try whether one is able not to fear temporal loss; they caress with exquisite allurements to see if one cannot be softened by the inducement of various pleasures. You are being exercised, O virgin, whilst you are being urged. And the anxious entreaties of your parents are your first battles. Conquer your affection first, O maiden. If you conquer your home, you conquer the world.

64. But suppose that the loss of your patrimony awaits you; are not the future realms of heaven a compensation for perishable and frail possessions? For if we believe the heavenly message, "there is no one who has forsaken house, or parents, or brethren, or wife, or children, for the kingdom of God's sake, who shall not receive sevenfold more in this present time, and in the world to come shall have everlasting life." Entrust your faith to God, who entrust your money to man; lend to Christ. The faithful keeper of the deposit of your hope pays the talent of your faith with manifold interest. The Truth does not deceive, Justice does not circumvent, Virtue does not deceive. But if you believe not God's word, at least believe instances.65. Within my memory a girl once noblein the world, now more noble in the sight of God, being urged to a marriage by her parents and kinsfolk, took refuge at the holy altar. Whither could a virgin better flee, than thither where the Virgin Sacrifice is offered? Nor was even that the limit of her boldness. She, the oblation of modesty, the victim of chastity, was standing at the altar of God,

now placing upon her head the right hand of the priest, asking his prayers, and now impatient at the righteous delay, placing the top of her head under the altar. "Can any better veil," she said, "cover me better than the altar which consecrates the veils themselves? Such a bridal veil is most suitable on which Christ, the Head of all, is daily consecrated. What are you doing, my kinsfolk? Why do you still trouble my mind with seeking marriage? I have long since provided for that. Do you offer me a bridegroom? I have found a better. Make the most you can of my wealth, boast of his nobility, extol his power, I have Him with Whom no one can compare himself, rich in the world, powerful in empire, noble in heaven. If you have such an one, I do not reject the choice; if you do not find such, you do me not a kindness, my relatives, but an injury."

66. When the others were silent, one burst forth somewhat roughly: "If," he said, "your father were alive, would he suffer you to remain unmarried?" Then she replied with more religion and more restrained piety: "And perchance he is gone that no one may be able to hinder me. Which answer concerning her father, but warning as to himself, he made good by his own speedy death. So the others, each of them, fearing the same for himself, began to assist and not to hinder her as before, and her virginity involved not the loss of the property due to her, but also received the reward of her integrity. You see, maidens, the reward of devotion, and do you, parents, be warned by the example of transgression.

BOOK II.

Chapter I.

In this book St. Ambrose purposes to treat of the training of virgins, using examples rather than precepts, and explains why he does so in writing rather than by word of mouth.

1. In the former book I wished(though I was not able) to set forth how great is the gift of virginity, that the grace of the heavenly gift might of itself invite the reader. In the second book it is fitting that the virgin should be instructed and, as it were, be educated by the teaching of suitable precepts.

2. But, inasmuch as I am feeble in advising and unequal to teaching(for he who teaches ought to excel him who is taught), lest I should seem to have abandoned the task I have undertaken, or to have taken too much upon myself, I thought it better to instruct by examples than by precepts; for more progress may be made by means of an example, inasmuch as that which has been already done is considered to be not difficult, and that which has been tried to be expedient, and that which has been transmitted in sucession to us by a kind of hereditary practice of ancestral virtue to be binding in religion.

3. But if any one rebukes me for presumption, let him rather rebuke me for zeal, because I thought that I ought not to refuse even this to the virgins who asked it of me. For I preferred rather to run the risk of perilling my own modesty, than not to fulfil the wish of those whose pursuits even our God favours with kindly approbation.

4. Nor can the mark of presumption be set on my task, since, when they had those from whom they could learn, they sought my good-will rather than my teaching, and my zeal may be excused, since when they had the guidance of a martyr for the observance of discipline, I did not think it superfluous if I could turn the persuasion of my discourse into an allurement to profession. He who teaches with facility restrains fault with severity; I, who cannot teach, entice.

5. And because many who were absent desired to have the use of my discourse, I compiled this book, in order that holding in their hands the substance of what my voice had uttered to them, they might not think that he whom they were holding failed them. But let us go on with our plan.

Chapter II.

The life of Mary is set before virgins as an example, and her many virtues are dwelt upon, her chastity, humility, hard life, love of retirement, and the like; then her kindness to others, her zeal in learning, and love of frequenting the temple. St. Ambrose then sets forth how she, adorned with all these virtues, will come to meet the numberless bands of virgins and lead them with great triumph to the bridal chamber of the Spouse.

6. Let, then, the life of Mary be as it were virginity itself, set forth in a likeness, from which, as from a mirror, the appearance of chastity and the form of virtue is reflected. From this you may take your pattern of life, showing, as an example, the clear rules of virtue: what you have to correct, to effect, and to hold fast.

7. The first thing which kindles ardour in learning is the greatness of the teacher. What is greater than the Mother of God? What more glorious than she whom Glory Itself chose? What more chaste than she who bore a body without contact with another body? For why should I speak of her other virtues? She was a virgin not only in body but also in mind, who stained the sincerity of its disposition by no guile, who was humble in heart, grave in speech, prudent in mind, sparing of words, studious in reading, resting her hope not on uncertain riches, but on the prayer of the poor, intent on work, modest in discourse; wont to seek not man but God as the judge of her thoughts, to injure no one, to have goodwill towards all, to rise up before her elders, not to envy her equals, to avoid boastfulness, to follow reason, to love virtue. When did she pain her parents even by a look? When did she disagree with her neighbours? When did she despise the lowly? When did she avoid the needy? Being wont only to go to such gatherings of men as mercy would not blush at, nor modesty pass by. There was nothing gloomy in her eyes,

393

nothing forward in her words, nothing unseemly in her acts, there was not a silly movement, nor unrestrained step, nor was her voice petulant, that the very appearance of her outward being might be the image of her soul, the representation of what is approved. For a well-ordered house ought to be recognized on the very threshold, and should show at the very first entrance thatno darkness is hidden within, as our soul hindered by no restraints of the body may shine abroad like a lamp placed within.

8. Why should I detail her spareness of food, her abundance of services—the one abounding beyond nature, the other almost insufficient for nature? And there were no seasons of slackness, but days of fasting, one upon the other. And if ever the desire for refreshment came, her food was generally what came to hand, taken to keep off death, not to minister to comfort. Necessity before inclination caused her to sleep, and yet when her body was sleeping her soul was awake, and often in sleep either went again through what had been read, or went on with what had been interrupted by sleep, or carried out what had been designed, or foresaw what was to be carried out.

9. She was unaccustomed to go from home, except for divine service, and this with parents or kinsfolk. Busy in private at home, accompanied by others abroad, yet with no better guardian than herself, as she, inspiring respect by her gait and address, progressed not so much by the motion of her feet as by step upon step of virtue. But though the Virgin had other persons who were protectors of her body, she alone guarded her character; she can learn many points if she be her own teacher, who possesses the perfection of all virtues, for whatever she did is a lesson. Mary attended to everything as though she were warned by many, and fulfilled every obligation of virtue as though she were teaching rather than learning.

10. Such has the Evangelist shown her, such did the angel find her, such did the Holy Spirit choose her. Why delay about details? How her parents loved her, strangers praised her, how worthy she was that the Son of God should be born of her. She, when the angel entered, was found at home in privacy, without a companion, that no one might interrupt her attention or disturb her; and she did not desire any women as companions, who had the companionship of good thoughts. Moreover, she seemed to herself to be less alone when she was alone. For how should she be alone, who had with her so many books, so many archangels, so many prophets?11. And so, too, when Gabriel visited her, did he find her, and Mary trembled, being disturbed, as though at the form of a man, but on hearing his name recognized him as one not unknown to her. And so she was a stranger as to men, but not as to the angel; that we might know that her ears were modest and her eyes bashful. Then when saluted she kept silence, and when addressed she answered, and she whose feelings were first troubled afterwards promised obedience.

12. And holy Scripture points out how modest she was towards her neighbours. For she became more humble when she knew herself to be chosen of God, and went forthwith to her kinswoman in the hill country, not in order to gain belief by anything external, for she had believed the word of God. "Blessed," she said, "art thou who didst believe." And she abode with her three months. Now in such an interval of time it is not that faith is being sought for, but kindness which is being shown. And this was after that the child, leaping in his mother's womb, had saluted the mother of the Lord, attaining to reason before birth.

13. And then, in the many subsequent wonders, when the barren bore a son, the virgin conceived, the dumb spake, the wise men worshipped, Simeon waited, the stars gave notice. Mary, who was moved by the angel's entrance, was unmoved by the miracles. "Mary," it is said, "kept all these things in her heart," Though she was the mother of the Lord, yet she desired to learn the precepts of the Lord, and she who brought forth God, yet desired to know God.

14. And then, how she also went every year to Jerusalem at the solemn day of the passover, and went with Joseph. Everywhere is modesty the companion of her singular virtues in the Virgin. This, without which virginity cannot exist, must be the inseparable companion of virginity. And so Mary did not go even to the temple without the guardianship of her modesty.

15. This is the likeness of virginity. For Mary was such that her example alone is a lesson for all. If, then, the author displeases us not, let us make trial of the production, that whoever desires its reward for herself may imitate the pattern. How many kinds of virtues shine forth in one Virgin! The secret of modesty, the banner of faith, the service of devotion, the Virgin within the house, the companion for the ministry, the mother at the temple.

16. Oh! how many virgins shall she meet, how many shall she embrace and bring to the Lord, and say: "She has been faithful to her espousal, to my Son; she has kept her bridal couch with spotless modesty." How shall the Lord Himself commend them to His Father, repeating again those words of His: "Holy Father, these are they whom I have kept for Thee, on whom the Son of Man leant His head and rested; I ask that where I am there they may be with Me." And if they ought to benefit not themselves only, who lived not for themselves alone, one virgin may redeem her parents, another her brothers. "Holy Father, the world hath not known Me, but these have known Me, and have willed not to know the world."

17. What a procession shall that be, what joy of applauding angels when she is found worthy of dwelling in heaven who lived on earth a heavenly life! Then too Mary, taking her timbrel, shall stir up the choirs of virgins, singing to the Lord because they have passed through the sea of this world without suffering from the waves of this world. Then each shall rejoice, saying: "I will go to the altar of God; to God Who maketh my youth glad;" and, "I will offer unto God thanksgiving, and pay my vows unto the Most High."

18. Nor would I hesitate to admit you to the altars of God, whose souls I would without hesitation call altars, on which Christ is daily offered for the redemption of the body. For if the virgin's body be a temple of God, what is her soul, which, the ashes, as it were, of the body being shaken off, once more uncovered by the hand of the Eternal Priest, exhales the vapour of the divine fire. Blessed virgins, who emit a fragrancethrough divine grace as gardens do through flowers, temples through religion, altars through the priest.

Chapter III.
St. Ambrose having set forth the Virgin Mary as a pattern for life, adduces Thecla as a model for learning how to die. Thecla suffered not from the beasts to whom she was condemned, but on the contrary received from them signs of reverence. He then proceeds to introduce a more recent example.

19. Let, then, holy Mary instruct you in the discipline of life, and Thecla teach you how to be offered, for she, avoiding nuptial intercourse, and condemned through her husband's rage, changed even the disposition of wild beasts by their reverence for virginity. For being made ready for the wild beasts, when avoiding the gaze of men, she offered her vital parts to a fierce lion, caused those who had turned away their immodest looks to turn them back modestly.

20. The beast was to be seen lying on the ground, licking her feet, showing without a sound that it could not injure the sacred body of the virgin. So the beast reverenced his prey, and forgetful of his own nature, put on that nature which men had lost. One could see, as it were, by some transfusion of nature, men clothed with savageness, goading the beast to cruelty, and the beast kissing the feet of the virgin, teaching them what was due from men. Virginity has in itself so much that is admirable, that even lions admire it. Food did not induce them though kept without their meal; no impulse hurried them on when excited;anger did not exasperate them when stirred up, nor did their habits lead them blindly as they were wont, nor their own natural disposition possess them with fierceness. They set an example of piety when reverencing the martyr; and gave a lesson in favor of chastity when they did nothing but kiss the virgin's feet, with their eyes turned to the ground, as though through modesty, fearing that any male, even a beast, should see the virgin naked.

21. Some one will say: "Why have you brought forward the example of Mary, as if any one could be found to imitate the Lord's mother? And why that of Thecla, whom the Apostle of the Gentiles trained? Give us a teacher of our own sort if you wish for disciples." I will, therefore,

set before you a recent example of this sort, that you may understand that the Apostle is the teacher, not of one only, but of all.

Chapter IV.

A virgin at Antioch, having refused to sacrifice to idols, was condemned to a house of ill-fame, whence she escaped unharmed, having changed clothes with a Christian soldier. Then when he was condemned for this, she returned and the two contended for the prize of martyrdom, which was at last given to each.

22. There was lately at Antioch a virgin who avoided being seen in public, but the more she shrank from men's eyes, the more they longed for her. For beauty which is heard of but not seen is more desired, there being two incentives to passion, love and knowledge—so long as nothing is met with which pleases less; and that which pleases is thought to be of more worth, because the eye is not in this case the judge by investigation, but the mind inflamed with love is full of longing. And so the holy virgin, lest their passions should be longer fed by the desire of gaining her, professed her intention of preserving her chastity, and so quenched the fires of those wicked men, that she was no longer loved, but informed against.

23. So a persecution arose. The maiden, not knowing how to escape, and afraid lest she might fall into the hands of those who were plotting against her chastity, prepared her soul for heroic virtue, being so religious as not to fear death, so chaste as to expect it. The day of her crown arrived. The expectation of all was at its height. The maiden is brought forward, and makes her twofold profession, of religion and of chastity. But when they saw the constancy of her profession, her fear for her modesty, her readiness for tortures, and her blushes at being looked on, they began to consider how they might overcome her religion by setting chastity before her, so that, having deprived her of that which was the greatest, they might also deprive her of that which they had left. So the sentence was that she should either sacrifice, or be sent to a house of ill-fame. After what manner do they worship their gods who thus avenge them, or how do they live themselves who give sentence after this fashion?

24. And the virgin, not hesitating about her religion, but fearful as to her chastity, began to reflect, What am I to do? Each crown, that of martyrdom and that of virginity, is grudged me to-day. But the name of virgin is not acknowledged where the Author of virginity is denied. How can one be a virgin who cherishes a harlot? How can one be a virgin who loves adulterers? How a virgin if she seeks for a lover? It is preferable to have a virgin mind than a virgin body. Each is good if each be possible; if it be not possible, let me be chaste, not to man but to God. Rahab, too, was a harlot, but after she believed in God, she found salvation. And Judith adorned herself that she might please an adulterer, but because she did this for religion and not for love, no one considered her an adulteress. This instance turned out well. For if she who entrusted herself to religion both preserved her chastity and her country, perhaps I, by preserving my religion, shall also preserve my chastity. But if Judith had preferred her chastity to her religion, when her country had been lost, she would also have lost her chastity.

25. And so, instructed by such examples, and at the same time bearing in mind the words of the Lord, where He says: "Whosoever shall lose his life for My sake, shall find it," she wept, and was silent, that the adulterer might not even hear her speaking, and she did not choose the wrong done to her modesty, but rejected wrong done to Christ. Consider whether it was possible for her to suffer her body to be unchaste, who guarded even her speech.

26. For some time my words have been becoming bashful, and fear to laud on or describe the wicked series of what was done. Close your ears, ye virgins! The Virgin of God is taken to a house of shame, But now unclose your ears, ye virgins, The Virgin of Christ can be exposed to shame, but cannot be contaminated. Everywhere she is the Virgin of God, and the Temple of God, and houses of ill-fame cannot injure chastity, but chastity does away with the ill-fame of the place.

27. A great rush of wanton men is made to the place. Listen, ye holy virgins, to the miracles of the martyr, forget the nameof the place. The door is shut within, the hawks cry without; some

are contending who shall first attack the prey. But she, with her hands raised to heaven, as though she had come to a house of prayer, not to a resort of lust, says: "O Christ, Who didst tame the fierce lions for the virgin Daniel, Thou canst also tame the fierce minds of men. Fire became as dew to the Hebrew children, the water stood up for the Jews, of Thy mercy, not of its own nature. Susanna knelt down for punishment and triumphed over her adulterous accusers, the right hand withered which violated the gifts of Thy temple; and now thy temple itself is violated; suffer not sacrilegious incest, Thou Who didst not suffer theft. Let Thy Name be now again glorified in that I who came here for shame, may go away a virgin!"

28. Scarcely had she finished her prayer, when, lo! a man with the aspect of a terrible warrior burst in. How the virgin trembled before him to whom the trembling people gave way. But she did not forget what she had read. "Daniel," said she, "had gone to see the punishment of Susanna, and alone pronounced her guiltless, whom the people had condemned. A sheep may be hidden in the shape of this wolf. Christ has His soldiers also, Who is Master of legions. Or, perchance, an executioner has come in. Fear not, my soul, such an one makes martyrs. O Virgin! thy faith has saved thee."

29. And the soldier said to her: "Fear not, sister, I pray you. I, a brother, am come hither to save life, not to destroy it. Save me, that you yourself may be saved. I came in like an adulterer, to go forth, if you will, as a martyr. Let us change our attire, mine will fit you, and yours will fit me, and each for Christ. Your robe will make me a true soldier, mine will make you a virgin. You will be clothed well, I shall be unclothed even better that the persecutor may recognize me. Take the garment which will conceal the woman, give me that which shall consecrate me a martyr. Put on the cloak which will hide the limbs of a virgin, but preserve her modesty. Take the cap which will cover your hair and conceal your countenance. They who have entered houses of ill-fame are wont to blush. When you have gone forth, take care not to look back, remembering Lot's wife, who lost her very nature because she looked back at what was unchaste, though with chaste eyes. And be not afraid lest any part of the sacrifice fail. I will offer the victim to God for you, do you offer the soldier to Christ for me. You have served the good service of chastity, the wages of which are everlasting life; you have the breastplate of righteousness, which protects the body with spiritual armour, the shield of faith with which to ward off wounds, and the helmet of salvation, for there is the defence of our salvation where Christ is, since the man is the head of the woman. and Christ of the virgin.

30. Whilst saying this he put off his cloak. This garment has been up to this time suspected of being that of a persecutor and adulterer. The virgin offered her neck, the soldier his cloak. What a spectacle that was, what a manifestation of grace when they were contending for martyrdom in a house of ill-fame! Let the characters be also considered, a soldier and a virgin, that is, persons unlike in natural disposition, but alike by the mercy of God, that the saying might be fulfilled: "Then the wolves and the lambs shall feed together." Behold the lamb and the wolf not only feed together but are also offered together. Why should I say more? Having changed her garment, the maiden flies from the snare, not now with wings of her own, seeing she was borne on spiritual wings, and(a sight which the ages had never seen) she leaves the house of ill-fame a virgin, but a virgin of Christ.

31. But they who were looking with their eyes, yet saw not, raged like robbers for prey, or wolves for a lamb. One who was more shameless went in. But when he took in the state of the matter with his eyes, he said, What is this? A maiden entered, now a man is to be seen here. This is not the old fable of a hind instead of a maiden, but in truth a virgin become a soldier. I had heard but believed not that Christ changed water into wine; now He has begun also to change the sexes. Let us depart hence whilst we still are what we were. Am I too changed who see things differently from what I believe them to be? I came to a house of ill-fame, and see a surety. And yet I go forth changed, for I shall go out chaste who came in unchaste.

32. When the affair was known, because a crown was due to such a conqueror, he was condemned for the virgin who was seized for the virgin, and so not only a virgin but a martyr

came forth from the house of ill-fame. It is reported that the maiden ran to the place of punishment, and that they both contended for death. He said: "I am condemned to death, the sentence let you go free when it retained me." And she replied: "I did not choose you as my surety on pain of death, but as a guarantee for my chastity. If chastity be attacked, my sex remains; if blood is sought, I desire none to give bail for me, I have the means to pay. The sentence was pronounced on me, which was pronounced for me. Undoubtedly, if I had offered you as security for my debt, and in my absence the judge had assigned your property to the creditor, you would share the sentence with me, and I should pay your obligations with my patrimony. Were I to refuse, who would not judge me worthy of a shameful death? How much more am I bound where there is a question of death? Let me die innocent, that I may not die guilty. In this matter there is no middle course; today I shall either be guilty of your blood or a martyr in my own. If I came back quickly, who dares to shut me out? If I delayed, who dares acquit me? I owe a greater debt to the laws who am guilty not only of my own flight, but also of the death of another. My limbs are equal to death, which were not equal to dishonour. A virgin can accept a wound who could not accept contumely. I avoided disgrace, not martyrdom. I gave up my robe to you; I did not alter my profession. And if you deprive me of death, you will not have rescued but circumvented me. Beware, pray, of resisting, beware of venturing to contend with me. Take not away the kindness you have conferred on me. In denying me the execution of this sentence, you are setting up again the former one. For the sentence is changed for a former one. If the latter binds me not, the former one does. We can each satisfy the sentence if you suffer me to be slain first. From you they can exact no other penalty, but her chastity is in danger with a virgin. And so you will be more glorious if you are seen to have made a martyr of an adulteress. than to have made again an adulteress of a martyr."

33. What do you think was the end? The two contended, and both gained the victory, and the crown was not divided, but became two. So the holy martyrs, conferring benefits one on the other, gave the one the impulse and the other the result to their martyrdom.

Chapter V.

The story of the two Pythagorean friends, Damon and Pythias, is related by St. Ambrose, who points out that the case mentioned in the last chapter is more praiseworthy. A comparison is instituted between the treatment of their gods by heathen without any punishment, and Jeroboam's irreverence with its punishment.

34. And the schools of the philosophers laud Damon and Pythias—the Pythagoreans—to the skies, of whom one, when condemnned to death, asked for time to set his affairs in order. whereupon, the tyrant, in his cunning, not supposing that such could be found, asked for a bondsman who should suffer the penalty if the other delayed his return. I do not know which act of the two was the more noble. The one found the bondsman, the other offered himself. And so while he who was condemned met with some delay, the bondsman with calm countenance did not refuse death. As he was being led forth his friend returned, and offered his neck to the axe. Then the tyrant, wondering that friendship was dearer to philosophers than life, asked himself to be received into friendship by those whom he had condemned. The grace of Virtue was so great that it moved even a tyrant.

35. These things are worthy of praise; but are inferior to our instance. For those two were men, with us one was a virgin, who had first to be superior to her sex; those were friends, these were unknown to each other; those offered themselves to one tyrant, these to many tyrants; and these more cruel, for in the former case the tyrant spared them, these slew them; with the former one was bound by necessity, with these the will of each was free. In this, too, the latter were the wiser, that with those the end of their zeal was the pleasure of friendship, with these the crown of martyrdom, for they strove for men, these for God.

36. And since we have mentioned that man who was condemned, it is fitting to add what he thought of his gods, that you may judge how weak they are whom their own followers deride. For he, having come into the temple of Jupiter, bade them take off the fillet of gold with which

his image was crowned, and to put on one of wool instead, saying that the golden fillet was cold in winter and heavy in summer. So he derided his god as being unable to bear either a weight or cold. He, too, when he saw the golden beard of Aesculapius, bade them remove it, saying that it was not fit for the son to have a beard when the father had none. Again, he took away the golden bowls from the images which held them, saying that he ought to receive what the gods gave. For, said he, men make prayers to receive good things from the gods, and nothing is better than gold; if, however, gold be evil, the gods ought not to have it; if it be good, it is better that men should have it who know how to use it.

37. Such objects of ridicule were they, that neither could Jupiter defend his garment, nor Aesculapius his beard, for Apollo had not yet begun to grow one; nor could all those who are esteemed gods keep the golden bowls which they were holding, not fearing the charge of theft so much as not having any feeling. Who, then, would worship them, who can neither defend themselves as gods nor hide themselves as men?

38. But when in the temple of our God, that wicked king Jeroboam took away the gifts which his father had laid up, and offered to idols upon the holy altar, did not his right hand, which he stretched out, wither, and his idols, which he called upon, were not able to help him? Then, turning to the Lord, he asked for pardon, and at once his hand which had withered by sacrilege was healed by true religion. So complete an example was there set forth in one person, both of divine mercy and wrath when he who was sacrificing suddenly lost his right hand, but when penitent received forgiveness.

Chapter VI.

St. Ambrose, in concluding the second book, ascribes any good there may be in it to the merits of the virgins, and sets forth that it was right before laying down any severe precepts to encourage them by examples, as is done both in human teaching and in holy Scripture.

39. I, Who have been not yet three years a bishop, have prepared this offering for you, holy virgins, although untaught by my own experience, yet having learnt much from your mode of life. For what experience could have grown up in so short a time of being initiated in religion? If you find any flowers herein, gather them together in the bosom of your lives. These are not precepts for virgins, but instances taken from virgins. My words have sketched the likeness of your virtue, you may see the reflection of your gravity, as it were, in the mirror of this discourse. If you have received any pleasure from my ability, all the fragrance of this book is yours. And since there are as many opinions as there are persons, if there be anything simple in my treatise let all read it; if anything stronger, let the more mature prove it; if anything modest, let it cleave to the breast and tinge the cheeks; if there be anything flowery, let the flowery age of youth not disdain it.

40. We ought to stir up the love of the bride, for iris written: "Thou shalt love the Lord thy God." At bridal feasts we ought to adorn the hair at least with some ornaments of prayer, for it is written: "Smite the hands together, and strike with the foot." We ought to scatter roses on those uninterrupted bridals. Even in these temporal marriages the bride is received with acclamation before she receives commands, lest hard commands should hurt her, before love cherished by kindness grows strong.

41. Horses learn to love the sound of patting their necks, that they may not refuse the yoke, and are first trained with words of enticement before the stripe of discipline. But when the horse has submitted its neck to the yoke, the rein pulls in, and the spur urges on, and its companions draw it, and the driver bids it. So, too, our virgin ought first to play with pious love, and admire the golden supports of the heavenly marriage couch on the very threshold of marriage, and to see the door-posts adorned with wreaths of leaves, and to taste the delight of the musicians playing within; that she may not through fear withdraw herself from the Lord's yoke, before she obeys His call.

42. "Come, then, hither from Lebanon, My spouse, come hither from Lebanon, thou shalt pass and pass through." This verse must be often repeated by us, that at least being called by the words of the Lord, she may follow if there be any who will not trust the words of man. We have not formed this power for ourselves, but have received it; this is the heavenly teaching of the mystic song: "Let Him kiss me with the kisses of His mouth, for Thy breasts are better than wine, and the odor of Thy ointments is above all spices. Thy name is as ointment poured forth." The whole of that place of delights sounds of sport, stirs up approval, calls forth love. "Therefore," it continues, "have the maidens loved Thee and have drawn Thee, let us run after the odour of Thy ointments. The King hath brought me into His chamber." She began with kisses, and so attained to the chamber.

43. She, now so patient of hard toil, and of practised virtue, as to open the bars with her hand, go forth into the field, and abide in strongholds, at the beginning ran after the odour of the ointment; soon when she is come into the chamber the ointment is changed. And see whither she goes: "If it be a wall," it is said, "we will build upon it towers of silver." She who sported with kisses now builds towers that, encircled with the precious battlements of the saints, she may not only render fruitless the attacks of the enemy, but also erect the safe defences of holy merits.

BOOK III.

Chapter I.

St. Ambrose now goes back to the address of Liberius when he gave the veil to Marcellina. Touching on the crowds pressing to the bridal feast of that Spouse Who feeds them all, he passes on to the fitness of her profession on the day on which Christ was born of a Virgin, and concludes with a fervent exhortation to love Him.

1.Inasmuch as I have digressed in what I have said in the two former hooks, it is now time, holy sister, to reconsider those precepts of Liberius of blessed memory which you used to talk over with me, as the holier the man the more pleasing is his discourse. For he, when on the Nativity of the Saviour in the Church of St. Peter you signified your profession of virginity by your change of attire (and what day could be better than that on which the Virgin received her child?) whilst many virgins were standing round and vying with each other for your companionship. "You," said he, "my daughter, have desired a good espousal. You see how great a crowd has come together for the birthday of your Spouse, and none has gone away without food. This is He, Who, when invited to the marriage feast, changed water into wine. He, too, will confer the pure sacrament of virginity on you who before were subject to the vile elements of material nature. This is He Who fed four thousand in the wilderness with five loaves and two fishes." He could have fed more; if more had been there to be fed, they would have been. And now He has called many to your espousal, but it is not now barley bread, but the Body from heaven which is supplied.

2. To-day, indeed, He was born after the manner of men, of a Virgin, but was begotten of the Father before all things, resembling His mother in body, His Father in power. Only-begotten on earth, and Only-begotten in heaven. God of God, born of a Virgin, Righteousness from the Father, Power from the Mighty One, Light of Light, not unequal to His Father; nor separated inpower, not confused by extension of the Word or enlargement as though mingled with the Father, but distinguished from the Father by virtue of His generation. He is your Brother, without Whom neither things in heaven, nor things in the sea, nor things on earth consist. The good Word of the Father, Which was, it is said, "in the beginning," here you have His eternity. "And," it is said, "the Word was with God." Here you have His power, undivided and inseparable from the Father. "And the Word was God." Here you have His unbegotten Godhead, for your faith is to be drawn from the mutual relationship.

3. Love him, my daughter, for He is good. For, "None is good save God only." For if there be no doubt that the Son is God, and that God is good, there is certainly no doubt that God the Son is good. Love Him I say. He it is Whom the Father begat before the morning star, as being eternal, He brought Him forth from the womb as the Son; He uttered him from His heart, as the Word. He it is in Whom the Father is well pleased; He is the Arm of the Father, for He is Creator of all, and the Wisdom of the Father, for He proceeded from the mouth of God; the Power of the Father, because the fulness of the Godhead dwelleth in Him bodily. And the Father so loved Him, as to bear Him in His bosom, and place Him at His right hand, that you may learn His wisdom, and know His power.

4. If, then, Christ is the Power of God, was God ever without power? Was the Father ever without the Son? If the Father of a certainty always was, of a certainty the Son always was. So He is the perfect Son of a perfect Father. For he who derogates from the power, derogates from Him Whose is the power. The Perfection of the Godhead does not admit of inequality. Love, then, Him Whom the Father loves, honour Him Whom the Father honours, for "he that honoureth not the Son, honoureth not the Father," and "whoso denieth the Son, hath not the Father." So much as to the faith.

Chapter II.

Touching next upon the training of a virgin, he speaks of moderation in food and drink, and of restraint upon the impulses of the mind, introducing some teaching upon the fable of the death and resurrection of Hippolytus, and advises the avoidance of certain meats.

5. But sometimes even when faith is to be relied upon, youth is not trusted. Use wine, therefore, sparingly, in order that the weakness of the body may not increase, not for pleasurable excitement, for each alike kindles a flame, both wine and youth. Let fasts also put a bridle on tender age, and spare diet restrain the unsubdued appetites with a kind of rein. Let reason check, hope subdue, and fear curb them. For he who knows not how to govern his desires, like a man run away with by wild horses, is overthrown, bruised, torn, and injured.

6. And this is said to have happened to a youth for his love of Diana. But the fable is coloured with poet's tales, that Neptune, stirred with grief at his rival being preferred, sent madness upon his horses, whereby his great power might be set forth in that he overcame the youth, not by strength, but by fraud. And from this event a yearly sacrifice is celebrated for Diana, when a horse is offered at her altar. And they say that she was a virgin, and (of which even harlots would be ashamed) yet could love one who did not love her. But as far as I am concerned let their fables have authority, for though each be criminal, it is yet a less evil that a youth should have been so enamoured of an adulteress as to perish, than that two gods should, as they relate, contend for committing adultery, and that Jupiter avenged the grief of his daughter who played the harlot on the physician who cured the wound of him who had violated Diana in the woods, a most excellent huntress, no doubt, not of wild beasts, but of lust: yet also of wild beasts, so that she was worshipped naked.

7. Let them ascribe, then, to Neptune the mastery over madness, in order to fix on him the crime of unchaste love. Let them ascribe to Diana the rule over the woods, wherein she dwelt, so as to establish the adultery which she practised. Let them ascribe to Aesculapius the restoration of the dead so long as they confess that when struck by lightning he himself escaped not. Let them also ascribe to Jupiter the thunderbolts which he did not possess, so that they witness to the disgrace with which he was laden.

8. And I think that one should sparingly eat all kinds of food which cause heat to the limbs, for flesh drags down even eagles as they fly. But within you let that bird of which we read, "Thy youth shall be renewed like the eagle's," holding its course on high, swift in its virgin flight, be ignorant of the desire for unnecessary food. The gathering of banquets and salutations must be avoided.

Chapter III.

Virgins are exhorted to avoid visits, to observe modesty, to be silent during the celebration of the Mysteries after the example of Mary. Then after narrating the story of a heathen youth, and saying of a poet, St. Ambrose relates a miracle wrought by a holy priest.

9. I Will, too, that visits amongst the younger, except such as may be due to parents and those of like age, be few. For modesty is worn away by intercourse, and boldness breaks forth, laughter creeps in, and bashfulness is lessened, whilst politeness is studied. Not to answer one who asks a question is childishness, to answer is nonsense. I should prefer, therefore, that conversation should rather be wanting to a virgin, than abound. For if women are bidden to keep silence in churches, even about divine things, and to ask their husbands at home, what do we think should be the caution of virgins, in whom modesty adorns their age, and silence commends their modesty.

10. Was it a small sign of modesty that when Rebecca came to wed Isaac, and saw her bridegroom, she took a veil, that she might not be seen before they were united? Certainly the fair virgin feared not for her beauty, but for her modesty. What of Rachel, how she, when Jacob's kiss had been taken, wept and groaned, and would not have ceased weeping had she not known him to be a kinsman? So she both observed what was due to modesty, and omitted not

kindly affection. But if it is said to a man: "Gaze not on a maid, lest she cause thee to fall," what is to be said to a consecrated virgin, who, if she loves, sins in mind; if she is loved, in act also?

11. The virtue of silence, especially in Church, is very great. Let no sentence of the divine lessons escape you; if you give ear, restrain your voice, utter no word with your lips which you would wish to recall, but let your boldness to speak be sparing. For in truth in much speaking there is abundance of sin. To the murderer it was said: "Thou hast sinned, be silent," that he might not sin more; but to the virgin it must be said, "Be silent lest thou sin." For Mary, as we read, kept in heart all things that were said concerning her Son, and do you, when any passage is read where Christ is announced as about to come, or is shown to have come, not make a noise by talking, but attend. Is anything more unbecoming than the divine words should be so drowned by talking, as not to be heard, believed, or made known, that the sacraments should be indistinctly heard through the sound of voices, that prayer should be hindered when offered for the salvation of all?

12. The Gentiles pay respect to their idols by silence, of which this instance is given: As Alexander, the king of the Macedonians, was sacrificing, the sleeve of a barbarian lad who was lighting the lamp for him caught fire and burnt his body, yet he remained without moving and neither betrayed the pain by a groan, nor showed his suffering by silent tears. Such was the discipline of reverence in a barbarian lad that nature was subdued. Yet he feared not the gods, who were no gods, but the king. For why should he fear those who if the same fire had caught them would have burnt?

13. How much better still is it where a youth at his father's banquet is bidden not to betray by coarse gestures his unchaste loves. And do you, holy virgin, abstain from groans, cries, coughing, and laughter at the Mystery. Can you not at the Mystery do what he did at a banquet? Let virginity be first marked by the voice, let modesty close the mouth, let religion remove weakness, and habit instruct nature. Let her gravity first announce a virgin to me, a modest approach, a sober gait, a bashful countenance, and let the march of virtue be preceded by the evidence of integrity. That virgin is not sufficiently worthy of approval who has to be enquired about when she is seen.

14. There is common story how, when the excessive croaking of frogs was resounding in the ears of the faithful people, the priest of God bade them be silent, and show reverence to the sacred words, and then at once the noise was stilled. Shall then the marshes keep silence and not the frogs? And shall irrational animals re-acknowledge by reverence what they know not by nature? While the shamelessness of men is such, that many care not to pay that respect to the religious feelings of their minds, which they do to the pleasure of their ears.

Chapter IV.

Having summed up the address of Liberius, St. Ambrose passes on to the virtues of his sister, especially her fasts, which however he advises her to moderate to some extent, and to exercise herself in other matters, after the example which he adduces. Especially he recommends the Lord's Prayer, and the repetition of Psalms by night, and the recitation of the Creed before daylight.

15. After such a fashion did Liberius of holy memory address you, in words beyond the reality of practice in most cases, but coming short of your performance, who have not only attained to the whole of discipline by your virtue, but have surpassed it in your zeal. For we are bidden to practise fasting, but only for single days; but you, multiplying nights and days, pass untold periods without food, and if ever requested to partake of some, and to lay aside your book a little while, you at once answer: "Man doth not live by bread alone, but by every word of God." Your very meals consisted but of what food came to hand, so that fasting is to be preferred to eating what was repugnant; your drink is from the spring, your weeping and prayer combine, your sleep is on your book.

16. These kings were suited to younger years, whilst he was ripening with the gray hairs of age; but when a virgin has gained the triumph over her subdued body, she should lessen her toil,

that she may be preserved as teacher for a younger age. The vine laden with the fruitful branches of full growth soon breaks unless it be from time to time kept back. But whilst it is young let it grow rank, and as it grows older be pruned, so as not to grow into a forest of twigs, or die deprived of life by its exceptive produce. A good husbandman by tending the soil keeps the vine in excellent order, protects it from cold, and guards it from being parched by the mid-day sun. And he works his land by turns, or if he will not let it lie fallow, he alternates his crops, so that the fields may rest through change of produce. Do you too, a veteran in virginity, at least sow the fields of your breast with different seeds, at one time with moderate sustenance, at another with sparing fasts, with reading, work, and prayer, that change of toil may be as a truce for rest.

17. The whole land does not produce the same harvest. On one side vines grow on the hills, on another you can see the purple olives, elsewhere the scented roses. And after leaving the plough, the strong husbandman with his fingers scrapes the soil to plant the roots of flowers, and with the rough hands wherewith he turns the bullocks striving amongst the vines, he gently presses the udders of the sheep. The land is the better the more numerous are its fruits. So do you, following the example of a good husbandman, avoid cleaving your soil with perpetual fastings as if with deep ploughings. Let the rose of modesty bloom in your garden, and the lily of the mind, and let the violet beds drink from the source of sacred blood. There is a common saying, "What you wish to perform abundantly, sometimes do not do at all." There ought to be something to add to the days of Lent, but so that nothing be done for the sake of ostentation, but of religion.

18. Frequent prayer also commends us to God. For if the prophet says, "Seven times a day have I praised Thee," though he was busy with the affairs of a kingdom, what ought we to do, who read: "Watch and pray that ye enter not into temptation"? Certainly our customary prayers ought to be said with giving of thanks, when we rise from sleep, when we go forth, when we prepare to receive food, after receiving it, and at the hour of incense, when at last we are going to rest.

19. And again in your bed-chamber itself, I would have you join psalms in frequent interchange with the Lord's prayer, either when you wake up, or before sleep bedews your body, so that at the very commencement of rest sleep may find you free from the care of worldly matters, meditating upon the things of God. And, indeed, he who first found out the name of Philosophy itself, every day before he went to rest, had the flute-player play softer melodies to soothe his mind disturbed by worldly cares. But he, like a man washing tiles, fruitlessly desired to drive away worldly things by worldly means, for he was, indeed, rather besmearing himself with fresh mud, in seeking a reward from pleasure, but let us, having wiped off the filth of earthly vices, purify our utmost souls from every defilement of the flesh.

20. We ought, also, specially to repeat the Creed, as a seal upon our hearts, daily, before light, and to recur to it in thought whenever we are in fear of anything. For when is the soldier in his tent or the warrior in battle without his military oath?

Chapter V.

St. Ambrose, speaking of tears, explains David's saying, "Every night wash I my couch with my tears," and goes on to speak of Christ bearing our griefs and infirmities. Everything should be referred to His honour, and we ought to rejoice with spiritual joy, but not after a worldly fashion.

21. And who can now fail to understand that the holy prophet said for our instruction: "Every night will I wash my couch and water my bed with my tears"? For if you take it literally for his bed, he shows that such abundance of tears should be shed as to wash the bed and water it with tears, the couch of him who is praying, for weeping has to do with the present, rewards with the future, since it is said: "Blessed are ye that weep, for ye shall laugh;" or if we take the word of the prophet as applied to our bodies, we must wash away the offences of the body with tears of penitence. For Solomon made himself a bed of wood from Lebanon, its pillars were of silver, its bottom of gold, its back strewn with gems. What is that bed but the fashion of our

body? For by gems is set forth the splendour of the brightness of the air, fire is set forth by the gold, water by silver, and earth by wood, of which four elements the human body consists, in which our soul rests, if it do not exist deprived of rest by the roughness of hills or the damp ground, but raised on high, above vices, supported by the wood. For which reason David also says: "The Lord will send him help upon his bed of pain." For how can that be a bed of pain which cannot feel pain, and which has no feeling? But the body of pain is like the body of that death, of which it is said: "O wretched man that I am, who shall deliver me from the body of this death?"

22. And since I have inserted a clause in which mention is made of the Lord's Body, lest any one should be troubled at reading that the Lord took a body of pain, let him remember that the Lord grieved and wept over the death of Lazarus, and was wounded in His passion, and that from the wound there went forth blood and water, and that He gave up His Spirit. Water for washing, Blood for drink, the Spirit for His rising again. For Christ alone is to us hope, faith, and love—hope in His resurrection, faith in the layer, and love in the sacrament.

23. And as He took a body of pain, so too He turned His bed in His weakness. for He converted it to the benefit of human flesh. For by His Passion weakness was ended, and death by His resurrection. And yet you ought to mourn for the world but to rejoice in the Lord, to be sad for penitence but joyful for grace, though, too, the teacher of the Gentiles by a wholesome precept has bidden to weep with them that weep, and to rejoice with them that do rejoice.

24. But let him who desires to solve the whole difficulty of this question have recourse to the same Apostle. "Whatsoever ye do," says he, "in word or deed, do all in the Name of our Lord Jesus Christ, giving thanks to God the Father by Him." Let us then refer all our words and deeds to Christ, Who brought life out of death, and created light out of darkness. For as a sick body is at one time cherished by warmth, at another soothed by cool applications, and the variation of remedies, if carried out according to the direction of the physician, is healthful, but if done in opposition to his orders increases the sickness; so whatever is paid to Christ is a remedy, whatever is done by our own will is harmful.

25. There ought then to be the joy of the mind, conscious of right, not excited by unrestrained feasts, or nuptial concerts, for in such modesty is not safe, and temptation may be suspected where excessive dancing accompanies festivities. I desire that the virgins of God should be far from this. For as a certain teacher of this world has said: "No one dances when sober unless he is mad." Now if, according to the wisdom of this world, either drunkenness or madness is the cause of dancing, what a warning is given to us amongst the instances mentioned in the Divine Scriptures, where John, the forerunner of Christ, being beheaded at the wish of a dancer, is an instance that the allurements of dancing did more harm than the madness of sacrilegious anger.

Chapter VI.

Having mentioned the Baptist, St. Ambrose enters into a description of the events concerning his death, and speaks against dancing and the festivities of the wicked.

26. And since we must not cursorily pass by the mention of so great a man, let us consider who he was, by whom, on what account, how, and at what time he was slain. A just man, he is put to death by adulterers, and the penalty of a capital crime is turned off by the guilty on to the judge. Again the reward of the dancer is the death of the prophet. Lastly (a matter of honour even to all barbarians), the cruel sentence is given in the midst of banqueting and festivities, and the news of the deadly crime is carried from the banquet to the prison, and then from the prison to the banquet. How many crimes are there in one wicked act!

27. A banquet of death is set out with royal luxury, and when a larger concourse than usual had come together, the daughter of the queen, sent for from within the private apartments, is brought forth to dance in the sight of men. What could she have learnt from an adulteress but loss of modesty? Is anything so conducive to lust as with unseemly movements thus to expose

in nakedness those parts of the body which either nature has hidden or custom has veiled, to sport with the looks, to turn the neck, to loosen the hair? Fitly was the next step an offence against God. For what modesty can there be where there is dancing and noise and clapping of hands?

28. "Then," it is said, "the king being pleased, said unto the damsel, that she should ask of the king whatsoever she would. Then he swore that if she asked he would give her even the half of his kingdom." See how worldly men themselves judge of their worldly power, so as to give even kingdoms for dancing. But the damsel, being taught by her mother, demanded that the head of John should be brought to her on a dish. That which is said that "the king was sorry, " is not repentance on the part of the king, but a confession of guilt, which is, according to the wont of the divine rule, that they who have done evil condemn themselves by their own confession. "But for their sakes which sat with him," it is said. What is more base than that a murder should be committed in order not to displease those who sat at meat? "And," it follows, "for his oath's sake." What a new religion! He had better have forsworn himself. The Lord therefore in the Gospel bids us not to swear at all, that there be no cause for perjury, and no need of offending. And so an innocent man is slain that an oath be not violated. I know which to have in the greatest horror. Perjury is more endurable than are theoaths of tyrants.

29. Who would not think when he saw some one running from the banquet to the prison, that orders had been given to set the prophet free? Who, I say, having heard that it was Herod's birthday, and of the state banquet, and the choice given to the damsel of choosing whatever she wished, would not think that the man was sent to set John free? What has cruelty in common with delicacies? What have death and pleasure in common? The prophet is hurried to suffer at a festal time by a festal order, by which he would even wish to be set free; he is slain by the sword, and his head is brought on a platter. This dish was well suited to their cruelty, in order that their insatiate savageness might be feasted.

30. Look, most savage king, at the sights worthy of thy feast. Stretch forth thy right hand, that nothing be wanting to thy cruelty, that streams of holy blood may pour down between thy fingers. And since the hunger for such unheard-of cruelty could not be satisfied by banquets, nor the thirst by goblets, drink the blood pouring from the still flowing veins of the cut-off head. Behold those eyes, even in death, the witnesses of thy crime, turning away from the sight of the delicacies. The eyes are closing, not so much owing to death, as to horror of luxury. That bloodless golden mouth, whose sentence thou couldst not endure, is silent, and yet thou fearest. Yet the tongue, which even after death is wont to observe its duty as when living, condemned, though with trembling motion, the incest. This head is borne to Herodias: she rejoices, she exults as though she had escaped from the crime, because she has slain her judge.

31. What say you, holy women? Do you see what you ought to teach, and what also to unteach your daughters? She dances, but she is the daughter of an adulteress. But she who is modest, she who is chaste, let her teach her daughter religion, not dancing. And do you, grave and prudent men, learn to avoid the banquets of hateful men. If such are the banquets, what will be the judgment of the impious?

Chapter VII.

In reply to Marcellina, who had asked what should be thought of those who to escape violence killed themselves, St. Ambrose replies by narrating the history of Pelagia, a virgin, with her mother and sister, and goes on to speak of the martyrdom of the blessed Sotheris, one of their own ancestors.

32. As I am drawing near the close of my address, you make a good suggestion, holy sister, that I should touch upon what we ought to think of the merits of those who have cast themselves down from a height, or have drowned themselves in a river, lest they should fall into the hands of persecutors, seeing that holy Scripture forbids a Christian to lay hands on himself. And indeed as regard; virgins placed in the necessity of preserving their purity, we have a plain answer, seeing that there exists an instance of martyrdom.

33. Saint Pelagia lived formerly at Antioch, being about fifteen years old, a sister of virgins, and a virgin herself. She shut herself up at home at the first sound of persecution, seeing herself surrounded by those who would rob her of her faith and purity, in the absence of her mother and sisters, without any defence, but all the more filled with God. "What are we to do, unless," says she to herself, "thou, a captive of virginity, takest thought? I both wish and fear to die, for I meet not death but seek it. Let us die if we are allowed, or if they will not allow it, still let us die. God is not offended by a remedy against evil, and faith permits the act. In truth, if we think of the real meaning of the word, how can what is voluntary be violence? It is rather violence to wish to die and not to be able. And we do not fear any difficulty. For who is there who wishes to die and is not able to do so, when there are so many easy ways to death? For I can now rush upon the sacrilegious altars and overthrow them, and quench with my blood the kindled fires. I am not afraid that my right hand may fail to deliver the blow, or that my breast may shrink from the pain. I shall leave no sin to my flesh. I fear not that a sword will be wanting. I can die by my own weapons, I can die without the help of an executioner, in my mother's bosom."

34. She is said to have adorned her head, and to have put on a bridal dress, so that one would say that she was going to a bridegroom, not to death. But when the hateful persecutors saw that they had lost the prey of her chastity, they began to seek her mother and sisters. But they, by a spiritual flight, already held the field of chastity, when, as on the one side, persecutors suddenly threatened them, and on the other, escape was shut off by an impetuous river, they said, what do we fear? See the water, what hinders us from being baptized? And this is the baptism whereby sins are forgiven, and kingdoms are sought. This is a baptism after which no one sins. Let the water receive us, which is wont to regenerate. Let the water receive us, which makes virgins. Let the water receive us, which opens heaven, protects the weak, hides death, makes martyrs. We pray Thee, God, Creator of all things, let not the water scatter our bodies, deprived of the breath of life; let not death separate our obsequies, whose lives affection has always conjoined; but let our constancy be one, our death one, and our burial also be one.

35. Having said these words, and having slightly girded up the bosom of their dress, to veil their modesty without impeding their steps, joining hands as though to lead a dance, they went forward to the middle of the river bed, directing their steps to where the stream was more violent, and the depth more abrupt. No one drew back, no one ceased to go on, no one tried where to place her steps, they were anxious only when they felt the ground, grieved when the water was shallow, and glad when it was deep. One could see the pious mother tightening her grasp, rejoicing in her pledges, afraid of a fall test even the stream should carry off her daughters from her. "These victims, O Christ," said she, "do I offer as leaders of chastity, guides on my journey, and companions of my sufferings."

37. But who would have cause to wonder that they had such constancy whilst alive, seeing that even when dead they preserved the position of their bodies unmoved? The water did not lay bare their corpses, nor did the rapid course of the river roll them along. Moreover, the holy mother, though without sensation, still maintained her loving grasp, and held the sacred knot which she had tied, and loosed not her hold in death, that she who had paid her debt to religion might die leaving her piety as her heir. For those whom she had joined together with herself for martyrdom, she claimed even to the tomb.

38. But why use instances of people of another race to you, my sister, whom the inspiration of hereditary chastity has taught by descent from a martyred ancestor? For whence have you learnt who had no one from whom to learn, living in the country, with no virgin companion, instructed by no teacher? You have played the part then not of a disciple, for this cannot be done without teaching, but of an heir of virtue.

39. For how could it come to pass that holy Sotheris should not have been the originator of your purpose, who is an ancestor of your race? Who, in an age of persecution, borne to the heights of suffering by the insults of slaves, gave to the executioner even her face, which is usually free from injury when the whole body is tortured, and rather beholds than suffers

torments; so brave and patient that when she offered her tender cheeks to punishment, the executioner failed in striking before the martyr yielded under the injuries. She moved not her face, she turned not away her countenance, she uttered not a groan or a tear. Lastly, when she had overcome other kinds of punishment, she found the sword which she desired.

Concerning Widows. Introduction.

The writer informs us himself at the beginning of his treaise that he felt moved by the example of St. Paul, after speaking about virgings, to continue with the subject of widows. But there was also another matter in his own diocese which touched him personally, and caused him at once to take up the matter. A certain widow who had several daughters, some married already and others of marriageable age, began to think of a second marriage for herself. St. Ambrose, partly for her own sake, partly that it might not be supposed that he had in any way advised the step, published the following treatise.

In the frst place he affirms that the profession of widowhood comes very closed to that of virginity, and is to be esteemed far above the married state. He proves this by the testimony of St. Paul and by his description of one who is a widow indeed; also by many examples taken both from the old and New Testament. Having mentioned St. Peter's wife's mother, he trun more particularly to the widow for whose sake he is writing, though he avoids mentioning her name, pointing out how really empty and insufficient are all the reasons she is setting before herself for marrying again. The marriage bond is, indeed, he says, holy and good, and the married and single are as various kinds of flowers in the field of the church. There is, However, more corn produced than lilies, more that is married than virgin. He points out that widowhood has been held in dishonour by idolaters alone, for which reason it may well be held in honour by Christians. St. Ambrose does not condemn a second marriage, though placing widowhood befere it, as being bound to aim at leading those committed to his loving carc to the highest possible degree of perfection.

The treatise was written not long after that concerning Virgins, that is, soon after a.d. 337

THE TREATISE CONCERNING WIDOWS.

Chapter I.

After having written about virgins, it seemed needful to say something concerning widows, since the Apostle joins the two classes together, and the latter are as it were teachers of the former, and far superior to those who are married. Elijah was sent to a widow, a great mark of honour; yet widows are not honourable like her of Sarepta, unless they copy her virtues, notably hospitality. The avarice of men is rebuked, who forfeit the promises of God by their grasping.

1. Since I have treated of the honour of virgins in three books, it is fitting now, my brethren, that a treatise concerning widows should come in order; for I ought not to leave them without honour, nor to separate them from the commendation belonging to virgins, since the voice of the Apostle has joined them to virgins, according to what is written: "The unmarried woman and the virgin careth for the things of the Lord, that she may be holy both in body and in spirit." For in a certain manner the inculcation of virginity is strengthened by the example of widows. They who have preserved their marriage bed undefiled are a testimony to virgins that chastity is to be preserved for God. And it is almost a mark of no less virtue to abstain from marriage, which was once a delight, than to remain ignorant of the pleasures of wedlock. They are strong in each point, in that they regret not wedlock, the faith of which they keep, and entangle not themselves with wedded pleasures, lest they appear weak and not able to take care of themselves.

2. But in this particular virtue is contained also the prizes of liberty. For: "The wife is bound as long as her husband liveth; but if her husband fall asleep she is freed: let her marry whom she will, only in the Lord. But she will be happier if she so abide, after my judgment, for I think I also have the Spirit of God." Evidently, then, the Apostle has expressed the difference, having said that the one is bound, and stated that the other is happier, and that he asserts not so much as the result of his own judgment, as of the infusion of the Spirit of God; that the decision should be seen to be heavenly, not human.

3. And what is the teaching of the fact that at that time when the whole human race was afflicted by famine and Elias was sent to the widow? And see how for each is reserved her own special grace. An angel is sent to the Virgin, a prophet to the widow. Notice, farther, that in one case it is Gabriel, in the other Elisha. The most excellent chiefs of the number of angels and prophets are seen to be chosen. But there is no praise simply in widowhood, unless there be added the virtues of widowhood. For, indeed, there were many widows, but one is preferred to all, in which fact it is not so much that others are called back from their pursuit as that they are stimulated by the example of virtue.

4. What is said at first makes the ears attentive, although the simplicity itself of the understanding has weight to attract widows to the pattern of virtue; since each seems to excel, not according to her profession, but her merit, and the grace of hospitality is not lost sight of by God, Who, as He Himself related in the Gospel, rewards a cup of cold water with the exceeding recompense of eternity, and compensates the small measure of meal and oil by an unfailing abundance of plenty ever coming in. For if one of the heathen has said that all the possessions of friends should be common, how much more ought those of relatives to be common! For we are relatives who are bound into one body.

5. But we are not bound by any prescribed limit of hospitality. For why do you think that what is of this world is private property when this world is common? Or why do you consider the fruits of the earth are private, when the earth itself is common property? "Behold," He said, "the fowls of the air, they sow not, neither do they reap." For to those to whom nothing is private property nothing is wanting, and God, the master of His own word, knows how to keep His promise. Again, the birds do not gather together, and yet they eat, for our heavenly Father feeds them. But we turning aside the warnings of a general utterance to our private advantage, God says: "Every tree which has in it the fruit of a tree yielding seed shall be to you for meat,

and to every beast, and to every bird, and to everything that creepeth upon the earth." By gathering together we come to want, and by gathering together we are made empty. For we cannot hope for the promise, who keep not the saying. It is also good for us to attend to the precept of hospitality, to be ready to give to strangers, for we, too, are strangers in the world.

6. But how holy was that widow, who, when pinched by extreme hunger. observed the reverence due to God, and was not using the food for herself alone, but was dividing it with her son, that she might not outlive her dear offspring. Great is the duty of affection, but that of religion brings more return. For as no one ought to be set before her son, so the prophet of God ought to be set before her son and her preservation. For she is to be believed to have given to him not a little food, but the whole support of her life, who left nothing for herself. So hospitable was she that she gave the whole, so full of faith that she believed at once.

Chapter II.

The precepts of the Apostle concerning a widow indeed are laid down, such as, that she bring up children, attend to her parents, desire to please God, show herself irreproachable, set forth a ripeness of merits, have been the wife of one man. St. Ambrose notes, however, that a second marriage was not condemned by St. Paul, and adds that widows must have a good report for virtue with all. The reasons why younger widows are to be avoided, and what is meant by its being better to marry than to burn. St. Ambrose then goes on to speak of the dignity of widows, shown by the fact that any injury done to them is visited by the anger of God.

7. So, then, a widow is not only marked off by bodily abstinence, but is distinguished by virtue, to whom I do not give commandments, but the Apostle. I am not the only person to do them honour, but the Doctor of the Gentiles did so first, when he said: "Honour widows that are widows indeed. But if any widow have children or nephews, let her first learn to govern her own house, and to requite her parents." Whence we observe that each inclination of affection ought to exist in a widow, to love her children and to do her duty to her parents. So when discharging her duty to her parents she is teaching her children, and is rewarded herself by her own compliance with duty, in that what she performs for others benefits herself.

8. "For this," says he, "is acceptable with God." So that if thou, O widow, carest for the things of God, thou oughtest to follow after that which thou hast learnt to be well pleasing to God. And, indeed, the Apostle somewhat farther back, exhorting widows to the pursuit of continence, said that they mind the things of the Lord. But elsewhere, when a widow who is approved is to be selected, she is bidden not only to bear in mind but also to hope in the Lord: "For she that is a widow indeed," it is said, "and desolate, must hope in God, and be instant in supplications and prayers night and day." And not without reason does he show that these ought to be blameless, to whom, as virtuous works are enjoined, so, too, great respect is paid, so that they are honoured even by bishops.

9. And of what kind she ought to be who is chosen the description is given in the words of the teacher himself: "Not less than threescore years old, having been the wife of one man." Not that old age alone makes the widow, but that the merits of the widow are the duties of old age. For she certainly is the more noble who represses the heat of youth, and the impetuous ardour of youthful age, desiring neither the tenderness of a husband, nor the abundant delights of children, rather than one who, now worn out in body, cold in age, of ripe years, can neither grow warm with pleasures, nor hope for offspring.

10. Nor in truth is any one excluded from the devotion of widowhood, if after entering upon a second marriage, which the precepts of the Apostle certainly do not condemn as though the fruit of chastity were lost, if she be again loosed from her husband. She will have, indeed, the merit of her chastity, even if it be tardy, but she will be more approved who has tried a second marriage, for the desire of chastity is conspicuous in her, for the other old age or shame seems to have put an end to marrying.

11. Nor yet is bodily chastity alone the strong purpose of the widow, but a large and most abundant exercise of virtue. "Well reported of for good works, if she have brought up children;

if she have lodged strangers; if she have washed the saints' feet; if she have ministered to those suffering tribulation; if, lastly, she have followed after every good work." You see how many practices of virtue he has included. He demands, first of all, the duty of piety; secondly, the practice of hospitality and humble service; thirdly, the ministry of mercy and liberality in assisting; and, lastly, the performance of every good work.

12. And he, therefore, that the younger should be avoided, because they are not able to fulfil the requirements of so high a degree of virtue. For youth is prone to fall because the heat of various desires is inflamed by the warmth of glowing youth, and it is the part of a good doctor to keep off the materials of sin. For the first exercise in training the soul is to turn away sin, the second to implant virtue. Yet, since the Apostle knew that Anna, the widow of fourscore years, from her youth was a herald of the works of the Lord, I do not think that he thought that the younger should be excluded from the devotion of widowhood, especially as he said: "It is better to marry than to burn." For certainly he recommended marriage as a remedy, that she who would else perish might be saved; he did not prescribe the choice that one who could contain should not follow chastity, for it is one thing to succour one who is falling, another to persuade to virtue.

13. And what shall I say of human judgments, since in the judgments of God the Jews are set forth as having offended the Lord in nothing more than violating what was due to the widow and the rights of minors? This is proclaimed by the voices of the prophets as the cause which brought upon the Jews the penalty of rejection. This is mentioned as the only cause which will mitigate the wrath of God against their sin. if they honour the widow, and execute true judgment for minors, for thus we read: "Judge the fatherless, deal justly with the widow, and come let us reason together, saith the Lord." And elsewhere: "The Lord shall maintain the orphan and the widow." And again: "I will abundantly bless her widow." Wherein also the likeness of the Church is foreshadowed. You see, then, holy widows, that that office which is honoured by the assistance of divine grace must not be degraded by impure desire.

Chapter III.

St. Ambrose returns to the story of the widow of Sarepta, and shows that she represented the Church, hence that she was an example to virgins, married women, and widows. Then he refers to the prophet as setting forth Christ, inasmuch as he foretold the mysteries and the rain which was to come. Next he touches upon and explains the twofold sign of Gideon, and points out that it is not in every one's power to work miracles, and that the Incarnation of Christ and the rejection of the Jews were foreshadowed in that account.

14. To return to what was treated of above, what is the meaning of the fact that when there was a very great famine in all the land, yet the care of God was not wanting to the widow, and the prophet was sent to sustain her? And when in this story the Lord warns me that He is about to speak in truth, He seems to bid my ears attend to a mystery. For what can be more true than the mystery of Christ and the Church? Not, then, without a purpose is one preferred amongst many widows. Who is such an one, to whom so great a prophet who was carried up into heaven, should be guided, especially at that time when the heaven was shut for three years and six months, when there was a great famine in the whole land? The famine was everywhere, and yet notwithstanding this widow did not want. What are these three years? Are they not, perchance, those in which the Lord came to the earth and could not find fruit on the fig-tree, according to that which is written: "Behold, there are three years that I came seeking fruit on this fig-tree, and find none."

15. This is assuredly that widow of whom it was said: "Rejoice, thou barren that bearest not, break forth and cry, thou that availest not with child; for many are the children of the desolate, more than of her who hath an husband." And well is she a widow of whom it is well said: "Thou shalt not remember thy shame and thy widowhood, for I am the Lord Who make thee." And perchance therefore is she a widow who has lost her Husband indeed in the suffering of His body, but in the day of judgment shall receive again the Son of Man Whom she seemed to

have lost. "For a short time have I forsaken thee," He says, in order that, being forsaken, she may the more gloriously keep her faith.

16. All, then, have an example to imitate, virgins, married women, and widows. And perchance is the Church therefore a virgin, married, and a widow, because they are one body in Christ. She is then that widow for Whose sake when there was a dearth of the heavenly Word on earth, the prophets were appointed, for there was a widow who was barren, yet reserved her bringing forth for its own time.

17. So that his person does not seem to us of small account, who by his word moistened the dry earth with the dew of heaven, and unlocked the closed heavens certainly not by human power. For who is he who can open the heavens except Christ, for Whom daily out of sinners food is gathered, an increase for the Church? For it is not in the power of man to say: "The barrel of meal shall not waste, and the cruse of oil shall not fail, until the day on which the Lord shall send rain on the earth," For though it be the rule of the prophets to speak thus, the voice is in truth that of the Lord. And so it is stated first: "For thus saith the Lord." For it is of the Lord to vouch for a continuance of heavenly sacraments, and to promise that the grace of spiritual joy shall not fail, to grant the defences of life, the seals of faith, the gifts of virtues.

18. But what does this mean: "Until the day on which the Lord shall send rain on the earth"? except that He, too, "shall come down like rain upon a fleece, and like the drops that water the earth." In which passage is disclosed the mystery of the old history where Gideon, the warrior of the mystic conflict, receiving the pledge of future victory, recognized the spiritual sacrament in the vision of his mind, that that rain was the dew of the Divine Word, which first came down on the fleece, when all the earth was parched with continual drought, and by a second true sign, moistened the floor of all the earth with a shower, whilst dryness was upon the fleece.

19. For the prescient man observed the sign of the future growth of the Church. For first in Judaea the dew of the divine utterance began to give moisture (for "in Jewry is God known"), whilst the whole earth remained without the dew of faith. But when Joseph's flock began to deny God, and by venturing on various enormous offences to incur guilt before God, then when the dew of the heavenly shower was poured on the whole earth, the people of the Jews began to grow dry and parched in their own unbelief, when the clouds of prophecy and the healthful shower of the Apostles watered the holy Church gathered together from all parts of the world. This is that rain, now condensed from earthly moisture, now from mountain mists, but diffused throughout the whole world in the salutary shower of the heavenly Scriptures.

20. By this example, then, it is shown that not all can merit the miracles of divine power, but they who are aided by the pursuits of religious devotion, and that they lose the fruits of divine working who are devoid of reverence for heaven. It is also shown in a mystery that the Son of God, in order to restore the Church, took upon Himself the mystery of a human body, casting off the Jewish people, from whom the counsellor and the prophet and the miracles of the divine benefits were taken away, because that as it were by a kind of national blemish they were not willing to believe in the Son of God.

Chapter IV.

By the example of Anna St. Ambrose shows what ought to be the life of widows, and shows that she was an example of chastity at every age. From this he argues that there are three degrees of the same virtue, all of which are included in the Church, and sets forth several examples in Mary, in Anna, and in Susanna. But, he adds, the state of virginity is superior to either of the others, but that a widow ought to take greater care for the preservation of her good name.

21. Scripture then teaches as how much grace is conferred by unity, and how great is the gift of divine blessing in widows. And since such honour is given them by God, we must observe what mode of life corresponds thereto; for Anna shows what widows ought to be, who, left destitute by the early death of her husband, yet obtained the reward of full praise, being intent not less on the duties of religion than on the pursuit of chastity. A widow, it is said, of fourscore

and four years, a widow who departed not from the temple, a widow who served God night and day with fastings and with prayers.

22. You see what sort of person a widow is said to be, the wife of one man, tested also by the progress of age, vigorous in religion, and worn out in body, whose resting-place is the temple, whose conversation is prayer, whose life is fasting, who in the times of day and night by a service of unwearied devotion, though the body acknowledge old age, yet knows no age in her piety. Thus is a widow trained from her youth, thus is she spoken of in her age, who has kept her widowhood not through the chance of time, nor through weakness of body, but by large-heartedness in virtue. For when it is said that she was for seven years from her virginity with her husband, it is a setting forth that the things which are the support of her old age began in the aims of her youth.

23. And so we are taught that the virtue of chastity is threefold, one kind that of married life, a second that of widowhood, and the third that of virginity, for we do not so set forth one as to exclude others. These result each in that which belongs to each. The training of the Church is rich in this, that it has those whom it may set before others, but has none whom it rejects, and would that it never could have any! We have so spoken of virginity as not to reject widowhood, we so reverence widows as to reserve its own honour for wedlock. It is not our precepts but the divine sayings which teach this.

24. Let us remember then how Mary, how Anna, and how Susanna are spoken of. But since not only must we celebrate their praises but also follow their manner of life, let us remember where Susanna, and Anna, and Mary are found, and observe how each is spoken of with her special commendation, and where each is mentioned, she that is married in the garden, the widow in the temple, the virgin in her secret chamber.

25. But in the former the fruit is later, in virginity it is earlier; old age proves them, virginity is the praise of youth, and does not need the help of years, being the fruit of every age. It becomes early years, it adorns youth, it adds to the dignity of age, and at all ages it has the gray hairs of its righteousness, the ripeness of its gravity, the veil of modesty, which does hinder devotion and increases religion. For we see by what follows that holy Mary went every year with Joseph to Jerusalem on the solemn day of the passover. Everywhere in company with the Virgin is eager devotion and a zealous sharer of her chastity. Nor is the Mother of the Lord puffed up, as though secure of her own merits, but the more she recognized her merit, the more fully did she pay her vows, the more abundantly did she perform her service, the more fully did she discharge her office, the more religiously did she perform her duty and fill up the mystic time.

26. How much more then does it beseem you to be intent on the pursuit of chastity, lest you leave any place for unfavourable opinion who have the evidence of your modesty and your behaviour alone. For a virgin, though in her also character rather than the body has the first claim, puts away calumny by the integrity of her body, a widow who has lost the assistance of being able to prove her virginity undergoes the inquiry as to her chastity not according to the word of a midwife, but according to her own manner of life. Scripture, then, has shown how attentive and religious should be the disposition of a widow.

Chapter V.

Liberality to the poor is recommended by the example of the widow the Gospel, whose two mites were preferred to the large gifts of the rich. The two mites are treated as mystically representing the two Testaments. What that treasure is for which we are taught to offer, after the example of the wise men, three gifts, or after that of the widow, two. St. Ambrose concludes the chapter by an exhortation to widows to be zealous in good works.

27. In the same book, too, but in another place, we are taught how fitting it is to be merciful and liberal towards the poor, and that this feeling should not be checked by the consideration of our poverty, since liberality is determined not by the amount of our possessions, but by the disposition of giving. For by the voice of the Lord that widow is preferred to all of whom it was said: "This widow hath cast in more than all." In which instance the Lord characteristically

teaches all, that none should be held back from giving assistance through shame at his own poverty, and that the rich should not flatter themselves that they seem to give more than the poor. For the piece of money out of a small stock is richer than treasures out of abundance, because it is not the amount that is given but the amount that remains which is considered. No one gives more than she who has left nothing for herself.

28. Why do you, rich woman, boast yourself by comparison with the poor, and when you are all loaded with gold, and drag along the ground a costly robe, desire to be honoured as though she were inferior and small in comparison with your riches, because you have surpassed the needy with your gifts? Rivers too overflow, when they are too full, but a draught from a brook is more pleasant. New wine foams while fermenting, and the husbandman does not consider as lost that which runs over. While the harvest is being threshed out, grains of corn fall from the groaning floor; but though the harvests fail, the barrel of meal wastes not, and the cruse full of oil gives forth. But the draught emptied the casks of the rich, while the tiny cruse of oil of the widow gave abundance. That, then, is to be reckoned which you give for devotion, not what you cast forth disdainfully. For in fine, no one gave more than she who fed the prophet with her children's nourishment. And so since no one gave more, no one had greater merit. This has a moral application.

29. And considering the mystical sense, one must not despise this woman casting in two mites into the treasury. Plainly the woman was noble who in the divine judgment was found worthy to be preferred to all. Perchance it is she who of her faith has given two testaments for the help of man, and so no one has done more. Nor could any one equal the amount of her gift, who joined faith with mercy. Do you, then, whoever you are, who exercise your life the practice of widowhood, not hesitate to cast into the treasury the two mites, full of faith and grace.

30. Happy is she who out of her treasure brings forth the perfect image of the King. Your treasure is wisdom, your treasure is chastity and righteousness, your treasure is a good understanding, such as was that treasure from which the Magi, when they worshipped the Lord, brought forth gold, frankincense, and myrrh; setting forth by gold the power of a king, venerating God by the frankincense, and by myrrh acknowledging the resurrection of the body. You too have this treasure if you look into yourself: "For we have this treasure in earthen vessels." You have gold which you can give, for God does not exact of you the precious gift of shining metal, but that gold which at the day of judgment the fire shall be unable to consume. Nor does He require precious gifts, but the good odour of faith, which the altars of your heart send forth and the disposition of a religious mind exhales.

31. From this treasure, then, not only the three gifts of the Magi but also the two mites of the widow are taken, on which the perfect image of the heavenly King shines forth, the brightness of His glory and the image of His substance. Precious, too, are those hardly earned gains of chastity which the widow gives of her labour and daily task, continually night and day working at her task, and by the wakeful labour of her profitable chastity gathering treasure; that she may preserve the couch of her deceased husband unviolated, be able to support her dear children, and to minister to the poor. She is to be preferred to the rich, she it is who shall not fear the judgment of Christ.

32. Strive to equal her, my daughters: "It is good to be zealously affected in a good thing." "Covet earnestly the best gifts" The Lord is ever looking upon you, Jesus looks upon you when He goes to the treasury, and you think that of the gain of your good works assistance is to be given to those in need. What is it, then, that you should give your two mites and gain in return the Lord's Body? Go not, then, empty into the sight of the Lord your God, empty of mercy, empty of faith, empty of chastity; for the Lord Jesus is wont to look upon and to commend not the empty, but those who are rich in virtues. Let the maiden see you at work, let her see you ministering to others. For this is the return which you owe to God, that you should make your return to God from the progress of others. No return is more acceptable to God than the offerings of piety.

Chapter VI.

Naomi is an instance of a widow receiving back from her daughter-in-law the fruits of her own good training, and is a token that necessary support will never fail the good widow. And if her life appears sad, she is happy, since the promises of the Lord are made to her. St. Ambrose then touches upon the benefits of weeping.

33. Does the widow Naomi seem to you of small account, who supported her widowhood on the gleanings from another's harvest, and who, when heavy with age, was supported by her daughter-in-law? It is a great benefit both for the support and for the advantage of widows, that they so train their daughters-in-law as to have in them a support in full old age, and, as it were, payment for their teaching and reward for their training. For to her who has well taught and well instructed her daughter-in-law a Ruth will never be wanting who will prefer the widowed life of her mother-in-law to her father's house, and if her husband also be dead, will not leave her, will support her in need, comfort her in sorrow, and not leave her if sent away; for good instruction will never know want. So that Naomi, deprived of her husband and her two sons, having lost the offspring of her fruitfulness, lost not the reward of her pious care, for she found both a comfort in sorrow and a support in poverty.

34. You see, then, holy women, how fruitful a widow is in the offspring of virtues, and the results of her own merits, which cannot come to an end. A good widow, then, knows no want, and if she be weary through age, in extreme poverty, yet she has as a rule the reward of the training she has given. Though the nearest to herself have failed, she finds those not so near akin to cherish their mother, revere their parent, and by the trifling gifts for her support desire to gain the fruit of their own kindness, for richly are gifts to a widow repaid. She asks food and pays back treasures.

35. But she seems to spend sad days, and to pass her time in tears. And she is the more blessed in this, for by a little weeping she purchases for herself everlasting joys, and at the cost of a few moments gains eternity. To such it is well said: "Blessed are ye that weep, for ye shall laugh." Who then would prefer the deceitful appearances of present joys to the pleasure of future freedom from anxiety? Does he seem to us an insignificant authority, the elect forefather of the Lord after the flesh, who ate ashes as it were bread, and mingled his drink with weeping, and by his tears at night gained for himself the joy of redemption in the morning? Whence did he gain that great joy except that he greatly wept, and, as it were, at the price of his tears obtained the grace of future glory for himself.

36. The widow has, then, this excellent recommendation, that while she mourns her husband she also weeps for the world, and the redeeming tears are ready, which shed for the dead will benefit the living. The weeping of the eyes is fitted to the sadness of the mind, it arouses pity, lessens labour, relieves grief, and preserves modesty, and she no longer seems to herself so wretched, finding comfort in tears Which are the pay of love and proofs of pious memory.

Chapter VII.

By the example of Judith is shown that courage is not wanting in widows; her preparation for her visit to Holofernes is dwelt upon, as also her chastity and her wisdom, her sobriety and moderation. Lastly, St. Ambrose, after demonstrating that she was no less brave than prudent, sets forth her modesty after her success.

37. But bravery also is usually not wanting to a good widow. For this is true bravery, which surpasses the usual nature and the weakness of the sex by the devotion of the mind, such as was in her who was named Judith, who of herself alone was able to rouse up from utter prostration and defend from the enemy men broken down by the siege, smitten with fear, and pining with hunger. For she, as we read, when Holofernes, dreaded after his success in so many battles, had driven countless thousands of men within the walls; when the armed men were afraid, and were already treating about the final surrender, went forth outside the wall, both excelling that army which she delivered, and braver than that which she put to flight.

38. But in order to learn the dispositions of ripe widowhood, run through the course of the Scriptures. From the time when her husband died she laid aside the garments of mirth, and took

those of mourning. Every day she was intent on fasting except on the Sabbath and the Lord's Day and the times of holy days, not as yielding to desire of refreshment, but out of respect for religion. For this is that which is said: "Whether ye eat or drink, all is to be done in the name of Jesus Christ," that even the very refreshment of the body is to have respect to the worship of holy religion. So then, holy Judith, strengthened by lengthened mourning and by daily fasting, sought not the enjoyments of the world regardless of danger, and strong in her contempt for death. In order to accomplish her stratagem she put on that robe of mirth, wherewith in her husband's lifetime she was wont to be clothed, as though she would give pleasure to her husband, if she freed her country. But she saw another man whom she was seeking to please, even Him, of Whom it is said: "After me cometh a Man Who is preferred before me." And she did well in resuming her bridal ornaments when about to fight, for the reminders of wedlock are the arms of chastity, and in no other way could a widow please or gain the victory.

39. Why relate the sequel? How she amongst thousands of enemies, remained chaste. Why speak of her wisdom, in that she designed such a scheme? She chose out the commander, to ward off from herself the insolence of inferiors, and prepare an opportunity for victory. She reserved the merit of abstinence and the grace of chastity. For unpolluted, as we read, either by food or by adultery, she gained no less a triumph over the enemy by preserving her chastity than by delivering her country.

40. What shall I say of her sobriety? Temperance, indeed, is the virtue of women. When the men were intoxicated with wine and buried in sleep, the widow took the sword, put forth her hand, cut off the warrior's head. and passed unharmed through the midst of the ranks of the enemy. You notice, then, how much drunkenness can injure a woman, seeing that wine so weakens men that they are overcome by women. Let a widow, then, be temperate, pure in the first place from wine, that she may be pure from adultery. He will tempt you in vain, if wine tempts you not. For if Judith had drunk she would have slept with the adulterer. But because she drank not, the sobriety of one without difficulty was able both to overcome and to escape from a drunken army.

41. And this was not so much a work of her hands, as much more a trophy of her wisdom. For having overcome Holofernes by her hand alone, she overcame the whole army of the enemies by her wisdom. For hanging up the head of Holofernes, a deed which the wisdom of the men had been unable to plan, she raised the courage of her countrymen, and broke down that of the enemy. She stirred up her own friends by her modesty, and struck terror into the enemy so that they were put to flight and slain. And so the temperance and sobriety of one widow not only subdued her own nature, but, which is far more, even made men more brave.

42. And yet she was not so elated by this success, though she might well rejoice and exult by right of her victory, as to give up the exercises of her widowhood, but refusing all who desired to wed her she laid aside her garments of mirth and took again those of her widowhood, not caring for the adornments of her triumph, thinking those things better whereby vices of the body are subdued than those whereby the weapons of an enemy are overcome.

Chapter VIII.

Though many other widows came near to Judith in virtue, St. Ambrose proposes to speak of Deborah only. What a pattern of virtue she must have been for widows, who was chosen to govern and defend men. It was no small glory to her that when her son was over the host he refused to go forth to battle unless she would go also. So that she led the army and foretold the result. In this story the conflicts and triumphs of the Church, and her spiritual weapons, are set forth, and every excuse of weakness is taken from women.

43. And in order that it may not seem as if only one widow had fulfilled this inimitable work, it seems in no Way doubtful that there were many others of equal or almost equal virtue, for good seed corn usually bears many ears filled with grains. Doubt not. then, that that ancient seed-time was fruitful in the characters of many women. But as it would be tedious to include all, consider some, and especially Deborah, whose virtue Scripture records for us.

44. For she showed not only that widows have no need of the help of a man, inasmuch as she, not at all restrained by the weakness of her sex, undertook to perform the duties of a man, and did even more than she had undertaken. And, at last, when the Jews were being ruled under the leadership of the judges, because they could not govern them with manly justice, or defend them with manly strength, and so wars broke out on all sides, they chose Deborah, by whose judgment they might be ruled. And so one widow both ruled many thousands of men in peace, and defended them from the enemy. There were many judges in Israel, but no woman before was a judge, as after Joshua there were many judges but none was a prophet. And I think that her judgeship has been narrated, and her deeds described, that women should not be restrained from deeds of valour by the weakness of their sex. A widow, she governs the people; a widow, she leads armies; a widow, she chooses generals; a widow, she determines wars and orders triumphs. So, then, it is not nature which is answerable for the fault or which is liable to weakness. It is not sex, but valour which makes strong.

45. And in time of peace there is no complaint, and no fault is found in this woman whereas most of the judges were causes of no small sins to the people. But when the Canaanites, a people fierce in battle and rich in troops, successively joined them, showed a horrible disposition against the people of the Jews, this widow, before all others, made all the preparations for war. And to show that the needs of the household were not dependent on the public resources, but rather that public duties were guided by the discipline of home life, she brings forth from her home her son as leader of the army, that we may acknowledge that a widow can train a warrior; whom, as a mother, she taught, and, as judge, placed in command, as, being herself brave, she trained him, and, as a prophetess, sent to certain victory.

46. And lastly, her son Barak shows the chief part of the victory was in the hands of a woman when he said: "If thou wilt not go with me I will not go, for I know not the day on which the Lord sendeth His angel with me." How great, then, was the might of that woman to whom the leader of the army says, "If thou wilt not go I will not go." How great, I say, the fortitude of the widow who keeps not back her son from dangers through motherly affection, but rather with the zeal of a mother exhorts her son to go forth to victory, while saying that the decisive point of that victory is in the hand of a woman!

47. So, then, Deborah foretold the event of the battle. Barak, as he was bidden, led forth the army; Jael carried off the triumph, for the prophecy of Deborah fought for her, who in a mystery revealed to us the rising of the Church from among the Gentiles, for whom should be found a triumph over Sisera, that is, over the powers opposed to her. For us, then, the oracles of the prophets fought, for us those judgments and arms of the prophets won the victory. And for this reason it was not the people of the Jews but Jael who gained the victory over the enemy. Unhappy, then, was that people which could not follow up by the virtue of faith the enemy, whom it had put to flight. And so by their fault salvation came to the Gentiles, by their sluggishness the victory was reserved for us.

48. Jael then destroyed Sisera, whom however the band of Jewish veterans had put to flight under their brilliant leader, for this is the interpretation of the name Barak; for often, as we read, the sayings and merits of the prophets procured heavenly aid for the fathers. But even at that time was victory being prepared over spiritual wickedness for those to whom it is said in the Gospel: "Come, ye blessed of My Father, take possession of the kingdom prepared for you from the foundation of the world." So the commencement of the victory was from the Fathers, its conclusion is in the Church.

49. But the Church does not overcome the powers of the enemy with weapons of this world, but with spiritual arms, "which are mighty through God to the destruction of strongholds and the high places of spiritual wickedness." And Sisera's thirst was quenched with a bowl of milk, because he was overcome by wisdom, for what is healthful for us as food is deadly and weakening to the power of the enemy. The weapons of the Church are faith, the weapons of the Church are prayer, which overcomes the enemy.

50. And so according to this history a woman, that the minds of women might be stirred up, became a judge, a woman set all in order, a woman prophesied, a woman triumphed, and joining in the battle array taught men to war under a woman's lead. But in a mystery it is the battle of faith and the victory of the Church.

51. You, then, who are women have no excuse because of your nature. You who are widows have no excuse because of the weakness of your sex, nor can you attribute your changeableness to the loss of the support of a husband. Every one has sufficient protection if courage is not wanting to the soul. And the very advance of age is a common defence of chastity for widows; and grief for the husband who is lost, regular work, the care of the house, anxiety for children, frequently ward off wantonness hurtful to the soul; while the very mourning attire, the funeral solemnities, the constant weeping, and grief impressed on the sad brow in deep wrinkles, restrains wanton eyes, checks lust, turns away forward looks. The sorrow of regretful affection is a good guardian of chastity, guilt cannot find an entrance if vigilance be not wanting.

Chapter IX.

To an objection that the state of widowhood might indeed be endurable if circumstances were pleasant, St. Ambrose replies that pleasant surroundings are more dangerous than even trouble; and goes to show by examples taken from holy Scripture, that widows may find much happiness in their children and their sons-in-law. They should have recourse to the Apostles, who are able to help us, and should entreat for the intercessions of angels and martyrs. He touches then on certain complaints respecting loneliness, and care of property, and ends by pointing out the unseemliness of a widow marrying who has daughters either married already or of marriageable age.

52. You have learnt, then, you who are widows, that you are not destitute of the help of nature, and that you can maintain sound counsel. Nor, again, are you devoid of protection at home, who are able to claim even the highest point of public power.

53. But perhaps some one may say that widowhood is more endurable for her who enjoys prosperity, but that widows are soon broken down by adversity, and easily succumb. On which point not only are we taught by experience that enjoyment is more perilous for widows than difficulties, but by the examples in the Scriptures that even in weakness widows are not usually without aid, and that divine and human support is furnished more readily to them than to others, if they have brought up children and chosen sons-in-law well. And, finally, when Simon's mother-in-law was lying sick with violent fever, Peter and Andrew besought the Lord for her: "And He stood over her and commanded the fever and it left her, and immediately she arose and ministered unto them."

54. "She was taken," it is said, "with a great fever, and they besought him for her." You too have those near you to entreat for you. You have the Apostles near, you have the Martyrs near; if associated with the Martyrs in devotion, you draw near them also by works of mercy. Do you show mercy and you will be close to Peter. It is not relationship by blood but affinity of virtue which makes near, for we walk not in the flesh but in the Spirit. Cherish, then, the nearness of Peter and the affinity of Andrew, that they may pray for you and your lusts give way. Touched by the word of God you, who lay on the earth, will then forthwith rise up to minister to Christ. "For our conversation is in heaven, whence also we look for the Saviour, the Lord Jesus Christ." For no one lying down can minister to Christ. Minister to the poor and you have ministered to Christ. "For what ye have done unto one of these," He says, "ye have done unto Me." You, widows, have then assistance, if you choose such sons-in-law for yourselves, such patrons and friends for your posterity.

55. So Peter and Andrew prayed for the widow. Would that there were some one who could so quickly pray for us, or better still, they who prayed for the mother-in-law, Peter and Andrew his brother. Then they could pray for one related to them, now they are able to pray for us and for all. For you see that one bound by great sin is less fit to pray for herself, certainly less likely to obtain for herself. Let her then make use of others to pray for her to the physician. For the sick, unless the physician be called to them by the prayers of others, cannot pray for themselves.

The flesh is weak, the soul is sick and hindered by the chains of sins, and cannot direct its feeble steps to the throne of that physician. The angels must be entreated for us, who have been to us as guards; the martyrs must be entreated, whose patronage we seem to claim for ourselves by the pledge as it were of their bodily remains. They can entreat for our sins, who, if they had any sins, washed them in their own blood; for they are the martyrs of God, our leaders, the beholders of our life and of our actions. Let us not be ashamed to take them as intercessors for our weakness, for they themselves knew the weaknesses of the body, even when they overcame.

56. So, then, Peter's mother-in-law found some to pray for her. And you, O widow, find those who will pray for you, if as a true widow and desolate you hope in God, continue instant in supplications, persist in prayers, treat your body as dying daily, that by dying you may live again; avoid pleasures, that you, too, being sick, may be healed. "For she that liveth in pleasure is dead while she liveth."

57. You have no longer any reason for marrying, you have some to intercede for you. Say not, "I am desolate." This is the complaint of one who wishes to marry. Say not, "I am alone." Chastity seeks solitude: the modest seek privacy, the immodest company. But you have necessary business; you have also one to plead for you. You are afraid of your adversary; the Lord Himself will intervene with the judge and say: "Judge for the fatherless, and justify the widow."

58. But you wish to take care of your inheritance. The inheritance of modesty is greater, and this a widow can guard better than one married. A slave has done wrong. Forgive him, for it is better that you should bear with another's fault than expose it. But you wish to marry. Be it so. The simple desire is no crime. I do not ask the reason, why is one invented? If you think it good, say so; if unsuitable, be silent. Do not blame God, do not blame your relatives, saying that protection fails you. Would that the wish did not fail! And say not that you are consulting the interests of your children, whom you are depriving of their mother.

59. There are some things permissible in the abstract, but not permissible on account of age. Why is the bridal of the mother being prepared at the same time with that of the daughters, and often even afterwards? Why does the grown-up daughter learn to blush in the presence of her mother's betrothed rather than her own? I confess that I advised you to change your dress, but not to put on a bridal veil; to go away from the tomb, not to prepare a bridal couch. What is the meaning of a newly-married woman who already has sons-in-law? How unseemly it is to have children younger than one's grand-children!

Chapter X.

St. Ambrose returns again to the subject of Christ, speaking of His goodness in all misery. The various ways in which the good Physician treats our diseases, and the quickness of the healing if only we do not neglect to call upon Him. He touches upon the moral meaning of the will, which he shows was manifested in Peter's mother-in-law, and lastly points out what a minister of Christ and specially a bishop ought to be, and says that they specially must rise through grace.

60. But let us return to the point, and not, while we are grieving over the wounds of our sins, leave the physician, and whilst ministering to the sores of others, let our own go on increasing. The Physician is then here asked for. Do not fear, because the Lord is great, that perhaps He will not condescend to come to one who is sick, for He often comes to us from heaven; and is wont to visit not only the rich but also the poor and the servants of the poor. And so now He comes, when called upon, to Peter's mother-in-law. "And He stood over her and rebuked the fever, and it left her, and immediately she arose and ministered unto them." As He is worthy of being remembered, so, too, is He worthy of being longed for, worthy, too, of love, for His condescension to every single matter which affects men, and His marvellous acts. He disdains not to visit widows, and to enter the narrow rooms of a poor cottage. As God He commands, as man He visits.

61. Thanks be to the Gospel, by means of which we also, who saw not Christ when He came into this world, seem to be with Him when we read His deeds, that as they, to whom He drew near, borrowed faith from Him, so may He, when we believe His deeds, draw near to us.

62. Do you see what kinds of healing are with Him? He commands the fever, He commands the unclean spirits, at another place He lays hands on them. He was wont then to heal the sick, not only by word but also by touch. And do you then, who burn with many desires, taken either by the beauty or by the fortune of some one, implore Christ, call in the Physician, stretch forth your right hand to Him, let the hand of God touch your inmost being, and the grace of the heavenly Word enter the veins of your inward desires, let God's right hand strike the secrets of your heart. He spreads clay on the eyes of some that they may see, and the Creator of all teaches us that we ought to be mindful of our own nature, and to discern the vileness of our body; for no one can see divine things except one who through knowledge of his vileness cannot be puffed up. Another is bidden to show himself to the priest, that he may for ever be free from the scales of leprosy. For he alone can preserve his purity, both of body and soul, who knows how to show himself to that priest, Whom we have received as an Advocate for our sins, and to Whom is plainly said: "Thou art a priest for ever after the order of Melchisedech."

63. And be not afraid that there will be any delay in healing. He who is healed by Christ has no hindrances. You must use the remedy which you have received; and as soon as He has given the command, the blind man sees, the paralytic walks, the dumb speaks, the deaf hears, she that has a fever ministers, the lunatic is delivered. And do you, then, who ever after an unseemly fashion languish for desire of anything, entreat the Lord, show Him your faith, and fear no delay. Where there is prayer, the Word is present, desire is put to flight, lust departs. And be not afraid of offending by confession, take it rather as a right, for you who were before afflicted by an intense disease of the body will begin to minister to Christ.

64. And in this place can be seen the disposition of the will of Peter's mother-in-law, from which she received for herself, as it were, the seed corn of what was to come, for to each his will is the cause of that which is to come. For from the will springs wisdom, which the wise man takes in marriage to himself, saying: "I desire to make her my spouse." This will, then, which at first was weak and languid under the fever of various desires, afterwards by the office of the apostles rose up strong to minister unto Christ.

65. At the same time it is also shown what he ought to be who ministers to Christ, for first he must be free from the enticements of various pleasures, he must be free from inward languor of body and soul, that he may minister the Body and Blood of Christ. For no one who is sick with his own sins, and far from being whole, can minister the remedies of the healing of immortality. See what thou doest, O priest, and touch not the Body of Christ with a fevered hand. First be healed that thou mayest be able to minister. If Christ bids those who are now cleansed, but were once leprous, to show themselves to the priests, how much more is it fitting for the priest himself to be pure. That widow, then, cannot take it ill that I have not spared her, since I spare not myself.

66. Peter's mother-in-law, it is written, rose up and ministered to them. Well is it said, rose up, for the grace of the apostleship was already furnishing a type of the sacrament. It is proper to the ministers of Christ to rise, according to that which is written: "Awake, thou that sleepest, and arise from the dead."

Chapter XI.

Having shown that the pretexts usually alleged for second marriages have no weight, St. Ambrose declares that he does not condemn them, though from the Apostle's words he sets forth their inconveniences, though the state of those twice married is approved in the Church, and he takes occasion to advert to those heretics who forbid them. And he says that it is because the strength of different persons varies that chastity is not commanded, but only recommended.

67. I say, then, that widows who have been in the habit of giving neither are in want of their necessary expenses, nor of help, who in very great dangers have often guarded the resources of their husbands; and further, I think that the good offices of a husband are usually made up for to them by sons-in-law and other relatives, and that God's mercy is more ready to help them, and therefore, when there is no special cause for marrying, the desire of so doing should not exist.

68. This, however, I say as a counsel, we do not order it as a precept, stirring up the wills of widows rather than binding them. for I do not forbid second marriages, only I do not advise them. The consideration of human weakness is one thing, the grace of chastity is another. I say more, I do not forbid second, but do not approve of often repeated marriages, for not everything is expedient which is lawful: "All things are lawful to me," says the Apostle, "but all things are not expedient." As, also, to drink wine is lawful, but, for the most part. it is not expedient.

69. It is then lawful to marry, but it is more seemly to abstain, for there are bonds in marriage. Do you ask what bonds? "The woman who is under a husband is bound by the law so long as her husband liveth; but if her husband be dead she is loosed from the law of her husband." It is then proved that marriage is a bond by which the woman is bound and from which she is loosed. Beautiful is the grace of mutual love, but the bondage is more constant. "The wife hath not power of her own body, but the husband." And lest this bondage should seem to be rather one of sex than of marriage, there follows: "Likewise, also, the husband hath not power of his own body, but the wife." How great; then, is the constraint in marriage, which subjects even the stronger to the other; for by mutual constraint each is bound to serve. Nor if one wishes to refrain can he withdraw his neck from the yoke, for he is subject to the incontinence of the other. It is said: "Ye are bought with a price, be not ye servants of men." You see how plainly the servitude of marriage is defined. It is not I who say this, but the Apostle; or, rather. it is not he, but Christ, Who spoke in him. And he spoke of this servitude in the case of good married people. For above you read: "The unbelieving husband is sanctified by his believing wife; and the unbelieving wife by her believing husband." And further on: "But if the unbelieving depart, let him depart. A brother or a sister is not bound in such cases." If, then, a good marriage is servitude, what is a bad one, when they cannot sanctify, but destroy one another?

70. But as I exhort widows to keep the grace of their gift, so, too, I incite women to observe ecclesiastical discipline, for the Church is made up of all. Though it be the flock of Christ, yet some are fed on strong food, others are still nourished with milk, who must be on their guard against those wolves who are hidden in sheep's clothing, pretending to all appearance of continence, but inciting to the foulness of incontinence. For they know how severe are the burdens of chastity, since they cannot touch them with the tips of their fingers; they require of others that which is above measure, when they themselves cannot even observe any measure, but rather give way under the cruel weight. For the measure of the burden must always be according to the strength of him who has to bear it; otherwise, where the bearer is weak, he breaks down with the burden laid upon him; for too strong meat chokes the throats of infants.

71. And so as in a multitude of bearers their strength is not estimated by that of a few; nor do the stronger receive their tasks in accordance with the weakness of others, but each is allowed to bear as great a burden as he desires, the reward increasing with the increase of strength; so, too, a snare is not to be set for women, nor a burden of continence beyond their strength to be taken up, but it must be left to each to weigh the matter for herself, not compelled by the authority of any command, but incited by increase of grace. And so for different degrees of virtue a different reward is set forth, and one thing is not blamed that another may be praised; but all are spoken of, in order that what is best may be preferred.

Chapter XII.

The difference between matters of precept and of counsel is treated of, as shown in the case of the young man in the Gospel, and the difference of the rewards set forth both for counsels and precepts is spoken of.

72. Marriage, then, is honourable, but chastity is more honourable, for "he that giveth his virgin ill marriage doeth well, but he that giveth her not in marriage doeth better." That, then, which is good need not be avoided, but that which is better should be chosen. And so it is not laid upon any, but set before him. And, therefore, the Apostle said well: "Concerning virgins I have no commandment of the Lord, yet I give my counsel." For a command is issued to those subject, counsel is given to friends. Where there is a commandment, there is a law; where counsel, there is grace. A commandment is given to enforce what is according to nature, a counsel to incite us to follow grace. And, therefore, the Law was given to the Jews, but grace was reserved for the elect. The Law was given that, through fear of punishment, it might recall those who were wandering beyond the limits of nature, to their observance, but grace to incite the elect both by the desire of good things, and also by the promised rewards.

73. You will see the difference between precept and counsel, if you remember the case of him in the Gospel, to whom it is first commanded to do no murder, not to commit adultery, not to bear false witness; for that is a commandment which has a penalty for its transgression. But when he said that he had fulfilled all the commandments of the Law, there is given to him a counsel that he should sell all that he had and follow the Lord, for these things are not imposed as commands, but are offered as counsels. For there are two ways of commanding things, one by way of precept, the other by way of counsel. And so the Lord in one way says: "Thou shalt not kill," where He gives a commandment; in the other He says: "If thou wilt be perfect, sell all that thou hast." He is, then, not bound by a commandment to whom the choice is left.

74. And so they who have fulfilled the commandments are able to say: "We are unprofitable servants, we have done that which was our duty to do." The virgin does not say this, nor he who sold all his goods, but they rather await the stored-up rewards like the holy Apostle who says: "Behold we have forsaken all and followed Thee, what shall we have therefore?" He says not, like the unprofitable servant, that he has done that which was his duty to do, but as being profitable to his Master, because he has multiplied the talents entrusted to him by the increase he has gained, having a good conscience, and without anxiety as to his merits he expects the reward of his faith and virtue. And so it is said to him and the others: "Ye which have followed Me, in the regeneration, when the Son of Man shall sit in the throne of His glory, shall also yourselves sit upon twelve thrones, judging the tribes of Israel." And to those who had faithfully preserved their talents He promises rewards indeed, though smaller saying: "Because thou hast been faithful over a few things, I will make thee ruler over many things." Good faith, then, is due, but mercy is in the rewards. He who has kept good faith has deserved that good faith should be kept with him; he who has made good profit, because he has not sought his own benefit, has gained a claim to a heavenly reward.

Chapter XIII.

St. Ambrose, treating of the words in the Gospel concerning eunuchs, condemns those who make themselves such. Those only deserve praise who have through continence gained the victory over themselves, but no one is to be compelled to live this life, as neither Christ nor the Apostle laid down such a law, so that the marriage vow is not to be blamed, though that of chastity is better.

75. So, then, a commandment to this effect is not given, but a counsel is. Chastity is commanded, entire continence counselled. "But all men cannot receive this saying, but they to whom it is given. For there are eunuchs which were so born from their mothers womb," in whom exists a natural necessity not the virtue of chastity. "And there are eunuchs who have made themselves eunuchs," of their own will, that is, not of necessity. "And there are eunuchs which were made eunuchs of men. …" And, therefore, great is the grace of continence in them, because it is the will, not incapacity, which makes a man continent. For it is seemly to preserve

the gift of divine working whole. And let them not think it too little not to be impeded by the inclination of the body, for if the reward for going through that conflict is taken from their reach, the matter of sin is also removed, and though they cannot receive the crown, no more can they be overcome. They have other kinds of virtues by which they ought to commend themselves if their faith be firm, their mercifulness abundant, avarice far from them, grace abundant. But in them there is no fault, for they are ignorant of the act of sin.

76. The case is not the same of those who mutilate themselves, and I touch upon this point advisedly, for there are some who look upon it as a holy deed to check by the evil violence of this sort. And though I am not willing to express my own opinion concerning them, though decisions of our forefathers are in existence; but then consider whether this tends not rather to a declaration of weakness than to a reputation for strength. On this principle no one should fight lest he be overcome, nor make use of his feet, fearing the danger of stumbling, nor let his eyes do their office because he fears a fall through lust. But what does it profit to cut the flesh, when there may be guilt even in a look? "For whosoever looketh on a woman to lust after her hath committed adultery already with her in his heart." And likewise she who looks on a man to lust after him commits adultery. It becomes us, then, to be chaste, not weak, to have our eyes modest, not feeble.

77. No one, then, ought, as many suppose, to mutilate himself, but rather gain the victory; for the Church gathers in those who conquer, not those who are defeated. And why should I use arguments when the words of the Apostle's command are at hand? For you find it thus written: "I would that they were mutilated who desire that you should be circumcised." For why should the means of gaining a crown and of the practice of virtue be lost to a man who is born to honour, equipped for victory? how can he through courage of soul mutilate himself? "There be eunuchs which have made themselves eunuchs for the kingdom of heaven's sake."

78. This, however, is not a commandment given to all, but a wish set before all. For he who commands must always keep to the exact scope of the commandments, and he who distributes tasks must observe equity in looking into them, for: "A false balance is abomination to the Lord." There is, then, an excess and a defect in weight, but the Church accepts neither, for: "Excessive and defective weights and divers measures, both of them are alike abominable in the sight of the Lord." There are tasks which wisdom apportions, and apportions according to the estimate of the virtue and strength of each. "He that is able to receive it let him receive it."

79. For the Creator of all knows that the dispositions of each are different, and therefore incited virtue by rewards, instead of binding weakness by chains. And he, the teacher of the Gentiles, the good guide of our conduct, and instructor of our inmost affections, who had learnt in himself that the law of the flesh resists the law of the mind, but yields to the grace of Christ, he knows, I say, that various movements of the mind are opposed to each other; and, therefore, so expresses his exhortations to chastity, as not to do away with the grace of marriage, nor has he so exalted marriage as to check the desire of chastity. But beginning with the recommendation of chastity, he goes on to remedies against incontinence, and having set before the stronger the prize of their high calling, he suffers no one to faint by the way; approving those who take the lead so as not to make little of those who follow. For he, himself, had learnt that the Lord Jesus gave to some barley bread lest they should faint by the way, and administered His Body to others, that they might strive for the kingdom.

80. For the Lord Himself did not impose this commandment, but invited the will, and the Apostle did not lay down a rule, but gave a counsel. But this not a man's counsel as to things within the compass of man's strength, for he acknowledges that the gift of divine mercy was bestowed upon him, that he might know how faithfully to set first the former, and to arrange the latter. And, therefore, he says: "I think," not, I order, but, "I think that this is good because of the present distress."

81. The marriage bond is not then to be shunned as though it were sinful, but rather declined as being a galling burden. For the law binds the wife to bear children in labour and in

sorrow, and is in subjection to her husband, for that he is lord over her. So, then, the married woman, but not the widow, is subject to labour and pain in bringing forth children, and she only that is married, not she that is a virgin, is under the power of her husband. The virgin is free from all these things, who has vowed her affection to the Word of God, who awaits the Spouse of blessing with her lamp burning with the light of a good will. And so she is moved. by counsels, not bound by chains.

Chapter XIV.

Though a widow may have received no commandment, yet she has received so many counsels that she ought not to think little of them. St. Ambrose would be sorry to lay any snare for her, seeing that the field of the Church grows richer as a result of wedlock, but it is absolutely impossible to deny that widowhood, which St. Paul praises, is profitable. Consequently, he speaks severely about those who have proscribed widowhood by law.

82. But neither has the widow received any command, but a counsel; a counsel, however, not given once only but often repeated. For, first, it is said: "It is good for a man not to touch a woman." And again: "I would that all men were even as I myself;" and once more: "It is good for them if they remain even as I;" and a fourth time: "It is good for the present distress." And that it is well pleasing to the Lord, and honourable, and, lastly, that perseverance in widowhood is happier, he lays down not only as his own judgment, but also as an aspiration of the Holy Spirit. Who, then, can reject the kindness of such a counsellor? Who gives the reins to the will, and advises in the case of others that which he has found advantageous by his own experience, he who is not easy to catch up, and is not hurt at being equalled. Who, then, would shrink from becoming holy in body and spirit, since the reward is far above the toil, grace beyond need, and the wages above the work?

83. And this, I say, not in order to lay a snare for others, but that as a good husbandman of the land entrusted to me, I may see this field of the Church to be fruitful, at one time blossoming with the flowers of purity, at another time strong in the gravity of widowhood, and yet again abounding with the fruits of wedlock. For though they be diverse, yet they are the fruits of one field; there are not so many lilies in the gardens as ears of corn in the fields, and many more fields are prepared for receiving seed than lie fallow after the crops are gathered in.

84. Widowhood is, then, good, which is so often praised by the judgment of the apostles, for it is a teacher of the faith and a teacher of chastity. Whereas they who honour the adulteries and the shame of their gods appointed penalties for celibacy and widowhood; that zealous in pursuit of crimes they might punish the study of virtues; under the pretext, indeed, of seeking increase of the population, but in reality that they might put an end to the purpose of chastity. For the soldier, when his time is ended, lays aside his arms, and leaving the rank which he held, is dismissed as a veteran to his own land, that he may obtain rest after the toils of a laborious life, and cause others to be more ready to undergo labour in the hope of future repose. The labourer, too, as he grows too old, entrusts the guiding of the plough to others, and worn out by the toil of his youth, enjoys in his old age that which his foresight has cared for, still ready to prune the vine rather than to press the grapes, so as to check the luxuriance of early life, and to cut off with his pruning knife the wantonness of youth, teaching, as it were, that blessed fruitfulness is to be aimed at even in the vine.

85. In like manner the widow, as a veteran, having served her time, though she lays aside the arms of married life, yet orders the peace of the whole house: though now freed from carrying burdens, she is yet watchful for the younger who are to be married; and with the thoughtfulness of old age she arranges where more pains would be profitable, where produce would be more abundant, which is fitted for the marriage bond. And so, if the field is entrusted to the elder rather than to the younger, why should you think that it is more advantageous to be a married woman than a widow? But, if the persecutors of the faith have also been the persecutors of widowhood, most certainly by those who hold the faith, widowhood is not to be shunned as a penalty, but to be esteemed as a reward.

Chapter XV.

St. Ambrose meets the objection of those who make the desire of having children an excuse for second marriage, and especially in the case of those who have children of their former marriage; and points out the consequent troubles of disagreements amongst the children, and even between the married persons, and gives a warning against a wrong use of Scripture instances in this matter.

86. Perhaps, however, it may seem good to some that marriage should again be entered upon for the sake of having children. But if the desire of children be a reason for marrying, certainly where there are children, the reason does not exist. And is it wise to wish to have a second trial of that fruitfulness which has already been tried in vain, or to submit to the solitude which you have already borne? This is the case of those who have no children.

87. Then, too, she who has borne children, and has lost them (for she who has a hope of bearing children will have an intenser longing), does not she, I say, seem to herself to be covering over the deaths of her lost children by the celebration of a second marriage? Will she not again suffer what she is again seeking? and does she not shrink at the graves of her hopes, the memories of the bereavements she has suffered, the voices of the mourners? Or, when the torches are lit and night is coming on, does she not think rather that funeral rites are being prepared than a bridal chamber? Why, then, my daughter, do you seek again those sorrows which you dread, more than you look for children whom you no longer hope for? If sorrow is so grievous, one should rather avoid than seek that which causes it.

88. And what advice shall I give to you who have children? What reason have you for marrying? Perhaps foolish light-mindedness, or the habit of incontinence, or the consciousness of a wounded spirit is urging you on. But counsel is given to the sober, not to the drunken, and so my words are addressed to the free conscience which is whole in each respect. She that is wounded has a remedy, she that is upright a counsel. What do you intend to do then, my daughter? Why do you seek for heirs from without when you have your own? You are not desiring of children, for you have them, but servitude from which you are free. For this true servitude, in which love is exhausted, which no longer the charm of virginity, and early youth, full of holy modesty and grace, excites; when offences are more felt, and rudeness is more suspected, and agreement less common, which is not bound fast by love deeply rooted by time, or by beauty in its prime of youth. Duty to a husband is burdensome, so that you are afraid to love your children and blush to look at them; and a cause of disagreement arises from that which ordinarily causes mutual love to increase the tender affections of parents. You wish to give birth to offspring who will be not the brothers but the adversaries of your children. For what is to bring forth other children other than to rob the children which you have, who are deprived alike of the offices of affection and of the profit of their possessions.

89. The divine law has bound together husband and wife by its authority, and yet mutual love remains a difficult matter. For God took a rib from the man, and formed the woman so as to join them one to the other, and said: "They shall be one flesh." He said this not of a second marriage but of the first, for neither did Eve take a second husband, nor does holy Church recognize a second bridegroom. "For that is a great mystery in Christ and in the Church." Neither, again, did Isaac know another wife besides Rebecca, nor bury his father, Abraham, with any wife but Sarah."

90. But in holy Rachel there was rather the figure of a mystery than a true order of marriage. Notwithstanding, in her, also, we have something which we can refer to the grace of the first marriage, since he loved her best whom he had first betrothed, and deceit did not shut out his intention, nor the intervening marriage destroy his love for his betrothed. And so the holy patriarch has taught us, how highly we ought to esteem a first marriage, since he himself esteemed his first betrothal so highly. Take care, then, my daughter, lest you be both unable to hold fast the grace of marriage, and also increase your own troubles.

Note on the Letters of St. Ambrose.

Of the 91 Epistles considered genuine by the Benedictine Editors, sixty-three are referred by them to fairly certain dates, and a large number of these would well be worth translation, throwing as they do so clear a light on the events of St. Ambrose's life, and in many cases on the history of the period. Only a few are here presented to the reader.

Perhaps some others might have been better selected, but if they were to be so few, it seemed as if these would give the best general impression of the indomitable energy and fearless constancy of the great Bishop.

SELECTIONS FROM THE LETTERS OF ST. AMBROSE.

MEMORIAL OF SYMMACHUS, THE PREFECT OF THE CITY.

Symmachus in the name of the heathen members of the Senate asks that the Altar of Victory, which had been removed by Gratian, should be restored in the Senate House, and that oaths should be taken there as of old. He argues that the example of former Emperors should be followed as to the things which they retained, not which their abolished. Rome expects this of them, and no injury can accrue to the treasury in consequence, whereas it is unjust to confiscate legacies to the Vestal Virgins and ancient rites.

There was a determined move on the part of Symmachus, Prefect of the city, and other heathen to regain the observances of their religion. He was perhaps the leading man of the day at Rome, equally renowned as a statesman, a scholar, and an orator. In a.d. 382 he headed a deputation of the Senate to the Emperor Gratian to request the replacement of the Altar of Victory in the Senate House, and the restoration of their endowments to the Vestal Virgins and the colleges of priests. There was a counterpetition on the part of the Christian senators forwarded through Pope Damasus, and Gratian refused to receive the deputation. In 384 the attempt was repeated, and these letters or memorials have to do with this application to Valentinian II., the brother of Gratian, who was now Emperor of the West; this attempt was also foiled.

It would seem that he took part in missions for the same purpose to Theodosius after the defeat of Maximus, and to Valentinian II. in a.d. 392, and again unsuccessfully. In the next year, Eugenius, who had been made Emperor by Flavian and Arbogastes, restored the Altar of Victory, which however was finally removed by Theodosius after the defeat of Eugenius and Arbogastes. Probably Symmachus made a final attempt in 403 or 404, but fruitlessly.[See *Dict. Christ. Biog.* s.v. Symmachus.]

The statue and Altar of Victory in question had been first removed by Constantius, son of Constantine, when at Rome, a.d. 356, but were restored by Julian with other heathen symbols and rites. Valentinian I. tolerated them, but possibly(at any rate for some time), as St. Ambrose says, did so in ignorance[Ep. XVII. 16]. They were once more removed by Gratian, and then the action of Symmachus comes in. It may be mentioned that though a heathen he was on intimate terms with Damasus, St. Ambrose, and many leading Christians.

The three Epistles or rather "Memorials" which follow refer to this part of the death-struggle of paganism.

EPISTLE XVII.

This Epistle was written when Symmachus sent his memorial to Valentinian II. St. Ambrose presses on the Emperor the consideration that it is his business to defend religion, and not superstition. The memorial was sent without the adhesion of the Christian senators, and therefore did not represent that body. He warns Valentinian that if he accedes to the request he will incur the censures of the Church, besides acting in a manner derogatory to the memory of his father and brother.

Ambrose, Bishop, to the most blessed Prince and most Christian Emperor Valentinian.

I. As all men who live under the Roman sway engage in military service under you, the Emperors and Princes of the world, so too do you yourselves owe service to Almighty God and our holy faith. For salvation is not sure unless everyone worship in truth the true God, that is the God of the Christians, under Whose sway are all things; for He alone is the true God, Who is to be worshipped from the bottom of the heart; for "the gods of the heathen," as Scripture says, "are devils,"

2. Now everyone is a soldier of this true God, and he who receives and worships Him in his inmost spirit, does not bring to His service dissimulation, or pretence, but earnest faith and devotion. And if, in fine, he does not attain to this, at least he ought not to give any countenance

to the worship of idols and to profane ceremonies. For no one deceives God, to whom all things, even the hidden things of the heart, are manifest.

3. Since, then, most Christian Emperor, there is due from you to the true God both faith and zeal, care and devotion for the faith, I wonder how the hope has risen up to some, that you would feel it a duty to restore by your command altars to the gods of the heathen, and furnish the funds requisite for profane sacrifices; for whatsoever has long been claimed by either the imperial or the city treasury you will seem to give rather from your own funds, than to be restoring what is theirs.

4. And they are complaining of their losses, who never spared our blood, who destroyed the very buildings of the churches. And they petition you to grant them privileges, who by the last Julian law denied us the common right of speaking and teaching, and those privileges whereby Christians also have often been deceived; for by those privileges they endeavoured to ensnare some, partly through inadvertence, partly in order to escape the burden of public requirements; and, because all are not found to be brave, even under Christian princes, many have lapsed.

5. Had these things not been abolished I could prove that they ought to be done away by your authority; but since they have been forbidden and prohibited by many princes throughout nearly the whole world, and were abolished at Rome by Gratian of august memory, the brother of your Clemency, in consideration of the true faith, and rendered void by a rescript; do not, I pray you, either pluck up what has been established in accordance with the faith, nor rescind your brother's precepts. In civil matters if he established anything, no one thinks that it ought to be treated lightly, while a precept about religion is trodden under foot.

6. Let no one take advantage of your youth; if he be a heathen who demands this, it is not right that he should bind your mind with the bonds of his own superstition; but by his zeal he ought to teach and admonish you how to be zealous for the true faith, since he defends vain things with all the passion of truth. I myself advise you to defer to the merits of illustrious men, but undoubtedly God must be preferred to all.

7. If we have to consult concerning military affairs, the opinion of a man experienced in warfare should be waited for, and his counsel be followed; when the question concerns religion, think upon God. No one is injured because God is set before him. He keeps his own opinion. You do not compel a man against his will to worship what he dislikes. Let the same liberty be given to you, O Emperor, and let every one bear it with patience, if he cannot extort from the Emperor what he would take it ill if the Emperor desired to extort from him. A shuffling spirit is displeasing to the heathen themselves, for everyone ought freely to defend and maintain the faith and purpose of his own mind.

8. But if any, Christians in name, think that any such decree should be made, let not bare words mislead your mind, let not empty words deceive you. Whoever advises this, and whoever decrees it, sacrifices. But that one should sacrifice is more tolerable than that all should fall. Here the whole Senate of Christians is in danger.

9. If to-day any heathen Emperor should build an altar, which God forbid, to idols, and should compel Christians to come together thither, in order to be amongst those who were sacrificing, so that the smoke and ashes from the altar, the sparks from the sacrilege, the smoke from the burning might choke the breath and throats of the faithful; and should give judgment in that court where members were compelled to vote after swearing at the altar of an idol(for they explain that an altar is so placed for this purpose, that every assembly should deliberate under its sanction, as they suppose, though the Senate is now made up with a majority of Christians), a Christian who was compelled with a choice such as this to come to the Senate, would consider it to be persecution, which often happens, for they are compelled to come together even by violence. Are these Christians, when you are Emperor, compelled to swear at a heathen altar? What is an oath, but a confession of the divine power of Him Whom you invoke as watcher over your good faith? When you are Emperor, this is sought and demanded. that you should command an altar to be built, and the cost of profane sacrifices to be granted.

10. But this cannot be decreed without sacrilege, wherefore I implore you not to decree or order it, nor to subscribe to any decrees of that sort. I, as a priest of Christ, call upon your faith, all of us bishops would have joined in calling upon you, were not the report so sudden and incredible, that any such thing had been either suggested in your council, or petitioned for by the Senate. But far be it from the Senate to have petitioned this, a few heathen are making use of the common name. For, nearly two years ago, when the same attempt was being made, holy Damasus, Bishop of the Roman Church, elected by the judgment of God, sent to me a memorial, which the Christian senators in great numbers put forth, protesting that they had given no such authority, that they did not agree with such requests of the heathen, nor give consent to them, and they declared publicly and privately that they would not come to the Senate, if any such thing were decreed. Is it agreeable to the dignity of your, that is Christian, times, that Christian senators should be deprived of their dignity, in order that effect should be given to the profane will of the heathen? This memorial I sent to your Clemency's brother, and from it it was plain that the Senate had made no order about the expenses of superstition.

11. But perhaps it may be said, why were they not before present in the Senate when those petitions were made? By not being present they sufficiently say what they wish, they said enough in what they said to the Emperor. And do we wonder if those persons deprive private persons at Rome of the liberty of resisting, who are unwilling that you should be free not to command what you do not approve, or to maintain your own opinion?

12. And so, remembering the legation lately entrusted to me, I call again upon your faith. I call upon your own feelings not to determine to answer according to this petition of the heathen, nor to attach to an answer of such a sort the sacrilege of your subscription. Refer to the father of your Piety, the Emperor Theodosius, whom you have been wont to consult in almost all matters of greater importance. Nothing is greater than religion, nothing more exalted than faith.

13. If it were a civil cause the right of reply would be reserved for the opposing party; it is a religious cause, and I the bishop make a claim. Let a copy of the memorial which has been sent be given me, that I may answer more fully, and then let your Clemency's father be consulted on the whole subject, and vouchsafe an answer. Certainly if anything else is decreed, we bishops cannot contentedly suffer it and take no notice; you indeed may come to the church, but will find either no priest there, or one who will resist you.

14. What will you answer a priest who says to you, "The church does not seek your gifts, because you have adorned the heathen temples with gifts. The Altar of Christ rejects your gifts, because you have made an altar for idols, for the voice is yours, the hand is yours, the subscription is yours, the deed is yours. The Lord Jesus refuses and rejects your service, because you have served idols, for He said to you: 'Ye cannot serve two masters.' The Virgins consecrated to God have no privileges from you, and do the Vestal Virgins claim them? Why do you ask for the priests of God, to whom you have preferred the profane petitions of the heathen? We cannot take up a share of the errors of others."

15. What will you answer to these words? That you who have fallen are but a boy? Every age is perfect in Christ, every age is full of God. No childhood is allowed in faith, for even children have confessed Christ against their persecutors with fearless mouth.

16. What will you answer your brother? Will he not say to you, "I did not feel that I was overcome, because I left you as Emperor; I did not grieve at dying, because I had you as my heir; I did not mourn at leaving my imperial command, because I believed that my commands, especially those concerning divine religion, would endure through all ages. I had set up these memorials of piety and virtue, I offered up these spoils gained from the world, these trophies of victory over the devil, these I offered up as gained from the enemy of all, and in them is eternal victory. What more could my enemy take away from me? You have abrogated my decrees, which so far he who took up arms against me did not do. Now do I receive a more terrible wound in that my decrees are condemned by my brother. My better part is endangered by you,

that was but the death of my body, this of my reputation. Now is my power annulled, and what is harder, annulled by my own family, and that is annulled, which even my enemies spoke well of in me. If you consented of your own free will, you have condemned the faith which was mine; if you yielded unwillingly, you have betrayed your own. So, too, which is more serious, I am in danger in your person.

16. What will you answer your father also? who with greater grief will address you, saying, "You judged very ill of me, my son, when you supposed that I could have connived at the heathen. No one ever told me that there was an altar in the Roman Senate House, I never believed such wickedness as that the heathen sacrificed in the common assembly of Christians and heathen, that is to say that the Gentiles should insult the Christians who were present, and that Christians should be compelled against their will to be present at the sacrifices. Many and various crimes were committed whilst I was Emperor. I punished such as were detected; if any one then escaped notice, ought one to say that I approved of that of which no one informed me? You have judged very ill of me, if a foreign superstition and not my own faith preserved the empire."

17. Wherefore, O Emperor, since you see that if you decree anything of that kind, injury will be done, first to God, and then to your father and brother, I implore you to do that which you know will be profitable to your salvation before God.

THE MEMORIAL OF SYMMACHUS, PREFECT OF THE CITY.

Symmachus addresses his memorial in the name of the Senate, nominally to the three Emperors, Valentinian, Theodosius, and Arcadius, though really to the first of these alone, who was sole Emperor of the West. The memorial sets forth a request that the old religion should be restored, and the Altar of Victory again erected in the Senate House, that the ancient customs might be observed. The example of the late emperors should be followed in what they maintained, not in what they did away. The treasury Would suffer no loss, whilst it is unjust that the Vestal Virgins and priests should be deprived of ancient legacies, a sacrilege which the gods punished by a famine. The memorial is drawn up with consummate skill, both in what is brought forward and in what is left unsaid.

1. As soon as the most honourable Senate, always devoted to you, knew that crimes were made amenable to law, and that the reputation of late times was being purified by pious princes, it, following the example of a more favourable time, gave utterance to its long suppressed grief, and bade me be once again the delegate to utter its complaints. But through wicked men audience as refused me by the divine Emperor, otherwise justice would not have been wanting, my lords and emperors, of great renown, Valentinian, Theodosius, and Arcadius, victorious and triumphant, ever august.

2. In the exercise, therefore, of a twofold office, as your Prefect I attend to public business, and as delegate I recommend to your notice the charge laid on me by the citizens. Here is no disagreement of wills, for men have now ceased to believe that they excel in courtly zeal, if they disagree. To be loved, to be reverenced, to be esteemed is more than imperial sway. Who could endure that private disagreement should injure the state? Rightly does the Senate censure those who have preferred their own power to the reputation of the prince.

3. But it is our task to watch on behalf of your Graces. For to what is it more suitable that we defend the institutions of our ancestors, and the rights and destiny of our country, than to the glory of these times, which is all the greater when you understand that you may not do anything contrary to the custom of your ancestors? We demand then the restoration of that condition of religious affairs which was so long advantageous to the state. Let the rulers of each sect and of each opinion be counted up; a late one practised the ceremonies of his ancestors, a later did not put them away. If the religion of old times does not make a precedent, let the connivance of the last do so.

4. Who is so friendly with the barbarians as not to require an Altar of Victory? We will be careful henceforth, and avoid a show of such things. But at least let that honour be paid to the

name which is refused to the goddess—your fame, which will last for ever, owes much and will owe still more to victory. Let those be averse to this power, whom it has never benefited. Do you refuse to desert a patronage which is friendly to your triumphs? That power is wished for by all, let no one deny that what he acknowledges is to be desired should also be venerated.

5. But even if the avoidance of such an omen were not sufficient, it would at least have been seemly to abstain from injuring the ornaments of the Senate House. Allow us, we beseech you, as old men to leave to posterity what we received as boys. The love of custom is great. Justly did the act of the divine Constantius last but for a short time. All precedents ought to be avoided by you, which you know were soon abolished. We are anxious for the permanence of your glory and your name, that the time to come may find nothing which needs correction.

6. Where shall we swear to obey your laws and commands? by what religious sanction shall the false mind be terrified, so as not to lie in bearing witness? All things are indeed filled with God, and no place is safe for the perjured, but to be urged in the very presence of religious forms has great power in producing a fear of sinning. That altar preserves the concord of all, that altar appeals to the good faith of each, and nothing gives more authority to our decrees than that the whole of our order issues every decree as it were under the sanction of an oath. So that a place will be opened to perjury, and this will be determined by my illustrious Princes, whose honour is defended by a public oath.

7. But the divine Constantius is said to have done the same. Let us rather imitate the other actions of that Prince, who would have undertaken nothing of the kind, if any one else had committed such an error before him. For the fall of the earlier sets his successor right, and amendment results from the censure of a previous example. It was pardonable for your Grace's ancestor in so novel a matter to fail in guarding against blame. Can the same excuse avail us if we imitate what we know to have been disapproved?

8. Will your Majesties listen to other actions of this same Prince, which you may more worthily imitate? He diminished none of the privileges of the sacred virgins, he filled the priestly offices with nobles, he did not refuse the cost of the Roman ceremonies, and following the rejoicing Senate through all the streets of the eternal city, he contentedly beheld the shrines with unmoved countenance, he read the names of the gods inscribed on the pediments, he enquired about the origin of the temples, and expressed admiration for their builders. Although he himself followed another religion, he maintained its own for the empire, for everyone has his own customs, everyone his own rites. The divine Mind has distributed different guardians and different cults to different cities. As souls are separately given to infants as they are born, so to peoples the genius of their destiny. Here comes in the proof from advantage, which most of all vouches to man for the gods. For, since our reason is wholly clouded, whence does the knowledge of the gods more rightly come to us, than from the memory and evidence of prosperity? Now if a long period gives authority to religious customs, we ought to keep faith with so many centuries, and to follow our ancestors, as they happily followed theirs.

9. Let us now suppose that Rome is present and addresses you in these words: "Excellent princes, fathers of your country, respect my years to which pious rites have brought me. Let me use the ancestral ceremonies, for I do not repent of them. Let me live after my own fashion, for I am free. This worship subdued the world to my laws, these sacred rites repelled Hannibal from the walls, and the Senones from the capitol. Have I been reserved for this, that in my old age I should be blamed? I will consider what it is thought should be set in order, but tardy and discreditable is the reformation of old age."

10. We ask, then, for peace for the gods of our fathers and of our country. It is just that all worship should be considered as one. We look on the same stars, the sky is common, the same world surrounds us. What difference does it make by what pains each seeks the truth? We cannot attain to so great a secret by one road; but this discussion is rather for persons at ease, we offer now prayers, not conflict.

11. With what advantage to your treasury are the prerogatives of the Vestal Virgins diminished? Is that refused under the most bountiful emperors which the most parsimonious have granted? Their sole honour consists in that, so to call it, wage of chastity. As fillets are the ornament of their heads, so is their distinction drawn from their leisure to attend to the offices of sacrifice. They seek for in a measure the empty name of immunity, since by their poverty they are exempt from payment. And so they who diminish anything of their substance increase their praise, inasmuch as virginity dedicated to the public good increases in merit when it is without reward.

12. Let such gains as these be far from the purity of your treasury. Let the revenue of good princes be increased not by the losses of priests, but by the spoils of enemies. Does any gain compensate for the odium? And because no charge of avarice falls upon your characters, they are the more wretched whose ancient revenues are diminished. For under emperors who abstain from what belongs to others, and resist avarice, that which does not move the desire of him who takes it, is taken solely to injure the loser.

13. The treasury also retains lands bequeathed to virgins and ministers by the will of dying persons. I entreat you, priests of justice, let the lost right of succession be restored to the sacred persons and places of your city. Let men dictate their wills without anxiety, and know that what has been written will be undisturbed under princes who are not avaricious. Let the happiness in this point of all men give pleasure to you, for precedents in this matter have begun to trouble the dying. Does not then the religion of Rome appertain to Roman law? What name shall be given to the taking away of property which no law nor accident has made to fail. Freedmen take legacies, slaves are not denied the just privilege of making wills; only noble virgins and the ministers of sacred rites are excluded from property sought by inheritance. What does it profit the public safety to dedicate the body to chastity, and to support the duration of the empire with heavenly guardianship, to attach the friendly powers to your arms and to your eagles, to take upon oneself vows efficacious for all, and not to have common rights with all? So, then, slavery is a better condition, which is a service rendered to men. We injure the State, whose interest it never is to be ungrateful.

14. And let no one think that I am defending the cause of religion only, for from deeds of this kind have arisen all the misfortunes of the Roman race. The law of our ancestors honoured the Vestal Virgins and the ministers of the gods with a moderate maintenance and just privileges. This grant remained unassailed till the time of the degenerate money-changers, who turned the fund for the support of sacred chastity into hire for common porters. A general famine followed upon this, and a poor harvest disappointed the hopes of all the provinces. This was not the fault of the earth, we impute no evil influence to the stars. Mildew did not injure the crops, nor wild oats destroy the corn; the year failed through the sacrilege, for it was necessary that what was refused to religion should be denied to all.

15. Certainly, if there be any instance of this evil, let us impute such a famine to the power of the season. A deadly wind has been the cause of this barrenness, life is sustained by trees and shrubs, and the need of the country folk has betaken itself once more to the oaks of Dodona. What similar evil did the provinces suffer, so long as the public charge sustained the ministers of religion? When were the oaks shaken for the use of men, when were the roots of plants torn up, when did fertility on all sides forsake the various lands, when supplies were in common for the people and for the sacred virgins? For the support of the priests was a blessing to the produce of the earth, and was rather an insurance than a bounty. Is there any doubt that what was given was for the benefit of all, seeing that the want of all has made this plain?

16. But some one will say that public support is only refused to the cost of foreign religions. Far be it from good princes to suppose that what has been given to certain persons from the common property can be in the power of the treasury. For as the State consists of individuals, that which goes out from it becomes again the property of individuals. You rule over all; but you preserve his own for each individual; and justice has more weight with you than arbitrary will.

Take counsel with your own liberality whether that which you have conferred on others ought to be considered public property. Sums once given to the honour of the city cease to be the property of those who have given them, and that which at the commencement was a gift, by custom and time becomes a debt. Any one is therefore endeavouring to impress upon your minds a vain fear, who asserts that you share the responsibility of the givers unless you incur the odium of withdrawing the gifts.

17. May the unseen guardians of all sects be favourable to your Graces, and may they especially, who in old time assisted your ancestors, defend you and be worshipped by us. We ask for that state of religious matters which preserved the empire for the divine parent of your Highnesses, and furnished that blessed prince with lawful heirs. That venerable father beholds from the starry height the tears of the priests, and considers himself censured by the violation of that custom which he willingly observed.

18. Amend also for your divine brother that which he did by the counsel of others, cover over the deed which he knew not to be displeasing to the Senate. For it is allowed that that legation was denied access to him, lest public opinion should reach him. It is for the credit of former times, that you should not hesitate to abolish that which is proved not to have been the doing of the prince.

EPISTLE XVIII.

Reply of St. Ambrose to the Memorial of Symmachus, in which after complimenting Valentinian he deals with three points of the Memorial. He replies to his opponent's personification of Rome in a singularly telling manner, and proves that the famine spoken of by Symmachus had nothing to do with the cessation of heathen rites.

Ambrose, Bishop, to the most blessed prince and most gracious Emperor Valentinianus, the august.

1. Since the illustrious Symmachus, Prefect of the city, has sent petition to your Grace that the altar, which was taken away from the Senate House of the city of Rome, should be restored to its place; and you, O Emperor, although still young in years and experience, yet a veteran in the power of faith, did not approve the prayer of the heathen, I presented a request the moment I heard of it, in which, though I stated such things as it seemed necessary to suggest, I requested that a copy of the Memorial might be given to me.

2. So, then, not being in doubt as to your faith, but anxiously considering the risk, and sure of a kindly consideration, I am replying in this document to the assertions of the Memorial, making this sole request, that you will not expect elegance of language but the force of facts. For, as the divine Scripture teaches, the tongue of wise and studious men is golden, which, gifted with glittering words and shining with the brilliancy of splendid utterance as if of some rich colour, captivates the eyes of the mind with the appearance of beauty and dazzles with the sight. But this gold, if you consider it carefully, is of value outwardly but within is base metal. Ponder well, I pray you, and examine the sect of the heathen, their utterances, sound, weighty, and grand, but defend what is without capacity for truth. They speak of God and worship idols.

3. The illustrious Prefect of the city has in his Memorial set forth three propositions which he considers of force: that Rome, as he says, asks for her rites again, that pay be given to her priests and Vestal Virgins, and that a general famine followed upon the refusal of the priests' stipends.

4. In his first proposition Rome complains with sad and tearful words, asking, as he says, for the restoration of the rites of her ancient ceremonies. These sacred rites, he says, repulsed Hannibal from the walls, and the Senones from the Capitol. And so at the same time that the power of the sacred rites is proclaimed, their weakness is betrayed. So that Hannibal long insulted the Roman rites, and while the gods were fighting against him, arrived a conqueror at the very walls of the city. Why did they suffer themselves to be besieged, for whom their gods were fighting in arms?

5. And why should I say anything of the Senones, whose entrance into the inmost Capitol the remnant of the Romans could not have prevented, had not a goose by its frightened cackling betrayed them? See what sort of protectors the Roman temples have. Where was Jupiter at that time? Was he speaking in the goose?

6. But why should I deny that their sacred rites fought for the Romans? For Hannibal also worshipped the same gods. Let them choose then which they will. If these sacred rites conquered in the Romans, then they were overcome in the Carthaginians; if they triumphed in the Carthaginians, they certainly did not benefit the Romans.

7. Let, then, that invidious complaint of the Roman people come to an end. Rome has given no such charge. She speaks with other words. "Why do you daily stain me with the useless blood of the harmless herd? Trophies of victory depend not on the entrails of the flocks, but on the strength of those who fight. I subdued the world by a different discipline. Camillus was my soldier, who slew those who had taken the Tarpeian rock, and brought back the standards taken from the Capitol; valour laid those low whom religion had not driven off. What shall I say of Attilius [Regulus], who gave the service of his death? Africanus found his triumphs not amongst the altars of the Capitol, but amongst the lines of Hannibal. Why do you bring forward the rites of our ancestors? I hate the rites of Neros. Why should I speak of the Emperors of two months, and the ends of rulers closely joined to their commencements. Or is it perchance a new thing for the barbarians to cross their boundaries? Were they, too, Christians in whose wretched and unprecedented cases, the one, a captive Emperor, and, under the other, the captive world made manifest that their rites which promised victory were false. Was there then no Altar of Victory? I mourn over my downfall, my old age is tinged with that shameful bloodshed. I do not blush to be converted with the whole world in my old age. It is undoubtedly true that no age is too late to learn. Let that old age blush which cannot amend itself. Not the old age of years is worthy of praise but that of character. There is no shame in passing to better things. This alone was common to me with the barbarians, that of old I knew not God. Your sacrifice is a rite of being sprinkled with the blood of beasts. Why do you seek the voice of God in dead animals? Come and learn on earth the heavenly warfare; we live here, but our warfare is there. Let God Himself, Who made me, teach me the mystery of heaven, not man, who knew not himself. Whom rather than God should I believe concerning God? How can I believe you, who confess that you know not what you worship?

8. By one road, says he, one cannot attain to so great a secret. What you know not, that we know by the voice of God. And what you seek by fancies, we have found out from the very Wisdom and Truth of God. Your ways, therefore, do not agree with ours. You implore peace for your gods from the Emperors, we ask for peace for the Emperors themselves from Christ. You worship the works of your own hands, we think it an offence that anything which can be made should be esteemed God. God wills not that He should be worshipped in stones. And, in fine, your philosophers themselves have ridiculed these things.

9. But if you deny Christ to be God, because you believe not that He died (for you are ignorant that death was of the body not of the Godhead, which has brought it to pass that now no one of those who believe dies), what is more thoughtless than you who honour with insult, and disparage with honour, for you consider a piece of wood to be your god. O worship full of insult! You believe not that Christ could die, O perversity rounded on respect!

10. But, says he, let the altars be restored to the images, and their ornaments to the shrines. Let this demand be made of one who shares in their superstitions; a Christian Emperor has learnt to honour the altar of Christ alone. Why do they exact of pious hands and faithful lips the ministry to their sacrilege? Let the voice of our Emperor utter the Name of Christ alone, and speak of Him only, Whom he is conscious of, for, "the King's heart is in the hand of the Lord." Has any heathen Emperor raised an altar to Christ? While they demand the restoration of things which have been, by their own example they show us how great reverence Christian Emperors

ought to pay to the religion which they follow, since heathen ones offered all to their superstitions.

11*a*. We began long since, and now they follow those whom they excluded. We glory in yielding our blood, an expense moves them. We consider these things in the place of victories, they think them loss. Never did they confer on us a greater benefit than when they ordered Christians to be beaten and proscribed and slain. Religion made a reward of that which unbelief thought to be a punishment. See their greatness of soul! We have increased through loss, through want, through punishment; they do not believe that their rites can continue without contributions.

11. Let the Vestal Virgins, he says, retain their privileges. Let those speak thus, who are unable to believe that virginity can exist without reward, let those who do not trust virtue, encourage by gain. But how many virgins have the promised rewards gained for them? Hardly are seven Vestal Virgins received. See the whole number whom the fillets and chaplets for the head, the dye of the purple robes, the pomp of the litter surrounded by a company of attendants, the greatest privileges, immense profits, and a prescribed time of virginity have gathered together.

12. Let them lift up the eyes of soul and body, let them look upon a people of modesty, a people of purity, an assembly of virginity. Not fillets are the ornament of their heads, but a veil common in use but ennobled by chastity, the enticement of beauty not sought out but laid aside, none of those purple insignia, no delicious luxuries, but the practice of fasts, no privileges, no gains; all things, in fine, of such a kind that one would think them restrained from enjoyment whilst practising their duties. But whilst the duty is being practised the enjoyment of it is aroused. Chastity is increased by its own sacrifices. That is not virginity which is bought with a price, and not kept through a love of virtue; that is not purity which is bought by auction for money, which is bid for a time. The first victory of chastity is to conquer the desire of wealth, for the pursuit of gain is a temptation to modesty. Let us, however, lay down that bountiful provision should be granted to virgins. What an amount will overflow upon Christians! What treasury will supply such riches? Or if they think that gifts should be conferred on the Vestals alone, are they not ashamed that they who claimed the whole for themselves under heathen Emperors should think that we ought to have no common share under Christian Princes?

13. They complain, also, that public support is not considered due to their priests and ministers. What a storm of words has resounded on this point! But on the other hand even the inheritance of private property is denied us by recent laws, and no one complains; for we do not consider it an injury, because we grieve not at the loss. If a priest seeks the privilege of declining the municipal burdens, he has to give up his ancestral and all other property. If the heathen suffered this how would they urge their complaint, that a priest must purchase the free time necessary for his ministry by the loss of all his patrimony, and buy the power to exercise his public ministry at the expense of all his private means; and, alleging his vigils for the public safety, must console himself with the reward of domestic want, because he has not sold a service but obtained a favour.

14. Compare the cases. You wish to excuse a decurio, when it is not allowed the Church to excuse a priest. Wills are written on behalf of ministers of the temples, no profane person is excepted, no one of the lowest condition, no one shamelessly immodest, the clergy alone are excluded from the common right, by whom alone common prayer is offered for all, and common service rendered, no legacies even of grave widows, no gifts are permitted. And where no fault can be found in the character, a penalty is notwithstanding imposed on the office. That which a Christian widow has bequeathed to the priests of a temple is valid, her legacy to the ministers of God is invalid. And I have related this not in order to complain, but that they may know what I do not complain of; for I prefer that we should be poorer in money than in grace.

15. But they say that what has been given or left to the Church has not been touched. Let them also state who has taken away gifts from the temples, which has been done to Christians,

If these things had been done to the heathen the wrong would have been rather a requital than an injury. Is it now only at last that justice is alleged as a pretext, and a claim made for equity? Where was this feeling when, after plundering the goods of all Christians, they grudged them the very breath of life, and forbade them the use of that last burial nowhere denied to any dead? The sea restored those whom the heathen had thrown into it. This is the victory of faith, that they themselves now blame the acts of their ancestors whose deeds they condemn. But what reason is there in seeking benefits from those whose deeds they condemn?

16. No one, however, has denied gifts to the shrines, and legacies to the soothsayers, their land alone has been taken away, because they did not use religiously that which they claimed in right of religion. Why did they not practise what we did if they allege our example? The Church has no possessions of her own except the Faith. Hence are her returns, her increase. The possessions of the Church are the maintenance of the poor. Let them count up how many captives the temples have ransomed, what food they have contributed for the poor, to what exiles they have supplied the means of living. Their lands then have been taken away, not their rights.

17. See what was done, and a public famine avenged, as they say, the sad impiety that what was before profitable only for the comfort of the priests began to be profitable to the use of all. For this reason then, as they say, was the bark shipped from the copses, and fainting men's mouths supped up the unsavoury sap. For this reason changing corn for the Chaonian acorn, going back once more to the food of cattle and the nourishment of wretched provisions, they shook the oaks and solaced their dire hunger in the woods. These, forsooth, were new prodigies on earth, which had never happened before, while heathen superstition was fervent throughout the world! When in truth before did the crop mock the prayers of the grasping husbandman with empty straw, and the blade of corn sought in the furrows fail the hope of the rustic crew?

18. And from what did the Greeks derive the oracles of their oaks except from their thinking that the support of their sylvan food was the gift of heavenly religion? For such do they believe to be the gifts of their gods. Who but heathen people worshipped the trees of Dodona, when they gave honour to the sorry food of the woodland? It is not likely that their gods in anger inflicted on them as a punishment that which they used when appeased to confer as a gift. And what justice would there be if, being grieved that support was refused to a few priests, they denied it to all, since the vengeance would be more unbearable than the fault? The cause, then, is not adequate to bring such suffering on a failing world, as that the full-grown hope of the year should perish suddenly while the crops were green.

19. And, certainly, many years ago the lights of the temples were taken away throughout the world; has it only now at length come into the mind of the gods of the heathen to avenge the injury? And did the Nile fail to overflow in its accustomed course, in order to avenge the losses of the priests of the city, whilst it did not avenge its own?

20. But let it be that they suppose that the injuries done to their gods were avenged in the past year. Why have they been unnoticed in the present year? For now neither do the country people feed upon torn up roots, nor seek refreshment from the berries of the wood, nor pluck its food from thorns, but joyful in their prosperous labours, while wondering at their harvest, made up for their fasting by the full accomplishment of their wishes; for the earth rendered her produce with interest.

21. Who, then, is so unused to human matters as to be astonished at the differences of years? And yet even last year we know that many provinces abounded with produce. What shall I say of the Gauls which were more productive than usual? The Pannonias sold corn which they had not sown, and Phaetia Secunda experienced harm of her own fertility, for she who was wont to be safe in her scarcity, stirred up an enemy against herself by her fertility. The fruits of the autumn fed Liguria and the Venetias. So, then, the former year did not wither because of sacrilege, and the latter flourished with the fruits of faith. Let them too deny if they can that the

vineyards abounded with an immense produce. And so we have both received a harvest with interest and possess the benefit of a more abundant vintage.

22. The last and most important point remains, whether, O Emperors, you ought to restore those helps which have profited you; for he says: 'Let them defend you, and be worshipped by us.' This it is, most faithful princes, which we cannot endure, that they should taunt us that they supplicate their gods in your names, and without your commands, commit an immense sacrilege, interpreting your shutting your eyes as consent. Let them have their guardians to themselves, let these, if they can, protect their worshippers. For, if they are not able to help those by whom they are worshipped, how can they protect you by whom they are not worshipped?

23. But, he says, the rites of our ancestors ought to be retained. But what, seeing that all things have made progress towards what is better? The world itself, which at first was compacted of the germs of the elements throughout the void, in a yielding sphere, or was dark with the shapeless confusion of the work as yet without order, did it not afterwards receive (the distinction between sky, sea, and earth being established), the forms of things whereby it appears beautiful? The lands freed from the misty darkness wondered at the new sun. The day does not shine in the beginning, but as time proceeds, it is bright with increase of light, and grows warm with increase of heat.

24. The moon herself, by which in the prophetic oracles the Church is represented, when first rising again, she waxes to her monthly age, is hidden from us in darkness, and filling up her horns little by little, so completing them opposite to the sun, glows with the brightness of clear shining.

25. The earth in former times was without experience of being worked for fruits; afterwards when the careful husbandman began to lord it over the fields, and to clothe the shapeless soil with vines, it put off its wild disposition, being softened by domestic cultivation.

26. The first age of the year itself, which has tinged us with a likeness to itself as things begin to grow, as it goes on becomes springlike with flowers soon about to fall, and grows up to full age in fruits at the end.

27. We too, inexperienced in age, have an infancy of our senses, but changing as years go on, lay aside the rudiments of our faculties.

28. Let them say, then, that all things ought to have remained in their first beginnings, that the world covered with darkness is now displeasing, because it has brightened with the shining of the sun. And how much more pleasant is it to have dispelled the darkness of the mind than that of the body, and that the ray of faith should have shone than that of the sun. So, then, the primeval state of the world as of all things has passed away, that the venerable old age of hoary faith might follow. Let those whom this touches find fault with the harvest, because its abundance comes late; let them find fault with the vintage, because it is at the close of the year; let them find fault with the olive, because it is the latest of fruits.

29. So, then, our harvest is the faith of souls; the grace of the Church is the vintage of merits, which from the beginning of the world flourished in the Saints, but in the last age has spread itself over the people, that all might notice that the faith of Christ has entered minds which were not rude (for there is no crown of victory without an adversary), but the opinion being exploded which before prevailed, that which was true is rightly preferred.

30. If the old rites pleased, why did Rome also take up foreign ones? I pass over the ground hidden by costly building, and shepherds' cottages glittering with degenerate gold. Why, that I may reply to the very matter which they complain of, have they eagerly received the images of captured cities, and conquered gods, and the foreign rites of alien superstition? Whence is the pattern for Cybele washing her chariots in a stream counterfeiting the Almo? Whence were the Phrygian bards, and the deities of unjust Carthage always hateful to the Romans? And her whom the Africans worship as Celestis, the Persians as Nitra, and the greater number as Venus, according to a difference of name, not a variety of deities. So they believed that Victory was a goddess, which is certainly a gift, not a power; is granted and does not rule, results from the aid

of legions not the power of religions. Is that goddess then great whom the number of soldiers claims, or the event of battle gives?

31. They ask to have her altar erected in the Senate House of the city of Rome, that is where the majority who meet together are Christians! There are altars in all the temples, and an altar also in the temple of Victories. Since they take pleasure in numbers they celebrate their sacrifices everywhere. To claim a sacrifice on this one altar, what is it but to insult the Faith? Is it to be borne that a heathen should sacrifice and a Christian be present? Let them imbibe, he says, let them imbibe, even against their will, the smoke with their eyes, the music with their ears, the ashes with their throats, the incense with their nostrils, and let the dust stirred up from our hearths cover their faces though they detest it. Are not the baths, the colonnades, the streets filled with images sufficient for them? Shall there not be a common lot in that common assembly? The faithful portion of the senate will be bound by the voices of those that call upon the gods, by the oaths of those that swear by them. If they oppose they will seem to exhibit their falsehood, if they acquiesce, to acknowledge what is sacrilege.

32. Where, says he, shall we swear obedience to your Grace's laws and decrees? Does then your mind, which is contained in the laws, gain assent and bind to faithfulness by heathen ceremonies? The faith is attacked, not only of those who are present but also of those who are absent, and what is more, O Emperors, your faith, too, is attacked, for you compel if you command. Constantius of august memory, though not yet initiated in the sacred Mysteries, thought that he would be polluted if he saw that altar. He commanded it to be removed, he did not command it to be replaced. The removal has the authority of an act, the restoration has not that of a command.

33. Let no one flatter himself because he is absent. He who joins himself to others in mind is more present than he whose assent is given by bodily presence. For it is more to be united in mind than to be joined in body. The Senate has you as the presidents who convene the assembly, it comes together for you; it gives its conscience to you, not to the gods of the heathen; it prefers you to its children, but not to its faith. This is a love to be desired, this is a love greater than any dominion, if faith which preserves dominion be secure.

34. But perhaps it may move some that if this be so, a most faithful Emperor has been forsaken, as if forsooth the reward of merits were to be estimated by the transitory measure of things present. For what wise man is ignorant that human affairs are ordered in a kind of round and cycle, for they have not always the same success, but their state varies and they suffer vicissitudes.

35. Whom have the Roman temples sent out more prosperous than Cneius Pompeius? Yet, when he had encompassed the earth with three triumphs, defeated in battle, a fugitive from war, and an exile beyond the bounds of his own empire, he fell by the hand of an eunuch of Canopus.

36. Whom has the whole land of the East given to the world more noble than Cyrus, king of the Persians? He too, after conquering the most powerful princes who opposed him, and retaining them, when conquered, as prisoners, perished, overthrown by the arms of a woman. And that king who was acknowledged to have treated even the vanquished with honour, had his head cut off, placed in a vessel full of blood, and was bidden to be satiated, being thus subject to the mocking of a woman's power. So in the course of that life of his like is not repaid by like, but far otherwise.

37. And whom do we find more devoted to sacrificing than Hamilcar, leader of the Carthaginians? Who, having offered sacrifice between the ranks during the whole time of the battle, when he saw that his side was conquered, threw himself into the fire which he was feeding, that he might extinguish even with his own body those fires which he had found to profit him nothing.

38. What, then, shall I say of Julian? Who, having credulously trusted the answers of the soothsayers, destroyed his own means of retreat. Therefore even in like cases there is not a like offence, for our promises have deceived no one.

39. I have answered those who provoked me as though I had not been provoked, for my object was to refute the Memorial, not to expose superstition. But let their very memorial make you, O Emperor, more careful. For after narrating of former princes, that the earlier of them practised the ceremonies of their fathers, and the later did not abolish them; and saying in addition that, if the religious practice of the older did not make a precedent, the connivance of the later ones did; it plainly showed what you owe, both to your faith, viz., that you should not follow the example of heathen rites, and to your affection, that you should not abolish the decrees of your brother. For if for their own side alone they have praised the connivance of those princes, who, though Christians, yet in no way abolished the heathen decrees, how much more ought you to defer to brotherly love, so that you, who ought to overlook some things even if you did not approve them in order not to detract from your brother's statutes, should now maintain what you judge to be in agreement both with your own faith, and the bond of brotherhood.

EPISTLE XX.

St. Ambrose relates to his sister the events at Milan connected with the demand of the Arians for a basilica, and how the people rose up in opposition. Then that on the second day the basilica had been occupied by soldiers, who however fraternized with the Catholics. He gives a sketch of his address, comparing their trials to those of Job, more particularly those caused by his wife, and other cases owing to women. Though the basilica was surrendered, he himself had been threatened by a notary, but this did not trouble him. He adapts the story of Jonah to the present circumstances, relates the joy of the people at recovering their church, Valentiuian's words to his courtiers, and the behaviour of Calligonus to himself. The date of the letter is Easter, a.d. 385.

1. Since in almost all your letters you enquire anxiously about the Church, you shall hear what is taking place. The day after I received your letter, in which you said you were troubled by dreams, the pressure of heavy troubles began to be felt. And this time it was not the Portian basilica, that is the one outside the walls, which was demanded, but the new basilica, that is the one within the walls, which is larger.

2. First of all some great men, counsellors of state, begged of me to give up the basilica, and to manage that the people should make no disturbance. I replied, of course, that the temple of God could not be surrendered by a Bishop.

3. On the following day this answer was approved by the people in the Church; and the Prefect came there, and began to persuade us to give up at least the Portian basilica, but the people clamoured against it. He then went away implying that he should report to the Emperor.

4. The day after, which was Sunday, after the lessons and the sermon, when the Catechumens were dismissed, I was teaching the creed to certain candidates in the baptistery of the basilica. There it was reported to me that they had sent decani from the palace, and were putting up hangings, and that part of the people were going there. I, however, remained at my ministrations, and began to celebrate mass.

5. Whilst offering the oblation, I heard that a certain Castulus, who, the Arians said, was a priest, had been seized by the people. Passers-by had come upon him in the streets. I began to weep bitterly, and to implore God in the oblation that He would come to our aid, and that no one's blood be shed in the Church's cause, or at least that it might be my blood shed for the benefit not of my people only, but also for the unbelievers themselves. Not to say more, I sent priests and deacons and rescued the man from violence.

6. Thereupon the heaviest sentences were decreed, first upon the whole body of merchants. And so during the holy days of the last week of Lent, when usually the bonds of debtors are loosed, chains were heard grating, were being placed on the necks ofinnocent persons, and two hundred pounds' weight of gold was required within three days' time. They replied that they

would give as much or twice as much, if demanded, so that only they might preserve their faith. The prisons were full of trades-people.

7. All the officials of the palace, that is the recorders, the commissioners, the apparitors of the different magistrates, were commanded to keep away from what was going on, on the pretence that they were forbidden to take part in any sedition; many very heavy penalties were threatened against men of position, if they did not surrender the basilica. Persecution was raging, and had they but opened the floodgates, they seemed likely to break out into every kind of violence.

8. The Counts and Tribunes come and urged me to cause the basilica to be quickly surrendered, saying that the Emperor was exercising his rights since everything was under his power. I answered that if he asked of me what was mine, that is, my land, my money, or whatever of this kind was my own, I would not refuse it, although all that I have belonged to the poor, but that those things which are God's are not subject to the imperial power. "If my patrimony is required, enter upon it, if my body, I will go at once. Do you wish to cast me into chains, or to give me to death? it will be a pleasure to me. I will not defend myself with throngs of people, nor will I cling to the altars and entreat for my life, but will more gladly be slain myself for the altars."

9. I was indeed Struck with horror when I learnt that armed men had been sent to take possession of the basilica, lest while the people were defending the basilica, there might be some slaughter which would tend to the injury of the whole city. I prayed that I might not survive the destruction of so great a city, or it might be of the whole of Italy. I feared the odium of shedding blood, I offered my own neck. Some Gothic tribunes were present, whom I accosted, and said, "Have you received the gift of Roman rights in order to make yourselves disturbers of the public peace? Whither will you go, if things here are destroyed?"

10. Then I was desired to restrain the people; I answered that it was in my power not to excite them; but in God's hands to quiet them. And that if they thought that I was urging them on, they ought at once to punish me, or that I ought to be sent to any desert part of the earth they chose. After I had said this, they departed, and I spent the whole day in the old basilica, and thence went home to sleep, that if any one wanted to carry me off he might find me ready.

11. Before day when I left the house the basilica was surrounded by soldiers. It is said that the soldiers had intimated to the Emperor that if he wished to go forth he could do so; that they would be in attendance, if they saw him go to join the Catholics; if not that they would go to the assembly which Ambrose had convened.

12. None of the Arians dared to go forth, for there was not one among the citizens, only a few of the royal family, and some of the Goths. And they as of old they made use of their waggons as dwellings, now make the Church their waggon. Wherever that woman goes, she carries with her all assemblage.

13. I heard that the Basilica was surrounded by the groaning of the people, but whilst the lessons were being read, I was informed that the new Basilica also was full of people, that the crowd seemed greater than when they were all free, and that a Reader was being called for. In short, the soldiers themselves who seemed to have occupied the Basilica, when they knew that I had ordered that the people should abstain from communion with them, began to come to our assembly. When they saw this, the minds of the women were troubled, and one rushed forth. But the soldiers themselves said that they had come for prayer not for fighting. The people uttered some cries. With great moderation, with great instancy, with great faithfulness they begged that we would go to that Basilica. It was said, too, that the people in that Basilica were demanding my presence.

14. I then commenced the following address. You have heard, my children, the reading of the book of Job, which, according to the appointed order and season, is being gone through. By experience the devil also knew that this book would be explained, in which all the power of his temptations is shown and made clear, and so to-day he roused himself with greater vigour. But

thanks be to our God, who has so established you with faith and patience. I had mounted the pulpit to praise Job alone, and I have found in you all Jobs to praise. In each of you Job lives again, in each the patience and valour of that saint has shone forth again. For what more resolute could have been said by Christian men, than what the Holy Spirit has to-day spoken in you? We request, O Augustus, we do not fight, we do not fear, but we request. This beseems Christians both to wish for peace and tranquillity, and not to suffer constancy of faith and truth to be checked by fear. For the Lord is our Leader, "Who is the Saviour of them that hope in Him."

15. But let us come to the lessons before us. You see that permission is given to the devil, that the good may be tested. The evil one envies all progress in good, he tempts us in divers way. He tried holy Job in his possessions, in his children, in pain of body. The stronger is tried in his own person, the weaker in that of another. And he was desirous of carrying off my riches which I possess in you, and wished to dissipate this patrimony of your tranquillity. And he strove to deprive me of yourselves also, my good children, for whom I daily renew the Sacrifice, you he endeavoured to involve in the ruin as it were of a public disturbance. I have then already been assailed by two kinds of temptation. And perhaps because the Lord our God knows me to be too weak, He has not yet given him power over my body. Though myself may desire it, though I offer myself, He deems me yet it may be unequal to this conflict, and exercises me with divers labours. And Job did not begin with that conflict but finished with it.

16. But Job was tried by accumulated tidings of evils, he was also tried by his wife, who said, "Speak a word against God and die." You see what terrible things are of a sudden stirred up, the Goths, armed men, the heathen, the fines of the merchants, the sufferings of the Saints. You observe what was commanded, when the order was given "surrender the Basilica;" that is "speak a word against God and die. And not only, speak against God," but, Do something against Him. For the command was, surrender the altars of God.

17. So, then, we are prepared by the imperial commands, but are strengthened by the words of Scripture, which replies: "Thou hast spoken as one of the foolish." That temptation then is no light one, for, we know that those temptations are more severe which arise through women. For even Adam was overthrown by Eve, whereby it came to pass that he erred from the Divine commandments. And when he recognized his error, feeling the reproach of a guilty conscience, he would fain have hidden himself, but he could not be hidden, and so God said to him: "Adam, where art thou?" that is, what wast thou before? where hast thou now begun to be? Where had I placed thee? Whither hast thou wandered? Thou ownest that thou art naked because thou hast lost the robe of a good faith. Those are leaves with which thou now seekest to veil thyself. Thou hast rejected the fruit, thou desired to hide under the leaves of the Law, but thou art betrayed. Thou hast desired to depart from the Lord thy God for the sake of one woman, therefore thou fleest from Him Whom thou soughtest before to see. Thou hast chosen to hide thyself with one woman, to forsake the Mirror of the world, the abode in Paradise, the grace of Christ.

18. Why should I relate that Jezebel, also persecuted Elisha after a bloodthirsty fashion? or that Herodias caused John the Baptist to be slain? Individuals persecuted individuals; but for me, whose merits are far inferior, the trials are all the harder. My strength is less, but I have more danger. Of women change follows on change, their hatreds alternate, their falsehoods vary, elders assemble together, wrong done to the Emperor is made a pretence. What is then the reason of such severe temptation against me, a mere worm; except that they are attacking not me but the Church?

19. At last the command was given: Surrender the Basilica. My reply was, it is not lawful for me to surrender it, nor advantageous for you, O Emperor, to receive it. By no right can you violate the house of a private person, and do you think that the House of God may be taken away It is asserted that everything is lawful for the Emperor, that all things are his. My answer is: Do not, O Emperor, lay on yourself the burden of such a thought as that you have any imperial

power over those things which belong to God. Exalt not yourself, but if you desire to reign long, submit yourself to God, It is written: "The things which are God's to God, those which are Caesar's to Caesar." The palaces belong to the Emperor, the churches to the Bishop. Authority is committed to you over public, not over sacred buildings. Again the Emperor was stated to have declared: I also ought to have one Basilica. My answer was: It is not lawful for you to have it. What have you to do with an adulteress? For she is an adulteress who is not joined to Christ in lawful wedlock.

20. Whilst I was treating on this matter, tidings were brought me that the royal hangings were taken down, and the Basilica filled with people, who were calling for my presence, so I at once turned my discourse to this, and said: How high and how deep are the oracles of the Holy Spirit! We said at Matins, as you, brethren, remember, and made the response with the greatest grief of mind: "O God, the heathen are come into Thine inheritance," And in very deed the heathen came, and even worse than the heathen came; for the Goths came, and men of different nations; they came with weapons and surrounded and occupied the Basilica. We in our ignorance of Thy greatness mourned over this, but our want of foresight was in error.

21. The heathen are come, and in very truth are come into Thine inheritance, for they who came as heathen have become Christians. Those who came to invade Thine inheritance, have been made coheirs with God. I have those as protectors whom I considered to be adversaries. That is fulfilled which the Prophet sang of the Lord Jesus that "His dwelling is in peace," and "There brake He the horns of the bows, the shield, the sword and the battle." For whose girl is this, whose work is this but Thine, Lord Jesus? Thou sawest armed men coming to Thy temple; on the one hand the people wailing and coming in throngs so as not to seem to surrender the Basilica of God, on the other hand the soldiers ordered to use violence. Death was before my eyes, lest madness should gain any footing whilst things were thus. Thou, O Lord, didst come between, and madest of twain one. Thou didst restrain the armed men, saying, If ye run together to arms, if those shut up in My temple are troubled, "what profit is there in My blood." Thanks then be unto Thee, O Christ. No ambassador, no messenger, but Thou, O Lord, hast saved Thy people, "Thou hast put off my sackcloth and girded me with gladness."

22. I said these things, wondering that the Emperor's mind could be softened by the zeal of the soldiers, the entreaties of the Counts, and the supplication of the people. Meanwhile I was told that a notary had been sent to me, to bring me orders. I retired a little, and he intimated the order to me. What were you thinking of, he said, in acting against the Emperor's decree? I replied: I do not know what has been decreed, and I have not been informed of what has been unadvisedly done. He asked: Why did you send priests to the Basilica? If you are a tyrant I wish to know it, that I may know how to prepare against you. I replied by saying that I had done nothing hastily regarding the Church. That at the time when I heard that the Basilica was occupied by soldiers, I only gave freer utterance to groans, and that when many were exhorting me to go thither, I said: I cannot surrender the basilica, but I may not fight. But after I heard that the royal hangings had been taken away, when the people were urging me to go thither, I sent some priests; that I would not go myself, but said, I believe in Christ that the Emperor himself will treat with us.

23. If these acts looked like tyranny, that I had arms, but only in the Name of Christ, that I had the power of offering my own body. Why, I said, did he delay to strike, if he thought me a tyrant? That by ancient right imperial power had been given by bishops, never assumed, and it was commonly said that emperors had desired the priesthood, rather than priests the imperial power. That Christ withdrew lest He should be made a king. That we had our own power; for the power of a bishop was his weakness. "When I am weak," says the Apostle, "then I become strong." But let him against whom God has not stirred up an adversary beware lest he make a tyrant for himself. That Maxim us did not say that I was the tyrant of Valentinian, he complained that by the intervention of my legation he had been unable to cross over into Italy. And I added that priests had never been tyrants, but had often suffered from them.

24. We passed that whole day in sadness, but the imperial hangings were cut by boys in derision. I could not return home, because the soldiers who were guarding the basilica were all around. We repeated Psalms with the brethren in the smaller basilica of the Church.

25. On the following day the Book of Jonah was read according to custom, after the completion of which I began this discourse. A book has been read, brethren, in which it is foretold that sinners shall be converted. Their acceptance takes place because that which is to happen is looked forward to at present. I added that the just man had been willing even to incur blame, in order not to see or denounce the destruction of the city. And because the sentence was mournful he was also saddened that the gourd had withered up. God too said to the prophet: "Art thou sad because of the gourd?" and Jonah answered: "I am sad." And the Lord then said, that if he grieved that the gourd was withered, how much should He Himself care for the salvation of so many people. And therefore that He had put away the destruction which had been prepared for the whole city.

26. And without further delay, tidings are brought that the Emperor had commanded the soldiers to retire from the basilica, and that the sums which had been exacted of the merchants should be restored. How great then was the joy of the whole people!how just their applause! and how abundant their thanks! And it was the day on which the Lord was delivered up for us, on which penance is relaxed in the Church. The soldiers vied with each other in bringing in these tidings, rushing to the altars, giving kisses, the mark of peace. Then I recognized that God had smitten the early worm that the whole city might be preserved.

27. These things were done,and would that all was at an end! but the Emperor's words full of excitement foreshadow future and worse troubles. I am called a tyrant, and even more than a tyrant. For when the Counts were entreating the Emperor to go to the Church, and said that they were doing this at the request of the soldiers, he answered: If Ambrose bade you, you would deliver me up to him in chains. You can think what may be coming after these words. All shuddered when they heard them, but he has some by whom he is exasperated.

28. Lastly, too, Calligonus, the chief chamberlain, ventured to address me in peculiar language. Do you, said he, whilst I am alive treat Valentinian with contempt? I will take your head from you. My reply was, God grant you to fulfil your threat; for then I shall suffer as bishops do, you will act as do eunuchs. Would that God might turn them away from the Church, let them direct all their weapons against me, let them satisfy their thirst with my blood.

LETTER XXI.

St. Ambrose excuses himself for not having gone to the consistory when summoned, on the ground that in matters of faith no one but bishops could rightly judge, and that he was not contumacious because he would not suffer wrong to be done to his own order. And he adds that Auxentius would perhaps choose as judges either Jews or unbelievers, that is, persons hostile to Christ. He says further that he is willing to discuss the matters in dispute at a synod, and that he would have told the Emperor his word of mouth what he is now writing, but that his fellow bishops and the people would not suffer him to do so.

Ambrose, Bishop, to the most gracious Emperor and blessed Augustus, Valentinian.

1. Dalmatius, the tribune and notary, summoned me by the orders of your Clemency, as he asserted, demanding that I should also choose judges, as Auxentius had done. He did not mention the names of those who had been asked for, but he added that there was to be a discussion in the consistory, and that the judgment of your piety would give the decision.

2. To this I make, as I think, a suitable answer. No one ought to consider me contumacious when I affirm what your father of august memory not only replied by word of mouth, but also sanctioned by his laws, that, in a matter of faith, or any ecclesiastical ordinance, he should judge who was not unsuited by office, nor disqualified by equity, for these are the words of the rescript. That is, it was his desire that priests should judge concerning priests. Moreover, if a bishop were accused of other matters also, and a question of character was to be enquired into, it was also his will that this should be reserved for the judgment of bishops.

3. Who, then, has answered your Clemency contumaciously? He who desires that you should be like your father, or he that wishes you to be unlike him? Unless, perhaps, the judgment of so great an Emperor seems to any persons of small account, whose faith has been proved by the constancy of his profession, and his wisdom declared by the continual improvement of the State.

4. When have you heard, most gracious Emperor, that laymen gave judgment concerning a bishop in a matter of faith? Are we so prostrate through the flattery of some as to be unmindful of the rights of the priesthood, and do I think that I can entrust to others what God has given me? If a bishop is to be taught by a layman, what will follow? Let the layman argue, and the bishop listen, let the bishop learn of the layman. But undoubtedly, whether we go through the series of the holy Scriptures, or the times of old, who is there who can deny that, in a matter of faith,—in a matter I say of faith,—bishops are wont to judge of Christian emperors, not emperors of bishops.

5. You will, by the favour of God, attain to a riper age, and then you will judge what kind of bishop he is who subjects the rights of the priesthood to laymen. Your father, by the favour of God a man of riper age, used to say: It is not my business to judge between bishops. Your Clemency now says: I ought to judge. And he, though baptized in Christ, thought himself unequal to the burden of such a judgment, does your Clemency, who have yet to earn for yourself the sacrament of baptism, arrogate to yourself a judgment concerning the faith, though ignorant of the sacrament of that faith?

6. I can leave it to be imagined what sort of judges he will have chosen. since he is afraid to publish their names. Let them simply come to the Church, if there are any to come; let them listen with the people, not for every one to sit as judge, but that each may examine his own disposition, and choose whom to follow. The matter is concerning the bishop of that Church: if the people hear him and think that he has the best of the argument, let them follow him, I shall not be jealous.

7. I omit to mention that the people have themselves already given their judgment. I am silent as to the fact that they demanded of your father him whom they now have. I am silent as to the promise of your father that if he who was chosen would undertake the bishopric there should be tranquillity. I acted on the faith of these promises.

8. But if he boasts himself of the approval of some foreigners, let him be bishop there from whence they are who think that he ought to receive the name of bishop. For I neither recognize him as a bishop, nor know I whence he comes.

9. And how, O Emperor, are we to settle a matter on which you have already declared your judgment, and have even promulgated laws, so that iris not open to any one to judge otherwise? But when you laid down this law for others, you laid it down for yourself as well. For the Emperor is the first to keep the laws which he passes. Do you, then, wish me to try how those who are chosen as judges will either come, contrary to your decision, or at least excuse themselves, saying that they cannot act against so severe and so stringent a law of the Emperor?

10. But this would be the act of one contumacious, not of one who knew his position. See, O Emperor, you are already yourself partially rescinding your law, would that it were not partially but altogether! for I would not that your law should be set above the law of God. The law of God has taught us what to follow; human laws cannot teach us this. They usually extort a change from the fearful, but they cannot inspire faith.

11. Who, then, will there be, who when he reads that at one instant through so many provinces the order was given, that whoever acts against the Emperor shall be beheaded, that whoever does not give up the temple of God shall at once be put to death; who, say, is there who will be able either alone or with a few others to say to the Emperor: I do not approve of your law? Priests are not allowed to say this, are then laymen allowed? And shall he judge concerning the faith who either hopes for favour or is afraid of giving offence?

12. Lastly, shall I myself choose laymen for judges, who, if they upheld the truth of their faith, would be either proscribed or put to death, as that law passed concerning the faith decrees? Shall I then expose these men either to denial of the truth or to punishment?

13. Ambrose is not of sufficient importance to degrade the priesthood on his own account. The life of one is not of so much value as the dignity of all priests, by whose advice I gave those directions, when they intimated that there might perchance be some heathen or Jew chosen by Auxentius, to whom I should give a triumph over Christ, if I entrusted to him a judgment concerning Christ. What else pleases them but to hear of some insult to Christ? What else can please them unless(which God forbid) the Godhead of Christ should be denied? Plainly they agree well with the Arian who says that Christ is a creature, which also heathen and Jews most readily acknowledge.

14. This was decreed at the Synod of Ariminum, and rightly do I detest that council, following the rule of the Nicene Council, from which neither death nor the sword can detach me, which faith the father of your Clemency also. Theodosius, the most blessed Emperor, both approved and follows. The Gauls hold this faith, and Spain, and keep it with the pious confession of the Divine Spirit.

15. If anything has to be discussed I have learnt to discuss it in church as those before me did. If a conference is to be held concerning the faith, there ought to be a gathering of Bishops, as was done under Constantine, the Prince of august memory, who did not promulgate any laws beforehand, but left the decision to the Bishops. This was done also under Constantius, Emperor of august memory, the heir of his father's dignity. But what began well ended otherwise, for the Bishops had at first subscribed an unadulterated confession of faith, but since some were desirous of deciding concerning the faith inside the palace, they managed that those decisions of the Bishops should be altered by fraud. But they immediately recalled this perverted decision, and certainly the larger number at Ariminum approved the faith of the Nicene Council and condemned the Arian propositions.

16. If Auxentius appeals to a synod, in order to discuss points concerning the faith(although it is not necessary that so many Bishops should be troubled for the sake of one man, who, even if he were an angel from heaven, ought not to be preferred to the peace of the Church), when I hear that a synod is gathering, I, too, will not be wanting. Repeal, then, the law if you wish for a disputation.

17. I would have come, O Emperor, to your consistory, and have made these remarks in your presence, if either the Bishops or the people had allowed me, but they said that matters concerning the faith ought to be treated in the church, in presence of the people.

18. And I wish, O Emperor, that you had not given sentence that I should go into banishment whither I would. I went out daily. No one guarded me. You ought to have appointed me a place wherever you would, for I offered myself for anything. But now the clergy say to me, "There is not much difference whether you voluntarily leave the altar of Christ or betray it, for if you leave it you will betray it."

19. And I wish it were clearly certain to me that the Church would by no means be given over to the Arians. I would then willingly offer myself to the will of your piety. But if I only am guilty of disturbance, why is there a command to invade all other churches? I would it were established that no one should trouble the churches, and then I could wish that whatever sentence seems good should be pronounced concerning me.

20. Vouchsafe, then, O Emperor, to accept the reason for which I could not come to the consistory. I have never learned to appear in the consistory except on your behalf, and I am not able to dispute within the palace, who neither know nor wish to know the secrets of the palace.

21. I, Ambrose, Bishop, offer this memorial to the most gracious Emperor, and most blessed Augustus Valentinian.

SERMON AGAINST AUXENTIUS ON
THE GIVING UP OF THE BASILICAS.

To calm the anxiety of the people over the imperial decree, he lays his answer before them, and adds that he did not go to the consistory, because he was afraid of losing the basilica. Then, first challenging his opponents to a discussion in the church, he says that he is not terrified at their weapons; and also, after recalling his answer on the subject of the sacred vessels, declares that he is ready for the contest. The will of God, he maintains, cannot be frustrated, nor can His protection be overcome, yet He is ready too to suffer in His servants. Since he has not already been taken before this, it is plain that the heretics are causing this disturbance for no reason whatever. Next, after applying Naboth's history and Christ's entry into Jerusalem to the present state of affairs, he censures Auxentius' cruel law, answers the Arians' objections, and states that he will gladly discuss the matter in the presence of the people. Auxentius, he adds, has been already condemned by the pagans, whom he had chosen to sit as judges, as he had been condemned by Paul and by Christ. The heretic had forgotten the year before, when he had made the same appeal to Caesar; and the Arians, in stirring up ill-will against the servants of Christ, are much worse than the Jews: for the Church does not belong to Caesar, but displays the image of Christ. Then adding to these a few more words on his answer and his hymns, he declares that he is not disobedient, that the Emperor is a son of the Church, and that Auxentius is worse than a Jew.

1. I See that you are unusually disturbed, and that you are closely watching me. I wonder what the reason is? Is it that you saw or heard that I had received an imperial order at the hands of the tribunes, to the effect that I was to go hence, whither I would, and that all who wished might follow me? Were you afraid that I should desert the Church and forsake you in fear for my own safety? But you could note the message I sent, that the wish to desert the Church had never entered my mind; for I feared the Lord of the universe more than an earthly emperor; and if force were to drag me from the Church, my body indeed could be driven out, but not my mind. I was ready, if he were to do what royal power is wont to do, to undergo the fate a priest has to bear.

2. Why, then, are you disturbed? I will never willingly desert you, though if force is used, I cannot meet it. I shall be able to grieve, to weep, to groan; against weapons, soldiers, Goths, my tears are my weapons, for these are a priest's defence. I ought not, I cannot resist in any other way; but to fly and forsake the Church is not my way; lest any one should suppose I did so from fear of some heavier punishment. You yourselves know that I am wont to show respect to our emperors, but not to yield to them, to offer myself freely to punishment, and not to fear what is prepared for me.

3. Would that I were sure the Church would never be given over to heretics. Gladly would I go to the Emperor's palace, if this but fitted the office of a priest, and so hold our discussion in the palace rather than the church. But in the consistory Christ is not wont to be the accused but the judge. Who will deny that the cause of faith should be pleaded in the church? If any one has confidence let him come hither; let him not seek the judgment of the Emperor, which already shows its bias, which clearly proves by the law that is passed that he is against the faith; neither let him seek the expected goodwill of certain people who want to stand well with both sides. I will not act in such a way as to give any one the chance of making money out of a wrong to Christ.

4. The soldiers around, the clash of the arms wherewith the church is surrounded, do not alarm my faith, but they disquiet me from fear that in keeping me here you might meet with some danger to your lives. For I have learnt by now not to be afraid, but I do begin to have more fear for you. Allow, I beg you, your bishop to meet his foes. We have an adversary who assails us, for our adversary "the devil goeth about, as a roaring lion, seeking whom he may devour," as the Apostle said. He has received, no doubt, he has received(we are not deceived, but warned of this) the power to tempt in this wise, lest I might perhaps by the wounds of my body be drawn away from the earnestness of my faith. You have read how the devil tempted

holy Job in these many ways, and how at last he sought and obtained power to try his body, which he covered with sores.

5. When it was suggested that I should give up the vessels of the Church, I gave the following answer: I will willingly give up whatever of my own property is demanded, whether it is estates, or house, or gold, or silver—anything, in fact, which is in my power. But I cannot take aught away from the temple of God; nor can I give up what I have received to guard and not to give up. In doing this I am acting for the Emperor's good, for it would neither be right for me to give it up, nor for him to receive it. Let him listen to the words of a free-spoken bishop, and if he wishes to do what is best for himself, let him cease to do wrong to Christ.

6. These words are full of humility, and as I think of that spirit which a bishop ought to show towards the Emperor. But since "our contest is not against flesh and blood, but also"(which is worse) "against spiritual wickedness in high places," that tempter the devil makes the struggle harder by means of his servants, and thinks to make trial of me by the wounds of my flesh. I know, my brethren, that these wounds which we receive for Christ's sake are not wounds that destroy life, but rather extend it. Allow, I pray, the contest to take place. It is for you to be the spectators. Reflect that if a city has an athlete, or one skilled in some other noble art, it is eager to bring him forward for a contest. Why do you refuse to do in a more important matter what you are wont to wish in smaller affairs? He fears not weapons nor barbarians who fears not death, and is not held fast by any pleasures of the flesh.

7. And indeed if the Lord has appointed me for this struggle, in vain have you kept sleepless watch so many nights and days. The will of Christ will be fulfilled. For our Lord Jesus is almighty, this is our faith: and so what He wills to be done will be fulfilled, and it is not for us to thwart the divine purpose.

8. You heard what was read to-day: The Saviour ordered that the foal of an ass should be brought to Him by the apostles, and bade them say, if any one withstood them: "The Lord hath need of him." What if now, too, He has commanded that foal of an ass, that is, the foal of that animal which is wont to bear a heavy burden, as man must, to whom is said: "Come unto Me all ye that labour and are heavy laden, and I will give you rest; take My yoke upon you, for it is easy;" what if, I say, He has commanded that foal to be brought to Him now, sending forth those apostles, who, having put off their body, wear the semblance of the angels unseen by our eyes? If withstood by any, will they not say: The Lord hath need of him? If, for instance, love of this life, or flesh and blood, or earthly intercourse(for perhaps we seem pleasing to some), were to withstand them? But he who loves me here, would show his love much more if he would suffer me to become Christ's victim, for "to depart and be with Christ is much better, though to abide in the flesh is more needful for you." There is nothing therefore for you to fear, beloved brethren. For I know that whatever I may suffer, I shall suffer for Christ's sake. And I have read that I ought not to fear those that can kill the flesh. And I have heard One Who says: "He that loseth his life for My sake shall find it."

9. Wherefore if the Lord wills, surely no one will resist. And if as yet He delay my struggle, what do you fear? It is not bodily guardianship but the Lord's providence that is wont to fence in the servant of Christ.

10. You are troubled because you have found the double doors open, which a blind man in seeking his chamber is said to have unfastened. In this you learn that human watchfulness is no defence. Behold! one who has lost the gift of sight has broken through all our defences, and escaped the notice of the guards. But the Lord has not lost the guard of His mercy. Was it not also discovered two days ago, as you remember, that a certain entrance on the left side of the basilica was open, which you thought had been shut and secured? Armed men surrounded the basilica, they tried this and the other entrance, but their eyes were blinded so that that could not see the one that was open. And you know well that it was open many nights. Cease, then, to be anxious; for that will take place which Christ commands and which is for the best.

11. And now I will put before you examples from the Law. Eiiseus was sought by the king of Syria; an army had been sent to capture him; and he was surrounded on all sides. His servant began to fear, for he was a servant, that is, he had not a free mind, nor had he free powers of action. The holy prophet sought to open his eyes, and said: "Look and see how many more are on our side than there are against us." And he beheld, and saw thousands of angels. Mark therefore that it is those that are not seen rather than those that are seen that guard the servants of Christ. But if they guard you, they do it in answer to your prayers: for you have read that those very men, who sought Eliseus, entered Samaria, and came to him whom they desired to take. Not only were they unable to harm him, but they were themselves preserved at the intercession of the man against whom they had come.

12. The Apostle Peter also gives you an example of either case. For when Herod sought him and took him, he was put into prison. For the servant of God had not got away, but stood firm without a thought of fear. The Church prayed for him, but the Apostle slept in prison, a proof that he was not in fear. An angel was sent to rouse him as he slept, by whom Peter was led forth out of prison, and escaped death for a time.

13. And Peter again afterwards, when he had overcome Simon, in sowing the doctrine of God among the people, and in teaching chastity, stirred up the minds of the Gentiles. And when these sought him, the Christians begged that he would withdraw himself for a little while. And although he was desirous to suffer, yet was he moved at the sight of the people praying, for they asked him to save himself for the instruction and strengthening of his people. Need I say more? At night he begins to leave the town, and seeing Christ coming to meet him at the gate, and entering the city, says: Lord, whither goest Thou? Christ answers: I am coming to be crucified again. Peter understood the divine answer to refer to his own cross, for Christ could not be crucified a second time, for He had put off the flesh by the passion of the death which He had undergone; since: "In that He died, He died unto sin once, but in that He liveth, He liveth unto God." So Peter understood that Christ was to be crucified again in the person of His servant. Therefore he willingly returned; and when tile Christians questioned him, told them the reason. He was immediately seized, and glorified the Lord Jesus by his cross.

14. You see, then, that Christ wills to suffer in His servants. And what if He says to this servant, "I will that he tarry, follow thou Me," and wishes to taste the fruit of this tree? For if His meat was to do the will of His Father, so also is it His meat to partake of our sufferings. Did He not, to take an example from our Lord Himself,—did He not suffer when He willed, and was He not found when He was sought? But when the hour of His passion had not yet come, He passed through the midst of those that sought Him, and though they saw Him they could not hold Him fast. This plainly shows us that when the Lord wills, each one is found and taken, but because the time is put off, he is not held fast, although he meets the eyes of those who seek him.

15. And did not I myself go forth daily to pay visits, or go to the tombs of the martyrs? Did I not pass by the royal palace both in going and returning? Yet no one laid hands on me, though they had the intention of driving me out, as they afterwards gave out, saying, Leave the city, and go where you will. I was, I own, looking for some great thing, either sword or fire for the Name of Christ, yet they offered me pleasant things instead of sufferings; but Christ's athlete needs not pleasant things but sufferings. Let no one, then, disturb you, because they have provided a carriage, or because hard words, as he thinks them, have been uttered by Auxentius, who calls himself bishop.

16. Many stated that assassins had been despatched, that the penalty of death had been decreed against me. I do not fear all that, nor am I going to desert my position here. Whither shall I go, when there is no spirit that is not filled with groans and tears; when throughout the Churches Catholic bishops are being expelled, or if they resist, are put to the sword, and every senator who does not obey the decree is proscribed. And these things were written by the hand and spoken by the mouth of a bishop who, that he might show himself to be most learned,

omitted not an ancient warning. For we read in the prophet that he saw a flying sickle. Auxentius, to imitate this, sent a flying sword through all cities. But Satan, too, transforms himself into an angel of light, and imitates his power for evil.

17. Thou, Lord Jesus, hast redeemed the world in one moment of time: shall Auxentius in one moment slay, as far as he can, so many peoples, some by the sword, others by sacrilege? He seeks my basilica with bloody lips and gory hands. Him to-day's chapter answers well: "But unto the wicked said God: Wherefore dost thou declare My righteousness?" That is, there is no union between peace and madness, there is no union between Christ and Belial. You remember also that we read to-day of Naboth, a holy man who owned his own vineyard, being urged on the king's request to give it up. When the king after rooting up the vines intended to plant common herbs, he answered him: "God forbid that I should give up the inheritance of my fathers." The king was grieved, because what belonged by right to another had been refused him on fair grounds, but had been unfairly got by a woman's device. Naboth defended his vines with his own blood. And if he did not give up his vineyard, shall we give up the Church of Christ?

18. Was the answer that I gave then contumacious? For when summoned I said: God forbid that I should give up the inheritance of Christ. If Naboth gave not up the inheritance of his fathers, shall I give up the inheritance of Christ? And I added further: God forbid that I shall give up the inheritance of my fathers, that is, the inheritance of Dionysius, who died in exile in the cause of the faith; the inheritance of the Confessor Eustorgius, the inheritance of Mysocles and of all the faithful bishops of bygone days. I answered as a bishop ought to answer: Let the Emperor act as an emperor ought to. He must take away my life rather than my faith.

19. But to whom shall I give it up? Today's lesson from the Gospel ought to teach us what is asked for and by whom it is asked. You have heard read that when Christ sat upon the foal of an ass, the children cried aloud, and the Jews were vexed. At length they spoke to the Lord Jesus, bidding Him to silence them. He answered: "If these should hold their peace, the stones will cry out." Then on entering the temple, He cast out the money-changers, and the tables, and those that sold doves in the temple of God. That passage was read by no arrangement of mine, but by chance; but it is well fitted to the present time. The praises of Christ are ever the scourges of the unfaithful. And now when Christ is praised, the heretics say that sedition is stirred up. The heretics say that death is being prepared for them, and truly they have their death in the praises of Christ. For how can they bear His praises, Whose weakness they maintain. And so to-day, when Christ is praised, the madness of the Arians is scourged.

20. The Gerasenes could not bear the presence of Christ; these, worse than the Gerasenes, cannot endure the praises of Christ. They see boys singing of the glory of Christ, for it is written: "Out of the mouths of babes and sucklings Thou hast perfected praise." They mock at their tender age, so full of faith, and say: "Behold, why do they cry out?" But Christ answers them: "If these should hold their peace, the stones will cry out," that is, the stronger will cry out, both youths and the more mature will cry out, and old men will cry out; these stones now firmly laid upon that stone of which it is written: "The stone which the builders rejected is become the head of the corner."

21. Invited, then, by these praises, Christ enters His temple, and takes His scourge and drives the money-changers out of the temple. For He does not allow the slaves of money to be in His temple, nor does He allow those to be there who sell seats. What are seats but honours? What are the doves but simple minds or souls that follow a pure and clear faith? Shall I, then, bring into the temple him whom Christ shuts out? For he who sells dignities and honours will be bidden to go out. He will be bidden to go out who desires to sell the simple minds of the faithful.

22. Therefore, Auxentius is cast out. Mercurius is shut out. The portent is one, the names are two! That no one might know who he was, he changed his name so as to call himself Auxentius, because there had been here an Arian bishop, named Auxentius. He did this to deceive the people over whom the other had had power. He changed his name, but he did not change his

falseness. He puts off the wolf, yet puts on the wolf again. It is no help to him that he has changed his name; whatever happens he is known. He is called by one name in the parts of Scythia, he is called by another here. He has a name for each country he lives in. He has two names already, and if he were to go elsewhere from here, he will have yet a third. For how will he endure to keep a name as a proof of such wickedness? He did less in Scythia, and was so ashamed that he changed his name. Here he has dared to do worse things, and will he be ready to be betrayed by his name wherever he goes? Shall he write the death warrant of so many people with his own hand, and yet be able to be unshaken in mind?

23. The Lord Jesus shut a few out of His temple, but Auxentius left none. Jesus with a scourge drove them out of His temple, Auxentius with a sword; Jesus with a scourge, Mercurius with an axe. The holy Lord drives out the sacrilegious with a scourge; the impious man pursues the holy with a sword. Of him you have well said to-day: Let him take away his laws with him. He will take them, although he is unwilling; he will take with him his conscience, although he takes no writing; he will take with him his soul inscribed with blood although he will not take a letter inscribed with ink. It is written: "Juda, thy sin is written with a pen of iron and with the point of a diamond, and it is graven upon thy heart," that is, it is written there, whence it came forth.

24. Does he, a man full of blood and full of murder, dare to make mention to me of a discussion? He who thinks that they whom he could not mislead by his words are to be slain with the sword, giving bloody laws with his mouth, writing them with his hand, and thinking that the law can order a faith for man to hold. He has not heard what was read to-day: "That a man is not justified by the works of the law," or "I, through the law, am dead to the law, that I may live unto God," that is, by the spiritual law he is dead to the carnal interpretation of the law. And we, by the law of our Lord Jesus Christ, are dead to this law, which sanctions such perfidious decrees. The law did not gather the Church together, but the faith of Christ. For the law is not by faith, but "the just man lives by faith." Therefore, faith, not the law, makes a man just, for justice is not through the law, but through the faith of Christ. But he who casts aside his faith and pleads for that the claims of the law, bears witness that he is himself unjust; for the just man lives by faith.

25. Shall any one, then, follow this law, whereby the Council of Ariminum is confirmed, wherein Christ was said to be a creature. But say they: "God sent forth His Son, made of a woman, made under the law." And so they say "made," that is, "created." Do they not consider these very words which they have brought forward; that Christ is said to have been made, but of a woman; that is, He was "made" as regards his birth from a Virgin, Who was begotten of the Father as regards His divine generation? Have they read also to-day, "that Christ redeemed us from the curse of the law, being made a curse for us"? Was Christ a curse in His Godhead? But why He is called a curse the Apostle tells us, saying that it is written: "Cursed is every one that hangeth on a tree," that is, He Who in his flesh bore our flesh, in His body bore our infirmities and our curses, that He might crucify them; for He was not cursed Himself, but was cursed in thee. I So it is written elsewhere: "Who knew no sin, but was made sin for us, for He bore our sins, that he might destroy them by the Sacrament of His Passion."

26. These matters, my brethren, I would discuss more fully with him in your presence; but knowing that you are not ignorant of the faith, he has avoided a trial before yon, and has chosen some four or five heathen to represent him, if that is he has chosen any, whom I should like to be present in our company, not to judge concerning Christ, but to hear the majesty of Christ. They, however, have already given their decision concerning Auxentius, to whom they gave no credence as he pleaded before them day by day. What can be more of a condemnation of him than the fact, that without an adversary he was defeated before his own judges? So now we also have their opinion against Auxentius.

27. And that he has chosen heathen is rightly to be condemned; for he has disregarded the Apostle's command, where he says: "Dare any of you, having a matter against another, go to law

before the unjust and not before the saints? Do ye not know the saints shall judge the world?" And below he says: "Is it so, that there is not a wise man among you, who can judge between heathen? But brother goeth to law with brother, and that before the unbelievers." You see, then, that what he has introduced is against the Apostle's authority. Do you decide, then, whether we are to follow Auxentius or Paul as our master.

28. But why speak of the Apostle, when the Lord Himself cries through the prophet: "Hearken unto Me, My people, ye who know judgment, in whose heart is My law." God says: "Hearken unto Me, My people, ye that know judgment." Auxentius says: Ye know not judgment. Do you see how he condemns God in you, who rejects the voice of the heavenly oracle: "Hearken unto Me, My people," says the Lord. He says not, "Hearken, ye Gentiles," nor does He say, "Hearken, ye Jews." For they who had been the people of the Lord have now become the people of error, and they who were the people of error have begun to be the people of God; for they have believed on Christ. That people then judges in whose heart is the divine, not the human law, the law not written in ink, but in the spirit of the living God; not set down on paper, but stamped upon the heart. Who then, does you a wrong, he who refuses, or he who chooses to be heard by you?

29. Hemmed in on all sides, he betakes himself to the wiles of his fathers. He wants to stir up ill-will on the Emperor's side, saying that a youth, a catechumen ignorant of the sacred writings, ought to judge, and to judge in the consistory. As though last year when I was sent for to go to the palace, when in the presence of the chief men the matter was discussed before the consistory, when the Emperor wished to seize the basilica, I was cowed then at the sight of the royal court, and did not show the firmness a bishop should, or departed with diminished claims. Do they not remember that the people, when they knew I had gone to the palace, made such a rush that they could not resist its force; and all offered themselves to death for the faith of Christ as a military officer came out with some light troops to disperse the crowd? Was not I asked to calm the people with a long speech? Did I not pledge my word that no one should invade the basilica of the church? And though my services were asked for to do an act of kindness, yet the fact that the people came to the palace was used to bring ill-will upon me. They wish to bring me to this now again.

30. I recalled the people, and yet I did not escape their ill-will, which ill-will, however, I think we ought rather to tempt than fear. For why should we fear for the Name of Christ? Unless perchance I ought to be troubled because they say: "Ought not the Emperor to have one basilica, to which to go, and Ambrose wants to have more power than the Emperor, and so refuses to the Emperor the opportunity of going forth to church?" When they say this, they desire to lay hold of my words, as did the Jews who tried Christ with cunning words, saying: "Master, is it lawful to give tribute to Caesar or not?" Is ill-will always stirred up against the servants of God on Caesar's account, and does impiety make use of this with a view to starting a slander, so as to shelter itself under the imperial name? and can they say that they do not share in the sacrilege of those whose advice they follow?

31. See how much worse than the Jews the Arians are. They asked whether He thought that the right of tribute should be given to Caesar; these want to give to Caesar the right of the Church. But as these faithless ones follow their author, so also let us answer as our Lord and Author has taught us. For Jesus seeing the wickedness of the Jews said to them: Why tempt ye Me? show Me a penny. When they had given it, He said: "Whose image and superscription hath it?" They answered and said: Caesar's. And Jesus says to them: "Render unto Caesar the things that are Caesar's, and to God the things that are God's." So, too, I say to these who oppose me: Show me a penny. Jesus sees Caesar's penny and says: Render unto Caesar the things that are Caesar's, and unto God the things that are God's. Can they in seizing the basilicas of the church offer Caesar's penny?

32. But in the church I only know of one Image, that is the Image of the unseen God, of Which God has said: "Let us make man in Our image and Our likeness;" that Image of Which it

is written, that Christ is the Brightness of His glory and the Image of His Person. In that Image I perceive the Father, as the Lord Jesus Himself has said: "He that seeth Me seeth the Father." For this Image is not separated from the Father, which indeed has taught me the unity of the Trinity, saying: "I and My Father are One," and again: "All things that the Father hath are Mine." Also of the Holy Spirit, saying that the Spirit is Christ's, and has received of Christ, as it is written: "He shall receive of Mine, and shall declare it unto you."

33. How, then, did we not answer humbly enough? If he demand tribute, we do not refuse it. The lands of the Church pay tribute. If the Emperor wants the lands, he has the power to claim them, none of us will interfere. The contributions of the people are amply sufficient for the poor. Do not stir up ill-will in the matter of the lands. Let them take them if it is the Emperor's will. I do not give them, but I do not refuse them. They ask for gold. I can say: Silver and gold I do not ask for. But they stir up ill-will because gold is spent. I am not afraid of such ill-will as this. I have dependents. My dependents are Christ's poor. I know how to collect this treasure. On that they may even charge me with this crime, that I have spent money on the poor I and if they make the charge that I seek for defence at their hands, I do not deny it; nay, I solicit it. I have my defence, but it consists in the prayers of the poor. The blind and the lame, the weak and the old, are stronger than hardy warriors. Lastly, gifts to the poor make God indebted to us, for it is written: "He that giveth to the poor, lendeth to God." The guards of warriors often do not merit divine grace.

34. They declare also that the people have been led astray by the strains of my hymns. I certainly do not deny it. That is a lofty strain, and there is nothing more powerful than it. For what has more power than the confession of the Trinity which is daily celebrated by the mouth of the whole people? All eagerly vie one with the other in confessing the faith, and know how to praise in verse the Father, Son, and Holy Spirit. So they all have become teachers, who scarcely could be disciples.

35. What could show greater obedience than that we should follow Christ's example, "Who, being found in fashion as a man, humbled Himself and became obedient even unto death?" Accordingly He has freed all through His obedience. "For as by one man's disobedience many were made sinners, so by the obedience of One shall many be made righteous." If, then, He was obedient, let them receive the rule of obedience: to which we cling, saying to those who stir up ill-will against us on the Emperor's side: We pay to Caesar what is Caesar's, and to God what is God's. Tribute is due to Caesar, we do not deny it. The Church belongs to God, therefore it ought not to be assigned to Caesar. For the temple of God cannot be Caesar's by right.

37. That this is said with respectful feeling for the Emperor, no one can deny. For what is more full of respect than that the Emperor should be called the son of the Church. As it is said, it is said without sin, since it is said with the divine favour. For the Emperor is within the Church, not above it. For a good emperor seeks the aid of the Church and does not refuse it. As I say this with all humility, so also I state it with firmness. Some threaten us with fire, sword, exile; we have learnt as servants of Christ not to fear. To those who have no fear, nothing is ever a serious cause of dread. Thus too is it written: "Arrows of infants their blows have become."

37. A sufficient answer, then, seems to have been given to their suggestion. Now I ask them, what the Saviour asked: "The baptism of John, was it from heaven or men?" The Jews could not answer Him. If the Jews did not make nothing of the baptism of John, does Auxentius make nothing of the baptism of Christ? For that is not a baptism of men, but from heaven, which the angel of great counsel has brought to us, that we might be justified to God. Wherefore, then, does Auxentius hold that the faithful ought to be rebaptized, when they have been baptized in the name of the Trinity, when the Apostle says: "One faith, one baptism"? And wherefore does he say that he is man's enemy, not Christ's, seeing that he despises the counsel of God and condemns the baptism which Christ has granted us to redeem our sins.

LETTER XXII.

St. Ambrose in a letter to his sister gives an account of the finding of the bodies of SS. Gervasius and Protasius, and of his addresses to the people on that occasion. Preaching from Psalm xix., he allegorically expounded the "heavens" to represent the martyrs and apostles, and the "day" he takes to be their confession. They were humbled by God, and then raised again. He then gives an account of the state in which their bodies were found, and of their translation to the basilica. In another address he speaks of the joy of the Catholics and the malice of the Arians who denied the miracles that were being wrought, as the Jews used to do, and points out that their faith is quite different from that of the martyrs, and that since the devils acknowledge the Trinity, and they do not, they are worse than the very devils themselves.

To the lady, his sister, dearer to him than his eyes and life, Ambrose Bishop.

1. As I do not wish anything which takes place here in your absence to escape the knowledge of your holiness, you must know that we have found some bodies of holy martyrs. For after I had dedicated the basilica, many, as it were, with one mouth began to address me, and said: Consecrate this as you did the Roman basilica. And I answered: "Certainly I will if I find any relics of martyrs." And at once a kind of prophetic ardour seemed to enter my heart.

2. Why should I use many words? God favoured us, for even the clergy were afraid who were bidden to clear away the earth from the spot before the chancel screen of SS. Felix and Nabor. I found the fitting signs, and on bringing in some on whom hands were to be laid, the power of the holy martyrs became so manifest, that even whilst I was still silent, one was seized and thrown prostrate at the holy burial-place. We found two men of marvellous stature, such as those of ancient days. All the bones were perfect, and there was much blood. During the whole of those two days there was an enormous concourse of people. Briefly we arranged the whole in order, and as evening was now coming on transferred them to the basilica of Fausta, where watch was kept during the night, and some received the laying on of hands. On the following day we translated the relics to the basilica called Ambrosian. During the translation a blind man was healed. I addressed the people then as follows:

3. When I considered the immense and unprecedented numbers of you who are here gathered together, and the gifts of divine grace which have shone forth in the holy. martyrs, I must confess that I felt myself unequal to this task, and that I could not express in words what we can scarcely conceive in our minds or take in with our eyes. But when the course of holy Scripture began to be read, the Holy Spirit Who spake in the prophets granted me to utter something worthy of so great a gathering, of your expectations, and of the merits of the holy martyrs.

4. "The heavens," it is said, "declare the glory of God." When this Psalm is read, it occurs to one that not so much the material elements as the heavenly merits seem to offer praise worthy of God. And by the chance of this day's lessons it is made clear what "heavens" declare the glory of God. Look at the holy relics at my right hand and at my left, see men of heavenly conversation, behold the trophies of a heavenly mind. These are the heavens which declare the glory of God, these are His handiwork which the firmament proclaims. For not worldly enticements, but the grace of the divine working, raised them to the firmament of the most sacred Passion, and long before by the testimony of their character and virtues bore witness of them, that they continued steadfast against the dangers of this world.

5. Paul was a heaven, when he said: "Our conversation is in heaven." James and John were heavens, and then were called "sons of thunder"; and John, being as it were a heaven, saw the Word with God. The Lord Jesus Himself was a heaven of perpetual light, when He was declaring the glory of God, that glory which no man had seen before. And therefore He said: "No man hath seen God at any time, except the only-begotten Son, Who is in the bosom of the Father, He hath declared Him." If you seek for the handiwork of God, listen to Job when he says: "The Spirit of God Who hath made me." And so strengthened against the temptations of the devil, he kept his footsteps constantly without offence. But let us go on to what follows.

6. "Day," it is said, "unto day uttereth speech." Behold the true days, where no darkness of night intervenes. Behold the days full of life and eternal brightness, which uttered the word of God, not in speech which passes away, but in their inmost heart, by constancy in confession, and perseverance in their witness.

7. Another Psalm which was read says: "Who is like unto the Lord our God, Who dwelleth on high, and regardeth lowly things in heaven and in the earth?" The Lord regarded indeed lowly things when He revealed to His Church the relics of the holy martyrs lying hidden under the unnoted turf, whose souls were in heaven, their bodies in the earth: "raising the poor out of the dust, and lifting the needy from the mire," an d you see how He hath "set them with the princes of His people." Whom are we to esteem as the princes of the people but the holy martyrs? amongst whose number Protasius and Gervasius long unknown are now enrolled, who have caused the Church of Milan, barren of martyrs hitherto, now as the mother of many children, to rejoice in the distinctions and instances of her own sufferings.

8. Nor let this seem at variance with the true faith: "Day unto day uttereth the word;" soul unto soul, life unto life, resurrection unto resurrection; "and night unto night showeth knowledge;" that is, flesh unto flesh, they, that is, whose passion has shown to all the true knowledge of the faith. Good are these nights, bright nights, not without stars: "For as star differeth from star in brightness, so too is the resurrection of the dead."

9. For not without reason do many call this the resurrection of the martyrs. I do not say whether they have risen for themselves, for us certainly the martyrs have risen. You know—nay, you have yourselves seen—that many are cleansed from evil spirits, that very many also, having touched with their hands the robe of the saints, are freed from those ailments which oppressed them; you see that the miracles of old time are renewed, when through the coming of the Lord Jesus grace was more largely shed forth upon the earth, and that many bodies are healed as it were by the shadow of the holy bodies. How many napkins are passed about! how many garments, laid upon the holy relics and endowed with healing power, are claimed! All are glad to touch even the outside thread, and whosoever touches will be made whole.

10. Thanks be to Thee, Lord Jesus, that at this time Thou hast stirred up for us the spirits of the holy martyrs, when Thy Church needs greater protection. Let all know what sort of champions I desire, who are able to defend, but desire not to attack. These have I gained for you, O holy people, such as may help all and injure none. Such defenders do I desire, such are the soldiers I have, that is, not soldiers of this world, but soldiers of Christ. I fear no ill-will on account of them, the more powerful their patronage is the greater safety is there in it. And I wish for their protection for those very persons who grudge them to me. Let them come, then, and see my attendants. I do not deny that I am surrounded by such arms: "Some trust in chariots, and some in horses, but we will boast in the Name of the Lord our God."

11. The course of divine Scripture relates that Elisha, when surrounded by the army of the Syrians, told his servant, who was afraid, not to fear; "for," said he, "they that be for us are more than those against us;" and in order to prove this, he prayed that the eyes of Gehazi might be opened, and when they were opened, he saw that numberless hosts of angels were present. And we, though we cannot see them, yet feel their presence. Our eyes were shut, so long as the bodies of the saints lay hidden. The Lord opened our eyes, and we saw the aids wherewith we have been often protected. We used not to see them, but yet we had them. And so, as though the Lord had said to us when trembling, "See what great martyrs I have given you," so we with opened eyes behold the glory of the Lord, which is passed in the passion of the martyrs, and present in their working. We have escaped, brethren, no slight lead of shame; we had patrons and knew it not. We have found this one thing, in which we seem to excel those who have gone before us. That knowledge of the martyrs, which they lost, we have regained.

12. The glorious relics are taken out of an ignoble burying-place, the trophies are displayed under heaven. The tomb is wet with blood. The marks of the bloody triumph are present, the relics are found undisturbed in their order, the head separated from the body. Old men now

repeat that they once heard the names of these martyrs and read their titles. The city which had carried off the martyrs of other places had lost her own. Though this be the gift of God, yet I cannot deny the favour which the Lord Jesus has granted to the time of my priesthood, and since I myself am not worthy to be a martyr, I have obtained these martyrs for you.

13. Let these triumphant victims be brought to the place where Christ is the victim. But He upon the altar, Who suffered for all; they beneath the altar, who were redeemed by His Passion. I had destined this place for myself, for it is fitting that the priest should rest there where he has been wont to offer, but I yield the right hand portion to the sacred victims; that place was due to the martyrs. Let us, then, deposit the sacred relics, and lay them up in a worthy resting-place, and let us celebrate the whole day with faithful devotion.

14. The people called out and demanded that the deposition of the martyrs should be postponed until the Lord's day, but at length it was agreed that it should take place the following day. On the following day again I preached to the people on this sort.

15. Yesterday I handled the verse, "Day unto day uttereth speech," as my ability enabled me; to-day holy Scripture seems to me not only to have prophesied in former times, but even at the present. For when I behold your holy celebration continued day and night, the oracles of the prophet's song have declared that these days, yesterday and to-day, are the days of which it is most opportunely said: "Day unto day uttereth speech;" and these the nights of which it is most fittingly said that "Night unto night showeth knowledge." For what else but the Word of God have you during these two days uttered with inmost affection, and have proved yourselves to have the knowledge of the faith.

16. And they who usually do so have a grudge against this solemnity of yours; and since because of their envious disposition they cannot endure this solemnity, they hate the cause of it, and go so far in their madness as to deny the merits of the martyrs, whose deeds even the evil spirits confess. But this is not to be wondered at since such is the faithlessness of unbelievers that the confession of the devil is often more easy to endure. For the devil said: "Jesus, Son of the living God, why art Thou come to torment us before the time?" And the Jews hearing this, even themselves denied Him to be the Son of God. And at this time you have heard the devils crying out, and confessing to the martys that they cannot bear their sufferings, and saying, "Why are ye come to torment us so severely?" And the Arians say: "These are not martys, and they cannot torment the devil, nor deliver any one, while the torments of the devils are proved by their own words, and the benefits of the martyrs are declared by the restoring of the healed, and the proof of those that are loosed.

17. They deny that the blind man received sight, but he denies not that he is healed. He says: I who could not see now see. He says: I ceased to be blind, and proves it by the fact. They deny the benefit, who are unable to deny the fact. The man is known: so long as he was well he was employed in the public service; his name is Severus, a butcher by trade. He had given up his occupation when this hindrance betel him. He calls for evidence those persons by whose kindness he was supported; he adduces those as able to affirm the truth of his visitation whom he had as witnesses of his blindness. He declares that when he touched the hem of the robe of the martyrs, wherewith the sacred relics were covered, his sight was restored.

18. Is not this like that which we read in the Gospel? For we praise the power of the same Author in each case, nor does it be a work or a gift, since He confers a gift in His works, and works in His gift. For that which He gave to others to be done, this His Name effects in the work of others. So we read in the Gospel, that the Jews, when they saw the gift of healing in the blind man, called for the testimony of his parents, and asked: "How doth your son see?" when he said: "Whereas I was blind, now I see." And in this case the man says, "I was blind and now I see." Ask others if you do not believe me; ask strangers if you think his parents are in collusion with me. The obstinacy of these men is more hateful than that of the Jews, for the latter, when they doubted, at least asked his parents; the others enquire in secret and deny in public, incredulous not as to the work, but as to its Author.

455

19. But I ask what it is that they do not believe; is it whether any one can be aided by the martyrs? This is the same thing as not to believe Christ, for He Himself said: "Ye shall do greater things than these." How? By those martyrs whose merits have been long efficacious, whose bodies were long since found? Here I ask, do they bear a grudge against me, or against the holy martyrs? If against me, are any miracles wrought by me? by my means or in my name? Why, then, grudge me what is not mine? If it be against the martyrs (for if they bear no grudge against me, it can only be against them), they show that the martyrs were of another faith than that which they believe. For otherwise they would not have any feeling against their works, did they not judge that they have not the faith which was in them, that faith established by the tradition of our forefathers, which the devils themselves cannot deny, but the Arians do.

21. We have to-day heard those on whom hands were laid say, that no one can be saved unless he believe in the Father, the Son, and the Holy Spirit; that he is dead and buried who denies the Holy Spirit, and believes not the almighty power of the Trinity. The devil confesses this, but the Arians refuse to do so. The devil says: Let him who denies the Godhead of the Holy Spirit be so tormented as himself was tormented by the martyrs.

22. I do not accept the devil's testimony but his confession. The devil spoke unwillingly, being compelled and tormented. That which wickedness suppresses, torture extracts. The devil yields to blows, and the Arians have not yet learned to yield. How great have been their sufferings, and yet. like Pharaoh, they are hardened by their calamities! The devil said, as we find it written: "I know Thee Who Thou art, Thou art the Son of the living God." And the Jews said: "We know not whence He is." The evil spirits said to-day, yesterday, and during the night, We know that ye are martyrs. And the Arians say, We know not, we will not understand, we will not believe. The evil spirits say to the martyrs, Ye are come to destroy us. The Arians say, The torments of the devils are not real but fictitious and made-up tales. I have heard of many things being made up, but no one has ever been able to feign that he was an evil spirit. What is the meaning of the torment we see in those on whom hands are laid? What room is there here for fraud? what suspicion of pretence?

23. But I will not make use of the voice of evil spirits in support of the martyrs. Their holy sufferings are proved by the benefits they confer. These have persons to judge of them, namely, those who are cleansed, and witnesses, namely, those who are set free. That voice is better than that of devils, which the soundness of those utters who came infirm; better is the voice which blood sends forth, for blood has a loud voice reaching from earth to heaven. You have read how God said: "Thy brother's blood crieth unto Me." This blood cries by its colour, the blood cries by the voice of its effects, the blood cries by the triumph of its passion. We have acceded to your request, and have postponed till to-day the deposition of the relics which was to have taken place yesterday.

LETTER XL.

St. Ambrose begs Theodosius to listen to him, as he cannot be silent without great risk to both. He points out that Theodosius though God-fearing may be led astray, and points out that his decision respecting the restoration of the Jewish synagogue is full of peril, exposing the bishop to the danger of either acting against the truth or of death. The case of Julian is referred to, and the reasons given for the imperial rescript are met, especially by the plea that the Jews had burnt many churches. St. Ambrose touches on the temple of the Valentinians, whom he declares to be worse than heathen, and points out what a door would be opened to the calumnies of the Jews and a triumph over Christ Himself. The Emperor is lastly warned by the example of Maximus not to take the part of Jews or heretics, and is urged to clemency.

Ambrose, Bishop, to the most clement prince, and blessed Emperor, Theodosius the Augustus.

1. I am continually harassed by almost incessant cares, most blessed Emperor, but I have never been in such anxiety as at present, since I see that I must take heed that there be nothing which may be ascribed to me savouring even of sacrilege. And so I entreat you to listen with

patience to what I say. For, if I am unworthy to be heard by you, I am unworthy to offer for you, who have been entrusted by you with your vows and prayers. Will you not yourself hear him whom you wish to be heard for you? Will you not hear him pleading his own cause whom you have heard for others? And do you not fear for your own decision, lest by thinking him unworthy to be heard by you, you make him unworthy to be heard for you?

2. But it is neither the part of an emperor to refuse liberty of speech, nor of a priest not to say what he thinks. For there is nothing in you emperors so popular and so estimable as to appreciate freedom in those even who are in subjection to you by military obedience. For this is the difference between good and bad princes, that the good love liberty, the bad slavery. And there is nothing in a priest so full of peril as regards God, or so base in the opinion of men, as not freely to declare what he thinks. For it is written: "I spoke of Thy testimonies before kings, and was not ashamed;" and in another place: "Son of man, I have set Thee a watchman unto the house of Israel, in order," it is said, "that if the righteous doth turn from his righteousness, and commit iniquity, because thou hast not given him warning," that is, hast not told him what to guard against, "the memory of his righteousness shall not be retained, and I will require his blood at thine hand. But if thou warn the righteous that he sin not, and he doth not sin, the righteous shall surely live because thou hast warned him, and thou shalt deliver thy soul."

3. I had rather then, O Emperor, have fellowship with you in good than in evil, and therefore the silence of the priest ought to displease your Clemency, and his freedom to please you. For you are involved in the risk of my silence, but are aided by the benefit of my freedom. I am not, then, officiously intruding in things where I ought not, nor interfering in the affairs of others. I am obeying the commands of God. And I do this first of all out of love for you, good-will toward you, and desire of preserving your well-doing. If I am not believed in this, or am forbidden to act on this feeling, I speak in very truth for fear of offending God. For if my peril would set you free, I would patiently offer myself for you, though not willingly, for I had rather that without my peril you might be acceptable to God and glorious. But if the guilt of silence and dissimulation on my part would both weigh me down and not set you free, I had rather that you should think me too importunate, than useless and base. Since it is written, as the holy Apostle Paul says, whose teaching you cannot controvert: "Be instant, in season, out of season, reprove, entreat, rebuke with all patience and doctrine."

4. We, then, also have One Whom it is even more perilous to displease, especially since even emperors are not displeased when every one discharges his own office, and you patiently listen to every one making suggestions in his own sphere, nay, you rebuke him if he act not according to the order of his service. Can this, then, seem to you offensive in priests, which you willingly accept from those who serve you; since we speak not what we wish, but what we are bidden? For you know the passage: "When ye shall stand before kings and rulers, take no thought what ye shall speak, for it shall be given you in that hour what ye shall speak; for it is not ye that speak, but the Spirit of your Father Who speaketh in you." And if I were speaking in state causes, although justice must be observed even in them, I should not feel such dread if I were not listened to, but in the cause of God whom will you listen to, if not to the priest, at whose greater peril sin is committed? Who will dare to tell you the truth if the priest dare not?

5. I know that you are Godfearing, merciful, gentle, and calm, having the faith and fear of God at heart, but often some things escape our notice. "Some have a zeal of God, but not according to knowledge." And I think that we ought to take care lest this also come upon faithful souls. I know your piety towards God, your lenity towards men, I myself am bound by the benefits of your favour. And therefore I fear the more, I am the more anxious; lest even you condemn me hereafter by your own judgment, because through my want of openness or my flattery you should not have avoided some fault. If I saw that you sinned against me, I ought not to keep silence, for it is written: "If thy brother sin against thee, rebuke him at first, then chide him sharply before two or three witnesses. If he will not hear thee, tell the Church." Shall I, then, keep silence in the cause of God? Let us, then, consider what I have to fear.

6. A report was made by the military Count of the East that a synagogue had been burnt, and that this was done at the instigation of the Bishop. You gave command that the others should be punished, and the synagogue be rebuilt by the Bishop himself. I do not urge that the Bishop's account ought to have been waited for, for priests are the calmers of disturbances, and anxious for peace, except when even they are moved by some offence against God, or insult to the Church. Let us suppose that that Bishop was too eager in the matter of burning the synagogue, and too timid at the judgment-seat, are not you afraid, O Emperor, lest he comply with your sentence, lest he fail in his faith?

7. Are you not also afraid, lest, which will happen, he oppose your Count with a refusal? He will then be obliged to make him either an apostate or a martyr, either of these alien to the times, either of them equivalent to persecution, if he be compelled either to apostatize or to undergo martyrdom. You see in what direction the issue of the matter inclines. If you think the Bishop firm, guard against making a martyr of a firm man; if you think him vacillating, avoid causing the fall of one who is frail. For he has a heavy responsibility who has caused the weak to fall.

8. Having, then, thus stated the two sides of the matter, suppose that the said Bishop says that he himself kindled the fire, collected the crowd, gathered the people together, in order not to lose an opportunity of martyrdom, and instead of the weak to put forward a stronger athlete. O happy falsehood, whereby one gains for others acquittal, for himself grace! This it is, O Emperor, which I, too, have requested, that you would rather take vengeance on me, and if you consider this a crime, would attribute it to me. Why order judgment against one who is absent? You have the guilty man present, you hear his confession. I declare that I set fire to the synagogue, or at least that I ordered those who did it, that there might not be a place where Christ was denied. If it be objected to me that I did not set the synagogue on fire here, I answer, it began to be burnt by the judgment of God, and my work came to an end. And if the very truth be asked, I was the more slack because I did not expect that it would be punished. Why should I do that which as it was unavenged would also be without reward? These words hurt modesty but recall grace, lest that be done whereby an offence against God most High may be committed.

9. But let it be granted that no one will cite the Bishop to the performance of this task, for I have asked this of your Clemency, and although I have not yet read that this edict is revoked, let us notwithstanding assume that it is revoked. What if others more timid offer that the synagogue be restored at their cost; or that the Count, having found this previously determined, himself orders it to be rebuilt out of the funds of Christians? You, O Emperor, will have an apostate Count, and to him will you entrust the victorious standards? Will you entrust the labarum, consecrated as it is by the Name of Christ, to one who restores the synagogue which knows not Christ? Order the labarum to be carried into the synagogue, and let us see if they do not resist.

10. Shall, then, a place be made for the unbelief of the Jews out of the spoils of the Church, and shall the patrimony, which by the favour of Christ has been gained for Christians, be transferred to the treasuries of unbelievers? We read that Of old temples were built for idols of the plunder taken from Cimbri, and the spoils of other enemies. Shall the Jews write this inscription on the front of their synagogue: "The temple of impiety, erected from the plunder of Christians"?

11. But, perhaps, the cause of discipline moves you, O Emperor. Which, then, is of greater importance, the show of discipline or the cause of religion? It is needful that judgment should yield to religion.

12. Have you not heard, O Emperor, how, when Julian had commanded that the temple of Jerusalem should be restored, those who were clearing the rubbish were consumed by fire? Will you not beware lest this happen now again? For you ought not to have commanded what Julian commanded.

13. But what is your motive? Is it because a public building of whatever kind has been burnt, or because it was a synagogue? If you are moved by the burning of a building of no importance (for what could there be in so mean a town?), do you not remember, O Emperor, how many prefects' houses have been burnt at Rome, and no one inflicted punishment for it? And, in truth, if any emperor had desired to punish the deed sharply, he would have injured the cause of him who had suffered so great a loss. Which, then, is more fitting, that a fire in some part of the buildings of Callinicum, or of the city of Rome, should be punished, if indeed it were right at all? At Constantinople lately, the house of the bishop was burnt and your Clemency's son interceded with his father, praying that you would not avenge the insult offered to him, that is, to the son of the emperor, and the burning of the episcopal house. Do you not consider, O Emperor, that if you were to order this deed to be punished, he would again intervene against the punishment? That favour was, however, fittingly obtained by the son from the father, for it was worthy of him first to forgive the injury done to himself. That was a good division in the distribution of favour, that the son should be entreated for his own loss, the father for that of the son. Here there is nothing for you to keep back for your son. Take heed, then, lest you derogate aught from God.

14. There is, then, no adequate cause for such a commotion, that the people should be so severely punished for the burning of a building, and much less since it is the burning of a synagogue, a home of unbelief, a house of impiety, a receptacle of folly, which God Himself has condemned. For thus we read, where the Lord our God speaks by the mouth of the prophet Jeremiah: "And I will do to this house, which is called by My Name, wherein ye trust, and to the place which I gave to you and to your fathers, as I have done to Shiloh, and I will cast you forth from My sight, as I cast forth your brethren, the whole seed of Ephraim. And do not thou pray for that people, and do not thou ask mercy for them, and do not come near Me on their behalf, for I will not hear thee. Or seest thou not what they do in the cities of Judah?" God forbids intercession to be made for those.

15. And certainly, if I were pleading according to the law of nations, I could tell how many of the Church's basilicas the Jews burnt in the time of the Emperor Julian: two at Damascus, one of which is scarcely now repaired, and this at the cost of the Church, not of the Synagogue; the other basilica still is a rough mass of shapeless ruins. Basilicas were burnt at Gaza, Ascalon, Berytus, and in almost every place in those parts, and no one demanded punishment. And at Alexandria a basilica was burnt by heathen and Jews, which surpassed all the rest. The Church was not avenged, shall the Synagogue be so?

16. Shall, then, the burning of the temple of the Valentinians be also avenged? But what is but a temple in which is a gathering of heathen? Although the heathen invoke twelve gods, the Valentinians worship thirty-two Aeons whom they call gods. And I have found out concerning these alsothat it is reported and ordered that some monks should be punished, who, when the Valentinians were stopping the road on which, according to custom and ancient use, they were singing psalms as they went to celebrate the festival of the Maccabees, enraged by their insolence, burnt their hurriedly-built temple in some country village.

17. How many have to offer themselves to such a choice, when they remember that in the time of Julian, he who threw down an altar, and disturbed a sacrifice, was condemned by the judge and suffered martyrdom? And so the judge who heard him was never esteemed other than a prosecutor, for no one thought him worthy of being associated with, or of a kiss. And if he were not now dead, I should fear, O Emperor, that you would take vengeance on him, although he escaped not the vengeance of heaven, outliving his own heir.

18. But it is related that the judge was ordered to take cognizance of the matter, and that it was written that he ought not to have reported the deed, but to have punished it, and that the money chests which had been taken away should be demanded. I will omit other matters. The buildings of our churches were burnt by the Jews, and nothing was restored, nothing was asked back, nothing demanded. But what could the Synagogue have possessed in a far distant town,

when the whole of what there is there is not much; there is nothing of value, and no abundance? And what then could the scheming Jews lose by the fire? These are artifices of the Jews who wish to calumniate us, that because of their complaints, an extraordinary military inquiry may be ordered, and a soldier sent, who will, perhaps, say what one said once here, O Emperor, before your accession: "How will Christ be able to help us who fight for the Jews against Christ, who are sent to avenge the Jews? They have destroyed their own armies, and wish to destroy ours."

19. Further, into what calumnies will they not break out, who by false witness calumniated even Christ? Into what calumnies will not men break out who are liars, even in things belonging to God? Whom will they not say to have been the instigators of that sedition? Whom will they not assail, even of those whom they recognize not, that may gaze upon the numberless ranks of Christians in chains, that they may see the necks of the faithful people bowed in captivity, that the servants of God may be concealed in darkness, may be beheaded, given over to the fire, delivered to the mines, that their sufferings may not quickly pass away?

20. Will you give this triumph over the Church of God to the Jews? this trophy over Christ's people, this exultation, O Emperor, to the unbelievers? this rejoicing to the Synagogue, this sorrow to the Church? The people of the Jews will set this solemnity amongst their feast-days, and will doubtless number it amongst those on which they triumphed either over the Amorites, or the Canaanites, or were delivered from the hand of Pharaoh, King of Egypt, or of Nebuchodonosor, King of Babylon. They will add this solemnity, in memory of their having triumphed over the people of Christ.

21. And whereas they deny that they themselves are bound by the Roman laws, and repute those laws as criminal, yet now they think that they ought to be avenged, as it were, by the Roman laws. Where were those laws when they themselves set fire to the roofs of the sacred basilicas? If Julian did not avenge the Church because he was an apostate, will you, O Emperor, avenge the injury done to the Synagogue, because you are a Christian?

22. And what will Christ say to you afterwards? Do you not remember what He said by the prophet Nathan to holy David? "I have chosen thee the youngest of thy brethren, and from a private man have made thee emperor. I have placed of the fruit of thy seed on the imperial throne. I have made barbarous nations subject unto thee, I have given thee peace, I have delivered thine enemy captive into thy power. Thou hadst no corn for provision for thine army, I opened to thee the gates, I opened to thee their stores by the hand of the enemies themselves. Thy enemies gave to thee their provisions which they had prepared for themselves. I troubled the counsels of thy enemy, so that he made himself bare. I so lettered the usurper of the empire himself and bound his mind, that whilst he still had means of escape, yet with all belonging to him, as though for fear lest any should escape thee, he shut himself in. His officer and forces on the other element, whom before I had scattered, that they might not join to fight against thee, I brought together again to complete thy victory. Thy army, gathered together from many unsubdued nations, I bade keep faith, tranquillity, and concord as if of one nation. When there was the greatest danger lest the perfidious designs of the barbarians should penetrate the Alps, I conferred victory on thee within the very wall of the Alps, that thou mightest conquer without loss. Thus, then, I caused thee to triumph over thy enemy, and thou givest My enemies a triumph over My people."

23. Is it not on this account that Maximus was forsaken, who, before the days of the expedition, hearing that a synagogue had been burnt in Rome, had sent an edict to Rome, as if he were the upholder of public order? Wherefore the Christian people said, No good is in store for him. That king has become a Jew, we have heard of him as a defender of order, and Christ, Who died for sinners, soon tested him. If this was said of words, what will be said of punishment? And then at once he was overcome by the Franks and the Saxons, in Sicily, at Siscia, at Petavio, in a word everywhere. What has the believer in common with the unbeliever? The instances of his unbelief ought to be done away with together with the unbeliever himself.

That which injured him, that wherein he who was conquered offended, the conqueror ought not to follow but to condemn.

24. I have, then, recounted these things not as to one who is ungrateful, but have enumerated them as rightly bestowed, in order that, warned by them, you, to whom more has been given, may love more. When Simon answered in these words the Lord Jesus said: "Thou hast judged rightly." And straightway turning to the woman who anointed His feet with ointment, setting forth a type of the Church, He said to Simon: "Wherefore I say unto thee, her sins which are many are forgiven, since she loved much. But he to whom less is forgiven loveth less." This is the woman who entered into the house of the Pharisee, and cast off the Jew, but gained Christ. For the Church shut out the Synagogue, why is it now again attempted that in the servant of Christ the Synagogue should exclude the Church from the bosom of faith, from the house of Christ?

25. I have brought these matters together in this address, O Emperor, out of love and zeal for you. For I owe it to your kindnesses (whereby, at my request, you have liberated many from exile, from prison, from the extreme penalty of death) that I should not fear even offending your feelings for the sake of your own salvation (no one has greater confidence than he who loves from his heart, certainly no one ought to injure him who takes thought for him); that I may not lose in one moment that favour granted to every priest and received by me for so many years; and yet it is not the loss of favour which I deprecate but the peril to salvation.

26. And yet how great a thing it is, O Emperor, that you should not think it necessary to enquire or to punish in regard to a matter as to which up to this day no one has enquired, no one has ever inflicted punishment. It is a serious matter to endanger your salvation for the Jews. When Gideon had slain the sacred calf, the heathen said, The gods will themselves avenge the injury done to them. Who is to avenge the Synagogue? Christ, Whom they slew, Whom they denied? Will God the Father avenge those who do not receive the Father, since they have not received the Son? Who is to avenge the heresy of the Valentinians? How can your piety avenge them, seeing it has commanded them to be excluded, and denied them permission to meet together? If I set before you Josiah as a king approved of God, will you condemn that in them which was approved in him?

27. But at any rate if too little confidence is placed in me, command the presence of those bishops whom you think fit, let it be discussed, O Emperor, what ought to be done without injury to the faith, If you consult your officers concerning pecuniary causes, how much more just is it that you should consult the priests of God in the cause of religion.

28. Let your Clemency consider from how many plotters, how many spies the Church suffers. If they come upon a slight crack, they plant a dart in it. I speak after the manner of men, but God is feared more than men, Who is rightly set before even emperors. If any one thinks it right that deference should be paid to a friend, a parent, or a neighbour, I am right in judging that deference should be paid to God, and that He should be preferred to all. Consult, O Emperor, your own advantage, or suffer me to consult mine.

29. What shall I answer hereafter, if it be discovered that, by authority given from this place, Christians have been slain by the sword, or by clubs, or thongs knotted with lead? How shall I explain such a fact? How shall I excuse it to those bishops, who now mourn bitterly because some, who have discharged the office of the priesthood for thirty and many more years, or other ministers of the Church, are withdrawn from their sacred office, and set to discharge municipal duties? For if they who war for you serve for a stated time of service, how much more ought you to consider those who war for God. How, I say, shall I excuse this to the bishops, who make complaint concerning the clergy, and write that the Churches are wasted by a serious attack upon them?

30. I was desirous that this should come to the knowledge of your Clemency. You will, when it pleases you, vouchsafe to consider and give order according to your will, but exclude and cast out that which troubles me, and troubles me rightly. You do yourself whatever you order to be

done, even if he, your officer, do not do it. I much prefer that you should be merciful, than that he should not do what he has been ordered.

31. You have those for whom you ought yet to invite and to merit the mercy of the Lord in regard to the Roman Empire; you have those for whom you hope even more than for yourself; let the grace of God for them, let their salvation appeal to you in these words of mine. I fear that you may commit your cause to the judgment of others. Everything is still unprejudiced before you. On this point I pledge myself to our God for you, do not fear your oath. Is it possible that that should displease God which is amended for His honour? You need not alter anything in that letter, whether it be sent or is not yet sent. Order another to be written, which shall be full of faith, full of piety. For you it is possible to change for the better, for me it is not possible to hide the truth.

32. You forgave the Antiochians the insult offered to you; you have recalled the daughters of your enemy, and given them to be brought up by a relative; you sent sums of money to the mother of your enemy from your own treasury. This so great piety, this so great faith towards God, will be darkened by this deed. Do not you, then, I entreat, who spared enemies in arms, and preserved your adversaries, think that Christians ought to be punished with such eagerness.

33. And now, O Emperor, I beg you not to disdain to hear me who am in fear both for yourself and for myself, for it is the voice of a Saint which says: "Wherefore was I made to see the misery of my people?" that I should commit an offence against God. I, indeed, have done what could be done consistently with honour to you, that you might rather listen to me in the palace, lest, if it were necessary, you should listen to me in the Church.

LETTER XLI.

St. Ambrose in this letter to his sister continues the account of the matters contained in his letter to Theodosius, and of a sermon which he subsequently delivered before the Emperor, with the result that the Emperor, when St. Ambrose refused to offer the Sacrifice before receiving a promise that the objectionable order should be revoked, yielded.

The Brother TO His Sister.

1. You were good enough to write me word that your holiness was still anxious, because I had written that I was so, so that I am surprised that you did not receive my letter in which I wrote word that satisfaction had been granted me. For when it was reported that a synagogue of the Jews and a conventicle of the Valentinians had been burnt by Christians at the instigation of the bishop, an order was made while I was at Aquileia, that the synagogue should be rebuilt, and the monks punished who had burnt the Valentinian building. Then since I gained little by frequent endeavours, I wrote and sent a letter to the Emperor, and when he went to church I delivered this discourse.

2. In the book of the prophet it is written: "Take to thyself the rod of an almond tree." We ought to consider why the Lord said this to the prophet, for it was not written without a purpose, since in the Pentateuch too we read that the almond rod of Aaron the priest, after being long laid up, blossomed. For the Lord seems to signify by the rod that the prophetic or priestly authority ought to be straightforward, and to advise not so much what is pleasant as what is expedient.

3. And so the prophet is bidden to take an almond rod, because the fruit of this tree is bitter in its rind, hard in its shell, and inside it is pleasant, that after its likeness the prophet should set forth things bitter and hard, and should not fear to proclaim harsh things. Likewise also the priest; for his teaching, though for a time it may seem bitter to some, and like Aaron's rod be long laid up in the ears of dissemblers, yet after a time, when it is thought to have dried up, it blossoms.

4. Wherefore also the Apostle says: "What will ye, shall I come to you with a rod, or in love and in the spirit of gentleness?" First he made mention of the rod, and like the almond rod struck those who were wandering, that he might afterwards comfort them in the spirit of

meekness. And so meekness restored him whom the rod had deprived of the heavenly sacraments. And to his disciple he gave similar injunctions, saying: "Reprove, beseech, rebuke." Two of these are hard, one is gentle, but they are hard only that they may soften; for as to suffering from excess of gall, bitter food or drink seems sweet, and on the other hand sweet food is bitter, so where the mind is wounded it grows worse under the influence of pleasurable flattery, and again is made sound by the bitterness of correction.

5. Let thus much be gathered from the passage of the prophet, and let us now consider what the lesson from the Gospel contains: "One of the Pharisees invited the Lord Jesus to eat with him, and He entered into the Pharisee's house and sat down. And behold a woman, who was a sinner in the city, when she knew that Jesus sat at meat in the Pharisee's house, brought an alabaster box of ointment, and standing behind at His feet, began to wash His feet with her tears." And then he read as far as this place: "Thy faith hath saved thee, go in peace." How simple, I went on to say, is this Gospel lesson in words, how deep in its counsels! And so because the words are those of the "Great Counsellor," let us consider their depth.

6. Our Lord Jusus Christ judged that men could more readily be bound and led on to do the things that are right by kindness than by fear, and that love avails more than dread for correction. And so, when He came, being born of a Virgin, He sent forth His grace, that sin might be forgiven in baptism in order to make us more grateful to Himself. Then if we repay Him by services befitting men who are grateful, He has declared in this woman that there will be a reward for this grace itself to all men. For if He had forgiven only our original debt, He would have seemed more cautious than merciful, and more careful for our correction than magnificent in His rewards. It is only the cunning of a narrow mind that tries to entice, but it is fitting for God that those whom He has invited by grace He should lead on by increase of that grace. And so He first bestows on us a gift by baptism, and afterwards gives more abundantly to those who serve Him faithfully. So, then, the benefits of Christ are both incentives and rewards of virtue.

7. And let no one be startled at the word "creditor." We were before under a hard creditor, who was not to be satisfied and paid to the full but by the death of the debtor. The Lord Jesus came, He saw us bound by a heavy debt. No one could pay his debt with the patrimony of his innocence. I could have nothing of my own wherewith to free myself. He gave to me a new kind of acquittance, changing my creditor because I had nothing wherewith to pay my debt. But it was sin, not nature, which had made us debtors, for we had contracted heavy debts by our sins, that we who had been free should be bound, for he is a debtor who received any of his creditor's money. Now sin is of the devil; that wicked one has, as it were, these riches in his possession. For as the riches of Christ are virtues, so crimes are the wealth of the devil. He had reduced the human race to perpetual captivity by the heavy debt of inherited liability, which our debt-laden ancestor had transmitted to his posterity by inheritance. The Lord Jesus came, He offered His death for the death of all, He poured out His Blood for the blood of all.

8. So, then, we have changed our creditor, not escaped wholly, or rather we have escaped, for the debt remains but the interest is cancelled, for the Lord Jesus said, "To those who are in bonds, Come out, and to those who are in prison, Go forth;" so your sins are forgiven. All, then, are forgiven, nor is there any one whom He has not loosed. For thus it is written, that He has forgiven "all trangressions, doing away the handwriting of the ordinance that was against us." Why, then, do we hold the bonds of others, and desire to exact the debts of others, while we enjoy our own remission? He who forgave all, required of all that what every one remembers to have been forgiven to himself, he also should forgive others.

9. Take care that you do not begin to be in a worse case as creditor than as debtor, like the man in the Gospel, to whom his lord forgave all his debt, and who afterwards began to exact from his fellow-servant that which he himself had not paid, for which reason his master being angry, exacted from him, with the bitterest reproaches, that which he had before forgiven him. Let us, therefore, take heed lest this happen to us, that by not forgiving that which is due to ourselves, we should incur the payment of what has been forgiven us, for thus is it written in the

words of the Lord Jesus: "So shall My Father, Which is in heaven, do also unto you, if ye from your hearts forgive not every one his brother." Let us, then, forgive few things to whom many have been forgiven, and understand that the more we forgive the more acceptable shall we be to God, for we are the more well pleasing to God, the more we have been forgiven.

10. And, finally, the Pharisee, when the Lord asked him, "which of them loved him most," answered, "I suppose that he to whom he forgave most." And the Lord replied. "Thou hast judged rightly." The judgment of the Pharisee is praised, but his affection is blamed. He judges well concerning others, but does not himself believe that which he thinks well of in the case of others. You hear a Jew praising the discipline of the Church, extolling its true grace, honouring the priests of the Church; if you exhort him to believe he refuses, and so follows not himself that which he praises in us. His praise, then, is not full, because Christ said to him: "Thou hast rightly judged," for Cain also offered rightly, but did not divide rightly, and therefore God said to him: "If thou offerest rightly, but dividest not rightly, thou hast sinned, be still." So, then, this man offered rightly, for he judges that Christ ought to be more loved by Christians, because He has forgiven us many sins; but he divided not rightly, because he thought that He could be ignorant of the sins of men Who forgave the sins of men.

11. And, therefore, He said to Simon: "Thou seest this woman. I entered into thine house, and thou gavest Me no water for My feet, but she hath washed My feet with her tears." We are all the one body of Christ, the head of which is God, and we are the members; some perchance eyes, as the prophets; others teeth, as the apostles, who have passed the food of the Gospel preached into our breasts, and rightly is it written: "His eyes shall be bright with wine. and his teeth whiter than milk." And His hands are they who are seen to carry out good works, His belly are they who distribute the strength of nourishment on the poor. So, too, some are His feet, and would that I might be worthy to be His heel! He, then, pours water upon the feet of Christ, who forgives the very lowest their offences, and while delivering those of low estate, yet is washing the feet of Christ.

12. And he pours water upon the feet of Christ, who purifies his conscience from the defilement of sin, for Christ walks in the breast of each. Take heed, then, not to hare your conscience polluted, and so to begin to defile the feet of Christ. Take heed lest He encounter a thorn of wickedness in you, whereby as He walks in you His heel may be wounded. For this was why the Pharisee gave no water for the feet of Christ, that he had not a soul pure from the filth of unbelief. For how could he cleanse his conscience who had not received the water of Christ? But the Church both has this water and has tears. For faith which mourns over former sins is wont to guard against fresh ones. Therefore, Simon the Pharisee, who had no water, had also, of course, no tears. For how should he have tears who had no penitence? For since he believed not in Christ he had no tears. For if he had had them he would have washed his eyes, that he might see Christ, Whom, though he sat at meat with Him, he saw not. For had he seen Him, he would not have doubted of His power.

13. The Pharisee had no hair, inasmuch as he could not recognize the Nazarite; the Church had hair, and she sought the Nazarite, Hairs are counted as amongst the superfluities of the body, but if they be anointed, they give forth a good odour, and are an ornament to the head; if they be not anointed with oil, are a burden. So, too, riches are a burden if you know not how to use them, and sprinkle them not with the odour of Christ. But if you nourish the poor, if you wash their wounds and wipe away their filth, you have indeed wiped the feet of Christ.

14. "Thou gavest Me no kiss, but she from the time she came in hath not ceased to kiss My feet." A kiss is the sign of love. Whence, then, can a Jew have a kiss, seeing he has not known peace, nor received peace from Christ when He said: "My peace I give you, My peace I leave you." The Synagogue has not a kiss, but the Church has, who waited for Him, who loved Him, who said: "Let Him kiss me with the kisses of His mouth." For by His kisses she wished gradually to quench the burning of that long desire, which had grown with looking for the coming of the Lord, and to satisfy her thirst by this gift. And so the holy prophet says: "Thou

shalt open my mouth, and it shall declare Thy praise." He, then, who praises the Lord Jesus kisses Him, he who praises Him undoubtedly believes. Finally, David himself says: "I believed, therefore have I spoken;" and before: "Let my mouth be filled with Thy praise, and let me sing of Thy glory."

15. And the same Scripture teaches you concerning the infusion of special grace, that he kisses Christ who receives the Spirit, where the holy prophet says: "I opened my mouth and drew in the Spirit." He, then, kisses Christ who confesses Him: "For with the heart man believeth unto righteousness, and with the mouth confession is made unto salvation." He, again, kisses the feet of Christ who, when reading the Gospel, recognizes the acts of the Lord Jesus, and admires them with pious affection, and so piously he kisses, as it were, the footprints of the Lord Jesus as He walks. We kiss Christ, then, with the kiss of communion: "Let him that readeth understand."

16. Whence should the Jew have this kiss? For he who believed in His coming, believed not in His Passion. For how can he believe that He has suffered Whom he believes not to have come? The Pharisee, then, had no kiss except perchance that of the traitor Judas. But neither had Judas the kiss; and so when he wished to show to, the Jews that kiss which he had promised as the sign of betrayal, the Lord said to him: "Judas, betrayest thou the Son of Man with a kiss?" that is, you, who have not the love marked by the kiss, offer a kiss. You offer a kiss who know not the mystery of the kiss. It is not the kiss of the lips which is sought for, but that of the heart and soul.

17. But you say, he kissed the Lord. Yes, he kissed Him indeed with his lips. The Jewish people has this kiss, and therefore it is said: "This people honoureth Me with their lips, but their heart is far from Me." So, then, he who has not faith and charity has not the kiss, for by a kiss the strength of love is impressed. When love is not, faith is not, and affection is not, what sweetness can there be in kisses?

18. But the Church ceases not to kiss the feet of Christ, and therefore in the Song of Songs she desires not one but many kisses, and like Holy Mary she is intent upon all His sayings, and receives all His words when the Gospel or the Prophets are read, and "keeps all His sayings in her heart." So, then, the Church alone has kisses as a bride, for a kiss is as it were a pledge of espousals and the prerogative of wedlock. Whence should the Jew have kisses, who believes not in the Bridegroom? Whence should the Jew have kisses, who knows not that the Bridegroom is come?

19. And not only has he no kisses, but neither has he oil wherewith to anoint the feet of Christ, for if he had oil he would certainly, before now, soften his own neck.

Moses says: "This people is stiff-necked," and the Lord says that the priest and the Levite passed by, and neither of them poured oil or wine into the wounds of him who had been wounded by robbers; for they had nothing to pour in, since if they had had oil they would have poured it into their own wounds. But Isaiah declares: "They cannot apply ointment nor oil nor bandage."

20. But the Church has oil wherewith she dresses the wounds of her children, lest the hardness of the wound spread deeply; she has oil which she has received secretly. With this oil Asher washed his feet as it is written: "A blessed son is Asher, and he shall be acceptable to his brothers, and shall dip his feet in oil." With this oil, then, the Church anoints the necks of her children, that they may take up the yoke of Christ; with this oil she anointed the Martyrs, that she might cleanse them from the dust of this world; with this oil she anointed the Confessors, that they might not yield to their labours, nor sink down through weariness; that they might not be overcome by the heat of this world; and she anointed them in order to refresh them with the spiritual oil.

21.The Synagogue has not this oil, inasmuch as she has not the olive, and understood not that dove which brought back the olive branch after the deluge. For that Dove descended afterwards when Christ was baptized, and abode upon Him, as John testified in the Gospel, saying: "I saw the Spirit descending from heaven like a dove, and He abode upon Him." But how could he see the Dove, who saw not Him, upon Whom the Spirit descended like a dove?

22. The Church, then, both washes the feet of Christ and wipes them with her hair. and anoints them with oil, and pours ointment upon them, because not only does she care for the wounded and cherish the weary, but also sprinkles them with the sweet odour of grace; and pours forth the same grace not only on the rich and powerful, but also on men of lowly estate. She weighs all with equal balance, gathers all in the same bosom, and cherishes them in the same lap.

23. Christ died once, and was buried once, and nevertheless He wills that ointment should daily be poured on His feet. What, then, are those feet of Christ on which we pour ointment? The feet of Christ are they of whom He Himself says: "What ye have done to one of the least of these ye have done to Me." These feet that woman in the Gospel refreshes, these feet she bedews with her tears; when sin is forgiven to the lowliest, guilt is washed away, and pardon granted. These feet he kisses, who loves even the lowest of the holy people. These feet he anoints with ointment, who imparts the kindness of his gentleness even to the weaker. In these the martyrs, in these the apostles, in these the Lord Jesus Himself declares that He is honoured.

24. You see how ready to teach the Lord is, that He may by His own example provoke you to piety, for He is ready to teach when He rebukes. So when accusing the Jews, He says: "O My people, what have I done to thee, or wherein have I troubled thee, or wherein have I wearied thee? Answer Me. Is it because I brought thee out of the land of Egypt, and delivered thee from the house of bondage?" adding: "And I sent before thy face Moses and Aaron and Miriam." Remember what Balaam conceived against thee, seeking the aid of magic art, but I suffered him not to hurt thee. Thou wast indeed weighed down an exile in foreign lands, thou wast oppressed with heavy burdens. I sent before thy face Moses and Aaron and Miriam, and he who spoiled the exile was first spoiled himself. Thou who hadst lost what was thine, didst obtain that which was another's, being freed from the enemies who were hedging thee in, and safe in the midst of the waters thou sawest the destruction of thine enemies, when the same waves which surrounded and carried thee on thy way, pouring back, drowned the enemy. Did I not, when food was lacking to thee passing through the desert, supply a rain of food, and nourishment around thee, whithersoever thou wentest? Did I not, after subduing all thine enemies, bring thee into the region of Eshcol? Did I not deliver up thee Sihon, King of the Amorites (that is, the proud one, the leader of them that provoked thee)? Did I not deliver up to thee alive the King of Ai, whom after the ancient curse thou didst condemn to be fastened to the wood and raised upon the cross? Why should I speak of the troops of the five kings which were slain in endeavouring to deny thee the land given to thee? And now what is required of thee in return for all this, but to do judgment and justice, to love mercy, and to be ready to walk with the Lord thy God?

25. And what was His expostulation by Nathan the prophet to King David himself, that pious and gentle man? I, He said, chose thee the youngest of thy brethren, I filled thee with the spirit of meekness, I anointed thee king by the hand of Samuel, in whom I and My Name dwelt. Having removed that former king, whom an evil spirit stirred up to persecute the priests of the Lord, I made thee triumph after exile. I set upon thy throne of thy seed one not more an heir than a colleague. I made even strangers subject to thee, that they who attacked might serve thee, and wilt thou deliver My servants into the power of My enemies, and wilt thou take away that which was My servant's, whereby both thyself wilt be branded with sin, and My adversaries will have whereof to rejoice.

26. Wherefore, O Emperor, that I may now address my words not only about you, but to you, since you observe how severely the Lord is wont to censure, see that the more glorious you are become, the more utterly you submit to your Maker. For it is written: "When the Lord thy God shall have brought thee into a strange land, and thou shalt eat the fruits of others, say not, My power and my righteousness hath given me this, for the Lord thy God hath given it to thee;"

for Christ in His mercy hath conferred it on thee, and therefore, in love for His body, that is, the Church, give water for His feet, kiss His feet, so that you may not only pardon those who have been taken in sin, but also by your peaceableness restore them to concord, and give them rest Pour ointment upon His feet that the whole house in which Christ sits may be filled with thy ointment, and all that sit with Him may rejoice in thy fragrance, that is, honour the lowest, so that the angels may rejoice in their forgiveness, as over one sinner that repenteth, the apostles may be glad, the prophets be filled with delight. For the eyes cannnot say to the hand: "We have no need of thee, nor the head to the feet, Ye are not necessary to me." So, since all are necessary, guard the whole body of the Lord Jesus, that He also by His heavenly condescension may preserve your kingdom.

27. When I came down from the pulpit, he said to me: "You spoke about me." I replied: "I dealt with matters intended for your benefit." Then he said: "I had indeed decided too harshly about the repairing of the synagogue by the bishop, but that has been rectified. The monks commit many crimes." Then Timasius the general began to be over-vehement against the monks, and I answered him: "With the Emperor I deal as is fitting, because I know that he has the fear of God, but with you, who speak so roughly, one must deal otherwise."

28. Then, after standing for some time, I said to the Emperor: "Let me offer for you without anxiety, set my mind at ease." As he continued sitting and nodded, but did not give an open promise, and I remained standing, he said that he would amend the edict. I went on at once to say that he must end the whole investigation, lest the Count should use the opportunity of the investigation to do any injury to the Christians. He promised that it should be so. I said to him, "I act on your promise," and repeated, "I act on your promise." "Act," he said, "on my promise." And so I went to the altar, whither I shouldnot have gone unless he had given me a distinct promise. And indeed so great was the grace attending the offering, that I felt myself that that favour granted by the Emperor was very acceptable to our God, and that the divine presence was not wanting. And so everything was done as I wished.

LETTER LI.

Addressed to the Emperor Theodosius after the massacre at Thessalonica. St. Ambrose begins by stating his reasons for not having met the Emperor on his return to Milan. He then mentions the sentiments of the bishops with regard to the slaughter at Thessalonica, and points out that repentance for that deed is necessary to obtain forgiveness and a victory over the devil, the instigator to that crime. St. Ambrose could not offer the sacrifice in the Emperor's presence, and, as truly loving the Emperor, grieves and yet hopes.

1. The memory of your old friendship is pleasant to me, and I gratefully call to mind the kindnesses which, in reply to my frequent intercessions, you have most graciously conferred on others. Whence it may be inferred that I did not from any ungrateful feeling avoid meeting you on your arrival, which I had always before earnestly desired. And I will now briefly set forth the reason for my acting as I did.

2. I saw that from me alone in your court the natural right of hearing was withdrawn, so that I was deprived also of the office of speaking; for you were frequently troubled because certain matters which had been decided in your consistory had come to my knowledge. I, therefore, am without a part in the common privilege, since the Lord Jesus says: "That nothing is hidden, which shall not be made known." I, therefore, as reverently as I could, complied with the imperial will, and took heed that neither yourself should have any reason for displeasure, when I effected that nothing should be related to me of the imperial decrees; and that I, when present, either should not hear, through fear of all others, and so incur the reputation of connivance, or should hear in such a fashion that my ears might be open, my utterance prevented, that I might not be able to utter what I had heard lest I should injure and bring in peril those who had incurred the suspicion of treachery.

3. What, then, could I do? Should I not hear? But I could not close my ears with the wax of the old fables. Should I utter what I heard? But I was bound to be on my guard in my words

467

against that which I feared in your commands, namely, lest some deed of blood should be committed. Should I keep silence? But then my conscience would be bound, my utterance taken away, which would be the most wretched condition of all. And where would be that text? If the priest speak not to him that erreth, he who errs shall die in his sin, and the priest shall be liable to the penalty because he warned not the erring.

4. Listen, august Emperor. I cannot deny that you have a zeal for the faith; I do confess that you have the fear of God. But you have a natural vehemence, which, if any one endeavours to soothe, you quickly turn to mercy; if any one stirs it up, you rouse it so much more that you can scarcely restrain it. Would that if no one soothe it, at least no one may inflame it! To yourself I willingly entrust it, you restrain yourself, and overcome your natural vehemence by the love of piety.

5. This vehemence of yours I preferred to commend privately to your own consideration, rather than possibly raise it by any action of mine in public. And so I have preferred to be somewhat wanting in duty rather than in humility, and that other, should rather think me wanting in priestly authority than that you should find me lacking in most loving reverence, that having restrained your vehemence your power of deciding on your counsel should not be weakened. I excuse myself by bodily sickness, which was in truth severe, and scarcely to be lightened but by great care. Yet I would rather have died than not wait two or three days for your arrival. But it was not possible for me to do so.

6. There was that done in the city of the Thessalonians of which no similar record exists, which I was not able to prevent happening; which, indeed, I had before said would be most atrocious when I so often petitioned against it, and that which you yourself show by revoking it too late you consider to be grave, this I could not extenuate when done. When it was first heard of, a synod had met because of the arrival of the Gallican Bishops. There was not one who did not lament it, not one who thought lightly of it; your being in fellowship with Ambrose was no excuse for your deed. Blame for what had been done would have been heaped more and more on me, had no one said that your reconciliation to our God was necessary.

7. Are you ashamed, O Emperor, to do that which the royal prophet David, the forefather of Christ, according to the flesh, did? To him it was told how the rich man who had many flocks seized and killed the poor man's one lamb, because of the arrival of his guest, and recognizing that he himself was being condemned in the tale, for that he himself had done it, he said: "I have sinned against the Lord." Bear it, then, without impatience, O Emperor, if it be said to you: "You have done that which was spoken of to King David by the prophet. For if you listen obediently to this, and say: "I have sinned against the Lord," if you repeat those words of the royal prophet: "O come let us worship and fall down before Him, and mourn before the Lord our God. Who made us," it shall be said to you also: "Since thou repentest, the Lord putteth away thy sin, and thou shalt not die,"

8. And again, David, after he had commanded the people to be numbered, was smitten in heart, and said to the Lord: "I have sinned exceedingly, because I have commanded this, and now, O Lord, take away the iniquity of Thy servant, for I have transgressed exceedingly." And the prophet Nathan was sent again to him, to offer him the choice of three things, that he should select the one he chose—famine in the land for three years, or that he should flee for three months before his enemies, or mortal pestilence in the land for three days. And David answered: "These three things are a great strait to me, but let me fall into the hand of the Lord, for very many are His mercies, and let me not fall into the hands of man." Now his fault was that he desired to know the number of the whole of the people which was with him, which knowledge he ought to have left to God alone.

9. And, we are told, when death came upon the people, on the very first day at dinner time, when David saw the angel smiting the people, he said: "I have sinned, and I, the shepherd, have done wickedly, and this flock, what hath it done? Let Thine hand be upon me, and upon my father's house." And so it repented the Lord, and He commanded the angel to spare the people,

and David to offer a sacrifice, for sacrifices were then offered for sins; sacrifices are now those of penitence. And so by that humbling of himself he became more acceptable to God, for it is no matter of wonder that a man should sin, but this is reprehensible, if he does not recognize that he has erred, and humble himself before God.

10. Holy Job, himself also powerful in this world, says: "I hid not my sin, but declared it before all the people." His son Jonathan said to the fierce King Saul himself: "Do not sin against thy servant David;" and: "Why dost thou sin against innocent blood, to slay David without a cause?" For, although he was a king, yet he would have sinned if he slew the innocent. And again, David also, when he was in possession of the kingdom, and had heard that innocent Abner had been slain by Joab, the leader of his host, said: "I am guiltless and my kingdom is guiltless henceforth and for ever of the blood of Abner, the son of Ner," and he fasted for sorrow.

11. I have written this, not in order to confound you, but that the examples of these kings may stir you up to put away this sin from your kingdom, for you will do it away by humbling your soul before God. You are a man, and it has come upon you, conquer it. Sin is not done away but by tears and penitence. Neither angel can do it, nor archangel. The Lord Himself, Who alone can say, "I am with you," if we have sinned, does not forgive any but those who repent.

12. I urge, I beg, I exhort, I warn, for it is a grief to me, that you who were an example of unusual piety, who were conspicuous for clemency, who would not suffer single offenders to be put in peril, should not mourn that so many have perished. Though you have waged battle most successfully, though in other matters, too, you are worthy of praise, yet piety was ever the crown of your actions. The devil envied that which was your most excellent possession. Conquer him whilst you still possess that wherewith you may conquer. Do not add another sin to your sin by a course of action which has injured many.

13. I, indeed, though a debtor to your kindness, for which I cannot be ungrateful, that kindness which has surpassed that of many emperors, and has been equalled by one only; I, I say, have no cause for a charge of contumacy against you, but have cause for fear; I dare not offer the sacrifice if you intend to be present. Is that which is not allowed after shedding the blood of one innocent person, allowed after shedding the blood of many? I do not think so.

14. Lastly, I am writing with my own hand that which you alone may read. As I hope that the Lord will deliver me from all troubles, I have been warned, not by man, nor through man, but plainly by Himself that this is forbidden me. For when I was anxious, in the very night in which I was preparing to set out, you appeared to me in a dream to have come into the Church, and I was not permitted to offer the sacrifice. I pass over other things, which I could have avoided, but I bore them for love of you, as I believe. May the Lord cause all things to pass peaceably. Our God gives warnings in many ways, by heavenly signs, by the precepts of the prophets; by the visions even of sinners He wills that we should understand, that we should entreat Him to take away all disturbances, to preserve peace for you emperors, that the faith and peace of the Church, whose advantage it is that emperors should be Christians and devout, may continue.

15. You certainly desire to be approved by God. "To everything there is a time," as it is written: "It is time for Thee, Lord, to work." "It is an acceptable time, O Lord." You shall then make your offering when you have received permission to sacrifice, when your offering shall be acceptable to God. Would it not delight me to enjoy the favour of the Emperor, to act according to your wish, if the case allowed it? And prayer by itself is a sacrifice, it obtains pardon, when the oblation would bring offence, for the one is a sign of humility, the other of contempt. For the Word of God Himself tells us that He prefers the performance of His commandments to the offering of sacrifice. God proclaims this, Moses declares it to the people, Paul preaches it to the Gentiles. Do that which you understand is most profitable for the time. "I prefer mercy," it is said, "rather than sacrifice." Are they not, then, rather Christians in truth who condemn their own sin, than they who think to defend it? "The just is an accuser of

himself in the beginning of his words." He who accuses himself when tie has sinned is just, not he who praises himself.

16. I wish, O Emperor, that before this I had trusted rather to myself, than to your habits. When I consider that you quickly pardon, and quickly revoke your sentence, as you have often done; you have been anticipated, and I have not shunned that which I needed not to fear. But thanks be to the Lord, Who willeth to chastise His servants, that He may not lose them. This I have in common with the prophets, and you shall have it in common with the saints.

17. Shall I not value the father of Gratian more than my very eyes? Your other holy pledges also claim pardon. I conferred beforehand a dear name on those to whom I bore a common love. I follow you with my love, my affection, and my prayers. If you believe me, be guided by me; if, I say, you believe me, acknowledge what I say; if you believe me not, pardon that which I do, in that I set God before you. May you, most august Emperor, with your holy offspring, enjoy perpetual peace with perfect happiness and prosperity.

LETTER LVII.

St. Ambrose informs the Emperor Eugenius why he was absent from Milan. He then proceeds to reprove him for his conduct with regard to heathen worship. This was, he says, the reason why he did not write sooner, and he promises that for the future he will treat him with the same freedom as the other emperors.

Ambrose, Bishop, to the most gracious Emperor Eugenius.

1. The cause of my departure was the fear of the Lord, to Whom, so far as I am able, I am accustomed to refer all my acts, and never to turn away my mind from Him, nor to make more of any man than of the grace of Christ. For I do no one an injury, if I set God before all, and, trusting in Him, I am not afraid to tell you emperors my thoughts, such as they are. And so I will not keep silence before you, O Emperor, as to things respecting which I have not kept silence before other emperors. And that I may keep the order of the matters, I will go through, one by one, the things which have to do with this matter.

2. The illustrious Symmachus, when prefect of the city, had memorialized the Emperor Valentinian the younger of august memory, requesting that he would command that what had been taken away should be restored to the temples. He performed his part in accordance with his zeal and his religion. And I also, as Bishop, was bound to recognize my part. I presented two petitions to the Emperors, in which I pointed out that a Christian man could not contribute to the cost of the sacrifices; that I indeed had not been the cause of their being abolished, but I certainly did urge that they should not be decreed; and lastly, that he himself would seem to be giving not restoring those sums to the images. For what he had not himself taken away, he could not, as it were, restore, but of his own will to grant towards the expenses of superstition. Lastly, that, if he did it, either he must not come to the Church, or, if he came, he would either not find a priest there, or he would find one withstanding him in the Church. Nor could it be alleged in excuse that he was a catechumen, seeing that catechumens are not allowed to contribute to the idols' expenses.

3. My letters were read in the consistory. Count Bauto, a man of the highest rank of military authority was present, and Rumoridus, himself also of the same dignity, addicted to the worship of the gentile nations from the first years of his boyhood. Valentinian at that time listened to my suggestion, and did nothing but what the rule of our faith required. And they yielded to his officer.

4. Afterwards I plainly addressed the most clement Emperor Theodosius, and hesitated not to speak to his face. And he, having received a similar message from the Senate, though it was not the request of the whole Senate, at length assented to my recommendation, and so I did not go near him for some days, nor did he take it ill, for he knew that I was not acting for my own advantage, but was not ashamed to say in the sight of the king that which was for the profit of himself and of my own soul.

5. Again a legation sent into Gaul from the Senate to the Emperor Valentinian of august memory could procure nothing; and then I was certainly absent, and had not written anything at that time to him.

6. But when your Clemency took up the reins of government it was afterwards discovered that favours of this kind had been granted to men, excellent indeed in matters of state but in religion heathens. And it may, perhaps, be said, august Emperor, that you did not make any restitution to temples, but presented gifts to men who had deserved well of you. But you know that we must constantly act in the cause of God, as is often done in the cause of liberty, also not only by priests, but also by those who are in your armies, or are reckoned in the number of those who dwell in the provinces. When you became Emperor envoys requested that you would make restitution to the temples, and you did not do it; others came a second time and you resisted, and afterwards you thought fit that this should be granted to those very persons who made the petition.

7. Though the imperial power be great, yet consider, O Emperor, how great God is. He sees the hearts of all, He questions the inmost conscience, He knows all things before they happen, He knows the inmost things of your breast. You do not suffer yourselves to be deceived, and do you desire to conceal anything from God? Has not this come into your mind? For although they acted with such perseverance, was it not your duty, O Emperor, to resist with still greater perseverance because of the reverence due to the most high and true and living God, and to refuse what was an offence against His holy law?

8. Who grudges your having given what you would to others? We are not scrutinizers of your liberality, nor envious of the advantages of others, but are interpreters of the faith. How will you offer your gifts to Christ? Not many but will put their own estimate on what you have done, all will do so on your intentions. Whatever they do will be ascribed to you; whatever they do not do, to themselves. Although you are Emperor, you ought to be all the more subject to God. How shall the ministers of Christ dispense your gifts?

9. There was a question of this sort in former times, and yet persecution itself yielded to the faith of our fathers, and heathendom gave way. For when in the city of Tyre the quinquennial game was being kept, and the intensely wicked King of Antioch had come to witness it, Jason appointed officers of sacred rites, who were Antiochians, to carry three hundred didrachms of silver from Jerusalem, and give them to the sacrifice of Hercules. But the fathers did not give the money to the heathen, but having sent faithful men declared that that money should not be spent on sacrifices to the gods, because it was not fitting, but on other expenses, And it was decreed that because he had said that the money was sent for the sacrifice of Hercules, it ought to be taken for that for which it was sent; but, because they, who had brought it, because of their zeal and religion, pleaded that it should not be used for the sacrifice, but for other expenses, the money was given for the building of ships. Being compelled they sent it, but it was not used for sacrifice, but for other expenses of the state.

10. Now they who had brought the money might, no doubt, have kept silence, but would have done violence to their faith, because they knew whither the money was being carried, and therefore they sent men who feared God to contrive that what was sent should be assigned, not to the temple, but to the cost of ships. For they entrusted the money to those who should plead the cause of the sacred Law, and He Who absolves the conscience was made judge of the matter. If they when in the power of another were so careful, there can be no doubt what you, O Emperor, ought to have done. You, at any rate, whom no one compelled, whom no one had in his power, ought to have sought counsel from the priest.

11. And I certainly when I then resisted, although I was alone in resistance, was not alone in what I wished, and was not alone in what I advised. Since, then, I am bound by my own words both before God and before all men, I felt that nothing else was allowable or needful for me but to act for myself, because I could not well trust you. I kept back and concealed my grief for a long time; I thought it not right to intimate anything to anybody, now I may no longer

dissemble, nor is it open to me to keep silence. For this reason also at the commencement of your reign I did not reply when you wrote to me, because I foresaw that this would happen. Then at last, when you required a letter, because I had not written a reply, I said: This is the reason that I think this will be extorted from him.

12. But when a reason for exercising my office arose, I both wrote and petitioned for those who were in anxiety about themselves, that I might show that in the canse of God I felt a righteous fear, and that I did not value flattery above my own soul; but in those matters in which it is fitting that petitions should be addressed to you. I also pay the deference due to authority, as it is written: "Honour to whom honour is due, tribute to whom tribute." For since I deferred from the bottom of my heart to a private person, how could I not defer to the Emperor? But do you who desire that deference be paid to you suffer us to pay deference to Him Whom you are desirous to be proved the Author of your power.

LETTER LXI.

St. Ambrose explains his absence from Milan on the arrival of the Emperor Theodosius after his victory over Eugenius, and after expressing his thankfulness for that success he promises obedience to the Emperor's will, and while commending his piety urges him to be merciful to the conquered.

Ambrose, to the Emperor Theodosius.

1. You thought, most blessed Emperor, so far as I gathered from your letter, that I kept away from the city of Milan, because I believed that your cause was forsaken by God. But I was not so wanting in foresight, nor so unmindful in my absence of your virtue and merits, as not to anticipate that the aid of Heaven would be with your piety, with which you would rescue the Roman Empire from the cruelty of a barbarian robber, and the dominion of an unworthy usurper.

2. I therefore made haste to return thither, as soon as I knew that he, whom I thought it right to avoid, was now gone, for I had not deserted the Church of Milan, entrusted to me by the judgment of God, but avoided the presence of him who had involved himself in sacrilege. I returned, therefore, about the Calends of August, and have resided here since that day. Here, too, O Augustus, your letter found me.

3. Thanks be to our Lord God, Who responded to your faith and piety, and has restored the form of ancient sanctity, suffering us to see in our time that which we wonder at in reading the Scriptures, namely, such a presence of the divine assistance in battle, that no mountain heights delayed the course of your approach, no hostile arms were any hindrance.

4. For these mercies you think that I ought to render thanks to the Lord our God, and being conscious of your merits, I will do so willingly, Certainly that offering will be acceptable to God which is offered in your name, and what a mark of faith and devotion is this l Other emperors, immediately upon a victory, order the erection of triumphal arches, or other monuments of their triumphs; your Clemency prepares an offering for God, and desires that oblation and thanksgiving should be presented by the priests to the Lord.

5. Though I be unworthy and unequal to such an office and the offering of such acknowledgments, yet will I describe what I have done. I took the letter of your Piety with me to the altar. I laid it upon the altar. I held it in my hand whilst I offered the Sacrifice; so that your faith might speak by my voice, and the Emperor's letter discharge the function of the priestly oblation.

6. In truth, the Lord is propitious to the Roman Empire, since He has chosen such a prince and father of princes, whose virtue and power, established on such a triumphant height of dominion, rests on such humility, that in valour he has surpassed emperors and priests in humility. What can I wish? What can I desire? You have everything, and therefore I will endeavour to gain the sum of my desires. You, O Emperor, are pitiful, and of the greatest clemency.

7. And for yourself, I desire again and again an increase of piety, than which God has given nothing more excellent, that by your clemency the Church of God, as it delights in the peace and tranquillity of the innocent, so, too, may rejoice in the pardon of the guilty. Pardon especially those who have not offended before. May the Lord preserve your Clemency. Amen.

LETTER LXII.

St. Ambrose excuses himself for having omitted an opportunity of writing to the Emperor, but is now sending a letter by the hands of a deacon, requesting forgiveness for some of Eugenius' followers who had sought the protection of the Church, especially in consideration of the miraculous aid which had been vouchsafed to the Emperor.

Ambrose, to the Emperor Theodosius.

1. Although I lately wrote to your Clemency even a second time, it did not seem to me that I had responded sufficiently to the duty of intercourse by answering as it were in turn, for I have been so bound by frequent benefits from your Clemency, that I cannot repay what I owe by any services, most blessed and august Emperor.

2. And so just as the first opportunity was not to be lost by me, when, through your chamberlain, I was able to thank your Clemency and to pay the duty of an address, especially lest my not having written before should seem to have been owing to sloth rather than necessity, so, too, I had to seek some manner of rendering to your Piety my dutiful salutations.

3. And rightly do I send my son, the deacon Felix, to bear my letter, and, at the same time, to present to you my duty, in my place, and also a memorial on behalf of those who have fled to the Church, the Mother of your Piety, seeking mercy. I have been unable to endure their tears without anticipating by my entreaty the coming of your Clemency.

4. It is a great boon that I ask, but I ask it from him to whom the Lord has granted great and unheard-of things, from him whose clemency I know, and whose piety I have as a pledge. For your victory is considered to have been granted to you after the ancient manner, and with the old miracles, a victory such as was granted to holy Moses, and holy Joshua, son of Nave, and Samuel, and David, not by human calculations, but by the outpouring of heavenly grace. Now we expect an equal amount of gentleness with that by virtue of which so great a victory has been gained.

EPISTLE LXIII.

Limenius, Bishop of Vercellae, having died, the see remained long vacant owing to domestic factions. St. Ambrose, therefore, as Exarch, writes to the Christians at Vercellae, and commences by reference to the speedy and unanimous election of Eusebius, a former Bishop, and reminds them of the presence of Christ as a reason for concord, He refers next to two apostate monks, Sarmatio and Barbatianus, and inveighs against sensuality, which degrades men below the beasts. Thence he passes to the virtues required in a bishop, referring again to Eusebius, and to Dionysius, Bishop of Milan, comparing the clerical and monastic lives, and ends with exhortations to Christian virtue. The letter seems to have been written a.d. 396.

Ambrose, a servant of Christ, called to be a Bishop, to the Church of Vercellae, and to those who call on the Name of our Lord Jesus Christ, Grace be fulfilled unto you in the Holy Spirit from God the Father and His only-begotten Son.

1. I am spent with grief that the Church of God which is among you is still without a bishop, and now alone of all the regions of Liguria and Aemilia, and of the Venetiae all the and other neighbouring parts of Italy needs that care which other churches were wont to ask for themselves from it; and what is a greater source of shame to myself, the tension amongst you which causes the obstacle is laid to my charge. Now since there are dissensions among you, how can we decree anything, or you elect, or anyone agree to undertake this office amongst those who are at variance which he could hardly sustain amongst those who are at unity.

2. Is this the training of a confessor, are these the offspring of those righteous fathers who, as soon as they saw, approved of holy Eusebius, whom they had never known before, preferring

him to their fellow-citizens, and he was no sooner amongst them than he was approved, and much more when they had observed him. Justly did he turn out so great a man, whom the whole Church elected, justly was it believed that he whom all had demanded was elected by the judgment of God. It is fitting then that you follow the example of your parents, especially since you who have been instructed by a holy confessor ought to be so much better than your fathers, as a better teacher has taught and instructed you, and to manifest a sign of your moderation and concord by agreeing in your request for a Bishop.

3. For if according to the Lord's saying, that which two shall have agreed upon on earth concerning anything which they shall ask, shall be done for them, as He says, by My Father, Who is in heaven, for: "Where two or three are gathered together in My Name, there am I in the midst of them, how much less, where the full congregation is gathered in the Name of the Lord. Where the demand of all is unanimous, ought we to doubt that the Lord Jesus is there as the Author of that desire, and the Hearer of the petition, the Presider over the ordination, and the Giver of the grace?

4. Make yourselves then to appear worthy that Christ should be in your midst. For where peace is, there is Christ, for Christ is Peace; and where righteousness is, there is Christ, for Christ is Righteousness. Let Him be in the midst of you, that you may see Him, lest it be said to you also: "There standeth One in the midst of you, Whom ye see not." The Jews saw not Him in Whom they believed not; we look upon Him by devotion, and behold Him by faith.

5. Let Him therefore stand in your midst, that the heavens, which declare the glory of God, may be opened to you, that you may do His will, and work His works. He who sees Jesus, to him are the heavens opened as they were opened to Stephen, when he said: "Behold I see the heavens opened and Jesus standing at the right hand of God." Jesus was standing as his advocate, He was standing as though anxious, that He might help His athlete Stephen in his conflict, He was standing as though ready to crown His martyr.

6. Let Him then be standing for you, that you may not be afraid of Him sitting; for when sitting He judges, as Daniel says: "The thrones were placed, and the books were opened, and the Ancient of days did sit." But in the eighty-first[second] Psalm it is written: "God stood in the congregation of gods, and decideth among the gods." So then when He sits He judges, when He stands He decides, and He judges concerning the imperfect, but decides among the gods. Let Him stand for you as a defender, as a good shepherd, lest the fierce wolves assault you.

7. And not in vain is my warning turned to this point; for I hear that Sarmatio and Barbatianus are come to you, foolish talkers, who say that there is no merit in abstinence no grace in a frugal life, none in virginity, that all are valued at one price, that they are mad who chasten their flesh with fastings, that they may bring it into subjection to the spirit. But if he had thought it madness, Paul the Apostle would never himself have acted thus, nor written to instruct others. For he glories in it, saying: "But I chasten my body, and bring it into bondage, lest, after preaching to others, I myself should be found reprobate." So they who do not chasten their body, and desire to preach to others, are themselves esteemed reprobates.

8. For is there anything so reprobate as that which excites to luxury, to corruption, to wantonness, as the incentive to lust, the enticer to pleasure, the fuel of incontinence, the firebrand of desire?What new school has sent out these Epicureans?Not a school of philosophers, as they themselves say, but of unlearned men who preach pleasure, persuade to luxury, esteem chastity to be of no use. They were with us, but they were not of us, for we are not ashamed to say what the Evangelist John said. But when settled here they used to fast at first, they were enclosed within the monastery, there was no place for luxury, the opportunity of mocking and disputing was cut off.

9. This these dainty men could not endure. They went abroad, then when they desired to return they were not received; for I had heard many thinks which necessitated my being cautious; I admonished them, but effected nothing. And so boiling over they began to disseminate such things as made them the miserable enticers to all vices. They utterly lost the

benefit of having fasted; they lost the fruits of their temporary continence. And so now they with Satanic eagerness envy the good works of others, the fruit of which themselves have failed to keep.

10. What virgin can hear that there is no reward for her chastity and not groan?Far be it from her to believe this easily, and still more to lay aside her zeal, or change the intention of her mind. What widow, when she learnt that there was no profit in her widowhood, would choose to preserve her marriage faith and live in sorrow, rather than give herself up to a happier condition?Who, bound by the marriage-bond, if she hear that there is no honour in chastity, might not be tempted by careless levity of body or mind?And for this reason the Church in the holy lessons, and in the addresses of her priests, proclaims the praise of chastity and the glory of virginity.

11. In vain, then, does the Apostle say: "I wrote to you, in an Epistle, not to mingle with fornicators;" and lest perchance they should say, We are not speaking of all the fornicators of the world, but we say that he who has been baptized in Christ ought not now to be esteemed a fornicator, but his life, whatever it is, is accepted of God, the Apostle has added "Not at all[meaning] with the fornicators of this world," and farther on, "If any that is named a brother be a fornicator, or covetous, or an idolator, or a reviler, or a drunkard, or an extortioner, with such an one not even to eat. For what have I to do with judging them that are without?" And to the Ephesians: "But fornication, and all uncleanness, and covetousness let it not even be named among you, as becometh saints." And immediately he adds: "For this ye know, that no immodest person, nor unclean, nor covetous, which is an idolator, hath any inheritance in the kingdom of Christ and of God." It is clear that this is said of the baptized, for they receive the inheritance, who are baptized into the death of Christ and are buried together with Him, that they may rise again with Him. Therefore they are heirs of God, and joint heirs with Christ: heirs of God, because the grace of Christ is conveyed to them; joint-heirs with Christ, because they are renewed into His life; heirs also of Christ; because to them is given by His death as it were the inheritance of the testator.

12. These then ought to take heed to themselves who have that which they may lose, rather than they who have it not. These ought to act with greater care, these ought to guard against the allurements of vice, or incentives to error, which arise chiefly from food and drink. For "the people sat down to eat and drink, and rose up to play."

13. Epicurus himself also, whom these persons think they should follow rather than the apostles, the advocate of pleasure, although he denies that pleasure brings in evil, does not deny that certain things result from it from which evils are generated; and asserts in fine that the life of the luxurious which is filled with pleasures does not seem to be reprehensible, unless it be disturbed by the fear either of pain or of death. But how far he is from the truth is perceived even from this, that he asserts that pleasure was originally created in man by God its author, as Philomarus his follower argues in his Epitomae, asserting that the Stoics are the authors of this opinion.

14. But Holy Scripture refutes this, for it teaches us that pleasure was suggested to Adam and Eve by the craft and enticements of the serpent. Since, indeed, the serpent itself is pleasure, and therefore the passions of pleasure are various and slippery, and as it were infected with the poison of corruptions, it is certain then that Adam, being deceived by the desire of pleasure, fell away from the commandment of God and from the enjoyment of grace. How then can pleasure recall us to paradise, seeing that it alone deprived us of it?

15. Wherefore also the Lord Jesus, wishing to make us more strong against the temptations of the devil, fasted when about to contend with him, that we might know that we can in no other way overcome the enticements of evil. Further, the devil himself hurled the first dart of his temptations from the quiver of pleasure, saying: "If Thou be the Son of God, command that these stones become bread." After which the Lord said: "Man doth not live by bread alone, but by every word of God;" and would not do it, although He could, in order to teach us by a

salutary precept to attend rather to the pursuit of reading than to pleasure. And since they say that we ought not to fast, let them prove for what cause Christ fasted, unless it were that His fast might be an example to us. Lastly, in His later words He taught us that evil cannot be easily overcome except by our fasting, saying: "This kind of devils is not cast out but by prayer and fasting."

16. And what is the intention of the Scripture which teaches us that Peter fasted, and that the revelation concerning the baptism of Gentiles was made to him when fasting and praying, except to show that the Saints themselves advance when they fast. Finally, Moses received the Law when he was fasting; and so Peter when fasting was taught the grace of the New Testament. Daniel too by virtue of his fast stopped the mouths of the lions and saw the events of future times. And what safety can there be for us unless we wash away our sins by fasting, since ScriptUre says that fasting and alms do away sin?

17. Who then are these new teachers who reject the merit of fasting? Is it not the voice of heathen who say, "Let us eat and drink?" whom the Apostle well ridicules, when he says: "If after the manner of men I have fought with beasts at Ephesus, what advantageth it me if the dead rise not?Let us eat and drink, for to-morrow we die." That is to say, What profited me my contention even unto death, except that I might redeem my body?And it is redeemed in vain if there is no hope of the resurrection. And, consequently, if all hope of the resurrection is lost, let us eat and drink, let us not lose the enjoyment of things present, who have none of things to come. It is then for them to indulge in meats and drinks who hope for nothing after death.

18. Rightly then does the Apostle, arguing against these men, warn us that we be not shaken by such opinions, saying: "Be not deceived, evil communications corrupt good manners. Be ye righteously sober and sin not, for some have no knowledge of God." Sobriety, then, is good, for drunkenness is sin.

19. But as to that Epicurus himself, the defender of pleasure, of whom, therefore, we have made frequent mention in order to prove that these men are either disciples of the heathen and followers of the Epicurean sect or himself, whom the very philosophers exclude from their company as the patron of luxury, what if we prove him to be more tolerable than these men? He declares, as Demarchus asserts, that neither drinking, nor banquets, nor offspring, nor embraces of women, nor abundance of fish, and other such like things which are prepared for the service of a sumptuous banquet, make life sweet, but sober discussion. Lastly, he added that those who do not use the banquets of society in excess, use them with moderation. He who willingly makes use of the juices of plants alone together with bread and water, despises feasts on delicacies, for many inconveniences arise from them. In another place they also say: It is not excessive banquets, nor drinking which give rise to the enjoyment of pleasure, but a life of temperance.

20. Since, then, philosophy has disowned those men, is the Church not to exclude them?Seeing, too, that they, because they have a bad cause, frequently fall foul of themselves by their own assertions. For, although their chief opinion is that there is no enjoyment of pleasure except such as is derived from eating and drinking, yet understanding that they cannot, without the greatest shame, cling to so disgraceful a definition, and that they are forsaken by all, they have tried to colour it with a sort of stain of specious arguments; so that one of them has said: Whilst we are aiming at pleasure by means of banquets and songs, we have lost that which is infused into us by the reception of the Word, whereby alone we can be saved.

21. Do not they by these various arguments show themselves to us as differing and disagreeing one with the other? And Scripture too condemns them, not passing over those whom the Apostle refuted, as Luke, who wrote the book as a history, tells us in the Acts of the Apostles, "And certain also of the Epicurean and Stoic philosophers disputed with him. And some said, What does this babbler mean?And others said, He seemeth to be a setter forth of new gods."

22. Yet from this hand too the Apostle did not go forth without success, since even Dionysius the Areopagite together with his wife Damaris and many others believed. And so that

company of most learned and eloquent men showed themselves overcome in a simple discussion by the example of those who believed. What then do those men mean, who endeavour to prevent those whom the Apostle has gained, and whom Christ has redeemed with His own blood? asserting that the baptized ought not to give themselves to the discipline of the virtues, that revellings injure them not, nor abundance of pleasures; that they are foolish who go without them, that virgins ought to marry, bear children, and likewise widows to repeat that converse with man which they have once experienced with ill results; and that even if they can contain, they are in error who will not again enter the marriage bond.

23. What then? Would you have us put off the man in order to put on the beast, and stripping ourselves of Christ, clothe ourselves or be superclothed with the garments of the devil? But since the very teachers of the heathen did not think that honour and pleasure could be joined together, because they would seem thus to class beasts with men, shall we as it were infuse the habits of beasts into the human breast, and inscribe on the reasonable mind the unreasoning ways of wild beasts?

24. And yet there are many kinds of animals, which, when they have lost their fellow, will not mate again, and spend their time as it were in solitary life; many too live on simple herbs, and will not quench their thirst except at a pure stream; one can also often see dogs refrain from food forbidden them, so that they close their famishing mouths if restraint is bidden them. Must men then be warned against that wherein brutes have learned not to transgress?

26. But what is more admirable than abstinence, which makes even the years of youth to ripen, so that there is an old age of character? For as by excess of food and by drunkenness even mature age is excited, so the wildness of youth is lessened by scanty feasts and by the running stream. An external fire is extinguished by pouring on water, it is then no wonder if the inward heat of the body is cooled by draughts from the stream, for the flame is fed or fails according to the fuel. As hay, straw, wood, oil, and such like things are the nourishment which feeds fire, if you take them away, or do not supply them, the fire is extinguished. In like manner then the heat of the body is supported or lessened by food, it is excited by food and lessened by food. Luxury then is the mother of lust.

27. And is not temperance agreeable to nature, and to that divine law, which in the very beginning of all created things gave the springs for drink and the fruits of the trees for food? After the Flood the just man found wine a source of temptation to him. Let us then use the natural drink of temperance, and would that we all were able to do so. But because all are not strong the Apostle said: "Use a little wine because of thy frequent infirmities." We must drink it then not for the sake of pleasure, but because of infirmity, and therefore sparingly as a remedy, not in excess as a gratification.

28. Lastly, Elijah, whom the Lord was training to the perfection of virtue, found at his head a cake and a cruse of water; and then fasted in the strength of that food forty days and forty nights. Our fathers, when they passed across the sea on foot, drank water not wine. Daniel and the Hebrew children, fed with their peculiar food, and with water to drink, overcame, the former the fury of the lions; the latter saw the burning fire play around their limbs with harmless touch.

26. And why should I speak of men? Judith, in no way moved by the luxurious banquet of Holophernes, carried off the triumph of which men's arms despaired, solely in right of her temperance; delivered her country from occupation and slew the leader of the expedition with her own hands. A clear proof both that his luxury had enervated that warrior, terrible to the nations, and that temperance made this woman stronger than men. In this case it was not in her sex that nature was surpassed, but she overcame by her diet. Esther by her fasts moved a proud king. Anna, who for eighty-four years in her widowhood had served God with fasts and prayers day and night in the temple, recognized Christ, Whom John, the master of abstinence, and as it were a new angel on earth, announced.

30. O foolish Elisha, for feeding the prophets with wild and bitter gourds! O Ezra forgetful of Scripture, though he did restore the Scriptures from memory! foolish Paul, who glories in fastings, if fastings profit nothing.

31. But how should that not be profitable by which our sins are purged? And if you offer this with humility and with mercy, your bones, as Isaiah said, shall be fat, and you shall be like a well-watered garden. So, then, your soul shall grow fat and its virtues also by the spiritual richness of fasting, and your fruits shall be multiplied by the fertility of your mind, so that there may be in you the inebriation of soberness, like that cup of which the Prophet says: "Thy cup which inebriates, how excellent it is!"

32. But not only is that temperance worthy of praise which moderates food, but also that which moderates lust. Since it is written: "Go not after thy lusts, and deny thy appetite. If thou givest her desires to thy soul, thou wilt be a joy to thine enemies;" and farther on; "Wine and women make even wise men to fall away;" So that Paul teaches temperance even in marriage itself; for he who is incontinent in marriage is a kind of adulterer, and violates the law of the Apostle.

33. And why should I tell how great is the grace of virginity, which was found worthy to be chosen by Christ, that it might be even the bodily temple of God, in which as we read the fulness of the Godhead dwelt bodily. A Virgin conceived the Salvation of the world, a Virgin brought forth the life of all. Virginity then ought not to be left to itself, seeing that it benefited all in Christ. A Virgin bore Him Whom this world cannot contain or support. And when He was born from His mother's womb, He yet preserved the fence of her chastity and the inviolate seal of her virginity. And so Christ found in the Virgin that which He willed to make His own, that which the Lord of all might take to Himself. Further, our flesh was cast out of Paradise by a man and woman and was joined to God through a Virgin.

34. What shall I say concerning the other Mary, the sister of Moses, who as leader of the women passed on foot the straits of the sea? By the same gift Thecla also was reverenced by the lions, so that the unfed beasts stretched at the feet of their prey prolonged a holy fast, and harmed the virgin neither with wanton look nor claw, since virginity is injured even by a look.

35. Again, with what reverence for virginity has the holy Apostle spoken: "Concerning virgins I have no commandment of the Lord, but I give my counsel, as having obtained mercy of the Lord." He has received no commandment, but a counsel, for that which beyond the law is not commanded, but is rather advised by way of counsel. Authority is not assumed but grace is shown, and this is not shown by anyone, but by him who obtained mercy from the Lord. Are then the counsels of these men better than those of the apostles? The Apostle says, "I give my counsel," but they think it right to dissuade any from cultivating virginity.

36. And we ought to recognize what commendation of it the prophet, or rather Christ in the prophet, has uttered in a short verse; "A garden enclosed," says He, "is My sister, My spouse, a garden enclosed, a sealed fountain." Christ says this to the Church, which he desires to be a virgin, without spot, without a wrinkle. A fertile garden is virginity, which can bear many fruits of good odour. A garden enclosed, because it is everywhere shut in by the wall of chastity. A sealed fountain, because virginity is the source and origin of modesty, having to keep inviolate the seal of purity, in which source the image of God is reflected, since the purity of simplicity agrees also with chastity of the body.

37. And no one can doubt that the Church is a virgin, who also in the Epistle to the Corinthians is espoused and presented as a chaste virgin to Christ. So in the first Epistle he gives his counsel, and esteems the gift of virginity as good, since it is not disturbed by any troubles of the present time, nor polluted by any of its defilements, nor shaken by any storms; in the later Epistle he brings a spouse to Christ, because he is able to certify the virginity of the Church in the purity of that people.

38. Answer me now, O Paul, in what way thou givest counsel for the present distress. "Because he that is without a wife is careful," he says, "for the things of the Lord, how he may

please God." And he adds, "The unmarried woman and the virgin think of the things of the Lord, that they may be holy in body and spirit." She has then her wall against the tempests of this world, and so fortified by the defence of divine protection she is disturbed by none of the blasts of this world. Good then is counsel, because there is advantage in counsel, but there is a bond in a commandment. Counsel attracts the willing, commandment binds the unwilling. If then anyone has followed counsel, and not repented, she has gained an advantage; but if she has repented, she has no ground for blaming the Apostle, for she ought herself to have judged of her own weakness; and so she is responsible for her own will, inasmuch as she bound herself by a bond and knot beyond her power to bear.

39. And so like a good physician, desiring to preserve the stability of virtue in the strong, and to give health to the weak, he gives counsel to the one, and points out the remedy to the others: "He that is weak eateth herbs," let him take a wife; he that has more power let him seek the stronger meat of virtue. And rightly he added: "For he who being steadfast hath settled in his own heart, having no necessity, but hath power over his own will, and hath determined this in his own heart, to keep his own virgin, doeth well. So then both he who giveth his own virgin in marriage, doeth well; and he that giveth her not in marriage, doeth better. A woman is bound by the law, for so long a time as her husband liveth. But if her husband have fallen asleep, she is freed, let her marry whom she will, only in the Lord. But she will be more happy if she abide as she is, after my counsel, for I think that I also have the Spirit of the Lord." This is to have the counsel of God, to search diligently into all things, and to advise things that are best, and to point out those that are safest.

40. A careful guide points out many paths, that each may walk along the one which he prefers and considers suitable to himself, so long as he comes upon one by which he can reach the camp. The path of virginity is good, but being high and steep requires the stronger wayfarers. Good also is that of widowhood, not so difficult as the former, but being rocky and rough, it requires more cautious travellers. Good too is that of marriage; being smooth and even it reaches the camp of the saints by a longer circuit. This way is taken by most. There are then the rewards of virginity, there are the merits of widowhood, there is also a place for conjugal modesty. There are steps and advances in each and every virtue.

41. Stand therefore firm in your hearts, that no one overthrow you, that no one be able to make you fall. The Apostle has taught us what it is "to stand," that is what was said to Moses: "The place whereon thou standest is holy ground;" for no one stands unless he stand by faith, unless he stands fixed in the determination of his own heart. In another place also we read: "But do thou stand here with Me." Each sentence was spoken by the Lord to Moses, both "Where thou standest is holy ground," and "Stand here with Me," that is, thou standest with Me, if thou stand firm in the Church. For the very place is holy, the very ground is fruitful with sanctity and fertile with harvests of virtues.

42. Stand then in the Church, stand where I appeared to thee, where I am with thee. Where the Church is, there is the most solid resting place for thy mind, there the support of thy soul, where I appeared to thee in the bush. Thou art the bush, I am the fire; the fire in the bush, I in the flesh. Therefore am I the fire, that I may give light to thee, that I may consume thy thorns, that is, thy sins. and show thee My grace.

43. Standing firm then in your hearts, drive away from the Church the wolves which seek to carry off prey. Let there be no sloth in you, let not your mouth be evil nor your tongue bitter. Do not sit in the council of vanity; for it is written, "I have not sat in the council of vanity." Do not listen to those who speak against their neighbours, lest whilst you listen to others, you be stirred up yourselves to speak against your neighbours, and it be said to each of you "Thou satest and spakest against thy brother."

44. Men sit when speaking against others, they stand when they praise the Lord, to whom it is said: "Behold now, praise the Lord, all ye servants of the Lord, ye that stand in the house of the Lord." He who sits, to speak of the bodily habit, is as it were loosened by ease, and relaxes

the energy of his mind. But the careful watchman, the active searcher, the watchful guardian, who keeps the outposts of the camp, stands. The zealous warrior, too, who desires to anticipate the designs of the enemy, stands in array before he is expected.

45. "Let him that standeth take heed lest he fall." He who stands does not give way to detraction, for it is the tales of those at ease in which detraction is spread abroad, and malignity betrayed. So that the prophet says: "I have hated the congregation of the malignant, and will not sit with the ungodly." And in the thirty-sixth Psalm, which he has filled with moral precepts, he has put at the very beginning: "Be not malignant amongst the malignant, neither be envious of those who do iniquity." Malignancy is more harmful than malice, because malignancy has neither pure simplicity nor open malice, but a hidden ill-will. And it is more difficult to guard against what is hidden than against what is known. For which reason too our Saviour warns us to beware of malignant spirits, because they would catch us by the appearance of sweet pleasures and a show of other things, when they hold forth honour to entice us to ambition, riches to avarice, power to pride.

46. And so both in every action, and especially in the demand for a bishop, by whom [as a pattern] the life of all is formed; malignity ought to be absent; so that the man who is to be elected out of all, and to heal all, may be preferred to all by a calm and peaceful decision. For "the meek man is the physician of the heart." And the Lord in the Gospel called Himself this, when He said: "They that be whole need not a physician, but they that are sick."

47. He is the good Physician, Who has taken upon Him our infirmities, has healed our sicknesses, and yet He, as it is written, honoured not Himself to be made a High Priest, but He Who spake to Him. The Father said: "Thou art My Son, this day have I begotten Thee." As He said in another place: "Thou art a Priest for ever after the order of Melchisedech." Who, since He was the type of all future priests, took our flesh upon Him, that "in the days of His flesh He might offer prayers and supplications with a loud voice and tears; and by those things which He suffered, though He was the Son of God, might seem to learn obedience, which He taught us, that He might be made to us the Author of Salvation?" And at last when His sufferings were completed, as though completed and made perfect Himself, He gave health to all, He bore the sin of all.

48. And so He Himself also chose Aaron as priest, that not the will of man but the grace of God should have the chief part in the election of the priest; not the voluntary offering of himself, nor the taking it upon himself, but the vocation from heaven, that he should offer gifts for sins who could be touched for those who sinned, for He Himself, it is said, bears our weakness. No one ought to take this honour upon himself but they are called of God, as was Aaron, and so Christ did not demand but received the priesthood.

49. Lastly, when the succession derived through family descent from Aaron, contained rather heirs of the family than sharers in his righteousness, there came, after the likeness of that Melchisedech, of whom we read in the Old Testament, the true Melchisedech, the true King of peace, the true King of righteousness, for this is the interpretation of the Name, "without father, without mother, without genealogy, having neither beginning of days nor end of life," which also refers to the Son of God, Who in His Divine Generation had no mother, was in His Birth of the Virgin Mary without a father; begotten before the ages of the Father alone, born in this age of the Virgin alone, and certainly could have no beginning of days seeing He "was in the beginning." And how could He have any end of life, Who is the Author of life to all? He is "the Beginning and the Ending." But this also is referred to Him as an example, that a priest ought to be without father and without mother, since in him it is not nobility of family, but holiness of character and pro-eminence in virtue which is elected.

50. Let there be in him faith and ripeness of character, not one without the other, but let both meet together in one with good works and deeds. For which reason the Apostle Paul wishes that we should be imitators of them, who, as he says, "by faith and patience" possess the promises made to Abraham, who by patience was found worthy to receive and to possess the

grace of the blessing promised to him. David the prophet warns us that we should be imitators of holy Aaron, and has set him amongst the Saints of God to be imitated by us, saying: "Moses and Aaron among his priests, and Samuel among those that call upon His Name."

51. A man clearly worthy to be proposed that all should follow him was he, for when a terrible death on account of the rebels was spreading over the people, he offered himself between the dead and the living, that he might arrest death, and that no more should perish. A man truly of priestly mind and soul, who as a good shepherd with pious affection offered himself for the Lord's flock. And so he broke the sting of death, restrained its violence, refused it further course. Affection aided his deserts, for he offered himself for those who were resisting him.

52. Let those then who dissent learn to fear to rouse up the Lord, and to appease His priests. What! did not the earthquake swallow up Dathan, Abiron, and Korah because of their dissension? For when Korah, Dathan, and Abiron had stirred up two hundred and fifty men against Moses and Aaron to separate themselves from them, they rose up against them and said: "Let it suffice you that all the congregation are holy, every one, and the Lord is amongst them."

53. Whereupon the Lord was angry and spoke to the whole congregation. The Lord considered and knew those that were His, and drew His saints to. Himself; and those whom He chose not, He did not draw to Himself. And the Lord commanded that Korah and all those who had risen up with him against Moses and Aaron the priests of the Lord should take to themselves censers, and put on incense, that he who was chosen of the Lord might be established as holy among the Levites of the Lord,54. And Moses said to Korah: "Hear me, ye sons of Levi: Is this a small thing unto you, that God hath separated you from the congregation of Israel, and brought you near to Himself, to minister the service of the Tabernacle of the Lord." And farther on, "Seek ye the priesthood also, so that thou and all thy congregation are gathered against the Lord. And what is Aaron that ye murmur about him?"

55. Considering, then, what causes of offence existed, that unworthy persons desired to discharge the offices of the priesthood, and therefore were causing dissensions; and were murmuring in censure of the judgment of God in the choice of His priest, the whole people were seized with a great fear, and dread of punishment came upon them all. But when all implore that all perish not for the insolence of few, those guilty of the wickedness are marked out; and two hundred and fifty men with their leaders are separated from the whole body of the people; and then the earth with a groan cleaves asunder in the midst of the people, a deep gulf opens, the offenders are swallowed up, and are so removed from all the elements of this world, as neither to pollute the air by breathing it, nor the heavens by beholding them, nor the sea by their touch, nor the earth by their sepulchres.

56. The punishment ceased, but the wickedness ceased not; for from this very thing a murmuring rose among them that the people had perished through the priests. In His wrath at this, the Lord would have destroyed them all, had He not been moved first by the prayers of Moses and Aaron, and afterwards also at the intervention of His priest Aaron (the humiliation of their forgiveness being thereby greater), He willed to give their lives to those whose privilege they had repudiated.

57. Miriam the prophetess herself, who with her brothers had crossed the straits of the sea on foot, because, being still ignorant of the mystery of the Ethiopian woman, she had murmured against her brother Moses, broke out with leprous spots, so that she would scarcely have been freed from so great a plague, unless Moses had prayed for her. Although this murmuring refers to the type of the Synagogue, which is ignorant of the mystery of that Ethiopian woman, that is the Church gathered out of the nations, and murmurs with daily reproaches, and envies that people through whose faith itself also shall be delivered from the leprosy of its unbelief, according to what we read that: "blindness in part has happened unto Israel, until the fulness of the Gentiles be come in, and so all Israel shall be saved.

58. And that we may observe that divine grace rather than human works in priests, of the many rods which Moses had received according to the Tribes, and had laid up, that of Aaron alone blossomed. And so the people saw that the gift of the Divine vocation is to be looked for in a priest, and ceased from claiming equal grace for a human choice though they had before thought that a similar prerogative belonged to themselves. But what else does that rod show, but that priestly grace never decays, and in the deepest lowliness has in its office the flower of the power committed to it, or that this also is refered to in mystery? Nor do we think that it was without a purpose that this took place near the end of the life of Aaron the priest. It seems to be shown that the ancient people, full of decay through the oldness of the long-continued unfaithfulness of the priests, being fashioned again in the last times to zeal in faith and devotion by the example of the Church, will again send forth with revived grace its flowers dead through so many ages.

59. But what does this signify, that after Aaron was dead, the Lord commanded, not the whole people, but Moses alone, who is amongst the priests, to clothe Aaron's son Eleazar with the priest's garments, except that we should understand that priest must consecrate priest, and himself clothe him with the vestments, that is, with priestly virtues; and then, if he has seen that nothing is wanting to him of the priestly garments, and that all things are perfect, should admit him to the sacred altars. For he who is to supplicate for the people ought to be chosen of God and approved by the priests, lest there be anything which might give serious offence in him whose office it is to intercede for the offences of others. For the virtue of a priest must be of no ordinary kind, since he has to guard not only from nearness to greater faults, but even the very least. He must also be prompt to have pity, not recall a promise, restore the fallen, have sympathy with pain, preserve meekness, love piety, repel or keep down anger, must be as it were a trumpet to excite the people to devotion, or to soothe them to tranquillity.

60. It is an old saying: Accustom yourself to be consistent, that your life may set forth as it were a picture, always preserving the same representation which it has received. How can he be consistent who at one time is inflamed by anger, at another blazes up with fierce indignation, whose face now burns, and now again is changed to paleness, varying and changing colour every moment? But let it be so, let it be natural for one to be angry, or that there is generally a cause, it is a man's duty to restrain anger, and not to be carried away like a lion by fury, so as not to know to be quieted, not to spread tales, nor to embitter family quarrels; for it is written: "A wrathful man diggeth up sin" He will not be consistent who is double-minded; he cannot be consistent who cannot restrain himself when angry, as to which David well says: "Be ye angry and sin not." He does not govern his anger, but indulges his natural disposition, which a man cannot indeed prevent but may moderate. Therefore even though we are angry, let our passion admit only such emotion as is according to nature, not sin contrary to nature. For who would endure that he should not be able to govern himself, who has undertaken to govern others?

61. And so the Apostle has given a pattern, saying that a bishop must be blameless, and in another place: "A bishop must be without offence, as a steward of God, not proud, not soon angry, not given to wine, not a striker, not greedy of filthy lucre." For how can the compassion of a dispenser of alms an the avarice of a covetous man agree together?

62. I have set down these things which I have been told are to be avoided, but the Apostle is the Master of virtues, and he teaches that gainsayers are to be convicted with patience, who lays down that one should be the husband of a single wife, not in order to exclude him from the right of marriage (for this is beyond the force of the precept), but that by conjugal chastity he may preserve the grace of his baptismal washing; nor again that he may be induced by the Apostle's authority to beget children in the priesthood; for the speaks of having children, not of begetting them, or marrying again.

63. And I have thought it well not to pass by this point, because many contend that having one wife is said of the time after Baptism; so that the fault whereby any obstacle would ensue would be washed away in baptism. And indeed all faults and sins are washed away; so that if

anyone have polluted his body with very many whom he has bound to himself by no law of marriage, all the sins are forgiven him, but if any one have contracted a second marriage it is not done away; for sin not law is loosed by the laver, and as to baptism there is no sin but law. That then which has to do with law is not remitted as though it were sin, but is retained. And the Apostle has established a law, saying: "If any man be without reproach the husband of one wife." So then he who is without blame the husband of one wife comes within the rule for undertaking the priestly office; he, however, who has married again has no guilt of pollution, but is disqualified for the priestly prerogative.

64. We have stated what is according to the law, let us state in addition what is according to reason. But first we must notice that not only has the Apostle laid down this rule concerning a bishop or priest, but that the Fathers in the Nicene Council added that no one who has contracted a second marriage ought to be admitted amongst the clergy at all. For how can he comfort or honour a widow, or exhort her to preserve her widowhood, and the faith pledged to her husband, which he himself has not kept in regard to his former marriage? Or what difference would there be between people and priest, if they were bound by the same laws? The life of a priest ought to excel that of others as does his grace, for he who binds others by his precepts ought himself to keep the precepts of the law.

65. How I resisted my ordination, and lastly, when I was compelled, endeavoured that it might at least be deferred, but the prescribed rule did not prevail against the popular eagerness. Yet the Western Bishops approved of my ordination by their decision, the Eastern by an example of the same kind. And yet the ordination of a neophyte is forbidden, lest he should be lifted up by pride. If the ordination was not postponed it was because of constraint, and if humility suitable to the priestly office be not wanting, where there is no reason blame will not be imputed to him.

66. But if so much consideration is needed in other churches for the ordination of a bishop, how much care is required in the Church of Vercellae, where two things seem to be equally required of the bishop, monastic rule and church discipline? For Eusebius of holy memory was the first in Western lands to bring together these differing matters, both while living in the city observing the rules of the monks, and ruling the Church with fasting and temperance. For the grace of the priesthood is much increased if the bishop constrain young men to the practice of abstinence, and to the rule of purity; and forbid them though living in the city, the manners and mode of life of the city.

67. From such a rule sprang those great men, Elijah, Elisha, John the son of Elizabeth, who clothed in sheepskins, poor and needy, and afflicted with pain, wandered in deserts, in hollows and thickets of mountains, amongst pathless rocks, rough caves, pitfalls and marshes, of whom the world was not worthy. From the same, Daniel, Ananias, Azarias, and Misael, who were brought up in the royal palace, were fed meagrely as though in the desert, with coarse food, and ordinary drink. Rightly did those royal slaves prevail over kingdoms, despise captivity, shaking off its yoke, subdue powers, conquer the elements, quench the nature of fire, dull the flames, blunt the edge of the sword, stop the mouths of lions; they were found most strong when esteemed to be most weak, and did not shrink from the mockings of men, because they looked for heavenly rewards; they did not dread the darkness of the prison, on whom was shining the beauty of eternal light.

68. Following these, holy Eusebius went forth out of his country, and from his own relatives, and preferred a foreign wandering to ease at home. For the faith also he preferred and chose the hardships of exile, in conjunction with Dionysius of holy memory, who esteemed a voluntary exile above an Emperor's friendship. And so these illustrious men, surrounded with arms, closed in by soldiers, when torn away from the larger Church, triumphed over the imperial power, because by earthly shame they purchased fortitude of soul, and kingly power; they from whom the band of soldiers and the din of arms could not tear away the faith subdued the raging

of the brutal mind, which was unable to hurt the saints. For, as you read in Proverbs, "the king's wrath is as the wrath of a lion."

69. He confessed that he was overcome when he asked them to change their determination, but they thought their pen stronger than swords of iron. Then it was unbelief which was wounded so that it fell, not the faith of the saints; they did not desire a tomb in their own country, for whom was reserved a home in the heavens. They wandered over the whole earth, "having nothing and yet possessing all things." Wherever they were sent, they esteemed it a place full of delights, for nothing wanting to them in whom the riches of faith abounded. Lastly, they enriched others, being themselves poor as to earthly means, rich in grace. They were tried but not killed, in fasting, in labours, in watchings, in vigils. Out of weakness they came forth strong. They did not wait for the enticements of pleasure who were satiated by fasting; the burning summer did not parch those whom the hope of eternal grace refreshed, nor did the cold of icy regions break them down, whose devotion was ever budding afresh with glowing devotion; they feared not the chains of men whom Jesus had set free; they desired not to be rescued from death, who expected to be raised again by Christ.

70. And at last holy Dionysius requested in his prayers, that he might end his life in exile, for fear that he might, if he returned home, find the minds of the people or the clergy disturbed through the teaching or practice of the unbelievers, and he obtained this favour, so that he bore with him the peace of the Lord with a quiet mind. Thus as holy Eusebius first raised the standard of confessorship, so blessed Dionysius in his exile gave up his life with honour higher even than martyrs.

71. Now this patience in holy Eusebius grew strong by the discipline of the monastery, and from the custom of hard endurance he derived the power of enduring hardships. For who doubts that in stricter Christian devotion these two things are the most excellent, the offices of the clergy and the rule of the monks? The former is a discipline which accustoms to courteousness and good morals, the latter to abstinence and patience; the former as it were on an open stage, the latter in secret; the one is visible, the other hidden. And so he who was a good athlete said: "We are made a spectacle to this world and to Angels." Worthy indeed was he to be gazed upon by Angels, when he was striving to attain the prize of Christ, when he was striving to lead on earth the life of Angels, and overcome the wickedness of spirits in heaven, for he wrestled with spiritual wickedness. Rightly did the world gaze upon him, that it might imitate him.

72. The one life, then, is on the open arena, the other hidden as in a cave; the one is opposed to the confusion of the world, the other to the desires of the flesh; the one subdues, the other shuns the pleasures of the body; the one was more agreeable, the other more safe; the one ruling, the other restraining itself, in order to be wholly Christ's, for to the perfect it is said: "He who will come after Me, let him deny himself, and take up his cross and follow Me." Now he follows Christ who is able to say: "It is no longer I that live, but Christ liveth in me."

73. Paul denied himself, when, knowing that chains and tribulations awaited him in Jesusalem, he willingly offered himself to danger, saying: "Nor do I count my life dear to myself, if only I can accomplish my course, and the ministry of the Word, which I have received of the Lord Jesus." And at last, though many were standing round, weeping and beseeching him, he did not change his mind, so stern a censor of itself is ready faith.

74. The one then contends, the other retires; the one overcomes incitements, the other flees from them; by the one the world is triumphed over, the other rejoices over it; to the one the world is crucified, or itself is crucified to the world, to the other it is unknown; the one endures more frequent temptations, and so has the greater victory, the other falls less often, and keeps guard more easily.

75. Elijah himself too, that the word spoken by his mouth might be confirmed, was sent by the Lord to hide himself by the brook Cherith. Ahab threatened, Jezebel threatened, Elijah was afraid and rose up, and then "went in the strength of that spiritual meat forty days and forty

nights unto Horeb the mount of God;" and entered into a cave and rested there; and afterwards was sent to anoint kings. He was then inured to patience by dwelling in solitude, and, as though fed to the fatness of virtue by the homely food, went on more strong.

76. John, too, grew up in the desert, and baptized the Lord, and there first practised constancy, that afterwards he might rebuke kings.

77. And since in speaking of holy Elijah's dwelling in the desert, we have passed by without notice the names of places which were not given without a purpose, it seems well to go back to what they signify. Elijah was sent to the brook Cherith, and there the ravens nourished him, bringing him bread in the morning, for it "strengthens man's heart." For how should the prophet be nourished except by mystical food? At evening flesh was supplied. Understand what you read, for Cherith means "understanding," Horeb signifies "heart" or "as a heart," Beersheba also is interpreted "the well of the seventh," or "of the oath."

78. Elijah went first to Beersheba, to the mysteries and sacraments of the divine and holy Law, next he is sent to the brook, to the stream of the river which makes glad the City of God. You perceive the two Testaments of the One Author; the old Scripture as a well deep and obscure, whence you can only draw with labour; it is not full, for He Who was to fill it was not yet come, Who afterwards said: "I am come not to destroy but to fulfil the Law." And so the Saint is bidden of the Lord to pass over to the stream, for he who has drunk of the New Testament, not only is a river, but also "from his belly shall flow rivers of living water," rivers of understanding, rivers of meditation, spiritual rivers, which, however, dried up in the times of unbelief, lest the sacrilegious and unbelieving should drink.

79. At that place the ravens recognized the Prophet of the Lord, whom the Jews did not recognize. The ravens fed him, whom that royal and noble race were persecuting. What is Jezebel, who persecuted him but the Synagogue, vainly fluent, vainly abounding in the Scriptures, which it neither keeps nor understands? What ravens fed him but those whose young call upon Him, to whose cattle He gives food as we read; "to the young ravens that call upon Him." Those ravens knew whom they were feeding, who were close upon understanding, and brought food to that stream of sacred knowledge.

80. He feeds the prophet, who understands and keeps the things that are written. Our faith gives him sustenance, our progress gives him nourishment; he feeds upon our minds and senses, his discourse is nourished by our understanding. In the morning we give him bread, who, being placed in the light of the Gospel, bestow on him the settled strength of our hearts. By these things he is nourished, by these he is strong, with these he fills the mouths of those who fast, to whom the unbelief of the Jews supplied no food of faith. To them every prophetic utterance is but fasting diet, the interior richness of which they do not see; empty and thin, such as cannot fatten their jaws.

81. Perhaps they brought him flesh in the evening, as it were stronger food, such as the Corinthians, whose minds were weak, could not take, and were therefore fed by the Apostle with milk. So, stronger meat was brought in the evening of the world, in the morning bread. And so, because the Lord commanded this food to be supplied, that word of prophecy may be suitably addressed to Him in this place: "Thou wilt give joy in the outgoings of morning and evening;" and, farther on: "Thou hast prepared their food, for so is its preparation."

82. But I think that enough has been said of the Master, let us now go on to the lives of the disciples, who have given themselves to His praise and celebrate it with hymns day and night. For this is the service of the Angels, to be always occupied in the praises of God, to propitiate and entreat the Lord with frequent prayers. They attend to reading, or occupy their minds with continual labours, and separated from the companionship of women, afford safe protection to each other. What a life is this, in which is nothing to fear, much to imitate! The pain of fasting is compensated by tranquillity of mind, is lightened by practice, aided by leisure, or beguiled by occupation; is not burdened with worldly cares, nor occupied with uncongenial troubles, nor weighed down with the distractions of the city.

83. You perceive what kind of teacher must be found for the preservation or teaching of this gift, and we can find him, if you assist by unanimity, if you forgive one another should any one think himself injured by another. For it is not the only kind of justice, not to injure him who has not injured us, but also to forgive him who has most injured us. We are often injured by the fraud of another, by the guile of a neighbour; do we consider it a mark of virtue, to avenge guile by guile, or to repay fraud by fraud? For if justice is a virtue it should be free from offence, and should not repel wickedness by wickedness. For what virtue is it that the same thing should be done by you which you yourself punish in another? That is the spreading of wickedness not its punishment, for it makes no difference whom one injures, whether a just man or an unjust, seeing one ought not to injure anyone. Nor does it make any difference in what way one bears ill will, whether from a desire of revenging oneself, or from a wish to injure, since in neither case is ill will free from blame. For to bear ill will is the same thing as to be unjust, and so it is said to thee: "Bear not ill will amongst those that bear ill will, and emulate not those that do unrighteousness;" and above; "I have hated the congregation of them that bear ill will." He clearly comprehends all and makes no exception, he lays hold of ill will and asks not the cause.

84. But what better pattern can there be than that of Divine justice? For the Son of God says: "Love your enemies;" and again: "Pray for those that persecute you and speak against you." So far does He remove the desire of vengeance from the perfect that He commands charity towards those who injure them. And since He had said in the Old Testament: "Vengeance is Mine, I will repay." He says in the Gospel, that we are to pray for those who have injured us, that He Who has said that He will avenge, may not do so; for it is His will to pardon at your desire with which according to His promise He agrees. But if you seek for you know that the unjust is more severely punished by his own convictions than by judicial severity.

85. And since no one can be without some adversities, let us take care that they do not happen to us through our own fault. For no one is more severely condemned by the judgment of others, than a foolish man, who is the cause of his misfortunes, is condemned by his own. For which reason we should decline matters which are full of trouble and contention, which have no advantage, but cause hindrances. Although we ought to take care not to have to repent our decisions or acts. For it is the part of a prudent man to look forward, so as not often to have to repent, for never to repent belongs to God alone. But what is the fruit of righteousness, but tranquillity of mind? Or what is to live righteously but to live with tranquility? Such as is the pattern of the master, such is the condition of the whole house. But if these things are requisite in a house, how much more in the Church, "where we, both rich and poor, bond and free, Greek anti Scythian, noble and common, are all one in Christ Jesus."

86. Let no man suppose that because he is rich, more deference is to be paid him. In the Church he is rich who is rich in faith, for the faithful has a whole world of riches. What wonder is it if the faithful possesses the world, who possesses the inheritance of Christ, which is of more value than the world? "Ye were redeemed with the Precious Blood," was certainly said to all, not to the rich only. But if you will be rich, obey him who says: "Be ye holy in all your conversation." He is speaking not to the rich only but to all; for He judges without respect of persons, as the Apostle His faithful witness says. And therefore says he: "Spend the time of your sojourning here," not in luxury, or fastidiousness, nor haughtiness of heart, but in fear. On this earth you have time not eternity, do you use the time as those who must pass hence.

87. Do not trust in riches; for all such things are left here, faith alone will accompany you. And righteousness indeed will go with you if faith has led the way. Why do riches entice you? "Ye were not redeemed with gold and silver," with possessions, or silk garments, "from your vain conversation, but with the precious Blood of Christ." He then is rich who is an heir of God, a joint heir with Christ. Despise not the poor man, he has made you rich. "This poor man cried, and the Lord heard him." Do not reject a poor man, Christ when He was rich became poor, and became poor because of you, that by His poverty He might make you rich. Do not then as though rich exalt yourself, He sent forth His apostles without money.

88. And the first of them said: "Silver and gold have I none." He glories in poverty as though shunning contamination. "Silver and gold," he says, "I have none,"—not gold and silver. He knows not their order in value who knows not the use of them. "Silver and gold have I none," but I have faith. I am rich enough in the Name of Jesus, "which is above every name." I have no silver, neither do I require any; I have no gold, neither do I desire it, but I have what you rich men have not, I have what even you would consider to be of more value, and I give it to the poor, namely that I say in the Name of Jesus: "Be strengthened, ye weak hands, and ye feeble knees."

89. But if you will be rich, you must be poor. Then shall you in all things be rich, if you are poor in spirit. It is not property which makes rich, but the spirit.

90. There are those who humble themselves in abundance of riches, and they act rightly and prudently, for the law of nature is sufficiently rich for all, according to which one may soon find what is more than enough; but for lust any abundance of riches is still penury. Again, no one is born poor but becomes so. Poverty then is not in nature but in our own feelings, and so to find oneself rich is easy for nature, but hard for lust. For the more a man has gained the more he thirsts for gain, and burns as it were with a kind of intoxication from his lusts.

91. Why do you seek for a heap of riches as though it were necessary? Nothing is so necessary as to know that this is not necessary. Why do you throw the blame on the flesh? It is not the belly in the body but avarice in the mind which makes a man insatiable. Does the flesh take away the hope of the future? Does the flesh destroy the sweetness of spiritual grace? Does the flesh hinder faith? Is it the flesh which attributes any weight to vain opinions as it were to insane masters? The flesh prefers frugal moderation, by which it is freed from burdens, is clothed with health, because it has laid aside its care and has obtained tranquillity.

92. But riches themselves are not blameable. For "the ransom of a man's life are his riches," since he that gives to the poor redeems his soul. So that even in these material riches there is place for virtue. You are like steersmen in the vast sea. If a man steers his course well, he quickly passes over the sea so as to attain to the port, but one who knows not how to direct his property is drowned together with his freight. And so it is written: "The wealth of rich men is a most strong city."

93. And what is that city but Jerusalem which is in heaven, in which is the kingdom of God? This is a good possession which brings eternal fruit. A good possession which is not left here, but is possessed there. He who possesses this says: "The Lord is my portion." He says not, My portion stretches and extends from this boundary to that. Nor does he say, My portion is amongst such and such neighbours, except perchance amongst the apostles, amongst the prophets, amongst the saints of the Lord, for this is the righteous man's portion. He does not say, My portion is in the meadows, or in the woods, or the plains, except perchance those wooded plains in which the Church is found, of which it is written: "We found it in the wooded plains." He does not say, My portion consists of herds of horses, for "a horse is a vain thing for safety." He does not say, My portion consists of herds of oxen, asses, or sheep; except perchance he reckons himself amongst those which know their Owner, and wishes to company with the ass which does not shun the crib of Christ; and that Sheep is his portion which was led to the slaughter, and that Lamb which was dumb before the shearer, and opened not His mouth, in Whose humiliation judgment has been exalted. Well does he say "before the shearer," for He laid aside what was additional, not His own essence, on the cross, when He laid aside His Body, but lost not His Divinity.

94. It is not then everyone who can say, "The Lord is my portion." The covetous man cannot, for covetousness draws near and says: Thou art my portion, I have thee in subjection, thou hast served me, thou hast sold thyself to me with that gold, by that possession thou hast adjudged thyself to me. The luxurious man says not: Christ is my portion, for luxury comes and says: Thou art my portion, I made thee mine in that banquet, I caught thee in the net of that feast, I hold thee by the bond of thy gluttony. Dost thou not know that thy table was more

valued by thee than thy life? I refute thee by thine own judgment, deny if thou canst, but thou canst not. And in fine thou hast reserved nothing for thy life, thou hast spent it all for thy table. The adulterer cannot say: "The Lord is my portion;" for lust comes and says: I am thy portion, thou didst bind thyself to me in the love of that maiden, by a night with that harlot thou hast come under my laws and into my power. The traitor cannot say: "Christ is my portion," for at once the wickedness of his sin rushes on him and says: He is deceiving Thee, Lord Jesus, he is mine.

95. We have an example of this, for when Judas had received the bread from Christ the devil entered into his heart, as though claiming his own property, as though retaining his right to his own portion, as though saying: He is not Thine but mine; clearly he is my servant, Thy betrayer, plainly he is mine. He sits at table with Thee, and serves me; with Thee he feasts, but is fed by me; from Thee he receives bread, from me money; with Thee he drinks, and has sold Thy Blood to me. And he proved how truly he spoke. Then Christ departed from him, Judas also himself left Jesus and followed the devil.

96. How many masters has he who has forsaken the One! But let us not forsake Him. Who would forsake Him Whom they follow bound with chains indeed, but chains of love, which set free and do not bind, those chains in which they who are bound boast, saying: "Paul the bondservant of Jesus Christ, and Timothy." It is more glorious for us to be bound by Him, than to be set free and loosed from others. Who then would flee from peace? Who would flee from salvation? Who would flee from mercy? Who would flee from redemption?

97. You see, my sons, what has been the end of those who followed these things, how being dead they yet work. Let us study to gain the diligence of those the glory of whose virtues we admire, and what we praise in others, let us silently recognize in ourselves. Nothing effeminate, nothing feeble attains to praise. "The kingdom of heaven suffereth violence, and the violent take it by force." The fathers ate the lamb in haste. Faith hastens, devotion is quick, hope is active, it loves not objections of the mind, but to pass from fruitless ease to the fruits of toil. Why do you put off till tomorrow? You can gain to-day; and must guard against not attaining the one and losing the other. The loss even of one hour is no slight one, one hour is a portion of our whole life.

98. There are young persons who desire quickly to attain to old age, so as no longer to be subject to the will of their elders; and there are also old men who would wish if they could to return again to youth. And I approve of neither desire, for the young, disdainful of things present, as it were ungratefully desire a change in their way of living, the old wish for its lengthening, whereas youth can grow old in character, and old age grow green with action. For it is discipline as much as age which brings amendment of character. How much the more then ought we to raise our hopes to the kingdom of God, where will be newness of life, and where will be a change of grace not of age!

99. Reward is not obtained by ease or by sleep. The sleeper does no work, ease brings no profit, but rather loss. Esau by taking his ease lost the blessing of the first-born, for he preferred to have food given to him rather than to seek it. Industrious Jacob found favour with each parent.

100. And yet although Jacob was superior in virtue and favour, he yielded to his brother's anger, who grieved that his younger brother was preferred to him. And so it is written: "Give place to wrath," lest the wrath of another draw you also into sin, when you wish to resist, and to avenge yourself. You can put away sin both from him and from yourself, if you think well to yield. Imitate the patriarch who by his mother's counsel went far away. And who was the mother? Rebecca, that is, Patience. For who but Patience could have given this counsel? The mother loved her son, but preferred that he should be cut off from herself rather than from God. And so because the mother was good, she benefited both her sons, but to the youngest she gave a blessing which he could keep; yet she preferred not one son to the other as sons; but the active to the easy-going, the faithful to the unbelieving.

101. And so since he was separated from his parents through piety not on account of impiety, he talked with God, he increased in riches, in children, and in favour. Nor was he elated by these things when he met his brother; but humbly bowed down to him, not indeed considering him the pitiless, the furious, the degenerate, but Him Whom he reverenced in him. And so he bowed down seven times, which is the number of remission, for he was not bowing down to man, but to Him Whom he foresaw in the Spirit, as hereafter to come in human flesh to take away the sins of the world. And this mystery is unfolded to you in the answer given to Peter, when he said: "If my brother trespass against me how often shall I forgive him? Until seven times?" You see that remission of sins is a type of that great Sabbath, of that rest of everlasting grace, and therefore is given by contemplation.

102. But what is the meaning of his having arranged his wives and children and all his servants, and ordered that they should bow down to the earth? It was certainly not to the element of earth, which is often filled with blood, in which is the workshop of all crimes, which often is rough with huge rocks, or broken cliffs, or barren and hungry soil, but as to that Flesh which is to be for our salvation. And perchance this is that mystery which the Lord taught, when He said: "Not only seven times, but even seventy times seven."

103. Do you then forgive injuries done to you that you may be children of Jacob. Be not provoked as was Esau. Imitate holy David, who as a good master left us what we should follow, saying: "Instead of loving me they spake against me, but I prayed," and when he was reviled, he prayed. Prayer is a good shield, wherewith contumely is kept away, cursing is repelled and often is turned back on those who utter it, so that they are wounded by their own weapons. "Let them curse," he says, "but bless Thou." The curse of man is to be sought for, which procures the blessing of the Lord.

104. And for the rest, most dear brethren, consider that Jesus suffered without the gate, and do you go forth out of this earthly city, for your city is Jerusalem which is above. Let your conversation be there, that you may say: "But our conversation is in heaven." Therefore did Jesus go forth out of the city, that you going out of this world may be above the world. Moses alone, who saw God, had his tabernacle without the camp when he talked with God; and the blood indeed of the victims which were offered for sin, was brought to the altar, but the bodies were burnt without the camp; for no one placed amidst the evil of this world can lay aside sin, nor is his blood accepted of God, except he go forth from the defilement of this body.

105. Love hospitality, whereby holy Abraham found favour, and received Christ as his guest, and Sarah already worn with age gained a son; Lot also escaped the fire of the destruction of Sodom. You too can receive Angels if you offer hospitality to strangers. What shall I say of Rahab who by this means found safety?

106. Compassionate those who are bound with chains, as though bound with them. Comfort those in sorrow; for, "It is better to go into the house of mourning than into the house of rejoicing." From the one is gained the merit of a good work, from the other a lapse into sin. Lastly, in the one case you still hope for the reward, in the other you have already received it. Feel with those who are afflicted as if also afflicted with them.

107. Let a wife show deference, not be a slave to her husband; let her show herself ready to be ruled not coerced. She is not worthy of wedlock who deserves chiding. Let a husband also guide his wife like a steersman, honour her as the partner of his life, share with her as a joint heir of grace.

108. Mothers, wean your children, love them, but pray for them that they may long live above this earth, not on the earth but above it, for there is nothing long-lived on this earth, and that which lasts long is but short and very frail. Warn them rather to take up the Cross of the Lord than to love this life.

109. Mary, the mother of the Lord stood by her Son's Cross; no one has taught me this but the holy Evangelist St. John. Others have related how the earth was shaken at the Lord's passion, the sky was covered with darkness, the sun withdrew itself; that the thief was after a

faithful confession received into paradise. John tells us what the others have not told, how the Lord fixed on the Cross called to His mother, esteeming it of more worth that, victorious over His sufferings, He rendered her the offices of piety, than that lie gave her a heavenly kingdom. For if it be according to religion to grant pardon to the thief, it is a mark of much greater piety that a mother is honoured with such affection by her Son. "Behold," He says, "thy Son".... "Behold thy mother." Christ testified from the Cross, and divided the offices of piety between the mother and the disciple. The Lord made not only a public but also a private testament, and John signed this testament of His, a witness worthy of so great a Testator. A good testament not of money but of eternal life, which was written not with ink but with the Spirit of the living God, Who says: "My tongue is the pen of a quickly writing scribe."

110. Nor was Mary below what was becoming the mother of Christ. When the apostles fled, she stood at the Cross, and with pious eyes beheld her Son's wounds, for she did not look for the death of her Offspring, but the salvation of the world. Or perchance, because that "royal hall" knew that the redemption of the world would be through the death of her Son, she thought that by her death also she might add something to the public weal. But Jesus did not need a helper for the redemption of all, Who saved all without a helper. Wherefore also He says: "I am become like a man without help, free among the dead." He received indeed the affection of His mother, but sought not another's help.

111. Imitate her, holy mothers, who in her only dearly beloved Son set forth so great an example of maternal virtue; for neither have you sweeter children, nor did the Virgin seek the consolation of being able to bear another son.

112. Masters, command your servants not as being below you in rank, but as remembering that they are sharers of the same nature as yourselves. Servants, serve your masters with good will, for each ought patiently to support that to which he is born, and be obedient not only to good but also to froward masters. For what thanks has your service if you zealously serve good masters? But if you thus serve the froward also you gain merit; for the free also have no reward, if when they transgress they are punished by the judges, but this is their merit to suffer without transgressing. And so you, if contemplating the Lord Jesus you serve even difficult masters with patience, will have your reward. Since the Lord Himself suffered, the just at the hand of the unjust, and by His wonderful patience nailed our sins to His Cross, that he who shall imitate Him may wash away his sins in His Blood.

113. In fine, turn all to the Lord Jesus. Let your enjoyment of this life be with a good conscience, your endurance of death with the hope of immortality, your assurance of the resurrection through the grace of Christ; let truth be with simplicity, faith with confidence, abstinence with holiness, industry with soberness, conversation with modesty, learning without vanity; let there be soberness of doctrine, faith without the intoxication of heresy. The grace of our Lord Jesus Christ be with you all. Amen.parparpar

Made in the USA
Middletown, DE
13 December 2019